Philosophical Perspectives, 5
Philosophy of Religion, 1991

*Previously Published Volumes*
Volume 1, Metaphysics, 1987
Volume 2, Epistemology, 1988
Volume 3, Philosophy of Mind and Action Theory, 1989
Volume 4, Action Theory and Philosophy of Mind, 1990


*Forthcoming Volumes*
Volume 6, Ethics, Fall 1992
Additional Titles to be announced.

# Philosophical Perspectives, 5
# Philosophy of Religion, 1991

Edited by
JAMES E. TOMBERLIN
*California State University, Northridge*

Ridgeview Publishing Company ● Atascadero, California

Paper Text: ISBN 0-924922-03-6
Cloth Text: ISBN 0-924922-53-2

The typesetting and illustrations were done by the CSUN Graphics Department (James W. Reese, Manager). The typesetter was Robert Olsen.

Published in the United States of America
by Ridgeview Publishing Company
P. O. Box 686
Atascadero, California 93423

Printed in the United States of America

Philosophical Perspectives, 5, Philosophy of Religion, 1991

# Contents

*Omniscience and Foreknowledge*

*The Nature of God*

*God and Nature*

# PREFACE

The problem of evil, omniscience, foreknowledge and free will, omnipotence, the rationality of religious belief, God's simplicity, the ontological argument, creation, causation and occasionalism, souls, substances, and dualism, theism and moral dilemmas—these are some of the central issues addressed in twenty-three original essays included in the present volume devoted to the philosophy of religion.

A new series of topical philosophy studies, *Philosophical Perspectives* aims to publish original essays by foremost thinkers in their fields, with each volume confined to a main area of philosophical research. The intention is to publish volumes annually.

*Philosophical Perspectives* could not have come to fruition without the precious encouragement it received from Administrative Officials at California State University, Northridge. I am particularly grateful to Dr. James W. Cleary, President of this institution, and Dr. Bob H. Suzuki, Vice President for Academic Affairs, who provided essential financial support through the Special Projects Fund of the California State University Foundation, Northridge. I also thank Dr. Jorge Garcia, Dean, School of Humanities, and Dr. Daniel Sedey, Chair, Department of Philosophy, for their consistent efforts in advancing this project. Pat Boles, Administrative Program Specialist, School of Humanitites, maintained logistical supervision and arranged for many valuable services. Dorothy Johnson, Irene Yarmak, and Sally Brenneman contributed ever so many hours of invaluable clerical assistance and support.

*March 1991*                    **JAMES E. TOMBERLIN**

Philosophical Perspectives, 5, Philosophy of Religion, 1991

# SIN AS UNCLEANNESS

## Marilyn McCord Adams
## University of California, Los Angeles

### I. What is Sin?

Sin was a rare topic during the first twenty of the last thirty years of analytic philosophy of religion. That it came up at all was due to the popularity of Free Will approaches to the problem of evil, which fix on traditional doctrines of the Fall and assert their logical possibility or truth as the explanation of evil's origin and/or Divine permission of it. Such Free Will approaches envision an "original position" in which incompatibilist free creatures are competent choosers placed in a utopian environment: that is, they have enough cognitive and emotional maturity to grasp and accurately apply relevant normative principles, while (on the occasion of choice) their exercise of these abilities is unfettered by unruly passions or external determinants of any kind. The possibility envisioned is that such creatures should choose contrary to their normative judgments, thereby introducing evil into the world. Even so, Free-Will-Defending philosophers such as Alvin Plantinga[1] have chosen not to speak of *sin*, but of *moral* agency and responsibility, of **moral** goodness or turpitude. And this preference is of a piece with the widespread but unspoken agreement to discuss both the concept of God and the problem of evil within the parameters of religion neutral value-theory.[2] Little wonder if the relation between the concepts of sin and immorality should seem puzzling now![3]

One obvious way to connect them starts with a religion-neutral view of human beings and the norms pertaining to them, and then identifies sin with violations of some or any of these norms, with or without the stipulation that to call them 'sin' adds a reference to God.[4] With Basil Mitchell's "Plain Moralist,"[5] many Free-Will-Defenders readily identify the normative principles relevant to sin with moral principles (and so conceive of sin *moralistically*). Agreeing that 'moral-ought' implies 'can', they readily conclude that sin is, in the first instance and the primary sense, a matter of wrongful choices by fully competent, incompatibilist free creatures (and so to think of sin *voluntaristically*).

This straightforward strategy for dealing with the concept of sin has the vices of its virtues. For if it renders the concept of sin palatable to secular thinkers, it runs the risk of being religiously inadequate. First of all, the Biblical catalog of sins includes, not only (i) conscious voluntary actions, but also (ii) emotions (e.g., anger) and cognitive states (e.g., belief) not within our (direct) voluntary control, (iii) dispositions, habits, inclinations that resist the normative ordering of the self,[6] and (iv) states or conditions of uncleanness (e.g., the abominations of Leviticus). Plain Moralists with the courage of their convictions dismiss (iv) uncleanness as a primitive category deservedly supplanted by the ethical,[7] while refusing to count us responsible for any of (ii) or (iii) that are not within our power.[8] And in general, among those who equate sin with the immoral, disagreements about which (if any) of (ii) or (iii) count as sin would parallel disputes about which are genuinely morally wrong, morally vicious or bad. Second and more importantly, this strategy makes the notion of sin *anthropocentric*, by conceding that the norms relevant to sin lie within the province of religion-neutral value theory. One implication is that a human being who conformed to all such norms would be sinless; where the standards are moral principles for (i) voluntary action, Pelagianism is ready in the wings.[9]

My own contention is that 'sin' is a fundamentally theological notion, signifying some sort of impropriety in the relation between created persons and God. The difficulty cannot be moral *at bottom*, because (as I have maintained in other papers[10]) the network of moral considerations, rights and obligations is *not* one that connects God with His free creatures. Rather morality is a human institution, roughly the best framework humans generally can master and/or apply on a large scale to promote friendly and curtail anti-social behavior and attitudes.[11] Moreover, the network of *moral* considerations, rights, and obligations presupposes a commensuration among the agents connected thereby. But God and creatures are ontologically incommensurate. This is why God has no *obligations* to creatures, and why creatures' obligation to obey God cannot be *moral* strictly speaking.[12] To identify sin with moral wrong-doing thus threatens either to trivialize sin or to make an idol of morality.

My purpose here is to commend the alternative view, that *the fundamental obstacle to Divine-human relations lies in the very incommensuration of Divine and created natures.* To lend vivacity and plausibility to this idea, I will begin with category (iv), by exploring three accounts of sin as uncleanness. With the first two—drawn from Rudolf Otto's justly famous book *The Idea of the Holy* and from Mary Douglas' work in the social anthropology of religion—I follow out the methodological axiom of John Locke and David Hume: that considerable insight into a concept is gained by reflecting on its genetic origins. The third reflects on religious experience a different way, and is found in Julian of Norwich's *Revelation of Divine Love*. I will consider this breaking of disciplinary ranks justified if it manages to dislodge philosophical myopia regarding the nature of sin.

## II. Sin as Uncleanness and the Idea of the Holy

In *The Idea of the Holy*, Rudolf Otto offers a rational reconstruction of our supposed derivation of the idea of God ("the Holy" or "the numen") from religious experience.[13] Otto's approach is particularly apt for our purposes, because it results describe the Holy, and human relationship to the Holy at one and the same time. Since sin is a sometime feature of the latter, Otto's search for the genetic roots of the idea of the Holy promise to identify those of our notion of sin as well.[14] *(2.1) Otto's Procedure*: (i) Recall how Otto identifies as paradigm religious experience which content-wise is *of* God (the Holy, the numen), in which God is presented as something other than the self, and which is attended by a full range of feeling accompaniments.[15] By analogy, one might identify a paradigm experience of a tiger as a visual experience in which the tiger is presented to me as something other than myself, and which is accompanied by a wide range of feelings, such as terror, awe, and admiration. (ii) My experience provides with two sources of tiger-descriptions. Most obviously, I can read off a characterization of the tiger from its visual appearance (e.g., as being huge in size, and as having orange and black stripes, long claws, and sharp teeth). In addition, I can infer features of the tiger from the feeling accompaniments, according to the following pattern: 'Feeling $\phi$ accompanies my experience of $x$; therefore I experience $x$ as the logically appropriate object of feeling $\phi$'. For example, terror accompanies my vision of the tiger chasing me; therefore I experience the tiger as a logically appropriate object of terror—i.e., as terrifying and terrible! Where ordinary objects are concerned, information from the one source can be checked against and/or corrected by that from the other. For example, I may be terrified of lady bugs, but they (as harmless to human well-being) are not logically appropriate objects of terror. Or a detective may have a funny feeling that something is wrong, although everything looks fine. Otto insists, however, that because God (the Holy, the numen) is so different from and so much bigger than we are, we cannot read off a characterization of God from the "visual" content of religious experience; instead, we can characterize God *only* as the logically appropriate object of the feelings that normally accompany paradigm religious experiences that are content-wise of Him. For present purposes, we need not accept this strong thesis, that religious feelings are our only root to God-characterizations. We can profit from his remarks so long as we concede the weaker claim that religious feelings *contribute* to the content of our idea in the way he describes.

(iii) According to Otto, our efforts thus to articulate our idea of the Holy are further complicated by the fact that such religious feelings are *sui generis* and only analogically related to those that accompany our experience of ordinary objects (e.g., our fear of loose tigers versus our dread of grave yard ghosts on Halloween). This means we will have to proceed by comparison and contrast, and must be alert to the fact that feeling-vocabulary will often be used analogically.

(iv) Finally, Otto hypothesizes that, in addition to reason and the five senses, humans are endowed with a special faculty for religious experience, a faculty for having experiences in which God is presented as something other than the self, and for having a wide range of feeling-accompaniments.[16] Moreover, such religious feelings can be triggered in different degrees by situations other than paradigm religious experience (e.g., by telling ghost stories or watching horror movies). Thus, Otto expects most (if not all) of his readers to have had the feelings to which he refers in his reconstruction.

*(2.2) Otto's Results*: Drawing on various religious texts including the Bible, Otto identifies and classifies religious feelings and infers the consequent God-characterizations as follows:

| *Feeling Experience of Myself* | *Characterization of God/Holy/Numen* |
|---|---|
| A. *Tremendum* | |
| 1. Fear, dread | 1. Aweful, eerie, weird, dreadful |
| 2. Creature-feeling | 2. Powerful, plenitude of being |
| 3. Radically threatened | 3. Living, urgent, active |
| B. *Mysterium* | |
| 1. Angst, stupor | 1. Wholly other |
| 2. Attracted | 2. *Fascinans* |
| C. *Augustus* | |
| 1. Profane, unclean | 1. August, holy |

*(A)* First, God is experienced as a worthy object of trembling and terror. For, Otto claims, *(A1)* paradigm religious experiences would be accompanied with something like my fear of a loose tiger, but different from it in the direction of my reactions to graveyard ghosts on Halloween. Stories of ghosts and active corpses make flesh creep and blood run cold; they seem eerie, uncanny, and weird.[17] Biblical examples include God's smoking pot covenant with Abraham in Genesis 15:7-12. Abraham splits and arranges the animals for the ratification ceremony, and shoos the birds away all day long. Then, "as the sun was going down, a deep sleep fell on Abram; and lo, a dread and great darkness fell upon him" (Gen. 15:12) and "behold, a smoking fire pot and flaming torch passed between these pieces. On that day the Lord made a covenant with Abraham, saying, 'To your descendants I give this land...'" (Gen. 15:17-18).

Again, *(A2)* paradigm religious experiences would be accompanied by creature-feeling, the sense of being radically weak and impotent in relation to something overwhelmingly efficacious; of being (in Anselm's words) "almost nothing" in relation to an infinite ocean of being (Damascene's words). In Biblical language, it is the experience of hearts melting, of strength draining out, of being utterly undone at the very sight of the other.[18] Moreover, *(A3)* in paradigm religious experience, I would not only experience myself as utterly unable to affect what has an overwhelming capacity to affect me; I would experience myself as *on the verge* of being ruined, done in, or annihilated, and accordingly experience the Holy as living, urgent, active.[19] Thus, the voice of the Lord is said to shake the wilderness (Ps.29:8), to make the oak trees writhe, and to strip the forests bare (Ps.29:9); His presence, to make mountains skip like rams and little hills like young sheep (Ps.114:4,6) and to cause seas and rivers to flee (Ps.114:3,5). Again, in preparation for the Sinai summit, God warns Moses that the people must consecrate themselves and not touch the mountain, lest the Lord "break out against them" (Exodus 19:12-15, 21-24) as He later did against Uzzah who reached forth his hand to steady the ark (II Samuel 6:1-11). When the time came for the Sinai meeting, the people were so terrified at the thunder and lighting, the trumpet blasts, and smoking mountain that they insisted on dealing with God only through mediators like Moses (Exodus 20:18-20).

*(B)* Otto's second category, the *Mysterium*, breaks down into two parts. On the one hand, in paradigm religious experience, I would experience *(B1)* great anxiety, I would feel stupefied, at a loss for words. Thus, when God finally grants Job a hearing, Job stammers, "Behold, I am of small account; what shall I answer thee? I lay my hand on my mouth. I have spoken once, and I will not answer; twice, but I will proceed no further" (Job 40:3-5). And, seeing Jesus transfigured, Peter suggests three tents "not knowing what he said" (Luke 9:33). Otto infers, one experiences God as wholly other, utterly unique and unlike the ordinary objects of our experience.[20] On the other hand, *(B2)* I would feel powerfully attracted to the Holy.[21] For instance, the psalmist writes, "As a deer longs for the water-brooks, so longs my soul for you, O God. My soul is athirst for God, athirst for the living God; when shall I come to appear before the presence of God?" (Ps.42:1-2) Or again, "O God, you are my God; eagerly I seek you; my soul thirsts for you, my flesh faints for you, as in a barren and dry land where there is no water" (Ps. 63:1). And, "How dear to me is your dwelling, O Lord of hosts! My soul has a desire and longing for the courts of the Lord; my heart and my flesh rejoice in the living God" (Ps.84:1). Accordingly, the Holy is experienced as fascinating and enticing.

*(C)* Finally, Otto claims, in paradigm religious experience, I would experience myself as profane, unclean, sinful. Thus, when Isaiah sees the Lord in the temple, he cries, "Woe is me! For I am lost; for I am a man of unclean lips, and I dwell in the midst of a people of unclean lips; for my eyes have seen the King, the Lord of hosts!" (Isaiah 6:5) Likewise, faced with God, Job gasps, "I had heard of thee by the

hearing of the ear, but now my eye sees thee; therefore I despise myself and repent in dust and ashes" (Job 42:5-6). And Peter, seeing the miraculous draught of fishes, falls down before Jesus, saying, "Depart from me, for I am a sinful man, O Lord" (Luke 5:8). Conversely, God is experienced as pure and holy.[22]

Drawing Otto's conclusions together, we see that feelings in category *(B1)* reveal God to us as "separate" in the sense of being radically unlike anything else in our experience. Those in category *(A)* tell us that this Wholly Other is radically dangerous to the health of beings of our kind, while category *(C)* shows normative priority to lie on the side of God. As Otto himself insists, all of these characterizations are pre-moral,[23] because what, in the first instance, evokes the feelings from which the descriptions are derived, is the sheer presence of Divine *nature* to human *nature*, quite apart from any exercise of agency on either side. For Otto, it is a further step—what he styles a *"moralizing"* of the concepts—when the feelings arising from the interaction of the natures are projected onto the personal characters, policies, and choices of God and creatures (so that, e.g., so that 'powerful' in *(A2)* and 'threatening' in *(A3)* are transmuted into 'wrathful'; 'fascinating' and 'attractive' in *(B2)* into 'gracious' and 'benevolent'). Thus, the devaluations of creatures in *(A2)* and *(C1)* have nothing to do with the unique conditions or behavior of individuals; but pertain to individuals *qua* members of a certain kind. *(A2)* simply expresses the ontological incommensuration between God and creatures, while *(C1)* is a relative devaluation consequent upon it. It follows that on Otto's analysis, the notion of sin is, in its genetic origin, pre-moral. Creatures are to be characterized as sinful or unclean, because the radical incommensuration of Divine and created natures obstructs relations between God and creatures, and the problem lies, not in any flaw in the Divine nature, but in the radical limitation and finitude of created natures in comparison to God.[24]

## III. Sin and the Sociology of Uncleanness

Even if we agree that Otto's focus on religious feeling catches something fundamental and *Uralt* that should not be lost sight of in our attempts to understand God and Divine-human relationships; and that part of the soul of religion is lost, when theological concepts are entirely cut off from these feeling roots, we might consider Otto's reflections on genetic origins inconclusive. After all, so much Biblical attention to Divine-human relationships revolves around themes of covenant, commandments, obedience and disobedience—notions which seem prima facie congruent with the voluntaristic/ moralistic common-places about sin mentioned in section I. To undermine this objection, I turn now to the work of Mary Douglas, which provides a framework of ideas relative to which the Biblical structure of covenants and commandments emerge as a solution to the more fundamental problem of the incommensuration between Divine and created natures. Theoretically, her conceptual apparatus has the advantage over the Plain Moralists'. For Douglas can provide a *unified* sociological explanation of why Biblical legislation ranges over, not only morally wrong acts, but also conditions of ritual uncleanness. Not only does her account make the notion of uncleanness foundational; it sheds light on the legal/anti-nomian controversy in the New Testament as well.

In her fascinating book *Purity and Danger*, Douglas offers a sociological explanation of the function of cleanliness metaphors and institutions in terms of twin ideas: *that dirt is stuff out of order,*[25] and *that stuff out of order is both powerful and dangerous.*[26] (i) Order and boundaries come in many varieties. Within society, social classes or castes, governmental, social, and familial roles give definition and create order. In the world at large, national boundaries, treaties, and international agreements give structure and definition to relations among nation states. Likewise, in nature, genus and species boundaries give structure and definition to plant and animal worlds. (ii) Disorder is experienced as doubly dangerous: fundamentally, because order confers identity on individuals and groups by giving them definition—what compromises identity threatens existence[27]; pragmatically, because order makes reality predictable and so enables individuals and groups to plot survival- and prosperity-strategies. At the same time, disorderly elements seem powerful, not only because they threaten to disrupt the old, but also because they symbolize creative potential for the new. Again, powers outside the order may bring super-structural blessing as well as curse, and so may be objects of admiration as well as terror.[28]

*(3.1) Sample Applications*: Thus, Douglas remarks, the numen or numenal individuals (such as, witches, medicine men, pregnant women, ghosts, madmen, saints) are felt to be *powerful, dangerous,*

*and/or attractive*, because they fall between the cracks of social, political, and/or natural categories.[29]

Again, Douglas explains, where group boundaries (whether social, political, or natural) are under assimilative pressure, communities tend to meet the threats to group identity by evolving codes and regulations that clarify and strengthen group definition. And such institutions often metaphorically express the resolution of the problem, by positing sharp distinctions between the clean and the polluted. Douglas sees "the abominations of Leviticus" in this light.[30] *Etymologically, 'holy' means separate*,[31] so that, on the one hand, holiness involves the clear and distinct separation of one thing from another. Thus, animals are clean or unclean, insofar as they perfectly conform to or compromise the species boundaries of rudimentary zoology. Those which fall between the taxonomical cracks or blur them by participating partly in one category and partly in another are unclean (Lev.11:3-7, 26-28). Similarly, swarming things are unclean, because their motion is indeterminate, no more of one sort than another (Lev.11:10-11, 29-38, 41-43).[32] Likewise, *because 'holy' symbolizes the whole, complete, or perfect*,[33] things which are defective members of their kind (such as the lame, the blind, those with crushed limbs or sex organs; Lev.21:17-21; 22:20-25; cf. Lev.1:3,10) are unclean.[34] And *because holiness implies purity, being of the same kind all over and through and through*, it follows that hybrids (such as mules; Lev.19:19), mixtures (such as linsey-woolsey), and those with blotchy or blemished surfaces (people who are partially leprous, partially mildewed walls or cloth, etc.; Lev.13; Lev.22:4) are unclean. Again, *because the human body is itself an image of society*, bodily emissions symbolize ruptured group definition. Hence, bodily discharges of whatever sort (including menstrual blood, Lev. 12:1, Lev.15; and semen; Lev. 22:4) render one unclean.[35]

*(3.2) Douglas Adapted*: It is not clear to me whether Douglas intends a sociological *reduction* of religion generally, or of such institutions of purity and danger in particular. Happily, we need not embrace any reductive program to accept her generic thesis—that human perceptions and responses to others are profoundly shaped, both individually and collectively, by social context and institutions— or to profit from her more precise observations about how a thing's relation to social structure, or a group's position in its wider context, affect ascriptions of purity and pollution, danger and power. Adapting

Douglas' ideas, I want now to propose an account of the function of covenants and commandments in ancient Israel, which harmonizes with my contention that, at the most basic level, sin is a disorder arising in Divine-human relationships because of the incommensuration of natures.

The application is straightforward. Because Divine and created natures are incommensurate, God will be unclassifiable relative to any merely human order (social, political, international) or to any human perception of natural order. Since we are unable to fit Him into any of our categories, we experience God as *(B1)* wholly other, and therefore as utterly unpredictable, as arbitrary power *(A2)*, at once dangerous *(A3)* and attractive *(B2)*. Given that roles not only confer identity, but define relationships, the possibility of Divine-human interactions seems likewise jeopardized.

However intimidating the Divine *nature* ("no one can see God and live"), Biblical religion insists on a relentless Divine will to intimate, beneficial relations with His human creatures, a goal which requires Him to overcome human terror at His presence. One Biblical solution has *God* create an order, which assigns God and creatures roles, and issue a set of laws and commandments that define and structure Divine-human relations, thereby making them possible, tolerably safe, and potentially wholesome. In doing so, God accommodates Himself to the human condition by using analogues of human institutions: the Genesis 15:7-16 covenant with Abraham is modelled on ancient business deals; the Sinai covenant on international treaties (Exodus 20; Deuteronomy 5-8); and various liturgical rules on courtroom etiquette. On the other hand, the incommensuration between God and creatures accounts for a certain arbitrariness (e.g., which clan is eligible for priesthood, Temple decorations, etc.) and historical relativity in the content of the rules (e.g., pork and honeyed sacrifices are forbidden (Lev.2:11-13) because they were typical of Canaanite religion, which was exerting assimilative pressure on Israelite culture).

Since only God can assign God a role, the *norm* for God-creature interactions is God's social order, the Divinely imposed suzerainty covenant. Cast in the language of purity and pollution, since God is Holy, His people must be metaphorically holy; and God takes the initiative to make this possible by providing covenant obligations in terms of which to "separate" Israel from other nations (cf. Lev.19:2; 20:7, 26; 22:31-33). Thus, creatures are out of order and so unclean, when they fail to conform to God's laws. The notion that disobedience to Divine laws has bad consequences for the human violator and/or his community, remains legal on the surface—the Sinai covenant is sealed with conditional curses (Deuteronomy 28:1-14) , and specific penalties for law-breakers are prescribed in the code itself. Nevertheless, the laws themselves are not invariably voluntaristic/moralistic (cf. Levitical laws regarding *unintentional* sins which must nevertheless be expiated by sacrifice, and pollution legislation which concerns states and conditions outside the agent's voluntary control).[36] And underneath lies the fact that the Law was God's gift, a protective shield and framework; to break it, exposes the creature to the terrors of unstructured contact with the Divine.

*3.3. A Christian Alternative*: The Christian answer to the incommensuration problem is different: in a word, it is Christ Jesus Himself! *The person of Christ* declares that, despite Douglas-Ottonian appearances, created proximity to the Divine is *not metaphysically ruinous*. Christ is the eternal Word made flesh (John 1:14), the One who "bears the very stamp" of God's nature (Hebrews 1:3) and at the same time is "like us in every respect" (Hebrews 2:17), partaking of the same flesh and blood nature (Hebrews 2:14). In Chalcedonian language, Divine nature and human nature are united in one person or *suppositum*, without confusion, change, division, or separation. According to medieval theology, the *suppositum* that is the Divine Word (God the Son) assumes and "supposits" an individual human nature. And although the Divine Word assumed the human nature contingently and could shed it at will, the Divine Word will remain united to that human nature forever.[37]

*The work of Christ* proclaims that God is an extra-structural figure relationship with whom will involve trials and suffering but be dominated by blessing. Because of the incommensuration problem, God will be experienced by any human consciousness as powerful and dangerous if also attractive (see sections 2 and 3.1 above). Because God's ways are higher than our ways, both beyond and contrary to our comprehension, "yes" to Divine vocation means exchanging citizenship in the earthly homeland for that in a heavenly country (Hebrews 11:8-16) and accepting to become "strangers and exiles upon the earth" (Hebrews 11:13). Although God is the ideal city-planner, the Christian should not expect to grasp the structure of the Kingdom of God in a more than fragmentary way—enough to know that it so fails to be congruent with human social divisions—e.g., between Jew and Greek, male and female, slave and free, rich and poor—as to explode them. On Douglas' model, the disciple risks becoming a displaced person who falls between the cracks of human social organization, oneself a liminal figure liable to evoke fear and hostility from others who remain imbedded in the merely human social institutions.

The letter to the Hebrews implies that Christ, in His human nature, reacted to His vocation with all the normal human fears and anxieties: He learned obedience through suffering (Hebrews 5:8; cf. 2:10), was tempted in all respects as we are (Hebrews 4:15), even prayed with loud cries and tears in Death's dark hour (Hebrews 5:7). Nevertheless, He chose to tolerate these psychic storms of Ottonian feelings and to trust God for goods as yet unseen. The incongruity between earthly and heavenly cities brought Him trials, and eventually failure and ruin by human standards, but God exalted Him to a position of intimacy and honor at God's right hand (Hebrews 8:1-2). Similarly, the letter-writer explains, such trials are the discipline by which God the Father teaches human beings how to be citizens of the city which He has prepared (Hebrews 12:7, 10, 13). The resurrection and exaltation of Christ are offered as assurance that blessing has the last word!

Finally, the letter-writer concludes, human approach to God is not, as for the Israelites at Mt. Sinai, towards "naked" Divinity, but through Jesus (Hebrews 12:18-24), a person of our own nature, our pioneer (Hebrews 2:10) and companion, a priest who knows how to sympathize with us (Hebrews 4:15), who intercedes for us at God's right hand (Hebrews 7:24-25). Jesus Himself furnishes human beings safe passage into the holy of holies through the curtain of His flesh (Hebrews 10:19-20).

## IV. Sin as Uncleanness and the Tender Loving Care of Mother Jesus

If the Bible represents God as overcoming the barrier of ontological incommensuration by taking the initiative to establish a covenant relationship with human beings, the problem of sin re-arises with human non-compliance to its terms (from a Christian point of view, summarized in the First and Second Great "Love" commandments). Julian of Norwich analyzes this failure, not as rebellion that results in guilt, but as incompetence issuing in uncleanness, requiring a Divine Mother's loving care.

*(4.1) Psychological Prototypes*: Since Julian's account of Divine-human relationships emphasizes family as well as courtly models, we can best harvest her insights by taking a brief detour through developmental psychology. Beginning with Freud, psychologists have argued that (T1) religious belief reflects a projection of childhood models of parent-child relationships. Freud himself took the psychodynamics of the little boy's Oedipal struggle as the psychological prototype of human religion. God is a projection of the primal horde father within every human male, and the God thus projected is omnipotent, harsh, and demanding, threatening violent punishment of the slightest infractions of his arbitrary commands. As an atheist, Freud wanted to work (T2) a psychological reduction of religious belief, and so maintained that as therapy undid unconscious ego strategies, unconscious projections would be withdrawn, resulting in the end of religious delusion.

Others, influenced by Freud but uninterested in (T2) a psychological reduction of religion, have thought that Freudian dynamics nevertheless help to explain why people conceive of God as they do. Anna Maria Rizutto has documented striking parallels between people's pictures of God and their view of parent and family figures, and sees this psychic interference as explaining why some people believe in God and others don't. For her, therapy can help transform one's picture of God. But (not-T2) the psychodynamic explanation of people's conceptions of God is logically compatible with the reality of God as a spiritual being who is more or less different from these conceptions.

If humans inevitably conceive of the God-creature relationship on analogy with some developmental model or other of human relationships, the *theologian's* question becomes which developmental prototype would be the least inaccurate. This choice is crucial for soteriology, because the meaning of sin and suffering varies so considerably from model to model.

To appreciate this point, we must review briefly what these earlier phases are. (i) According to developmental psychologists, to begin with, a child's psyche is bombarded with stimuli from within and from without, and is a booming, buzzing confusion with no center or organizational principle. The child does not at first distinguish self from world (or not-self), but actively gropes for some way to center or organize this psychic material. (ii) At the age of three months, the child is able to focus on a human face (or just a drawing of one) and use that to center himself and his world. The presence of the face is a major organizer of the personality. We may call this the stage of **semi-differentiation**. In a way, the child differentiates the face as an object within the matrix of his psyche. But insofar as the face is the center of *the child's* personality and world, the child does not fully distinguish the face from the matrix which is itself. Usually, the face is that of the mother or adult care-taker, and so is experienced as an identity-conferring, loving other who orders the cosmos. To be sure, the child experiences heat and cold, wet and dry, hunger and digestive pains, and—to put it mildly—it does not understand why the psyche "has" to include these things. But insofar as the mother is indeed nurturing, the child will experience the face-centered world as a place made hospitable through the agency of the face.

(iii) At the age of six months, the child learns to recognize the absence of the face, and so experiences the face as something not entirely reliable. This makes the child realize it has to fend for itself, and here begins a long process of ego-development.

(iv) In the course of this ego-development, the child learns to move and walk, etc.etc. And if the mother continues to be nurturing, she will respect and support the child in its moves towards independence. When the child takes the first step and then falls at the second, the mother will admire and be delighted in the first, and will in no way blame the child for the fall but will encourage it to get up and try again. The nurturing mother will thus exercise a kind of delicate courtesy and respect for the child's developing ego, and will not blame or shame it but will seek to provide a context of unconditional love and support within which these competencies can grow.

(v) Not until a year and a half or so later does the child reach the stage on which Freudian history of religions fixated, the stage at which the child is mature enough to construct the world as a place containing the big powerful authority figure who holds it accountable for obedience and disobedience with rewards and punishments.

Julian's dominant conception of God as a loving and nurturing heavenly Mother draws on psychological prototype from phases of child-development earlier than Freud's.

*(4.2) Metaphysical Mothering*: Julian agrees with Otto about the ontological incommensuration between God and creatures, and acknowledges a deep human propensity to fear the Divine presence. Nevertheless, she insists, the enormous metaphysical difference does

not show itself in the need for separation or distance between God and creatures, but rather the radical metaphysical dependence of creatures on Him. For Julian, the developmental prototype of this dependence relation is the relation of semi-differentiation between a three to six-month old infant and its mother/adult care taker. Thus, she describes the relationship between God and the human soul in terms of *mutual indwelling*.[38] The human soul is a "glorious city," "a resting place"[39] where Christ makes Himself completely at home[40] and where the Blessed Trinity lives eternally.[41] Again, God is "the foundation of our nature"[42] and "the ground of our life and existence,"[43] in such a way that "all souls to be saved in heaven forever are joined and united in this union and made holy in this holiness."[44] Bringing her metaphysical remarks into explicit juxtaposition with the mother-image, Julian declares, "the Trinity is our Mother, in whom we are enfolded"[45]; Christ's "the tender love" that "enfolds," "embraces," and "completely surrounds us, never to leave us."[46] From a metaphysical point of view, human beings never get beyond the stage of semi-differentiation: for "our Saviour himself is our Mother"; "we are forever being born of him, and we shall never be delivered."[47]

Of course, human adults do not invariably *experience* themselves in relation to God the way a six month old does in relation to its mother. But Julian insists that those who pursue the path of self-knowledge will find it so. For it is

> "easier for us to get to know God than to know our own soul. For our soul is so deeply set in God, and so deeply valued, that we cannot come to know it until we first know God, its Creator, to whom it is joined."[48]

Inevitably, "we come to know both together," because

> "God is nearer to us than our own soul, for he is the ground in which it stands, and he is the means by which substance and sensuality are held together so that they can never separate."[49]

If the child finds a center for its personality in the mother's face and so does not know itself apart from knowing the mother, so also it cannot know the mother in the stage of semi-differentiation apart from knowing itself.

*(4.3) Sin as Incompetence and Uncleanness*: According to Julian, the evaluative truth about the human condition finds its developmental prototype in the pre-Oedipal stages, where the emotional

developmental agenda is to establish a favorable balance of trust over mistrust, of autonomy over shame and doubt.

Following tradition, Julian analyzes sin as a disordering of two parts of human nature: an essential/inward/higher/godly nature which is superior to and ought to govern the sensual/outward/lower/animal nature.[50] Implicitly drawing on Romans 7, she insists that sin does not occur in the higher nature, but rather is a defect of the lower nature in not conforming to the higher.[51] Unruly desires and sinful inclinations are rooted in our sensuality.[52] Nevertheless, God regards both parts of human nature as good, and willed from eternity that they should be created and joined to one another. The soul's higher essential nature, both Christ's and ours, were created simultaneously and immediately united to God and hence to God the Son. But sensuality was joined to God the Son at His Incarnation,[53] so that God Himself is the means whereby our two natures are inseparably united.[54] The Divinely purposed conformity of the lower to the higher nature occurs first in the person of Christ; their realignment in us, perfected in heaven, is His saving work.[55]

Julian's picture is distinctive because of her contention that psychological bad government results, not from rebellion, which would make the sinner guilty, but from incompetence, which threatens autonomy and produces shame. This diagnosis is already implicit in the Parable of the Lord and the Servant, which Julian received after persistent inquiries into the origin and purpose of pain and sin:

> "...I saw physically before me two people, a lord and his servant. And God showed me its spiritual meaning. The lord is sitting down quietly, relaxed and peaceful: the servant is standing by his lord, humble and ready to do his bidding. And then I saw the lord look at his servant with rare love and tenderness, and quietly send him to a certain place to fulfil his purpose. Not only does that servant go, but he starts off at once, running with all speed, in his love to do what his master wanted. And without warning he falls head-long into a deep ditch, and injures himself very badly. And though he groans and cries and struggles, he is quite unable to get up or to help himself in any way. To crown all, he could get no relief of any sort: he could not even turn his head to look at the lord who loved him, and who was so close to him. The sight of him would have been of real comfort, but he was temporarily so weak and bemused that he gave vent to his feelings as he suffered his pains."[56]

The fall is sin and is incurred in the course of trying to obey God's will. It is a result of our "blindness,"[57] "weakness,"[58] and "ineffectiveness."[59] When we sin, we are like two-year olds who fail the competence-test in toilet training. Sins are "foul, black, shameful,"[60] "vile"[61] deeds, which leave us "befouled"[62] and "really unclean."[63] "Our heavenly Mother Jesus" wants us to run to Him and cry

> "with the humility of a child, 'Kind, thoughtful, dearest Mother, do be sorry for me. I have got myself into a filthy mess, and am not a bit like you. I cannot begin to put it right without your special and willing help."[64]

We need to be "purged"[65] or "cleansed"[66] to arrive at a sinless state, "clean,"[67] "pure,"[68] and "holy."[69] In other words, "Mommy, please change my diaper!"

*(4.4.) Love in Place of Blame*: Human beings respond to sin three ways. We feel *grief*[70] at the pain it causes[71]; *shame* because it prevents us from doing what we, in our essential nature, want[72]; and *fear* that God will be angry with us, blame us, punish if He does not forgive us.[73] Holy Mother Church encourages the last, and it would be appropriate if sin were a matter of the creature's autonomous (and hence guilty) rebellion.

Yet, Julian reports, she *saw* something different. God's love for us is eternal and entirely undisturbed by our sin.[74] God judges us according to our essential nature, and His first verdict was to join human nature to Himself.[75] Further, as much as she looked, Julian found no anger in God[76]: for anger is inconsistent with peace and contrary to "the integrity of His love," "to the nature of his power, wisdom, and goodness."[77] As angerless, God cannot strictly speaking forgive us, if 'forgiveness' signifies the removal of anger[78]; if it means that sin is not held against us, our forgiveness is guaranteed.[79] Instead of blaming us,[80] God "overlooks"[81] and "excuses"[82] our sin and "never faults those who are going to praise Him forever."[83] He regards our incompetence with sympathy and pity.[84] Julian is convinced that the worst punishment the elect will ever have to suffer is enduring our weakened condition and the struggles between our higher and lower natures, during our lives in this world.[85]

*(4.5) Sanctification as Development*: God gauges His expectations to our condition, as children[86] whom it will take the whole of this passing life to rear up.[87] Our developmental goal is to become

persons who can enjoy God's astonishing love for us; our developmental agenda in this world is to learn to love God and trust Him humbly and wholeheartedly.[88] The first step is to appreciate the ontological incommensuration between God and creatures: "...to realize the littleness of creation and to see it for the nothing that it is."[89] If theophany convinced Mary,[90] our humility grows when we meet awareness of our incompetence with hatred of whatever makes us sin, and the choice to trust God's love instead of accusing Him for our pains.[91] For Julian, the contrast between Divine and human reactions to sin estimate the wideness of God's love: awareness of sin moves us to fear of God's anger and repentance in hope of forgiveness, all which yields to surprise at His "friendly welcome"[92] and the recognition that our sin "has made no difference at all to his love."[93] Moreover, this lesson repeats; it spirals and deepens, so that the more the soul sees of Divine courtesy and love, the more it hates sin and the greater its sense of shame; the humbler it becomes, the broader its appreciation of Divine love.[94]

*(4.6) The Motherhood of Jesus*: Childhood growth and development needs a mother's tender loving care. According to Julian, Jesus Christ is the paradigm-case Mother:

> "A mother's is the most intimate, willing, and dependable of all services, because it is the truest of all. None has been able properly to fulfil it but Christ."[95]

In His divine nature, Mother Jesus *creates* us and joins us inseparably to the Godhead forever; God the Son is Mother of our sensual nature, by taking it on Himself in the Incarnation.[96] Mother Jesus *"carries us within himself in love."*[97] Julian was allowed mystically to enter the wound in His side into a place "large enough for all saved mankind to rest in peace and love,"[98] like baby kangaroos in their mother's pouch. Mother Jesus *bears* us with the labor pangs of His suffering and death on the cross.[99] Yet, we are never more than semi-differentiated from Mother Jesus: "our Saviour himself is our Mother for we are ever *being born* of him, and shall never be delivered!"[100] If only we could see this truth, we should be as satisfied and content as the three to six month old infant, enfolded in its mother's arms and gazing into her face.[101] Where earthly mothers feed with their own milk, Mother Jesus *feeds* us with Himself, and leads us to His breast through His open side.[102] Mother Jesus "functions as a kindly nurse who has no other business than to care for the well-being of her charge,"[103] to rear us up in those virtues which will enable us to enjoy Him forever.[104] Mother Jesus *guides* us by His laws,[105] and sometimes *punishes to correct* faults.[106] Like any mother, Jesus sometimes allows His children to learn the hard way, but never allows the situation to become dangerous or life-threatening for them.[107] When we fall, it is the gracious touch of Mother Jesus that enables us to get up and try again.[108] Whenever we are frightened, whether by suffering or our own disobedience and failures, Mother Jesus wants us to run to Him at once and cling to Him forever.[109] Thus, Julian declares,

> "...Jesus Christ who sets good against evil is our real Mother. We owe our being to Him—and this is the essence of motherhood!—and all the delightful, loving protection which ever follows."[110] "Jesus is the true Mother of our nature, for he made us. He is our Mother, too, by grace, because he took our created nature upon himself."[111]

And she invites us to find blessed assurance in those bonds of motherly love which sin and death cannot break.[112]

*(4.7) Honor Cancels Shame*: According to Julian, God will finally solve the problem of sin, not by a debt-moratorium lifting the burden of guilt, but by Divine courtesy canceling shame. Strictly, "courtesy" signifies an elaborate etiquette governing royal courts and conventionally defining behaviors as symbolic of worth and valor. Julian retains the heraldic imagery of the Parable of the Lord and the Servant, but interprets it kenotically, reversing lordly and servant roles. She envisions God as a great king who pays His creatures the unsurpassable honor of genuine and spontaneous, intimate and loving friendship.[113] Not at all condescending,[114] Our Lord is so "utterly kind and unassuming"[115] that He does not hesitate to become human in order to serve us.[116] The passion of Christ is a deed of knightly valor, which Lord Jesus gladly undertook to honor and please His Lady, the soul. Julian reports on her vision of the crucifixion that

> "...our good Lord Jesus Christ said, 'Are you well satisfied with my suffering for you?' 'Yes, thank you, good Lord,' I replied. 'Yes, good Lord, bless you.' And the kind Lord Jesus said, 'If you are satisfied, I am satisfied too. It gives me great happiness and joy and, indeed, eternal delight ever to have suffered for you. If I could possibly have suffered more, I would have done so.'"[117]

Calculating the magnitude of the deed, Julian reckons that the hypostatic union between Divine and human natures strengthened the manhood of Christ to suffer more than the whole human race could suffer.[118] In comparison with other feats possible for Him (such as the creation of countless worlds), Julian estimates His "willingness to die times without number" and yet "count it as nothing for the love of us"[119] "the greatest gesture our Lord God could make to the soul of man."[120] Lord Jesus Christ, our knight in shining armor, will present elect souls to the Father in worship, whereupon the Father will gratefully receive them and grant them to the Son[121] as His happy reward.[122]

During this passing life, God shows His royal friendship for us, by the great courtesy with which He corrects us: "he holds on to us so tenderly when we are in sin" and exposes our "foul" condition "by the gentle light of mercy and grace," to protect us from despair.[123] He greets our repentance with "friendly welcome" as to loved ones released from prison.[124] Our entrance into heaven will not begin with court flattery and thanksgiving from servants to the Lord; rather God will honor His servants by showing His gratitude to them: "Thank you for all your suffering, the suffering of your youth!"[125] Julian observes, not even the whole history of human suffering could have merited such heavenly gratitude; moreover, it will be public, and the pleasure of it will last eternally. Further, not only will the wounds of sin finally heal into honorable battle scars, but also God will compensate us for suffering through them with a "great, glorious, and honorable reward."[126] "So shall shame be turned to greater honour and joy."[127]

## V. Conclusion

I want now to draw the threads of the above discussion together, to sketch a Christian account of sin, which I find preferable to its moralistic competitors and worthy of further development.

Theologically, sin is an impropriety in the relation between God and created persons. My three exhibits—from Rudolf Otto, Mary Douglas, and Julian of Norwich—suggest a two-tiered understanding, where sin is to be identified, at both levels, with uncleanness rooted in incompetence, and seen as a problem for Divine-human relations to which Divine love is an indispensable solution.

*Fundamentally*, sin is uncleanness arising from the incommensuration of Divine and created natures, in the incapacity of any finite
being to do or to be anything, naturally or intrinsically, worthy of
God. The latter claim divides into two: that finite creatures are not
naturally or intrinsically valuable enough either to command God's
love or to be or do anything that could render Him fitting honor.
Developing the first point, the great Franciscan theologians, Scotus
and Ockham, measure the gap between finite and infinite by their
intuition that if it is rational to love valuable things in proportion
to their intrinsic worth, yet it is not necessarily irrational not to love
finite goods even a little bit, not always foolish to love the lesser more
than the greater.[128] As for the second claim, to be natural signs of
value, by nature the currency of honor, things have to be sufficiently
valuable in themselves. Cardboard crowns and plastic rings are not
naturally suited to honor kings, but rather gold and diamonds.

This ontological incommensuration of natures is a metaphysically
necessary consequence of what God and creatures are, not the
outcome of the free and contingent exercise of anyone's agency,
created or Divine. It follows that the disproportion between finite
and infinite can never change: there neither is, was, nor could be
a time, whether in the mythological past or the eschatological future,
in which God and creatures existed and were of metaphysically
comparable size. Likewise, if sin is fundamentally a consequence of
what God and creatures *are*, and the normative priority lies with God,
then the logically appropriate feeling response for creatures is not
guilt (which befits a rebellious use of free agency) but a sense of taint
and shame.

Immutable as the ontological incommensuration itself is, the
resultant *formal* obstacles to relationship can be easily overcome by
Divine fiat: just as governments confer value on relatively worthless
paper through legislation stipulating a value-equivalence to silver and
gold; so God, the creator and governor of the universe, can simply
count finite creatures as valuable by loving them, declare *ex officio*
certain conditions and deeds of creatures to be honorific of Him. The
result is to create *at the second level a "stipulative" or "statutory"
contrast* among created beings and doings between what is sinful
and what is worthy and acceptable and righteous in God's sight.

Specific items—the sorts and conditions of ritual uncleanness,
morally wrong actions and moral vices, thoughts, emotions, and
unconsciously acquired habits—enter the Biblical catalog of sins at

the second, stipulative or statutory level. If some second-level sins are within our power to do or withhold in the sense normally required for moral responsibility, others just happen to us (e.g., states of ritual uncleanness) and still others, while caused by our substance, lie outside the conscious control of mature agency (e.g., neurotic childhood adaptations). Since, from a Biblical point of view, the *content* of Divine stipulations is summarized in the First and Second Great Commandments (to love God with one's whole self, and to love one's neighbor as oneself), human agency is once again reduced to a posture before God of incompetence and shame! Some (e.g., Aquinas and Julian of Norwich) diagnose our difficulty as the incapacity of the higher, intellectual or spiritual nature to subordinate the lower, sensual nature. Others (e.g., Reinhold Niebuhr and Basil Mitchell; cf. St. Anselm on post-lapsarian condition of rational creatures) locate it in a dominant psycho-biological drive toward self-centeredness.

At the secondary content level, as much as the foundational formal level, gratuitous Divine Love is the solution to created incompetence, uncleanness, and shame. For Divine Love guarantees the being and well-being of each created person. And Divine pedagogy trains the soul, guiding its unlearning of ego-centricity, teaching it new skills, making trust and self-giving love possible. The soteriological syllabus spirals through stages in which God creates structures to house the relationship until the creature believes enough in Divine Love to do without such definitive structures. The ultimate cure for shame is not the achievement of natural competence (although we grow towards it in this passing life, and its fulfillment is promised in the eschatological future), because even at our created best, our finitude would leave us, naturally and intrinsically, unworthy to appear in the presence of God. Rather the Love of the Infinite Creator, identifying with His creature in the Incarnation, serving His creature in His passion, showing eternal gratitude to His creature for the earthly service of a created life—God Himself many ways honoring His creature, finally overcomes our shame!

### Notes

1. *The Nature of Necessity*, Oxford at the Clarendon Press, 1974, ch. IX, pp. 164-93. John Hick, writing as a theologian and proceeding historically from Augustine, does talk about **sin**. Cf. *Evil and the God of Love*, Harper and Row, 1966, 1978, pp. 64-69, 87-89.

2. Cf. my "Problems of Evil: More Advice to Christian Philosophers," *Faith and Philosophy* 5 (1988), pp. 121-43; esp. pp. 127-135.

3. In the lead paper of a recent symposium, Basil Mitchell remarks: "The word 'sin' is unlikely to be found in the index of a book on moral philosophy. It belongs to the vocabulary of theology. But the serious student of both subjects is bound to wonder how the concept of sin is to be related to the topics that interest moral philosophers. The problem is complicated by the evident fact that 'sin' is what W. B. Gallie has called an 'essentially contested concept' and that unanimity is as rare among moral philosophers as it is among theologians. It is not a matter, therefore, of applying an agreed philosophical method to a clearly defined theological concept, but of looking for a way of thinking about sin which is theologically defensible and which can approve itself to a reasonably sympathetic moral philosopher." ("How is the Concept of Sin related to the Concept of Moral Wrongdoing?" *Religious Studies* 20, pp. 165-73; quoted passage on p. 165.)

4. Thus, Mitchell (*op.cit.*, p. 165) and co-symposiast David G. Attfield ("The Morality of Sins," *Religious Studies* 20, p. 228) agree that 'sin' connotes a reference to Divine disapproval. By contrast, Robert Merrihew Adams, who does not in general follow the strategy I am sketching, offers the term 'sin' to secular as well as religious moralists ("Involuntary Sins," *Philosophical Review* XCIV (1985), 3-31).

5. Cf. Mitchell, "How is the Concept of Sin related to the Concept of Moral Wrongdoing?" *Religious Studies* 20, pp. 165-68.

6. The rabbis spoke of the evil *yezer* or evil heart (cf. 2 Esdras 3:20-26). Reinhold Niebuhr speaks more concretely of an innate anxiety over finitude which leads to individual and collective self-deception and prideful self-assertion at the expense of others (*The Nature and Destiny of Man*, Charles Scribners' Sons, 1941, chapter vi, pp. 164-69; chapter vii, pp. 179-88; chapter viii, pp. 209-210; chapter ix, pp. 247, 249. Basil Mitchell remarks on an insidious self-centeredness that leads to self-deception ("How is the Concept of Sin related to the Concept of Moral Wrongdoing?" *Religious Studies* 20, pp. 168-67).

7. As Mitchell notes ("How is the Concept of Sin related to the Concept of Moral Wrongdoing?" *loc.cit.*, p. 165: "It is...the definitive stage in the development of ethical monotheism when men came to see that it was *unrighteousness* rather than *ritual uncleanness* that incurred the wrath of God."

8. David G. Attfield measures the category of "inward thoughts and emotions," failures to exemplify ideals, collective or public sins, and cultic acts, against Tennant's criterion that "sin must be a violation of a moral law" and excludes those that are not within our direct voluntary control ("The Morality of Sins," *Religious Studies* 20, pp. 227-32).

9. Note that those who, like Reinhold Niebuhr, locate the root of sin in a built-in self-centeredness arising from anxiety over finitude, still take an anthropocentric approach to sin. For this diagnosis of the human condition is one shared by atheistic and theistic existentialists alike. Likewise, those who would characterize sin as sickness or defection from

a norm naturalistically conceived. For the diagnosis is arrived at on religion-neutral territory; the reference to God is still secondary in the order of explanation.

10. Viz., "Problems of Evil: More Advice to Christian Philosophers," *Faith and Philosophy* Vol. 5, No. 2 (1988), pp. 121-43; and "Theodicy without Blame," *Philosophical Topics* Vol. XVI (1988), pp. 215-245.

11. Cf. my "Theodicy without Blame," *Philosophical Topics* (Fall 1988), sec. 5.3, pp. 230-33. Mitchell seems to agree, when he distinguishes "what other people have a right to blame us for" from "what we should be ready to confess as a sin to God" as follows: "I am answerable to other men, that is to say morally responsible for, my failure to fulfil my duties and obligations towards them, but I am answerable to God for my failure to love my neighbor as myself." ("How is the Concept of Sin related to the Concept of Moral Wrongdoing?" loc.cit., pp. 169.)

12. "Theodicy without Blame," sec. 5, passim.

13. *Idea of the Holy*, Oxford University Press: New York, 1958, ch. III, pp. 8-11. I am particularly indebted in this section to Nelson Pike, who used regularly to begin his courses on the nature and attributes of God with a unit on Otto. For years, I have followed Pike's practice (as well as many interpretive details) in my own teaching.

14. *The Idea of the Holy*, ch. VII, pp. 41-49.

15. *The Idea of the Holy*, ch. III, pp. 8-11.

16. *The Idea of the Holy*, ch. XIV, pp. 112-116; ch. XVII, pp. 136-42.

17. *The Idea of the Holy*, ch. IV, pp. 13-17.

18. *The Idea of the Holy*, ch. III, pp. 8-11, 20-21.

19. *The Idea of the Holy*, ch. IV, pp. 23-24.

20. *The Idea of the Holy*, ch. V, pp. 25-26, 29; Appendix I, pp. 179-86.

21. *The Idea of the Holy*, ch. VI, pp. 31-32.

22. *The Idea of the Holy*, ch. VIII, pp. 50-57.

23. *The Idea of the Holy*, ch. VIII, pp. 50-59.

24. Commenting on the difference between moral devaluation and that involved in (A2) and (C1), Otto writes, "Mere morality is not the soil from which grows either the need of 'redemption' and deliverance or the need for that other unique good which is likewise altogether and specifically numinous in character, 'covering', and 'atonement'. There would perhaps be less disputing as to the warrant and value of these later in Christian doctrine *if dogmatic theology itself had not transferred them from their mystical sphere into that of rational ethics and attenuated them into moral concepts.*" (*The Idea of the Holy*, ch. VIII, p. 53) Again, "'Atonement'...is a 'sheltering' or 'covering', but a profound form of it...Mere awe, mere need for shelter from the *tremendum*, has been elevated to the feeling that man in his 'profaneness' is not *worthy* to stand in the presence of the holy one, and that his own entire personal unworthiness might defile even the holy itself..." Cf. *ibid.*, pp. 55-56.

25. Mary Douglas, *Purity and Danger: An analysis of concepts of pollution and taboo.* Routledge & Kegan Paul: London, 1966, Introduction, p. 2; ch. 2, pp. 35-36; ch. 10, pp. 160-61.

26. *Purity and Danger*, ch. 3, pp. 49-50; ch. 6, pp. 94-113.

27. *Purity and Danger*, ch. 1, pp. 2-3; ch. 2, p. 36.
28. *Purity and Danger*, ch. 6, pp. 109-13; ch. 10, pp. 160-79.
29. *Purity and Danger*, ch. 6, pp. 95-98.
30. *Purity and Danger*, ch. 3, pp. 49-57.
31. *Purity and Danger*, ch. 3, pp. 49-51.
32. Likewise for rules about sexuality (Lev. 18:6-20): "...Holiness means keeping distinct the categories of creation. It therefore involves correct definition, discrimination, and order. Under this head all the rules of sexual morality exemplify the holy. Incest and adultery (Lev. xviii, 6-20) are against holiness, in the simple sense of right order. Morality does not conflict with holiness, but holiness is more a matter of separating that which should be separated than of protecting the rights of husbands and brothers." (Cf. *Purity and Danger*, ch. 3, p. 53.)
33. *Purity and Danger*, ch. 3, pp. 51-2.
34. *Purity and Danger*, ch. 3, p. 53.
35. *Purity and Danger*, ch. 7, pp. 114-28.
36. For a discussion of this legislation, see Jacob Milgrom, *Cult and Conscience: The Asham and the Priestly Doctrine of Repentance*, E.J.Brill: Leiden, 1976.
37. Cf. my paper "The Metaphysics of the Incarnation in Some Fourteenth Century Franciscans," in *Essays Honoring Allan B. Wolter*. Edited by William A. Frank and Girard J. Etzkorn. The Franciscan Institute, St. Bonaventure University: St. Bonaventure, N.Y. 1985, pp. 21-57.
38. *Revelations of Divine Love*, translated by Clifton Wolters, Penguin Books, 1966, ch. 54, p. 157. (Hereafter *RDL* followed by chapter number, period, then page number: e.g., *RDL* 54.157.) Cf. *RDL* 9.75.
39. *RDL* 81.206.
40. *RDL* 67.183.
41. *RDL* 1.63.
42. *RDL* 56.162.
43. *RDL* 78.201.
44. *RDL* 53.157.
45. *RDL* 54.158.
46. *RDL* 5.67-68; cf. *RDL* 5.69.
47. *RDL* 57.164.
48. *RDL* 56.160.
49. *RDL* 56.161.
50. *RDL* 19.93; cf. *RDL* 37.118, 57.163.
51. *RDL* 51.144; 57.163.
52. *RDL* 37.118.
53. *RDL* 57.163; 158.166.
54. *RDL* 56.161.
55. *RDL* 56.161.
56. *RDL* 51.141.
57. *RDL* 11.80-81; 64.178, 66.181-82; 72.190.
58. *RDL* 51.144, 64.178, 66.181-82, 74.194.
59. *RDL* 51.144, 62.174.
60. *RDL* 10.78, 40.121.

61. *RDL* 40.122, 78.201.
62. *RDL* 39.120.
63. *RDL* 63.175.
64. *RDL* 61.172-73.
65. *RDL* 27.104.
66. *RDL* 27.104, 39.120.
67. *RDL* 12.82-83, 27.103, 28.105, 40.123.
68. *RDL* 20.94.
69. *RDL* 28.105.
70. *RDL* 13.83.
71. *RDL* 27.104.
72. *RDL* 13.83, 29.120, 40.122, 66.181.
73. *RDL* 45.131, 46.133-34.
74. *RDL* 53.155, 82.207.
75. *RDL* 45.131.
76. *RDL* 13.84, 45.131, 46.133, 49.137-38.
77. *RDL* 48.136, 46.133.
78. *RDL* 49.137.
79. *RDL* 41.121.
80. *RDL* 27.104, 39.120, 45.131.
81. *RDL* 28.105.
82. *RDL* 52.154.
83. *RDL* 53.155.
84. *RDL* 28.105, 51.144-45, 82.207.
85. *RDL* 39.120, 40.122, 63.175, 77.199.
86. *RDL* 28.105, 63.176.
87. *RDL* 52.153, 56.161, 58.165, 82.207.
88. *RDL* 61.173; cf. 7.72-73, 10.79, 52.151-52.
89. *RDL* 5.68.
90. *RDL* 7.71; cf. Otto's account in section (2.2) above.
91. *RDL* 36.117, 52.153, 79.202, 81.206.
92. *RDL* 40.121-22; cf. 38.118-19, 39.120.
93. *RDL* 61.172.
94. *RDL* 40.122.
95. *RDL* 60.169,170.
96. *RDL* 58.165.
97. *RDL* 60.169; cf. 57.163.
98. *RDL* 25.100
99. *RDL* 60.169-70.
100. *RDL* 57.164.
101. *RDL* 47.134-35; 54.158; 72.191.
102. *RDL* 60.170.
103. *RDL* 61.173.
104. *RDL* 58.166-67.
105. *RDL* 55.158.
106. *RDL* 61.171-72.
107. *RDL* 61.172.
108. *RDL* 52.153.

109. *RDL* 61.172.
110. *RDL* 59.168.
111. *RDL* 59.168.
112. *RDL* 78.201.
113. *RDL* 5.67, 7.72.
114. *RDL* 7.72.
115. *RDL* 10.79.
116. *RDL* 6.70; 7.72-73.
117. *RDL* 22.96.
118. *RDL* 20.94.
119. *RDL* 22.96-97.
120. *RDL* 22.97.
121. *RDL* 23.98-99.
122. *RDL* 23.98-99.
123. *RDL* 40.121.
124. *RDL* 40.121.
125. *RDL* 14.86.
126. *RDL* 14.85, 39.120-21.
127. *RDL* 39.121.
128. Cf. my "The Structure of Ockham's Moral Theory," *Franciscan Studies* 46 (1986), pp. 1-35; esp. pp. 5-6, 18-23.

Philosophical Perspectives, 5, Philosophy of Religion, 1991

# THE INDUCTIVE ARGUMENT FROM EVIL AND THE HUMAN COGNITIVE CONDITION

William P. Alston
Syracuse University

i

The recent outpouring of literature on the problem of evil has materially advanced the subject in several ways. In particular, a clear distinction has been made between the "logical" *argument against the existence of God* ("atheological argument") from evil, which attempts to show that evil is logically incompatible with the existence of God, and the "inductive" ("empirical", "probabilistic") argument, which contents itself with the claim that evil constitutes (sufficient) empirical evidence against the existence of God. It is now acknowledged on (almost) all sides that the logical argument is bankrupt, but the inductive argument is still very much alive and kicking.

In this paper I will be concerned with the inductive argument. More specifically, I shall be contributing to a certain criticism of that argument, one based on a low estimate of human cognitive capacities in a certain application. To indicate the point at which this criticism engages the argument, I shall use one of the most careful and perspicuous formulations of the argument in a recent essay by William Rowe (1979).

1. There exist instances of intense suffering which an omnipotent, omniscient being could have prevented without thereby losing some greater good or permitting some evil equally bad or worse.
2. An omniscient, wholly good being would prevent the

occurrence of any intense suffering it could, unless it could not do so without thereby losing some greater good or permitting some evil equally bad or worse.
3. There does not exist an omnipotent, omniscient, wholly good being (p. 336).

Let's use the term 'gratuitous suffering' for any case of intense suffering, E, that satisfies premise 1, that is, which is such that an omnipotent, omniscient being could have prevented it without thereby losing some greater good or permitting some evil equally bad or worse.[1] 2 takes what we might call the "content" of 1 (losing a greater good or permitting some worse or equally bad evil) as a necessary condition for God to have a sufficient reason for permitting E. E's being gratuitous, then, is the contradictory of the possibility of God's having a sufficient reason to permit it, and equivalent to the impossibility of God's having a sufficient reason for permitting it. I will oscillate freely between speaking of a particular case of suffering, E, being gratuitous, and speaking of the impossibility of God's having a sufficient reason for permitting E. I shall call a proponent of an inductive argument from evil the "critic".

The criticism I shall be supporting attacks the claim that we are rationally justified in accepting 1, and it does so on the grounds that our epistemic situation is such that we are unable to make a sufficiently well grounded determination that 1 is the case. I will call this, faute de mieux, the *agnostic* thesis, or simply *agnosticism*. The criticism claims that the magnitude or complexity of the question is such that our powers, access to data, and so on are radically insufficient to provide sufficient warrant for accepting 1. And if that is so, the inductive argument collapses.[2]

How might one be justified in accepting 1? The obvious way to support an existential statement is to establish one or more instantiations and then use existential generalization. This is Rowe's tack, and I don't see any real alternative. Thus Rowe considers one or another case of suffering and argues, in the case of each, that it instantiates 1. I will follow him in this approach. Thus to argue that we cannot be justified in asserting 1, I shall argue that we cannot be justified in asserting any of its instantiations, each of which is of the form

1A. E is such that an omnipotent, omniscient being could have prevented it without thereby losing some greater good or permitting some evil equally bad or worse.

In the sequel when I speak of being or not being justified in accepting 1, it must be remembered that this is taken to hang on whether one is, or can be justified, in accepting propositions of the form 1A.

Does the agnostic thesis, in my version, also claim that we are unable to justifiably assert the denial of 1, as we would have to do to develop a successful theodicy? It is no part of my task in this paper to address this question, but I will make a couple of remarks. First, my position is that we could justifiably believe, or even know, the denial of 1, and that in one of two ways. We might have sufficient grounds for believing in the existence of God—whether from arguments of natural theology, religious experience or whatever—including sufficient grounds for taking God to be omnipotent, omniscient, and perfectly good, and that could put us in a position to warrantedly deny 1. Or God might reveal to us that 1 is false, and we might be justified in accepting the message as coming from God. Indeed, revelation might not only provide justification for denying 1, but also justification for beliefs about what God's reasons are for permitting this or that case of suffering or type of suffering, thereby putting us in a position to construct a theodicy of a rather ambitious sort.[3] If, however, we leave aside the putative sources just mentioned and restrict ourselves to what we can do by way of tracing out the interconnections of goods and evils in the world by the use of our natural powers, what are we to say? Well, the matter is a bit complicated. Note that 1 is an existential statement, which says that there are instances of intense suffering of which a certain negative claim is true. To deny 1 would be to say that this negative claim is false for *every* case of intense suffering. And even if we could establish the non-gratuitousness of certain cases by tracing out interconnections—and I don't *see* that this is necessarily beyond our powers—that would not be sufficient to yield the denial of 1. To sum up: I think that examining the interconnections of good and evil in the world by our natural powers cannot suffice to establish either 1 or its negation.[4] For particular cases of suffering we might conceivably be able to establish non-gratuitousness in this way, but what I shall argue in this paper is that no one can justifiably assert gratuitousness for any case.

## ii

Before setting out the agnostic thesis in more detail and adding my bit to the case for it, let me make some further comments about the argument against which the criticism is directed and variants thereof.

A. The argument is stated in terms of intense suffering, but it could just as well have appealed to anything else that can plausibly be claimed to be undesirable in itself. Rowe focuses on intense suffering because he thinks that it presents the greatest difficulty for anyone who tries to deny a premise like 1. I shall follow him in this, though for concision I shall often simply say 'suffering' with the 'intense' tacitly understood.

B. Rowe doesn't claim that all suffering is gratuitous, but only that some is. He takes it that even one case of gratuitous suffering is incompatible with theism. I go along with this assumption (though in E, I question whether Rowe has succeeded in specifying necessary and sufficient conditions for gratuitousness, and for God's having a sufficient reason for permitting suffering). As already noted, Rowe does not argue for 1 by staying on its level of unspecificity; rather he takes particular examples of suffering and argues in the case of each that it is gratuitous; from there it is a short step of existential generalization to 1. In (1979) and subsequent papers Rowe focuses on the case of a fawn trapped in a forest fire and undergoing several days of terrible agony before dying ( hereinafter 'Bambi'). In (1988) he adds to this a (real life) case introduced by Bruce Russell (1989), a case of the rape, beating, and murder by strangulation of a 5-year-old girl ('Sue') by her mother's boyfriend. Since I am specifically interested in criticizing Rowe's argument I will argue that we are not justified, and cannot be justified, in judging these evils to be gratuitous. It will turn out that some of my discussion pertains not to Rowe's cases but to others. I will signal the reader as to how to understand the dummy designator, 'E', in each part of the paper.

C. The argument deals with a classical conception of God as omnipotent, omniscient and perfectly good; it is designed to yield the conclusion that no being with those characteristics exists. I shall also be thinking of the matter in this way. When I use 'God' it will be to refer to a being with these characteristics.

D. There are obvious advantages to thinking of the inductive argument from evil as directed against the belief in the existence of God as God is thought of in some full blown theistic religion, rather than as directed against what we may call "generic theism". The main advantage is that the total system of beliefs in a religion gives us much more to go on in considering what reasons God might possibly have for permitting E. In other terms, it provides much more of a basis for distinguishing between plausible and implausible theodicies. I shall construe the argument as directed against the traditional Christian belief in God.[5] I choose Christianity for this purpose because (a) I am more familiar with it than other alternatives, as most of my readers will be, and (b) most of the philosophical discussions of the problem of evil, both historically and currently, have grown out of Christian thought.

E. Rowe does not claim to know or to be able to prove that 1 is true. With respect to his fawn example he acknowledges that "Perhaps, for all we know, there is some familiar good outweighing the fawn's suffering to which that suffering is connected in a way we do not see" (1979, p. 337). He only claims that we have sufficient rational grounds for believing that the fawn's suffering is gratuitous, and still stronger rational grounds for holding that at least some of the many cases of suffering that, so far as we can see, instantiate 1 actually do so.[6] Not all of Rowe's fellow atheologians are so modest, but I will concentrate my fire on his weaker and less vulnerable version.

F. A final comment will occupy us longer. Rowe obviously supposes, as premise 2 makes explicit, that cases of "gratuitous" evil count decisively against the existence of God. That is, he takes it that an omnipotent, omniscient, and perfectly good God would not permit any gratuitous evil; perhaps he regards this as conceptually or metaphysically necessary. Thus he holds that God could have no other reason for permitting suffering except that preventing it would involve losing some greater good or permitting some equally bad or worse evil.[7] But this is highly controversial. It looks as if there are possible divine reasons for permitting evil that would be ruled out by (2). (i) Suppose that God could bring about a greater good only by permitting any one of several equally bad cases of suffering. Then no one is such that by preventing it He would lose that greater good. And if we stipulate that God has a free choice as to whether to permit any of these disjuncts, it is not the case that to prevent it would be to permit something equally bad or worse; that might or might not ensue, depending on God's choice. But if we are to allow that being necessary for a greater good can justify permission of evil, it looks as if we will have to allow this case as well. (ii) More importantly, human free will complicates God's strategies for carrying out His purposes. As we will be noting later in the paper, if God has a policy of respecting human free will, He cannot guarantee human responses to His initiatives where those responses would be freely made if at all.[8] Hence if God visits suffering on us in an attempt to turn us from our sinful ways, and a particular recipient doesn't make the desired response, God could have prevented that suffering without losing any greater good (no such good was forthcoming), even though we might reasonably take God to be justified in permitting the suffering, provided that was His best strategy in the situation, the one most likely to get the desired result. (iii) Look at "general policy" theodicies.[9] Consider the idea that God's general policy of, e.g., usually letting nature take its course and not interfering, even when much suffering will ensue, is justified by the overall benefits of the policy. Now consider a particular case of divine non-intervention to prevent intense suffering. Clearly, God could have intervened in this case without subverting the general policy and losing its benefits. To prevent this particular suffering would not be to lose some greater good or permit something worse or equally bad. And yet it seems that general policy considerations of the sort mentioned could justify God in refraining from intervening in this case. For if it couldn't, it could not justify His non-intervention in any case, and so He would be inhibited from carrying out the general policy.[10]

Since my central aim in this paper is not to refine principles like 2 in microscopic detail, I will take a shortcut in dealing with these difficulties. (i) can be handled by complicating the formula to allow the permission of any member of a disjunction, some member of which is necessary for a greater good. Consider it done. (ii) and (iii) can be accommodated by widening the sphere of goods for which the evil is necessary. For cases of the (ii) sort, take the greater good to be having as great a chance as possible to attain salvation, and let's say that this good is attained whatever the response. As for (iii), we can say that E is permitted in order to realize the good of maintaining a beneficial general policy except where there are overriding reasons to make an exception, and the reasons in this case are not overriding. With these modifications we can take Rowe to have provided a plausible formulation of necessary conditions for divine sufficient reasons for permitting E. But if you don't think I have successfully defended my revision of Rowe, then you may think in terms of an unspecific substitute for 1 like "There are instances of suffering such that there is no sufficient reason for God to allow them". That will still enable me to argue that no one is in a position to justifiably assert that God could have no sufficient reason for allowing E.

### iii

Clearly the case for 1 depends on an inference from "So far as I can tell, p" to "p" or "Probably, p". And, equally clearly, such inferences are sometimes warranted and sometimes not. Having carefully examined my desk I can infer 'Jones' letter is not on my desk' from 'So far as I can tell, Jones' letter is not on my desk'. But being ignorant of quantum mechanics I cannot infer 'This treatise on quantum mechanics is well done' from 'So far as I can tell, this treatise on quantum mechanics is well done'. I shall be contending that our position vis-a-vis 1 is like the latter rather than like the former.

I am by no means the first to suggest that the atheological argument from evil is vitiated by an unwarranted confidence in our ability to determine that God could have no sufficient reason for permitting some of the evils we find in the world. A number of recent writers have developed the theme.[11] I endorse many of the reasons they give for their pessimism. Wykstra points out that our cognitive capacities are much more inferior to God's than is a small child's to his parents; and in the latter case the small child is often unable to understand the parents' reasons for inflicting punishment or for requiring him to perform tasks that are distasteful to him. (88). Ahern points out that our knowledge of the goods and evils in the world (54-5) and of the interconnections between things (57, 72-3) are very limited. Fitzpatrick adduces the deficiencies in our grasp of the divine nature (25-28). This is all well taken and, I believe, does provide support for the agnostic thesis. But then why am I taking pen in hand to add to this ever swelling stream of literature? For several reasons. First, I will not be proceeding on the basis of any general skepticism about our cognitive powers either across the board or generally with respect to God. I will, rather, be focusing on the peculiar difficulties we encounter in attempting to provide adequate support for a certain very ambitious negative existential claim, viz., that there is (can be) no sufficient divine reason for permitting a certain case of suffering, E.[12] I will be appealing to the difficulties of defending a claim of this particular kind, rather than to more generalized human cognitive weaknesses. Second, much of the literature just alluded to has centered around Wykstra's claim that to be justified in asserting 1 it would have to be the case that if 1 were false that would be indicated to one in some way.[13] By contrast I will not be proceeding on the basis of any such unrestrictedly general epistemological principle. Third, I will lay out in much more detail than my predecessors the range of conceivable divine reasons we would have to be able to exclude in order to be justified in asserting 1. Fourth, I can respond to some of the defenses the likes of Rowe have deployed against the agnostic criticism.

## iv

Now, at last, I am ready to turn to my central project of arguing that we cannot be justified in accepting 1A. As already noted, I will be emphasizing the fact that this is a negative existential claim. It will be my contention that to be justified in such a claim one must be justified in excluding all the live possibilities for what the claim denies to exist. What 1A denies is that there is any reason God could have for permitting it. I will argue that we are not, and cannot, be justified in asserting that none of these possibilities are realized. I will draw on various theodicies to compile a (partial) list of the reasons God might conceivably have for permitting E. That will provide me with a partial list of the suggestions we must have sufficient reason to reject in order to rationally accept 1. Note that it is no part of my purpose here to develop or defend a theodicy. I am using theodicies only as a source of *possibilities* for divine reasons for evil, possibilities the realization of which the atheologian will have to show to be highly implausible if his project is to succeed.

Since I am criticizing Rowe's argument I am concerned to argue that we are not justified in asserting 1A for the particular kinds of suffering on which Rowe focuses. And we should not suppose that God would have the same reason for permitting every case of suffering.[14] Hence it is to be expected that the reasons suggested by a given theodicy will be live possibilities for some cases of evil and not others. I am, naturally, most interested in suggestions that constitute live possibilities for divine reasons for permitting Bambi's and Sue's suffering. And many familiar theodicies do not pass this test. (This is, no doubt, why these cases were chosen by Rowe and Russell.) Bambi's suffering, and presumably Sue's as well, could hardly be put down to punishment for sin, and neither case could seriously be supposed to be allowed by God for the sake of character building. Nevertheless, I shall not confine the discussion to live possibilities for these two cases. There are two reasons for this. First, a discussion of other theodicies will help to nail down the general point that we are typically unable to exclude live possibilities for divine reasons in a particular case. Second, these discussions will provide ammunition against atheological arguments based on other kinds of suffering.

Thus I shall first consider theodical suggestions that seem clearly not to apply to Bambi or Sue. Here I shall be thinking instead of an adult sufferer from a painful and lengthy disease (fill in the details as you like) whom I shall call 'Sam'. Having argued that we are not in a position to exclude the possibility that God has reasons of these sorts for permitting Sam's suffering, I shall pass on to other suggestions that do constitute genuine possibilities for Bambi and/or Sue.

## V

I begin with a traditional theme, that human suffering is God's punishment for sin. Though it hardly applies to Bambi or Sue, it may be a live possibility in other cases, and so I will consider it. The punishment motif has tended to drop out of theodicies in our "soft-on-criminals" and "depravity-is-a-disease" climate, but it has bulked large in the Christian tradition.[15] It often draws the criticism that, so far as we can see, degree or extent of suffering is not nicely proportioned to degree of guilt. Are the people of Vietnam, whose country was ravaged by war in this century, markedly more sinful than the people of Switzerland, whose country was not? But, remembering the warnings of the last section, that does not show that this is never God's reason for permitting suffering, and here we are concerned with a particular case, Sam. Let's say that it seems clear, so far as we can tell, that Sam's suffering is not in proportion to his sinfulness. Sam doesn't seem to have been a bad sort at all, and he has suffered horribly. Can we go from that to "Sam's suffering was not a punishment for sin", or even to "It is reasonable to suppose that Sam's suffering was not a punishment for sin". I suggest that we cannot.

First, we are often in a poor position to assess the degree and kind of a certain person's sinfulness, or to compare people in this regard. Since I am thinking of the inductive argument from evil as directed against Christian belief in God, it will be appropriate to understand the punishment-for-sin suggestion in those terms. Two points about sin are particularly relevant here. (1) Inward sins—one's intentions, motives, attitudes—are more serious than failings in outward behavior.[16] (2) The greatest sin is a self-centered refusal or failure to make God the center of one's life. (2) is sharply at variance with standard secular bases for moral judgment and evaluation. Hence the fact that X does not seem, from that standpoint, more wicked than Y, or doesn't seem wicked at all, does nothing to show that God, on a Christian understanding of God, would make the same judgment. Because of (1) overt behavior is not always a good indication of a person's condition, sin-wise. This is not to say that we could not make a sound judgment of a person's inner state if we had a complete record of what is publicly observable concerning the person. Perhaps in some instances we could, and perhaps in others we could not. But in any event, we rarely or never have such a record. Hence, for both these reasons our judgments as to the relation between S's suffering and S's sinfulness are usually of questionable value.

Second, according to Christianity, one's life on earth is only a tiny proportion of one's total life span. This means that, knowing nothing about the immeasurably greater proportion of Sam's life, we are in no position that deny that the suffering qua punishment has not had a reformative effect, even if we can see no such effect in his earthly life.[17]

I might be accused of begging the question by dragging in Christian convictions to support my case. But that would be a misunderstanding. I am not seeking to prove, or give grounds for, theism or Christianity. I am countering a certain argument against Christian theism. I introduce these Christian doctrines only to spell out crucial features of what is being argued against. The Christian understanding of sin, human life, God's purposes, and so on, go into the determination of what the critic must be justified in denying if she is to be justified in the conclusion that Sam's suffering would not have been permitted by God.

**vi**

I have led off my survey of theodical suggestions with the punishment motif, despite the fact that it is highly controversial and the reverse of popular. Nor would I want to put heavy emphasis on it were I constructing a theodicy. I have put my worst foot forward in order to show that even here the critic is in no position to show that Sam's suffering is not permitted by God for this reason. If the critic can't manage even this, he will presumably be much worse off with more plausible suggestions for divine reasons, to some of which I now turn.

One of the most prominent theodical suggestions is that God allows suffering because He is interested in a "vale of soul making". He takes it that by confronting difficulties, hardships, frustrations, perils, and even suffering and only by doing this, we have a chance to develop such qualities of character as patience, courage, and compassion, qualities we would otherwise have no opportunity to develop. This line has been set forth most forcefully in our time by John Hick in *Evil and the God of Love* (revised edition, 1978), a book that has evoked much discussion. To put the point most generally, God's purpose is to make it possible for us to grow into the kind of person that is capable of an eternal life of loving communion with Himself. To be that kind of person one will have to possess traits of character like those just mentioned, traits that one cannot develop without meeting and reacting to difficulties and hardships, including suffering. To show that E would not be permitted by God, the critic has to show that it does not serve the "soul-making" function.

To get to the points I am concerned to make I must first respond to some standard objections to this theodicy. (1) God could surely just create us with the kind of character needed for fellowship with Himself, thereby rendering the hardships and suffering unnecessary. Hick's answer is that what God aims at is not fellowship with a suitably programmed robot, but fellowship with creatures who freely choose to work for what is needed and to take advantage of the opportunity thus engendered. God sees the realization of this aim for some free creatures[18], even at the cost of suffering and hardship for all, as being of much greater value than any alternative, including a world with no free creatures and a world in which the likes of human beings come off the assembly line pre-sanctified. As usual, I am not concerned to defend the claim that this is the way things are, but only to claim that we are in no position to deny that God is correct in this judgment. (For a discussion of difficulties in carrying out comparative evaluation of total universes, see the end of section ix.)

(2) "If God is using suffering to achieve this goal, He is not doing very well. In spite of all the suffering we undergo, most of us don't get very far in developing courage, compassion, etc." There are two answers to this. First, we are in no position to make that last judgment. We don't know nearly enough about the inner springs of peoples' motivation, attitudes, and character, even in this life. And we know nothing about any further development in an after-life. Second, the theism under discussion takes God to respect the free will of human beings. No strategy consistent with that can guarantee that all, or perhaps any, creatures will respond in the way intended. Whether they do is ultimately up to them. Hence we cannot argue from the fact that such tactics often don't succeed to the conclusion that God wouldn't employ them. When dealing with free creatures God must, because of self-imposed limitations, use means that have some considerable likelihood of success, not means that cannot fail. It is amazing that so many critics reject theodicies like Hick's on the grounds of a poor success rate. I don't say that a poor success rate could not, under any circumstances, justify us in denying that God would permit E for the sake of soul making. If we really did know enough to be reasonably sure that the success rate is very poor *and* that other devices open to God would be seen by omniscience to have a significantly greater chance of success, *then* we could conclude that Hick's line does not get at what God is up to. But we are a very long way indeed from being able to justifiably assert this.

We cannot take the kind of reason stressed by Hick to be a live possibility for the Bambi and Sue cases. The former is much more obvious than the latter, but even in the latter case Sue has no chance to respond to the suffering in the desired way, except in an after life, and it strains credulity to suppose that God would subject a 5-year old to *that* for the sake of character building in the life to come. Hence once more, and until further notice, we will stick with Sam.

Let's stipulate that Sam's suffering does not appear, on close examination, to be theistically explainable as aimed by God at "soul-making". He seems already to have more of the qualities of character in question than most of us, or the amount of suffering seems to be too much for the purpose, or to be so great as to overwhelm him and make character development highly unlikely. And so our best judgment is that God wouldn't be permitting his suffering for that reason. But that judgment is made in ignorance of much relevant information. Perhaps a more penetrating picture of Sam's spiritual condition would reveal that he is much more in need of further development than is apparent to us from our usual superficial perspective on such matters. Since we don't see his career after death, we are in a poor position to determine how, over the long run, he reacts to the suffering; perhaps if we had that information we would see that this suffering is very important for his full development. Moreover, we are in a poor position, or no position, to determine what is the most effective strategy for God to use in His pursuit of Sam. We don't know what alternatives are open to God, while respecting Sam's freedom, or what the chances are, on one or another alternative, of inducing the desired responses. We are in a poor position to say that this was too much suffering for the purpose, or to say how much would be just right. And we will continue to be in that position until our access to relevant information is radically improved.

Thus we cannot be justified in holding that Sam's suffering is not permitted by God in order to further His project of soul-making. There is an allied, but significantly different theodical suggestion by Eleonore Stump concerning which I would make the same points. Briefly, and oversimply, Stump's central suggestion is that the function of natural evil in God's scheme is to bring us to salvation, or, as she likes to put it, to contribute to the project of "fixing our wills", which have been damaged by original sin. Natural evil tends to prod us to turn to God, thereby giving Him a chance to fix our wills.

> Natural evil—the pain of disease, the intermittent and unpredictable destruction of natural disasters, the decay of old age, the imminence of death—takes away a person's satisfaction with himself. It tends to humble him, show him his frailty, make him reflect on the transience of temporal goods, and turn his affections towards other-worldly things, away from the things of this world. No amount of moral or natural evil, of course, can *guarantee* that a man will seek God's help. If it could, the willing it produced would not be free. But evil of this sort is the best hope, I think, and maybe the only effective means, for bringing men to such a state (Stump, 1985, p. 409).

Objections will be raised somewhat similar to those that have been made to Hick. A perfectly good God wouldn't have let us get in this situation in the first place. God would employ a more effective technique.[19] There's too much suffering for the purpose. It is not distributed properly. And so on. These will answered in the same way as the analogous objections to Hick. As for Sam, if we cannot see how his suffering was permitted by God for the reason Stump suggests, I will do a rerun of the parallel points concerning Hick's soul making suggestion.

Closely related suggestions have been made by Marilyn McCord Adams in her essay, "Redemptive Suffering: A Christian Solution to the Problem of Evil" (1986). She takes martyrdom as her model for redemptive suffering, though she by no means wishes to limit her discussion to martyrdom strictly so called. "...the redemptive potential of many other cases that, strictly speaking, are not martyrdoms can be seen by extrapolation" (p. 261). In other words her suggestion is that the benefits for the martyr and others that can flow from martyrdom in the strict sense, can also flow from suffering that does not involve undergoing persecution for the faith. Her bold suggestion is that "martyrdom is an expression of God's righteous love toward the onlooker, the persecutor, and even the martyr himself" (257). Here I want to focus on her account of the benefits to the martyr. "...the threat of martyrdom is a time of testing and judgment. It makes urgent the previously abstract dilemma of whether he loves God more than the temporal goods that are being extracted as a price...the martyr will have had to face a deeper truth about himself and his relations to God and temporal goods than ever he could in fair weather...the time of trial is also an opportunity for building a relationship of trust between the martyr and that to which he testifies. Whether because we are fallen or by the nature of the case, trusting relationships have to be built up by a history of interactions. If the martyr's loyalty to God is tested, but after a struggle he holds onto his allegiance to God and God delivers him (in his own time and way), the relationship is strengthened and deepened" (259). Adams is modest in her claims. She does not assert that all cases of suffering are analogous to martyrdom in these respects. "Some are too witless to have relationships that can profit and mature through such tests of loyalty. Some people are killed or severely harmed too quickly for such moral struggles to take place. At other times the victim is an unbeliever who has no explicit relationship with God to wrestle with."[20] However none of these disqualifications apply to her boldest suggestion, that given the Christian doctrine of the suffering of God incarnate on the cross, "temporal suffering itself is a vision into the inner life of God" (264), a theme that she takes from Christian mysticism. That value of suffering, if such it be, can be enjoyed by any sufferer, whatever the circumstances. To be sure, one might not realize at the time that the suffering has that significance. But if one reaches the final term of Christian development, "he might be led to reason that the good aspect of an experience of deep suffering [the aspect just pointed to] is great enough that, from the standpoint of the beatific vision, the victim would not wish the experience away from his life history, but would, on the contrary, count it as an extremely valuable part of his life" (265). It should also be noted that Adams does not suggest that God's reasons for permitting suffering in any particular case are restricted to one of the considerations she has been presenting, or indeed to all of the points she makes.

If we were to try to decide whether Sam's suffering is permitted by God for any of these reasons, we would be in a poor position to make a negative judgment for reasons parallel to those brought out in the discussion of Hick. Given the limits of our access to the secrets of the human heart and the course of the after life, if any, we are, in many instances, in no position to assert with any confidence that this suffering does not have such consequences, and hence that God does not permit it (at least in part) for the sake of just those consequences.

## vii

Thus far I have been restricting myself to conceivable divine reasons for suffering that involve the use of that suffering to bring about good for the sufferer. This is obvious except for the punishment reason. As for that one, this claim is equally obvious if we are thinking of punishment in terms of reformation of the punishee,[21] but what about a "retributive" theory, according to which the rationale of punishment is simply that the sinner *deserves* to suffer for his sin, that justice demands this, or that a proportionate suffering for wickedness is intrinsically good? Well, though one might balk at describing this as a *good* for the sufferer, it remains that such good as is aimed at and effected by the punishment, on this conception, terminates with the sufferer and does not extend to the welfare of others.

Where divine reasons are restricted this narrowly, the critic is operating on the most favorable possible terrain. If he has any hope of making his case it will be here, where the field of possibilities that must be excluded is relatively narrow. What we have seen is that wherever the reasons we have canvassed are live possibilities, even this is too much for his (our) powers. Our ignorance of relevant facts is so extensive, and the deficiencies in our powers of discernment are so fundamental, as to leave us without any sufficient basis for saying, with respect to a particular case of suffering, that God does not permit it for reasons such as these.

To be sure, this is cold comfort for the critic of Rowe's argument since, as noted earlier, the possibilities we have been canvassing do not seem to be live possibilities for Bambi or Sue. The only real chance for an exception is Adams' suggestion that the experience of suffering constitutes a vision of the inner life of God. Since this is not confined to those who identify it as such, it could apply to Sue, and perhaps to Bambi as well, though presumably only Sue would have a chance to recognize it and rejoice in it, retrospectively, in the light of the beatific vision. However, I don't want to insist on this exception. Let us say that a consideration of the theodicies thus far canvassed does nothing to show that we can't be justified in affirming an instantiation of 1 for Bambi or Sue.

Nevertheless, that does *not* show that we can be justified in excluding the possibility that God has no patient-centered reason for permitting Bambi's or Sue's suffering. It doesn't show this because we are not warranted in supposing that the possible reasons we have been extracting from theodicies exhaust the possibilities for patient-centered reasons God might have for permitting Bambi's or Sue's suffering. Perhaps, unbeknownst to us, one or the other of these bits of suffering is necessary, in ways we cannot grasp, for some outweighing good of a sort with which we are familiar, e.g., supreme fulfillment of one's deepest nature. Or perhaps it is necessary for the realization of a good of which we as yet have no conception. And these possibility are by no means remote ones. "There are more things in heaven and earth, Horatio, than are dreamt of in your philosophy." Truer words were never spoken. They point to the fact that our cognitions of the world, obtained by filtering raw data through such conceptual screens as we have available for the nonce, acquaint us with only some indeterminable fraction of what is there to be known. The progress of human knowledge makes this evident. No one explicitly realized the distinction between concrete and abstract entities, the distinction between efficient and final causes, the distinction between knowledge and opinion, until great creative thinkers adumbrated these distinctions and disseminated them to their fellows. The development of physical science has made us aware of a myriad of things hitherto undreamed of, and developed the concepts with which to grasp them—gravitation, electricity, electromagnetic fields, space-time curvature, irrational numbers, and so on. It is an irresistible induction from this that we have not reached the final term of this process, and that more realities, aspects, properties, structures remain to be discerned and conceptualized. And why should values, and the conditions of their realization, be any exception to this generalization? A history of the apprehension of values could undoubtedly be written, parallel to the history just adumbrated, though the archeology would be a more difficult and delicate task.

Moreover, remember that our topic is not the possibilities for future human apprehensions, but rather what an omniscient being can grasp of modes of value and the conditions of their realization. Surely it is eminently possible that there are real possibilities for the latter that exceed anything we can anticipate, or even conceptualize. It would be exceedingly strange if an omniscient being did not immeasurably exceed our grasp of such matters. Thus there is an unquestionably live possibility that God's reasons for allowing human suffering may have to do, in part, with the appropriate connection of those sufferings with goods in ways that have never been dreamed of in our theodicies. Once we bring this into the picture, the critic is seen to be on shaky ground in denying, of Bambi's or Sue's suffering, that God could have any patient-centered reason for permitting it, even if we are unable to suggest what such a reason might be.[22]

This would be an appropriate place to consider Rowe's argument that we can be justified in excluding the possibility that God permits one or another case of suffering in order to obtain goods of which we have no conception. In his latest article on the subject (1988) Rowe claims that the variant of 1 there put forward:

Q. No good state of affairs is such that an omnipotent, omniscient being's obtaining it would morally justify that being in permitting E1 or E2 (p. 120).[23]

can be derived probabilistically from:

P. No good state of affairs we know of is such that an

omnipotent, omniscient being's obtaining it would morally justify that being's permitting E1 or E2 (p. 121).

I have been arguing, and will continue to argue, that Rowe is not justified in asserting P, since he is not justified in supposing that none of the particular goods we have been discussing provide God with sufficient reason for permitting the suffering of Bambi and Sue. But even if Rowe were justified in asserting P, what I have just been contending is that the argument from P to Q does not go through. In defending the argument Rowe says the following.

> My answer is that we are justified in making this inference in the same way we are justified in making the many inferences we constantly make from the known to the unknown. All of us are constantly inferring from the A's we know of to the A's we don't know of. If we observe many A's and all of them are B's we are justified in believing that the A's we haven't observed are also B's. If I encounter a fair number of pit bulls and all of them are vicious, I have reason to believe that all pit bulls are vicious (1988, pp. 123-24).

But it is just not true that Rowe's inference from known goods to all goods is parallel to inductive inferences we "constantly make". Typically when we generalize from observed instances, at least when we are warranted in doing so, we know quite a lot about what makes a sample of things like that a good base for general attributions of the properties in question. We know that temperamental traits like viciousness or affectionateness are often breed-specific in dogs, and so when a number of individuals of a breed are observed to exhibit such a trait it is a good guess that it is characteristic of that breed. If, on the other hand, the characteristic found throughout the sample were a certain precise height or a certain sex, our knowledge indicates that an inference that all members of that breed are of that height or of that sex would be foolhardy indeed. But, as I have been arguing, an inference from known goods lacking J to all goods (including those we have never experienced and even those of which we have no conception) is unlike both the sorts just mentioned in the way they resemble one another, viz., our possession of knowledge indicating which characteristics can be expected to be (fairly) constant in the larger population. We have no background knowledge that tells us the chances of J's being a "goods-specific" characteristic, one that can reasonably be expected to be present in all or most goods if it is found in a considerable sample. Hence we cannot appeal to clearly warranted generalizations in support of this one. Rowe's generalization is more like inferring from the fact that no one has yet produced a physical theory that will unify relativity and quantum mechanics, to the prediction that no one will ever do so, or inferring, in 1850, from the fact no one has yet voyaged to the moon that no one will ever do so. We have no way of drawing boundaries around the total class of goods; we are unable to anticipate what may lie in its so-far-unknown sub-class, just as we are unable to anticipate future scientific developments and future artistic innovations. This is not an area in which induction by simple enumeration yields justified belief.[24]

## viii

It is now time to move beyond the restriction on divine reasons to benefits to the sufferer. The theodical suggestions we will be discussing from here on do not observe this restriction. Since I am moving onto territory less favorable to my opponent, I must give some indication of what might justify dropping the restriction. For my central purposes in this paper I do not need to show that the restriction is unjustified. I take myself to have already shown that the critic is not entitled to his "no sufficient divine reasons" thesis even with the restriction. But I do believe that the restriction is unwarranted, and I want to consider how the land lies with respect to conceivable divine reasons of other sorts. As a prelude to that I will point out the main reasons for and against the restriction to benefits to the sufferer.

On the pro side by far the main consideration is one of justice and fairness. Why should suffering be laid on me for the sake of some good in which I will not participate, or in which my participation is not sufficient to justify my suffering? Wouldn't God be sacrificing me to His own ends and/or to the ends of others if that were His modus operandi, and in that case how could He be considered perfectly good?

> Undeserved suffering which is uncompensated seems clearly unjust; but so does suffering compensated only by benefits to someone other than the sufferer...other things being equal, it seems morally permissible to allow someone to suffer involuntarily only in case doing so is a necessary means or the best possible means in the circumstances to keep the sufferer from incurring even greater harm.[25]

I agree with this to the extent of conceding that a perfectly good God would not wholly sacrifice the welfare of one of His intelligent creatures simply in order to achieve a good for others, or for Himself. This would be incompatible with His concern for the welfare of each of His creatures. Any plan that God would implement will include provision for each of us having a life that is, on balance, a good thing, and one in which the person reaches the point of being able to see that his life as a whole is a good for him. Or at least, where free creaturely responses have a significant bearing on the overall quality of the person's life, any possible divine plan will have to provide for each of us to have the chance (or perhaps many chances) for such an outcome, if our free responses are of the right sort. Nevertheless, this is compatible with God having as part of his reason for permitting a given case of suffering that it contributes to results that extend beyond the sufferer.[26] So long as the sufferer is amply taken care of, I can't see that this violates any demands of divine justice, compassion, or love. After all, parents regularly impose sacrifices on some of their children for the overall welfare of the family. Of course, in doing so they are acting out of a scarcity of resources, and God's situation is enormously different in this respect. Nevertheless, assuming that Sue's suffering is necessary even for God to be able to achieve a certain good state of affairs, then, provided that Sue is taken care of in such a way that she will eventually come to recognize the value and justifiability of the proceeding and to joyfully endorse it (or at least has ample opportunities to get herself into this position), I cannot see that God could be faulted for setting things up this way.[27]

From now on I will be considering possible divine reasons that extend beyond benefit to the sufferer. Though in line with the previous paragraph I will not suppose that any of these (so far as they exclusively concern persons other than the sufferer) could be God's whole reason for permitting a bit of suffering, I will take it as a live possibility that they could contribute to a sufficient divine reason. The theodicies to be considered now will give us more specific suggestions for Bambi and Sue.

I will begin with the familiar free will theodicy, according to which God is justified in permitting creaturely wickedness and its consequences because he has to do so if he is bestow on some of his creatures the incommensurable privilege of being responsible agents who have, in many areas, the capacity to choose between alternatives as they will, without God, or anyone or anything else (other than themselves), determining which alternative they choose. The suggestion of this theodicy is that it is conceptually impossible for God to create free agents and also determine how they are to choose, within those areas in which they are free. If He were so to determine their choices they would, ipso facto, not be free. But this being the case, when God decided to endow some of His creatures, including us, with free choice, He thereby took the chance, ran the risk, of our sometimes or often making the wrong choice, a possibility that has been richly realized. It is conceptually impossible for God to create free agents and not subject Himself to such a risk. Not to do the latter would be not to do the former. But that being the case, He, and we, are stuck with whatever consequences ensue. And this is why God permits such horrors as the rape, beating, and murder of Sue. He does it not because that particular wicked choice is itself necessary for the realization of some great good, but because the permission of such horrors is bound up with the decision to give human beings free choice in many areas, and that (the capacity to freely choose) is a great good, such a great good as to be worth all the suffering and others evils that it makes possible.[28]

This theodicy has been repeatedly subjected to radical criticisms that, if sound, would imply that the value of creaturely free will is not even a possible reason for God's allowing Sue's attacker to do his thing. For one thing, it has been urged that it is within God's power to create free agents so that they always choose what is right. For another, it has been denied or doubted that free will is of such value as to be worth all the sin and suffering it has brought into the world. In accord with my general policy in this paper, I will not attempt to argue that this theodicy does succeed in identifying God's reasons for permitting wrongdoing and its results, but only that the possibility of this cannot be excluded. Hence I can confine myself to arguing that these criticisms do not dispose of that possibility. Though lack of space prevents a proper discussion, I will just indicate what I would say in such a discussion. On the first point, if we set aside middle knowledge as I am doing in this paper, it is logically impossible for God to create beings with genuine freedom of choice and also guarantee that they will always choose the right. And even granting middle knowledge Plantinga (1974) has established the *possibility* that God could not actualize a world containing free creatures that always do the right thing. As for the second point, though it may be beyond our powers to show that free will has sufficient value to carry the theodical load, it is surely equally beyond our powers to show that it does not.[29]

Thus we may take it to be a live possibility that the maintenance of creaturely free will is at least part of God's reason for permitting wrongdoing and its consequences. But then the main reason one could have for denying that this is at least part of why God would allow the attack on Sue is that God could, miraculously or otherwise, prevent any one incipient free human action without losing the value of human free will. Clearly a divine interference in normal human operations in this one instance is not going to prevent even Sue's attacker from being a free moral agent in general, with all that that involves. This point is supported by the consideration that, for all we know, God does sometimes intervene to prevent human agents from doing wicked things they would otherwise have done, and, so the free will theodicist will claim, even if that is the case we do enjoy the incommensurable value of free choice. We can also think of it this way. It is perfectly obvious that the scope of our free choice is not unlimited. We have no effective voluntary control over, e.g., our genetic constitution, our digestive and other biological processes, and much of our cognitive operations. Thus whatever value the human capacity for free choice possesses, that value is compatible with free choice being confined within fairly narrow limits. But then presumably a tiny additional constriction such as would be involved in God's preventing Sue's attacker from committing that atrocity would not render things radically different, free-will-wise, from what they would have been without that. So God could have prevented this without losing the good emphasized by this theodicy. Hence we can be sure that this does not constitute a sufficient reason for His not preventing it.

To be sure, if God were to act on this principle in every case of incipient wrongdoing, the situation would be materially changed. Human agents would no longer have a real choice between good and evil, and the surpassing worth that attaches to having such a choice would be lost. Hence, if God is to promote the values emphasized by the free will theodicy, He can intervene in this way in only a small proportion of cases. And how are these to be selected? I doubt that we are in a position to give a confident answer to this question, but let's assume that the critic proposes that the exceptions are to be picked in such a way as to maximize welfare, and let's go along with that. Rowe's claim would then have to be that Sue's murder was so horrible that it would qualify for the class of exceptions. But that is precisely where the critic's claims far outrun his justification. How can we tell that Sue falls within the most damaging n% of what would be cases of human wrongdoing apart from divine intervention. To be in a position to make such a judgment we would have to survey the full range of such cases and make reliable assessments of the deleterious consequences of each. Both tasks are far beyond our powers. We don't even know what free creaturely agents there are beyond human beings, and with respect to humans the range of wickedness, past, present, and future, is largely beyond our ken. And even with respect to the cases of which we are aware we have only a limited ability to assess the total consequences. Hence, by the nature of the case, we are simply not in a position to make a warranted judgment that Sue's case is among the n% worst cases of wrongdoing in the history of the universe. No doubt, it strikes us as incomparably horrible on hearing about it, but so would innumerable others. Therefore, the critic is not in a position to set aside the value of free will as at least part of God's reason for permitting Sue's murder.

## ix

Next I turn to theodicies that stress benefit to human beings other than the sufferer or to humanity generally.[30] And first let's return to Marilyn Adams' discussion of martyrdom in (1986). In addition to her account, already noted, of martyrdom as a vehicle of God's goodness to the martyr, she discusses "Martyrdom as a vehicle of God's goodness to the onlooker". " For onlookers, the event of martyrdom may function as a prophetic story, the more powerful for being brought to life. The martyr who perseveres to the end presents an inspiring example. Onlookers are invited to see in the martyr the person they ought to be and to be brought to a deeper level of commitment. Alternatively, onlookers may see themselves in the persecutor and be moved to repentance. If the onlooker has ears to hear the martyr's testimony, he may receive God's redemption through it" (p. 257). She also suggests that martyrdom may be redemptive for the persecutor. "First of all, the martyr's sacrifice can be used as an instrument of divine judgment, because it draws the persecutor an external picture of what he is really like—the more innocent the victim, the clearer the focus...In attempting to bring reconciliation out of judgment, God may find no more promising vehicle than martyrdom for dealing with the hard-hearted" (p. 258). (Again, in making these suggestions for a theodicy of suffering, Adams is not restricting their scope to martyrdom strictly so called.) To be sure, sometimes there is no persecutor, but often there is, as in child and wife abuse. And there is always the possibility, and usually the actuality, of onlookers.[31]

Can the critic be justified in holding that Sue's suffering, e.g., would not be permitted by God at least in part for reasons of these sorts? Once more, even if we cannot see that Sue's suffering brings these kinds of benefits to her attacker or to onlookers, our massive ignorance of the recesses of the human heart and of the total outcomes, perhaps through eternity, for all such people, renders us poor judges of whether such benefits are indeed forthcoming. And, finally, even if no goods of these sorts eventuate, there is once more the insoluble problem of whether God could be expected to use a different strategy, given His respect for human free will. Perhaps that was (a part of) the strategy that held out the best chance of evoking the optimal response from these particularly hard-hearted subjects.

Next I want to consider a quite different theodicy that also sees God's reasons for permitting suffering in terms of benefits that are generally distributed, viz., the appeal to the benefits of a lawlike natural order, and the claim that suffering will be an inevitable byproduct of any such order. I choose the exposition of this theodicy in Bruce Reichenbach in *Evil and a Good God* (1982).

> ...creation, in order to make possible the existence of moral agents...had to be ordered according to some set of natural laws (p. 101).

The argument for this is that if things do not happen in a lawlike fashion, at least usually, agents will be unable to anticipate the consequences of their volitions, and hence will not be able to effectively make significant choices between good and evil actions. Reichenbach continues:

> Consequently, the possibility arises that sentient creatures like ourselves can be negatively affected by the outworkings of these laws in nature, such that we experience pain, suffering, disability, disutility, and at times the frustration of our good desires. Since a

world with free persons making choices between moral good and evil and choosing a significant amount of moral good is better than a world without free persons and moral good and evil, God in creating had to create a world which operated according to natural laws to achieve this higher good. Thus, his action of creation of a natural world and a natural order, along with the resulting pain and pleasure which we experience, is justified. The natural evils which afflict us—diseases, sickness, disasters, birth defects—are all the outworking of the natural system of which we are a part. They are the byproducts made possible by that which is necessary for the greater good (100-01).

This is a theodicy for natural evil, not for the suffering that results from human wickedness. Hence it has possible application to Bambi, but not to Sue, and possible application to any other suffering that results from natural processes that are independent of human intentional action.

Let's agree that significant moral agency requires a natural lawful order. But that doesn't show that it is even possible that God had a sufficient reason to allow Bambi's suffering. There are two difficulties that must be surmounted to arrive at that point.

First, a natural order can be regular enough to provide the degree of predictability required for morally significant choice even if there are exceptions to the regularities. Therefore, God could set aside the usual consequences of natural forces in this instance, so as to prevent Bambi's suffering, without thereby interfering with human agents' reasonable anticipations of the consequences of their actions. So long as God doesn't do this too often, we will still have ample basis for suppositions as to what we can reasonably expect to follow what. But note that by the same line of reasoning God cannot do this too often, or the desired predictability will not be forthcoming. Hence, though any one naturally caused suffering could have been miraculously prevented, God certainly has a strong prima facie reason in each case to refrain from doing this; for if He didn't He would have no reason for letting nature usually take its course. And so He has a possible reason for allowing nature to take its course in the Bambi case, a reason that would have to be overridden by stronger contrary considerations.

This means that in order to be justified in supposing that God would not have a sufficient reason to refrain from intervening in this case, we would have to be justified in supposing that God would have a sufficient reason to make, in this case, an exception to the general policy. And how could we be justified in supposing that? We would need an adequate grasp of the full range of cases from which God would have to choose whatever exceptions He is going to make, if any, to the general policy of letting nature take its course. Without that we would not be in a position to judge that Bambi is among the n% of the cases most worthy of being miraculously prevented.[32] And it is abundantly clear that we have and can have no such grasp of this territory as a whole. We are quite unable, by our natural powers, of determining just what cases, or even what kinds of cases, of suffering there would be throughout the history of the universe if nature took its course. We just don't know enough about the constituents of the universe even at present, much less throughout the past and future, to make any such catalogue. And we could not make good that deficiency without an enormous enlargement of our cognitive capacities. Hence we are in no position to judge that God does not have sufficient reason (of the Reichenbach sort) for refraining from interfering in the Bambi case.[33]

But all this has to do with whether God would have interfered with the natural order, as it actually exists, to prevent Bambi's suffering. And it will be suggested, secondly, that God could have instituted a quite different natural order, one that would not involve human and animal suffering, or at least much less of it. Why couldn't there be a natural order in which there are no viruses and bacteria the natural operation of which results in human and animal disease, a natural order in which rainfall is evenly distributed, in which earthquakes do not occur, in which forests are not subject to massive fires? To be sure, even God could not bring into being just the creatures we presently have while subjecting their behavior to different laws. For the fact that a tiger's natural operations and tendencies are what they are is an essential part of what makes it the kind of thing it is.[34] But why couldn't God have created a world with different constituents so as to avoid subjecting any sentient creatures to disease and natural disasters? Let's agree that this is possible for God. But then the critic must also show that at least one of the ways in which God could have done this would have produced a world that is better on the whole than the actual world. For even if God could have instituted a natural order without disease and natural disasters, that by itself doesn't show that He would have done so if He existed. For if that world had other undesirable features and/or lacked desirable features in such a way as to be worse, or at least no better than, the actual world, it still doesn't follow that God would have chosen the former over the latter. It all depends on the overall comparative worth of the two systems. Once again I am not concerned to argue for Reichenbach's theodicy, which would, on the rules by which we are playing, require arguing that no possible natural order is overall better than the one we have. Instead I merely want to show that the critic is not justified in supposing that some alternative natural order open to God that does not involve suffering (to the extent that we have it) is better on the whole.

There are two points I want to make about this, points that have not cropped up earlier in the paper. First, it is by no means clear what possibilities are open to God. Here it is important to remember that we are concerned with metaphysical possibilities (necessities...), not merely with conceptual or logical possibilities in a narrow sense of 'logical'. The critic typically points out that we can consistently and intelligibly conceive a world in which there are no diseases, no earthquakes, floods, or tornadoes, no predators in the animal kingdom, while all or most of the goods we actually enjoy are still present. He takes this to show that it is possible for God to bring about such a world. But, as many thinkers have recently argued,[35] consistent conceivability (conceptual possibility) is by no means sufficient for metaphysical possibility, for what is possible given the metaphysical structure of reality. To use a well worn example, it may be metaphysically necessary that the chemical composition of water is $H_2O$ since that is what water essentially is, even though, given the ordinary concept of water, we can without contradiction or unintelligibility, think of water as made of up of carbon and chlorine. Roughly speaking, what is conceptually or logically (in a narrow sense of 'logical') possible depends on the composition of the concepts, or the meanings of the terms, we use to cognize reality, while metaphysical possibility depends on what things are like in themselves, their essential natures, regardless of how they are represented in our thought and language.

It is much more difficult to determine what is metaphysically possible or necessary than to determine what is conceptually possible or necessary. The latter requires only careful reflection on our concepts. The former requires—well, it's not clear what will do the trick, but it's not something we can bring off just by reflecting on what we mean by what we say, or on what we are committing ourselves to by applying a certain concept. To know what is metaphysically possible in the way of alternative systems of natural order, we would have to have as firm a grasp of this subject matter as we have of the chemical constitution of familiar substances like water and salt. It is clear that we have no such grasp. We don't have a clue as to what essential natures are within God's creative repertoire, and still less do we have a clue as to which combinations of these into total lawful systems are doable. We know that you can't have water without hydrogen and oxygen and that you can't have salt without sodium and chlorine. But can there be life without hydrocarbons? Who knows? Can there be conscious, intelligent organisms with free will that are not susceptible to pain? That is, just what is metaphysically required for a creature to have the essential nature of a conscious, intelligent, free agent? Who can say? Since we don't have even the beginnings of a canvass of the possibilities here, we are in no position to make a sufficiently informed judgment as to what God could or could not create by way of a natural order that contains the goods of this one (or equal goods of other sorts) without its disadvantages.

One particular aspect of this disability is our inability to determine what consequences would ensue, with metaphysical necessity, on a certain alteration in the natural order. Suppose that predators were turned into vegetarians. Or rather, if predatory tendencies are part of the essential natures of lions, tigers, and the like, suppose that they were replaced with vegetarians as much like them as possible. How much like them is that? What other features are linked to predatory tendencies by metaphysical necessity? We may know something of what is linked to predation by natural necessity, e.g., by the structure and dispositional properties of genes. But to what extent does metaphysical possibility go beyond natural possibility here? To what extent could God institute a different system of heredity such that what is inseparable from predation in the actual genetic code is separable from it instead? Who can say? To take another example, suppose we think of the constitution of the earth altered so that the subterranean tensions and collisions involved in earthquakes are ruled out. What would also have to be ruled out, by metaphysical necessity? (Again, we know something of what goes along with this by natural necessity, but that's not the question.) Could the earth still contain soil suitable for edible crops? Would there still be mountains? A system of flowing streams? We are, if anything, still more at a loss when we think of eradicating all the major sources of suffering from the natural order. What metaphysical possibilities are there for what we could be left with? It boggles the (human) mind to contemplate the question.[36]

The second main point is this. Even if we could, at least in outline, determine what alternative systems of natural order are open to God, we would still be faced with the staggering job of comparative evaluation. How can we hold together in our minds the salient features of two such total systems sufficiently to make a considered judgment of their relative merits? *Perhaps* we are capable of making a considered evaluation of each feature of the systems (or many of them), and even capable of judicious comparisons of features two-by-two. For example, we might be justified in holding that the reduction in the possibilities of disease is worth more than the greater variety of forms of life that goes along with susceptibility to disease. But it is another matter altogether to get the kind of overall grasp of each system to the extent required to provide a comprehensive ranking of those systems. We find it difficult enough, if not impossible, to arrive at a definitive comparative evaluation of cultures, social systems, or educational policies. It is far from clear that even if I devoted my life to the study of two primitive cultures, I would thereby be in a position to make an authoritative pronouncement as to which is better on the whole. How much less are we capable of making a comparative evaluation of two alternative natural orders, with all the indefinitely complex ramification of the differences between the two.[37]

Before leaving this topic I want to emphasize the point that, unlike the theodicies discussed earlier the natural law theodicy bears on the question of animal as well as human suffering. If the value of a lawful universe justifies the suffering that results from the operation of those laws, that would apply to suffering at all levels of the great chain of being.

## X

I have been gleaning suggestions from a variety of theodicies as to what reasons God might have for permitting suffering. I believe that each of these suggestions embody one or more sorts of reasons that God might conceivably have for some of the suffering in the world. And I believe that I have shown that none of us are in a position to warrantedly assert, with respect to any of those reasons, that

God would not permit some cases of suffering for that reason. Even if I am mistaken in supposing that we cannot rule out some particular reason, e.g. that the suffering is a punishment for sin, I make bold to claim that it is extremely unlikely that I am mistaken about all those suggestions. Moreover, I have argued, successfully I believe, that some of these reasons are at least part of possible divine reasons for Rowe's cases, Bambi and Sue, and that hence we are unable to justifiably assert that God does not have reasons of these sorts for permitting Rowe-like cases.

However that does not suffice to dispose of Rowe's specific argument, concerned as it is with the Bambi and Sue cases in particular. For I earlier conceded, for the sake of argument, that (1) none of the sufferer-centered reasons I considered could be any part of God's reasons for permitting the Bambi and Sue cases, and (2) that non-sufferer-centered reasons could not be the whole of God's reasons for allowing any case of suffering. This left me without any specific suggestions as to what might be a fully sufficient reason for God to permit those cases. And hence showing that no one can be justified in supposing that reasons of the sort considered are not at least part of God's reasons for one or another case of suffering does not suffice to show that no one can be justified in supposing that God could have no sufficient reason for permitting the Bambi and Sue cases. And hence it does not suffice to show that Rowe cannot be justified in asserting 1.

This lacuna in the argument is remedied by the point that we cannot be justified in supposing that there are no other reasons, thus far unenvisaged, that would fully justify God in permitting Rowe's cases. That point was made at the end of section vii for sufferer-centered reasons, and it can now be made more generally. Even if we were fully entitled to dismiss all the alleged reasons for permitting suffering that have been suggested, we would still have to consider whether there are further possibilities that are undreamt of in our theodicies. Why should we suppose that the theodicies thus far excogitated, however brilliant and learned their authors, exhaust the field. The points made in the earlier discussion about the impossibility of anticipating future developments in human thought can be applied here. Just as we can never repose confidence in any alleged limits of future human theoretical and conceptual developments in science, so it is here, even more so if possible. It is surely reasonable to suppose that God, if such there be, has more tricks up His sleeve than we can envisage. Since it is in principle impossible for us to be justified in supposing that God does not have sufficient reasons for permitting E that are unknown to us, and perhaps unknowable by us, no one can be justified in holding that God could have no reasons for permitting the Bambi and Sue cases, or any other particular cases of suffering.[38]

This last point, that we are not warranted in supposing that God does not have sufficient reasons unknown to us for permitting E, is not only an essential part of the total argument against the justifiability of 1. It would be sufficient by itself. Even if all my argumentation prior to that point were in vain and my opponent could definitively rule out all the specific suggestions I have put forward, she would still face the insurmountable task of showing herself to be justified in supposing that there are no further possibilities for sufficient divine reasons. That point by itself would be decisive.

## xi

In the case of each of the theodical suggestions considered I have drawn on various limits to our cognitive powers, opportunities, and achievements in arguing that we are not in a position to deny that God could have that kind of reason for various cases of suffering. In conclusion it may be useful to list the cognitive limits that have formed the backbone of my argument.

1. *Lack of data*. This includes, inter alia, the secrets of the human heart, the detailed constitution and structure of the universe, and the remote past and future, including the afterlife if any.

2. *Complexity greater than we can handle*. Most notably there is the difficulty of holding enormous complexes of fact—different possible worlds or different systems of natural law—together in the mind sufficiently for comparative evaluation.

3. *Difficulty of determining what is metaphysically possible or necessary*. Once we move beyond conceptual or semantic modalities (and even that is no piece of cake) it is notoriously difficult to find any sufficient basis for claims as to what is metaphysically possible, given the essential natures of things, the exact character of which is often obscure to us and virtually always controversial. This difficulty is many times multiplied when we are dealing with total possible worlds or total systems of natural order.

4. *Ignorance of the full range of possibilities.* This is always crippling when we are trying to establish negative conclusions. If we don't know whether or not there are possibilities beyond the ones we have thought of, we are in a very bad position to show that there can be no divine reasons for permitting evil.

5. *Ignorance of the full range of values.* When it's a question of whether some good is related to E in such a way as to justify God in permitting E, we are, for the reason mentioned in 4., in a very poor position to answer the question if we don't know the extent to which there are modes of value beyond those of which we are aware. For in that case, so far as we can know, E may be justified by virtue of its relation to one of those unknown goods.

6. *Limits to our capacity to make well considered value judgments.* The chief example of this we have noted is the difficulty in making comparative evaluations of large complex wholes.

It may seem to the reader that I have been making things too difficult for the critic, holding him to unwarrantedly exaggerated standards for epistemic justification. "If we were to apply your standards across the board", he may complain, "it would turn out that we are justified in believing little or nothing. That would land us in a total skepticism. And doesn't that indicate that your standards are absurdly inflated?" I agree that it would indicate that if the application of my standards did have that result, but I don't agree that this is the case. The point is that the critic is engaged in attempting to support a particularly difficult claim, a claim that there isn't something in a certain territory, while having a very sketchy idea of what is in that territory, and having no sufficient basis for an estimate of how much of the territory falls outside his knowledge. This is very different from our more usual situation in which we are forming judgments and drawing conclusions about matters concerning which we antecedently know quite a lot, and the boundaries and parameters of which we have pretty well settled. Thus the attempt to show that God could have no sufficient reason for permitting Bambi's or Sue's suffering is quite atypical of our usual cognitive situation; no conclusion can be drawn from our poor performance in the former to an equally poor performance in the latter.[39]

I want to underline the point that my argument in this paper does not rely on a general skepticism about our cognitive powers, about our capacity to achieve knowledge and justified belief. On the contrary, I have been working with what I take to be our usual non-skeptical standards for these matters, standards that I take to be satisfied by the great mass of our beliefs in many areas. My claim has been that when these standards are applied to the kind of claim exemplified by Rowe's 1, it turns out this claim is not justified and that the prospects for any of us being justified in making it are poor at best. This is because of the specific character of that claim, its being a negative existential claim concerning a territory about the extent, contents, and parameters of which we know little. My position no more implies, presupposes, or reflects a general skepticism than does the claim that we don't know that there is no life elsewhere in the universe.

This completes my case for the "agnostic thesis", the claim that we are simply not in a position to justifiably assert, with respect to Bambi or Sue or other cases of suffering, that God, if He exists, would have no sufficient reason for permitting it. And if that is right, the inductive argument from evil is in no better shape that its late lamented deductive cousin.

### Notes

1. The term 'gratuitous' is used in different ways in the literature. Lately it has sprouted variations (Hasker, forthcoming). My use of the term is strictly tied to Rowe's 1.
2. In (1979) Rowe considers this criticism. He says of it: "I suppose some theists would be content with this rather modest response...But given the validity of the basic argument and the theist's likely acceptance of (2), he is thereby committed to the view that (1) is false, not just that we have no good reasons for accepting (1) as true" (338). No doubt, the theist is committed to regarding (1) as false, at least on the assumption that it embodies necessary conditions for God's having sufficient reason for permitting suffering (on which see F in the next section). But Rowe does not explain why he thinks that showing that we are not justified in asserting 1 does not constitute a decisive reason for rejecting his argument.
3. There is considerable confusion in the literature over what it takes to have a theodicy, or, otherwise put, what a reasonable level of aspiration is for theodicy. Even if we were vouchsafed an abundance of divine revelations I cannot conceive of our being able to specify God's reason for permitting each individual evil. The most that could be sensibly be aimed at would be an account of the sorts of reasons God has for various sorts of evil. And a more modest, but still significant, ambition would be to make suggestions as to what God's reasons might be, reasons that

are plausible in the light of what we know and believe about God, His nature, purposes, and activities. See Stump, 1990.

4. In arguing for 1 in (1979) Rowe proceeds as if he supposed that the only alternatives are (a) its being reasonable to believe 1 and (b) its being reasonable to believe not-1. "Consider again the case of the fawn's suffering. Is it reasonable to believe that there is some greater good so intimately connected to that suffering that even an omnipotent, omniscient being could not have obtained that good without permitting that suffering or some evil at least as bad? It certainly does not appear reasonable to believe this. Nor does it seem reasonable to believe that there is some evil at least as bad as the fawn's suffering such that an omnipotent being simply could not have prevented it without permitting the fawn's suffering. But even if it should somehow be reasonable to believe either of these things of the fawn's suffering, we must then ask whether it is reasonable to believe either of these things of *all* the instances of seemingly pointless human and animal suffering that occur daily in our world. And surely the answer to this more general question must be no...It seems then that although we cannot *prove* that (1) is true, it is nevertheless, altogether *reasonable* to believe that (1) is true, that (1) is a *rational* belief" (337-38). The form of this argument is: "It is not rational to believe that p. Therefore it is rational to believe that not-p." But this is patently lacking in force. There are many issues on which it is rational to believe neither p nor not-p. Take p to be, e.g, the proposition that it was raining on this spot exactly 45,000 years ago.

5. The qualifier 'traditional' adheres to the restrictions laid down in D and excludes variants like process theology. Admittedly, "traditional Christianity" contains a number of in-house variants, but in this paper I will appeal only to what is common to all forms of what could reasonably be called "traditional Christianity".

6. Rowe does not often use the term 'justified belief', but instead usually speaks of its being *rational* to hold a belief. I shall ignore any minor differences there may be between these epistemic concepts.

7. The point at issue here is whether being non-gratuitous in this sense is necessary for divine permission. But there is also a question as to whether it is sufficient. Would any outweighing good for which a particular bit of suffering is necessary, however trivial and insignificant that good, justify that suffering? Suppose that some minor suffering on my part is necessary for my enjoying my dinner to the extent I did, and that the enjoyment outweighs the suffering? Would that give God a reason for permitting the suffering? I doubt it. Again, suppose that E is necessary for some greater good, but that the universe as whole would be better without E and the greater good than with them? Would God be justified in permitting E? (Note that in (1986) Rowe's substitute for 1 is in terms of the world as a whole: "There exists evils that O [God] could have prevented, and had O prevented them the world as a whole would have been better") ( 228). However I am not concerned here with what is sufficient for God to have a reason for permitting evil, only with what is necessary for this.

8. This presupposes that God does not enjoy "middle knowledge". For if He did, He could see to it that suffering would be imposed on people only where they will in fact make the desired response. I owe this point to William Hasker.

9. Such a theodicy will be discussed in section ix.

10. There are also more radical objections to Rowe's 2. I think particularly of those who question or deny the principle that God would, by virtue of His nature, create the best possible universe or, in case there can be no uniquely best possible universe, would create a universe that comes up to some minimal evaluative level. See, e.g., R. Adams (1987). On these views an argument like Rowe's never gets out of the starting gate. Though I have some sympathy with such views I will not take that line in this paper.

11. See, e.g., Ahern (1971), Fitzpatrick (1981), Reichenbach (1982), Wykstra (1984).

12. To be sure, 1 is in the form of a positive existential statement. However when we consider an instantiation of it with respect to a particular case of suffering, E, as Rowe does in arguing for it, it turns out to be a negative existential statement about E, that *there is no sufficient divine reason for permitting E*. It is statements of this form that, so I claim, no one can be justified in making.

13. Wykstra labors under the additional burden of having to defend a thesis as to the conditions under which one is justified in making an assertion of the form "It appears that p", and much of the considerable literature spawned by his article is taken up with this side-issue.

14. Hence the very common procedure of knocking down theodical suggestions, one by one, by pointing out, in the case of each, that there are evils it does not cover, will not suffice to make the critic's case. For it may be that even though no one divine reason covers all cases each case is covered by some divine reason.

15. It is often dismissed nowadays on the grounds that it presupposes a morally unacceptable theory of punishment, viz., a retributive conception. But it need not make any such presupposition; whatever the rationale of punishment, the suggestion is that (in some cases) God has that rationale for permitting suffering. Though it must be admitted that the "retributive" principle that *it is intrinsically good that persons should suffer for wrongdoing* makes it easier to claim that suffering constitutes justifiable punishment than a reformatory theory does, where a necessary condition for the justification of punishment is the significant chance of an improvement of the punishee. For purposes of this discussion I will not choose between different theories of punishment.

16. I don't mean to suggest that a person's inner sinfulness or saintliness cannot be expected to manifest itself in behavior. Still less do I mean to suggest that one could be fully or ideally living the life of the spirit, whatever her outward behavior.

17. Rowe writes: "Perhaps the good for which *some* intense suffering is permitted cannot be realized until the end of the world, but it certainly seems likely that much of this good could be realized in the lifetime

of the sufferer...In the absence of any reason to think that O [God] would need to postpone these good experiences, we have reason to expect that many of these goods would occur in the world we know" (1986, 244-45). But why suppose that we are entitled to judge that justifying goods, if any, would be realized during the sufferer's earthly life, unless we have specific reasons to the contrary? Why this initial presumption? Why is the burden of proof on the suggestion of the realization of the goods in an after-life? Rowe doesn't say, nor do I see what he could say.

18. Actually, Hick is a universalist and believes that all free creatures will attain this consummation; but I do not take this thesis as necessary for the soul making theodicy.

19. Stump gives her answer to this one in the passage quoted.

20. All these disclaimers may well apply to Sue.

21. Here, of course, as in the other cases in which God's action is designed to evoke a free response from the patient, there is no guarantee that the reformation will be effected. But it still remains true that the good aimed at is a good for the sufferer.

22. There is, to be sure, a question as to why, if things are as I have just suggested they may be, God doesn't fill us in on His reasons for permitting suffering. Wouldn't a perfectly benevolent creator see to it that we realize why we are called upon to suffer? I acknowledge this difficulty; in fact it is just another form taken by the problem of evil. And I will respond to it in the same way. Even if we can't see why God would keep us in the dark in this matter, we cannot be justified in supposing that God does not have sufficient reason for doing so.

23. E1 is Bambi's suffering and E2 is Sue's suffering. There are, of course, various differences between Q and 1. For one thing, Q, unlike 1 makes reference to God's being morally justified. For another, Q has to do with God's *obtaining* particular goods, apparently leaving out of account the cases in which cooperation from human free choice is required. However these differences are not germane to the present point.

24. Cf. the criticism of Rowe's move from P to Q in Christlieb (forthcoming). Note too that Rowe restricts his consideration of the unknown to "good states of affairs" we do not know of. But, as is recognized in my discussion, it is an equally relevant and equally live possibility that we do not grasp ways in which good states of affairs we know of are connected with cases of suffering so to as to provide God with a reason for permitting the latter. Both types of unknown factors, if realized, would yield divine reasons for permitting suffering of which we are not cognizant.

25. Stump (1990), p. 66. Many other thinkers, both theistic and atheistic, concur in this judgment.

26. Note that we are assuming (what seems to be obvious) that God might have a number of reasons for permitting a particular case of suffering, no one of which reasons is sufficient by itself though the whole complex is. This obvious possibility is often ignored when critics seek to knock down theodical suggestions one by one.

27. In "Victimization and the Problem of Evil" [forthcoming], Thomas F.

Tracy persuasively argues that although "God must not actualize a world that contains persons whose lives, through no fault of their own, are on balance an evil (i.e., an intrinsic disvalue) for them rather than a good" (20), nevertheless, we cannot also claim that "God must not actualize a world in which a person suffers some evil E if the elimination of E by God would result in a better balance *for this individual* of the goods God intends for persons and the evils God permits" (23).

28. The reader may well wonder why it is only now that I have introduced the free will theodicy, since it has such an obvious application to Sue's case. The reason is that I wanted at first to focus on those suggestions that confined the rationale of suffering to benefit to the sufferer.

29. On this point, see the discussion in the next section of our inability to make evaluative comparisons on the scale required here.

30. Or to other creatures. Most discussions of the problem of evil are markedly anthropocentric, in a way that would not survive serious theological scrutiny.

31. These suggestions will draw many of the objections we have already seen to be levelled against Hick's, Stump's, and Adams' sufferer-centered points. See section vi for a discussion of these objections.

32. There are also questions as to whether we are capable of making a reasonable judgment as to which cases from a given field have the strongest claim to being prevented. Our capacity to do this is especially questionable where incommensurable factors are involved, e.g., the worth of the subject and the magnitude of the suffering. But let this pass.

33. The reader will, no doubt, be struck by the similarity between this problem and the one that came up with respect to the free will theodicy. There too it was agreed that God can occasionally, but only occasionally, interfere with human free choice and its implementation without sacrificing the value of human free will. And so there too we were faced with the question of whether we could be assured that a particular case would be a sufficiently strong candidate for such interference that God would have sufficient reason to intervene.

34. Reichenbach, 110-11.

35. See, e.g., Kripke (1972), Plantinga (1974).

36. I hope it is unnecessary to point out that I am not suggesting that we are incapable of making any reasonable judgments of metaphysical modality. Here, as elsewhere, my point is that the judgments required by the inductive argument from evil are of a very special and enormously ambitious type and that our cognitive capacities that serve us well in more limited tasks are not equal to this one. (For more on this general feature of the argument see the final section.) Indeed, just now I contrasted the problem of determining what total systems of nature are metaphysically possible with the problem of the chemical composition of various substances, where we are in a much better position to make judgments of metaphysical modality.

37. This point cuts more than one way. For example, theodicists often confidently assert, as something obvious on the face of it, that a world with free creatures, even free creatures who often misuse their freedom,

is better than a world with no free creatures. But it seems to me that it is fearsomely difficult to make this comparison and that we should not be so airily confident that we can do so. Again, to establish a natural law theodicy along Reichenbach's lines one would have to show that the actual natural order is at least as beneficial as any possible alternative; and the considerations I have been adducing cast doubt on our inability to do this. Again, please note that in this paper I am not concerned to defend any particular theodicy.

38. For Rowe's objection to this invocation of the possibility of humanly unenvisaged divine reasons for permitting suffering, and my answer thereto, see the end of section vii.

39. See the end of section vii for a similar point.

## References

1. Adams, Marilyn McCord, "Redemptive Suffering: A Christian Approach to the Problem of Evil", in *Rationality, Religious Belief, and Moral Commitment*, ed. R. Audi & W. J. Wainwright (Ithaca, NY: Cornell U. Press, 1986).

2. Adams, Robert M., "Must God Create the Best?", in *The Virtue of Faith and Other Essays in Philosophical Theology* (New York: Oxford University Press, 1987).

3. Ahern, M. B., *The Problem of Evil* (London: Routledge & Kegan Paul, 1971)

4. Christlieb, Terry, "Which Theism's Face an Evidential Problem of Evil?", *Faith and Philosophy*, forthcoming.

5. Fitzpatrick, F. J., "The Onus of Proof in Arguments about the Problem of Evil", *Religious Studies*, 17 (1981).

6. Hasker, William, "The Necessity of Gratuitous Evil", *Faith and Philosophy*, forthcoming.

7. Hick, John, *Evil and the God of Love*, rev. ed. (New York: Harper & Row, 1978).

8. Keller, James, "The Problem of Evil and the Attributes of God", *Int. Journ. Philos Relig.*, 26 (1989).

9. Kripke, Saul A., "Naming and Necessity", in *Semantics of Natural Language*, ed. Donald Davidson & Gilbert Harman (Dordrecht: D. Reidel Pub. Co., 1972).

10. Plantinga, Alvin, *The Nature of Necessity* (Oxford: Clarendon Press, 1974).

11. Reichenbach, Bruce, *Evil and a Good God* (New York: Fordham U. Press, 1982).

12. Rowe, William L., "The Problem of Evil and Some Varieties of Atheism", *Amer. Philos. Quart.*, 16, no. 4 (October, 1979).

13. Rowe, William L., "The Empirical Argument from Evil", in *Rationality, Religious Belief, and Moral Commitment*, ed. R. Audi & W. J. Wainwright (Ithaca, NY: Cornell U. Press, 1986).

14. Rowe, William L., "Evil and Theodicy", *Philosophical Topics*, 16, no. 2 (Fall, 1988).

15. Russell, Bruce, "The Persistent Problem of Evil", *Faith and Philosophy*, 6, no. 2 (April, 1989).
16. Stump, Eleonore, "The Problem of Evil", *Faith and Philosophy*, 2, no. 4 (Oct., 1985).
17. Stump, Eleonore, "Providence and Evil", in *Christian Philosophy*, ed. Thomas P. Flint (Notre Dame, IN: U. of Notre Dame Press, 1990).
18. Tracy, Thomas F. "Victimization and the Problem of Evil", *Faith and Philosophy*, forthcoming.
19. Wykstra, Stephen, "The Humean Obstacle to Evidential Arguments from Suffering: On Avoiding the Evils of 'Appearance'", *Int. Journ. Philos. Relig.*, 16 (1984).

Philosophical Perspectives, 5, Philosophy of Religion, 1991

# RUMINATIONS ABOUT EVIL

## William L. Rowe
## Purdue University

Some years ago, in an effort to set forth an argument for atheism based on certain cases of intense human and animal suffering, I claimed that we have reason to believe that

1. There exist instances of intense suffering which an omnipotent, omniscient being could have prevented without thereby losing some greater good or permitting some evil equally bad or worse.

Now, if we have reason to believe (1), then since even many theists will accept

2. An omniscient, wholly good being would prevent the occurrence of any intense suffering it could, unless it could not do so without thereby losing some greater good or permitting some evil equally bad or worse.

we have reason to conclude that the God of traditional theism (an omnipotent, omniscient, wholly good being) does not exist.[1] Confronted with this argument, theists, I suggested, would be wise to acknowledge that it does provide some rational grounds for atheism. Whether atheism is the position that from the rational point of view we all ought to adopt, however, will depend on what else we know or have reason to believe that is relevant to whether theism or atheism is true.

While some philosophers may have been persuaded both of the strength of the argument and of the wisdom of the advice, others have taken a more critical position; they have argued *either* that the considerations given in support of premise (1) are wholly inadequate to provide it with rational support *or* that premise (2), despite its appearance of being a necessary truth, is a proposition of dubious intellectual merit. In this paper I want to examine two important attacks on the claim that we are rationally justified in accepting premise (1), and one important attack on premise (2). In the course of discussing these attacks, I hope to cast the original argument into a form that more clearly reveals why particular instances of evil count against the existence of the God of traditional theism.

# I

Alvin Plantinga raises the question of what makes (1) probable.[2] He then notes my answer.

> First, I think, is the fact that there is an enormous variety and profusion of intense human and animal suffering in our world. Second, is the fact that much of this suffering seems quite unrelated to any greater goods (or the absence of equal or greater evils) that might justify it. And, finally, there is the fact that such suffering as is related to greater good (or the absence of equal or greater evils) does not, in many cases, seem so intimately related as to require its permission by an omnipotent being bent on securing those goods (the absence of those evils) (561).

Putting these points of mine together into a single claim, Plantinga suggests that I take (1) to be probable with respect to

3. Many cases of evil are apparently pointless.

Suppose we agree that it is something like (3) that is being claimed to provide support for (1). Plantinga thinks there is a problem with (3), a problem of understanding what one is claiming in asserting (3). He suggests that on one reading (1) is probable with respect to (3), but on this reading (3) is not something we could know to be true. On a second reading, Plantinga notes that (3) turns out to be something of which we can be certain, but (1) is not in the least probable with respect to this reading of (3). Here is his discussion.

> But how shall we understand Rowe here? Shall we see him as holding that in fact there are many cases of evil such that it is apparent that an omnipotent and omniscient God, if he existed, would not have a reason for permitting them? But this is much too

strong; ...we could sensibly claim something like this only if we had reason to think that if such a God *did* have a reason for permitting such evils, we would be likely to have some insight into what it is. But if theism is true, then this is false; from the theistic perspective there is little or no reason to think that God would have a reason for a particular evil state of affairs only if we had a pretty good idea of what [that] reason might be. On the theistic conception our cognitive powers, as opposed to God's, are a bit slim for that. God might have reasons we cannot so much as understand; he might have reasons involving other free creatures—angels, devils, the principalities and powers of which St. Paul speaks—of which we have no knowledge. Shall we take (3) as pointing out, then, just that there are many evils such that we have no idea what God's reason, if any, is for permitting them? That seems right; but why suppose (1) is probable with respect to it? We could sensibly claim that (1) is probable with respect to (3) (taken thus) only if we had good reason to think we would be privy to God's reasons for permitting evil. (561)

The problem, as Plantinga sees it, is to understand (3). He poses a dilemma. Either (3) is to be understood as

3a. It is apparent to us that certain evils are pointless.[3]

or

3b. It is not apparent to us that certain evils have a point.

I agree with Plantinga that (3a) is too strong and (3b) too weak to provide proper support for (1). (3a) implies that we *know* that certain evils are pointless. And clearly this is something we do not know. (3b), as Plantinga rightly notes, would support (1) only if it is conjoined with some claim to the effect that if there were a God it is likely we would know what his reason is for permitting these evils.

But has Plantinga got it right? When we consider (3) are we driven to understand it as either (3a) or (3b)? I don't believe so. When I say:

His remark was apparently misleading.

must I be saying either that it is apparent to me that his remark was misleading or that it is not apparent to me that his remark wasn't misleading. No. For the first is stronger and the second weaker than what I said. What I said implies that there was something about the situation that makes it reasonable to believe that his remark was misleading. And what I'm saying about certain evils is that there is something about them and the situation in which they occur that makes it reasonable for us to believe that they are pointless.

What is it about certain cases of evil that makes it reasonable for us to believe that they are pointless? I might here simply reiterate the three points Plantinga quotes at the outset of his discussion. But it will be helpful, I think, to try to answer this question without using expressions like 'appears' or 'seems'.[4] Consider, for example, our hypothetical case of the fawn's intense suffering over several days as a result of being severely burned in a forest fire started by lightning. Or consider the actual case of a 5-year old girl who was raped, severely beaten over most of her body and strangled by her mother's boyfriend.[5] Let's refer to the first case as E1 and the second case as E2. Now about E1 and E2 I make the following judgment.

> P. No good state of affairs we know of is such that an omnipotent, omniscient being's obtaining it would morally justify that being's permitting E1 or E2.[6]

What am I implying in making this assertion? I am implying that we have *good reason* to believe that no good state of affairs we know of would justify an omnipotent, omniscient being in permitting either E1 or E2. I don't mean simply that we can't see how some good we know about (say, my enjoyment on smelling a fine cigar) would justify an omnipotent being's permitting E1 or E2. I mean that we can see how such a good would *not* justify an omnipotent being's permitting E1 or E2. For we can see that an omnipotent being wouldn't have to permit E1 or E2 in order to obtain the good of my enjoyment on smelling a fine cigar. And we can see that even were that not so, obtaining such a good wouldn't justify any being in permitting E1 or E2. Is there some other good state of affairs we know of that would justify an omnipotent being in permitting E1 or E2? I don't believe there is. The good states of affairs I know of, when I reflect on them, meet one or both of the following conditions: either an omnipotent being could obtain them without having to permit E1 or E2, or obtaining them wouldn't morally justify that being in permitting E1 or E2. And if this is so, I have reason to conclude that:

> Q. No good state of affairs is such that an omnipotent, omniscient being's obtaining it would morally justify that being in permitting E1 or E2.[7]

Since Q, slightly qualified, is tantamount to (1) in the earlier argument for atheism, if we are justified in accepting P and justified in inferring

Q from P, we are justified in accepting premise (1).

To simplify our discussion, I will use the letter 'J' to stand for the property a good has just in case obtaining that good would justify an omnipotent, omniscient being in permitting E1 or E2. If a good is such that obtaining it would justify an omnipotent, omniscient being in permitting E1 or E2, then that good has J; and if not, the good lacks J. In briefer terms, then, I have claimed P (no good we know of has J), inferred Q (No good has J), and concluded that since Q is tantamount to (1) we are justified in accepting (1).

The main point in Plantinga's earlier criticism is that we can get to (1) only if we have a good reason to think that if there is a good that has J, we would likely know of that good and likely see that it has J. Now since Q is tantamount to (1), we can take Plantinga to be claiming that we are justified in inferring Q (no good has J) from P (No good we know of has J) only if we have a *good reason* to think that if there were a good that has J it would be a good we are acquainted with and could see to have J. For the question can be raised: How can we have confidence in this inference unless we have a good reason to think that were a good to have J it would likely be a good within our ken? My answer is that we are justified in making this inference in the same way we are justified in making the many inferences we constantly make from the known to the unknown. All of us are constantly inferring from the A's we know of to the A's we don't know of. If we observe many A's and note that all of them are B's we are justified in believing that the A's we haven't observed are also B's. Of course, these inferences may be defeated. We may find some independent reason to think that if an A were not a B it would likely not be among the A's we have observed. But to claim that we cannot be justified in making such inferences unless we already know, or have good reason to believe, that were an A not to be a B it would likely be among the A's we've observed is simply to encourage radical skepticism concerning inductive reasoning in general.

In considering the inference from P to Q it is very important to distinguish two criticisms:

A. One is entitled to infer Q from P only if she has a good reason to think that if some good had J it would be a good that she knows of.
B. One is entitled to infer Q from P only if she has *no*

*reason* to think that if some good had J it would likely not
be a good that she knows of.

Plantinga's criticism is of type A. For the reason given, it is not a
cogent criticism. But a criticism of type B is entirely proper to advance
against any inductive inference of the sort we are considering. For
if one does have some independent, positive reason to think that
were an A not a B it would likely not be among the A's we've observed, then one's confidence in the inference must be diminished.
Thus one important route for the theist to explore is whether there
is some reason to think that were a good to have J it either would
not be a good within our ken or would be such that although we
apprehend this good we are incapable of determining that it has J.
Before we explore a criticism of type B, however, we need to consider
another point Plantinga makes against the view that it is likely that
(1) is true.

   It is part of the Free Will Defense to claim that it is logically possible
that an omnipotent, omniscient being could not have created a world
with less evil, but as much good, as our world contains. So long as
we accept (3) that a world with as much good as our world would
have to contain significantly free beings, and (4) that freely performing an action is not compatible with being causally necessitated to
perform that action, the argument Plantinga gives for this important
claim in the Free Will Defense is, I think, compelling.[8] Now if this
logical possibility were actually true then an omnipotent, omniscient
being would not have been able to improve on our world; our world
would be on balance as good as any that it was in his power to
actualize. All this, I think, is right. But how does it bear on our argument that it is in fact likely that an omnipotent, omniscient being
could have done a better job of things? For reasons that pass me
by, Plantinga thinks that this claim at the heart of the Free Will
Defense should lead us to reject the view that we have reason to
think it likely that an omnipotent, omniscient being could have done
better.

   I'm sure it strikes most of us as just plain reasonable to think that
if there were an omnipotent, omniscient being, then a bit more
activity on his part would have made the world somewhat better.
Suppose Hitler had been made to die in his sleep prior to carrying
out his plan to exterminate the Jews. Wouldn't this have made things
better? Probably, I would say. Perhaps, but perhaps not, Plantinga

would say. Now I grant that we don't *know* that things would have been better. It is possible that had Hitler died in his sleep some other person would have taken his place and brought about more evil than even Hitler did. But surely it is reasonable to believe that the number of German leaders who would have outdone Hitler in wickedness is relatively small. Or are all such conjectures just an epistemic toss-up? No one, I believe, really thinks this way. The mere fact that it is logically possible that an omnipotent, omniscient being couldn't have made things better is no real reason at all to doubt that such a being in fact could have made things better. Consider the proposition:

> If an omnipotent being had caused Hitler to die in his sleep, G. E. Moore would have been so distressed at the news of Hitler's death that he would have ended up promoting more evil than Hitler did.

This proposition, no less than the proposition at the heart of the Free Will Defense, is logically possible. But not much can be gained from that fact to make us doubtful of the future course of Moore's moral life, even had an omnipotent being caused Hitler to die in his sleep.

Perhaps, however, we are assuming the world's free creatures to consist of just human beings like us, with the possible exception of an omnipotent, omniscient being. And perhaps it is just this assumption that Plantinga is unwilling to make.

> For all we know, there is a great variety of free creatures involved in our history and in the history of our world—creatures of whose nature and activity we are at best but dimly aware. Perhaps there are angels and devils (Satan and his cohorts), perhaps there are the principalities, powers and dominions of whom St. Paul speaks. We know far too little about the world that is in fact actual, far too little about the sorts of creatures it contains and the counterfactuals of freedom that characterize them, to be justly confident of opinions about God's alternatives. (565)

The idea here, I take it, is that if it were only human beings and their freedom that we had to worry about, some reasonable judgments perhaps could be made to the effect that an omnipotent, omniscient being could have done better.[9] But who knows how Neptune or one of Satan's cohorts would have reacted if Hitler had been made to die in his sleep? And who among us is in a position to say what would have gone on in the principalities, powers and dominions, if such there be? The result, then, is that once we recognize the *possibility* that such beings as these are studying the daily twists and turns of our world, we really cannot make any rational judgments at all about what would have happened had an omnipotent being endeavored to make things better. But again, why should the mere logical possibility of the existence of Neptune, Satan's cohorts, etc., tell against our reasonable judgments of what would have transpired had an omnipotent, omniscient being caused Hitler to die in his sleep, prevented the fawn's agony, or prevented the mother's boyfriend from raping and savagely murdering the 5 yr. old girl?

## II

The second criticism I want to discuss is due to Stephen Wykstra.[10] This criticism consists of two related points. The first point may be viewed as an attack on our assertion that no good we know of has J. How do we tell whether a good has J? Well, Wykstra might suggest, we contemplate that good and find ourselves *unable to see* how it could morally justify an omniscient, omnipotent being in permitting E1 or E2. Having looked hard at that good and seeing no way in which it would justify such a being in permitting E1 or E2, we conclude that that good doesn't have J. But, Wykstra objects, this procedure is reliable only if *having J* has "seeability."[11] Our failure to see an elephant in a room is a good reason to conclude that one isn't there. But our failure, after careful inspection, to see a sand flea in a room is not a good reason to think that one isn't there. The reason for this is that the sand flea has what Wykstra calls "low seeability."[12]

Wykstra's second point is that there is good reason to think that were a good to have J it would likely be among the goods with which we are *not* acquainted. This is the point we need to consider carefully, for it is a type-B criticism of the inference from P to Q. If Wykstra is correct on this point, therefore, we have an effective attack against the argument for atheism based on the occurrence of certain types of evils. Before examining this point, however, it will be helpful to make a brief remark concerning his first point.

When we contemplate the good of my smelling a fine cigar, is it true that we *see* that this good lacks J, or do we simply fail to see that it has J? The answer, I think, is clearly the former. For we see clearly that this good is not good enough to justify any being in permitting E1 or E2. We also see clearly that obtaining this good would not require such a being to permit E1 or E2. So the absence of J is something we can determine, often with certainty, when we consider various goods with which we are acquainted. What is much more difficult, I believe, is to determine of some good *that it has J.* For suppose we do know of some good that far outweighs in value either E1 or E2. And suppose we see by the light of nature that even an omnipotent, omniscient being could not obtain that good without permitting E1 or E2. Would we be in a position to affirm for sure that the good in question has J? No. For it may be, for all we know, that there is some good state of affairs G* that significantly exceeds G in value and is such that an omnipotent, omniscient being can obtain it only by *preventing* E1 and E2. If this were so, then, even though an omnipotent being could obtain G only by permitting E1 or E2, G might very well lack J.[13]

I said earlier that Wykstra's main point is that there is reason to think that were a good to have J it would likely be among the goods with which we are *not* acquainted. In fact, however, this does not quite reflect his position. His view is that were a good not only such that obtaining it would justify an omnipotent, omniscient being in permitting E1 or E2, but also such that it is *purposed by the omnipotent, omniscient, creator of all things* as His reason for permitting E1 or E2, then that good would very likely be a good that is beyond our ken. Now we can ask what Wykstra's *purposed by the omnipotent, omniscient, creator of all things* adds to a good that has J. It adds, I think, two points. First, a good can have J even if there is no omnipotent, omniscient being. For to have J a good need only be such that obtaining it *would justify* an omnipotent, omniscient being in permitting E1 or E3. And that may be true of a good even though there is in fact no omnipotent, omniscient being. But, of course, if a good *is purposed* by an omnipotent, omniscient being as his reason for permitting E1 or E2, then there must be such a being. Second, a good that is purposed by the *creator of all things* would presumably be part of a large-scale plan that the creator has for the world as a whole. It would fit into some coherent plan that the creator has for his entire creation.

What kind of overall moral plan might such a creator have for his creation? Wykstra distinguishes between a "morally shallow" universe and a universe with "moral depth," arguing that such a being would likely plan the latter sort of universe.

> If God exists, then ...he would allow an evil only if doing so served some outweighing good. Such a good would be the "moral (or axiological) cause" for his allowing the evil. If God exists, there is some such cause for each of his allowings of evil. But here there are two options. We might think that if our universe is the creation of God, these moral causes would likely be "near the observable surface" of their effects. ...In contrast, we might judge that if our universe is the creation of God, it would likely have great "moral depth." By this I mean that many of the goods below its puzzling observable surface, many of the moral causes of God's current allowings and intervenings, would be "deep" moral goods. The question is this: if our universe is the creation of God, is it more likely to be morally shallow or morally deep? ...if our universe is the creation of God, a God with the sort of wisdom and vision entailed by theism, then it is eminently likely that it is morally deep rather than morally shallow.[14]

We might quarrel with Wykstra's way of framing the issue. What is "morally deep" sounds better than what is "morally shallow". But these are here only epistemic expressions. The difference is between a world in which it is understandable to us what the goods are (or might plausibly be) that justify God in permitting E1 or E2, and a world in which we are left without a clue. And what Wykstra is saying is that it is more likely that an omnipotent, omniscient, wholly good being who is the creator of everything would bring about the second kind of world, rather than the first. Unfortunately, Wykstra doesn't tell us why this is so.

Wykstra suggests that God may have had a choice about E1 and E2. On the one hand, he could have produced a world in which the goods for the sake of which he permits these evils—and others like them—are within our ken (the "morally shallow" world). On the other hand, he could have produced a world in which the goods for the sake of which he permits these evils are beyond our ken (the "morally deep" world). Faced with these alternatives, it is highly likely, so Wykstra thinks, that he would choose the latter. Why? Is it that the latter world is somehow better? If it is a better world, it must be that the goods that justify E1 and E2 in the deep world are much better, other things being equal, than the goods that justify E1 and E2 in the shallow world. For clearly, a good deal of suffering in this world is occasioned by the simple fact that so far as we can see there is no good that justifies an omnipotent, omniscient being in permitting E1 or E2. If we could see these goods occurring in our lives and could have some glimmer as to how they are obtainable by such a being only through permitting E1 and E2, it is quite likely that the grief and suffering occasioned by E1 and E2 would be less than it is.

Until we are provided with some reasons for thinking that if there were an omnipotent, omniscient, wholly good being who created our world, then the goods in virtue of which he permits E1 and E2 would be undetectable by us, we certainly are within our rights to infer Q from P and conclude that it is likely that there is no such being.[15]

If we take *standard theism* to be the view that there exists an omnipotent, omniscient, wholly good being who is the creator of the world, the question before us is whether the fact (or rational belief) that P (No good we know of has J) is a reason for thinking that standard theism is false. If we have some good reason to think that such a being would likely permit E1 and E2 only by virtue of goods that are *beyond our ken*, then P will not be a reason to think that no such being exists. For the reason for thinking that such a being would likely permit E1 and E2 only by virtue of goods that are beyond our ken will *diminish* the strength of our inference form P to Q. So the task for Wykstra is to show how standard theism implies (or makes it quite likely) that our world is morally deep (obscure). If we simply *attach* to standard theism the view that

> The goods for the sake of which an omnipotent, wholly good being must permit vast amounts of human and animal suffering are beyond our ken and will be realized only at the end of the world,

we can create an *expanded* version of theism that will not be rendered unlikely by P. For this expanded theism will make it likely that if Q were false, P would be true anyway. But as Wykstra and Russell point out, the danger here is that one may purchase immunity at the price of enlarging the original hypothesis, thus increasing (decreasing) its original implausibility (plausibility).[16]

## III

The final objection to be discussed is radical, if not revolutionary.

This objection is due to William Hasker.[17] Instead of attacking the reasoning in support of premise 1 (in the original argument) and the inference from P to Q (in the revised argument), Hasker attacks premise 2 (in the original argument) and the inference from Q to atheism (in the revised argument). For Hasker thinks that if theism is true then, given our moral obligations to refrain from harming others, there would have to be *gratuitous evils*. [A gratuitous evil is an instance of evil such that an omnipotent being could have prevented it without thereby preventing the occurrence of some greater good. (p. 2)] Hasker reasons as follows. If God prevents any evil that does not lead to a greater good, morality will be undermined —for no sense could then be made of principles prohibiting wrong-doing or the infliction of harm. Given, then, that morality is not to be undermined, God must permit evils that do not lead to any greater good. But for God to permit such evils is nothing more than for gratuitous evils to exist.

Although Hasker elaborates his view in terms of both consequentialist and deontological moral theories, his central point can best be grasped in terms of a consequentialist moral theory. If God prevents any evil that does not lead to a greater good then it will be impossible for anyone to act wrongly. For a wrong act would be among those that do not lead to a greater good. But what then becomes of morality? The whole fabric of moral principles prohibiting us from harming others and from wrongdoing would simply collapse. For moral principles prohibiting such actions are intelligible only if it is possible for us to perform them.

My answer to Hasker is twofold. First, if there is a God and he prevents all gratuitous evil, it hardly seems that we are deprived of the possibility of significantly harming others. We can still torture and murder the innocent. These are paradigm cases of harming, of wrongdoing. Of course, God would prevent these deeds unless He could not do so without thereby foregoing obtaining some good that justifies Him in permitting them. Do these actions then become morally right? It hardly seems so. The actions themselves do not produce the greater good. It is God in his freedom (according to theism) who is responsible for obtaining the justifying goods. But let's put this consideration aside, and pursue a second answer to Hasker's objection.

In commenting on an earlier version of Hasker's important paper,[18] I argued that if an evil is such that its prevention by an omnipotent, omniscient being would undermine morality, then if morality is a good to be preserved, God may permit that evil in order to achieve the good of sustaining morality. So evils whose permission is not justified by any other goods may be justified by the good of sustaining the application to us of fundamental moral principles. But if this is so, these evils are not after all gratuitous. I then concluded:

> And what this means, I'm afraid, is that Hasker's argument contains the seeds of its own destruction. A world suitable for significant morality would not require an omnipotent, omniscient, perfectly good being to permit any *gratuitous* evil at all.[19]

In the version of his paper now being considered, Hasker argues that my answer is inadequate because a person could still reason that any evil action he performs that serves no other good will be permitted by God *only if* it serves the greater good of maintaining significant morality.

> But now, surely, we have reached a situation exactly parallel to the one which led to our previous conclusion about the undermining of morality. The agent will be able to say to himself that if he performs the action in question, the resulting evil is *permitted by God* as the *most economical means* to an end of overriding importance—namely, the maintenance of significant morality. So once again, morality is undermined, ...(p. 28)

What Hasker is arguing here, I think, is this. Suppose God permits evils (otherwise gratuitous) so as to maintain significant morality. Presumably, there would be a threshold beyond which his permission of evils for this purpose (the maintenance of significant morality) would no longer be required. Beyond that threshold, such evils would be genuinely gratuitous and, therefore, God would not permit them to occur.[20] My point was that the evils permitted up to the threshold would *not be gratuitous*. Hasker acknowledges this, but argues that morality, nevertheless, would still be undermined. For a person contemplating performing some evil deed will know that *God's permitting the deed* will mean that some justifying good is obtained, either (a) a good unrelated to the maintenance of morality, or (b) the good of sustaining morality. If the person knows that (a) is the case, morality is undermined. The prohibition against doing the evil deed will make no sense. But the person doesn't know this. For all he knows, it is (b) that is the case. But here, Hasker argues, our agent can reason further. First, he can infer that if (b) is so then God will permit the evil so as to maintain the threshold of evils required for morality. And second, he can infer that if he were to refrain from his evil deed, God would have to permit some other evil no less severe in order to maintain the threshold at the level required to sustain morality. The result, in either case, is that the agent is powerless to make the world better by refraining from performing any putative evil deed. The prohibition against wrongdoing will make no sense. Morality is again undermined.

I'm inclined to think that this argument has some force if we are operating within a purely consequentialist ethical theory. Suppose, however, that we operate within a deontological moral theory. We may suppose that there are moral principles forbidding certain acts of harm to others. Consider an agent who contemplates an evil deed of seriously harming some other human being. Our agent may reason that if he refrains God will have to permit some other evil just as severe in order to sustain significant morality. So he may conclude that his evil action won't have consequences that make the world any worse than it will be if he refrains. But, of course, on a deonto- logical theory it won't follow that he has no duty to refrain. His duty to refrain does not depend merely on the consequences of his action. It depends on the fact that his proposed action is itself something that is at least prima facie wrong for him to do. Thus, it is intelligible that there would be moral principles prohibiting human actions that on occasion are permitted by God for the purpose of making such moral prohibitions a significant fact in human conduct. Given such a deontological moral theory, God could prevent all gratuitous evil without morality thereby being undermined.

Toward the end of his paper Hasker acknowledges that there may still be a problem with the existence of *natural evils* (like the fawn's suffering) that we have reason to believe are gratuitous. So, he endeavors to prove that the existence of gratuitous natural evils is fully consistent with the existence of an omnipotent, omniscient, perfectly good being.

Why would such a being permit natural evils that he could prevent without thereby losing some outweighing good? Hasker points out that there are goods that come about as a result of our having to deal with natural forces that bring about harm of various kinds. These threatening forces motivate us to develop knowledge of nature's workings, courage, cooperation, compassion for others, etc. Hasker claims that if God were to prevent all such evils, *and we knew it,* we would not be motivated to develop these goods.

> Surely the motivation to acquire and/or respond in accordance with any or all of these goods would be greatly reduced, if not eliminated entirely, if we *really believed* that God would prevent any natural evils which were not essential to the realization of still greater goods. (p. 34)

So, in order for humans to develop in these desirable ways, God must either massively deceive us about what is going on in nature (He makes it *seem* as though a good deal of gratuitous, natural evil occurs) or he must permit natural evils that serve no balancing or outweighing good at all.

My answer strikes a now familiar refrain. If God must permit natural evils that serve no *other goods* in order to obtain the goods of our developing ourselves into courageous, cooperative, compassionate, knowledgeable beings, then those natural evils are *not* gratuitous after all. What Hasker needs to establish is that God would be justified in permitting natural evils that he could prevent without losing any outweighing goods, *including* the goods of human knowledge, courage, compassion, etc. Hasker fails to do this.

From our earlier discussion, we can construct a Haskerian response to this criticism. Suppose a certain level of *actual*, otherwise gratuitous, natural evil must occur in order to provide rational motivation for humans to develop certain good qualities and dispositions in themselves. If so, God will then permit this level of otherwise gratuitous, natural evil in order to provide us with the requisite rational motivation to develop in these ways. But now consider some agent who is in a position to prevent some serious animal suffering that is about to be occasioned by natural forces. We will suppose our agent is in a position to rescue the fawn from the fire (occasioned by lightning) before it is severely burned. Our agent can reason that if she prevents this otherwise gratuitous, natural evil, God will have to permit the occurrence of some other equally severe, otherwise gratuitous, natural evil in order to maintain the level necessary to provide humans with rational motivation to develop in virtuous ways. Knowing this, our agent may well be deprived of *rational grounds* for her motivation to prevent this otherwise gratuitous, natural evil. Paradoxically, if God prevents all natural evils unless He cannot do so without losing some outweighing good (including the good of providing rational motivation for humans to develop knowledge, courage, compassion in relation to harmful effects of natural forces), *and we know this to be so*, then our motivation to prevent what appear to be gratuitous, natural evils would be diminished. Thus, we would be less likely to develop knowledge, courage, compassion, in relation to harmful effects of natural forces.[21]

Suppose there is a good demon with power and inclination to prevent any toothaches from occurring. The good demon, however, recognizes that it is good for human beings to develop and exercise their capacities to relieve their fellows of toothaches. The fostering of human motivation to achieve this good requires the demon to permit toothaches to occur every now and then. Moreover, achieving the good in question justifies the demon in permitting these toothaches. Potential toothaches not required for this end are prevented by the good demon. Now let's also suppose that, *knowing this*, I come upon you at the moment you are about to have a toothache. I might well reason that were I to struggle to find a way to prevent your toothache, the good demon will have to permit some other toothache to occur so that toothaches occur at the required rate to provide humans with the motivation to develop and exercise their capacities to relieve them. The result is that I am not rationally motivated to struggle to find a way to prevent your toothache. But it is precisely our efforts to find a way to prevent or relieve instances of toothache suffering that enable us to develop the knowledge we need to prevent or relieve them. Paradoxically, the policy of the good demon, once known by us, appears to render it somewhat unreasonable for us to develop the capacities for the sake of whose development and exercise the demon permits certain toothaches to occur. Even more paradoxically, it would seem that if the good demon is to accomplish the good of our developing and exercising our capacities to relieve others of toothaches, he must permit toothaches to occur that are not required for us to develop and exercise these capacities. But if they are not required for us to develop and exercise these capacities, why does he have to permit them? What is our good demon to do? His goodness inclines him to prevent any gratuitous toothaches. But it now seems that the only way he can achieve the end of humans developing the capacity to relieve others of toothaches is by allowing gratuitous toothaches.

The good demon's problem is like God's problem, as Hasker sees it. God's goodness, I would think, inclines him to prevent hideous moral evils and natural evils that involve extraordinary human and/or animal suffering. But some such evils must be permitted to achieve certain goods: a world with significant morality, a world in which human beings are motivated to develop courage, compassion, knowledge of the workings of nature, etc. These evils, therefore, are not genuinely gratuitous. But it seems that if we all know what policy God and the good demon are following, the achievement of the very goods for the sake of which these evils are permitted is undermined, if not defeated.

Let's suppose that the arguments for these conclusions are both rigorous and compelling. What are God and the good demon to do? Will they let gratuitous evils and gratuitous toothaches abound, so that (paradoxically) the various goods noted above can be achieved? Or is there a better way?

Consider again the good demon. The problem contains an essential element that is epistemic in nature: the knowledge human beings have that the good demon exists and is operating according to the policy described above. It is that knowledge that undermines my motivation to struggle to find a way to prevent your toothache. If the good demon is powerful enough, he then has two ways out of his plight. He can allow genuinely gratuitous toothaches to abound *or* he can refrain from making his presence and policy so decisively known that human beings become unmotivated to develop the capacity to relieve people of their toothaches. Is there any real doubt as to how a *good* demon would solve the problem?

If my son will be undergoing delicate and dangerous surgery in the morning and I have been advised that a sound night's rest is quite important to a successful outcome, what will I say if he asks me before sleep if the operation will be dangerous? Suppose I know that by telling him it is he will be so frightened that he will hardly sleep at all. Clearly, I need to assure him that all will be well. Similarly, for the good demon. Similarly, also for God. If God really is in the paradoxical corner that Hasker thinks He is in, then clearly the best course is not to make his presence and policy so decisively known that his very purposes for human life are undermined, if not defeated.[22] Hasker thinks this engages God in a "massive disinformation campaign." God will need to allow it to appear that gratuitous evils occur, even though they in fact do not. For so long as human beings believe that gratuitous evils occur, neither morality nor our motivation to develop courage, compassion, etc., will be diminished or undermined. Surely, other things being equal, God will judge that our lack of decisive knowledge of His presence and policy is better than letting horrendous, gratuitous evils abound in the world. As many theists believe, God will wait for the next life to provide us with a decisive knowledge of his nature and actions. This being so, Hasker's thesis fails. In a universe with significant morality, human courage, compassion, and knowledge of the workings of nature, there is no need whatever for God to permit evils that He could prevent without loss of any balancing or outweighing good.

Hasker might (but only for purpose of argument) be willing to concede all of the above. But he would then go on to argue that the concession is rather detrimental to the argument for atheism based on evil. For that argument presumed that if it is rational to believe that genuinely gratuitous evil exists then it is rational to believe that an omnipotent, omniscient perfectly good being does not exist. But this is no longer so. For if the reasoning above is correct such a being would have to make it (or allow it to) seem to us that gratuitous evils occur. Even though the being prevents all gratuitous evil, the realization of some of His good purposes for us (significant morality, knowledge of the workings of nature, compassion, etc.) depends on it being rational for us to believe that gratuitous evils exist. So we can't appeal to this point as our grounds for concluding that it is rational to believe that such a being does not exist.

My answer to this is that it is not only likely that evils occur that an omnipotent, omniscient being could have prevented without loss of any balancing or greater good, it also is likely that such evils occur far in excess of what such a being would have to permit in order for us to be *rational* in believing that such evils occur. Clearly, if there is an omnipotent being, such a being could have prevented a good deal of evil in our world without in the least altering the fact that the amount and intensity of evil makes it rational for us to believe that evils occur in excess of what an omnipotent being would need to permit to achieve a balancing or greater good (including the goods of significant morality, knowledge, compassion, etc.) Who would say that if only five million had been permitted by omnipotence to perish in the holocaust it would *not* have been rational to believe that evils occur that omnipotence could have prevented without loss of any greater good? So, even if the reasoning above is accepted, there remains plenty of space for a strong argument for atheism to be constructed.

## Notes

1. "The Problem of Evil and Some Varieties of Atheism," *American Philosophical Quarterly* 16 (1979): 335-341.
2. "Epistemic Probability and Evil," *Archivio Di filosofia* LVI (1988): 557-584.
3. An evil is pointless provided there is no good the obtaining of which would justify an omnipotent, omniscient being in permitting that evil.
4. The use of these expressions has led to some misunderstanding of the argument. For a good discussion of these problems see Stephen J. Wykstra, "The Humean Obstacle to Evidential Arguments From Suffering: On Avoiding the Evils of "Appearance," *International Journal for the Philosophy of Religion* 16 (1984): 73-93. Also see my reply, "Evil and the Theistic Hypothesis: A Response to Wykstra," *International Journal for the Philosophy of Religion* 16 (1984): 95-100.
5. For the details of this case and an excellent discussion of the problem of evil see Bruce Russell, "The Persistent Problem of Evil," *Faith and Philosophy* 6 (1989): 121-139.
6. For sake of simplicity, I shall ignore the possibility that such a being might permit E1 or E2 in order to prevent some equal or worse state from obtaining.
7. For a defense of P and the inference of Q from P see my "Evil and Theodicy," *Philosophical Topics* 16 (1988): 119-132.
8. Plantinga's lucid presentation of the argument for this claim may be found in *God, Freedom, and Evil*, (New York: Harper Torchbook, 1974).
9. This is what I am reading into Plantinga's discussion. He nowhere explicitly concedes this.
10. See his "The Humean Obstacle to Evidential Arguments From Suffering: On Avoiding the Evils of 'Appearance'." Also see his co-authored piece (with Bruce Russell), "The 'Inductive' Argument from Evil: A Dialogue," *Philosophical Topics* 16 (1988): 133-160.
11. I discuss Wykstra's first point here only in order not to have been thought to have intentionally refused to address it. Actually, his first point is not directed at the question of justifying the claim that a good lacks J. It is directed at the question of justifying the claim than an evil serves no justifying good.
12. "The "Inductive" Argument From Evil: A Dialogue," 143.
13. It is important to note that there are two ways in which the permission of an evil *may* be justified. First, it may be part of a good whole that has another part that is better than the whole. Second, it may be part of a good whole in which the other part is not better than the whole. In the first case, the evil is *outweighed*; in the second case, it is *defeated*. Here I only discuss the first way. For some remarks about the second way see 233-234 of my essay, "The Empirical Argument From Evil," *Rationality, Religious Belief, and Moral Commitment*, ed. by R. Audi and W. Wainwright, Cornell University Press, 1986. Also see Roderick Chisholm's analysis of the idea of evil being defeated in "The Defeat of Good and Evil," *Proceedings and Addresses of the American Philosophical Association* 42 (1968-69): 21-38.

14. "The "Inductive" Argument From Evil: A Dialogue," 146-147.
15. What I say here isn't quite right. It would be sufficient to weaken the inference from P to Q to show that if there were an omnipotent, wholly good being who created our world, then the goods in virtue of which he permits E1 and E2 would be as likely to be undetectable by us as to be detectable by us. (I owe this correction to Stephen Wykstra.)
16. "The "Inductive" Argument From Evil: A Dialogue," 157-160. Also see my discussion of this point in "The Empirical Argument from Evil," 239-241.
17. "The Necessity of Gratuitous Evil," forthcoming in *Faith and Philosophy*. References to the pages of this manuscript will be included in the text.
18. The comments were presented at the meeting of the Central Division of the APA, April, 1988.
19. Quoted in Hasker's paper, p. 22
20. I would argue that we have reason to believe that a good deal of evil could have been prevented by an omnipotent being without loss of any justifying good, including the good of sustaining morality. It is reasonable to believe, for example, that an omnipotent being could have prevented much of the horror of the holocaust without rendering senseless our prohibitions against harming others. Therefore, it is likely that genuinely gratuitous evil exists and, therefore, likely that an omnipotent, morally perfect being does not exist.
21. I've compressed this argument considerably. As it stands, I doubt that Hasker would endorse it. It is intended only to suggest a similar kind of response to my objection to his argument concerning gratuitous moral evil.
22. A position quite like this is held by John Hick, the foremost theodicist of our time. See the revised edition of *Evil and the God of Love*, (New York: Harper and Row, 1978).

Philosophical Perspectives, 5, Philosophy of Religion, 1991

# THE ARGUMENT FROM EVIL

Michael Tooley
The Australian National University

The problem that suffering and other evils pose for the rationality of belief in an omnipotent, omniscient, and morally perfect person has been the focus of intense discussion for a long time. The main thing that I want to do here is to consider whether recent discussions have significantly advanced our understanding of the underlying issues. I believe that they have, and I shall try to indicate the ways in which that is so.

The structure of my discussion is as follows. The first two sections constitute the main part of the paper. In the first section, I shall consider how the argument from evil might best be formulated. Among the topics that I shall discuss are, first, the distinction between abstract and concrete formulations of the argument from evil; secondly, the distinction between incompatibility and evidential formulations; thirdly, the distinction between subjective and objective formulations; and fourthly, the relevance to the argument from evil of traditional arguments in support of the existence of God.

One of my conclusions in the first section is that the argument from evil is best viewed as consisting of a core argument which is relatively straightforward—with the exception of one crucial premise—plus a subsidiary argument designed to support the premise in question. The second section will therefore be devoted to an examination of that subsidiary argument.

In the third section, I shall consider different types of responses to the argument from evil. One useful classification, I suggest, is in terms of whether the goal is that of a total refutation of the argument, a defense, or a theodicy.

In section four, I then consider various attempts to show that facts concerning evil do not constitute even *prima facie* evidence against the existence of God. The five attempts that I shall consider are, first, an appeal to the idea that there is no best of all possible worlds; secondly, Plantinga's initial attempt to refute evidential versions of the argument; thirdly, Plantinga's attack upon inductive logic; fourthly, an appeal to human epistemological limitations; and finally, an appeal to the ontological argument. I shall argue that none of these attempts at a total refutation of the argument from evil is satisfactory.

In section five, I consider two defenses that might be offered. The one appeals to the possibility of positive evidence for the existence of God, and the other to partial successes achieved by theodicies. I then conclude with a very brief look at the prospects for a successful theodicy.

## I. Formulating the Argument from Evil

How is the argument from evil best formulated? To answer that question, it is useful to consider three distinctions: (1) that between *abstract* and *concrete* formulations; (2) that between *incompatibility* and *evidential* formulations; (3) that between *subjective* and *objective* formulations. Two of these distinctions, I shall argue, are important, and have received insufficient attention. The other, in contrast, is not only less significant than it is often thought to be, but is potentially misleading with respect to the basic structure of the argument.

Of these three distinctions, the first is the crucial one. For, with it in mind, it is a relatively straightforward matter to set out a version of the argument from evil that avoids a number of rather widespread errors, and that seems generally satisfactory. I shall also argue, however, that there are two natural variants of the basic argument which are very useful for some purposes.

### 1.1 Abstract Formulations Versus Concrete Formulations

Any version of the argument from evil claims that there is some fact concerning the evil in the world such that the existence of God— understood as an omnipotent, omniscient, and morally perfect person—is either logically precluded, or rendered unlikely, by that fact. But versions of the argument differ radically with respect to what the relevant fact in question is. Sometimes the appeal is to the mere existence of any evil whatever. Sometimes it is to the existence of a certain amount of evil. And sometimes it is to the existence of evils of a certain specified sort.

To formulate the argument from evil either in terms of the mere existence of any evil at all, or in terms of the existence of a certain quantity of evil, is to advance an abstract version of the argument from evil. It is to assume that the detailed nature of the evils that there are in the world does not matter: all that is important is that there is at least some evil, or, alternatively, that the sum total of evils, of whatever sorts, is a certain amount.

The alternative is a concrete version of the argument from evil— one where it is important that there be instances of evil which possess certain further properties. In some cases, the further properties may be of a very general sort. Thus, some concrete formulations of the argument from evil, for example, appeal only to the fact that the world appears to contain natural evil. Others appeal to more detailed facts concerning the evil that is present in the world—such as the fact that innocent children suffer agonizing deaths, or that animals suffer, or that animals did so before there were any persons to observe their suffering, or that the suffering that people undergo apparently bears no relation to the moral quality of their lives, or that it bears a rather clear relation to the wealth and medical knowledge of the societies in which they live.

How should the argument from evil be formulated? Abstractly, or concretely? The answer is that a formulation that refers to specific sorts of evils is surely the natural choice. For consider, first of all, an abstract formulation that appeals to the mere existence of evil. One problem with such a formulation is that while one might well feel that the world would be better off without the vast majority of evils, it is not so clear that this is so for absolutely all evils. Some would argue, for example, that the frustration that one experiences in trying to solve a difficult problem is outweighed by the satisfaction of arriving at a solution, and therefore that the world is a better place because it contains such evils.

Another familiar objection is connected with the idea of libertarian free will. Many people would claim that the world is a better place if it contains individuals who possess libertarian free will, rather than individuals who are free only in a compatibilist sense. If this claim can be made plausible, one can then argue, first, that God would have a good reason for creating a world with individuals who possessed libertarian free will, but secondly, that if he did choose to create such a world, even he could not ensure that no one would ever choose to do something morally wrong. The good of libertarian free will requires, in short, the possibility of moral evil.

Neither of these lines of argument is unproblematic. The basic point here, however, is that the idea that either the actuality of certain undesirable states of affairs, or at least the possibility, may be logically necessary for goods that outweigh them, is not without some initial plausibility, and if some such claim can be sustained, it will follow immediately that the mere existence of evil cannot be *incompatible* with the existence of an omnipotent, omniscient, and morally perfect being. But, in addition, if there can be such evils, it also seems clear that the mere existence of evil cannot really provide much in the way of *evidence* against the existence of God.

Is the situation improved if one shifts to an abstract formulation which appeals, instead, to some fact concerning the *quantity* of evil to be found in the world? It is hard to see that it is. For as David Conway (1988) remarks, in a very important recent article on the argument from evil, if we ask how much evil we should expect there to be in the world if God exists, "the only halfway plausible candidates here would be 'none' and 'who knows'" (p. 58). The former will be right if the existence of evil is incompatible with the existence of God, whereas if it is not, it would seem that one will have no idea how much evil to expect. For if evil can be necessary for a greater good that outweighs it, the idea of worlds that are larger and larger, either in space or in time, strongly suggests that one cannot place any upper limit on the quantity of evil that might be found in a world created by God.

The prospects for a successful abstract version of the argument from evil would seem, therefore, rather problematic. It may be, of course, that it does follow from the correct moral principles that there cannot be any evils whose actuality or possibility makes for a better world, but to attempt to set out a version of the argument from evil that requires a defense of that thesis is certainly to swim upstream. A much more promising approach, surely, is simply to focus upon those evils that are thought, by the vast majority of people, to pose a problem for the rationality of belief in an omnipotent, omniscient, and morally perfect person.

Given that the preceding observations are rather obvious ones, one might have expected that discussions of the argument from evil would have centered mainly upon concrete formulations of the argument. Rather surprisingly, that has not been so. Indeed, some authors seem to focus almost exclusively upon abstract versions of the argument.

One of the more striking illustrations of this phenomenon is provided by Alvin Plantinga's discussions of the problem of evil. In *God and Other Minds*, in *The Nature of Necessity*, in *God, Freedom, and Evil*, for example, he focuses mainly on the question of whether the existence of God is compatible with the existence of evil, although there are also short discussions of whether the existence of God is compatible with the existence of a given quantity of evil, and of whether the existence of a certain amount of evil renders the existence of God unlikely. The latter topic is then the total focus of attention in his long article, "The Probabilistic Argument from Evil".

Not only does Plantinga concentrate exclusively on abstract versions of the argument from evil, but he seems to believe that if it can be shown that the existence of God is neither incompatible with, nor rendered improbable by, either (1) the mere existence of evil, or (2) the existence of a specified amount of evil, then no *philosophical* problem remains. People may find, of course, that they are still troubled by the existence of *specific* evils, but this, Plantinga seems to be believe, is a *religious* problem, and what is called for is not philosophical argument, but "pastoral care".[1]

This view is wrong, and seriously so. For not only can the argument from evil be formulated in terms of specific evils, but that is the natural way to do so, given that it is only certain types of evils that are generally viewed as raising a serious problem with respect to the rationality of belief in God. To concentrate on abstract versions of the argument from evil is to ignore the most plausible and challenging versions of the argument.

## 1.2 The Empirical, or Concrete, Version of the Argument from Evil

Contrary to what is sometimes claimed, most philosophers who have felt that evil poses a problem for the rationality of belief in God have appealed, I believe, to detailed facts concerning the evils that one encounters in the world. They did so, I suggest, because they thought that some evils—such as natural disasters, the intense sufferings of animals and innocent people, the deaths of young children—have a bearing upon belief in God that others evils—such as that of the unhappiness experienced by a mass murder when his most recent killing was less exciting than he had hoped—do not. Such philosophers were advancing, accordingly, concrete versions of the argument from evil, not abstract ones.

At the same time, however, the contrast between concrete and abstract versions of the argument from evil was rarely set out in an explicit way. One of the real advances, accordingly, in more recent presentations of the argument from evil is that this distinction has come to the forefront, with a number of philosophers realizing, clearly and explicitly, that the argument from evil needs to be formulated in terms of specific evils, or specific types of evil.

The result is a growing consensus concerning how the argument from evil should be formulated. Thus, if one considers recent discussions by philosophers such as David Conway (1988, pp. 40-1), R. K. Perkins (1983, pp. 230-40), William Rowe (1979, pp. 336-8, and 1986, pp. 222-35), and Richard Swinburne (1988, pp. 289-92), among others, it seems clear that, though there are some differences of detail, there is general agreement concerning the basic structure of the argument from evil.

The view that has gradually emerged is, I suggest, as follows. First, the argument from evil can be viewed as having two parts. On the one hand, there is the core argument, the conclusion of which is that there is no omnipotent, omniscient, and morally perfect person. On the other, there is a subsidiary argument, the aim of which is to defend a crucial premise of the core argument, and which focuses upon one or more specific evils, or types of evil, that are found in the world. Secondly, the core argument, carefully formulated, is deductively valid. Thirdly, in view of the problematic nature of abstract versions of the argument from evil, the core argument must achieve deductive validity at a price: the cost is that one of the premises, though it may well seem eminently plausible, is certainly open to question. Hence the need for the subsidiary argument. Fifthly, the subsidiary argument will involve both substantive moral claims and factual claims. Finally, the subsidiary argument is neither invariably deductive nor invariably inductive or probabilistic. Indeed, even given a particular statement of the argument from evil, the subsidiary argument may involve a number of parts, dealing with different specific evils or types of evil, and some of those parts may be purely deductive, while others involve inductive or evidential considerations.

How does the core argument run? The following, which is based upon formulations offered by Conway (1988, p. 40), and Rowe (1979, p. 336), illustrates the basic format:

(1) Cases where animals die agonizing deaths in forest fires, or where children undergo lingering suffering and eventual death due to cancer, are cases of intrinsically undesirable states of affairs that an omnipotent and omniscient person could have prevented without thereby either allowing an equal or greater evil, or preventing an equal or greater good.

(2) An omniscient and morally perfect person would prevent the existence of any intrinsically undesirable state of affairs whose prevention it could achieve without either allowing an equal or greater evil, or preventing an equal or greater good.

(3) There does not exist an omnipotent, omniscient, and morally perfect person.

Given that others have discussed this general type of argument in a very careful way, there is no need here to take a detailed look at this argument. The basic strategy, however, is worth noting. First, then, one guiding idea is that the core argument should turn upon the existence of what might be called *unjustified* evils, where an evil counts as unjustified, in the present context, if an omnipotent and omniscient being could have prevented it, and would not have been justified in not doing so. Secondly, another guiding idea is that the soundness of the argument should reduce to the question of the acceptability of one of its premises. For this to be so, the argument must be deductively valid, and all of the premises but one must be such as would be accepted by virtually everyone, regardless of his or her basic world view.

Since the above argument is deductively valid, the question is whether one of the two premises qualifies as clearly acceptable. The second premise is the one that is intended to play that role. Does it do so?

In thinking about this, it is important to notice the following two points. First, the second premise does not imply that an omnipotent, omniscient, and morally perfect person would create the best of all possible worlds. So it is not exposed to the objection that even such a person might not be able to ensure the existence of the best of all possible worlds, given that how good a world is depends upon the free choices of the other individuals it contains. Secondly, the second premise does not imply that an omniscient and morally perfect being will make whatever improvements it can. For the second premise refers only to actions that involve the prevention of intrinsically undesirable states of affairs, or evils, not to actions that involve the production of intrinsically desirable states of affairs.[2]

If premise two, properly understood, is acceptable, everything comes down to premise one. Can it be shown to be reasonable, and if so, how? This is the question that the subsidiary argument addresses, and, in section 2, I shall turn to the question of how that argument might best be formulated.

## 1.3 Incompatibility Formulations Versus Probabilistic Formulations

A very common view concerning the argument from evil is that it is important to distinguish between versions of the argument which claim that some facts about the evil in the world are logically incompatible with the existence of God, and versions which claim only that some such facts make belief in the existence of God irrational. Recently, however, David Conway has argued against the idea that this distinction is an important one.

Conway's basic argument may, I think, be put as follows. First, given the problematic nature of abstract versions of the argument from evil, it seems likely that a satisfactory version of the argument from evil will involve a core argument that has the structure indicated in the preceding section. It will, therefore, be a deductively valid argument. Accordingly, if the distinction between incompatibility formulations and evidential or probabilistic formulations is to have any application, it must be with respect to the subsidiary argument that is used to establish the crucial premise which asserts that there are evils that are unjustified in the relevant sense. Next, Conway argues, in effect, that this difference with respect to the subsidiary argument reduces to a difference with respect to the modal status of one of the premises.[3] Finally, Conway argues that the modal status of the proposition in question is not a significant feature of the argument. For, in the first place, if the proposition is true, then the argument is sound, and it does not matter whether the proposition is necessarily true or contingently true. Similarly, if the proposition is false, then the argument is unsuccessful, and it does not matter whether the proposition is necessarily false, or only contingently so. And in the second place, with regard to supporting the argument, one does not need either to show that the proposition in question is necessarily true or to show that it is contingently true: one need only show that it is true. Similarly, in order to refute the argument, one need only show that the proposition is false: its modal status may be left an open question.

The final step in this argument seems dubious. The problem is that, in general, it will not be possible to offer reasons for thinking that a proposition is true that are not also either reasons for thinking that it is necessarily true, or reasons for thinking that it is contingently true. For the modal status of a proposition determines what sort of argument is needed to support it: consider, for example, the very different support that is relevant in the cases of mathematical generalizations and scientific generalizations. So it would seem that it can be argued, against Conway, that the distinction between incompatibility formulations of the argument from evil and evidential formulations remains a relevant one, since it is a matter of the very different sorts of support that are required for a crucial proposition.

Another objection to Conway's argument here is that he has not considered the point that one reason the distinction between incompatibility and evidential formulations is important is because it bears upon how secure the argument is with respect to additional considerations. For whereas deductively valid arguments can only be undermined via considerations that show that one or more of the premises is suspect, good inductive arguments can also be undermined by evidence that merely supplements one's initial evidence. So a sound incompatibility formulation of the argument from evil would settle the issue, whereas a sound evidential version of the argument might always be overthrown.

These two considerations show that the distinction between incompatibility formulations and evidential formulations is not an irrelevant one. Nevertheless, I believe that Conway is essentially right. The distinction between incompatibility versions and evidential versions, although not irrelevant, is not really very important. Moreover, it can be potentially very misleading.

Consider the issue of security. It is true that there is a type of defeat to which inductive arguments are exposed, and to which deductive arguments are immune. But how important is that fact? Isn't the crucial question rather *how likely* it is that a given conclusion will be overthrown? Given a short, clear, deductive argument from premises that appear indubitable, the probability that the conclusion is false will surely be very low. But the same may be true with regard to the conclusions of merely inductive arguments—such as the conclusion that the earth is round rather than flat.

What is true, then, is that if a formulation of the argument from evil involves only evidential considerations, the likelihood that the conclusion is true may vary widely. It may be that it is only slightly more likely that there is no omnipotent, omniscient, and morally perfect being than that there is, in which case the argument is a rather tenuous one, and there is a real chance that it will be overthrown by additional information. But, on the other hand, the probability that there is no omnipotent, omniscient, and morally perfect person might instead be very high relative to one's total evidence, in which case the probability that the conclusion will be overthrown by additional evidence must, by definition, be very low. Thus, given a good evidential argument, a serious question does remain concerning how much support it provides for the conclusion. But if the answer to that question was, in a given case, that it was about as likely that God existed as that the earth was flat, the fact that the argument was merely an evidential one would not, I suggest, be very important.

I also said—in agreement with Conway (1988, p. 43)—that it was potentially very misleading to think in terms of a distinction between incompatibility formulations of the argument from evil and evidential or probabilistic formulations. The reason is that this way of thinking suggests that any version of the argument from evil can be classified as of either one type or the other. But that is not so. For as I mentioned in the previous section, and as we shall see in more detail in section 2, in the case of concrete versions of the argument from evil, the subsidiary argument may involve consideration of different instances of evil, and for some of these the thrust of the argument may be that it follows deductively from the relevant moral principles, and empirical facts, that the evil is unjustified, while for other cases the conclusion may only be that it is likely, or likely to a certain extent, that the evil is unjustified.

In the case of concrete versions of the argument from evil, the basic locus for the application of the incompatibility/evidential distinction is not to the subsidiary argument as a whole, but to the different parts of that argument which are concerned with the specific instances of evil that are being cited. Some versions of the argument may, of course, cite only instances of evil that, it is claimed, can be shown to be unjustified by means of a deductive argument from sound moral principles. Other versions may cite only instances of evil that, though they may be justified, are unlikely to be so. But still other versions may appeal to evils of both sorts. It would seem, then, that what one should think in terms of is a distinction between incompatibility and evidential *considerations*, rather than one between incompatibility and evidential *versions* of the argument.

## 1.4 Subjective Versus Objective Formulations

In this section and the next, I shall mention two alternatives to the core argument outlined in section 1.3—alternatives which seem very useful in certain contexts. The one to be considered in this section arises out of a distinction between what might be called subjective and objective formulations of the argument from evil.

A good place to begin is with the following passage:

> It will be important for me to distinguish among the inquirer's doubts between moral doubts and doubts about contingent non-moral fact, and for this purpose I need to establish a position on the status of moral judgments. I hold that they have truth-value; some are true and some are false. I do not need to argue for that aspect of my position in this context, since anyone who thinks that evil raises for theism the 'problem' which I have described must think this. There could only arise an issue as to whether certain evils were *compatible* with the existence of a good God if goodness and evil were properties which belonged to persons, actions, and states of affairs, and judgments which affirmed or denied their existence had a truth value (Swinburne, 1988, p. 290).

Embedded in what is otherwise a very thoughtful discussion, these claims by Swinburne that the problem of evil arises only if moral judgements are either true or false, and only if goodness and evil are real properties of persons, actions, and states of affairs, are rather jarring. For, in the first place, suppose that John Mackie's error theory is correct, and that, although we are ascribing non-natural properties to actions when we describe them as right or wrong, and to states of affairs when we describe them as good or bad, the world in fact contains no such properties (1977, pp. 15-49). All of our 'positive' ethical beliefs would be false in that case, but that would not be a barrier to some of John's ethical beliefs being logically inconsistent with some of Mary's, nor to some of John's ethical beliefs being mutually inconsistent, or to their giving rise to inconsistencies when combined with some of his non-moral beliefs about the world.

What about Swinburne's other claim—viz., that the problem of evil does not arise unless moral judgements have truth values? Swinburne does not spell out his grounds for this claim, but it appears to rest upon the idea that the only sentences that can stand in logical relations with one another are *statements*. But that, surely, is not so. The reason is that any number of psychological states can stand in logical relations to one another. Just as the belief that Peano's postulates are true is logically incompatible with the belief that there is a largest prime number, so the desire that Peano's postulates be true is logically incompatible with the desire that there be a largest prime number, and similarly for the corresponding hopes, fears, etc. And because various psychological states can exhibit this sort of inconsistency, sentences that 'express' those psychological states can also exhibit inconsistency. Thus the two optative sentences, "Would that all the windows were closed" and "Would that that window were open" are mutually incompatible.

This general point is central, of course, to R. M. Hare's account of the meaning of ethical language (1952). Hare maintains that any adequate account of the meaning of ethical language must be able to explain the logic of moral argument, and his response to this requirement involves arguing, first, that there is a logic of imperatives, and that arguments involving imperatives can be valid or invalid in precisely the same sense that arguments involving statements can be, and secondly, that the idea that moral language is related to what he refers to as "universalized" imperatives provides a good initial model for understanding the logic of moral discourse.

Suppose, then, that ethical judgements, rather than being either true or false, are really universalized imperatives. That will not affect the logical relations between ethical judgements, nor within sets of sentences, some of which are ethical, and some of which describe non-moral states of affairs. So whether or not some states of affairs which are characterized as evil are incompatible with the existence of a being that, in addition to being omnipotent and omniscient, is also characterized as perfectly good, cannot depend upon whether a cognitivist meta-ethics is correct.

But if the logical relations in question are unaffected by whether ethical judgements have truth values, then it would seem that it must be possible to formulate versions of the argument from evil that, rather than involving implicit reference to correct moral principles, refer instead to the moral principles that happen to be accepted by a given individual, or group of individuals. And surely this is so. For suppose that Jack is a philosopher who is a theist and a hedonistic utilitarian, while Mary is an atheist who accepts a slightly different ethical outlook. Does Mary have to convert Jack to her moral outlook before she can employ the argument from evil? Clearly not. She can point out that if there were a being that was omnipotent and omniscient and morally perfect as judged by Jack's own moral standards, then one would expect the world to be a hedonistic paradise. But that doesn't seem to be the case. Thus Mary can show that it is unlikely that there is any being that is omnipotent, omniscient, and morally perfect as judged by the principles of hedonistic utilitarianism. She will have shown, therefore, that there is something irrational about the system of beliefs and values that Jack accepts.

The general idea may be put as follows. Consider any objective formulation of the argument from evil. It can be changed into a subjective formulation by the following two steps. First, replace all of the moral terms by expressions that involve explicit reference to correct moral principles, so that, rather than referring to intrinsically undesirable states of affairs, one refers to states of affairs that are intrinsically undesirable as judged by correct moral principles, and rather than referring to a morally perfect person, one refers to a person who is morally perfect as judged by correct moral principles. Next, replace all references to correct moral principles by references to the moral principles accepted by some specific person, *A*. The first change will not affect the content. The second change will, but it will not affect the logical relations between statements. The result will be a subjective formulation which refers to the moral principles accepted by a specific person, but the logical relations within the argument will be precisely the same as those within the original, objective formulation of the argument.

Just as in the case of an objective formulation of the argument from evil, precisely what is established will depend upon the details of the subsidiary argument—an argument which will now be functioning to establish that there are evils that are unjustified, in the relevant sense, according to the moral principles accepted by individual *A*. If some of the evils cited in the subsidiary argument are the subject of incompatibility-style arguments, then the overall conclusion will be that there is no being that is omnipotent and omniscient, and morally perfect as judged by the moral principles accepted by *A*. On the other hand, if all of the evils give rise only to evidential arguments, then the conclusion will instead be that the existence of such a being is unlikely.

The possibility of subjective formulations of the argument from evil is, I believe, an important one, given that disagreements concerning fundamental values are not always easily resolved. The availability of subjective formulations means that it may be possible to show that a given person's belief in the existence of God is irrational without having to question the moral values that he or she accepts.

## 1.5 The Relevance of Traditional Arguments for the Existence of God

If a given, concrete formulation of the argument from evil appeals to cases of intrinsically undesirable states of affairs that give rise only to evidential considerations, rather than to incompatibility considerations, then, although the existence of God may be improbable relative to that evidence, it may not be improbable relative to one's total evidence. Theists, however, have often contended that there are a variety of arguments that, even if they do not prove that God exists, provide positive evidence. May not this positive evidence outweigh, then, the negative evidence of apparently unjustified evils?

Starting out from this line of thought, a number of philosophers have gone on to claim that in order to be justified in asserting that there are evils in the world that establish that it is unlikely that God exists, one would first have to examine *all* of the traditional arguments for the existence of God, and show that none of them is sound. Alvin Plantinga, for example, says that in order for the atheologian to show that the existence of God is improbable relative to one's total evidence, "he would be obliged to consider all the sorts of reasons natural theologians have invoked *in favor of* theistic belief—the traditional cosmological, teleological and ontological arguments, for example" (1979, p. 3). And in a similar vein, Bruce Reichenbach remarks:

> With respect to the atheologian's inductive argument from evil, the theist might reasonably contend that the atheologian's exclusion of the theistic arguments or proofs for God's existence advanced by the natural theologian has skewed the results (1980, p. 224).

Now it is certainly true that if one is defending a version of the argument from evil which supports only a probabilistic conclusion, one needs to *consider* what sort of positive reasons might be offered in support of the existence of God. But Plantinga and Reichenbach are advancing a rather stronger claim here, for they are saying that one needs to look at all of the traditional theistic arguments, such as the cosmological and the teleological. They are claiming, in short, that if one of those arguments turned out to be defensible, then it might well serve to undercut the argument from evil.

But this view seems mistaken. Consider the cosmological argument. In some versions, the conclusion is that there is an unmoved mover. In others, that there is a first cause. In others, that there is a necessary being, having its necessity of itself. None of these conclusions involve any claims about the moral character of the object in question, let alone the claim that it is a morally perfect person. But in the absence of such a claim, how could such arguments, even if they turned out to be sound, serve to undercut the argument from evil?

The situation is not essentially different in the case of the argument from order. For while that argument, if it were sound, would provide grounds for drawing some tentative conclusion concerning the moral character of the designer or creator of the universe, the conclusion in question would not be one that could be used to overthrow the argument from evil. For given the mixture of good and evil that one finds in the world, the argument from order can hardly provide support even for the existence of a designer or creator who is very good, let alone one who is morally perfect.[4] So it is very hard to see how the teleological argument, any more than the cosmological, can overturn the argument from evil.

A similar conclusion can be defended with respect to other arguments, such as those that appeal to purported miracles, or religious experiences. For while in the case of religious experiences it might be argued that personal contact with a being may provide additional evidence concerning the person's character, it is clear that the *primary* evidence concerning a person's character must consist of information concerning what the person does and does not do. So, contrary to the claim advanced by Robert Adams (1985, p. 245), even if there were veridical religious experiences, they would not provide one with a satisfactory defense against the argument from evil.

A good way of underlining the basic point here, I think, is to set out an alternative formulation of the argument from evil. The idea is to grant, for the sake of argument, that there is an omnipotent and omniscient person, and then to reformulate the argument from evil so that it includes that assumption. The result might be the following, 'hypothetical' version of the argument from evil:

(1) There is an omnipotent and omniscient person, and cases where animals die agonizing deaths in forest fires, or where children undergo lingering suffering and eventual death due to cancer, are cases of intrinsically undesirable states of affairs that the omnipotent and omniscient person could have prevented without thereby either allowing an equal or greater evil, or preventing an equal or greater good.

(2) An omniscient and morally perfect person would prevent the existence of any intrinsically undesirable state of affairs whose prevention it could achieve without either allowing an equal or greater evil, or preventing an equal or greater good.

(3) Although there is an omnipotent and omniscient person, there is no person who is omnipotent, omniscient, *and morally perfect*.

When the argument from evil is formulated in this way, it becomes clear that the vast majority of considerations that have been offered as reasons for believing in God can be of little assistance to the person who is trying to resist the argument from evil. For most of them provide, at best, very tenuous grounds for *any* conclusion concerning the moral character of any omnipotent and omniscient being who may happen to exist, and almost none of them provide any support for the hypothesis that there is an omnipotent and omniscient being who is also morally perfect.

The ontological argument is, of course, a notable exception, and, consequently, the advocate of the argument from evil certainly needs to be able to show that it is unsound. But almost all of the other standard arguments are not at all to the point.

## 2. Supporting the Crucial Premise: the Subsidiary Argument

We saw earlier that concrete formulations of the argument from evil typically involve two parts: first, a core argument, which is deductively valid, but which has one premise that stands in need of support; secondly, a subsidiary argument, the function of which is to establish the premise in question. In this section I shall turn to the crucial issue of the structure of the subsidiary argument.

The premise in the core argument that stands in need of support claims, first, that certain states of affairs are actual; secondly, that those states of affairs are intrinsically undesirable; thirdly, that an omnipotent and omniscient being could have prevented their existence; and fourthly, that he could have done so without either allowing an equal or greater evil to exist, or preventing the existence of an equal or greater good. Establishing the crucial premise, accordingly, with respect to any given instance of evil, will involve arguing for each of those four claims.

## 2.1 The First Three Claims

Consider a specific type of evil—say, the case, used by Rowe in his formulation of the argument from evil, of a fawn dying an agonizing death because of a forest fire. The first step would be to establish that such cases actually occur. Normally that claim would be readily conceded. But not always. Thus F. J. Fitzpatrick, in discussing Rowe's appeal to such cases of suffering, argues as follows:

> Since God is omnipotent, he can prevent animals from experiencing intense suffering in all those cases in which we should ordinarily expect such suffering to be felt. Whenever intense animal suffering would in fact be gratuitous, then, we may believe that God, being perfectly good, will intervene to prevent it from being experienced. Of course, God may still allow animals to display those bodily reactions which we should normally regard as the characteristic physiological and behavioral manifestations of intense pain; but since there is a clear ontological distinction between pain and its normal overt manifestations, it is quite possible for the latter to take place without the former. There is, of course, no positive evidence that God actually does intervene to produce this result, but equally there is no positive evidence that he does not. Hence the theist can conclude that Rowe's formulation of his 'unreasonableness' argument relies on a presupposition which is open to question; for in describing the fawn as being 'in terrible agony for some days' he is assuming the existence of a situation which may never exist, since it may be prevented by God's power (1981, p. 34).

Fitzpatrick's suggestion here may seem like a desperate one indeed. But it should be noted that Fitzpatrick speaks throughout as if one knew that God existed. If that were so, then I think it might very well be the case that the hypothesis he proposes would be the most reasonable one. The problem, however, as we saw in section 1.5, is that almost none of the considerations typically offered in support of belief in God would, even if they were sound, give us good reasons for believing in the existence of a being that was omnipotent, omniscient, and morally perfect. Thus, barring something like a victorious ontological argument, one is not justified in supporting the claim that there are no such cases of suffering by appealing to the belief that an omnipotent, omniscient, and morally perfect person exists. Moreover, given that that is so, one can offer very strong reasons for holding that animals, in such situations, do undergo enormous suffering. For we know that their brains are similar in the relevant respects to ours, and we know that there are, first of all, laws connecting brain states to states of consciousness, including pain, and secondly, other laws connecting states of consciousness to behavior, and both sorts of laws, when applied to animals in such situations, lead to the conclusion that such animals suffer greatly.

The next step involves arguing that such situations are intrinsically undesirable, or evil, so one needs to appeal to a relevant moral principle. One possible principle, accepted by many people, is the principle that all suffering is intrinsically bad. But that principle might be challenged. Someone who accepts a retributivist view of punishment might maintain, for example, that the suffering that people deservedly experience as punishment for morally wrong actions is not intrinsically bad—though I suspect that even most retributivists would reject this contention. But in any case, even if one were inclined to accept this view, it seems clear that one could formulate a more guarded moral principle that one would find satisfactory, and that would still apply to the case of the fawn. One might, for example, appeal to the more modest principle that suffering which is endured by sentient beings that are morally innocent is always intrinsically bad.

The third step involves arguing that an omnipotent and omniscient being could have prevented the existence of the state of affairs in question. In the case of the fawn, that is surely true: an omnipotent and omniscient being could either have intervened to save the fawn from the fire, or to end its life painlessly. It might be thought, moreover, that this would always be the case, that an omnipotent and omniscient person could always intervene to prevent the existence of any evil. For being omniscient, he would know that the evil would occur unless he intervened, and being omnipotent, he would have the power to intervene and prevent the evil from occurring.

But there is a problem with this argument. It concerns the case of worlds that involve indeterministic processes. Consider such a world, and consider a case where an omniscient being intervenes in an indeterministic process. Could that being possibly know that if he had not intervened, then, although it would not have been causally determined, the process would, as a matter of fact, have given rise to some specific evil? To know that would be to have known that a certain counterfactual was true. But according to the general truth-maker principle,[5] statements can be true only if there are *categorical* truth-makers for them, and the problem is what such a categorical truth-maker could be when it is a matter of how an indeterministic process would have gone if there had been no intervention.

This is a more general version of a problem which is familiar from discussions of the free will defense: the problem of counterfactuals concerning what agents possessing libertarian free will would have done if circumstances had been different. Robert M. Adams (1977) has claimed that such 'counterfactuals of freedom' cannot be true, and has supported this contention by means of a truth-maker argument. Alvin Plantinga, on the other hand, is unimpressed by Adams' arguments, and holds that counterfactuals of freedom can be true (1985b, pp. 372-9). Plantinga's response to Adams is, however, quite unconvincing: Plantinga simply rejects out of hand the idea that true statements require categorical truth-makers, neither offering any arguments against this thesis, nor considering the support that can be offered for it.

If, as seems very plausible, the general truth-maker argument is sound, then not even an omniscient being can always know what would happen in a given situation were he not to intervene. But such a being can know, in the vast majority of situations, whether a given type of evil would be *likely* to occur were he not to intervene. For even in an indeterministic world there can certainly be categorical truth-makers for subjunctive conditionals concerning what is likely to occur. So even if, in Rowe's example, it is not causally determined that the fawn will suffer an agonizing death, it will still be extraordinarily likely that this will occur if there is no intervention, and knowledge of this latter fact would enable an omnipotent and omniscient being to prevent the evil in question. The third step in the subsidiary argument does not involve, therefore, any real difficulty.

## 2.2 The Fourth, and Crucial Claim

This brings me to the fourth and final step, which really lies at the heart of the whole argument. Can it be established, or at least shown to be likely, that an omnipotent and omniscient being could have prevented the evil in question, and have done so without thereby either allowing an equal or greater evil, or preventing the existence of some desirable state of affairs whose desirability would have been at least as great as the undesirability of the evil?

A useful way of tackling this issue, I suggest, is as follows. First, consider the situation where, though one may be ignorant of many things, one is morally omniscient, at least with respect to *basic* moral principles, and try to determine what lines of argument would be open to one in that case. Then, having done that, consider how it affects the situation if one does not assume that one's knowledge of basic moral principles is complete.

### 2.2.1 From the Perspective of Moral Omniscience

Let us consider, then, the case where a person has complete knowledge of all basic moral principles. Given such knowledge, such a person would be able to specify all the types of states of affairs which are either intrinsically good or intrinsically bad. Next, he would also be able to consider all possible pairs of morally significant states of affairs, and determine, first, which types of evils are logically connected, so that an evil of the one type can be prevented only by allowing an evil of the other type, and secondly, which types of evils are logically connected with which types of goods in such a way that it is impossible to prevent the evil without also preventing the good. Finally, for all such cases, he would be able to determine, by considering relevant basic moral principles, when one ought to prevent a given sort of evil, either at the cost of allowing an evil of some other sort, or at the cost of preventing some type of good.

What are some possible outcomes of such an investigation, and what would be the relevance of each with respect to the final step in the subsidiary argument? One possible outcome might be the conclusion that there are some types of evils that are not logically connected, in the relevant ways, either to other evils or to goods. A little reflection suggests, however, that even if this outcome is possible, it is not likely to be helpful in the present context, for the following reason. Any evil that anyone is ever aware of would seem to be a logically necessary condition for at least one good state of affairs—that, namely, of someone's regarding the evil as something that, considered in itself, the world would be off without.

A second, more plausible outcome would be a conclusion to the effect that there are some types of evil that are logically connected, in the appropriate ways, with goods and/or evils, but where the relevant goods and evils do not constitute a sufficient reason for allowing an evil of the type in question. Consider, for example, the fawn's suffering. Such suffering makes possible feelings of sympathy in any individuals who are aware of the suffering. But it might well be the case that it follows from some of the basic moral principles that the goodness of such feelings could never justify one in allowing the suffering in question If that were the case, and if, moreover, the same were true with respect to all the desirable and undesirable states of affairs that are logically connected in the relevant ways with such a case of suffering, then it would follow that while there might be occasions where *we* would be justified in allowing such suffering, this could not be so for an omnipotent and omniscient being.

A third possible outcome would be a conclusion to the effect there are some types of evil that are logically connected, in the appropriate ways, with goods and/or evils, and where either the realization of the relevant goods, or the prevention of the relevant evils, would constitute a sufficient reason for allowing an evil of the type in question. Given knowledge of all basic moral principles, one could determine precisely which evils could be justified in this way, and under precisely what conditions they would be justified.

One could then make use of one's non-moral knowledge to see whether, where such evils had occurred, the relevant conditions which would make it permissible for an omnipotent and omniscient person to refrain from preventing those evils did in fact obtain. Suppose, for example, that it followed from basic moral principles that it would be permissible for an omnipotent and omniscient person to allow reasonably good people to endure great suffering only if such suffering resulted in substantial personal growth—or, at least, if it was likely to do so. If studies of people in such a situation showed that it was more likely, say, to embitter them, than to result in positive moral development, then one would, presumably, be justified in concluding that it would not be morally permissible for an omnipotent and omniscient being to allow such suffering. Or suppose that it followed from basic moral principles that it would be permissible for an omnipotent and omniscient person to allow there to be conscious, rational beings who sometimes fail to do what is morally right, only if the beings in question possess libertarian free will. If there were considerations that made it unlikely that people in this world possess libertarian free will, then one would be justified in concluding that our world probably contains undesirable states of affairs that an omnipotent and omniscient being would not have a morally sufficient reason for not preventing.

Up to this point, I have assumed, in effect, that our morally omniscient person is reasoning in a certain way in arriving at his conclusions concerning the conditions under which an omnipotent and omniscient person would be justified in not preventing some evil. For I have imagined him proceeding as follows. He is considering, say, whether an omnipotent and omniscient person could be justified in allowing an evil of type $E_1$ for the sake of some greater good. Examining all of the basic moral principles, he concludes that there are $n$ possible types of good states of affairs: $G_1$, $G_2$,...$G_n$. He asks which are logically connected with $E_1$ in the appropriate way. Let us suppose that only $G_1$ and $G_2$ are. He then asks whether the goodness of either is sufficient to outweigh the badness of $E_1$. If neither is, then he concludes that there are no conditions under which an omnipotent and omniscient person would be justified in not preventing an evil of type $E_1$, while if the goodness of $G_1$, say, is sufficiently great to outweigh the badness of $E_1$, whereas that of $G_2$ is not, then he concludes that an omnipotent and omniscient person is justified in not preventing an instance of $E_1$ only if it is accompanied by an instance of $G_1$—or at least, if it was sufficiently likely that it would be.

The important thing to notice about this reasoning is that it depends upon one's having a complete list of all basic moral principles, since if there could very well be types of states of affairs other than $G_1$, $G_2$,...$G_n$ that were intrinsically good, then one would not be justified in drawing the conclusions in question, in the way indicated.

But the above sort of reasoning is not the only way that those conclusions might be derived. For it might follow, for example, from one or more of the basic moral principles, either that it would be permissible for an omnipotent and omniscient person to allow an evil of type $E_1$ only if it was accompanied by a good of type $G_1$, or if it was sufficiently likely that it would be so accompanied. Alternatively, it might follow from one or more of the basic moral principles that it would never be permissible for an omnipotent and omniscient person to allow an evil of type $E_1$.

Consider, for example, the case of suffering. Mightn't it be plausibly claimed, for example, that an omnipotent and omniscient being would never be justified in allowing one innocent person to suffer in order to *benefit others*, that the only acceptable justification would be that there was some good logically connected with the suffering in an appropriate way—such as moral growth in response to suffering— which was a good for the individual who was suffering?

But, then, if an omnipotent and omniscient being would only be justified in not preventing the suffering of an innocent person if the individual in question was likely to benefit from it, it would seem to follow that there are also types of evils that an omnipotent and omniscient being would never be justified in not preventing. For in the case of sentient beings that are not persons, one is dealing with individuals who cannot undergo moral growth in response to suffering, and thus who can never benefit from their own suffering. So it follows from the previous conclusion that an omnipotent and omniscient person would never be justified in allowing non-persons to suffer.

## 2.2.2 From our Ordinary Perspective: the Relevance of Normative Ethics and Meta-ethics

Up to this point, I have been considering the justification of the fourth, and crucial claim of the subsidiary argument, from the perspective of a person with complete moral knowledge. How is the situation affected if one no longer explicitly assumes moral omniscience?

Given this shift, a theist may feel that an answer to the argument from evil is at last on the horizon. For if our moral knowledge is not necessarily complete, then there may be types of intrinsically good states of affairs that, first of all, we have not even conceived of; secondly, that could be logically connected with the problematic evils that we find in the world; and thirdly, that would be sufficiently weighty that an omnipotent and omniscient person would be justified in not preventing the evils in question for the sake of those goods. And if this is possible, may we not be able to argue that it is not only possible, but also sufficiently likely—given the gulf between our knowledge and omniscience—to undermine the final step in the subsidiary argument?

But this hope depends, I shall now argue, upon crucial assumptions, one in normative ethics, and one in meta-ethics—neither of which is, I believe, acceptable.

Recall that, given unlimited knowledge of basic moral principles, there are two very different ways in which one might arrive at conclusions concerning the conditions under which it would be morally permissible for an omnipotent and omniscient person to refrain from preventing certain evils. The one route involves considering all possible goods that might be connected with the evil in question, and, in view of this fact, it is natural to suppose that it requires knowledge of *all* moral truths. The second route, however, is a very different one, since there the relevant conclusions are being derived from one or more basic moral principles, and not from the total set. A successful answer to the argument from evil needs to block both routes. The attempt to block the first leads to unacceptable conclusions concerning the nature of morality, and our epistemic access to moral truths. The attempt to block the second involves unacceptable claims within normative ethics.

First, then, the second route, and the relevance of normative ethics. To block this route, one would have to maintain *either* that there are not, either for any specific types of evil, or for evil in general, any basic principles that, in isolation from the totality of moral truth, entail constraints concerning the conditions under which it is morally permissible for an omnipotent and omniscient person to refrain from preventing evil, or to refrain from preventing evil of some specific sort, *or else* that, while there may well be such principles, there are none of which we have any knowledge. Can either of these things be plausibly maintained?

I do not believe that they can. For it seems to me that the principles that support the conclusions in question are simply certain principles that are essential to the concept of *justice*. In deciding what to do, or to allow to happen, it is not enough simply to tally up the quantities of good and evil, and to see what the overall balance of good over evil is. Nor is it acceptable to decide upon a course of action by simply considering the average quality of life enjoyed by individuals.. One must consider the distribution of goods and evils; one must consider how individuals are affected. For it is unjust to impose evils upon some in order to provide goods for others.

Given only limited knowledge and power, one may be forced to allow some individuals to suffer who do not deserve to so, either because one cannot prevent the suffering, or because the only alternative is allowing others, who also do not deserve to suffer, to experience equal or greater suffering. But given unlimited knowledge and power, the situation is different: one need not allow anyone to suffer unjustly. Hence one has arrived at one of the conclusions advanced in the previous section: it is morally permissible for an omnipotent and omniscient being to allow a morally innocent individual to suffer only if that suffering will benefit the individual in question, or, at least, if it is sufficiently likely that it will do so.

What the theist needs to do, therefore, to block the second route, is to embrace a maximizing view within normative ethics—that is, a view according to which the rightness of an action is a matter of the resulting, overall balance of good over evil—or of some related quantity, such as the average—and according to which there are no basic moral principles concerning justice or fairness. Utilitarianism is one such normative view. In large measure, however, the widespread dissatisfaction with utilitarianism is due precisely to its conflict with very strong intuitions which most people have concerning justice. As a consequence, the prospects of blocking the second route do not appear at all promising.

What about the first route? Given that the reasoning involved in it, as that line of thought was developed above, rested upon the assumption that one had knowledge of all basic moral principles, it might seem obvious that once we cut back to the moral knowledge that we actually possess, the first route can no longer be negotiated. But before one draws that conclusion, one needs to consider the implications it would have with respect to the nature of morality, and with respect to moral epistemology.

In many areas, truth may well remain forever hidden from our gaze. In mathematics, one may contemplate a proposition, without even suspecting that it is a theorem, let alone discovering a proof of it. In physics, we may never arrive at a totally satisfactory theory of the physical world, with the result that we may be totally unable to describe the causes of events that are perfectly familiar to us. Can morality be just like that? Could there, for example, be some property with which we were all perfectly familiar, which was of great moral significance, but which never struck any human, at any time, as having any moral importance at all? Or could there be a property of states of affairs that was good-making, but which seemed to all humans, at all times, to be a bad-making property? Could there be a property of actions that was wrong-making, but which all humans firmly believed was right-making?

Though I cannot attempt to argue the matter here, the idea that any of these are genuine possibilities seems to me extremely problematic. The main ground of this feeling, I think, lies in the idea, first, that a property cannot be morally significant in itself unless the belief that something has that property, or the belief that some possible state of affairs or action would have that property, has the power to affect one's motivation in certain ways, and secondly, that the belief that a property is morally significant in itself arises out of an awareness of the intrinsically-motivating quality of the relevant beliefs.

If this is right, then the epistemological situation with respect to ethics differs in at least one very significant way from that with respect to other areas such as mathematics and science. No matter how many people consider some mathematical proposition, its truth may remain inaccessible. No matter how much time and thought is devoted to discovering the cause of some event, the answer may not be found. But if some property with which people are perfectly well acquainted is morally significant in itself, that fact cannot be, it would seem, epistemically inaccessible.

What is the significance of this epistemic accessibility with respect to the present argument? The answer is that if there could be properties with which people were perfectly familiar, but whose moral significance no one was aware of, then we would have virtually no grounds at all for drawing any conclusion concerning how complete or incomplete our moral knowledge is likely to be. But epistemic accessibility means that if it is true that some particular property is morally significant, the property must be one with which we are not acquainted. Is it possible that there are such properties? Yes, that is certainly possible, and because it is, it is possible that there are basic moral truths of which we have no knowledge. But is that possibility sufficient to block the first route? No, it is not.

The reason is this. The human race has become acquainted, over a long period of time, with a vast array of properties, any of which could have possessed intrinsic moral significance. Of that vast array, only a vanishingly small proportion have turned out to be possibly significant in themselves. In addition, when one looks back over the last few thousand years, to what extent are there properties whose moral significance was recognized by no one up until that time? Consider, for example, the sorts of things that people judge to be intrinsically good—things such as friendship, freedom, knowledge, pleasure, and so on. Must not these things have struck humans as good from the very earliest times? Or consider the sorts of things that people typically judge to be intrinsically bad—things such as pain, loneliness, the frustration of desires, deprivation of freedom, and death. How many of these represent recent discoveries, recent advances in our moral understanding?

What, then, are we to make of moral progress? The answer, I suggest, is that the moral progress that we see as we look back over human history does not consist in the recognition of more good-making and bad-making properties, or right-making and wrong-making properties. It consists, rather, in a gradually increasing ability on the part of humans to respond appropriately to those properties *wherever* they occur. Pain is intrinsically bad, and because it is a bad thing, it is a reason for being concerned not only about the suffering of humans, but also about the suffering of non-human animals. The property of being an act of killing a person is a wrong-making characteristic, and because it is, one has a reason not only to refrain from killing members of one's group, but outsiders as well.

The thrust of the argument, in short, is that the discovery of a new property which is morally significant in itself is an extremely rare occurrence. That being so, how likely is it, first of all, that new, morally significant properties will be discovered; secondly, that they will be logically connected in the appropriate ways to all of the evils in the world that, judged by our present moral knowledge, are unjustified; and thirdly, that they will also possess sufficient moral weight to make it the case that an omnipotent and omniscient being would be justified in not preventing any of those evils? In the light of the above, I believe that such an outcome is improbable in the extreme.

To sum up. I have been considering, in this section, the question of the justification of the fourth, and crucial step, of the subsidiary argument. I argued, first, that, given complete knowledge of basic moral principles, there are at least two ways in which one can arrive at conclusions concerning conditions that must be satisfied if an omnipotent and omniscient being is to be justified in preventing evils of a specified sort. We have now seen that neither of those routes is undercut if one assumes, instead, that our knowledge of basic moral principles is to some extent incomplete. I believe that one is justified in concluding, therefore, that the subsidiary argument can in principle be sustained.

## 3. Three Types of Responses: Total Refutations, Defenses, and Theodicies

The basic thrust of the argument from evil, as we have seen, is that it is rational to believe that there are a number of intrinsically undesirable states of affairs in the world that are such that there is no morally sufficient reason that an omnipotent and omniscient being would have for allowing those states of affairs to exist, and that, consequently, it is rational to believe that either there is no omnipotent and omniscient being, or that such a being exists, but is not morally perfect.

Given a formulation of the argument from evil along the lines indicated above, what sorts of responses are possible? I want to suggest that a useful way of dividing up possible responses is into what I shall refer to as total refutations, defenses, and theodicies. This classification is based upon the following line of thought. The advocate of the argument from evil is claiming, in the first place, that there are facts about evil in the world that make it *prima facie* unreasonable to believe in the existence of God, and, in the second place, that the situation is not altered when those facts concerning intrinsically undesirable states of affairs are conjoined with all the other things that one is justified in believing, both inferentially and non-inferentially: belief in the existence of God is also unreasonable *relative to the total evidence* available. In responding to the argument from evil, then, one might challenge either of these claims. That is to say, one might grant, at least for the sake of argument, that there are facts about evil that, other things being equal, render belief in God unreasonable, but then argue that when those considerations are embedded within one's total evidence, belief in the existence of God can be seen to be reasonable, all things considered. Alternatively, one might defend the more radical thesis that there are no facts about evil in the world that make it even *prima facie* unreasonable to believe in the existence of God.

If the latter thesis is correct, the argument from evil does not even get started. I shall therefore classify such attempts to answer the argument from evil as *total refutations* of the argument.

The proposition that relevant facts about evil do not make it even *prima facie* unreasonable to believe in the existence of God strikes most philosophers, of course, as rather implausible. We shall see, nevertheless, that a number of philosophers have attempted to mount this sort of attack upon the argument from evil.

The alternative course is to grant that there are facts about intrinsically undesirable states of the world that make it *prima facie* unreasonable to believe that God exists, but then to argue that belief in the existence of God is not unreasonable, all things considered. This response may take, however, two slightly different forms. One possibility is the offering of a complete *theodicy*. This involves, first of all, describing, for every actual evil found in the world, some state of affairs that it is reasonable to believe exists, and which is such that, if it exists, will provide an omnipotent and omniscient being with a morally sufficient reason for allowing the evil in question; and secondly, establishing that it is reasonable to believe that all evils, taken collectively, are thus justified.[6]

The other possibility is that of offering a *defense*. This I shall understand to be any argument which attempts to show that it is the case— or at least, that it is probably the case—that there are reasons which would justify an omnipotent and omniscient being in not preventing the evils that we find in the world. A defense differs from a theodicy in that it attempts to show only that *there are* such reasons: it does not attempt to specify what they are.[7]

## 4. Attempted Total Refutations

In this section, I shall consider five attempts to show that the argument from evil does not succeed in establishing even that evil is *prima facie* evidence against the existence of God, let alone that the existence of God is improbable relative to our total evidence. The first appeals to the claim that there is no best of all possible worlds. The second and third are two of Plantinga's attempts to refute probabilistic arguments from evil. The fourth attempt appeals to human epistemological limitations, and the fifth to the ontological argument.

### 4.1 The 'No Best of All Possible Worlds' Response

One way of attempting to show that the argument from evil does not even get started is by appealing to the proposition that there is no best of all possible worlds. For if for *every* possible world, however good, there is a better one, then the fact that this world could be improved upon does not give one any reason for concluding that, if there is an omnipotent and omniscient being, that being cannot be morally perfect.

This response to the argument from evil has been around for awhile. In recent years, however, it has been strongly advocated by George Schlesinger (1964, 1977), and, more recently, by Peter Forrest (1981)—though Forrest, curiously, describes the defense as one that has been "neglected", and refers neither to Schlesinger's well-known discussions, nor to the very strong objections that have been directed against this response to the argument from evil.

The decisive weakness in this attempt to refute the argument from evil was pointed out very clearly some years ago by Nicholas La Para (1965) and Haig Khatchadourian (1966) among others, and has been set out in an especially forceful and detailed way in a recent article by Keith Chrzan (1987). The basic point is simply that the argument from evil, properly formulated, does not turn upon the claim that this world could be improved upon, or upon the claim that it is not the best of all possible worlds: it turns upon the claim that there are good reasons for holding that the world contains evils, including instances of suffering, that an omnipotent and omniscient being would not have a morally sufficient reason for not preventing. As a consequence, the proposition that there might be better and better worlds without limit is simply irrelevant to the argument from evil.

### 4.2 Plantinga's Initial Attempts

In *God and Other Minds* (1967, pp. 151-5), in *The Nature of Necessity* (1974, pp. 193-5), and in *God, Freedom, and Evil* (1974, pp. 59-63), Plantinga dismissed probabilistic versions of the argument from evil very quickly. Since his arguments in all three places are very similar in structure and content, it will be sufficient here to look at only one of them.

Let us consider, then, the version offered in *God, Freedom, and Evil*.[8] After specifying that "a proposition *p confirms* a proposition *q* if *q* is more probable than not on *p* alone", and that "*p disconfirms q* if *p* confirms the denial of *q*" (pp. 62-3), Plantinga focuses upon the following two propositions:

(47) There are $10^{18}$ turps of evil

(41) All the evil in Kronos is broadly moral evil; and it was not within the power of God to create a world containing a better balance of broadly moral good and evil (pp. 63 and 59).

The argument that Plantinga offers then begins with the assertion that (47) does not disconfirm (41). He then says that (47) also fails to disconfirm:

(48) God is omniscient, omnipotent, and morally perfect; God has created the world; all the evil in the world is broadly moral evil; and there is no possible world God could have created that contains a better balance of broadly moral good with respect to broadly moral evil (p. 63).

But, then, in view of the fact, first, that (48) entails the proposition that God exists, and secondly, that a proposition *p* cannot disconfirm a proposition *q*—in the sense of "disconfirm" specified above—unless it disconfirms every proposition that entails *q*, it follows that (41) cannot disconfirm the proposition that God exists (p. 63).

There are two main objections to this argument. The first concerns the transition from the claim that (47) does not disconfirm (41) to the claim that (47) does not disconfirm (48). What one is to say about this transition depends upon how (41) is to be interpreted. In particular, does (41) entail the proposition that God exists? The natural reading, I suggest, is one where (41) does not entail that God exists. On that reading, the transition can be shown to be fallacious, by an argument precisely parallel to the one that I used in criticizing the version of the present argument that is offered in *The Nature of Necessity* (1980, pp. 366-70). Plantinga's reply to my objection there strongly suggests, however, that he would defend the transition by interpreting (41) in such a way that it entails the proposition that God exists (1981, p. 75). This saves the transition, but at the cost of rendering the whole argument question-begging, for now one is simply asserting, without any supporting argument, that a certain proposition which entails the proposition that God exists is not disconfirmed by (47).

The other main objection concerns the starting point—i.e., the claim that (47) does not disconfirm (41)—and it applies no matter which interpretation of (41) is adopted. Is it plausible to say that (41) is as likely as its denial, given only (47)? It is very hard to see how this can possibly be so. For one thing, (41) is a conjunction, one conjunct of which is the universal generalization that absolutely *all* the evil in the world is broadly moral evil, while (47) tells us that there is a tremendous amount of evil in the world—$10^{18}$ turps, to be precise. If even one of these turps of evil is not caused by the free action of some person, (41) will be false. It would be a rather unusual inductive logic in which it were true that (41) was as likely as its denial, given (47), and no other evidence.

### 4.3 The Attack upon Probability

Having perhaps realized that his earlier attempts to refute what he refers to as "the probabilistic argument from evil" were unsound, Plantinga published, in 1979, a fifty-three page article on the subject. In this section, I shall consider whether this longer discussion was any more successful than the earlier efforts.

The first comments that need to be made concern the version of the argument from evil upon which Plantinga chooses to focus. It is, once again, an abstract version of the argument from evil, rather than a concrete one, for its central claim is that the proposition

G God exists and is omniscient, omnipotent and wholly good

is improbable relative to the proposition:

E There are $10^{13}$ turps of evil.

David Conway makes three main points about this. First, Plantinga sometimes presents the above argument "as if it were *the* alternative to the logical version of the argument from evil" (1988, p. 58). But this is to ignore completely the much more important concrete formulations of the argument from evil.

Secondly, Plantinga contends that a number of contemporary atheologians are advancing the above argument. Conway argues that, on the contrary, it is not easy to make out a case that "skeptics have in fact frequently relied on a formulation that begins with the amount of evil in the world" (1988, p. 59).

Finally, and as I noted earlier, this particular version of the argument from evil does not seem especially promising. Or, as Conway puts it: "If that is the evidential version, we do not need extended discussion of probability theories to conclude that the evidential version poses little threat to theism" (1988, p. 58).

Let me now turn to Plantinga's argument. His strategy is to consider three interpretations of probability—namely, the subjective or personalist interpretation, the logical interpretation, and the relative frequency interpretation—and to argue that none of them can be used by the atheologian to formulate a satisfactory evidential version of the argument from evil. Indeed, Plantinga concludes that "the atheological probabilistic argument from evil is totally misconceived" (1979, p. 49).

I shall ignore Plantinga's discussion of the personalist and relative frequency interpretations of probability, since those interpretations are not fundamentally concerned with evidential support, and it is precisely the latter notion that is of course crucial in the present context.[9]

It is Plantinga's argument against the logical interpretation of probability that are, accordingly, crucial. What arguments does he offer? The answer is that there is one argument that he apparently regards as decisive. For he thinks that it shows that there is "no way to assign content and hence *a priori* probability in a way that is consistent both with the probability calculus and with intuition" (p. 25).

Plantinga's purportedly knockdown argument begins by asking us to consider the infinite set, $H$, that contains the following hypotheses:

$H_0$ There are no horses
$H_1$ There is just 1 horse
$H_2$ There are just 2 horses
. . . . . . . . . . . . . . . . . . . . . . . . . . . . . . . . . . . . . . . . . . . . . . . . . . . . . . .
$H_n$ There are just n horses
. . . . . . . . . . . . . . . . . . . . . . . . . . . . . . . . . . . . . . . . . . . . . . . . . . . . . . .

where $n$ ranges over all natural numbers. Plantinga then argues as follows:

> $H$ is a countably infinite set of propositions; for each natural number $n$, $H$ contains a member according to which there are just $n$ horses. All the members of $H$ are maximally specific with respect to the question how many horses there are; presumably, therefore, all have the same content. If so, they will have the same *a priori* probability. But the members of $H$ can have the *same a priori* probability only if they all have *a priori* probability *zero* (p. 26).

Given the conclusion that the *a priori* probability of any member of $H$ is zero, the next step is to argue that this has unacceptable consequences. To establish the first unacceptable consequence, Plantinga appeals to the proposition that if you have "a countable set of propositions that are mutually exclusive in pairs and jointly exhaustive," then the sum of their a priori probabilities should equal one (p. 26). But in the case of H, the sum of the a priori probabilities is not one, but zero, since each member of H, as we have just seen, has an a priori probability of zero.

This certainly seems bad enough. But, Plantinga argues, much worse is to come. For consider another infinite set of hypotheses that is just like H, except that its members, rather than being about the number of horses that there are, concern the number of non-black crows that there are. A precisely parallel argument will show that all of those hypotheses must have a priori probabilities equal to zero. One of those hypotheses, however, is the hypothesis that there are no non-black crows, so its a priori probability must be equal to zero. That hypothesis, however, is logically equivalent to the contingent universal proposition that that all crows are black. So the a priori probability of that hypothesis must also be equal to zero. And, in general, what one can show is that any (ordinary) contingent universal generalization must have an a priori probability of zero.

Since an ordinary existential proposition—such as that there is a horse—is true if and only if the corresponding universal proposition—that everything is a non-horse—is false, it follows that every existential proposition must have an a priori probability of one. Indeed, one can even show that the proposition that there are more that n horses has an a priori probability of one, no matter how large n is.

What is one to say about this argument? I shall confine myself to three points. The first focuses upon a fact concerning the probabilities of universal generalizations, and its relevance to Plantinga's argument. The second concerns a fallacy in the first part of Plantinga's argument, while the third is concerned with the fundamental error in the argument as a whole.

Universal generalizations can be true in two very different ways. They can be true simply because there happen never to be any counterexamples, at any time or place, or they can be true because there are relevant laws of nature, realistically conceived. The probability that a generalization is true is, consequently, the sum of the probability that it is accidentally true and the probability that it obtains in virtue of a law of nature.

The relevance of this to Plantinga's argument is as follows. Plantinga assumes that all of the propositions in H have equal a priori probability. It would seem, however, that one of them is special—namely, the proposition that there are no horses. For that proposition might be true because it was entailed by the existence of certain laws, whereas it is not easy to see how, for example, the proposition that there are just seven horses could be entailed by the existence of certain laws *alone*—that is, not in conjunction with boundary conditions. So there is a way in which $H_0$ could be true that is not open in the case of $H_n$, if $n$ has any value other than zero. So Plantinga is mistaken in claiming that, if one assigns *a priori* probabilities to the members of $H$, the value should be the same for all of them: the proposition $H_0$ should be assigned a higher probability than the other members of $H$.

The fact that it is $H_0$ that is odd man out, and that receives a higher probability, cripples the rest of the argument. For Plantinga's conclusions concerning the *a priori* probabilities of universal generalizations and existential generalizations all rest upon the assumption that the proposition $H_0$ must be assigned the same *a priori* probability as all the other members of $H$.[10]

My second point is that the first part of Plantinga's argument is fallacious. For in order to establish that the sum of the *a priori* probabilities of the hypotheses in $H$ should be one, rather than zero, he had to appeal to a principle that only applies when one has a set of hypotheses that are *jointly exhaustive*, and $H$ does not satisfy that condition. For $H$ does not contain any hypothesis that would be true if there were infinitely many horses.

Plantinga suggests in a footnote (p. 53, fn. 24) that one can revise the argument by simply adding that extra hypothesis to $H$. If so, why wasn't it included in $H$ all along? The answer is that one would then need to prove that that hypothesis should be assigned the same *a priori* probability as the other members of $H$, and the consideration to which Plantinga appealed with respect to the original set, $H$, does not work when $H$ is thus supplemented.

Either of above points suffices to refute Plantinga's argument as it stands. Readers who are familiar with discussions of the foundations of probability will be aware, however, that the general sort of argument that Plantinga has attempted to set out here could easily have been put in a more satisfactory way, and one which would avoid both of the above objections. Consider, then, darts and a dart board, where the darts have tips that are perfectly cylindrical in shape. Assume, further, that space is infinitely divisible. If a dart is thrown at the board, and hits it, what is the probability that the center of its tip will coincide with some specific point on the board? In the absence of further information, the center of the tip is as likely to coincide with one point as any other, so the probabilities in question should be equal. The question then is whether all of the probabilities are equal to zero or not, and it may seem that there is a problem no matter which answer one embraces. For on the one hand, if all the probabilities are zero, then the probability that the dart will hit the dart board will also be equal to zero. But this is unacceptable, since we are explicitly assuming that the dart will hit the board. The latter probability, therefore, must be equal to one. On the other hand, if the probability that the center of the tip of the dart will coincide with any specific point has any finite value other than zero, then, since the relevant probabilities are all equal, the sum of the probabilities of the uncountably many, pairwise exclusive and jointly exhaustive outcomes will be more than one, which once again is unacceptable.

What is the conclusion? Does this show something about *a priori* probabilities? In particular, does it show that the idea of such probabilities is incoherent? If the argument did show this, it would show much more. It would not be only *a priori* probabilities which were in trouble. For one can describe situations where the time when a dart is fired at a dart board depends upon radioactive decay, and where the trajectory of the dart depends upon the time when it is released in such a way that it is equally likely, given a detailed description of the experimental setup, that the dart will hit any one point as any other. As a consequence, unless one is prepared to hold that the idea of probabilities based on extensive evidence is also incoherent, one is forced to conclude that there must be a solution to this problem.

But what is the solution? Consider what the above argument shows. In some cases, one runs into trouble both if one assumes that certain probabilities are equal to zero, and if one assumes that they have some finite value other than zero. What one needs, accordingly, are numbers that are neither finite nor zero. In short, one needs infinitesimals.

The upshot is that all that Plantinga's argument establishes, even when reconstructed so as to avoid the earlier objections, is the perfectly familiar result that probabilities cannot always be adequately represented by means of the standard real numbers.[11] There are cases where one needs to employ non-standard reals as values of probabilities. But once that is done, the *a priori* probabilities of the hypotheses in *H*, rather than being either zero or some finite value, will be infinitesimals, and the whole argument then collapses.

## 4.4 The Appeal to Human Epistemological Limitations

A standard way of attempting to answer the argument from evil involves claiming that, because of our human, epistemological limitations, it is impossible for us to have grounds which would justify us in believing that the world contains evils which it would be morally wrong for an omnipotent and omniscient being not to prevent. This claim has been advanced by a number of writers, including F. J. Fitzpatrick (1981), Delmas Lewis (1983), and Stephen Wykstra (1984). The arguments that they offer in support of the above contention differ somewhat, and, in addition, Fitzpatrick's presentation is very brief in comparison with those of Lewis and Wykstra. Nevertheless, the underlying line of thought is essentially the same, and I shall, therefore, confine my attention to a critical examination of the basic argument. Readers who are interested in a detailed examination of different presentations of the argument, especially those by Lewis and Wykstra, should turn to the very careful and incisive critical discussion to be found in Rowe (1986).

In outline, the argument runs as follows. Granted, there are an enormous number of intrinsically bad states of affairs in the world where we know of no corresponding good that would outweigh the evil in question. Indeed, in many cases, try as we will, we cannot even imagine what form such a counterbalancing good could possibly take. But does this fact suffice to justify the belief that, for some of those evils, no such good exists, or even the belief that it is unlikely that such a good exists? Initially it may seem that it does. But consider the following. Given God's omniscience, and our limited knowledge, it is surely *possible* for God to conceive of great goods that we cannot. But is this only a possibility? Is it not rather the case that, if God exists, it is *very likely* that he has in mind goods that we have not even thought of? And if that is so, then given that he is also omnipotent, he will probably have the power to bring those goods into existence. The conclusion, in short, is that one would expect that, if God were to exist, the world would contain goods of which we have not the slightest conception. But if that is so, how can we ever be justified in concluding that there are evils in the world for which no counter-balancing goods exist?

Given this appeal to goods beyond our ken, the first question that needs to be asked is precisely what sort of human epistemological limitation is in question here. For there are two quite different possibilities, between which it is important to distinguish. On the one hand, the appeal may be to our limited knowledge concerning *non-moral facts*. Talk about goods beyond our ken would them come down to the idea that if God exists, he may very well have a long-range plan for the world, of which we have no knowledge, but which is such that, if only we did have knowledge of it, we would be able, by employing our present moral principles, to see not only that it was very good, but that the goods involved in it were sufficient to justify God's not having prevented any of the apparently problematic evils that we find in the world.

On the other hand, the appeal may instead be to the idea that our knowledge of *basic moral truths* is severely limited. Talk about goods beyond our ken then has a very different meaning, namely, that there are states of affairs—perhaps existing right now, perhaps in the distant future—that are intrinsically very good, and whose goodness justifies an omnipotent and omniscient being in not preventing any of the problematic evils that we see around us, but whose goodness we would not even recognize, given our present moral knowledge.

Neither Fitzpatrick, nor Lewis, nor Wykstra makes it at all clear whether the appeal is to human limitations with respect to knowledge of non-moral facts, or with respect to knowledge of basic moral truths. Wykstra, for example, talks vaguely about the discerning of goods, and never indicates whether what he is referring to is (1) knowing that certain states of affairs exist, or (2) knowing that states of affairs of a certain type are good (p. 88). It is, however, crucial to be clear on this matter, since the considerations that are relevant to an evaluation of the argument are very different in the two cases.

Let us consider, then, the two appeals in turn. First, suppose that the argument rests upon the idea that, if God exists, humans will have only very limited knowledge of certain non-moral facts—specifically, those concerning certain states of affairs that play an essential role in God's grand plan for the world. Can this be the basis of a serious objection to the argument from evil?

Suppose that certain intrinsically undesirable states of affairs are such that we cannot immediately detect the existence of any appropriately related goods that would justify the evils in question. We apply our knowledge of the relevant moral principles to the situation, and conclude that there could be a good that would justify an omnipotent and omniscient being in not preventing the evil only if some condition *C* is satisfied. Perhaps we conclude, for example, that the evil in question can only be justified if humans survive death, or if they have libertarian free will. Making use of the non-moral information that we have, we then determine that while it is possible that *C* is true, it is very unlikely that this is the case. We therefore conclude that it is very unlikely that there is a morally sufficient reason for the evil in question.

This reasoning is surely impeccable, given the assumptions, and cannot be undermined by the observation that *C might*, after all, turn out to be true. An appeal to ignorance of non-moral facts cannot, therefore, be used to rebut the argument from evil.

The other possibility is that the argument is appealing to the idea that humans may lack some crucial knowledge of basic moral truths. This version of the argument has already been considered in the discussion, in section 2.2, of the central step in the subsidiary argument. What I argued there—to recap very briefly—was that even if one does not assume that our moral knowledge is complete, one can still arrive at principles that specify conditions that must be satisfied if certain evils are to be justified, and this in two ways. First, the moral knowledge that we do possess involves principles concerning justice, and it is a consequence of those principles that an omnipotent and omniscient person would be justified in allowing an innocent individual to suffer only if the individual in question benefitted from that suffering. Secondly, ethics differs from other areas in that moral truths cannot be inaccessible in the way that truths in areas such as mathematics and physics may very well be. This fact, combined with information concerning the extreme infrequency of the discovery of new, morally significant properties by the human race, provides good grounds for concluding that it is very unlikely that our knowledge of good-making and bad-making properties is seriously incomplete. This, in turn, enables us to derive further conclusions concerning the conditions that must, in all probability, be satisfied, if certain evils are to be justified.

It does not matter, therefore, whether the appeal is to our limited knowledge of God's purposes, or other non-moral facts, or to limitations with respect to our knowledge of basic moral truths. Neither can provide the basis of a satisfactory response to the argument from evil.

## 4.5 The Appeal to the Ontological Argument

A final way in which one could attempt to show that facts about evil cannot constitute even *prima facie* evidence against the existence of God is by appealing to the ontological argument. Relatively few philosophers have held, of course, that the ontological argument is sound. But there have certainly been notable exceptions—such as Anselm and Descartes, and, in this century, Charles Hartshorne (1962), Normal Malcolm (1960), and Alvin Plantinga (1974a, 1974b).

If the ontological argument were sound, it would provide a rather decisive refutation of the argument from evil. For in showing not merely that there is an omnipotent, omniscient, and morally perfect being, but that it is necessary that such a being exists, it would entail that the proposition that God exists must have probability one on any body of evidence whatever.

The only question, accordingly, is whether the ontological argument is sound. In common with the vast majority of philosophers, I believe that it is not. For, as I have argued elsewhere, (1981) it seems to me that strengthened Gaunilo-type objections suffice to show that the argument *must* be unsound—where the idea behind a strengthened Gaunilo-type objection is that, rather than paralleling the ontological argument in order to show that there is a population problem in the form of perfect islands, perfect unicorns, and so on, one constructs versions that lead to mutually incompatible conclusions, such as the conclusion that there is a perfect solvent, together with the conclusion that there is a perfectly insoluble substance.

## 5. Defenses and Theodicies

## 5.1 Attempted Defenses

In this section I shall look very briefly at two attempts to show that it is reasonable to believe that every evil is such that an omnipotent and omniscient person would have a morally sufficient reason for not preventing its existence, even if one is not able to say, in every case, what that morally sufficient reason might be.

### 5.1.1 The Appeal to Positive Evidence for the Existence of God

The idea behind the first defense is that if one can point to sufficiently strong considerations in support of the existence of God, then that positive evidence may outweigh the negative evidence which consists in the existence of apparently unjustified evils, and, as a consequence, belief in God may be rational relative to one's total evidence.

This approach was discussed earlier, in section 1.5. The problem with it, as I noted there, is that virtually none of the arguments in support of the existence of God provides any grounds for concluding that there is an omnipotent, omniscient, *and morally perfect* person. Indeed, most of them provide only very tenuous ground for even very mild conclusions concerning the moral character of the being in question.

### 5.1.2 Induction Based on Partial Success

Swinburne (1988) argued in support of the conclusion that theism does need a theodicy. In doing so, however, he noted one minor qualification—namely, that if one could show, for a sufficiently impressive range of evils that initially seemed problematic, that it was likely that an omnipotent and omniscient person would be morally justified in not having prevented them, then one might well be justified in believing that the same would be true of other evils, even if one could not specify, in those other cases, what the morally sufficient reason for allowing them might be (pp. 297-8).

What Swinburne says here is surely very reasonable, and I can see no objection in principle to a defense of this sort This type of defense is, of course, very different from that discussed in the previous section. For if one could find a proof of the existence of God that had the required characteristics—namely, one that provided good reason for believing in the existence of a being who was morally perfect, as well as omnipotent and omniscient, and that was sufficiently strong not to be deluged by the counterevidence provided by the evils that are found in the world—then one would have a defense that would be compatible with one's not being able to say, for *any* of the problematic evils, what morally sufficient reason there is for allowing its existence. The partial defense mentioned by Swinburne, in contrast, rests upon a foundation that would have to be provided by a theodicy which, though incomplete, would have to be very extensive in its coverage, and thoroughly convincing with respect to the evils that it did cover.

## 5.2. Theodicies

What are the prospects for a complete, or nearly complete theodicy? Some philosophers, such as Swinburne, are optimistic, and believe that "the required theodicy can be provided" (1988, p. 311). Others, including many theists, are much less hopeful. Alvin Plantinga, for example remarks:

> ...we cannot see *why* our world, with all its ills, would be better than others we think we can imagine, or *what*, in any detail, is God's reason for permitting a given specific and appalling evil. Not only can we not see this, we can't think of any very good possibilities. And here I must say that most attempts to explain *why* God permits evil—*theodicies*, as we may call them—strike me as tepid, shallow and ultimately frivolous (1985a, p. 35).

I do not share Plantinga's view that most theodicies are "shallow and ultimately frivolous." On the contrary, for reasons that will be very clear from the discussion above, I believe that it is precisely in the work of philosophers who do attempt to develop satisfactory theodicies—such as John Hick (1966, 1978) and Richard Swinburne (1979)—that one is dealing with serious attempts to grapple with the argument from evil.

On the other hand, I do share Plantinga's pessimism concerning the prospects for a successful theodicy. To justify that pessimism would require, of course, a *very* detailed examination of the many proposals that have been advanced. But a number of important starts have certainly been made. I am thinking, for example, of Stanley Kane's critical discussion (1975) of Hick's soul-making theodicy; of criticism of Swinburne's approach by philosophers such as David O'Connor (1983) and Eleonore Stump (1983); of Michael Martin's very incisive criticisms (1988) of Bruce Reichenbach's attempt (1976) to provide a natural law theodicy for natural evils; and of Robert McKim's outstanding discussion (1984) of the attempt to justify evils by appealing to free will. These and other discussions suggest, at the very least, that there are enormous obstacles that stand in the way of any successful theodicy.

## 6. Summing Up

One moral that has emerged very clearly in recent discussions of the argument from evil is that the time and energy that has been lavished on abstract formulations of the argument has been more or less wasted: it is concrete formulations of the argument from evil which are crucial. A consensus also seems to be emerging concerning the basic structure of the argument: it consists of a core argument, which is deductively valid, together with a subsidiary argument.

By contrast, there has been only relatively limited discussion of precisely how the subsidiary argument is best set out. I therefore attempted to offer a reasonably detailed account both of the structure of that argument, and of the justification of the crucial steps.

I also suggested, however, that there are two variations on the basic argument that can be very useful for certain purposes: first, subjective formulations, which refer to the moral standards of a given individual, and which thus do not involve the assumption that there are objective values; and secondly, 'hypothetical' formulations, which incorporate the assumption that there is an omnipotent and omniscient person.

Finally, I considered a number of possible responses to the argument for evil, and among the conclusions for which I argued were, first, that the argument from evil cannot be refuted by an attack upon inductive logic; secondly, that an appeal to human epistemological limitations is also unsuccessful; and thirdly, that none of the traditional arguments in support of the existence of God provides the basis for an adequate defense. More generally, I attempted to show, in agreement with Swinburne, that nothing less than a reasonably complete theodicy will do.

### Notes

1. Alvin Plantinga, (1974a), pp. 63-4. For additional critical discussion of this, see Conway (1988), p. 35, and Robert Adams (1985), pp. 225 and 240.
2. This second remark is not true in the case of the formulation of the argument set out by R. K. Perkins, since he employs the premise that "God wishes to bring about as much good as He can" (1983, p. 240). But, as will emerge later, in section 4.1, this is a shortcoming of the formulation in question.
3. Conway puts the argument in a slightly different way, since he makes use of the idea that the crucial premise of the core argument can be viewed as a compound proposition, and focuses upon the modal status

of one of its parts, whereas I have put the point here in terms of the modal status of some of the premises of the underlying, subsidiary argument. For Conway's own statement of the argument, and his discussion of it, see Conway, (1988), pp. 41-50.

4. Compare David Hume's discussion in Part XI of his *Dialogues Concerning Natural Religion*.

5. The utilization of a general truth-maker principle seems much more common in Australian than in American philosophy. This difference is due in large measure to the influence of Charlie Martin, who, early on, convinced many Australian philosophers of the importance of this principle for metaphysics.

6. The term "theodicy" is sometimes used in a stronger sense, according to which one is attempting to show not only that such morally sufficient reasons exist, but that the reasons cited are in fact *God's* reasons. Alvin Plantinga (1974a. p. 10; 1985a, p. 35) and Robert Adams (1985, p. 242) use the term in that way, but that is to saddle the theodicist with an unnecessarily ambitious program, as has been pointed out by a number of writers, including Richard Swinburne (1988, p. 298), and William Hasker (1988, p. 5).

7. In the context of abstract, incompatibility versions of the argument from evil, the term "defense" is frequently used to refer to arguments which attempt to show that there is no logical incompatibility between the existence of evil and the existence of God. But as soon as one focuses upon concrete formulations of the argument from evil, a different interpretation is needed if the term is to remain a useful one.

8. In "Alvin Plantinga and the Argument from Evil", I criticized the version of the argument found in *The Nature of Necessity*, and essentially the same criticisms apply to that given in *God and Other Minds*. Plantinga's response can be found in Plantinga (1981). Two other authors who have recently criticized the former version of the argument are Keith Chrzan (1988) and Bruce Langtry (1989).

9. Compare Swinburne's comments in his discussion of Plantinga's argument (1988, p. 303).

10. Further discussion of the assignment of probabilities to universal generalizations, and of the relevance of a non-reductionist view of laws of nature can be found in Tooley (1977, pp. 687-93 and 1988, pp. 129-37).

11. I have discussed this matter in *Causation: A Realist Approach*, pp. 136-7.

## References

Adams, Robert M. (1977) "Middle Knowledge and the Problem of Evil", *American Philosophical Quarterly* 14: 109-17.

Adams, Robert M. (1985), "Plantinga on the Problem of Evil", in Tomberlin and van Inwagen, 225-55.

Chrzan, Keith (1987) "The Irrelevance of the No Best Possible World Defense", *Philosophia* 17: 161-7.

Chrzan, Keith (1988) "Plantinga on Atheistic Induction", *Sophia* 27:10-14.

Conway David A. (1988) "The Philosophical Problem of Evil", *Philosophy of Religion* 24: 35-66.

Fitzpatrick, F. J. (1981) "The Onus of Proof in Arguments about the Problem of Evil", *Religious Studies* 17: 19-38.

Forrest, Peter (1981) "The Problem of Evil: Two Neglected Defenses", *Sophia* 20: 49-54.

Hartshorne, Charles (1962) *The Logic of Perfection* (La Salle: Open Court Publishing).

Hare, R. M. (1952) *The Language of Morals* (Oxford: Oxford University Press).

Hasker, Wiliam (1988) "Suffering, Soul-Making, and Salvation", *International Philosophical Quarterly* 28: 3-19.

Hick, John (1966; revised edition 1978) *Evil and the God of Love* (New York: Harper and Row).

Kane, G. Stanley (1975) "The Failure of Soul-Making Theodicy", *International Journal for Philosophy of Religion* 6: 1-22.

Khatchadourian, Haig (1966) "God, Happiness and Evil", *Religious Studies* 2: 109-19.

La Para, Nicholas (1965) "Suffering, Happiness, Evil", *Sophia* 4: 10-16.

Langtry, Bruce (1989) "God, Evil and Probability", *Sophia* 28: 32-40.

Lewis, Delmas (1983) "The Problem with the Problem of Evil", *Sophia* 22: 26-35.

Mackie, J. L. (1977) *Ethics—Inventing Right and Wrong* (Harmondsworth: Penguin Books).

Malcolm, Norman (1960) "Anselm's Ontological Arguments", *The Philosophical Review* 69: 41-62.

Martin, Michael (1988) "Reichenbach on Natural Evil", *Religious Studies* 24: 91-9.

McKim, Robert (1984) "Worlds Without Evil", *International Journal for Philosophy of Religion* 15: 161-70.

O'Connor David, (1983) "Swinburne on Natural Evil", *Religious Studies* 19: 65-73.

Perkins, R. M. (1983) "An Atheistic Argument from the Improvability of the Universe", *Nous* 17: 239-50.

Plantinga, Alvin (1967) *God and Other Minds* (Ithaca: Cornell University Press).

Plantinga, Alvin (1974a) *God, Freedom, and Evil* (New York: Harper and Row).

Plantinga, Alvin (1974b) *The Nature of Necessity* (Oxford: Clarendon Press).

Plantinga, Alvin (1979) "The Probabilistic Argument from Evil", *Philosophical Studies*, 35: 1-53.

Plantinga, Alvin (1981) "Tooley and Evil: A Reply", *Australasian Journal of Philosophy* 60: 66-75.

Plantinga, Alvin (1985a) "Self-Profile", in Tomberlin and van Inwagen: 3-97.

Plantinga, Alvin (1985b) "Reply to Robert M. Adams", in Tomberlin and van Inwagen: 371-82.

Reichenbach, Bruce R. (1976) "Natural Evils and Natural Law: A Theodicy for Natural Evils", *International Philosophical Quarterly* 16: 179-96.

Reichenbach, Bruce R. (1980) "The Inductive Argument from Evil", *American Philosophical Quarterly* 17: 221-7.

Rowe, William (1979) "The Problem of Evil and Some Varieties of Atheism", *American Philosophical Quarterly* 16: 335-41.

Rowe, William (1984) "Evil and the Theistic Hypothesis: A Response to Wykstra", *International Journal for Philosophy of Religion* 16: 95-100.

Rowe, William (1986) "The Empirical Argument from Evil", in *Rationality, Religious Belief, and Moral Commitment*, edited by Robert Audi and William J. Wainwright, (Ithaca: Cornell University Press), 227-47.

Schlesinger, George (1964) "The Problem of Evil and the Problem of Suffering", *American Philosophical Quarterly* 1: 244-7.

Schlesinger, George (1977) *Religion and Scientific Method* (Boston: D. Reidel).

Stump, Eleonore (1983) "Knowledge, Freedom and the Problem of Evil", *International Journal for Philosophy of Religion* 14: 49-58.

Swinburne, Richard (1979) *The Existence of God* (Oxford: Clarendon Press).

Swinburne, Richard (1988) "Does Theism Need A Theodicy?", *Canadian Journal of Philosophy* 18: 287-312.

Tomberlin, James E. and van Inwagen, Peter, ed. (1985) *Alvin Plantinga*, (Dordrecht: D. Reidel).

Tooley, Michael (1977) "The Nature of Laws", *Canadian Journal of Philosophy* 7: 667-98.

Tooley, Michael (1980) "Alvin Plantinga and the Argument from Evil", *Australasian Journal of Philosophy* 58: 360-76.

Tooley, Michael (1981) "Plantinga's Defence of the Ontological Argument", *Mind* 90: 422-7.

Tooley, Michael (1988) *Causation: A Realist Approach* (Oxford: Oxford University Press).

Wykstra, Stephen J. (1984) "The Humean Obstacle to Evidential Arguments from Suffering: On Avoiding the Evils of 'Appearance'", *International Journal for Philosophy of Religion* 16: 73-93.

Philosophical Perspectives, 5, Philosophy of Religion, 1991

# THE PROBLEM OF EVIL, THE PROBLEM OF AIR, AND THE PROBLEM OF SILENCE

Peter van Inwagen
Syracuse University

It used to be widely held that evil—which for present purposes we may identify with undeserved pain and suffering—was incompatible with the existence of God: that no possible world contained both God and evil. So far as I am able to tell, this thesis is no longer defended. But arguments for the following weaker thesis continue to be very popular: Evil (or at least evil of the amounts and kinds we actually observe) constitutes evidence against the existence of God, evidence that seems decisively to outweigh the totality of available evidence *for* the existence of God.

In this paper, I wish to discuss what seems to me to be the most powerful version of the "evidential argument from evil." The argument takes the following form. There is a serious hypothesis $h$ that is inconsistent with theism and on which the amounts and kinds of suffering that the world contains are far more easily explained than they are on the hypothesis of theism. This fact constitutes a *prima facie* case for preferring $h$ to theism. Examination shows that there is no known way of answering this case, and there is good reason to think that no way of answering it will be forthcoming. Therefore, the hypothesis $h$ is (relative to the epistemic situation of someone who has followed the argument this far) preferable to theism. But if $p$ and $q$ are inconsistent and $p$ is (relative to one's epistemic situation) epistemically preferable to $q$, then it is not rational for one to accept $q$. (Of course, it does not follow either that it is rational for one to accept $p$ or that it is rational for one to reject $q$.) It is, therefore, not rational for one who has followed the argument up to this point to accept theism.[1]

In Section I, I shall present the version of the evidential argument from evil I wish to discuss. In Section II, I shall explain why I find the argument unconvincing. These two sections could stand on their own, and this paper might have consisted simply of the proposed refutation of the evidential argument from evil that they contain. But many philosophers will find the proposed refutation implausible, owing to the fact that it turns on controversial theses about the epistemology of metaphysical possibility and intrinsic value. And perhaps there will also be philosophers who find my reasoning unconvincing because of a deep conviction that, since evil just *obviously* creates an insoluble evidential problem for the theist, a reply to any version of the evidential argument can be nothing more than a desperate attempt to render the obvious obscure. Now if philosophers are unconvinced by one's diagnosis of the faults of a certain argument, one can attempt to make the diagnosis seem more plausible to them by the following method. One can try to find a "parallel" argument that is obviously faulty, and try to show that a parallel diagnosis of the faults of the parallel argument can be given, a diagnosis that seems plausible, and hope that some of the plausibility of the parallel diagnosis will rub off on the original. For example, if philosophers find one's diagnosis of the faults of the ontological argument unconvincing, one can construct an obviously faulty argument that "runs parallel to" the ontological argument—in the classical case, an argument for the existence of a perfect island. And one can then attempt to show that a diagnosis parallel to one's diagnosis of the faults of the ontological argument is a correct diagnosis of the faults (which, one hopes, will be so evident as to be uncontroversial) of the parallel argument. It is worth noting that even if an application of this procedure did not convince one's audience of the correctness of one's diagnosis of the faults of the original argument, the parallel argument might by itself be enough to convince them that there must be *something* wrong with the original argument.

This is the plan I shall follow. In fact, I shall consider *two* arguments that run parallel to the evidential argument from evil. In Section III, I shall present an evidential argument, which I feign is addressed to an ancient Greek atomist by one of his contemporaries, for the conclusion that the observed properties of air render a belief in atoms irrational. In Section IV, I shall present an evidential argument for the conclusion that the observed fact of "cosmic silence" renders a belief in "extra-terrestrial intelligence" irrational. Neither of these parallel arguments—at least this seems clear to me—succeeds in establishing its conclusion. In each case, I shall offer a diagnosis of the faults of the parallel argument that parallels my diagnosis of the faults of the evidential argument from evil.

Finally, in Section V, I shall make some remarks in aid of a proposed distinction between facts that raise *difficulties* for a theory, and facts that constitute *evidence* against a theory.

# I

Let 'S' stand for a proposition that describes in some detail the amount, kinds, and distribution of suffering—the suffering not only of human beings, but of all the sentient terrestrial creatures that there are or ever have been.[2] (We assume that the content of S is about what one would expect, given our own experience, the newspapers, history books, textbooks of natural history and paleontology, and so on. For example, we assume that the world was not created five minutes ago—or six thousand years ago—"complete with memories of an unreal past," and we assume that Descartes was wrong and that cats really do feel pain.)

Let "theism" be the proposition that the universe was created by an omniscient, omnipotent, and morally perfect being.[3]

The core of the evidential argument from evil is the contention that there is a serious hypothesis, inconsistent with theism, on which S is more probable than S is on theism. (The probabilities that figure in this discussion are epistemic. Without making a serious attempt to clarify this notion, we may say this much: $p$ has a higher epistemic probability on $h$ than $q$ does, just in the case that, given $h$, $q$ is more *surprising* than $p$. And here 'surprising' must be understood as having an epistemic, rather than a merely psychological, sense. It is evident that the epistemic probability of a proposition is relative to the "epistemic background" or "epistemic situation" of an individual or a community: the epistemic probability of $p$ on $h$ need not be the same for two persons or for the same person at two times.[4]) That hypothesis is "the hypothesis of indifference" (HI):

> Neither the nature nor the condition of sentient beings on earth is the result of benevolent or malevolent actions performed by non-human persons.[5]

Here is a brief statement of the argument that is built round this core. We begin with an epistemic challenge to the theist, the presentation of a *prima facie* case against theism: The truth of S is not at all surprising, given HI, but the truth of S is very surprising, given theism. (For the following propositions, if they are not beyond all dispute, are at least highly plausible. Suffering is an intrinsic evil; A morally perfect being will see to it that, insofar as it is possible, intrinsic evils, if they are allowed to exist at all, are distributed according to desert; An omniscient and omnipotent being will be able so to arrange matters that the world contains sentient beings among whom suffering, if it exists at all, is apportioned according to desert; the pattern of suffering recorded in S is well explained—insofar as it can be explained: many instances of suffering are obviously due to chance—by the biological utility of pain, which is just what one would expect on HI, and has little if anything to do with desert.) We have, therefore, a good *prima facie* reason to prefer HI to theism.

How shall the theist respond to this challenge? The "evidentialist" (as I shall call the proponent of the evidential argument from evil) maintains that any response must be of one of the following three types:

—the theist may argue that S is much more surprising, given HI, than one might suppose
—the theist may argue that S is much less surprising, given theism, than one might suppose
—the theist may argue that there are reasons for preferring theism to HI that outweigh the *prima facie* reason for preferring HI to theism that we have provided.

The first of these options (the evidentialist continues) is unlikely to appeal to anyone. The third is also unappealing, at least if "reasons" is taken to mean "arguments for the existence of God" in the traditional or philosophy-of-religion-text sense. Whatever the individual merits or defects of those arguments, none of them but the "moral argument" (and perhaps the ontological argument) purports to prove the existence of a morally perfect being. And neither the moral argument nor the ontological argument has many defenders these days. None of the "theistic" arguments that are currently regarded as at all promising is, therefore, really an argument for *theism*.[6] And, therefore, none of them can supply a reason for preferring theism to HI.

The second option is that taken by philosophers who construct *theodicies*. A theodicy, let us say, is the conjunction of theism with some "auxiliary hypothesis" *h* that purports to explain how S could be true, given theism. Let us think for a moment in terms of the probability calculus. It is clear that if a theodicy is to be at all interesting, the probability of S on the conjunction of theism and *h* (that is, on the theodicy) will have to be high—or at least not too low. But whether a theodicy is interesting depends not only on the probability of S on the conjunction of theism and *h*, but also on the probability of *h* on theism. Note that the higher P(*h*/theism), the more closely P(S/theism) will approximate P(S/theism & *h*). On the other hand, if P(*h*/theism) is low, P(S/theism) could be low even if P(S/theism & *h*) were high. (Consider, for example, the case in which *h* is S itself: even if P(S/theism) is low, P(S/theism & S) will be 1—as high as a probability gets.) The task of the theodicist, therefore, may be represented as follows: find an hypothesis *h* such that P(S/theism & *h*) is high, or at least not too low, and P(*h*/theism) is high. In other words, the theodicist is to reason as follows. "Although S might initially seem surprising on the assumption of theism, this initial appearance, like many initial appearances, is misleading. For consider the hypothesis *h*. The truth of this hypothesis is just what one would expect given theism, and S is just what one would expect [would not be all that surprising] given both theism and *h*. Therefore, S is just what one would expect [would not be all that surprising] given theism. And, therefore, we do not have a *prima facie* reason to prefer HI to theism, and the evidential argument from evil fails."[7]

But (the evidentialist concludes) the prospects of finding a theodicy that satisfies these conditions are not very promising. For any auxiliary hypothesis *h* that has actually been offered by the defenders of theism, it would seem that either no real case has been made for P(*h*/theism) being high, or else no real case has been made for P(S/theism & *h*) being high—or even not too low. Consider, for example, the celebrated Free Will Defense (FWD). Even if it is granted that P(FWD/theism) is high, there is every reason to think that P(S/theism & FWD) is low, since of all cases of suffering (a phenomenon that has existed for hundreds of millions of years), only a minuscule proportion involve, even in the most indirect way, beings with free will. And no one has the faintest idea of how to find a proposition that is probable on theism *and*, in conjunction with theism, renders S probable. Therefore, given the present state of the available evidence, our original judgment stands: we have a good *prima facie* reason to prefer HI to theism. And, as we have seen, we have no reason to prefer theism to HI that outweighs this *prima facie* reason. It is, therefore, irrational to accept theism in the present state of our knowledge.

## II

It will be noted that the evidential argument consists not only of an argument for the conclusion that there is a *prima facie* case for preferring HI to theism, but also of a list of options open to the theist who wishes to reply to that argument: the defender of theism must either refute the argument or else make a case for preferring theism to HI that outweighs the *prima facie* case for preferring HI to theism; if the defender chooses to refute the argument, he must do this by producing a theodicy in the sense explained in Section I.

This list of options seems to me to be incomplete. Suppose that one were successfully to argue that S was not surprising on theism—and not because S was "just what one should expect" if theism were true, but because no one is in a position to know whether S is what one should expect if theism were true. (Suppose I have never seen, or heard a description of, Egyptian hieroglyphs, although I am familiar with Chinese characters and Babylonian cuneiform and many other exotic scripts. I am shown a sheet of paper reproducing an ancient Egyptian inscription, having been told that it displays a script used in ancient Egypt. What I see cannot be described as "looking just the way one should expect a script used in ancient Egypt to look," but the fact that the script looks the way it does is not epistemically surprising on the hypothesis that it was a script used in ancient Egypt. I am simply not in a position to know whether *this* is the way one should expect a script that was used in ancient Egypt to look.[8]) If one could successfully argue that one simply could not know whether to expect patterns of suffering like those contained in the actual world in a world created by an omniscient, omnipotent, and morally perfect being, this would refute the evidentialist's case for the thesis that there is a *prima facie* reason for preferring HI to theism. If one is not in a position to assign any epistemic probability to S on theism—if one is not in a position even to assign a probability-range like 'high' or 'low' or 'middling' to S on theism—, then, obviously, one is not in a position to say that the epistemic probability of S on HI is higher than the probability of S on theism.[9]

The evidentialist's statement of the way in which the defender of theism must conduct his defense is therefore overly restrictive: it is false that the defender must either make a case for theism or devise a theodicy. At any rate, another option exists as a formal possibility. But how might the defender of theism avail himself of this other option? Are there reasons for thinking that the assumption of theism yields no *prima facie* grounds for expecting a pattern of suffering different from that recorded by S?

I would suggest that it is the function of what have come to be called "defenses" to provide just such reasons. The word 'defense' was first employed as a technical term in discussions of the "logical" version of the argument from evil. In that context, a defense is a story according to which both God and suffering exist, and which is possible "in the broadly logical sense"—or which is such that there is no reason to believe that it is impossible in the broadly logical sense. Let us adapt the notion of a defense to the requirements of a discussion of the evidential argument: a defense is a story according to which God and suffering of the sort contained in the actual world both exist, and which is such that (given the existence of God) there is no reason to think that it is false, a story that is not surprising on the hypothesis that God exists. A defense obviously need not be a theodicy in the evidentialist's sense, for the probability of a defense need not be high on theism.[10] (That is, a defense need not be such that its denial is surprising on theism.) In practice, of course, the probability of a defense will never be high on theism: if the defender of theism knew of a story that accounted for the sufferings of the actual world and which was highly probable on theism, he would employ it as a theodicy. We may therefore say that, in practice, a defense is a story that accounts for the sufferings of the actual world and which (given the existence of God) is true "for all anyone knows."

What does the defender of theism accomplish by constructing a defense? Well, it's like this. Suppose that Jane wishes to defend the character of Richard III, and that she must contend with evidence that has convinced many people that Richard murdered the two princes in the Tower. Suppose that she proceeds by telling a story—which she does not claim to be true, or even more probable than not—that accounts for the evidence that has come down to us, a story according to which Richard did not murder the princes. If my reaction to her story is, "For all I know, that's true. I shouldn't be at all surprised if that's how things happened," I shall be less willing to accept a negative evaluation of Richard's character than I might otherwise have been. (Note that Jane need not try to show that her story is highly probable on the hypothesis that Richard was of good character.) It would, moreover, strengthen Jane's case if she could produce not one story but many stories that "exonerated" Richard— stories that were not trivial variants on one another but which were importantly different.

This analogy suggests that one course that is open to the defender of theism is to construct stories that are true for all anyone knows— given that there is a God—and which entail both S and the existence of God. If the defender can do that, this accomplishment will undermine the evidentialist's case for the proposition that the probability of S is lower on theism than on HI. Of course, these stories will (presumably) be *false* for all anyone knows, so they will not, or should not, create any tendency to believe that the probability of S on theism is *not* lower than it is on HI, that it is about the same or higher. Rather, the stories will, or should, lead a person in our epistemic situation to refuse to make any judgment about the relation between the probabilities of S on theism and on HI.

I shall presently offer such a story. But I propose to simplify my task in a way that I hope is legitimate. It seems to me that the theist should not assume that there is a single reason, or tightly interrelated set of reasons, for the sufferings of all sentient creatures. In particular, the theist should not assume that God's reasons for decreeing, or allowing, the sufferings of non-rational creatures have much in common with His reasons for decreeing or allowing the sufferings of human beings. The most satisfactory "defenses" that have so far been offered by theists purport to account only for the sufferings of human beings. In the sequel, I will offer a defense that is directed towards the sufferings of non-rational creatures—"beasts," I shall call them. If this defense were a success, it could be combined with defenses directed towards the sufferings of human beings (like the Free Will Defense) to produce a "total" defense. This "separation of cases" does not seem to me to be an arbitrary procedure. Human beings are radically different from all other animals, and a "total" defense that explained the sufferings of beasts in one way and the sufferings of human beings in a radically different way would not be implausible on that account. Although it is not strictly to our purpose, I will point out that this is consonant with the most usual Christian view of suffering. Typically, Christians have held that human suffering is not a part of God's plan for the world, but exists only because that plan has gone awry. On the other hand:

> Thou makest darkness that it may be night; wherein all the beasts
> of the forest do move.
> The lions, roaring after their prey, do seek their meat from God.
> The sun ariseth, and they get them away together, and lay them
> down in their dens. (Ps. 104: 20-22)

This and many other Biblical texts seem to imply that the whole subrational natural world proceeds according to God's plan (except insofar as we human beings have corrupted nature). And this, as the Psalmist tells us in his great hymn of praise to the order that God has established in nature, includes the phenomenon of predation.

I will now tell a story, a story that is true for all I know, that accounts for the sufferings of beasts. The story consists of the following three propositions:

(1) Every possible world that contains higher-level sentient creatures either contains patterns of suffering morally equivalent to those recorded by S, or else is massively irregular.

(2) Some important intrinsic or extrinsic good depends on the existence of higher-level sentient creatures; this good is of sufficient magnitude that it outweighs the patterns of suffering recorded by S.

(3) Being massively irregular is a defect in a world, a defect at least as great as the defect of containing patterns of suffering morally equivalent to those recorded by S.

The four key terms contained in this story may be explained as follows.

*Higher-level sentient creatures* are animals that are *conscious* in the way in which (*pace* Descartes) the higher non-human mammals are conscious.

Two patterns of suffering are *morally equivalent* if there are no morally decisive reasons for preferring one to the other: if there are no morally decisive reasons for creating a world that embodies one pattern rather than the other. To say that A and B are in this sense morally equivalent is not to say that they are in any interesting sense comparable. Suppose, for example, that the Benthamite dream of a universal hedonic calculus is an illusion, and that there is no answer to the question whether the suffering caused by war is less than, the same as, or greater than the suffering caused by cancer. It does not follow that these two patterns of suffering are not morally equivalent. On the contrary: unless there is some "non-hedonic" morally relevant distinction to be made between a world that contains war and no cancer and a world that contains cancer and no war (i.e., a distinction that does not depend on comparing the amounts of suffering caused by war and cancer), it would seem to follow that the suffering caused by war and the suffering caused by cancer *are*, in the present technical sense, morally equivalent.

It is important to note that A and B may be morally equivalent even if they are comparable and one of them involves *less* suffering than the other. By way of analogy, consider the fact that there is no morally decisive reason to prefer a jail term of ten years as a penalty for armed assault to a term of ten years and a day, despite the indubitable facts that these two penalties would have the same deterrent effect and that one is lighter than the other. I have argued elsewhere that, for any amount of suffering that somehow serves God's purposes, it may be that some smaller amount of suffering would have served them as well.[11] It may be, therefore, that God has had to choose *some* amount of suffering as the amount contained in the actual world, and could, consistently with His purposes, have chosen any of a vast array of smaller or greater amounts, and that all of the members of this vast array of alternative amounts of suffering are morally equivalent. (Similarly, a legislature has to choose *some* penalty as the penalty for armed assault, and—think of penalties as jail terms measured in minutes—must choose among the members of a vast array of morally equivalent penalties.) Or it may be that God has decreed, with respect to this vast array of alternative, morally equivalent amounts of suffering, that *some* member of this array shall be the actual amount of suffering, but has left it up to chance which member that is.[12]

A *massively irregular world* is a world in which the laws of nature fail in some massive way. A world containing all of the miracles recorded in the New Testament would not, on that account, be massively irregular, for those miracles were too small (if size is measured in terms of the amounts of matter directly affected) and too few and far between. But a world would be massively irregular if it contained the following state of affairs:

God, by means of a continuous series of ubiquitous miracles, causes a planet inhabited by the same animal life as the actual earth to be a hedonic utopia. On this planet, fawns are (like Shadrach, Meshach, and Abednego) saved by angels when they are in danger of being burnt alive. Harmful parasites and microorganisms suffer immediate supernatural dissolution if they enter a higher animal's body. Lambs are miraculously hidden from lions, and the lions are compensated for the resulting restriction on their diets by physically impossible falls of high-protein manna. On this planet, either God created every species by a separate miracle, or else, although all living things evolved from a common ancestor, a hedonic utopia has existed at every stage of the evolutionary process. (The latter alternative implies that God has, by means of a vast and intricately coordinated sequence of supernatural adjustments to the machinery of nature, guided the evolutionary process in such a way as to compensate for the fact that a hedonic utopia exerts no selection pressure.)

It would also be possible for a world to be massively irregular in a more systematic or "wholesale" way. A world that came into existence five minutes ago, complete with memories of an unreal past, would be on that account alone massively irregular—if indeed such a world was metaphysically possible. A world in which beasts (beasts having the physical structure and exhibiting the pain-behavior of actual beasts) felt no pain would be on that account alone massively irregular—if indeed such a world was metaphysically possible.

A *defect in a world* is a feature of a world that (whatever its extrinsic value might be in various worlds) a world is intrinsically better for not having.

Our story comprises propositions (1), (2), and (3). I believe that we have no reason to assign any probability or range of probabilities to this story. (With the following possible exception: if we have a reason to regard the existence of God as improbable, then we shall have a reason to regard the story as improbable.)

We should have reason to reject this story if we had reason to believe that there were possible worlds—worlds that were not massively irregular—in which higher-level sentient creatures inhabited a hedonic utopia. Is there any reason to think that there are such worlds? I suppose that the only kind of reason one could have for believing that there was a possible world having a certain feature would be the reason provided by a plausible attempt to "design" a world having that feature. How does one go about designing a world?

One should start by describing in some detail the laws of nature that govern that world. (Physicists' actual formulations of quantum field theories and the general theory of relativity provide the standard of required "detail.") One should then go on to describe the boundary conditions under which those laws operate: the topology of the world's spacetime, its relativistic mass, the number of particle families, and so on. Then one should tell in convincing detail the story of cosmic evolution in that world: the story of the development of large objects like galaxies and stars and of small objects like carbon atoms. Finally, one should tell the story of the evolution of life. These stories, of course, must be coherent, given one's specification of laws and boundary conditions. Unless one proceeds in this manner, one's statements about what is intrinsically or metaphysically possible—and thus one's statements about an omnipotent being's "options" in creating a world—will be entirely subjective, and therefore without value. But I have argued for this view of the epistemology of modal statements (that is, of modal statements concerning major departures from actuality) elsewhere, and the reader is referred to those arguments. In fact, the argument of those papers should be considered a part of the argument of the present paper.[13]

Our own universe provides the only model we have for the formidable task of designing a world. (For all we know, in every possible world that exhibits any degree of complexity, the laws of nature are the actual laws, or at least have the same structure as the actual laws. There are, in fact, philosophically minded physicists who believe that there is only one possible set of laws of nature, and it is epistemically possible that they are right.) Our universe apparently evolved out of an initial singularity in accordance with certain laws of nature.[14] This evolution is not without its mysteries: the very early stages of the unfolding of the universe (the incredibly brief instant during which the laws of nature operated under conditions of perfect symmetry), the formation of the galaxies, and the origin of life on the earth are, in the present state of natural knowledge, deep mysteries. Nevertheless, it seems reasonable to assume that all of these processes involved only the non-miraculous operation of the laws of nature. One important thing that is known about the evolution of the universe into its present state is that it has been a very tightly structured process. A large number of physical parameters have apparently arbitrary values such that if those values had been only slightly different (very, *very* slightly different) the universe would contain no life, and *a fortiori* no intelligent life.[15] It may or may not be the "purpose" of the cosmos to constitute an arena in which the evolution of intelligent life takes place, but it is certainly true that this evolution did take place, and that if the universe had been different by an all but unimaginably minute degree it wouldn't have. My purpose in citing this fact—it is reasonable to believe that it is a fact—is not to produce an up-to-date version of the Design Argument. It is, rather, to suggest that (at least, for all we know) only in a universe very much like ours could intelligent life, or even sentient life, develop by the non-miraculous operation of the laws of nature. And the natural evolution of higher sentient life in a universe like ours essentially involves suffering, or there is every reason to believe it does. The mechanisms underlying biological evolution may be just what most biologists seem to suppose—the production of new genes by random mutation and the culling of gene pools by environmental selection pressure—or they may be more subtle. But no one, I believe, would take seriously the idea that conscious animals, animals conscious as a dog is conscious, could evolve naturally without hundreds of millions of years of ancestral suffering. Pain is an indispensable component of the evolutionary process after organisms have reached a certain stage of complexity. And, for all we know, the amount of pain that organisms have experienced in the actual world, or some amount morally equivalent to that amount, is necessary for the natural evolution of conscious animals. I conclude that the first part of our defense is true for all we know: Every possible world that contains higher-level sentient creatures either contains patterns of suffering morally equivalent to those recorded by S, or else is massively irregular.

Let us now consider the second part of our defense: Some important intrinsic or extrinsic good depends on the existence of higher-level sentient creatures; this good is of sufficient magnitude that it outweighs the patterns of suffering recorded by S. It is not very hard to believe (is it?) that a world that was as the earth was just before the appearance of human beings would contain a much larger amount of intrinsic good, and would, in fact, contain a better balance of good over evil, than a world in which there were no organisms higher than worms. (Which is not to say that there could not be worlds lacking intelligent life that contained a still better balance of good over evil—say, worlds containing the same organisms, but significantly less suffering.) And then there is the question of extrinsic value. One consideration immediately suggests itself: intelligent life— creatures made in the image and likeness of God—could not evolve directly from worms or oysters; the immediate evolutionary predecessors of intelligent animals must possess higher-level sentience.

We now turn to the third part of our defense: Being massively irregular is a defect in a world, a defect at least as great as the defect of containing patterns of suffering morally equivalent to those recorded by S. We should recall that a defense is not a theodicy, and that we are not required to argue at this point that it is *plausible to suppose* that massive irregularity is a defect in a world, a defect so grave that creating a world containing animal suffering morally equivalent to the animal suffering of the actual world is a reasonable price to pay to avoid it. We are required to argue only that *for all we know* this judgment is correct.

The third part of our defense is objectionable only if we have some *prima facie* reason for believing that the actual sufferings of beasts are a graver defect in a world than massive irregularity would be. Have we any such reason? It seems to me that we do not. To begin with, it does seem that massive irregularity is a defect in a world. One minor point in favor of this thesis is the witness of deists and other thinkers who have deprecated the miraculous on the ground that *any* degree of irregularity in a world is a defect, a sort of unlovely jury-rigging of things that is altogether unworthy of the power and wisdom of God. Presumably such thinkers would regard *massive* irregularity as a very grave defect indeed. And perhaps there is something to this reaction. It does seem that there is something right about the idea that God would include no more irregularity than was necessary in His creation. A second point is that many, if not all, massively irregular worlds are not only massively irregular but massively *deceptive*. This is obviously true of a world that looks like the actual world but which began five minutes ago, or a world that looks like the actual world but in which beasts feel no pain. (And this is not surprising, for our beliefs about the world depend in large measure on our habit of drawing conclusions that are based on the assumption that the world is regular.) But it is plausible to suppose that deception, and, *a fortiori*, massive deception, is inconsistent with the nature of a perfect being. These points, however, are no more than suggestive, and, even if they amounted to proof, they would prove only that massive irregularity was a defect; they would not prove that it was a defect in any way comparable with the actual suffering of beasts. In any case, proof is not the present question: the question is whether there is a *prima facie* case for the thesis that the actual sufferings of beasts constitute a graver defect in a world than does massive irregularity.

What would such a case be based on? I would suppose that someone who maintained that there was such a case would have to rely on his moral intuitions, or, more generally, on his intuitions of value. He would have to say something like this: "I have held the two states of affairs—the actual sufferings of beasts and massive irregularity—before my mind and carefully compared them. My considered judgment is that the former is worse than the latter." This judgment presupposes that these two states of affairs are, in the sense that was explained above, comparable: one of them is worse than the other, or else they are of the same value (or disvalue). It is not clear to me that there is any reason to suppose that this is so. If it is *not* so, then, as we have seen, it can plausibly be maintained that the two states of affairs are morally equivalent, and a Creator could not be faulted on moral grounds for choosing either over the other. But let us suppose that the two states of affairs are comparable. In that case, if the value-judgment we are considering is to be trusted, then human beings possess a faculty that enables them correctly to judge the relative values of states of affairs of literally cosmic magnitude, states of affairs, moreover, that are in no way (as some states of affairs of cosmic magnitude may be) connected with the practical concerns of human beings. Why should one suppose that one's inclinations to make judgments of value are reliable in this area? One's intuitions about value are either a gift from God or a product of evolution or socially inculcated or stem from some combination of these sources. Why should we suppose that any of these sources would provide us with the means to make correct value-judgments in matters that have nothing to do with the practical concerns of everyday life? (I do think we must be able to speak of *correct* value-judgments if the Problem of Evil is to be of any interest. An eminent philosopher of biology has said in one place that God, if He existed, would be indescribably wicked for having created a world like this one, and, in another place, that morality is an illusion, an illusion that we are subject to because of the evolutionary advantage it confers. These two theses do not seem to me to add up to a coherent position.) Earlier I advocated a form of modal skepticism: our modal intuitions, while they are no doubt to be trusted when they tell us that the table could have been placed on the other side of the room, are not to be trusted on such matters as whether there could be transparent iron or whether there could be a "regular" universe in which there were higher sentient creatures that did not suffer. And if this true, it is not surprising. Assuming that there are "modal facts of the matter," why should we assume that God or evolution or social training has given us access to modal facts knowledge of which is of no interest to anyone but the metaphysician? God or evolution has provided us with a capacity for making judgments about size and distance that is very useful in hunting mammoths and driving cars, but which is of no use at all in astronomy. It seems that an analogous restriction applies to our capacity for making modal judgments. How can we be sure that an analogous restriction does not also apply to our capacity for making *value*-judgments? My position is that we cannot be sure, and that for all we know our inclinations to make value-judgments are not veridical when they are applied to cosmic matters unrelated to the concerns of everyday life. (Not that our inclinations in this area are at all uniform. I myself experience no inclination to come down on one side or the other of the question whether massive irregularity or vast amounts of animal suffering is the graver defect in a world. I suspect that others do experience such inclinations. If they don't, of course, then I'm preaching to the converted.) But then there is no *prima facie* case for the thesis that the actual sufferings of beasts constitute a graver defect in a world than does massive irregularity. Or, at least, there is no case that is grounded in our intuitions about value. And in what else could such a case be grounded?

These considerations have to do with intrinsic value, with comparison of the intrinsic disvalue of two states of affairs. There is also the matter of extrinsic value. Who can say what the effects of creating a massively irregular world might be? What things of intrinsic value might be frustrated or rendered impossible in a massively irregular world? We cannot say. Christians have generally held that at a certain point God plans to hand over the government of the world to humanity. Would a massively irregular world be the sort of world that could be "handed over"? Perhaps a massively irregular world would immediately dissolve into chaos if an infinite being were not constantly making adjustments to it. We simply cannot say. If anyone insists that he has good reason to believe that nothing of any great value depends on the world's being regular, we must ask him why he thinks he is in a position to know things of that sort. We might remind him of the counsel of epistemic humility that was spoken to Job out of the whirlwind:

> Gird up now thy loins like a man; for I will demand of thee, and answer thou me.
> Where wast thou when I laid the foundations of the earth? Declare if thou hast understanding.
> Knowest thou it, because thou wast then born, or because the number of thy days is great?
> Canst thou bind the sweet influences of Pleiades, or loose the bands of Orion?
> Knowest thou the ordinances of heaven? Canst thou set the dominion thereof in the earth?[16]

I have urged extreme modal and moral skepticism (or, one might say, humility) in matters unrelated to the concerns of everyday life. If such skepticism is accepted, then we have no reason to accept the evidentialist's premise that "an omniscient and omnipotent being will be able so to arrange matters that the world contains sentient beings among whom suffering, if it exists at all, is apportioned according to desert." More exactly, we have no reason to suppose that an omniscient and omnipotent being could do this without creating a massively irregular world; and, for all we know, the intrinsic or extrinsic disvalue of a massively irregular world is greater than the intrinsic disvalue of vast amounts of animal suffering (which, presumably, are not apportioned according to desert). If these consequences of modal and moral skepticism are accepted, then there is no reason to believe that the probability of S on HI is higher than the probability of S on theism, and the evidential argument from evil cannot get started. Even if we assume that the probability of S on HI is high (that the denial of S is very surprising on HI), this assumption gives us no reason to prefer HI to theism. If there were such a reason, it could be presented as an argument:

> The probability of S on HI is high
> We do not know what to say about the probability of S on theism
> HI and theism are inconsistent
> Therefore, for anyone in our epistemic situation, the truth of S constitutes a *prima facie* case for preferring HI to theism.

This argument is far from compelling. If there is any doubt about this, it can be dispelled by considering a parallel argument. Let L be the proposition that intelligent life exists, and let G be the proposition that God wants intelligent life to exist. We argue as follows:

> The probability of L on G is high
> We do not know what to say about the probability of L on atheism
> G and atheism are inconsistent
> Therefore, for anyone in our epistemic situation, the truth of L constitutes a *prima facie* case for preferring G to atheism.

The premises of this argument are true. (As to the second premise, there has been considerable debate in the scientific community as to whether the natural evolution of intelligent life is inevitable or extremely unlikely or something in between; let us suppose that "we" are a group of people who have tried to follow this debate and have been hopelessly confused by it.) But I should be very surprised to learn of someone who believed that the premises of the argument entailed its conclusion.

I will close this section by pointing out something that is not strictly relevant to the argument it contains, but is, in my view, of more than merely autobiographical interest. I have not accepted the extreme modal skepticism that figures so prominently in the argument of this section as a result of epistemic pressures exerted by the evidential argument from evil. I was an extreme modal skeptic before I was a theist, and I have, on the basis of this skepticism, argued (and would still argue) against both Swinburne's attempt to show that the concept of God is coherent, and Plantinga's attempt to use the modal version of the ontological argument to show that theism is rational.[17]

## III

Imagine an ancient Greek, an atomist who believes that the whole world is made of tiny, indestructible, immutable solids. Imagine that an opponent of atomism (call him Aristotle) presents our atomist with the following argument: "If fire were made of tiny solids, the same solids earth is made of, or ones that differ from them only in shape, then fire would not be Absolutely Light—it would not rise toward the heavens of its own nature. But that fire is not Absolutely Light is contrary to observation."[18] From our lofty twentieth-century vantage-point, we might be inclined to regard Aristotle's argument as merely quaint. But this impression of quaintness rests on two features of the argument that can be removed without damage to what is, from one point of view anyway, its essential force. The two quaint features of Aristotle's argument, the idea that fire is a stuff, and the idea of the Absolutely Light, can be removed from the argument by substituting air for fire and by substituting the behavior we nowadays associate with the gaseous state for the defining behavior of the Absolutely Light (that is, a natural tendency to move upwards). The resulting argument would look something like this:

> Suppose air were made of tiny solid bodies as you say. Then air would behave like fine dust: it would eventually settle to the ground and become a mere dusty coating on the surface of the earth. But this is contrary to observation.

Well, what is wrong with this argument? Why *don't* the $O_2$, $N_2$, $CO_2$, and other molecules that make up the atmosphere simply settle to the ground like dust particles? The answer is that air molecules, unlike dust particles, push on one another; they are kept at average distances that are large in comparison with their own sizes by repulsive forces (electromagnetic in nature), the strength of these forces in a given region being a function of the local temperature. At the temperatures one finds near the surface of the earth (temperatures maintained by solar radiation and the internal heat of the earth), the aggregate action of these intermolecular forces produces the kind of aggregate molecular behavior that, at the macroscopic level of description, we call the gaseous state.

*We* can see where the improved version of Aristotle's argument goes wrong. (We can also see that in one minor respect it's better than an ancient Greek could know: if it weren't for intermolecular forces, air molecules would not simply settle slowly to the ground; they would drop like rocks.) But what about our imaginary ancient atomist, who not only doesn't know all these things about intermolecular forces and temperature and so on, but who couldn't even conceive of them as epistemic possibilities? What shall he say in response to the improved version of Aristotle's argument?

In order to sharpen this question, let us imagine that a Greek philosopher called A-prime has actually presented our atomist with the air-and-dust argument, and let us imagine that A-prime has at his disposal the techniques of a late-twentieth-century analytical philosopher. Having presented the atomist with the simple argument that I have given above (the primitive or "whence, then, is air?" version of the Argument from Air), he presses his point by confronting the atomist with a much more sophisticated argument, the *evidential* argument from air. "Let HI, the Hypothesis of Independence, be the thesis that there are four independent and continuous elements, air among them, each of which has *sui generis* properties (you can find a list of them in any reputable physics text) that determine its characteristic behavior. Let S be a proposition that records the properties of air. The simple air-and-dust argument is sufficient to establish that S is not surprising given HI, but is very surprising given atomism. There are only three ways for you to respond to this *prima facie* case against atomism: you may argue that S is much more surprising, given HI than one might suppose; or that S is much less surprising, given atomism, than one might suppose; or that there are reasons for preferring atomism to HI that outweigh the *prima facie* reason for preferring HI to atomism that is provided by the air-and-dust argument. The first I shall not discuss. The third is unpromising, unless you can come up with something better than the very abstract metaphysical arguments with which you have attempted to support atomism in the past, for they certainly do not outweigh the clear and concrete air-and-dust argument. The only course open to you is to construct an *atomodicy*. That is, you must find some auxiliary hypothesis *h* that explains how S could be true, given atomism. And you will have to show both that the probability of S is high (or at least not too low) on the conjunction of atomism and *h* and that the probability of *h* on atomism is high. While you may be able to find an hypothesis that satisfies the former condition, I think it very unlikely that you will be able to find one that satisfies the latter. In any case, unless you *can* find an hypothesis that satisfies both conditions, you cannot rationally continue to be an atomist."

Whatever else may be said about this argument, A-prime is certainly right about one thing: it is unlikely that the atomist will be able to produce a successful atomodicy. Even if he were told the modern story about air, he could not do it. At least, I don't think he could. What is the epistemic probability on atomism (relative to the epistemic situation of an ancient Greek) of our complicated modern story of intermolecular forces and the gaseous state? What probability should someone who knew nothing about the micro structure of the material world except that it was composed of atoms (it is, of course, our "elementary particles" and not our "atoms" or our "molecules" that correspond to the atoms of the Greeks) assign to the modern story? As far as I am able to judge, the only rational thing such a person could do would be to decline to assign any probability to the modern story on atomism. (The answer of modern science to the air-and-dust argument does not take the form of a story that, relative to the epistemic situation of an ancient Greek, is highly probable on atomism.)

Fortunately for the atomist, A-prime's demand that he produce an atomodicy is unreasonable. The atomist need do nothing more in response to the evidential argument from air than find a defense— or, better, several independent defenses. A defense, of course, is a story that explains how there could be a stuff that has the properties of air (those known to an ancient Greek), given that the material world is made entirely of atoms. A defense need *not* be highly probable on atomism. It is required only that, given atomism, the defense be true for all anyone (*sc.* any ancient Greek) knows.

Here is one example of a defense: air atoms (unlike earth atoms) are spheres covered with a "fur" of long, thin, flexible spikes that are, unless flexed by contact with another atom, perpendicular to the surface of the atom's "nucleus" (i.e., its central sphere); the length of the spikes is large in comparison with the diameters of nuclei, and their presence thus tends to keep nuclei far apart. Since, for all anyone (anyone in the epistemic situation of an ancient Greek) knows, some atoms have such features—if there are atoms at all—the observed properties of air are not surprising on the assumption of atomism. Since there are defenses that are true for all anyone (anyone in the epistemic situation of an ancient Greek) knows, no ancient Greek was in a position to say anything about the probability on atomism of S, the proposition that sums up the properties of air that were known to him. A-prime, therefore, is left with no better argument than the following:

> The probability of S on HI is high
> We do not know what to say about the probability of S on atomism
> HI and atomism are inconsistent
> Therefore, for anyone in our epistemic situation, the truth of S constitutes a *prima facie* case for preferring HI to atomism.

And this argument is manifestly invalid.

## IV

We know how it is that air can be composed of molecules and yet not drift to the ground like dust. This knowledge provides us with a certain rather Olympian perspective from which to view the "Problem of Air." I wish next to examine the epistemic situation of those of our contemporaries who believe that the Milky Way galaxy (ours) contains other intelligent species than humanity. (Since they are our contemporaries, we cannot view their situation from any such Olympian perspective.) Let us confront them with an argument analogous to the argument from evil and the argument from air. The essence of this argument is contained in a question of Enrico Fermi's, a question as pithy as 'Whence, then, is evil?': Where are they?

If there are other intelligent species in the galaxy, the overwhelming probability is that at least one intelligent species existed at least a hundred million years ago. There has been life on the earth for at least thirty times that long, and there is nothing magical about the present time. The universe was just as suitable for intelligent life a hundred million years ago, and if the pace of evolution on the earth had been just three or four percent faster, there would have been intelligent life *here* a hundred million years ago. An intelligent and technologically able species will attempt to send messages to other species elsewhere in the galaxy (as we have begun to do). The most efficient way to do this is to send out self-reproducing robotic probes to other stars: when such a probe reaches another star, it makes two or more duplicates of itself out of local materials, and these duplicates proceed to further stars. Then it waits, perhaps for hundreds of millions of years, till it detects locally produced radio signals, at which point it reveals itself and delivers its message. (There are no fundamental technological barriers to this program. At our present rate of scientific progress, we shall be able to set such a process in motion within the next century.) It is not hard to show that the descendants of the original probes will reach every star in the galaxy within fifty million years. (We assume that the probes are capable of reaching one-tenth the speed of light.) But no such probe has revealed itself to us. Therefore, any non-human intelligence in the galaxy came into existence less than fifty million years ago. But it is statistically very unlikely that there are non-human intelligences *all* of which came into existence within the last fifty million years. (The reasoning is like this: if you know that such people as there are in the Sahara Desert are distributed randomly, and if you know that there are no people in the Sahara except, possibly, within a circular area one hundred miles in diameter that is hidden from you, you can conclude that there are probably no people at all in the Sahara.) Furthermore, it is not merely the absence of robotic probes that should disturb the proponent of "extra-terrestrial intelligence." There are also the absence of radio signals from thousands of nearby stars and several of the nearer galaxies[19] and the absence of manifestations of "hypertechnology" like the wide-angle infrared source that would signal the presence of a star that has been surrounded with a "Dyson sphere." We may refer collectively to all of these "absences" as *cosmic silence*, or simply *silence*. (If there are other intelligent species in the galaxy, or even in nearby galaxies, they are *species absconditae*.) The obvious implication of these observations is that we are alone.[20]

Let us call the thesis that there is intelligent life elsewhere in the galaxy *noetism*. The above argument, the argument from cosmic silence, provides materials from which the anti-noetist may construct an evidential argument against noetism analogous to the evidential argument from evil: "Let the Hypothesis of Isolation (HI) be the hypothesis that humanity is the only intelligent species that exists or has ever existed in the Milky Way galaxy or any of the nearby galaxies. Let S be a proposition that records all of the observations that constitute a failure to discover any manifestation whatever of life, and, *a fortiori*, of intelligent life, elsewhere in the universe. The argument from cosmic silence is sufficient to establish that the truth of S (which, of course, is not at all surprising given HI) is very surprising, given noetism. There are only three ways for you to respond to the argument from cosmic silence: you may argue that S is much more surprising, given HI, than one might suppose; or that S is much less surprising, given noetism, than one might suppose; or that there are reasons for preferring noetism to HI that outweigh the *prima facie* reason for preferring HI to noetism that is provided by the argument from cosmic silence. The first is no more than a formal possibility. The third is unpromising, unless you can come up with something better than those facile arguments for the prevalence of life in the cosmos that are so popular with astronomers and physicists and so exasperating to evolutionary biologists.[21] The only course open to you is to construct a *noödicy*. That is, you must find some auxiliary hypothesis *h* that explains how S could be true, given noetism. And you will have to show both that the probability of S is high (or at least not too low) on the conjunction of noetism and *h* and that the probability of *h* on noetism is high. While you may be able to find an hypothesis that satisfies the former condition, I think it very unlikely that you will be able to find one that satisfies the latter. In any case, unless you *can* find an hypothesis that satisfies both conditions, you cannot rationally continue to be an noetist."

The anti-noetist is no doubt right in supposing that it is very unlikely that the noetist will be able to construct a successful noödicy. One example should suffice to make the point. Consider the elegantly simple, if rather depressing, Nuclear Destruction Scenario: intelligent species do not last long enough to make much of a mark on the cosmos; within at most a few decades of developing radio transmitters powerful enough to be detected across a distance of light-years (and long before they can make self-reproducing intersiderial robotic probes), they invariably destroy themselves in nuclear wars. It is clear that the Nuclear Destruction Scenario is a failure as a noödicy, for it is not highly probable on noetism. (That intelligent species invariably destroy themselves in nuclear wars is not highly probable on the hypothesis that intelligent species exist.) The proponents of extra-terrestrial intelligence have provided a wide range of possible explanations of "cosmic silence" (intelligence does not necessarily imply technology; the desire to communicate with other intelligent species is a human idiosyncrasy; the most efficient means of inter-siderial signaling, the one that all the extra-terrestrials actually employ, is one we haven't yet thought of), but it is clear that none of these possible explanations should be regarded as *highly probable* on noetism. We simply do not know enough to make any such probability judgment. Shall the noetist therefore concede that we have shown his position to be irrational? No, for the anti-noetist's demand that the noetist produce a noödicy is wholly unreasonable. The noetist need only produce one or more *defenses*, one or more explanations of the phenomenon of cosmic silence that entail noetism and are true for all we know. And this is just what the noetist has done. (I have already mentioned several of them.) Since there are defenses that for all anyone knows are true, no one knows what to say about the probability on noetism of S (the proposition that records all of our failed attempts to discover any manifestation of intelligent life elsewhere in the universe). The anti-noetist has therefore failed to show that the truth of S constitutes a *prima facie* case in favor of preferring HI to noetism.

## V

"This is all very well. But evil *is* a difficulty for the theist, and the gaseous state *was* a difficulty for the ancient atomist, and cosmic silence *is* a difficulty for the noetist. You seem to be saying that they can just ignore these difficulties."

Not at all. I have said that these difficulties (I accept the term 'difficulty') do not render their beliefs irrational—not even if they are unable to find arguments that raise the probabilities of their hypotheses relative to the probabilities of competing hypotheses that do not face the same difficulties, and are also unable to devise auxiliary hypotheses that enable them to construct "-dicies." It doesn't follow that they should simply ignore the difficulties.

"Well, what *should* they do?"

To begin with, they can acknowledge the difficulties. They can admit that the difficulties exist and that they're not sure what to say about them. They might go on to offer some speculations about the causes of the phenomena that raise the difficulties: mechanisms that would account for the gaseous state, possible conditions that would interfere with communications across light-years, reasons God might have for allowing evil. Such speculations need not be (they almost certainly will not be) highly probable on the "-ism" in whose defense they are employed. And they need not be probable on anything that is known to be true, although they should not be improbable on anything that is known to be true. They are to be offered as explanations of the difficult phenomena that are, *for all anyone knows*, the correct ones. In sum, the way to deal with such difficulties is to construct defenses.

"But if a phenomenon is a 'difficulty' for a certain theory, does that not mean that it is evidence against that theory? Or if it is not evidence against that theory, in what sense can it raise a 'difficulty' for the theory? Are you not saying that it can be right to accept a theory to which there is counterevidence when there are competing theories to which there is no counterevidence?"

That sounds good, but it is really a recipe for rejecting just about any interesting theory. Just about any interesting theory is faced with phenomena that make the advocates of the theory a bit uncomfortable, this discomfort being signalled by the tendency to speculate about circumstances consistent with the theory that might produce the phenomena. For any theory that faces such a difficulty, there will always be available another "theory," or at least another hypothesis, that does not face that difficulty: its denial. (The denial of an interesting theory will rarely if ever itself be an interesting theory; it will be too general and non-specific.) Your suggestion would therefore appear to constrain us never to accept any interesting theory, but always either to accept its denial or else neither the theory nor its denial. The latter will be the more common result, since the denial of a theory can usually be partitioned into interesting theories that face individual difficulties. (For example, the denial of atomism can be partitioned into the following hypotheses: matter is continuous; matter is neither continuous nor atomically structured; matter does not exist. Each of these hypotheses faces difficulties.) This result might be avoided if you placed some sort of restriction on what counted as a "competing theory," but it is not clear what sort of restriction would be required. It will not do simply to rule out the denial of a theory as a competing theory, for contraries of the theory that were very general and non-specific could produce equally counterintuitive results. If, moreover, you did produce a satisfactory solution to this problem, it is not clear what consequences your solution might have for the evidential argument from evil. Consider, for example, the Hypothesis of Indifference. This is not a very specific thesis: it tells us only that the nature and condition of sentient beings on earth do *not* have a certain (very narrowly delineated) cause. Perhaps it would not count as a proper "competitor" with the quite specific thesis we have called 'theism'. Perhaps it would be a consequence of your solution that only some proposition more specific than HI, some proposition that entailed but was not entailed by HI, could properly be in competition with theism. And this proposition might face difficulties of its own, difficulties not faced by HI.

But we may answer your question more directly and simply. A difficulty with a theory does not necessarily constitute evidence against it. To show that an acknowledged difficulty with a theory is not evidence against it, it suffices to construct a defense that accounts for the facts that raise the difficulty. (This thesis by no means provides an automatic "out" for a theory that is confronted with some recalcitrant observation, for a defense is not automatically available to the proponents of every theory that is confronted with a recalcitrant observation. A defense may not be improbable, either on the theory in whose cause it is employed, or on anything we know to be true. In a particular case, it may be that no one can think of any hypothesis that satisfies these two conditions, and what was a mere difficulty for a theory will thereby attain to the status of evidence against the theory. It is perhaps worth pointing out that two or more difficulties may jointly constitute evidence against a theory, even if none of them taken individually counts as evidence against it. This could be the case if the defenses that individually "handle" the difficulties are inconsistent, or if—despite the fact that none of the defenses taken individually is improbable—their conjunction is improbable.)

The central thesis of this paper may be usefully summarized in the terminology that has been introduced in the present section: While the patterns of suffering we find in the actual world constitute a *difficulty* for theism and do not constitute a difficulty for the competing hypothesis HI, they do not—owing to the availability of the defense[22] I have outlined—attain to the status of *evidence* that favors HI over theism. It follows that the evidential argument from evil fails, for it is essential to the evidential argument that those patterns of suffering be evidence that favors HI over theism.[23]

## Notes

1. My formulation of this argument owes a great deal to a recent article by Paul Draper ("Pain and Pleasure: An Evidential Problem for Theists," *Noûs* 23 (1989), 331-50). I do not, however, claim that the argument I shall present *is* Draper's intricate and subtle argument, or even a simplified version of it. (One important difference between the argument discussed in the present paper and Draper's argument is that the latter makes reference to the distribution of both pain and pleasure, while the former makes reference only to the distribution of pain.) Nevertheless, I hope that the version of the evidential argument from evil that I shall discuss is similar enough to Draper's that what I say about my version will at least suggest strategies that the theist can employ in dealing with Draper's argument. Draper (p. 332) credits Hume with being the first to ask the question whether there is "any serious hypothesis that is logically inconsistent with theism [and] explains some significant set of facts about evil...much better than theism does." (See *Dialogues Con-*

162 / Peter van Inwagen

cerning Natural Religion, Part XI.)

2. In Draper's argument, the role that corresponds to the role played by S in our argument is played by a proposition O that reports "both the observations one has made of humans and animals experiencing pain or pleasure and the testimony one has encountered concerning the observations others have made of sentient beings experiencing pain or pleasure" (p. 332). I find that the argument goes more easily if it is stated in terms of the probability (on various hypotheses) of the pattern of suffering that it is reasonable to believe the actual world exhibits, rather than in terms of the probability (on those hypotheses) of the observations and testimony on which our reasonable belief in that pattern rests. I do not think that this modification of Draper's strategy leaves me with an argument that is easier to refute than the argument that would have resulted if I had retained this feature of his strategy.

3. *Cf.* Draper, p. 331. Perhaps we should add that this being has not ceased to exist, and has never ceased to be omniscient, omnipotent, or morally perfect.

4. *Cf.* Draper, pp. 333 and 349 (note 2). Some difficulties with the notion of epistemic probability are discussed in note 7 below.

5. *Cf.* Draper, p. 332.

6. It is a currently popular view that one can have reasons for believing in God that are of a quite different kind from "arguments for the existence of God." For a sampling of versions of this view, see the essays by the editors and the essay by William P. Alston in Alvin Plantinga and Nicholas Wolterstorff, eds., *Faith and Rationality: Reason and Belief in God* (South Bend, Indiana: the University of Notre Dame Press, 1983). My own position on this matter is that some version of this view is right, and that there are reasons for believing in God that are of the general kind described by Plantinga, Wolterstorff, and Alston. I believe, moreover, that these reasons not only can provide one with adequate justification for being a theist in the absence of a *prima facie* case against theism, but are strong enough to override any conceivable *prima facie* case against theism. (For a contrary view—which I believe rests on a misunderstanding—see Draper, pp. 347-8.) But I shall not defend this thesis here, since the point of the present paper is that the patterns of suffering that exist in the actual world do not constitute even a *prima facie* case against theism.

7. I prefer to formulate the evidential argument from evil in terms of epistemic surprise, rather than in terms of high and low epistemic probability. (Draper's essay suggested this use of the concept of "surprise" to me. Although his "official" formulation of his argument is in terms of epistemic probability, he frequently employs the notion of "surprise" in his informal commentary on the argument. Indeed, at one place— see p. 333—he comes very close to explaining epistemic probability as I did in the text: by equating 'has a lower epistemic probability' with 'is more surprising'.) Let me attempt to explain why I am uneasy about formulating the argument in terms of probabilities. If the argument is

so formulated, it would appear to depend on the validity of the following inference-form: $p$; the probability of $p$ on $q$ is much higher than the probability of $p$ on $r$; $q$ and $r$ are inconsistent; therefore, there exists a *prima facie* reason (*viz*, that $p$) for preferring $q$ to $r$. The trouble with this inference-form is that the probability of $p$ may be very low on $q$ despite the fact that $p$ is not at all *surprising* on $q$. For example, the probability of the hypothesis that the unobservable card that Alice is holding is the four of clubs is quite low on the hypothesis that she drew the card at random from a standard deck, but the former hypothesis is not at all surprising on the latter. Now let S be some true proposition that has a low probability on theism, but is not at all surprising on theism. I should think that the proposition that states the exact number of dogs would do: in "most" possible worlds in which God exists, the number of dogs is not the actual number. It is clear that the following facts do not comprise a *prima facie* case for preferring 'S and God does not exist' to 'God exists': S; the probability of S on 'S and God does not exist' is much higher than the probability of S on 'God exists'; 'S and God does not exist' and 'God exists' are inconsistent.

These considerations show that the use of the language of high and low probabilities in formulating the evidential argument from evil is a source of possible confusion. Since, however, my criticisms of the argument have nothing to do with this point, I shall continue to employ this language. But I shall employ it only as a stylistic device: anything I say in this language could easily be restated in terms of epistemic surprise.

8. I can have *some* epistemically warranted expectations about how what I see displayed on the sheet of paper will look: it must in some sense "look like writing"—it can't be a detailed drawing of a cat or a series of a thousand identical marks. Similarly, I can have *some* epistemically warranted expectations about how suffering will be distributed if there is a God. I would suppose, for example, that it is highly improbable on theism that there be sentient creatures and that all of them be in excruciating pain at every moment of their existence.

9. Well, one might somehow know the probability of S on theism as a function of the probability of S on HI; one might know that the former probability was one-tenth the latter, and yet have no idea what either probability was. But that is not the present case. The evidentialist's argument essentially involves two independent probability-judgments: that the probability of S on HI is at least not too low, and that the probability of S on theism is very low.

10. Indeed, in *one* sense of probability, the probability of a defense may be very low on theism. We have said that a defense may not be *surprising* on theism, but, as we saw in note 7, there is a perfectly good sense of probability in which a proposition that is not at all surprising on theism may nevertheless be very improbable on theism. If the defender of theism had at his disposal a very large number of defenses, all of them inconsistent with the others, and none of them epistemically preferable to any of the others, it is hard to see why he should not conclude that

(relative to his epistemic situation) the probability of any given one of them was very low on theism.

11. "The Magnitude, Duration, and Distribution of Evil: A Theodicy," *Philosophical Topics*, Vol. 16, no. 2 (1988), pp. 161-87. See especially pp. 167-8. Failure to appreciate this consideration is a weak point in many versions of the evidential argument from evil. Consider, for example, William L. Rowe's much-discussed article, "The Problem of Evil and Some Varieties of Atheism" (*American Philosophical Quarterly* 16 (1979) pp. 335-41). In this article, Rowe employs the following premise:

> An omniscient, wholly good being would prevent the occurrence of any intense suffering it could, unless it could not do so without losing some greater good or permitting some evil equally bad or worse.

If there are alternative, morally equivalent amounts of (intense) suffering, then this premise is false. To make this point more concrete, let us consider Rowe's famous case of a fawn that dies in prolonged agony of burns that it suffers in a forest fire caused by lightning. God, I concede, could have miraculously prevented the fire, or miraculously saved the fawn, or miraculously caused its agony to be cut short by death. And, I will concede for the sake of argument, if He had done so, this would have thwarted no significant good and permitted no significant evil. But what of the hundreds of millions (at least) of similar incidents that have, no doubt, occurred during the long history of life? Well, I concede, He could have prevented any one of them, or any two of them, or any three of them...without thwarting any significant good or permitting any significant evil. But could he have prevented all of them? No—not without causing the world to be massively irregular. And, of course, there is no sharp cut-off point between a world that is massively irregular and a world that is not—just as there is no sharp cut-off point between a penalty that is an effective deterrent for armed assault and a penalty that is not. There is, therefore, no *minimum* number of cases of intense suffering that God could allow without forfeiting the good of a world that is not massively irregular—just as there is no shortest sentence that a legislature can establish as the penalty for armed assault without forfeiting the good of effective deterrence.

12. See my essay "The Place of Chance in a World Sustained by God" in Thomas V. Morris, ed., *Divine and Human Action: Essays in the Metaphysics of Theism* (Ithaca, N.Y.: Cornell University Press, 1988), pp. 211-35.

13. "Ontological Arguments," *Noûs* 11 (1977) pp. 375-95; Review of *The Coherence of Theism* by Richard Swinburne, *The Philosophical Review* LXXXVII (1979), pp. 668-72. See also George Seddon, "Logical Possibility," *Mind* LXXXI (1972), pp. 481-94.

14. These laws, being quantum-mechanical, are indeterministic. God could not, therefore, have "fine-tuned" the initial state of a universe like ours so as to render an eventual universal hedonic utopia causally inevitable. It would seem to be almost certain that, owing to quantum-mechanical

indeterminacy, a universe that was a duplicate of ours when ours was, say, $10^{-45}$ seconds old could have evolved into a very different universe from our present universe. (There is also the point to be considered that there probably *was* no initial state of the universe.) Would it be possible for an omniscient and omnipotent being to create a universe that evolved deterministically out of a carefully selected initial state into an hedonic utopia? This question raises many further questions, questions that mostly cannot be answered. Nevertheless, the following facts would seem to be relevant to an attempt to answer it: life depends on chemistry, and chemistry depends on atoms, and atoms depend on quantum mechanics (classically speaking, an atom cannot exist: the electrons of a "classical" atom would spiral inward, shedding their potential energy in the form of electromagnetic radiation, till they collided with the nucleus), and quantum mechanics is essentially indeterministic.

15. This fact has been widely remarked on. See, e.g., John Leslie, "Modern Cosmology and the Creation of Life" in Ernan McMullin, ed., *Evolution and Creation* (South Bend, Indiana: the University of Notre Dame Press, 1985), pp. 91-120.
16. This is not properly speaking a quotation; it is, rather, a selection of verses from Chapter 38 of the Book of Job. It comprises verses 3, 4, 21, 31, and 33.
17. See the article and review cited in note 13.
18. *Cf. De Cælo* IV, especially $309^{a}18$-$310^{a}13$.
19. This latter fact is very important in the debate about extra-terrestrial intelligence. If someone in our galaxy aimed a powerful signal at, say, the Andromeda galaxy, then, two million years later, anyone in the Andromeda galaxy who aimed a sensitive receiver precisely at our galaxy would detect that signal. When we aim a sensitive receiver precisely at the Andromeda galaxy, however, we detect no signal. Therefore, no one on any planet circling any of the hundred billion or more stars in the Andromeda galaxy was aiming a signal at the Milky Way galaxy two million years ago. (This argument actually depends on the false assumption that all of the stars in the Andromeda galaxy are equally distant from us, but the essential point of the argument is sound.)
20. For an excellent popular article on the search for extra-terrestrial intelligence, see Gregg Easterbrook, "Are We Alone?", *The Atlantic*, August 1988, pp.25-38.
21. See for example, Ernst Mayr, "The Probability of Extraterrestrial Intelligent Life," in Michael Ruse, ed., *Philosophy of Biology* (New York: Macmillan, 1989), pp. 279-85.
22. Are there other defenses—other defenses that cover the same ground as the defense I have presented in Section II? I should like to think so, although I have not had any very interesting ideas about how additional defenses might be constructed. I should welcome suggestions.
23. This paper was read at Brandeis University. The author wishes to thank the members of the Brandeis Philosophy Department, and especially Eli Hirsch, for their helpful comments and criticisms.

Philosophical Perspectives, 5, Philosophy of Religion, 1991

# ON THE SIMPLICITY OF THE SOUL

Roderick M. Chisholm
Brown University

"Gregory of Nyssa tells us Plato asserted that the intellectual substance which is called the soul is united to the body by a kind of spiritual contact; and this is understood in the sense in which a thing that moves or acts touches the thing that is moved or is passive, And hence Plato used to say, as the aforesaid Gregory relates, that man is not something that is composed of soul and body, but is a soul using a body, so that he is understood to be in a body in somewhat the same way as a sailor is in a ship." St. Thomas Aquinas.[1]

## The Soul as Incorporeal

I will defend the thesis according to which there is something that is metaphysically unique about persons: we have a nature wholly unlike anything that is known to be true of things that are known to be compound physical things. I will attempt to show how this thesis coheres with the traditional doctrine of "the simplicity of the soul." And I will argue that the doctrine of the simplicity of the soul is, in William James' terms, very much of a live option.

I am using the word "soul" in the way in which St. Augustine, Descartes, Bolzano and many others have used it: to mean the same thing as "person." In this use of the word, you and I and everyone else can be said to be souls. (This use of the term "soul" is one of two traditional philosophical uses. The other is the Aristotelian use, in which the term "soul" designates a *power*, or *principle*, by means of which certain substances think and perceive.)

According to the thesis of "the simplicity of the soul," we are substances but not compounds of substances; we are, therefore, monads. We are not like pieces of furniture, for such things are composed of other substances—as this chair is composed of back, seat and legs. Why, then, say that you and I are simple substances?

Using the first person, I will begin with the familiar question: "What is the relation between *me* and my body?" There are three possibilities. The first is that I am identical with my body. The second is that I am identical with a proper part of my body. And the third is that I am not identical with *any* body. (Surely, whatever else I may be, I am not identical with any bodily thing having parts that are not shared by *this* body.) Isn't the hypothesis that I am identical with some proper part of this body more plausible than the hypothesis that I am identical with the whole of this gross body? This hand, say, is not an essential part of me. I could have lost it, after all, just as I have lost other parts, without thereby ceasing to be.

What is an *incorporeal* substance? It is a substance that is *not* a bodily substance. What, then, is a *bodily* substance? St. Augustine raises this question in *Of the Soul and its Origin* and he tells us that bodily substances are *compound* substances:

> If that is not "body" which does not consist of limbs of flesh, then the earth cannot be a body, nor the sky, nor a stone, nor water, nor the stars, nor anything of the kind. If, however, a "body" is whatever consists of parts, whether greater or less, which occupy greater or smaller local spaces, then all the things which I have just mentioned are bodies.[2]

The thesis that we are, in this sense, *incorporeal* things is not the same as the thesis that we are things *composed of incorporeal stuff*. If we are composed of incorporeal stuff, then, of course, we are incorporeal. But we can be incorporeal without being composed of any stuff at all, as would be the case if we were simple substances. A simple substance, therefore, does not require a kind of stuff that is foreign to the world of physics. Indeed, there is very good reason to believe that every extended physical body contains inner and outer boundaries and therefore has constituents that are unextended.

## A Cartesian Approach

I propose that we treat these difficult questions from a Cartesian point of view.

This means, first, that we begin by considering the nature of our *mental* properties. We should begin here for the very good reason that our mental properties provide us with the most assured information that we have about *any* individual thing or substance. On the basis of what we know about our own thinking, we may derive certain conclusions about the nature of ourselves.

A Cartesian approach is also rationalistic. We presuppose that we are *rational* beings: we are able to "conceive things that are purely intelligible," such *entia rationis* as numbers and properties or attributes.[3] In conceiving these things, we are able to tell them apart and to see just what it is that they logically require in order to be exemplified. We can see, for example, that the property of *being a body*, if it is to be exemplified, logically requires an individual thing that has other individual things as proper parts.

We will consider the nature of mental properties, then, and ask ourselves what kind of entity *could* have such properties.

### The Qualitative Nature of Mental Properties

Our mental life, as many philosophers have said, has the property of being *qualitative*. To explicate what the relevant sense of "qualitative" is, I will list certain formal or structural marks of the property of thinking. These marks, in combination, will define a type of property which, so far as anyone knows, is exemplified only by things that are capable of thinking.

(1) If thinking is going on, then there is a *substance*, or *individual thing*, that is doing the thinking. Consider any familiar mental property—for example, judging, wondering, wishing, hoping, enjoying oneself, being sad, being depressed, having a sensation, or dreaming. In grasping the nature of such properties, we can see that they are properties that can be exemplified only by substances, or individual things. Judging, wondering, wishing, hoping cannot possibly be properties of *states* of things, or of *processes*. And they cannot be properties of *abstract objects* such as properties, numbers, and relations. *You* can hope for rain, but no state or process or number or property or relation can hope for rain.

In other words, the fact that a certain mental property is exemplified—the fact, say, that the property of hoping for rain is exemplified—logically implies that there is a *substance* that has that property. This is a fact about the property itself: the property of hoping for rain is necessarily such that the only things that can have it are substances. And similarly for the other mental properties.

These facts, of course, should be considered together with the *unity of consciousness*. If I can know that I see people who are running in time with the music that I hear, then the substance that knows this fact is identical with the substance that sees the people who are running and is identical with the substance that hears the music that is being played.[4]

What more does a mental property require in order to be exemplified? The answer is: very little—indeed astonishingly little. This brings us to a second feature of thinking, one that points in the direction of the simplicity of the soul.

(2) So far as *logical* requirements are concerned, mental properties are such that they may be exemplified by simple substances. Those of our activities that are not mental do not have this feature. The property of rowing a boat, for example, is not like that. The property of rowing a boat logically requires the existence of ever so many substances *in addition to* the person who is rowing the boat. But the property of *thinking about rowing a boat* doesn't logically require a single substance other than the person who is thinking. And this means that it doesn't *logically* require that the person who is thinking have any proper parts. You could think about rowing a boat even if you were a monad.

What I have just said is true of the relatively simple thought that you have when you think about rowing a boat. But the thought may be as complex as you like and yet not need a more complex substance in order to be exemplified. Let the content of the thought be one that would be normally expressed by a statement that is logically complex: a conditional, say, having a disjunction as antecedent and a conjunction as consequent. This thought, too, does not logically require any complexity on the part of the substance that thinks it. You could think in such a way even if you were only a simple substance.

But there are possible misunderstandings.

Presumably nothing can think unless it has a brain. The property of thinking, therefore, may causally require the existence of a brain. But this fact is quite consistent with what has just been said. When we say that thinking causally requires a brain, we mean that it is *causally* necessary—or *physically* necessary—that whatever thinks has a brain. But when we say that the property of thinking does not logically require that the things that have it have proper parts, we are saying only that it is *logically possible* that the thinker is an unextended thing. Clearly no *logical* contradiction is involved in saying that the thinker is unextended.

There is an elementary point here that is sometimes missed. I need a brain in order to think just as I need eyes in order to see and ears in order to hear. But I see *with*, or *by means of*, my eyes and I hear *with*, or *by means of* my ears. Those physical organs do not do my seeing and hearing *for* me. As Bishop Butler said, I see with my eyes in the same sense in which I see with my glasses.[5] And similarly in the case of my brain. *I* may want to take a walk tomorrow and *I* may wonder whether you are interested in this particular point. But *my brain* doesn't want to take a walk tomorrow. And *it* does not wonder whether you are interested in anything that I am asserting; unlike me it will not be in the least disappointed if you are not.

Mental properties, in order to be had, need no substances other than a single simple substance. And yet such properties are *open* to any number of substances. For any number you like, the mental properties that we have cited may be exemplified by just *that* number of things. Let us say that such properties are *"open"*:

D1 P is open =Df P is possibly such that, for any number $n$, there are $n$ substances that have P and $n$ substances that do not have P.

(3) Mental properties are *repeatable* in the following sense:

D2 P is repeatable =Df P is possibly such that there is something that does not have it but did have it and will have it.

I have recommended that we take a Cartesian approach to these questions. But so far as repeatability is concerned, I would say that Descartes went wrong. He had held, somewhat implausibly, that the property of *thinking*—the property of *being conscious*—is *not* repeatable. Once you lose it, according to him, you cease to be. This point is quite essential to what is called Cartesian philosophy, but it is not essential to what I have called a "Cartesian approach" to the mental.

May we say that the property of *being able to think* is repeatable? Not if we use "x is able to think" to mean that x is such that *no logical contradiction* is involved in saying that it thinks. But if one takes "x is able to think," as it is intended here, to mean that x has the *power* or *potentiality* of thinking, then one may say that the property it expresses is repeatable; for a person may lose such a power or potency and then take it on again.

I now list two structural features of some of the properties of *compound* substances—two features that are *not* shared by any mental property. These have to do with parts of substances—where the term "part" is so understood that we may say that a *part* of a substance is itself a substance.

(4) One feature that is known to characterize certain properties of compound things and that is also known *not* to hold of any mental property is that of being compositive.[6] Consider such properties as being magnetized, being warm, being heavy. If a physical thing is composed of two parts, each of which is magnetized or warm or heavy, then that physical thing itself is magnetized or warm or heavy. A *compositive* property is a property of this nature:

D3 P is compositive = Df P is necessarily such that whatever is composed of things that have P is itself a thing that has P.

Being extended and being green are also properties that are compositive.

Of course, not *all* properties of compounds are compositive. If a body is composed of two parts each of which weighs exactly 10 pounds, then it would be a mistake to suppose that that body itself weighs exactly 10 pounds. But although some physical properties are compositive and some are not, *no* mental property is compositive.

From the fact that an aggregate is composed of two persons each of whom is thinking, it does not follow that the aggregate is thinking. You could want the weather to be colder and I could want it to be warmer; but that heap or aggregate which is the pair of us (that thing that weighs 300 pounds if you and I each weigh 150 pounds) does not want anything at all.

(5) A closely related feature of mental properties is that of being what we may call "*divisive*":

D4 P is divisive = Df P is necessarily such that any compound thing that has it has a proper part that has it.

Any body that is extended also has a proper part that is extended. But the fact that I am hoping for rain does not imply that I have a proper part that is hoping for rain. That is to say, the fact that I am a substance that hopes for rain does not imply that there is *another* substance that is a proper part of me and that *that* substance *also* hopes for rain.

We now describe the final positive feature of mental properties.

(6) Mental properties are among those properties that have traditionally been called *internal*, or *nonrelational*. If an individual has properties that consist in *relating* that individual to *other* individuals, then that individual also has internal properties, properties that do *not* consist in relating it to other individuals.

Roughly speaking, we may say that my internal properties are those of my properties that would not tell you anything about any substance other than myself. If you know that I have the property of being married, then you are in a position to know that there is a person who has a property that I don't have—namely, that of having married me. But if I tell you that I feel well or that I do not feel well, then what I tell you does not logically imply anything about anyone else but me. We may put this point a little more precisely by saying that an *internal* property of a substance tells you something about the substance itself but doesn't tell you anything about the open and repeatable properties of any other substance.

> D5 P is an internal property of substances =Df (1) P is necessarily such that whatever has it is a substance; and (2) either P is necessary to whatever has it or P is necessarily such that whatever has it has every open and repeatable property that P implies.

The sense of "imply" intended in this definition may be defined this way:

> Property P implies Q =Df P is necessarily such that, if it is exemplified, then Q either was, is or will be exemplified.

(In saying that mental properties are internal to substances, we are taking account of the first of the six features of the mental that we singled out—namely, that mental properties are restricted to substances.)

With this concept of internality, we can assure ourselves that such properties as that of *being in the vicinity of a thinker* will not be counted as qualitative. Such properties, although they are exemplified by every thinker, are also exemplified by countless things that are not thinkers.

These five features, when taken together, yield the philosophical concept of being *qualitative*. They provide us with a sense of "qualitative property" which is such that, so far as we know, only substances that are capable of thinking may be said to have qualitative properties. But we must proceed with care in formulating just what the relevant sense of "qualitative" is. It will not be enough, for example, to say that a qualitative property is a property that has the features just singled out. The property of being *either thinking or moving* fulfills all five conditions, but this property, of course, is not restricted to things that are capable of thinking.

There *is* good reason to say that *thinking or moving*, unlike certain other properties, may be called a "disjunctive property." And disjunctive properties may be distinguished from conjunctive properties.[7] Thus we could say:

D is a property-disjunction of G and H =Df D is necessarily such that it is exemplified if and only if either G or H is exemplified; and G and H are such that neither implies the other and neither implies the negation of the other.
C is a property-conjunction of G and H =Df C implies G; C implies H; everything implied by C implies something that either G or H implies; and G and H are such that neither implies the other and neither implies the negation of the other.

Our definition of "qualitative property" should now go this way:

D6 P is qualitative =Df Consider the property Q of being both open and repeatable, being neither compositive nor divisive, and being an internal property of individuals: Q is exemplified by P and by either all or none of the disjuncts of any disjunctive property that is equivalent to P and by each conjunct of any conjunctive property equivalent to P.

The final qualification, pertaining to conjunctive properties, makes it clear that such conjunctive properties as *walking and (not-walking or thinking)* are not qualitative.

Anything that has a qualitative property, then, is a substance that is capable of thinking.

## Five Philosophical Arguments

Some philosophers have spoken about *proving* the simplicity of the soul. But, as one might reasonably expect, the attempts at such proofs usually presuppose something that is at least problematic. There are, however, philosophical arguments that may be said to *bear upon* the simplicity of the soul. I will consider five such arguments.

(A) The first is the argument that Kant presents in the second of his supposed "paralogisms of transcendental psychology." He formulates the argument this way:

> That, the action of which can never be regarded as the concurrence of several things, is *simple*. Now the soul, or the thinking 'I', is such a thing. Therefore, etc.[8]

Kant states that the argument "is no mere sophistical play...but an inference that appears to withstand even the closest scrutiny" (A351). Then he goes on to say:

> Suppose a compound thing were to think. Then every part of that compound would have a part of that thought. The thought that the compound would then have would be composed of the thoughts of the parts of that compound. But this would be contradictory. For thoughts that are distributed among different thinkers can never constitute a single thought. From the fact that the different words of a piece of poetry are thought of by different thinkers it does not follow that the aggregate of those thinkers has thought of the piece of poetry. It is, therefore, impossible for an aggregate to think.

Given the conclusion, it is a simple matter to complete the argument: I think; therefore I am not a compound.

But consider what is expressed by the second sentence: "Every part of that compound would have a part of that thought." What is the justification for saying that, if a compound thing has a certain thought, then one part of the compound has "a part" of that thought and another part of the compound has "another part" of the thought? One must *find* a sense for the use of "part" in the expression "a part of a thought," a sense that enables us to apply the expression to such a thought, say, as that of noting that a certain face is familiar. I would say that, having so such sense, we have no reason to accept the statement in question.

(B) The second argument is suggested in Maimonides' *Guide to the Perplexed*.[9] In discussing the incorporeality of God, Maimonides formulates—and rejects—an argument which could readily be re-stated as an argument for the simplicity of the soul. It is this:

> If God were corporeal, His true essence would necessarily either exist entirely in every part of the body, that is to say, in each of its atoms, or would be confined to one of the atoms. In the latter alternative the other atoms would be superfluous, and the existence of the corporeal being [with the exception of the one atom] would be of no purpose. If, on the other hand, each atom fully represented the Divine Being, the whole body would not be *one* deity, but a complex of deities, and this would be contrary to the doctrine adopted by the *kalâm* that God is one.

Maimonides rejects this argument on the ground that it has a false presupposition—namely, that God is composed of atoms. But in appli-cation to souls other the deity, it has at least this plausibility:

Consider the hypothesis, with respect to the soul and to some ex-tended proper part P of the gross physical body, that the soul is identical with P. However small P may be, there will be no sufficient reason for supposing that P itself, rather than some proper part of P, is identical with the soul. And so, to the question, "How small could I be?", the answer would seem, "Smaller than any dimension that one can specify."

(C) Bolzano's discussion, in the *Athanasia*, suggests a further possibility.[10]

(1) All compounds are necessarily such that they have parts.
(2) No bearers of psychological properties are necessarily such that they have parts.

Therefore

(3) No bearers of psychological properties are compounds.

The first premise seems to me to be beyond question. And the argument is formally valid. So what about the second premise?

A rational analysis of properties shows us that mental properties do not require that their bearers be compound things. But from the fact that psychological properties are possibly such that their bearers have no proper parts, it does not follow that the bearers of psycho-logical properties are possibly such that *they* have no proper parts.

(D) The doctrine of mereological essentialism may seem to provide another argument for the simplicity of the soul, but the argument, I believe, is subject to the same difficulties that we have just found in Bolzano's argument.

According to the principle of mereological essentialism, if a thing P is a part of a whole W, then W is necessarily such that P is a part of W. From this principle it follows that, if W is possibly such that it has no parts, then W has no parts and is, therefore, simple.[11] If this consequence is combined with the assumption that I am possibly such that I am a simple substance, then it yields the conclusion that I am a simple substance. But unfortunately this Cartesian conclusion does not enable us to deduce that *I* am possibly such that I am a simple substance.

(E) The final argument, which is somewhat more modest, has three premises. The first is an empirical proposition, stating certain things about our psychological properties. The second and third premises are Cartesian: they tell us what rational beings can know about the nature of the psychological properties that they have.

I will state the argument using the first person plural.

(1) We have qualitative properties.

(2) Every qualitative property that we are acquainted with is known to be possibly such that it is exemplified by simple substances.

(3) No qualitative property is known to be such that it may be exemplified by compound substances.

Hence

(4) Some of our properties are known to be such that simple substances can have them and are not known to be such that compound substances can have them.

Therefore

(5) We have a nature which is wholly unlike the nature that anything known to be a compound physical thing is known to have.

The conclusion of this argument leaves us with two possibilities: either (a) the soul is an unextended substance or (b) souls have a type of property that extended physical substances are not known to have. The latter option is defended by those who have argued that the fact of thinking indicates the presence of a peculiar type of "emergent property" in nature.[12]

## Souls and Complete Human Beings

I have said that we *are* souls and that souls are simple substances. But it is also said, even by those who have held that the soul is simple, that *persons* are compound things having souls as parts.[13] Can we have it both ways? Descartes, although he held that the soul is an unextended substance, felt compelled to say that a "complete man" is a compound consisting of the soul and the body.[14]

If the soul is simple and the person is a compound of soul and body, which would I be—the simple substance which is the soul or the compound substance which has the soul as one of its parts?

If we say (1) that I am a thinking being and (2) that thinking things and souls are the same, then we should also say (3) that I *am* a soul; and therefore (if we take "have" in its ordinary sense) we should say (4) that I do not *have* a soul. And this is what is suggested in the reference to Gregory of Nyssa, with which we began.

What, then, is the distinction between a boundary that has no dimensions and a monad? A boundary is an entity that depends for its existence upon being a boundary of *another* entity. It is necessarily such that there is a three-dimensional thing of which it *is* a boundary.[15] But a monad is a *simple substance*. This means, as Descartes had noted, that it is not ontologically dependent upon any other contingent thing. A substance is an entity which is possibly such that there is no other entity *in* which it exists.[16]

### Notes

1.  The citation is from pages 35-6 of the translation by M. C. Fitzpatrick and J. C. Wellmuth, of *On Spiritual Creatures*; (Milwaukee: Marquette University Press, 1949). The translators note that another version of the text reads: Plato "does not mean that man is made up of body and soul, but that he is a soul using a body and, as it were, clothed with a body" (P. 35n.).
2.  St. Augustine, *Of the Soul and its Origin*, Book IV, Ch. 17; in Marcus Dobs, ed., *The Anti-Pelagian Writings of St. Augustine*, Vol. II (Edinburgh: T. & T. Clark, 1874), p. 315.
3.  See René Descartes, *The Principles of Philosophy*, Part I, Section 32; in E.S.Haldane and G.R.T. Ross, *Philosophical Works of Descartes*, Vol. I, p. 232.
4.  Compare Chapter IV ("On the Unity of Consciousness"), in Franz Brentano, *Psychology from an Empirical Standpoint* (London: Routledge & Kegan Paul, 1973); this work first appeared in 1874.

5. Joseph Butler, *The Analogy of Religion*, Part I, Chapter 1 ("Of a Future Life"); in *The Whole Works of Joseph Butler, LL.D.* (London: Thomas Tegg, 1839), p. 7. Compare Bernard Bolzano, *Athanasia: oder Gründe für die Unsterblichkeit der Seele* (Sulzbach: J. G. v. Seidleschen Buchhandlung, 1838), p. 60. Bolzano's discussion of these questions (esp. pp. 21-68) is the best that is known to me.

6. The term "compositive" is suggested by the following sense of "being composed of." A compound object A may be said to be *composed of* two compound objects B and C, provided only that (i) B and C are parts of A, (ii) B and C have no parts in common and (iii) every part of A has a part in common either with B or with C. This definition was proposed, in somewhat different terms, by A. N. Whitehead, *The Organisation of Thought* (London: Williams and Norgate, 1917), pp. 159-60.

7. I have suggested a more rigid definition of "disjunctive property" in *On Metaphysics* (Minneapolis: The University of Minnesota Press, 1989), p. 146; but that definition, since it makes use of a mentalistic concept, cannot be used in the present context.

8. *Critique of Pure Reason*, A351. From the translation by Norman Kemp Smith in *Immanuel Kant's Critique of Pure Reason* (London: Macmillan and Company, 1933), p. 335.

9. Moses Maimonides, *The Guide to the Perplexed* (London: Routledge & Kegan Paul, Ltd., 1956), p. 142.

10. I have discussed Bolzano's reasoning in detail in "Bolzano on the Simplicity of the Soul," in *Traditionen und Perspektiven der analytischen Philosophie*, edited by W. Gombocz, H, Rutte, and W. Sauer, Vienna: Hölder-Pichler-Tempsky, 1989), pp. 79-88.

11. This consequence was pointed out by Gary Rosenkrantz, in "Reference, Intentionality, and Nonexistent Entities," in *Philosophical Studies*, Vol. 58 (1990), pp. 165-171, and discussed by me in "Monads, Nonexemplified Individuals, and Possible Worlds," in the same issue, pp. 173-5.

12. Compare James Van Cleve, "Mind-Dust or Magic? Panpsychism versus Emergence," *Philosophical Perspectives*, Vol. IV (1990), pp. 215-226. A useful discussion and bibliography of the doctrine of emergence may be found in Arthur Pap, *An Introduction to the Philosophy of Science* (Glencoe: The Free Press, 1962), pp. 364-72. Compare Leopold Stubenberg, "Chisholm, Fechner und das Geist-Körper Problem," *Grazer Philosophische Studien*, Vol. 28 (1986), pp. 187-210.

13. Two recent defenses of this approach may be found in: Richard Swinburne, *The Evolution of the Soul* (Oxford: The Clarendon Press, 1986), p. 145ff. and Josef Seifert, *Das Leib-Seele-Problem und die gegenwärtige philosophische Diskussion*, Second Edition, (Darmstadt: Wissenschaftliche Buchgesellschaft, 1989), pp. 35-72, 131-44.

14. See, for example, his reply to Gassendi's objections to the second *Meditation*; in E.S.Haldane and G.R.T.Ross, *Philosophical Works of Descartes*, Vol. II, p. 207-8. Descartes' expression was "*homme tout entier.*" St. Augustine noted that we have here a usage in which "a part is to be taken for the whole. For both the soul and the flesh, the component parts of man, can be used to signify the whole man; and so the

animal man and the carnal man are not two different things, but one and the same thing, viz., man living according to man." See *The City of God*, Book IV, Ch. 4; in Whitney J. Oates, ed., *Basic Writings of St. Augustine* (New York: Random House, 1948), Vol. II, p. 244.
15. I have discussed these points in detail in *On Metaphysics*, pp. 63-89, 162-8.
16. I am indebted to Earl Conee, Ernest Sosa and Barry Smith for criticisms of earlier versions of the discussion of mental properties.

**References**

Aquinas, St. Thomas, *On Spiritual Creatures*, ed. M. C. Fitzpatrick and J. C. Wellmuth (Milwaukee: Marquette University Press, 1949).

Augustine, St., *The Anti-Pelagian Writings of St. Augustine*, ed Marcus Dobs (Edinburgh: T. & T. Clark, 1874); and Whitney J. Oates, ed., *Basic Writings of St. Augustine* (New York: Random House, 1948).

Bolzano, Bernard, *Athanasia: oder Gründe für die Unsterblichkeit der Seele* (Sulzbach: J. G. v. Seidleschen Buchhandlung, 1838).

Brentano, Franz, *Psychology from an Empirical Standpoint* (London: Routledge & Kegan Paul, 1973).

Butler, Joseph, *The Whole Works of Joseph Butler, LL.D.* (London: Thomas Tegg, 1839).

Chisholm, Roderick M., "Bolzano on the Simplicity of the Soul," in *Traditionen und Perspektiven der analytischen Philosophie*, edited by W. Gombocz, H. Rutte, and W. Sauer, Vienna: Holder-Pichler-Tempsky, 1989), pp. 79-88.

Chisholm, Roderick M., *On Metaphysics* (Minneapolis: The University of Minnesota Press, 1989).

Chisholm, Roderick M., "Monads, Nonexemplified Individuals, and Possible Worlds," *Philosophical Studies*, Vol. 58 (1990), pp. 173-5.

Descartes, René, *The Philosophical Works of Descartes*, translated by E. S. Haldane and G. R. T. Ross, in two volumes (Cambridge: The University Press, 1931).

Kant, Immanuel, *Immanuel Kant's Critique of Pure Reason* (London: Macmillan and Company, 1933).

Maimonides, Moses, *The Guide to the Perplexed* (London: Routledge & Kegan Paul, Ltd., 1956).

Pap, Arthur *An Introduction to the Philosophy of Science* (Glencoe: The Free Press, 1962).

Rosenkrantz, Gary, "Reference, Intentionality, and Nonexistent Entities," in *Philosophical Studies*, Vol. 58 (1990), pp. 165-171.

Seifert, Josef, *Das Leib-Seele-Problem und die gegenwärtige philosophische Diskussion*, Second Edition, (Darmstadt: Wissenschaftliche Buchgesellschaft, 1989).

Stubenberg, Leopold, "Chisholm, Fechner und das Geist-Körper Problem," *Grazer Philosophische Studien*, Vol. 28 (1986), pp. 187-210.

Swinburne, Richard, *The Evolution of the Soul* (Oxford: The Clarendon Press, 1986).

Van Cleve, James, "Mind-Dust or Magic? Panpsychism versus Emergence," *Philosophical Perspectives*, Vol. IV (1990), pp. 215-226.

Whitehead, A. N., *The Organisation of Thought* (London: Williams and Norgate, 1917), pp. 159-60.

Philosophical Perspectives, 5, Philosophy of Religion, 1991

# ARE SOULS UNINTELLIGIBLE?

Joshua Hoffman
Gary Rosenkrantz
University of North Carolina at Greensboro

In asserting the existence of God, traditional Western theism asserts the existence of a purely spiritual being. According to this form of theism, God is a disembodied spirit, or soul, with the power to effect material things. In addition, many theists are committed to the existence of other souls that have this power, e.g., angels, devils, or human souls.

A variety of objections have been raised to the intelligibility of both the notion of a soul and the notion of a soul effecting a material thing. Since traditional Western theism presupposes the intelligibility of these notions, the soundness of any of these objections entails the unintelligibility of this form of theism. Our aim is to defend the intelligibility of the concepts of a soul and of dualistic interactionism against these objections.

## I.

What is a purely spiritual being or soul? We propose the following initial characterization.

(DI) $x$ is a soul $=$ df. (i) $x$ is a substance, and (ii) $x$ is unlocated, and (iii) $x$ is capable of consciousness.

Let us examine the rationale behind each of the three conditions in (DI). In the first condition of (DI), we employ the concept of an individual substance as ordinarily understood, paradigm cases of which seem to be particular material objects and persons. In one of its ordinary senses, the term 'thing' means individual substance. For example, the term 'thing' is being used in this sense in the following sentences:

> 'Jealousy is not a thing; it is a quality of a thing.'
> 'Edges and gaps are not things; they are limits and absences of them, respectively.'
> 'A spider's growing bigger is not a thing; it is a change in one.'[1]

We assume (plausibly, we think) that a thing in this ordinary sense, i.e., an individual substance, is not reducible to or identifiable with an entity of another kind or ontological category, e.g., a set or collection of either properties, ideas, sense-data, or events.[2] (This does not rule out the possibility that a substance can be *eliminated* in favor of an entity of another kind or ontological category.[3]) Elsewhere, we have argued that this intuitive notion of thinghood, i.e., the ontological category of substance, can be perspicuously analyzed in terms of an independence criterion.[4]

Since a soul is a person or a creature, and since a person or a creature is a substance, a soul is a substance. Thus, being a substance is a logically necessary condition of being a soul, and the inclusion of (i) in (DI) is warranted.

Clauses (i) and (ii) of (DI), which together say that a soul is an unlocated substance, entail that a soul is *unextended*. Being unextended and being unlocated are not equivalent. For example, Boscovichian point-particles are unextended but located; and places (other than points) are extended but unlocated. Finally, points are neither extended nor located. In other words, to be located is to occupy or be in a place. Although a place is unlocated, a place is not a substance.

It is not possible for a spiritual substance to be spatially extended, and it is a necessary truth that whatever is spatially extended is physical. Thus, a "ghost" that literally possesses spatial extension does not count as a soul. It would be either an exotic type of physical entity, or else a subtle type of physical stuff. (An extended but massless particle in physics is an example of an "exotic" physical entity, whereas a gas or plasma is a case of a "subtle" type of physical stuff.) It is arguable that there could be a substance that is conscious and unextended, but occupies a point of space. It can be further argued that such an entity is a soul or spirit. However, it is not obvious that either of these are genuine possibilities. But, even if there could be an unextended spiritual substance occupying a point of space, it would not be a *purely* spiritual being. That is, it would not be *wholly* outside of the physical world, inasmuch as it would occupy a point of space. When traditional Western theism affirms the existence of God, angels, etc., it is affirming the existence of purely spiritual beings, and this is what we mean by the term 'soul' or 'spirit.' For the foregoing reasons, we regard unlocatedness as a logically necessary condition of being a soul, as specified in clause (ii) of (DI).

Finally, in clause (iii) of (DI), we require that a soul be capable of consciousness. Descartes seems to hold that a soul is conscious at every moment that it exists. However, perhaps there could be a soul that is unconscious for a time. Clause (iii) of (DI) is compatible with this possibility. On the other hand, this clause is also logically consistent with what appears to be Descartes's overall position on souls. For Descartes maintains that any soul would be essentially conscious.[5] Thus, if Descartes is right, then there being a soul that is *capable* of consciousness entails that this soul *is* conscious. And of course, if a soul is conscious, then it must be capable of consciousness. Therefore, on Cartesian assumptions, consciousness and the capacity for consciousness are equivalent. It follows that clause (iii) of (DI) is logically compatible with Descartes's view that a soul is conscious at every moment of its existence.

But could there be a soul that is unconscious, yet capable of consciousness? Apparently, some capacities or dispositions of a physical thing are *basic*, that is, are not explained by any occurrent structural properties of that thing together with non-fundamental laws of nature. Rather, such capacities are grounded in some very general features of that thing, features involved in being the sort of thing that it is, together with some fundamental law or laws. For example, it seems that a material object has a basic capacity to move; it does not have this capacity in virtue of any of its structural characteristics, e.g., its shape, size, order and arrangement of parts, and so forth. Rather, it seems to be capable of motion simply in virtue of its being a spatial substance. Similarly, perhaps a soul has a basic capacity for consciousness simply in virtue of its being a *non*-spatial substance. On (DI), a soul has neither a structural nor any other plausible basis for its capacity for consciousness.

However, if there could be an unconscious soul that is capable of consciousness, then there seems to be an interesting difference between material and spiritual substances. This can be brought out in terms of the following comparison. It seems clear that a material object, $m$, that is currently stationary has a number of positive, occurrent, intrinsic qualities that are wholly in the present,[6] and these qualities of it are neither universal essential properties nor equivalent to ontic categories. For example, $m$ has a certain shape and size. In contrast, it is arguable that a currently unconscious soul would lack any such occurrent qualities. We agree with this point, unless the questionable Leibnizean view that a soul always has "unconscious mental states" were acceptable.

This having been said, the following somewhat plausible principle seems to create a challenge to the coherence of the notion of an unconscious soul.

> (P1)  A substance must have some positive, occurrent, intrinsic, wholly present quality that is neither a universal essential property nor equivalent to an ontic category.

We are not sure of the truth or falsity of (P1). (P1) would appear to rule out the possibility of an ontology of Boscovichian point-particles. This might be thought to cast some doubt on (P1). If, however, (P1) is true, and if unconscious mental states of souls are disallowed, then it would seem that a soul must be conscious at all times.[7] In that case, clause (iii) of (DI) should be replaced with 'x is conscious.' Otherwise, clause (iii) would be unnecessarily misleading. Call this revised characterization (DII).

For the purposes of this paper, we do not argue for specifically (DI) or (DII). One of them must be correct, though we do not display any preference.

## II.

It has been argued that the notion of a disembodied spirit or soul is unintelligible, on the ground that this notion can only be understood in *negative* terms. For example, a soul might be defined as a *non-physical* or *unlocated* thing. An argument of this kind seems to have been defended by Douglas Long.[8] Such an argument presupposes the following principle:[9]

(P2)  If a putative ontological category, *C*, stands in need of explication, and if *C* can only be explicated in terms of negative characteristics, then *C* is not an intelligible ontological category.

However, (P2) is ambiguous, and can be read in either of two ways. Let us designate the first such reading (P2A).

(P2A) If a putative ontological category, *C*, stands in need of explication, and if *C* can only be explicated in terms of a set of characteristics *all of which* are negative, then *C* is not an intelligible ontological category.

(P2A) has much intuitive plausibility. For example, in some places Plotinus says that the only way to "explicate" the transcendent "One" is in wholly negative terms, and his critics were rightly skeptical of the coherence of such a explication.[10] In general, to explicate an ontological category in wholly negative terms is, after all, not to distinguish it from other such categories which can also be described in those negative terms.[11] To explicate a category and to distinguish it from a different one, something must be said about the positive nature of that category. Thus, we accept principle (P2A), at least as it applies to the category of souls.

Nevertheless, an argument against the intelligibility of the notion of a soul based upon (P2A) is unsound, for as we have argued in terms of (DI) and (DII), this notion can be explicated in terms of a set of three characteristics *only one* of which is negative.

One arrives at the second reading of (P2), which we shall call (P2B), simply by replacing 'all of which are negative' in (P2A) with 'some of which are negative.' However, it appears that the explication of the notion of a soul must include a negative characteristic such as being unlocated.[12] Thus, we need to ask whether an argument against the intelligibility of the notion of a soul based upon (P2B) is successful. We maintain that such an argument is unsound. To begin with, (P2B) suffers in a comparison with (P2A). Unlike (P2A), (P2B) has no intuitive plausibility. There seems to be no objection to the inclusion of negative characteristics in an explication, provided that they are individually meaningful. Furthermore, there seem to be a variety of counter-examples to (P2B). For example, consider the following apparent cases of intelligible ontological categories that stand in need of explication, and which can only be explicated in terms of a set of characteristics that includes a negative feature. First, take photons. It seems that in order to explicate the notion of a photon, there must be reference to the negative characteristic of masslessness. Secondly, there is the category of number. To explicate this category, there must be reference to abstract entities whose nature involves a negative component, viz., zero, the empty set, or the like. Finally, what are the correct explications of the categories of instants of time and spatial points? They seem to be that an instant is an *unextended* time, and that a point is an *unextended* place.

For the foregoing reasons, (P2B) is implausible. Hence, it cannot be shown that the notion of a soul is unintelligible by appealing to either (P2A) or to (P2B). On either reading, (P2) cannot be utilized to show that the notion of a soul is unintelligible.

## III.

A second challenge to the intelligibility of the concept of a soul is based on the premise that for any intelligible ontological category, there must be an adequate criterion of individuation for entities of that category. Leibniz, for example, argued that any two entities must differ qualitatively.[13] Most philosophers now reject "Leibniz's Law," and allow for the possibility of two qualitatively indistinguishable concrete entities. Nevertheless, these philosophers often accept the premise that for such entities there must be a criterion of individuation. If they are correct, then it follows that the criterion of individuation for these entities is not solely in terms of qualitative universals, viz., the criterion involves either nonqualitative properties or relations to other concrete entities.

Let us assume that if there could be souls, then there could be two souls, each of which has the same qualitative properties as the other. Two such souls would exist at the same times, and at any given time of their existence, would be qualitatively indistinguishable in their thoughts, experiences, and so forth. Keith Campbell is representative of those philosophers who argue that since two souls of this kind would lack a criterion of individuation, the concept of a soul is unintelligible. Entities which are intelligible, Campbell assumes, do not lack such a criterion of individuation, for example, bodies, which are individuated by their different locations.

Note that Campbell is referring to synchronic individuation, or individuation at a time. As he says,

> "Atoms, and material things generally, are individuated and
> counted by their positions. Non-spatial spirits cannot, of course, be
> individuated and counted in this way. But then, in what way can
> they be individuated and counted? If there really is no difference
> between one spirit and two spirits of exactly similar history and
> contents, then spirits are a very suspect sort of thing indeed."[14]

The problem with this argument is that it presupposes that with
respect to Campbell's demand for a criterion of individuation, bodies
are *better off* than souls. Two bodies, he thinks, can be individuated
at a time by their different places, even if they are qualitatively
indistinguishable, while souls, lacking location, cannot be individuated
at a time when they are qualitatively indistinguishable.

Suppose that we have two qualitatively indistinguishable bodies,
$x$ and $y$, and that $x$ occupies place $p_1$ and $y$ occupies place $p_2$.
Campbell presupposes that $x$ differs from $y$ in that $x$ occupies place
$p_1$ while $y$ does not.

But if two qualitatively indistinguishable bodies must have a
criterion of synchronic individuation, then so must two qualitatively
indistinguishable places, i.e., $p_1$ and $p_2$. Thus, let us ask: what is the
criterion of individuation for two qualitatively indistinguishable
places?[15]

The answer to this question will depend on whether space is
relational or absolute. If space is relational, then the existence of
places depends on the existence of spatially located entities, and the
individuation of places must involve their relations to such entities.
Since Campbell assumes a substance ontology, so shall we. Thus, if
space is relational, and $p_1$ and $p_2$ are different places, then one of
these places has a relation to a body that the other lacks, and it is
this which individuates that place. This will not do for the purposes
of Campbell's argument, since it seems viciously circular to individuate bodies in terms of places, and places in terms of bodies.

The appearance of vicious circularity is more than a mere
appearance. The demand for a criterion of individuation is a demand
for an *explanation* of the diversity of entities of a certain category,
an explanation that is logically necessary and sufficient. In other
words, a criterion of individuation provides an *analysis* of the diversity of entities of that category.[16] Thus, the demand for a criterion
of individuation seems to rest on something like the following
premises:

*Argument A*

>   (A1) There could be two entities, each of which has the
>   same qualitative properties.
>   (A2) For each of these entities, there would be some fact
>   about it that accounts for or explains its diversity from
>   any other entity.
>   (A3) In the case of qualitatively indistinguishable entities, this
>   fact can only be that each entity has either a
>   nonqualitative property, or a relation to some other
>   entity, that any other entity lacks.

Since the demand for a criterion of individuation is based on the demand for a certain kind of explanation, and since explanations cannot be circular, the individuation of bodies in terms of places, combined with the individuation of places in terms of bodies, is *viciously* circular. The following general principle applies in this context: for diverse ontological categories, $F$ and $G$, it is viciously circular to individuate $F$s in terms of $G$s, and individuate $G$s in terms of $F$s.

The alternative is that space is absolute. If space is absolute, then places are not individuated by their relations to bodies, since places could exist without bodies. Thus, if space is absolute, and if bodies are individuated by their places, then what individuates places?[17] The only replies to this question that need to be considered are the following.

(1) Nothing individuates places. If this is the reply, then the diversity of places has no explanation. But if this is so, then why suppose that the diversity of souls is in need of an explanation? On the other hand, if places stand in need of a criterion of individuation, but do not have one, then places are unintelligible. Hence, if bodies stand in need of a criterion of individuation, but have no such criterion unless it is in terms of their locations, then bodies are unintelligible too.

(2) Places are individuated either by their exemplification of different nonqualitative properties or by their possession of different individual qualitative properties. An example of a nonqualitative property would be *being that* (where *that* = the place in question), and an example of an individual qualitative property (or trope) would be *a particular shape* (of the place in question). In either of these cases, souls could be individuated by the same sorts of properties, e.g., by the nonqualitative property, *being that* (where *that* = the

soul under discussion), or by an individual qualitative property, e.g., *a particular consciousness* (of the soul in question).

(3) Places are individuated by their parts, so that one place differs from another in that the former has different proper parts than the latter. Such parts, of course, would be places themselves. There is a serious problem with this approach. To begin with, the following general principle is highly plausible:

> (P3) For any entities, $x$ and $y$, belonging to the same ontological category, $F$, it is viciously circular to individuate $x$ by $x$'s bearing a relation, $R$, to $y$, where $R$ is a relation that nothing can bear to itself.

The problem with trying to individuate $x$ in terms of $R$ is that, necessarily, $R$ is a *relation* that $x$ can bear to $y$ only if $x$ is diverse from $y$. In this sense, the instantiation of $R$ presupposes the diversity of $x$ and $y$. Yet, $x$'s bearing $R$ to $y$ is supposed to *explain* in what $x$'s diversity from some other $F$ consists. It is viciously circular to explain the diversity of two $F$s in terms of a relation whose instantiation presupposes the diversity of $F$s. In the case at issue, the diversity of two entities, $x$ and $y$, belonging to the same ontological category, $F$, i.e., places, is to be explained in terms of a relation, $R$, that $x$ bears to another place which is a proper part of $x$, viz., the proper parthood relation between places. In this case, because no place can be a proper part of itself, the instantiation of $R$ entails the diversity of a place from a place which is a proper part of it. Hence, (P3) is satisfied, and the diversity of places cannot be explained in terms of $R$ upon pain of vicious circularity.

In conclusion, whether space is relational or absolute, the attempt to individuate bodies in terms of places does not yield any result that makes bodies any better off than souls with respect to individuation. Therefore, if bodies or places are intelligible, arguments like Campbell's do not establish any unintelligibility in the concept of a soul.

## IV.

In a subtle and interesting paper, Ernest Sosa discusses the argument from individuation against the intelligibility of souls. While criticizing this argument, Sosa argues that nevertheless, there is an important lesson to be learned from it.[18] According to Sosa, if there are two pieces of matter, then the relation of *spatial apartness* must hold between these two material objects. Generalizing from this case, Sosa argues that if *a* is diverse from *b*, then there must be some relation *other than diversity* that holds between them (such as spatial apartness), that nothing can bear to itself.[19] He calls this the Principle that Diversity Cannot Stand Alone (DCSA). Sosa maintains that for souls, there is no obviously acceptable relation to stand alongside diversity in the way that spatial apartness stands alongside diversity for pieces of matter. Note that Sosa, in setting out (DCSA), does not state that (DCSA) implies that an entity has a criterion of individuation, which, we have argued, must be explanatory. In this respect, Sosa's argument differs from Campbell's.

Thus, Sosa maintains that in the case of two material objects with all the same qualitative properties, their diversity does not stand alone, because the qualitative relation, x is spatially apart from y, stands alongside their diversity. On the other hand, in the case of two qualitatively indistinguishable souls (Sosa argues), no comparable qualitative relation stands alongside the diversity of the two souls. This, Sosa says, casts doubt on the intelligibility of souls.

A first response to Sosa is to question (DCSA). What reason is there to accept this principle? The only reason Sosa provides is the following:

> "Perhaps the lesson is simply that entities x and y cannot possibly *be related simply by diversity*. Otherwise, you might have not just one right foot but indefinitely many of them, all related only by diversity!"[20]

All this argument shows, if Sosa is right that no two pieces of matter can exhaustively coincide in space,[21] is that in the case of pieces of matter diversity cannot stand alone. Of course, this fact is explained by the spatial nature of such objects. Sosa generalizes from this case to get (DCSA), but it is not obvious why the generalization is warranted. He has not, for example, pointed out any unintelligibility in the supposition that there are indefinitely many souls, all qualitatively indistinguishable. Why can't there be indefinitely many souls of this kind?

On the other hand, if (DCSA) is correct, then the diversity of souls cannot stand alone. In that case, the defender of the intelligibility of souls must provide a irreflexive relation other than diversity which one soul must bear to another, and which does for souls what spatial apartness does for pieces of matter.

We think that such a relation in fact holds between any two souls, viz., the relation of being a soul x which is incapable of directly experiencing a mental state of a soul y. Thus, if we are right, then souls are "epistemically apart" in a way that parallels the spatial apartness of pieces of matter.[22] We assume that necessarily, a soul is capable of directly experiencing some of its own mental states, and that necessarily, no soul is capable of directly experiencing a mental state of another soul. On these assumptions, if there are two souls which are qualitatively indistinguishable, then this irreflexive relation will stand alongside their diversity in the way spatial apartness stands alongside the diversity of two pieces of matter.

Sosa considers and rejects this second reply to (DCSA).

"It might be suggested that no soul x could directly experience the mental states of another soul y and that this provides us with the desired relation to accompany with necessity every case of diversity among souls. But this seems to me to put things backwards. For the (transitive) *experiencing* done by substances like souls is a causal matter which is a form of 'causally registering a state of.' And direct experiencing is then a form of 'causally registering a state of, without reliance on causally intermediary states.' Now either *self*-registering states are allowed or they are not. If they are allowed, then the only states directly experienced would be those which are self-registering. And then it follows that one cannot directly experience states of anyone else. For to *register* a state X is to *have* a state Y with an appropriate causal relation to X. But if the only states directly registered by one are those states of one's own which are *self*-registering (as a limiting causal relation), then it follows trivially that one can only register directly states of one's own, and hence that these are the only states one can experience directly. But this follows only because of the way experiencing is understood as a form of registering and because of the way the *directness* of such registering is conceived."[23]

Sosa goes on to maintain that if self-registering states are *not* allowed, then it is arguable that a soul can directly experience a mental state of another soul, e.g., God would directly experience a mental state y of a human soul x if God has a mental state z such that z and y are qualitatively alike and God's having z is *directly* caused by x's having y. Since the epistemic apartness of souls, as we understand it, entails that a soul x directly experiences a mental state of a soul y only if that state is, in Sosa's terminology, 'self-registering', we shall just consider Sosa's objection to epistemic apartness of this kind. The crucial objection Sosa makes to this idea of epistemic apartness for souls is that it "puts things backwards," because of the "trivial" way that the epistemic apartness of souls follows from the conception of direct experience.

There are two responses we shall make to Sosa's criticism. The first is that his criticism introduces a new requirement that any relation must meet if it is to be a proper "accompaniment" to diversity, a requirement which Sosa never mentions until he voices this criticism. As we have indicated, Sosa complains that epistemic apartness is somehow not a proper accompaniment because of its triviality. This seems to be because

(S1) 'direct experience' must be defined in a certain way,

and consequently,

(S2) it "trivially follows" (i.e., logically follows from the definition) that a soul can only directly experience one of its own mental states.

Thus, it appears that Sosa's further requirement for a proper accompaniment to diversity is that it not be trivial as spelled out by the two conditions above. It is not clear why triviality in this sense is unacceptable. It seems that in condition (S1), Sosa implies that it is *analytic* that a soul can only directly experience its own mental states. Hence, Sosa appears to claim that his definition of 'direct experience' provides a *synonym* for it.

Given this reading of Sosa, there are two replies to his use of condition (S1) to criticize the epistemic apartness of souls. First, the rationale for the use of (S1), though unstated, is plausibly that if condition (S1) is met, then epistemic apartness cannot *explain* the diversity of souls.[24] However, a principle we defended earlier, i.e., (P4), implies that the spatial apartness of two bodies cannot explain their diversity either. Since spatial apartness is an irreflexive relation, (P4) implies that such an explanation would be viciously circular. Hence, bodies are no better off than souls in this regard. Secondly, there are serious doubts about the claim that Sosa's definition of 'direct experience' is really a synonymy. If, for example, the traditional view that souls can directly experience universals without causally interacting with them is correct, then Sosa's definition of 'direct experience' must be mistaken. Furthermore, if this traditional view, although false, is epistemically possible, then Sosa's definition of 'direct experience' cannot be a synonymy. But in any case, whatever triviality there is in the case of the epistemic apartness of souls appears to obtain as well in the case of the spatial apartness of two pieces of matter, $x$ and $y$.[25] Consider what their spatial apartness really is, after all. It is not just that $x$ is at some non-zero distance from $y$. This is true for two reasons: (a) $x$ can be at some non-zero distance from $x$ (as, for example, when $x$ is on the surface of a sphere, and a great circle is drawn from $x$ in any direction around the sphere and back to $x$);[26] and (b) $x$ can be spatially apart from $y$ even though $x$ is at zero distance from $y$ (in a case where $x$ and $y$ are touching). Furthermore, on certain plausible definitions of the concept of distance, a piece of matter is at zero distance from itself.[27] Thus, the notion of spatial apartness is not definable just in terms of the distance relation, and no dyadic spatial relation holding between material things seems to be adequate by itself to define it. What, then, is spatial apartness? We maintain that to define the spatial apartness of $x$ and $y$ one must presuppose the diversity of the places of $x$ and $y$. That is, to say that $x$ and $y$ are spatially apart is to say that $x$ and $y$ are in or occupy *different* places, or at least it is to say that $x$ is in a certain place, and that $y$ is not in that place.

Recall our earlier discussion of the individuation of places. We pointed out there that if space is relational, then places are individuated in terms of bodies. Moreover, if space is relational, then the concept of a place is defined in terms of certain relations between pieces or portions of matter. Hence, given that the definition of the spatial apartness of two bodies is in terms of the occupation of a place or places by those bodies, this definition involves a relation to a place or space, and the spatial apartness of two bodies is as trivial an accompaniment to their diversity as one could imagine.[28] If space is absolute, then the diversity of the two places which is presupposed by the relation of spatial apartness, and which accompanies the diversity of two bodies, will not *itself* be accompanied by any irreflexive relation of the required sort. Note that the two places will not be spatially apart, since spatial apartness presupposes that the entities which are apart occupy diverse places, and because places do not occupy places.

For all the above reasons, we conclude that Sosa has not shown that there is a relation of the required sort which accompanies the diversity of pieces of matter and that there is no such relation which accompanies the diversity of souls.

## V.

Sosa and others have challenged the intelligibility of causal interaction between souls and bodies.[29] In this argument, we are invited to consider the possibility of a world, $W_1$, in which there are two qualitatively indistinguishable souls, $s_1$ and $s_2$ and two qualitatively indistinguishable bodies, $b_1$ and $b_2$, such that: $s_1$ and $b_1$ causally interact, $s_2$ and $b_2$ causally interact, but $s_1$ does not interact with $b_2$, and $s_2$ does not interact with $b_1$. Sosa defends the plausible thesis that an object's causal properties *supervene upon* its noncausal properties. Sosa means by this that no single possible world, such as $W_1$, could contain two pairs of entities exactly alike noncausally but each differently interrelated causally. Therefore, it could not be the case that $s_1$ interacts with $b_1$ but not with $b_2$, while $s_2$ interacts with $b_2$, but not with $b_1$. In order for $s_1$, $s_2$, $b_1$, and $b_2$ to interact as described in $W_1$, there must be some noncausal relation between $s_1$ and $b_1$ which does not hold between $s_1$ and $b_2$, and so forth. Inasmuch as this relation cannot be a spatial one, and we have no idea what relation it might be, it is, Sosa says, "...a great mystery how souls could interact causally with bodies."[30]

This argument has the following key presupposition:

(P4) If souls and bodies could interact, then there is a possible world such as $W_1$.

But it is not clear why a defender of the intelligibility of dualistic interaction should grant (P4). After all, such a defender might reason as follows. Take a world, $W_2$, in which there is a pair of qualitatively indistinguishable souls, $s_1$ and $s_2$, and a pair of qualitatively indistinguishable bodies, $b_1$ and $b_2$, such that: $s_1$ and $b_1$ causally interact, and $s_2$ and $b_2$ causally interact. Since no single world could contain two pairs of entites exactly alike noncausally but each differently interrelated causally, and inasmuch as we have no hint of any relation holding between $s_1$ and $b_1$ which does not also hold between $s_1$ and $b_2$, and so forth, it is plausible that in $W_2$ $s_1$ must interact causally with *both* $b_1$ and $b_2$, and $s_2$ must interact causally with *both* $b_1$ and $b_2$. In other words, the situation in $W_2$ is one in which the effects of interaction in the respective bodies and souls are causally overdetermined. Admittedly, such a situation is strange, but then so is a symmetrical world containing a pair of qualitatively indistinguishable bodies and a pair of qualitatively indistinguishable souls. Nor does it seem to be *impossible* that a soul causally interacts with two bodies, and a body causally interacts with two souls. The foregoing argument entails the falsity of (P4).

On the other hand, suppose that there is a convincing argument that implies that it is impossible for a soul to causally interact with two bodies or a body to causally interact with two souls. Suppose, too, that no single world could contain two pairs of entities exactly alike noncausally but each differently interrelated causally. Now, if we consider a world, $W_3$, containing two qualitatively indistinguishable souls, $s_1$ and $s_2$, and two qualitatively indistinguishable bodies, $b_1$ and $b_2$, then we do not have the slightest hint of any relation holding between $s_1$ and $b_1$ which does not hold as well between $s_1$ and $b_2$, etcetera. In the light of this, and the foregoing two suppositions, it is plausible to conclude that in a world such as $W_3$, there simply could not be any causal interaction between either $s_1$ and $b_1$ or $b_2$, or $s_2$ and $b_1$ or $b_2$. And once again, we arrive at a conclusion incompatible with (P4).[31]

Since each of the foregoing lines of argument seems no less plausible than Sosa's argument against the intelligibility of dualistic interaction, we conclude that if Sosa's argument is to be convincing, then further substantive support for his key assumption (P4) is needed. At present, we have no idea of how such support might be provided. On the other hand, if no support of this kind is available, our reply to Sosa's argument reveals an interesting and hitherto unnoticed implication of dualistic interactionism, viz., that there are no possible worlds such as $W_1$, but only ones such as $W_2$ or $W_3$.

## VI.

The classical attack on the intelligibility of causal interaction between souls and bodies is based on the following premises:

*Argument B*

    (B1) Necessarily, a body, but not a soul, has spatial location.
    (B2) Necessarily, a soul and a body interact only if they both have spatial location.

(B1) is unquestionably true. However, it is not clear that (B2) is true. Sosa's argument from the supervenience of causal properties upon noncausal properties is example of an attempt to defend (B2). We have rejected that argument. However, there is another, more traditional, argument for (B2). In what follows, we try to show that this traditional argument, and certain related ones, are unsuccessful.

According to this traditional argument, the production of motion in a body can only be understood in terms of the transference of motion from one object to another. (Typically, this transference is characterized in terms of the collision of bodies and the transference of motion by impact.) This argument's assumption that the production of motion in a body can only be understood in terms of the transference of motion might be defended by appeal to the following principle of *transference*:

> Necessarily, if *a* brings it about that *b* is *F*, then *a* does so in virtue of the transference of *F*-ness from *a* to *b*.

Let *b* be a body, and let *F* be motion. In that case, the tranferrence principle implies that *a* could not bring it about that *b* is in motion unless *a* is in motion and transfers that motion to *b*.

However, body/soul interaction is possible only if it is possible for a soul to produce motion in a body. Hence, body/soul interaction is possible only if motion could be transferred from a soul to a body. Since the transference of motion from *a* to *b* requires that both *a* and *b* have spatial location, it follows that necessarily, a soul and a body interact only if they both have spatial location.

The transference principle presupposes the necessity of what Jonathan Barnes has called the *synonymy principle*:

> "If *a* brings it about that *b* is φ, then *a* is φ."[32]

However, as Barnes points out, the synonymy principle is false.[33] For example, a piece of clay can be caused to be square by an object which is not square, e.g., a rolling pin. It follows that the transference principle is false as well. Thus, neither the transference principle nor the synonymy principle can be used to provide a plausible defense of the crucial assumption that the production of motion in a body must be understood in terms of transference of motion.[34] It is not obvious that a plausible defense of this assumption can be provided in terms of some alternative principle. Is this assumption acceptable? We shall argue that it is not.

It is extremely plausible that causal interaction can be understood in terms of universally quantified general laws. If causal interaction is understood in terms of such general laws, then there can be functional or correlational causal relationships which do not involve the production of motion by the transference of motion. (This seems to be true whether or not a Humean is correct in denying that these laws express some kind of objective necessary connection.) For instance, consider the Law of Universal Gravitation. According to this law, there is mutual gravitational attraction between any two pieces of matter. As a result, two such pieces of matter accelerate toward each other. It is a law that each acquires a motion, but it is not the case that motion is *transferred* from one to the other. Must there be a deeper explanation of the accelerations in question in terms of transference of motion? Not necessarily. In a domain of causal activity, one could eventually arrive at laws or causal principles which are basic or fundamental, and which therefore describe interactions unexplainable in terms of any more general laws or principles. As far as we know, the Law of Gravitation is a basic principle or law, correlating one physical phenomenon with another, a principle or law which is *itself* physically inexplicable.[35]

Therefore, it seems that the aforementioned accelerations are causally related to one another in virtue of some functional law, but this causal interaction is neither a transference of motion, nor explainable in terms of other transferences of motion. Hence, production of motion in a body need not be understood in terms of the transference of motion. Since the argument for (B2) makes the key assumption that the production of motion in a body must be understood in terms of the tranferrence of motion, the argument for (B2) is unsuccessful. It seems that if a soul interacts with a body, then this entails that there is a psycho-physical correlation law which cannot be explained in terms of any more general or more basic physical law. However, it appears that a correlation law of this kind is unintelligible only if a physically inexplicable *physical*-physical correlation law is unintelligible. But, as we argued above, a correlation law of the latter kind is not unintelligible. In particular, it seems both that Universal Gravitation is such a law, and that Universal Gravitation is intelligible. Since a physically inexplicable physical-physical correlation law is not unintelligible, there seems to be no reason to reject the intelligibility of a physically inexplicable psycho-physical correlation law. (Although there is a sense in which an inexplicable psycho-physical correlation law is mysterious, an inexplicable physical-physical correlation law is no less mysterious.)

Is there another way to justify (B2) that is more plausible than the traditional argument we have criticized? We cannot think of one.[36] As far as we can tell, there is no good reason to accept (B2). Since the classical attack on the intelligibility of body/soul interaction is based on (B2), we conclude that this attack is ineffective.

## VII.

The following two premises together imply that body/soul interaction is unintelligible. *Argument C*

(C1) If it is possible that there is body/soul interaction, then it is possible that a physical law is violated.

(C2) It is not possible that a physical law is violated.

It would appear that (C2) is entailed by a plausible account of lawfulness. Necessarily, if $L$ is a law, then $L$ is a true universally quantified conditional. Necessarily, a universally quantified conditional is violated just when there exists a counter-instance to that conditional. For example, the conditional $(x)(Fx \rightarrow Gx)$ is violated iff $(\exists x)(Fx \ \& \ \sim Gx)$. Necessarily, there does not exist a counter-instance to a *true* universally quantified conditional. It follows that it is not possible that a law is violated. Therefore, (C2) is true. We shall not question (C2).

It might appear that (C1) is true; nevertheless, we shall argue that it is false. To begin, consider a typical physical law of the form: for any physical object, $x$, if $x$ is $F$, then $x$ is $G$. Unless the defender of *Argument C* is simply begging the question, he must concede that such a law says implicitly that for any physical object, $x$, if $Fx$ then $Gx$, provided that there is no true conjunction of a nonphysical law and initial conditions which implies that $x$ is both $F$ and $\sim G$. Since this law describes only interaction between physical states, it is appropriate to classify it as a *physical* law. An implicit *ceteris paribus* provision of the kind indicated guarantees the inviolability of a physical law of the form in question in the face of interventions by supernatural influences. It accomplishes this by limiting the scope of such a physical law to physical interactions. Parallel remarks apply to physical laws of any kind.

Suppose a physical state, $P_1$, is produced by a soul-state, $S_1$, and that if $S_1$ were to fail to exist, then there would be a true conjunction of a physical law, $L$, and physical initial conditions which implies that

$P_1$ fails to exist. Although, as we have argued, $L$ is not *violated* in such a case, it is accurate to say that $L$ is *superseded* or *overruled*. Observe that a law being superseded in this sense *does not* have the implication that a law is false. On the other hand, a law being violated *does* have this apparently absurd implication. Hence, a law being superseded does not imply that a law is violated, and it is a mistake to conflate the supersedence of a law with the violation of a law. If the supersedence of a law is assimilated to the violation of a law, a deceptive appearance is created that certain kinds of supernatural interventions would violate a physical law.

The foregoing considerations imply that (C1) is false. Hence, the argument for the unintelligibility of body/soul interaction based on (C1) is unsound.

## VIII.

The concept of a soul is the concept of a substance. A substance can endure through time. Thus, a soul can have identity over time. To say that an entity, $x$, has identity over time (*persistence*) is to say that $x$ exists at one time and is identical with something that exists at another time. Yet another challenge to the intelligibility of souls questions the coherence of the idea of a persisting soul. This challenge parallels the earlier one which claimed that the synchronic diversity of souls is unintelligible.

The premises of this argument are as follows:

*Argument D*

   (D1) A criterion for the identity over time of a soul must provide an explanation (and an analysis) of such identity.
   (D2) If an entity of a certain category can persist, then there must be a criterion of identity over time for entities of that category.
   (D3) A soul does not have a criterion for identity over time.[37]
   (D4) If it is possible that a soul exists, then it is possible that a soul persists.

Those who defend an argument of this sort are usually committed to the proposition that pieces of matter or bodies possess a criterion for persistence. This criterion is usually thought to involve spatio-temporal continuity, so we shall confine our attention to those who hold this view. Since souls are not in space, they obviously cannot possess a criterion of persistence involving spatiotemporal continuity.

Given the assumption that if bodies have a criterion of persistence, then that criterion involves spatiotemporal continuity, we will argue that if (D2) is true, then neither bodies nor places are intelligible. Hence, we will show that given this assumption souls are no worse off than bodies and places with respect to possessing a criterion of persistence.

Our argument is based on the following two claims. First, if a body persists in virtue of its momentary stages being spatiotemporally continuous, then this *entails* that places persist. Secondly, the notion of a body's persisting in virtue of its stages being spatiotemporally continuous *involves* the notion of a persisting place. The argument for these two claims goes as follows.

The notion of the stages of a body, $b$, being spatiotemporally continuous involves the idea that, necessarily, if a momentary stage of $b$ in a place $p_1$ at a moment of time $t_1$ is spatiotemporally continuous with a momentary stage of $b$ in a place $p_2$ at another moment of time $t_2$, then either (i) $p_1$ at $t_1$ = $p_2$ at $t_2$, or (ii) there exists a third place $p_3$ between $p_1$ and $p_2$, at a third time, $t_3$, between $t_1$ and $t_2$, and $p_3$ is occupied by a momentary stage of $b$. (i) is satisfied if $b$ is stationary from $t_1$ to $t_2$. (i) explicitly entails the identity of a place over time. (ii) is satisfied if $b$ is in motion at some time during $[t_1\text{-}t_2]$. In the case of (ii), since at time $t_3$, $p_3$ is *between* $p_1$ and $p_2$, it logically follows that $p_1$ exists at both $t_1$ and $t_3$, and $p_2$ exists at both $t_1$ and $t_3$. Consequently, if a body's stages exhibit spatiotemporal continuity, then this *entails* that places have identity across time.

Furthermore, if one says that an entity, $x$, exists (or has some property or bears some relation) at *two* times, then this is tantamount to saying that $x$ has identity across time. Let $x=p_1$. Since by hypothesis $p_1$ exists at $t_1$, and since (ii) says that at another time $t_3$, another place $p_3$ is between $p_1$ and $p_2$, it follows that in virtue of (ii) the notion of a body's stages being spatiotemporally continuous involves a notion tantamount to the persistence of a place. In addition, in virtue of (i) the notion of a body's stages being spatiotemporally continuous explicitly involves the idea that a place persists. Therefore, the notion of a body's persisting in virtue of its stages being spatiotemporally continuous involves the notion of a persisting place.

What, then, is the criterion of persistence for places? As in the case of synchronic diversity (or identity) of places, the answer to this question will depend on whether space is relational or absolute. If space is relational, then the existence of places depends on the existence of bodies, and the persistence of places must involve their relations to persisting bodies. Thus, if space is relational, and $p_1$ at $t_1$ is the same place as $p_2$ at $t_2$, then $p_1$ and $p_2$ must bear the same relations at the same times to bodies which persist from $t_1$ to $t_2$. Hence, if space is relational, then the criterion of persistence for places involves the persistence of bodies. However, as we have seen, if the criterion of persistence for bodies involves spatiotemporal continuity, then this criterion involves the persistence of places. It is circular to give a criterion for the persistence of bodies in terms of the persistence of places, and the persistence of places in terms of the persistence of bodies. As in the case of synchronic diversity, the demand for a criterion of the persistence of bodies is a demand for a certain kind of explanation. Since an explanation cannot be circular, if space is relational, then the circularity of a purported criterion of the persistence of bodies in terms of the persistence of places is vicious. In general, for diverse ontological categories $F$ and $G$, it is viciously circular to explain the persistence of $F$s in terms of a criterion involving the persistence of $G$s, and the persistence of $G$s in terms of a criterion involving the persistence of $F$s.

Even if space is absolute, it is viciously circular to explain the persistence of bodies in terms of a criterion involving the persistence of places, and the persistence of places in terms of a criterion involving the persistence of bodies. So, if space is absolute and the persistence of bodies is explained in terms of a criterion involving the persistence of places, then what explains the persistence of places?[38] The only replies to this question that need to be considered are the following.

(A) Places persist, but have no criterion of persistence. If this is the reply, then the persistence of a place has no explanation. But if this is so, why suppose that the persistence of a soul is in need of an explanation? Moreover, note that if persisting places have no criterion of persistence, then it is false that for any ontological category of persisting entity, there must be a criterion of persistence for entities of that category. This would mean that (D2) is false.

(B) Suppose (D2) is granted. In that case, since places lack a criterion of persistence, places are unintelligible. (Assuming that if it is possible for there to be places, then it is possible for places to persist.) In addition, given that bodies have no criterion of persistence unless they have one involving spatiotemporal continuity, and given that spatiotemporal continuity requires the persistence of places, it follows also that bodies are unintelligible.

(C) The persistence of a place can be explained in terms of a criterion involving either a nonqualitative haecceity or a trope that a place exemplifies or possesses at different times. An example of a nonqualitative haecceity would be the property of *being that* (where *that* = the place in question), and an example of a trope would be *that particular shape* (of the place in question). In this case, the persistence of a soul can be explained in terms of a criterion involving the same kind of property or trope, e.g., by the non-qualitative haecceity, *being that* (where *that* = the soul under discussion), or by the trope *that particular consciousness* (of the soul under discussion).

In conclusion, whether space is relational or absolute, the attempt to provide an explanatory criterion or analysis of the persistence of a body in terms of a criterion involving spatiotemporal continuity does not yield any result that makes bodies any better off than souls with respect to such an attempt. Therefore, if bodies or places are intelligible, the argument under discussion does not establish any unintelligibility in the concept of a soul.

## Appendix On Spatiotemporal Continuity

A *sequence of body-stages* is a densely ordered sequence of instantaneous temporal slices of a body or bodies, ordered so that each member of the sequence exists at a moment which is later than the moment at which any preceding member of the sequence exists and which is earlier than the moment at which any subsequent member of the sequence exists. The notion of a *spatiotemporally continuous* sequence of body-stages can be defined in three steps, as follows.

> $S$ is a *spatially discontinuous* sequence of body-stages =df. $S$ is a sequence of body-stages such that: (i) $S$ has a subsequence $S^*$, which has a member, $x$, which exists at a moment of time $t_1$ in a place $p_1$, and a member, $y$, which

exists at a moment of time $t_2$ in a place $p_2$, where $t_1$ is not identical with $t_2$ and $p_1$ is not identical with $p_2$; and (ii) no member of $S^*$ exists at a time between $t_1$ and $t_2$ in a place other than $p_1$ and other than $p_2$.

$S$ is a *temporally discontinuous* sequence of body-stages =df. $S$ is a sequence of body-stages such that: (i) $S$ has a subsequence $S^*$, and a member of $S^*$ exists at a time $t_1$ and a member of $S^*$ exists at a time $t_2$, where $t_1$ is not identical with $t_2$; and (ii) no member of $S^*$ exists at a time between $t_1$ and $t_2$.

$S$ is a *spatiotemporally continuous* sequence of body-stages =df. $S$ is a sequence of body-stages that is neither spatially discontinuous nor temporally discontinuous.

In this context, to say that a body is spatiotemporally continuous is to say that its stages constitute a spatiotemporally continuous sequence. We shall argue that a body lacks an analysis or criterion of persistence involving spatiotemporal continuity among a sequence of body-stages. (The following is a simple analysis of this kind: A body $x$ that exists at a moment $t_1$ is identical with a body $y$ that exists at another moment $t_2$ =df. the body-stage of $x$ at $t_1$ and the body-stage of $y$ at $t_2$ belong to a spatiotemporally continuous sequence of body-stages.)

Since the following case (*Case A*) seems possible, spatiotemporal continuity among some sequence of body-stages does not appear to be a logically necessary condition of the persistence of a body. Body $b$ occupies place $p_1$ at time $t_1$. There is another place $p_2$ such that at every time between $t_1$ and a later time $t_2$, $b$ occupies $p_2$. In this sort of case, $b$ instantaneously "jumps" in space. That is, $b$ persists, and although $b$'s stages belong to a temporally continuous sequence, some of these stages are spatially discontinuous. It also seems possible that $b$ persists, and some of its stages are temporally discontinuous. In such a case (*Case B*) an object "jumps" in time, for example as follows. A body $b$ occupies place $p_1$ at a moment of time $t_1$. At every time between $t_1$ and a later moment of time $t_2$, $b$ (and each of its parts) fails to exist. At $t_2$, $b$ occupies $p_1$. This case presupposes that possibly, a body is totally annihilated and then comes back into existence. The possibility of such a case also implies that the spatiotemporal continuity of some sequence of body-stages is not a logically necessary condition of the persistence of a body.

The possibility of a body making a spatial or temporal "jump" might be attacked as follows. This possibility presupposes that in some possible world someone has conclusive evidence (or at least justification) for believing that such a "jump" occurred. But, there is no such possible world.

Our reply is this. For an observer to re-identify even a spatio-temporally continuous body (other than himself), an *inductive* or *nonconclusive* justification is needed (at least implicitly). Such a justification is ultimately based on nonsimultaneous perceptions of a body which reveal a similarity in a body's sensory properties at diverse times. An inductive justification for such a re-identification may involve inference to the best explanation, causal reasoning, testimony, and so forth. An inductive justification for re-identifying a body need not involve the premise that the stages of this body form a spatiotemporally continuous sequence. Hence, assuming that an inductive justification is possible when an observer seeks to re-identify an external body whose stages form a spatiotemporally continuous sequence, an inductive justification is possible also when an observer seeks to re-identify an external body that "jumps" in space or time. For example, take a possible case of an apparent spatial "jump". Suppose that while you are staring at a ball of distinctive appearance, it disappears from its spot on the left hand end of your desk, and a ball which is indistinguishable in its sensible qualities instantly appears on the right hand end. Alternatively, in a possible case of an apparent temporal "jump", the ball vanishes from its spot, and two minutes later a ball that is indistinguishable in its sensible qualities appears in the same spot. In either of these cases, the following circumstances could obtain. First, the most sophisticated and exhaustive empirical tests fail to detect any spatiotemporally continuous sequence of body-stages connecting "pre-jump" and "post-jump" stages of the ball (or any of its parts). Secondly, the body-stages observed immediately before and after the apparent "jump" appear to be indistinguishable in their intrinsic qualitative properties and velocities when examined with our most accurate instruments, within the limits of experimental error. Thirdly, such an apparent "jump" invariably occurs under replicable conditions of a certain kind. In these circumstances, all other things being equal, one would possess an inductive justification for believing that the ball had made a "jump" in space or time.

Finally, it seems that there could be a case (*Case C*) which involves either the total annihilation of a body, and/or the total creation of another body, and/or one or more bodies that "jump" in space, and implies that the spatiotemporal continuity of a sequence of body-stages is not a logically sufficient condition for the persistence of a body. In this sort of case, a body $b$ occupies a place $p_1$ at time $t_1$, and $b$ occupies $p_1$ at every time after $t_1$ up to, but not including, $t_2$. In addition, at $t_2$, $b$ (and each of its parts) either fails to exist or makes a "jump" to another place. Lastly, at $t_2$, *another* body $b^*$ (together with each of its parts) either comes into being in $p_1$ or makes a "jump" into $p_1$ from another place. This implies both that there is a spatiotemporally continuous sequence of body-stages, and that the bodies to which these stages belong are diverse. Hence, if one observes a spatiotemporally continuous sequence of body-stages, this does not provide logically conclusive grounds for the re-identification of a body, even if in fact all of these stages do belong to the same body.

Although limitations of space preclude discussion of the foregoing arguments in full breadth and detail, enough has been said to make it plausible that spatiotemporal continuity among some sequence of body-stages is neither a logically necessary nor a logically sufficient condition for the persistence of a body. Hence, although souls lack an analysis or criterion of persistence involving spatiotemporal continuity among a sequence of stages, so do bodies.[39] Once again, souls turn out to be no worse off than bodies in this respect.[40]

## Notes

1. Accordingly, it is impossible for a thing or an object in this ordinary sense either to *occur* (as an event does) or be *exemplified* (as some properties are). To suppose otherwise is to commit what Ryle called a category mistake. This is the source of the apparent absurdity of saying, for example, that Gorbachev occurs or is exemplified by something.

2. We call a theory that identifies a substance with a set or collection of either properties, ideas, sensa-data, or events a *collectionist* theory. Such theories face two difficulties, sketched below. (i) There is the unity of qualities problem. Consider the collection of the greenness of an apple, the taste of a pickle, the sound of a ball being dropped, the shape of an orange, the smell of an onion, and so forth. (Alternatively, consider a collection of diverse psychological qualities of different persons.) Collections of this kind are *not* substances, but it is not clear that a collectionist or a bundle theorist can provide an adequate account of this fact. Notice that since such an account should distinguish a

nonsubstantial collection from a substance in any *possible* case, it appears that it ought do this *both* in the case of material objects and spirits. (ii) There is the problem of excessive essentialism. It seems that there could be individual substances that have accidental qualities and endure through changes in some of their intrinsic qualities. However, since it extremely plausible that a collection has its parts or elements essentially, it is hard to see how a collectionist can satisfactorily account for the full range of such accidental qualities and changes.

3. If an entity, *e*, is *reduced to* or *identified with* an entity, *e\**, then necessarily, *e* exists if and only if *e\** exists. If *e* is *eliminated* in favor of *e\**, then *e* fails to exist.

4. In "The Independence Criterion of Substance."

5. *Meditations*, II and VI.

6. For example, the property of being conscious is wholly present, but the property of having been conscious at some previous time is not.

7. Note that if a human person can exist when unconscious, it is open to one who agrees with Descartes that souls are conscious at all times, to respond that while human persons are not souls, souls are nevertheless possible. This response is not one Descartes himself would make, for he also holds that only souls are capable of consciousness.

8. In "Disembodied Existence, Physicalism, and the Mind-Body Problem," pp. 307-316.

9. Long never explicitly states this principle, but his argument against the intelligibility of the notion of a soul depends upon it.

10. *Enneads*.

11. The only kind of exception *may* occur in a case such as the explication of an *abstract entity* as a *non-concrete entity,* or vice-versa. This sort of exception may occur because this pair of ontological categories is at a certain very high level of generality. (On the other hand, this may not be an exception because it could be argued that the characterization of an abstract entity as a non-concrete entity is not a genuine explication of abstractness, but only an equivalence concept.) At lower levels of generality, purely negative characterizations do not serve to distinguish a genuine ontological kind from another, positively characterized one. For example, *non-substance* does not denote a genuine ontological kind, since it does not distinguish such categories of nonsubstantial entities as event, property, collection, time, place, and so forth. The category of soul is not at the very high level of generality which permits the negative characterization of a kind. For an explication of the notion of the levels of ontological categories, see our paper, "The Independence Criterion of Substance."

12. However, an explication of the concept of a soul needs to include a negative characteristic only if there could be a conscious material body.
    If, as Descartes supposed, it is impossible for a material body to be conscious, then the concept of a soul can be explicated in *wholly positive terms,* either as a substance that is capable of consciousness, or as a substance that is conscious.

13. According to "Leibniz's Law", necessarily, for any *x* and *y*, and any

property $P$, $x=y$ iff ($x$ has $P$ iff $y$ has $P$). '$P$' ranges over qualitative properties, including intrinsic and relational ones.

14. Campbell, *Body and Mind*, pp. 44-45.
15. Campbell and others who give his kind of argument never seem to pose this crucial question.
16. The analysis of the diversity of bodies at issue might be stated as follows. At a moment $t_1$, a body $x$ and a body $y$ are diverse $=$df. the places that $x$ and $y$ occupy at $t_1$ are diverse.
17. Note that a place cannot be individuated by its location, i.e., in terms of the place it occupies. Why? Because a place does not *occupy* (or is not *in*) a place, though of course every place is either a proper or improper *part* of some place, and stands in spatial relations to other places, e.g., relations of distance.
18. Ernest Sosa, "Subjects Among Other Things," pp. 160-164.
19. *Op. cit.*, p. 162.
20. *Ibid.*, p. 162.
21. Sosa also assumes that a piece of matter cannot be located in two different places at the same time.
22. This point was originally made by Gary Rosenkrantz in "Comments On 'Subjects Among Other Things'".
23. Sosa, *op. cit.*, p. 163.
24. Sosa might reply that a proper accompaniment to diversity need not explain diversity so long as it *analyzes* it. In our view, part of the difference between an analysans and a synonym is that the former, but not the latter, is explanatory.
25. We shall assume that $x$ and $y$ are spatially extended.
26. Moreover, apparently, there could be a curved universe, e.g., a three-dimensional spherical universe with a finite radius. In such a spherical universe, a body is at a finite nonzero distance from itself along *every* geodesic intersecting it, each of which is a great circle. Even in the case of a Euclidean universe, an object is at a nonzero distance from itself along every geodesic or straight line intersecting it, i.e., *an infinite distance*.
27. If we understand object $x$ being at zero distance from object $y$ in terms of there being a point on the surface of $x$ which is identical with a point on the surface of $y$, then it follows that an object can be at zero distance from itself. Given that between any two points there is a third point, $x$ being at zero distance from $y$ cannot be understood in terms of there being a point on the surface of $x$ that is *adjacent* to a point on the surface of $y$.

    As our examples have illustrated, an object $x$ is at a *nonzero* distance from an object $y$ only relative to a direction along some line that intersects $x$ and $y$. Of course, if $x$ is at *zero* distance from $y$, then this distance is in *not* relative to such a direction. Thus, there is no inconsistency in an object's both being at many nonzero distances from itself (relative to different directed lines) and being at a zero distance from itself.
28. We have employed 'distance' in its usual metrical sense. In the light of

our argument, it is interesting to observe that another sense of 'distance', now obsolete, was *diversity*.

29. Sosa, *op. cit.*, pp. 166-167. John Foster appears to have originated this type of argument against the intelligibility of interaction. See his "Psychophysical Causal Relations." Note, however, that Foster introduced the argument only to refute it. Below, we will cite his replies to the argument.

30. Sosa, *op. cit.*, p. 166.

31. Foster also has two replies to this kind of anti-interactionist argument. See Foster, *op. cit.*, and "In *Self*-Defense," pp. 168-70. The two replies are summarized in Foster, "A Defense of Dualism." Both of Foster's replies, however, involve the rejection of Sosa's premise that all causal relations supervene on purely qualitative non-causal facts. We do not reject this premise in making our two replies to Sosa.

32. Jonathan Barnes, *The Presocratics, Volume I*, page 119.

33. Barnes, *ibid*.

34. It should be noted that, unlike the transference principle, the synonymy principle says nothing about the *transference* of properties. The transference principle is based on the intuition that if *a* brings it about that *b* is *F*, then there is a transfer of *F*-ness from *a* to *b*—a transfer in which *F*-ness is *conserved*. It is logically consistent to reject this intuition, and yet affirm the synonymy principle based on another intuition, viz., that *like can only be produced by like*. Instead of appealing to the transference principle to defend (B2), one can appeal *instead* to the necessity of the synonymy principle. Such a defense of (B2) begins with the following observation. If the synonymy principle is necessarily true, then motion in a body can only be brought about by something that is in motion. But, if something is not located in space, then it cannot be in motion. It follows that motion in a body can only be brought about by something that is located in space. However, body/soul interaction is possible only if it is possible for a soul to produce motion in a body. Hence, (B2) is true.

    However, since the synonymy principle is false, the foregoing defense of (B2) is unsound. The defender of (B2) might retreat to the following *restricted* synonymy principle:

    If *a* brings it about that *b* is φ, then there is *some* property that *a* and *b* have in common.

    Although this restricted principle is necessarily true, it is only *trivially* so. Any two entities must have *some* property in common, for example, being self-identical. Since a soul and a body have a property in common, e.g., being concrete, being a substance, etc., the restricted synonymy principle cannot be used to support (B2).

35. Observe that the example of the law of gravitation seems to imply that even the following *restricted* transference principle is false (and in any case is not a necessary truth):

    (RTP) If *a* brings it about that *b* is φ, then *a* does so in virtue of the transference of *some* property from *a* to *b*.

In addition, it appears that (RTP) does not imply (B2). (RTP) implies (B2) only if the following lemma is true:

> (*Lemma*) There *could not* be a property, P, had by *both* a material substance, x, and an unlocated soul, y, such that P is transferred between x and y, and it is in virtue of the transference of P between x and y that x and y interact.

There appear to be two kinds of possible cases which refute (*Lemma*). First, it seems that *possibly*, a material substance and a soul *both* have the property of consciousness, and interaction between them occurs in virtue of a transfer of consciousness from a soul to a material substance, followed by a transfer of consciousness in the opposite direction. (It could happen that a transfer of consciousness from a soul *to a material substance* is the first link in a causal chain that results in the motion of that material substance, and that a transfer of consciousness *to a soul* from a material substance results in a change in the state of consciousness of that soul.) Thus, for example, a human soul could interact in this manner with certain living parts or cells of a human body, or a nonhuman spirit, e.g., an angel, could interact in this way with another life form that is a material substance, e.g., a human or some other creature. As a result, a soul would produce motion in a body, and a body would produce a change of consciousness in a soul.

In the second case, a body and a soul *both* have the property of having energy or the ability to do work, and interaction between them occurs in virtue of transfers of energy. In this context, *the ability to do work* can be taken to mean *either* the ability to produce some physical effect or a more generic ability, viz., *the ability to do something*. There are many things souls have the ability to do, e.g., solve mathematical problems, which a body could enhance by interaction with a soul. Clearly, the same holds for the enhancement of bodily abilities by souls.

36. See notes 34 and 35 for criticisms of certain related arguments for (B2).
37. For example, see John Perry, "A Dialogue on Personal Identity and Immortality."
38. Notice that a criterion of persistence for a place cannot be in terms of spatiotemporal continuity. The reasons for this are parallel to those which imply that a place cannot be individuated at a time by its location (see note 17).
39. Our criticisms of criteria of bodily persistence involving spatiotemporal continuity apply to *any* conceivable version of such a criterion, since in each of our examples *both* a body and all of its parts are spatially or temporally discontinuous. Thus, a criterion for the persistence of bodies cannot involve a spatiotemporally continuous sequence of stages of either *entire* bodies or any *proper parts* of bodies.
40. This appendix is based on "The Persistence of Physical Objects", by Joshua Hoffman.

## References

1. Barnes, Jonathan, *The Presocratics, Volume I* (Boston: Routledge and Kegan Paul, 1979).
2. Campbell, Keith, *Body and Mind* (Garden City: Anchor Books, 1970).
3. Descartes, Rene, *Meditations on First Philosophy*, in John Cottingham, *et. al.*, translators, *The Philosophical Works of Descartes, II*, (Cambridge: Cambridge University Press, 1984).
4. Foster, John, "A Defense of Dualism," in John Smythies and John Beloff, editors, *The Case For Dualism* (Charlottesville: University Press of Virginia, 1989), pp. 1-23.
5. Foster, John, "In *Self*-Defense," in G.F. MacDonald, editor, *Perception and Identity* (London: MacMillan, 1979), pp. 161-185.
6. Foster, John, "Psychophysical Causal Relations," *American Philosophical Quarterly* 5, 1968, pp, 64-70.
7. Hoffman, Joshua, "The Persistence of Physical Objects," unpublished manuscript.
8. Long, Douglas, "Disembodied Existence, Physicalism, and the Mind-Body Problem," *Philosophical Studies*, 31 (1977), pp. 307-16.
9. Perry, John, "A Dialogue on Personal Identity and Immortality," in Joel Feinberg, editor, *Reason and Responsibility*, 7th edition (Belmont: Wadsworth, 1989), pp. 323-341.
10. Plotinus, *Enneads*, 2nd edition revised, translated by Stephen Mackenna (London: Faber and Faber, 1969).
11. Rosenkrantz, Gary, "Comments on 'Subjects Among Other Things,'" delivered at the Tenth Annual Symposium in Philosophy at the University of North Carolina at Greensboro, April, 1986.
12. Rosenkrantz, Gary and Hoffman, Joshua, "The Independence Criterion of Substance," *Philosophy and Phenomenological Research*, forthcoming.
13. Sosa, Ernest, "Subjects Among Other Things," in *Philosophical Perspectives, 1, Metaphysics* (Atascadero, California: Ridgeview Publishing Company, 1987), pp. 155-187.

Philosophical Perspectives, 5, Philosophy of Religion, 1991

# FAITH, BELIEF, AND RATIONALITY

## Robert Audi
## University of Nebraska

Faith and reason are often taken to need reconciliation. They are viewed as not only contrasting, but also competing. The opposition is often seen as a tension between the spiritual and the rational, or between religion and science. I shall argue that, different though they are, faith and reason need not be put on opposing sides in human life. But there is a second mistake that concerns me even more. It is the attempt to reconcile faith and reason by assimilating faith, or at least the kind of faith regarded as consonant with reason, to rational belief. If this assimilation is a mistake, it is an important one. For if faith, or at least religious faith, is not reducible to a kind of belief, then the rationality of religious faith need not be decided on the basis of an account of rational belief. It may be, of course, that the relevant kinds of religious belief are rational and can be shown to be so. But I want to explore the possibility that faith, as a central element in religious commitment, can be rational even if theistic *beliefs* with the same content should turn out not to be. In doing this, I will distinguish between faith and belief in a way others have generally not done.[1]

## I. Dimensions of Rationality in Religious Commitment

By way of background, it is useful to distinguish three dimensions of religion to which questions of rationality apply. The first is *ontological*: it concerns what kind of purported reality we are talking about when we speak of God (or any spiritual being). The traditional view, at least as philosophers have tended to interpret it, is notoriously strong: God is omniscient, omnipotent, and omnibenevolent. (With process philosophers of religion, one might reduce the strength of theistic claims by qualifying this list, say in denying that omnipotence is essential to God, but I shall not pursue this possibility here.[2]) The second dimension—the *semantic*—is closely related to the first. The most notable contrast here is between cognitivism and non-cognitivism: the former maintains, and the latter denies, that sentences about God express propositions, hence truths or falsehoods as opposed to, say, spiritual attitudes or symbolic pictures.[3] Third, there is a wide range of *epistemic* dimensions. These concern both the cognitive—roughly, the proposition-expressive—attitude we take as central and the kinds of grounds, whether experiential or argumental or of some other sort, that must underlie that attitude if it is to be rationally held. We can make knowledge of God our main focus, or concentrate on justified theistic belief, or simply on rational belief. We might, on the other hand, choose an attitude like faith or hope and argue that the standards of rationality appropriate to it are distinctive.[4]

The ontological dimension, then, concerns *what* we hold; the semantic dimension, the *kind of meaning*—say, literal or figurative—appropriate to what we hold; and the epistemic dimension, the *kind of attitude* with which we hold it and the sorts of *grounds* appropriate to that attitude. Skepticism tends to push those concerned with the rationality of their religion toward weaker commitments in all three domains (and in others, such as the behavioral, which I discuss only briefly in this paper, in Section VII). I hope to indicate one way in which theists may resist skepticism without falling into the extremes toward which it may drive one, particularly *ontological attenuation* of the concept of God; *non-cognitivist transformation* of religious language; and *dogmatism* (or radical fideism) about the epistemic status of religious belief.

In the domain of cognitive religious commitment, there is not only the possibility of knowledge or justified belief regarding God, but of faith and hope. I especially want to clarify the notion of faith and to try to redirect some of the discussion of the rationality of cognitive religious commitment toward that of faith as opposed to belief. It is, then, the epistemic dimension of religious commitment that mainly concerns me, and my aim is to develop a position in this dimension which satisfies appropriate criteria for both faith and rationality.

## II. Faith, Belief, and Hope

There are apparently two main kinds of faith, and this distinction applies both to religious faith and to other kinds. One kind is faith *in*—which I shall call *attitudinal faith*. It may be illustrated by faith in other human beings, as well as by faith in God. The second is faith *that—propositional faith*. It is commonly exemplified by faith that a friend will recover from an illness. I intentionally use a secular example. While I think the concept of faith I shall clarify has a place— and doubtless a history—in religious parlance, I want to develop it independently of religious presuppositions and, from that vantage point, offer it as a useful focus of discussion in the philosophy of religion.[5]

Whether in secular or religious cases, neither kind of faith clearly requires belief of the proposition in question. I offer no analysis of 'belief' here, but what I have in mind is roughly this: simply and unqualifiedly believing the relevant proposition (*p*), as opposed to such things as believing *p* to be probable, believing it to be certain, half believing it, accepting it, in the sense of taking it as true,[6] being disposed to believe it, and believing it conditionally (even where one takes the condition to be satisfied). We may, to be sure, construe a person's believing that *p* is probable as a case of believing; but it is not equivalent to believing *that p*, which is the proposition in question. Believing that *p* is certain is not equivalent to believing that *p* either, though it may entail believing *p*, at least in a rational person. Half believing *p* may entail "going along with" *p* up to a certain point, but implies a lack of the overall *cognitive commitment*, as we might call it, characteristic of unqualifiedly believing. Accepting *p*—when this is not just a matter of believing it, as on many uses of 'accept'—can be a matter of something like forming an intention to use it as a basis of inference, or taking it as a basis for conduct. Neither kind of acceptance entails believing *p*. As for being disposed to believe *p*, for instance that there are more than ten words in this paragraph, this disposition is a readiness to *come* to believe *p* and is easily confused with actually believing it dispositionally rather than occurrently; but being disposed to believe is importantly different from dispositionally believing.[7] Finally, since a person can fail to put two and two together, believing that *p* is not implied even by believing both that *q* and that if *q* then *p*.

It is true that faith that, say, God loves us implies a disposition to believe that God exists, just as faith that a friend will recover from an illness implies a disposition to believe *that* proposition. Moreover, these dispositions tend to be realized by perceptions of certain positive signs, such as a pervasive sense of God's protecting one, or the discovery of the friend's improvement. But propositional faith does not entail having the corresponding belief. Indeed, at least in non-religious contexts the closer one comes to having that belief, the less natural it is to speak of faith rather than simply belief. It is doubtless possible to have faith that something is so when one also believes it is, but faith does not entail belief.[8]

One reason why (propositional) faith may seem to imply belief is that it is apparently incompatible with *dis*belief. If I believe that not-*p*, surely I cannot have faith that *p*, just as I cannot (at least normally) believe both that *p* and that not-*p*.[9] I *can* have faith compatibly with an absence of any feeling of certitude, and even with a belief that *p* is not highly probable. But if I disbelieve *p*, I do not have faith that it is so. Moreover, while I need not (and perhaps cannot) have a sense of certitude regarding the proposition, there are limits to how much doubt I can feel toward it. When the strength of doubt that *p* is true reaches a certain point, hope, but not faith, will likely be my attitude. Hope that *p* may be so desperate as to coexist with as much doubt as is possible consistently with not reaching certainty that not-*p*. Faith may alternate with such doubt, but cannot coexist with any doubt sufficient to undermine a basically positive overall outlook.

To be sure, there are uses of 'faith' for which the contrast with belief is inappropriate. Unqualified belief that God loves us may be an article of one's *religious faith* in a very common sense of that phrase—the *credal sense*—in which one can lay out one's religious faith by carefully formulating its content. But if one's cognitive attitude is belief that God loves us, it is at least not happily called faith *that* he does. The point is more easily grasped in a context in which no major philosophical issue is at stake: if, from previous experience (or indeed for whatever reason), I unqualifiedly believe that Janet will meet a certain challenge, I will tend not to express my attitude by saying I have faith that she will; for saying this would at least normally imply that I do not unqualifiedly believe it. Or, consider a case in which we are worrying about whether a student with a mixed record will be able to complete a dissertation. If I have faith that the student will do the job, then, while I cannot merely have a hope that the student will, must I believe it? And if, despite the mixed record, I urge my colleagues to have faith, must I be urging belief, or suggesting that the evidence warrants belief? The cognitive attitude I am urging must be strong enough to undergird positive behavior, such as giving the student another year of support; but it does not seem to imply belief that the dissertation will be completed.

The distinction I am drawing can be brought out further by noting three related contrasts. First, whereas if one believes that *p*, and *p* then turns out to be false, one has thereby been shown *mistaken* (or at least wrong) about *p*, this does not always hold for faith that *p*: one's faith might be shown to be *misplaced*, and it would be *disappointed*; but one might have had a kind or degree of doubt regarding *p*, or fear that not-*p*, rather different from the kind or degree of these consistent with belief. If the student never does the dissertation, then perhaps I should not have had the faith I did have, but I need not be shown to be mistaken by this failure, as is my optimistic colleague who simply believed the student would do it. A related contrast is this: other things being equal, for believing that *p* as opposed to having faith that *p* there is more tendency to be surprised upon discovering not-*p* to be the case. This contrast in turn goes well with a third: granting that strong faith that *p* tends to preclude doubt that *p*, and granting, too, that weak belief that *p* is compatible with a significant degree of such doubt, faith that *p*, as compared with belief that *p*, is compatible with a higher *degree* of doubt that *p*. I suggest, then, that propositional faith is neither reducible to nor entails belief.

This is not in the least to imply that belief and propositional faith are utterly different kinds of attitudes. Far from it: both are cognitive; both admit of rationality; both influence behavior; and both vary in many of the same dimensions, such as strength and centrality to the person's outlook on the world. Beyond that, I grant that in some cases change in a single dimension, notably that of confidence regarding the proposition in question, can cause faith that does not embody belief to evolve into faith that does. But all of this is consistent with treating faith as distinctive in the ways I suggest; and even if the only major difference between propositional faith that does, and propositional faith that does not, embody belief, should be one of confidence, that would be significant. It would *at least* affect the standards of rationality and justification appropriate to the faith. For other things being equal, the greater the confidence embodied in a cognitive attitude toward a proposition, the more is required for the rationality or justification of that attitude.

It might seem that even if propositional faith is not reducible to a kind of belief, it is reducible to a complex of beliefs and attitudes, for example to some degree of belief that *p* and a positive attitude toward *p*'s being the case. It is true that faith implies some degree of positive attitude toward the state of affairs in question; but adding such an attitude to belief is still not sufficient for propositional faith. Far from salvaging a reductionist strategy of analyzing faith in terms of belief, this move shows that in addition to finding an appropriate belief component, the reductionist would have to show this belief to imply an appropriate attitude. I doubt that either of these conditions can be met.

Attitudinal faith differs much from propositional faith. A true attribution of faith *in* God in some sense *presupposes* God's existence, in that—apart from inverted commas uses of the term—we cannot have faith in a non-existent being. But this ontological presupposition permits a person of faith to have associated cognitive attitudes as modest as presuming, rather than unqualifiedly believing, the relevant truths, as where someone with faith in a friend acts on the presumption that the friend will live up to an ideal. Presuming the truth of a proposition does not require holding it in the way characteristic of belief.

Perhaps even *strong* faith *in* God is compatible with cognitive presuppositions as modest as faith *that*, say, God is guiding humanity, where this propositional faith is of a kind incompatible *both* with doubting that tenet and with being sure of it in the way often appropriate to belief. Again, a non-religious analogy may help. Imagine that I cannot locate an old friend who, after many troubled years trying unsuccessfully to complete his Ph.D., has disappeared. Through what I remember of him, I might reject the thought that he has gone crooked and might instead have faith in him as a constructive human being. Still, being quite uncertain about whether he is alive and well, I would have propositional faith, and not belief, that he is leading a constructive life.

Religious *hope*, say the hope that this is a world in which God is sovereign and redemption is forthcoming, is like faith in some ways and different in others. Such hope is compatible with faith in God, and *religious* hope would tend to imply that faith. But this hope does not imply belief that God exists, and it is consistent with, though it does not require, believing that God's existence is likely. Even passionate hope may seem too thin to serve as the foundation of a cognitive outlook appropriate to religious commitment; but a case can surely be made that if such hope is, in a certain way, basic in one's life, it might be a sufficient foundation. I shall not argue for this, but my case for the suitability of faith as a foundation holds, to some degree, for hope. Two qualifications must be made here. First, the positive attitudinal component in hope may be only desire; this contrasts with a positive *evaluative* attitude in the case of faith. One could even hope incontinently, quite against one's better judgment, whereas no precise counterpart difficulty arises for faith.[10] Second, hope is also a cognitively weaker attitude than faith, as indicated by its compatibility with a higher degree of doubt. For these reasons, I discuss hope here only for purposes of comparison.[11]

We come now to one of my central points: the criteria for rational faith and rational hope, construed as cognitive attitudes (since they have truth-valued propositional objects), are less stringent than the criteria for rational belief. I can have rational faith, and certainly a rational hope, that a friend is leading a constructive life, even though I know I have little evidence for this. I might even realize that the evidence I have makes this at best an even bet; but I need not have any probability belief at all. Moreover, although rational faith that something is so requires much stronger grounds than does rational belief that it is *possible*, the former is achievable on the basis of considerably weaker grounds than those needed for rational belief that it *is* the case. Granted, *rational* faith implies that one not have good reasons for believing an obviously incompatible proposition— unless those counterreasons are ultimately defeated[12]—but rational faith still requires a lesser degree of positive grounding than does rational belief. Rational faith is epistemically less at risk, in the sense that it is less easily defeated, than rational belief. This point should not be exaggerated, however: the rationality of faith is still vulnerable to undermining evidence and typically implies an openness to dealing in some way with purported counterevidence. This openness and its often attendant sense of the possibility of error, is in part why having faith is sometimes associated with taking a risk.

## III. Rationality, Justification, and Internal Vs. External Reconciliations of Faith and Reason

It is important here that we take account of some often overlooked differences between justification and rationality. It may well be that the grounding required for rational faith—as opposed to irrational faith—is weaker than that required for justified—as opposed to unjustified—faith. The same holds for rational as opposed to justified belief. Skeptical influences tend to make us work with very high epistemic standards. These standards, in turn, tend to lead us to assimilate rationality to justification; for we become preoccupied not only with defending ourselves, but also with trying to provide grounds that would bring a neutral or even hostile party over to our side. There are, however, crucial differences between rationality and justification.

Rationality is the more global notion. Persons may be rational in an overall way, whereas they can be justified only with respect to something specific, such as a belief or action. We can attribute rationality to people independently of some proposition or issue they are rational *about*; but this does not hold for justification. And while rationality may be focal, since there are, for instance, rational beliefs, the notion of rational belief may well be derivative from that of a rational person: very roughly, rational beliefs—and rational faith— are a kind grounded in a way appropriate to a rational person's holding them, whereas justified beliefs and—I suspect—justified faith must rest on specific grounds of the kind such that, when cognitions based on them are true, they tend to (or at least typically do) constitute knowledge.[13]

There is also a difference between rationality and justification in relation to both sources and their role in discourse. Rationality is more a matter of minimal permissibility, justification more a matter of a kind of ground specifically connected with what we conceive as the basic *truth- conducive* sources, above all perception, introspection, memorial sense, and (a priori) reflection. This contrast may rest partly on the way justification of beliefs is anchored in our *practices* of justification, for example of citing perceptual grounds to justify beliefs about observables, for which there is no precise analogue in the case of rationality. We do rationalize beliefs, chiefly by giving what we take to be grounds for them; but—where this terminology is not simply used as a way of describing justification of beliefs—rationalizing beliefs is quite different from justifying them and indeed does *not* count toward either the epistemic rationality or the justifiedness of the person on whose behalf the rationalization is offered.[14]

The suggested contrast between rationality and justification goes with a distinction between what might be called *internal* and *external* reconciliations of faith (of any kind) and reason. An internal reconciliation shows their compatibility in the life of a religious person; it is thus both concrete, applying to particular *tokens* of cognitions and attitudes, and relative, depending on special features of the agent's experience. An external reconciliation shows that the rational grounds for faith are sufficient to render a rational, theistically neutral person justified (or at least rational) in adopting a theistic view on those grounds (even if not unjustified in suspending judgment on it). It is abstract, applying to *types* of cognitions and attitudes in relation to publicly accessible evidence or grounds, and non-relative, being independent of particular individuals. An internal reconciliation stresses rationality more than justification; an external one stresses justification more than rationality.

As compared with justification, rationality is more readily achieved by a cognitive outlook satisfactory by one's own lights, though some intersubjective standards, such as consistency, are clearly relevant; justification is more a matter of meeting a minimal intersubjective standard, including an appropriate cognitive grounding in the basic truth-conducive sources. If my beliefs are mutually consistent and not obviously disconfirmed in my own experience, this yields a presumption in favor of their rationality, even if I have no grounds that would constitute a justification of them; but it does not yield a presumption, or at least not as strong a presumption, of their justification.[15]

Connected with this, others may criticize me more harshly for having an attitude that is not rational than for having one which is not justified; and if I want to defend myself, I would owe them more if I claim to give a justification of my faith than if I seek only to vindicate its rationality. If we stress faith as a—or perhaps *the*—central cognitive attitude in religion, and rationality rather than justification as the focus of our concern to reconcile reason and religion, the prospects for reconciliation are surely improved.

Let me emphasize, however, that religious commitment of a full-blooded kind is never *just* cognitive, and hence even an eminently successful reconciliation of cognitive religious attitudes with the requirements of reason need not imply that such a reconciliation is possible for a religiously committed life as a whole. We must also remember the distinction between an internal and an external reconciliation of faith and reason: between reconciling them *in* the life of a religious person and, on the other hand, providing theistic beliefs with grounds that would satisfy a (moderate) skeptic, or at least provide a neutral non-theist with justification for adopting such beliefs. The demands of external reconciliation are greater, and my concern now is more with internal reconciliation.

On balance, it seems to me not clear that either natural theology or experientialism—the view that experience can non-inferentially warrant beliefs about God—provides an adequate account of how theistic belief, as opposed to faith, may be justified.[16] But suppose they do. Their success depends on a kind of justification not possessed by, and perhaps not even available to, *all* religious people, including many in the Hebraic-Christian tradition. Consider just the case of experientialism. Even those who open themselves to, for instance, God's speaking to them, cannot always count on his doing so—or, if they believe he often does—on being honestly able to *take* his doing so to be what it is. Divine deliverances may be misheard; deepseated desires may cause us to think we are spoken to when all we hear is our own voice in disguise; and quite apart from this, some religious people have much less spiritually rich lives than others. Experiential justification, then, varies greatly with the course of one's day-to-day life; and in a world of ugly buildings and pockmarked landscapes, of noisy motors and the intrusive sounds of radios and televisions, of crowded cities and competition for power and resources, of disease and famine and war, there are many people who cannot open themselves in the right way. For all that, some of them can have religious faith—indeed, such faith might normally be a precondition for the experiences that may justify theistic belief. How might their faith, and indeed their overall religious commitment, be rational?

## IV. Fiduciary Theistic Attitudes

In view of the difficulties confronting both experientialism and natural theology, it becomes quite important whether we are assessing theistic *belief* or other theistic attitudes. I have already argued that the standards of justification and rationality appropriate to faith and hope are less stringent. One might have strong faith in God and accompanying propositional faith that God is, say, sovereign, without having a belief that this is so, yet also without in any way doubting it. I propose, then, to concentrate on a kind of propositional faith that does not embody belief. For this reason, I call it *non-doxastic faith*. It may imply a disposition to believe its propositional object; it may even be a step on the way to belief; but as such it does not embody belief of its propositional object.

One might object that all non-doxastic faith comes to is weak belief, but I do not think so. The issue is not the strength, but the *kind*, of cognitive attitude in question. It is true that belief can be weak, in the usual sense that it is not marked by a sense of surety and, more important, is not strongly entrenched or highly resistant to dissipation through forgetting, or to being chipped away by time, or crushed by confrontation with counterevidence. Faith can also be weak, but weak (propositional) faith is not equivalent to faith accompanied by something like a low probability estimate of the truth of its object. Weakness in faith is more a matter of a lack of sustaining force in the agent's behavior, emotion, and cognition. As I conceive non-doxastic faith, say faith that God loves us, it is quite compatible with a kind of religious conviction, in the sense of that phrase illustrated by 'people of religious conviction'. Religious conviction as a general cognitive attitude or set of such attitudes is a matter of such things as the strength of one's faith, the depth of one's resolution to try to quell doubts one may have about God's love and goodness, and the extent of one's determination to make one's religious outlook central in one's life.[17] The non-doxastic character of the faith does not in the least prevent it from being strong both in the extent to which it pervades the person's life and in its resistance to being forgotten or given up too readily upon discovery of counterevidence.

Unlike belief, non-doxastic faith does not represent a definitely *accepted propositional object*; but it may far exceed belief in the role it gives to its *projected propositional object*. There is a sense in which the person of non-doxastic (propositional) faith and the person simply believing the same proposition have the same picture of the world; but they differ in their relation to that picture.

Since projection is typically something we do, the projective metaphor might suggest that projection is more nearly under direct voluntary control than acceptance. This may be so; but while faith may owe more, both genetically and in its ongoing life, to the will, *that* volitional difference between faith and belief is not entailed by the distinction I am drawing between projection and acceptance. The distinction is more a matter of inferential, assertive, and behavioral tendencies. All three tendencies are—other things being equal— stronger in the case of belief. It is noteworthy, however, that things are often not equal: one might stake one's life on faith that God will see one through a risky attempt to save a child from injury in a fail, yet refuse to stake it on a belief that, say, a car trip in a severe storm will succeed, even where one's sense of obligation is equal in the two cases. (A similar point holds for probability beliefs, but this analogy does not imply that faith *is* reducible to such a belief.)

Non-doxastic faith is also readily compatible with a kind of theistic *trust*; and at least when this faith is well developed, it implies such an attitude of trust in God, by which I mean in part a sense that God has seen to it, or will see to it, that ultimately things turn out as they should.[18] Wholehearted devotion to God is possible through such faith, even though unqualifiedly held theistic belief is not part of this faith. I take religious conviction to imply a number of cognitive commitments, yet not necessarily theistic beliefs; and an associated non-doxastic faith, while not embodying beliefs of propositions self-evidently entailing God's existence, does embody the kinds of beliefs required to understand one's religion and its implications for one's conduct, for instance beliefs about the divine nature and the implications of one's religion for daily life. If evidentialism is wrong even for religious *faith*, including non-doxastic faith—or if, alternatively, its evidential demands could be met by faith—that would be very significant. This point will be developed in the next section.

## V. The Rationality of Non-Doxastic Propositional Faith

Suppose evidentialists are right in insisting that, for cognitive religious commitments—including non-doxastic fiduciary commitments—justification, and even rationality, requires evidence. Still, the kind and amount of evidence required would differ for faith as opposed to belief. Theists tend to want to refute evidentialism across the board, for all the (normal) cognitive religious attitudes. But the rationality of religious commitment does not require doing so—even if, as I grant for the sake of argument—evidential considerations are insufficient to justify theistic beliefs. Non-doxastic religious *faith* might be warranted, whether experientially or evidentially, even if religious belief is not. Call this non-doxastic interpretation of the rationality of cognitive religious commitment *the non-doxastic approach*. I say 'cognitive' because, while the view stops short of claiming that religious belief is justified, it is cognitive in taking faith—at least faith that (which I have called propositional faith)—to have objects with truth value. It may indeed have the *same* propositional objects as the beliefs which experientialists take to be justified by religious experience, and it typically will have some of them, such as that God is present in certain moments of deep emotion, or on occasions of gratuitous-seeming sustenance in the face of stress. The non-doxastic view thus contrasts with non-cognitivism, which takes religious utterances to be expressive of attitudes and feelings, but not semantically statemental in a sense implying truth or falsity.

The way I have spoken so far may be misleading. It might suggest that the rationality of faith is just a matter of the rationality of its cognitive component. But it is in part because faith has a positive attitudinal component that I have resisted assimilating propositional faith to belief. It must be granted, then, that the rationality of such faith is partly determined by the rationality of that attitude. It may seem obvious that where religious faith is in question, the attitude is rational: how could it not be rational, for instance, to have a positive attitude toward the state of affairs, God's being sovereign, where this attitude by itself implies no existential belief and is as it were hypothetical? Even many atheists could agree that it *would* be good if God were sovereign. Still, given certain kinds of beliefs about what it is for God to be sovereign, it is not self-evidently rational to have a positive attitude here—unless, as is plausibly arguable, the relevant concept of God implies that God not have certain undesirable properties.

The general point that the rationality of faith is not wholly determined by its cognitive component is easier to see with other religious attitudes. Imagine someone who has faith that blasphemers will eternally burn in hell. If the punishment is as disproportionate to the crime as I think, this could fail to be a rational faith even apart from the probability of such retribution. There is no need here to develop an account of rationality for the attitudinal component of propositional faith. It should be clear that one can have a propositional faith regarding a number of theistic states of affairs without having any attitudes that lack rationality in the suggested way. The more pressing—though by no means the only—rationality issue for propositional faith concerns its cognitive component.

There are at least two important objections to this non-doxastic, fiduciary approach which we should consider before proceeding further. One directly challenges the truth of the non-doxastic view. The second questions the adequacy of the view to capture the cognitive aspects of religious commitment.

Here is the direct challenge. If you are justified in having faith, but not in believing, that $p$, then from your perspective not-$p$ is more probable than $p$: not in the sense that you must believe not-$p$—as a theist would surely not—but in the sense that your total relevant evidence justifies you in believing it. Otherwise, you *would* be justified in believing, even if in a tentative spirit, that $p$ is true. But if, from your perspective, not-$p$ is more probable than $p$, you are *not* justified in believing $p$, or even in having faith that $p$. I deny the premise: we are talking about justification, not probability, and justification for faith that, say, God loves us, implies no particular range of probabilities. Moreover, insofar as justification in the relevant sense may imply a probability, it would be one *greater* than .50; hence, unwillingness to assign such a probability to a theistic proposition would not imply that one should assign the proposition a probability *lower* than .50. In any case, the kind of justification we are considering is not only such as to make it rationally permissible to believe; it is also the sort of justification which, when possessed by a true belief, normally renders it knowledge. If this sort of justification is understandable in terms of probability at all, it is still not clear how to assign degrees of probability in the special case of theistic beliefs. We cannot play dice with the universe in that way. Similar points hold for rationality, to which the objection may be applied in a parallel fashion, but there is no need to treat rationality separately here.

The second objection is to the effect that unless faith *is* doxastic, it is not strong enough to bear the religious weight it must carry on the non-doxastic approach. If justified theistic faith is possible even where justified belief of the same proposition is not, the non-doxastic view may fail to do justice to religious commitment. How, it may be asked, can I center my life on a view not even really *believed*? The question is worrisome. But notice two points. First, religious *behavior* can flow from faith just as it can from belief: a cognitively projected conception of the world can structure one's behavior in essentially the same way that a definitely believed conception can.

This is in part because—and here is the second point by way of reply—a whole dimension of conviction is possible without beliefs of existential propositions about God: one can, for instance, grant that one does not know or believe that God exists, and that only one's faith is justified, without lacking a sense of surety, even a kind of certitude, *about* God, say about God's sovereignty over life and death. One form this sense could take is a certitude regarding the appropriateness of conceiving human life under the aspect of divine governance. This conception of life does not imply thinking that one perceives God's governance; having the conception is something like feeling certain of the appropriateness of perceiving much of what one does perceive *as* manifesting that governance. The existential propositions about God are objects of rational faith and not of belief; but normative propositions about God and many concerning how life should be lived in a world under God are objects of stronger cognitive attitudes. Even if one's theistic picture of the world is expressed by a fiduciary projection, and not by a definitely accepted set of propositions, one may unqualifiedly and rationally believe that the world so conceived, and human life conducted in accord with that conception, are good.

It might seem that this view substitutes a certainty that theism is *probably* true for a conviction that it *is* true. That is not so (though the suggested view is interesting in itself). While this probability belief is consistent with non-doxastic faith, having the belief is not what that faith comes to, nor does non-doxastic faith even imply a probability belief of this kind. A person who does not have a definite belief that God exists might find it inappropriate to say, and might neither believe nor disbelieve, that probably God exists. Moreover, non-doxastic faith can carry a conviction that the world is to be viewed as God's domain; and it can imply a deep, perhaps even unshakable, commitment to the hope that this is so, without the subject's having any probability beliefs on the matter. It is indeed possible to be religious without ever forming probability beliefs about such ultimate matters. To some people it may even seem irreverent or intellectually misguided to form them. Certainly their formation is not essential to a religious outlook.

A third reply deserves special emphasis. I begin with a concession. Because it is natural to *say*, publicly as well as privately, what one religiously holds, and because we typically do believe—and often think we *know*—what we put forward as our *stance* on a major matter, it is odd, even disconcerting, to think of religious views—or at least those central in a person's religious commitment—as not unqualifiedly believed. But this discomfort is misplaced. Religious affirmation must not be assimilated to ordinary, or even scientific, factual assertion. If there is a good scientific analogue, it is probably *theoretical* assertion, which also does not entail belief. The non-doxastic view of faith, then, does not imply that those for whom it is the primary cognitive religious attitude must abstain from publicly expressing their faith, or express it in a half-hearted or even tentative spirit. Moreover, avowal need not rest on evidence or proof in order to be rational. And if embracing a view as central in one's life may be warranted even apart from evidence sufficient to justify belief that it is true, then a rational person need not forbear from publicly affirming it.

Once again, we must prevent skepticism from biasing our conception of rationality. Just as, if we talk about what knowledge is while skepticism preoccupies us—or even lies in our peripheral vision—we tend to set our standards too high, or to require of ourselves a capacity to *show* that we know, as a condition of knowing itself, so also when we talk about the rationality of our religious outlook with the *assertive paradigm* in the background, we tend both to set our standard of rationality high and to require, as a condition for rationally holding our position, the ability to justify it to an uncommitted outsider. Even perceptual justification will not stand this second-order demand and can be distorted by the self-conscious standard we may adopt in the attempt to light our way out of the skeptical shadows. The rationality of religious belief should be analogously understood.

### VI. Propositional Faith, Attitudinal Faith, and Knowledge of God

My main focus so far has been propositional faith. But clearly where it is rational to have certain kinds of propositional faith, for instance that God is sovereign, it is rational to describe oneself as having faith *in* God. This is not an ontological point; granting that truly ascribing attitudinal faith to someone implies the existence of its object, sincerely expressing such faith in the first person does not imply it.

None of these points entails that theistic belief is *inappropriate* as a part of religious commitment. Indeed, doubtless there is, in most cases, at least, a kind of courage that is lacking in a religious person who cannot hold any theistic belief. My view acknowledges all this; the point here is simply that belief that *p* is not required for faith that *p* and is subject to different and more stringent criteria of rationality. A kind of faith that does not entail belief is a more appropriate attitude for many of those who are concerned with the rationality of their religious outlook. Above all, the possibility of such faith sets a different baseline for religious rationality (in the cognitive domain) than would be appropriate if theistic belief were a necessary condition of religious commitment.

If there is one way in which this fiduciary approach attenuates the cognitive aspect of religious commitment, there is also a respect in which it heightens the volitional dimension. If you take your grounds for a view to be conclusive, you normally have no choice but to accept it; if, on the other hand, you embrace a faith (partly) on the basis of indications you believe significant but far from conclusive, you may rationally choose to take some cognitive risk, hoping for further confirmation and allowing the faith to nurture the hope, while the hope—leading to an openminded search—may reinforce the faith. In this sense, faith that is aware of its own risks, and is nurtured by a steadfast religious devotion, can express a kind of religious commitment not possible for those to whom religious truths are obvious. Singlemindedness can be in tension with wholeheartedness. One can choose, and retain, one's religious commitment more freely when its rational grounds are less obvious and do not seem evidentially compelling.[19]

None of this implies that there cannot be directly justified or, more modestly, directly rational, religious beliefs. I leave this possibility open. It is at best very difficult to establish absolute restrictions on what sorts of beliefs can be directly justified. This holds even if the only way beliefs *can* be directly justified is by virtue of their grounding in the basic sources of justification. In any case, I have stressed that faith, though it is, by virtue of its propositional objects, cognitive, need not be, by virtue of entailing belief, doxastic; and even if there are few if any experientially justified theistic beliefs, there may yet be experientially justified religious faith.

Here it is instructive to make a brief comparison between the kind of faith I have been describing and some aspects of faith as understood by Aquinas.[20] It might seem that the two conceptions have little in common. It certainly appears that faith as Aquinas conceived it is doxastic. He speaks, for instance, of faith in relation to believing as if the former implied the latter: "'to believe' is the act of the intellect as it assents to the divine truth at the command of the will as moved by God through grace. . . The act of faith can therefore be meritorious" (*Secundum Secundae*, Question 2, Article Nine). Moreover, he at least appears to speak not only of beliefs held in faith but also of great confidence as appropriate to them. In addition, he takes the propositional objects of faith to be capable of certainty. This suggests (though it does not entail) that the attitude of faith may embody knowledge of its propositional objects, whether one knows one has this knowledge or not. He says, however, something rather different on this point: that "Faith is a mean between knowledge and opinion" (*Secundum Secundae*, Question 2). This suggests that faith (or at least the kind in question in the passage) is never a case of knowledge, and the point seems compatible with the possibility of propositional faith which does not embody belief.

There are, on the other hand, two definite points of similarity between Aquinas's view and the one I am developing. On both views, the will plays an important role. On his view, to be sure, it is pervasively involved in generating and sustaining faith in a way that it need not—though it certainly may—do on the non-doxastic approach. He says, "The assent of one who knows scientifically does not depend on his free will, since the cogency of demonstration compels him to give it. Hence in science, assent is not meritorious . . . In faith, on the other hand, both assent and practice depend on the free will" (*Secundum Secundae*, Question 2, Article Nine). Both assent and practice may also depend on the will in my view, though I do not stress this in the same way or for the same reasons. The second similarity concerns the relation between faith and certainty. Nothing I have said precludes the propositional object of faith, such as that God loves us, from *being certain*, in itself, as I think it is on Aquinas's view; all I have ruled out is that *one* be psychologically certain of it, since that would entail belief. An object of my faith (or belief) can *be* certain—say because it is either self-evident or can be decisively shown by readily accessible evidence—even if I am not certain *of* it.

Compare this second similarity with Aquinas's point that while "he who believes has a sufficient reason for believing. . . [and] Hence he does not believe lightly. . . he does not have a reason such as would suffice for scientific knowledge. Thus, the character of merit is not taken away" (*Secundum Secundae*, Question 2, Article Nine). This is certainly consistent with faith's embodying psychological certainty, but it is also consistent with a person of faith having a cognitive attitude that does not. Now suppose that, appropriately to the meritorious character of faith, whatever psychological certainty there is in it comes from the contribution of the will rather than from demonstration. We might compare that certainty to the strength of faith in the sense of its resistance to erosion and degree of influence on the subject's life *rather* than the doxastic confidence level of its cognitive component; and this kind of certainty seems consistent with non-doxastic faith. I do not claim that Aquinas had any such comparison in mind, but it is not inappropriate to some major elements in his view.[21]

Regarding the connection between faith and knowledge, *if* knowledge implies only a weak degree of cognition that falls short of belief, as opposed to implying an unqualified belief of the relevant proposition, which I think Aquinas required for faith, then my view even allows faith and knowledge to be compatible. Consider an unconfident but well prepared school child. The child can perhaps be said to know that the answer to a problem is A, while barely having enough cognitive inclination to believe this to write that answer down. Similarly, one might have grounds adequate for knowledge of a religious proposition, but take these grounds to be weaker than they are, and hold the proposition in faith, as opposed to believing it on the basis of the relevant evidence. If this can count as a kind of knowledge, then non-doxastic propositional faith that something is true is compatible with knowing its truth.

To be sure, while Aquinas apparently took faith to be compatible with the kind of psychological certainty about God consonant with his five ways, non-doxastic faith does not permit such certainty. But the faithful are surely not supposed to *need* the proofs in order to have faith; and, as we have seen, their faith is meritorious only if it is not grounded in a demonstration. For Aquinas, the proofs may best be seen as (among other things) confirmatory of faith and illustrative of God's relation to nature. They may evidentially warrant certainty, but should not be the grounds of fiduciary conviction. There may still be a kind of exclusion of psychological certainty required by the non-doxastic view and not by a Thomistic one, but if so it is compatible not only with the propositional objects of that faith having epistemic certainty (being certain), but with one's seeking to transform one's faith into the attitude of psychological certainty which is possible through what one sees as decisive grounds, whether demonstrative or experiential.

Non-doxastic faith is also compatible with "The assurance of things hoped for, the conviction of things not seen" (Hebrews 11:1), given two assumptions: that the assurance in question is a matter of a sense of surety, and conviction is not taken to imply belief, as opposed to a non-doxastic kind of positive expectation. The second assumption is perhaps not plausible, and it may be that the faith referred to in that text must be seen as doxastic. But it must at least be granted that the absence of fear which, in the New Testament and elsewhere, is often taken to be central to religious faith, does not require belief as opposed to the fiduciary attitude I have sketched as central in non-doxastic faith. Fear for one's future, for example, can be incompatible with non-doxastic faith that God is protecting one—at least where that faith is strong—even apart from one's believing that the protection will be given. The conquest of fear in the former case may take more participation by the will; but that conquest is possible without certainty and even without belief. It is, to be sure, easy not to fear an outcome one is certain will not materialize, and, other things being equal, less difficult where one believes this than where one has non-doxastic faith that it will not. But that faith, in calling as it does for a higher degree of voluntary participation, may be even more appropriate to a life of religious commitment than a more readily comforting doxastic counterpart.

## VII. Rationality and Religious Conduct: The Behavioral Dimension of Religious Commitment

Before closing, I want to return to the point that much of religious commitment is not cognitive in any narrow sense: while beliefs, or non-doxastic fiduciary cognitive attitudes, may in some way underlie it, it consists in dispositions to conduct oneself in a certain way, in and outside one's specifically religious life. Consider examples from two representative domains, the moral and the aesthetic.

Suppose my religious faith is in a God whom I take to command altruism and justice. Can faith, if itself justified and sufficiently rich in cognitive content, justify acting accordingly? I think that under certain conditions it can, though to be sure one's moral actions so motivated would, other things equal, be more extensively justified if, wherever one's justification extends only to non-doxastic faith, one had sufficient warrant for belief.

There is another point of the first importance: a rational person normally has *moral* grounds for ethical conduct, grounds that are evidentially (justificationally) independent of theistic commitments. Usually, these are themselves *sufficient* to warrant the relevant moral acts, in this case the altruistic and just actions. Indeed, even if this justificational overdetermination did not hold, rational persons *should* make some effort to find all the available major justifying grounds for important kinds of conduct they engage in. This not only yields better justified conduct; it helps one both to understand one's obligations and to fulfill them. It clarifies precisely what one should on balance do; it often provides a sense of why one should do it; and it strengthens one's motivation to do it.

Similar points hold in the aesthetic case. A cathedral built as a beautiful monument to God can also be so constructed as to serve secular needs sufficiently pressing to justify such a construction in their own right; and a rational builder will certainly try to make it safe enough to avoid crushing the huddled families who will take shelter there during storms. To be sure, the demands of beauty and utility can conflict, and a rational religious person can then face agonizing conflicts. But faith is no worse off than belief in such conflicts. Indeed, one lesson of history is that if one does not regard one's theistic beliefs and other religious beliefs as infallible or unassailably justified, one has a better chance of reconciling them with secular reasons that tend in a different direction.

If there is no antidote to skepticism about cognitive religious attitudes, the sting of that skepticism is greatly relieved when we grasp how much secular justification can be brought to bear in supporting the same non-religious attitudes and non-religious behavior that are among the central manifestations of much religious commitment: love of one's neighbor, charity towards the poor, the quest for world peace. This holds even if, psychologically, the agents in question are motivated by religious convictions more than by the secular—for instance, the moral—considerations that support their conduct.[22] One thing that should not escape us here is the coherence between behavioral requirements implicit in certain religious commitments and those implicit in a sound secular moral theory.

Arguably, this coherence provides some confirmation of the truth of, or at least the reasonableness of living in accord with, the underlying premises of the religious commitments. So far as there is independent confirmation of those premises, this coherence might also provide some confirmation of the secular moral theory.

## Conclusion

I have stressed the cognitive side of religious commitment, and I have argued that there is a conception of faith which is both psychologically strong enough to enable it to play a central part in the cognitive dimension of religious commitment and evidentially modest enough to be rational on the basis of substantially less grounding than is required for the rationality of belief with the same content. But faith alone, particularly propositional faith, does not exhaust religious commitment. A true religious commitment is both wide and deep. It is a commitment of the heart and not just the head, of a lifetime and not just its sabbaths. It affects moral and interpersonal conduct, as well as attitudes toward the universe and toward human existence within it. The rationality of this commitment does not reduce to that of religious belief or of any other religious attitude, alone.

Even if a religious commitment is central in one's life, it need not conflict with one's commitments as a rational agent simpliciter, and secular considerations may cooperate with religious ones in supporting moral and other conduct we justly regard as rational. The cooperation may be psychological, by virtue of religious and secular sources each providing motivation for certain conduct, as well as evidential, by way of each supplying justificatory grounds for certain behavior and attitudes. It is not clear to what extent experience, or arguments, can justify, or at least render rational, one's holding religious beliefs; but there are surely some lives in which the character of experience, taken together with supporting intellectual elements, justifies, or renders rational, at least a degree of theistic faith. I doubt that an account of rational religious commitment should demand more, natural though it is to impose stricter standards given the importance of the life commitments that are at stake.

Rational religious commitment lies somewhere between the safety of unshakable belief in the things that bombard the five senses, and headlong confidence in what we passionately wish to be true, between a merely aesthetic participation in religious practices and a dogmatic doctrinal codification, between apathy and conformism, between skepticism and credulity. Rational religious commitment may be elusive; it differs from one person to another; and, even in a single life, it may change much over time, for better or for worse. But if our notion of rationality is not too narrow, if our sense of the interconnection between the religious and the secular is sufficiently keen, and if we do not try to justify needlessly strong cognitive attitudes, we may well be able to construct an adequate theory of rational religious commitment and thereby reconcile faith and reason.[23]

## Notes

1. It is noteworthy that Robert M. Adams begins an excellent essay on faith with puzzlement about how faith can be regarded as a virtue given that "(1) Belief and unbelief seem to be mainly involuntary states, and it is thought that the involuntary cannot be ethically praised or blamed. (2) If belief is to be praised at all, we are accustomed to think that its praiseworthiness depends on its rationality, but the virtuousness of faith for Christians seems to be based on its correctness and independent of the strength of the evidence for it." See Adams (1987), p. 9. (The paper was first published in *Faith and Philosophy* 1 1984). While in the same essay he takes up the element of trust often thought to belong to faith, he is here speaking of faith as a kind of belief, and indeed elsewhere says that "Kierkegaard is surely right in placing religious faith in the category of beliefs for which 'probably' is not enough." See "The Leap of Faith" (1987), p. 45. I shall speak later to this doxastic conception of faith; and while I cannot take up the two problems Adams raises concerning faith as a virtue, I hope that the view I propose leaves us in a good position to deal with them.
2. Process theologians, such as Charles Hartshorne, deny that God is omnipotent in the traditional sense. For a sympathetic theological treatment of some of the pertinent issues which engages Hartshorne's views at various points, see Tracy (1975), esp. ch. 8. Cp. James M. Gustafson's (1981) conception of God as a power that bears down upon us; the conception does not seem meant to imply omnipotence (if indeed it is compatible with agency, which is plausibly thought to be implicit in omnipotence).
3. For a short statement of the picture preference view of religious avowal, see Anthony Flew's contribution to the Symposium on Theology and Falsification in Flew and MacIntyre (1960). R. M. Hare offers a different non-cognitivist view in the same place. John Hick's reply to Flew, in (1960) is interesting in itself and has generated much discussion.

4. The importance of hope as a religious attitude is developed by Muyskens 1979) and discussed in detail by Pojman (1986). Pojman also argues cogently for the importance of other religious attitudes and offers a conception of religious faith as hope. See esp. ch. XVI. Cp. Solomon's treatment of hope as faith: "Hope is faith uncertain, a passive anticipation of a positive fortune, beyond one's own control but always possible" (1976), p. 327.

5. For an indication of the great diversity of uses of 'faith' in theology, see Berkhof (1939), pp. 500-507. Much of relevance is also contained in Allen (1968), Reeder (1988), Wainwright (1988), and, especially, Penelhum (1989).

6. I hold that believing is not equivalent to believing true, and that, especially in discussions with someone whom one finds credible, one can accept something as true and not believe it. Much more could be said about belief, but nothing I say should turn on aspects of the notion left unresolved here. When I speak of taking as true, I do not mean having the semantic belief that the proposition is true, but something like treating the proposition as one does what one believes to be true, for instance as a basis of inference.

7. I introduced and defended this distinction in Audi (1982). Cf. Lycan's treatment of the distinction in (1988) and Moser's use of it in (1988).

8. Cf. L. J. Cohen's view that "Faith (in the everyday sense) that God exists is an example of belief, not acceptance," where "to accept that *p* is to have or adopt a policy of claiming positing or postulating that *p*..." and "Belief that *p* on the other hand, is a disposition to feel it true that *p*, whether or not one goes along with the proposition as a premise." See (1989), p. 386. I reject the suggested assimilation of propositional faith to belief, but it seems to me that such faith *is* something like what Cohen (mistakenly, I think) says belief is. Runzo quite explicitly treats faith *that* as "basically equivalent to the cognitive state of belief" (1990), p. 44, though on other points his treatment of the distinction between propositional and attitudinal faith is consistent with my construal of it.

9. I am distinguishing between separate beliefs of contradictories and beliefs of a contradiction. The case against the possibility of the former is less strong than that against the possibility of the latter, but I leave its possibility open. In Audi (1982b) I discuss why both are problematic. Perhaps we should, for similar reasons, leave open the possibility of having faith that *p* even while disbelieving it. It may be, however, that faith is *dominant* in a way belief is not, so that genuine faith that *p* rules out the kind of negative attitude toward *p* implicit in disbelieving it.

10. One could, to be sure, have faith toward which one has an attitude of disapproval, and certainly faith can be irrational. But that does not nullify the point that faith embodies a positive attitude, and hence, even if—say because the person justifiedly disapproves of it—it is inappropriate to its *subject*, it is not inappropriate to its *object*, provided its positive or negative quality suitably matches that object.

11. Compare Pojman's denial that "belief-in statements entail belief-that statements" and his suggestion that "if belief-in, or trusting, can be

analyzed in terms of commitment to a course of action or a disposition to act, then it seems that we do not need to believe-that $x$ exists in order to believe-in or deeply hope in the existence of $x$" (1986), p. 224. I agree with much of what Pojman says on this topic, but am inclined to take belief in God to entail, by virtue of presupposing, a cognitive commitment to God's existence. Since I do not take every kind of religious trust to entail this (such as trust regarding the occurrence of future states of affairs as prayed for), I would not treat belief in God as equivalent to religious trust (though the former implies the latter), but I agree with Pojman that, like hope, such trust does not entail what I call flat-out belief that God exists (or beliefs self-evidently entailing this, such as that God loves us). Granted, taken literally, trusting God, like trusting any being, entails the existence of the object of trust; I am assuming that there is a kind of religious trust that is not relational in this way. It is an attitude of trust regarding states of affairs associated with God, and could be internal to the faithful person.

12. I say "ultimately" because there can be an indefinitely long sequence of defeaters and defeaters of the defeaters, and what matters is the end result: an even number leaves the original justification intact.

13. They only *tend* to create knowledge because there are cases in which the justification, whatever its degree, is the wrong kind to render a true belief knowledge. For instance, even if I justifiedly and truly believe my ticket will loose a sweepstakes with a million coupons and one winner, I get no closer to knowledge if the number of coupons increases, even though my belief gains proportionately in probability.

14. In Audi (1988) I argue for the integration of the property of justifiedness with the practice of justification; and in (1986) I compare and contrast rationalization and justification. The former term, so far as it is non-pejorative, applies mainly to belief *types*; thus, even if I give a good rationalization for my instantiating the *type, believing that p*, I do not necessarily show that my *token* of that type, my *belief that p*, is rational. It may, e.g., be based on superstition, which is just the sort of reason why I want to rationalize it.

15. Perhaps we should also say 'not obviously inconsistent'; the general point is that where either inconsistency of disconfirming evidence is such that a rational person cannot be expected to notice it, its existence need not count against the rationality of the person in question. On the general issue cf. Wolterstorff (1983). On p. 163 he says, "A person is rationally justified in believing a certain proposition which he does believe unless he has adequate reason to cease from believing it. Our beliefs are rational unless we have reason for refraining..." He is not here distinguishing justification and rationality, but what he says about rational belief is similar to, though considerably stronger than, what I am suggesting.

16. For an indication of some of the problems with the experientialism approach see (Audi, 1986a). That paper does not discuss natural theology; but the difficulties besetting the traditional arguments for the existence of God are well known, and while I do not assume that they have no force I do take it to be important that the rationality of cognitive religious

commitment not be taken to depend on them, or at least on them alone.

17. Cp. Pojman's statement that "to believe-in God implies only that one regards such a being as possibly existing and that one is committed to live *as if* such a being does exist" (1986), p. 227). My conception is stronger in *at least* one way: the cognitive commitment to possibility is too weak (though Pojman does not have in mind here *mere* logical possibility). Depending on what it is to live as if God exists, my view may be stronger in a second way; for instance, one's reasons for religiously motivated action will not come from a kind of hypothetical commitment, but from a largely unconditional (though non-doxastic) commitment to one's religious view of the world. Compare living as if a missing spouse is alive: there are many ways to unpack this, and I am stressing that neither the merely behavioral interpretation (involving not marrying again), nor the interpretation with too weak a cognitive commitment (say, merely believing it possible that one's spouse is alive), nor the calculative (Pascalian) reading (one will do better, in case of her return, if one can believe her return is forthcoming), is adequate to the view I am developing (if indeed any reductive interpretation is).

18. Two points are in order here. I say 'ultimately' because, owing to evils such as those due to abuses of human freedom, things may not work out in the short run. Secondly, I do not speak of *trusting God* because I take this relationally, and so as obviously entailing God's existence.

19. This is not meant to imply that by choice one can directly determine what one will believe. But one can choose how one will lead the religious dimensions of one's life, and one can at least indirectly influence the attitudes one will take and, by these and other routes, indirectly influence one's beliefs.

20. Here I follow the *Summa Theologica*. For valuable discussion of Aquinas on faith see Eleonore Stump (forthcoming).

21. Compare the point stressed in Stump (forthcoming) that for Aquinas the most important point of faith is not its influence on the intellect but its effects on the will. Granted that this may imply that the intellect has to be guided by definite propositions, it seems to leave open much concerning the type and strength of the cognitive attitudes one must have towards those propositions.

22. I take it that a consideration justifies an action or propositional attitude only if the action or attitude is at least in part causally sustained or produced by it, but adequate justification may be derived from a consideration even if it is not a *main* reason for what it justifies. For discussion of a variety of cases of multiple reasons for an action and their connection with justification see my (1986a) and (1986c).

23. This paper grew out of two sources: a lecture on the wider topic of Rationality and Religious Commitment, delivered at the University of Chicago Divinity School, and a (later) paper on that same topic given at Wake Forest University's James Montgomery Hester Symposium on Faith, Reason, and Skepticism in 1989. I learned much on those occasions from the critical comments of colleagues. An earlier version of this essay benefitted from discussions at Georgetown University and, on other

occasions, with William Alston, Roger Ebertz, Hugh McCann, David Reiter, Lad Sessions, and Eleonore Stump.

**References**

Adams, Robert M.: 1987, "The Virtue of Faith," in his *The Virtue of Faith*, New York, Oxford University Press.

Allen, Diogenes: 1968, *The Reasonableness of Faith*, Washington and Cleveland, Corpus Books.

Audi, Robert: 1982a, "Believing and Affirming," *Mind* XCI.

Audi, Robert: 1982b, "Self-Deception, Action, and Will," *Erkenntnis* 18.

Audi, Robert: 1986a, "Acting for Reasons," *The Philosophical Review* XCV.

Audi, Robert: 1986b, "Direct Justification, Evidential Dependence, and Theistic Belief," in Robert Audi and William J. Wainwright, eds., *Rationality, Religious Belief, and Moral Commitment*, Cornell University Press, Ithaca and London.

Audi, Robert: 1986c, "Rationalization and Rationality," *Synthese* 65.

Audi, Robert: 1988, "Justification, Truth, and Reliability," *Philosophy and Phenomenological Research* XlIX.

Berkhof, L.: 1939, *Systematic Theology*, Grand Rapids, William B. Erdmans.

Cohen, L. J.: 1989, "Belief and Acceptance," *Mind* XCVIII.

Flew, Anthony and Alasdair MacIntyre, eds.: 1955, *New Essays in Philosophical Theology*, London, SCM Press.

Gustafson, James, M.: 1981, *Ethics from a Theocentric Perspective*, Vol. One, Chicago, The University of Chicago Press.

Hick, John: 1960, "Theology and Verification," *Theology Today*.

Lycan, William: 1988, *Judgement and Justification*, Cambridge and New York, Cambridge University Press.

Moser, Paul K.: 1988, *Knowledge and Evidence*, Cambridge and New York, Cambridge University Press, 1988.

Muyskens, James: 1979, *The Sufficiency of Hope*, Philadelphia, Temple University Press.

Penelhum, Terence (ed.): 1989, *Faith*, New York, Macmillan.

Pojman, Louis, P. :1986, *Religious Belief and the Will*, London and New York, Routledge and Kegan Paul.

Reeder, John P., Jr.: 1988, *Source, Sanction, and Salvation*, Englewood Cliffs, Prentice-Hall.

Runzo, Joseph: 1990. "World-Views and the Epistemic Foundations of Theism, *Religious Studies* 25.

Solomon, Robert C.: 1976, *The Passions*, New York, Doubleday.

Stump Eleonore: forthcoming, "Aquinas on Faith and Goodness."

Tracy, David: 1975, *Blessed Rage for Order*, Minneapolis, The Winston Seabury Press.

Wainwright, William J.: 1988, *Philosophy of Religion*, Belmont, California, Wadsworth Publishing Co.

Wolterstorff, Nicholas: 1983, "Can Belief in God Be Rational If It Has No Foundations," in Alvin Plantinga and Nicholas Wolterstorff, eds., *Faith and Rationality*, Notre Dame, University of Notre Dame Press.

Philosophical Perspectives, 5, Philosophy of Religion, 1991

# PRAGMATISM VERSUS MYSTICISM:
# THE DIVIDED SELF OF WILLIAM JAMES

## Richard M. Gale
## University of Pittsburgh

The best way to characterize the philosophy of William James is to say that it is basically deeply rooted in the blues. It is the soulful expression of someone who has "paid his dues;" someone who, like old wagonwheels, has "been through it all;" and, like good blues, the aim of his philosophy is therapeutic. While its immediate aim is to keep him sane and non-suicidal—"to help him make it through the night"—its larger one is to help him find his way to physical and spiritual health. In this respect he is very much in the Nietzschean mold, as is Wittgenstein also in my opinion. (The deep difference between James and Dewey is that Dewey couldn't sing the blues if his life depended on it.)

James's theme song is "Many Selves Blues." Part of the problem is that James is astonishingly complex and multi-faceted. He has a passion to be all things, to feel and understand everything. (Sometimes I think he succeeded!) Within him are all these different selves, each hungering after full actualization, but, having only finite time and resources, some of them must be denied or slighted. This gives rise to the "Actualization Blues," since every actualization denies an infinite number of possibilities that could have occurred in its place. (Maybe this was the deep cause of his notorious impatience and restlessness, which might explain his continual, almost obsessional, use of the "open doors" and "lowering of the dam" metaphors.) But far more serious is that the competing demands of these different selves are due to a serious rift within the man himself, this inspiring "Divided Self Blues." Thanks to Ralph Barton Perry's masterpiece,

242 / Richard M. Gale

*The Thought and Character of William James* (hereafter TC), it has become the "official" view that James's divided self involves a conflict between his scientific and religious-moral aspirations, the former involving his need to be "tough-minded" and the latter to be "tender-minded."[1] Pragmatism is seen as James's way of healing this breach within his divided self by showing that there is a method for determining both meaning and truth that these opposing selves share in common, thereby allowing him to actualize both of these selves with a clear conscience. For, if one of them is legitimate, so is the other; and, since no one wants to deny the legitimacy of science, religion and morality ride the coat tails of science to respectability, being subject to "all of the rights and privileges thereunto appertaining." Pragmatism, thereby, serves as the ultimate mediator or reconciler but, as we shall see, not synthesizer between his tough- and tender-minded selves.

I think this official account is fine as far as it goes, but this paper will try to show that it doesn't go far enough in unearthing the deepest source of James's "Divided Self Blues." It is not the science versus religion-morality conflict that is fundamental but a conflict that breaks out on an even deeper level within his religious aspirations themselves. There is a morbid side to James's nature, a *really* morbid side, that "can't get no satisfaction" in the sort of melioristic religion that pragmatism legitimates. For his sick self, pragmatism is not a methodologically neutral reconciler but an opponent to be conquered, being the expression of his tough-minded, promethean self. What this sick self needs to help it make it through the night is a mystical type religion that secures an absolute safety and peace that the promethean religion of meliorism can never supply. Thus, at the deepest level of James's divided self is the conflict between the promethean pragmatist and the mystic. I will attempt to support this novel view of James through a critical exposition of the connection between his pragmatism and philosophy of religion. I apologize for the shoddiness of my big picture effort, my excuse being that this topic requires (and eventually will receive) book-length treatment of at least two volumes. It will be shown that James's philosophy up until the late 1890's is almost exclusively promethean, being based on his brand of "humanistic" pragmatism, and that his later writings tend, though not without important exceptions, for James never succeeded in becoming a unified self, to give voice to a competing anti-promethean type of mysticism of the sort that will assuage his deep cosmic and personal anxieties by giving him absolute assurance that higher spiritual powers reign supreme and thus all is well.

## The Promethean Pragmatist

James characterizes his pragmatism as the doctrine that "the trail of the human serpent is...over everything," meaning that human interests and endeavors are omnipresent, coloring not only the way in which we depict reality but even the very being of this reality.[2] Everything—existence, truth, meaning, value, personal identity, the distinction between the mental and the physical, etc.—is relative to and, in part, created by human beings. He sometimes calls his pragmatism a version of Schiller's humanism according to which, as James quotes Schiller, "the world...is what we make of it" (P 117).[3] While James recognizes a given, he denies that there is any absolute, non-context relative distinction between what we contribute and what is presented. Our assignment of stars to different constellations involves a distinction between a perceptually given, the stars, and our contribution in organizing them into constellations. But in another context, that something qualifies as a star will involve an act of selection and construction on our part (which, I assume is what the lecherous producer had in mind when he promised to make her a star), in ways analogous to that in which we construct different axiomatic systems in mathematics. Thus, within any given context, there is a distinction between the given and what we do with it, but it is not an absolute distinction.[4] The trail of the human serpent doctrine is highly promethean in that it assigns to men the task of making the big buzzing blooming confusion into an articulate world that can be used to satisfy their deepest needs and longings.

This promethean theme informs James's philosophy from the very outset, long before he had explicitly formulated his pragmatic theory of meaning and truth. As Bruce Wilshire has properly stressed in his introduction to his anthology, *The Essential Writings of William James*, this theme clearly informs his early (1878) "Remarks on Spencer's Definition of Mind as Correspondence" (in EP).

> Mental interests, hypotheses, postulates, so far as they are bases for human action—action which to a great extent transforms the world—help to *make* the truth which they declare. In other words, there belongs to mind, from its birth upward, a spontaneity, a vote. It is in the game, and not a mere looker-on; and its judgments of

> the *should-be*, its ideals, cannot be peeled off from the body of the
> cognitandum as if they were excrescences, or meant, at most,
> survival. (21)

This human serpent doctrine, which fits James's need to believe in a world of unfolding novelties that provide a suitable arena for leading the morally strenuous life, is supported by his Darwinian-based view of the nature of consciousness which runs throughout his 1890 *Principles of Psychology* (hereafter PP). Consciousness is an instrument whose purpose is to help an organism come into the right sort of working relationships with its environment (PP 21). All of our classificatory systems, without exception, employ concepts that we have forged for the satisfaction of our purposes. Consciousness not only is selective but also impulsive (even explosive we are told in its chapter on "The Will" among the Celtic and Latin races, which mysteriously turns into the Celtic and Slavic races in the *Briefer Course* version published two years later[5]). James's very criterion for demarcating the mental is based on the selection of means for the realization of an end: "the pursuance of future ends and the choice of means for their attainment are thus the mark and criterion of the presence of mentality in a phenomenon" (PP 21).

The view of consciousness as an instrument of selection and emphasis, a fighter for ends, supports a promethean type view of man as creator at many places in PP. The most striking promethean consequence is in the chapter on "The Perception of Reality," where he develops the highly revisionary doctrine, though he is not aware that it is, that nothing exists (is real) simpliciter or absolutely (shades of David Lewis) but only in a person-relative manner. Everything is of some type, e.g. sensible object, theoretical entity, imaginary being, etc. and thus exists *qua* that type of being. "For, in the strict and ultimate sense of the word existence, everything which can be thought of at all exists as *some* sort of object..." (PP 923). (Notice the use of the tell-tale "in the strict and ultimate sense," which indicates that a disguised linguistic innovation is in the offing.) Each object, in addition to existing *qua* object of a certain kind, also inhabits a world of other objects of the same kind. It appears that for every one of James's many selves there is a corresponding world to which its interests and concerns are directed (See PP 295 for an enumeration of some of his many selves and the manner in which they conflict—the "Actualization Blues"). For the reader absorbed in *Ivanhoe*, the world of that novel is the real world, for the ardent platonist it is the world of abstract entities, and so on.

James begins by asking this question about the psychological causes of existential beliefs: "Under what circumstances do we think things real?" (PP 917), to which his answer is that we are caused to believe in the reality of that which has a dominant interest for us at that time. Immediately upon advancing this account of the psychological causes of an existential-belief, he says: "*reality means simply relation to our emotional and active life.* This is the only sense which the word ever has in the mouths of practical men" (PP 924). This is the semantic conclusion that he draws from his psychological account, judging by his use of "means." And he then draws the further ontological conclusion that "whatever excites and stimulates our interest is real." In other words, since it is a person's interests or purposes that cause her to take some world as *the* real world, be it the world of ordinary sensible objects, the theoretical entities of science, platonic abstracta, supernatural beings, fictional or mythical entities, etc., it follows that what person P means at time T by "x exists (is real)" is "x exists (is real) for person P at time T;" and, furthermore, this is what the being or reality of x consists in. Since James was fond of devising names for the "fallacies" committed by his adversaries, it is only fitting that a name be created for James's penchant to semanticize and ontologize his explanations of the psychological causes of belief—"The James Fallacy."[6]

The promethean nature of the doctrine that existence is relative to the interests of persons at a time becomes patent when it is realized that, for James, what interests us is what we attend to and what we attend to, within certain limits, is under the control of our will. "Will," he says, "consists in nothing but a manner of attending to certain objects, or consenting to their stable presence before the mind" (PP 947). And, since belief is nothing but an idea's stably filling the mind without any competitor, it follows that "Will and Belief...are two names for one and the same PSYCHOLOGICAL phenomenon" (PP 948). The upshot is that through our conscious will—our efforts to attend in a certain way, i.e. fill our consciousness in said manner—we determine what world exists or is real, and, the selectivity of consciousness also determines, at least in part, the internal nature of these worlds in the manner described above. For example, our efforts of attention or concentration create the indexical perspectives of here and there, now and then, myself and others. Furthermore, the many worlds together are supposed to constitute reality, but it

246 / Richard M. Gale

would seem that what unifies them is only their relation to ourselves, viz. that each is a possible object for our interest and relative to these interests interconnections between the worlds can be made in way that will help to further these interests. This is about as promethean a doctrine as one could imagine.

The promethean theme of creation-through-efforts-of-attention or concentration also underlies his account of the self. We make our own personal identity over time by "taking" or "appropriating" certain past and future states as our own on the basis of the sort of interest they have for us, the sort of concern and responsibility we show for them.[7] Not only do these efforts to attend create personal identity over time, they are what we really are. He speaks of "the source of effort and attention" as "the self of all the other selves" (PP 285).[8] "The voluntary effort to attend," which appears to be an original psychic force, is called "the star-performer" (PP 428). "...the effort seems...as if it were the substantive thing which we *are*..." (PP 1181). By identifying the true self with the source of our effort of attention and will James is glorifying man as creator—the promethean man. Each of us is that active force of will within us that is the determiner of what world is the "real" one, as well as of many features of these worlds and their interconnections.

The core doctrines of James's pragmatism, his theory of meaning and truth, are derived from the above Darwinian-inspired instrumentalist conception of the function of consciousness. From the fact that we pick out things from our environment that interest us because of their practical importance and conceive of them in terms of how they will interact with us, i.e. in terms of what experiences we can expect them to produce and accordingly what actions are appropriate for us to take in regard to them, it would seem to follow that our belief about an object will be, as Bain and Peirce urged, a certain habit or disposition to expect certain experiences and act accordingly. James's pragmatic theory of meaning falls out of this conception of belief: "the whole meaning of a conception expresses itself in practical consequences either in the shape of conduct to be recommended, or in that of experiences to be expected, if the conception be true," in which "the conduct to be recommended" are the actions that a believer in this conception is disposed to perform ("Pragmatism" in the 1902 Baldwin *Dictionary of Philosophy*, reprinted in EP, p. 94. See P 29 for a close paraphrase). James's pragmatic theory of truth is entailed by the conjunction of this theory of meaning with the correspondence theory of truth. The latter asserts that a conception (thought, etc.) is true if and only if it *corresponds* with reality; and, when we substitute into this formula the pragmatic account of *corresponds*, it yields the pragmatic theory of truth, viz. that a conception is true if and only if its practical consequences, in the sense specified in the above pragmatic account of meaning, obtain, i.e. the experiences that are supposed to occur if certain actions are performed occur. James claims that conceptions, etc. become true when verified, which has the promethean consequence that we create truth through our verificatory activities and not only in the cases in which we bring about the predicted event. In MT he supports this *making* doctrine of truth by first reducing truth to knowledge, and knowledge in turn to reference, which then is explicated in terms of our having a causal recipe for grabbing some object by the lapels, the latter being *made* the referent in virtue of our *taking* it to be. Since the conjunction of the pragmatic theory of meaning with the correspondence theory of truth entails the pragmatic theory of truth, it follows, on the reasonable assumption that the former is necessary, that the pragmatic theory of meaning alone entails the pragmatic theory of truth.

A very murky issue in James's philosophy concerns the relation between the pragmatic theory of meaning and truth and his radical empiricism. Radical empiricism, James says,

> consists first of a postulate, next of a statement of fact, and finally of a generalized conclusion. The postulate is that the only things that shall be debatable among philosophers shall be things definable in terms drawn from experience...The statement of fact is that the relations between things, conjunctive as well as disjunctive, are just as much matters of direct particular experience...than the things themselves. The generalized conclusion is that therefore the parts of experience hold together from next to next by relations that are themselves parts of experience. The directly apprehended universe needs...no extraneous trans-empirical connective support... .(MT 6-7)[9]

Since the postulate is a variant on the pragmatic theory of meaning, radical empiricism entails this theory, though not conversely; and, since the latter entails the pragmatic theory of truth, radical empiricism entails pragmatism, understood as encompassing both its theory of meaning and truth. But, strangely enough, James claims "that there is no logical connexion between pragmatism, as I understand it, and a doctrine which I have recently set forth as 'radical

empiricism'" (P 6). Yet at other places James says that the establishment of the pragmatist theory of truth "is a step of first-rate importance in making radical empiricism prevail," which could be
construed as the claim that pragmatism is a necessary condition of
radical empiricism (MT 6). It also is worth pointing out that both "the
statement of fact" and "generalized conclusion" are supposed to be
discovered by following the dictates of the phenomenalist "postulate"
and appealing to what is presented in immediate experience. We just
have to look and see, for example, whether we experience relations
or not.[10]

Another confusing issue concerns the relation between radical
empiricism and his doctrine of "pure experience" or "neutral monism"
as it often is called. James writes as if it were part of or entailed by
radical empiricism, but this must be a mistake, just as it would be
to say that the statement of fact and generalized conclusion of radical
empiricism is entailed by its methodological phenomenalist postulate.
Again, it is something that we are supposed to discover through the
use of this method. Let us see why.

Neutral monism really contains two tenets.

1. No event is mental or physical simpliciter but only in
   virtue of bearing certain sort of relations to other events.
2. Every event is both physical and mental in this relational
   sense.

Obviously, neither 1 nor 2 nor their conjunction is entailed by any
one of the three components of radical empiricism or by their conjunction. Rather, the truth of 1 is discovered by carefully attending
to our own percepts and discovering that we cannot detect any
distinction between a conscious act of sensing and its accusative, pace
G. E. Moore. In addition to this phenomenological support for neutral
monism, James recommends it as a way of dissolving traditional
philosophical puzzles about the relation between "inner" states of
consciousness and their "outer" physical accusatives. Thus, his
defense of 1 is both phenomenological and therapeutic.

There is a promethean upshot to 1, since the manner in which we
relate a given event to other events *makes* it physical or mental,
just as we determine whether a given letter in a crossword puzzle
belongs to the across or down word of which it is a common
constituent by how we *take* it. James initially characterizes the
difference between a physical and mental type order of events in

a viciously regressive manner, since he uses non-topically-neutral words to characterize the members of the order. He winds up saying, roughly, that an event qualifies as mental when it is placed in a succession of other mental events, i.e. anticipations, memories, etc. (An experience counts as mental if it "is the last term of a train of sensations, emotions, decisions, movements, classifications, expectations, etc., ending in the present, and the first term of a series of similar 'inner' operations extending into the future" and the very same experience counts as physical if it is the *"terminus ad quem* of a lot of previous physical operations, carpentering, papering, furnishing, warming, etc." (*Essays in Radical Empiricism*, hereafter ERE, pp. 8-9). But his later, more considered account is based on whether the events comprising the succession are connected in a stable, law-like manner or not, which is a close cousin of Kant's Second Analogy of Experience. (The percept of the pen counts as physical if "it is a stable feature, holds ink, marks paper...So far as it is unstable, on the contrary, coming and going with the movements of my eyes, altering with what I call my fancy" it counts as mental. ERE 61) One and the same event can be placed by us into these two different type of orders of succession, one of which displays law-like connections between its members and the other not.

Tenets 1 and 2 of neutral monism are logically independent. 1 holds that the difference between the mental and physical is functional, being based on the manner in which we relate it to other events. But, as James himself points out, it is possible for the world to be such that a given event can be fitted into only a physicalistic or mentalistic type series of events and thereby not qualify as both mental and physical.

> It is possible to imagine a universe of experiences in which the only alternative between neighbors would be either physical interaction or complete inertness. In such a word the mental or the physical *status* of any piece of experience would be unequivocal. (ERE 71)

Thus, 1 does not entail 2, since, in the above possible world in which 2 is false, 1 nevertheless is true because the mental or physical status of its events, although unequivocal, still depends on their relations to other events. Unfortunately, James does not present his neutral monism in a way that perspicuously distinguishes between tenets 1 and 2. Another serious difficulty for tenet 2 concerns events in the future and present that an individual does not experience. James seems to take the panpsychistic route with respect to them: "If not a future experience of our own or a present one of our neighbor, it must be...an experience *for* itself...," which seems to impute an inner consciousness to every physical event (ERE 43). There are other ways out of the problem of unperceived events that James pursues, such as relating them to possible experiences or placing them in other worlds within his menagerie of the "Many Worlds," but space does not permit further discussion. Thus, it appears that James waffles in his allegiance to 2. More will be said about this when we consider the mystical James.

This completes my very rough and admittedly shoddy overview of the promethean nature of pragmatism, broadly conceived so as to include both its core methods for determining meaning and truth, as well as the doctrines, such as radical empiricism and neutral monism, that are discovered through their employment. It now will be shown how James put his brand of pragmatism to work as a reconciler of science with religion, but with a highly promethean religion that stresses man's decisively creative role as a working partner of the forces within the universe that make for goodness.

**Pragmatism as Reconciler**

James, like Dewey, attempts to be a methodological univocalist by applying his pragmatic method across-the-board, though, possibly to his credit, there are some serious lapses, as we shall see. The above pragmatic method for determining meaning and truth informs all of our modes of action and thought, be they scientific, religious, moral, or esthetic. James, using Papini's simile, likens pragmatism to a hotel corridor "from which a hundred doors open into a hundred chambers" (EP 146) in each of which someone is doing something different—praying, performing a scientific experiment, etc. (It was a highclass hotel.) The connecting link between the diverse activities going on in these different rooms, the corridor, is the common method employed in them, that being pragmatism. Through this common method we can pass without obstruction, i.e. with a clear conscience, from the prayer room to the scientific laboratory. By allowing such a free passage between our scientific and religious endeavors, pragmatism is a reconciler, a mediator, even a harmonizer, although it presents no higher synthesis. (Only once, at P 144, does he speak of a *synthesis*.)

The fundamental point of similarity is that religious conceptions are just like scientific ones in that they must be understood in terms of how they are verified in our life. That is the corridor. Not all religious creeds will have such pragmatic meaning. So much the worse for them. The scholastic concept of God as a supernatural "omni"-man flunks the test, since there are no specific actions it requires of us nor experiences it predicts. Our conception of God must be an empirically grounded one that enables us to makes verifiable predictions and which therefore makes some difference in our practical affairs.

While James, *qua* pragmatist, recognizes a number of different meaningful religious creeds, they all are, what I will call, "moralistic religions," in that they make claims, often contingent upon our moral efforts, concerning the ultimate status or fate of goodness in the world. The pragmatic meaning of "God" in these creeds is that there is some assurance, going from being certain to being a real possibility, that the higher or better powers triumph over the lower ones. The most extreme form that this God-hypothesis takes is in those creeds or philosophies that give absolute assurance that all evils are overcome, *aufgehoben*, in a higher synthesis or get swallowed up in a tranquil mystical unity. For these absolutistic views, God means the assurance of safety and peace. "Nirvana means safety from this everlasting round of adventures of which the world of sense consists" (P 140). James makes it appear as if an absolutist would be committed to calling a pill "God" if it should cause those who ingest it to feel blissful and safe. Having identified their God with the assurance of safety, James next unearths the pragmatic meaning of their conception in terms of it licensing us to take an occasional moral holiday, since we are assured that good will triumph no matter what we do or that evil is only an illusion and thus not in need of elimination (P 41).

It is not surprising that James's absolutist opponents took offense at his pragmatic rendering of the cash-value of their conception of God. James, play-acting no doubt, expressed surprise that they were not grateful for his saving their doctrine from meaninglessness, apologized and took back his offering (MT 5). Certainly, they would not consider their God-hypothesis verified if those who believed it should find themselves turning into blissfully secure creatures. Rather, they would take it that such consequences served to verify only the *psychological* proposition that those who believe in some Absolute

252 / Richard M. Gale

or Nirvana become blissfully secure as a result. Such beneficial consequences might give one a *pragmatic reason* for believing that their God exists, i.e. a reason based on the beneficial consequence of believing this proposition, but it would not give them an *epistemological reason* for believing it, i.e. a reason that would help to justify a claim to know it, since these results do not confirm or verify it. Basically, the Royces are unhappy with James's pragmatic unpacking of the meaning of their Absolute or God because it seems to omit the star performer, the very content of their belief, being like a performance of *Hamlet* without the Prince of Denmark.

Fortunately, this is not all James had to say about moralistic religions. The pluralistic theist's use of "God exists" is given an alternative pragmatic rendering. Herein the claim is that good will win out over evil in the long run. James does not say how long the long run is, though at one place he says that the verification or falsification of the moralistic hypothesis might "take many centuries to come" ("Some Reflections on the Subjective Method," in EP, p. 337). Maybe he was just joshing, since there should not be any cut-off date in the future. He also does not go into much detail about what constitutes the eventual triumph of the higher forces of good but I assume he has in mind a denouement to history in which a just and benevolent social order comes to pass permanently, as in *Star Wars,* and all evils are triumphed over by being put to some outweighing good and noble end. Not only does there wind up being a favorable balance of moral good over moral evil, but, most important, most person's development shows a favorable vector, thus rendering their life a significant or worthwhile one—"All's well that ends well."

James's rendering of pluralistic theism is not as outlandish as is the one he gave of monism, though it still seems to leave out the star performer. But when he deals with the way in which future consequences are implicated in this doctrine he says things that seem to open him up to Lovejoy's charge that the pragmatic theory of meaning falls prey to "the paradox of the alleged futurity of yesterday" by converting the *whole* meaning of an idea or proposition into its future consequences if true.[11] (Recall that James claims that "the whole meaning of a conception expresses itself in practical consequences either in the shape of conduct to be recommended, or in that of experiences to be expected.") The difference between theism and atheism, misleadingly called "materialism" by him, consists in a difference in the future course of history they predict. Notice that James interprets the consequences to be quoad our making of a statement, and not quoad the event reported by the statement. Thus, the future in question is quoad now rather than the time of the reported event. From this James seems to infer the absurd consequence that if there were to be no future, these seemingly opposing theories would have the same meaning, viz. none.

> He asks us to imagine how the pragmatic test can be applied if there is no future. Concepts for him (the pragmatist) are things to come back into experience with, things to make us look for differences. But by hypothesis there is to be no more experience and no possible differences can now be looked for. Both theories have shown all their consequences and, by the hypothesis we are adopting, these are identical. The pragmatist must consequently say that the two theories, in spite of their different-sounding names, mean exactly the same thing, and that the dispute is purely verbal. (P 50-1)

He also says that "It makes not a single jot of difference so far as the *past* of the world goes, whether we deem it to have been the work of matter or whether we think a divine spirit was its author" (P 50). "Thus if no future detail of experience or conduct is to be deduced from our hypothesis, the debate between materialism and theism becomes quite idle and insignificant" ("The Pragmatic Method," in EP p. 127).[12]

What are we to make of these highly counter-intuitive claims? First, there is a minor problem of internal consistency. Elsewhere he says that God guarantees that "an ideal order...shall be permanently preserved" ("The Pragmatic Method" 130). That the world comes to an end, according to this rendering of theism, would settle the issue decisively against theism, pace what James says. Let us not worry about this, for, as used to be said at the end of a *Batman* show, the worst is yet to come.

When James says that if there is no future "the debate between materialism and theism becomes quite idle and insignificant," he seems to confound an hypothesis being interesting with its being meaningful. James seems to grant this very distinction when he claims that without prospective consciousness there would be no emotional interest, the issue being purely intellectual ("The Pragmatic Method" 126). But if it is intellectual, then, supposedly, it has some significant or meaningful content. Herein, I believe, James is granting more than he should, for it is in the promethean spirit of his pragmatism to embrace a theory of meaning that equates being meaningful with being of interest and practical importance to us human beings in our quest to remake reality. This promethean equation is seen in his analogy with the completed play. "When a play is once over, and the curtain down, you really make it no better by claiming an illustrious genius for its author, just as you make it no worse by calling him a common hack" ("The Pragmatic Method" 127). The proper response to this is that while your passing judgment on the worth of the author in no way alters the esthetic value of the completed play, the intrinsic qualities of the play itself do speak to whether it has an author at all, and, if so, how good a one. Thus, the choice between the author-no author hypotheses or the good author-hack author ones is decidable even if the world comes to an end when the curtain comes down. It is surprising that James should have used this play analogy, since it is so unfavorable for his purpose.

Another flaw in James's discussion is his claim that if there is no future then "no future detail of experience or conduct is to be deduced from our hypothesis" of theism (P 52). Whether there be a future or not does not make any difference in respect to what predictions an hypothesis logically entails, only in respect to the truth of these predictions, it being assumed by James that all predictions are false if there be no future.

Maybe the most decisive refutation of James's claim that there is no difference in meaning between atheism and theism in the no-future case is that it winds up violating the principle of the temporal homogeneity of *being evidence for*, i.e. if E counts as evidence for or confirms proposition p at time T, then, *ceteris paribus*, E counts as evidence for p at any time. Mere difference in time is irrelevant. The "*ceteris paribus*" restriction rules out all differences save temporal ones, such as a difference in background knowledge from one time to another. The manner in which James violates this principle is that he seems to be saying that a benevolent course of events in the future would serve as evidence for, even be verificatory of, theism, but this very same course of events in the past would not! It would be like saying with regard to the example by which James initially motivates his pragmatic account, that of the two senses in which someone goes around a squirrel, that I cannot determine whether or not someone went around a squirrel in either of these senses at some past time unless I know that there is a future.

There are indications that James saw serious difficulties with his discussion in the 1898 "Philosophical Conceptions and Practical Results." When he repeated eight years later its discussion of the dispute between theism and materialism in the no-future case he made an important qualification: "I am supposing, of course, that the theories *have* been equally successful in their explanations of what is" (P 51). Thus, James seems to be assuming, although he does not explicitly state it, that the past of the no-future world in his example is an ambiguous mixed-bag of moral good and evil that does not speak clearly either for atheism or for theism. But, if he is to hand pick his example in this manner, while he escapes the above charge of relativizing evidence to a time, he cannot generalize from his example, as he plainly does. For immediately after completing his discussion of the no-future example, he draws this general conclusion: "Accordingly, in *every* genuine metaphysical debate some practical issue, however conjectural and remote, is involved," in which the "issue," of course, concerns what is future quoad now (P 52 my italics).

We do not have to just infer that James saw a difficulty in his discussion of the no-future world in his 1898 address because in MT he comes right out and tells us what it is: "I had no sooner given the address than I perceived a flaw in that part of it; but I left the passage unaltered ever since, because the flaw did not spoil its illustrative value" (103).[13] James not only mislocates the source of the difficulty, failing to see that it temporally relativizes *being evidence for* and makes meaning wholly prospective, but makes a concession that in effect takes back his pragmatic theory of meaning. He finds the difficulty with his former identification of the whole meaning of theism with what is outwardly observable to be analogous to what we find missing in a mechanical sweetheart whose outwardly observable behavior is indistinguishable from that of a real woman. What we find woefully inadequate with the robot is its lack of inner conscious states, because its outward behavior "is valued mainly as an expression, as a manifestation of the accompanying consciousness believed in" (MT 103). Analogously what we sorely miss in his former pragmatic rendering of theism are the inner conscious states of God, for men desire a being "who will inwardly recognize them and judge them sympathetically." Herein, he seems to be giving up his former pragmatic theory of meaning in terms of observable consequences. A wedge is now being driven between the meaning of a proposition, e.g. the inner states of consciousness it describes, and its mode of empirical verification. The star performer now gets into the act. Content and verification fall apart. The same sort of taking it all back occurs when James later says (in SPP 38) that "In obeying this rule (the pragmatic one) we neglect the substantive content of the concept and follow its function only." These concessions should be viewed as careless aberrations, for if taken seriously they would greatly trivialize his philosophy, making all the controversies that his theory of meaning elicited a matter of a mere misunderstanding. The general rule to follow in James interpretation is: "When in doubt go with the radical version of James."

The version of moralistic religion that James personally favored, but only when his healthy self that craved an heroic moral challenge was ascendent over his morbid one, is that of "meliorism," according to which it is a real possibility that if we collectively exert our best moral effort good will win out over evil in the long run. A possibility for James is something that, relative to the actual circumstances, could well happen, though it is not assured that it will. This religion of meliorism, which steers a course midway between optimism and pessimism, is the one that James attempts to reconcile with science and tough-mindedness in general in the final lecture of P.

Its great emotional appeal is manifest in many things James says. He expressed sympathy with a soul-building type theodicy because it makes the universe to be a "great unending romance" that appeals to our healthy self ("Dilemma of Determinism," in WB p. 170). "Moral happiness is the greatest happiness known" ("Some Reflections on the Subjective Method" 334). The thought that there are genuine possibilities "is what gives the palpitating reality to our moral life and makes it tingle...with so strange and elaborate excitement" ("Dil of Det" 183). In his Introduction to *The Literary Remains of the Late Henry James* (hereafter LR, in EP), he rejects his father's optimism that all evils are overcome by contrasting it with his own emotional need to lead the morally strenuous life based on a melioristic outlook.

> The life we then feel tingling through us vouches sufficiently for itself, and nothing tempts us to refer it to a higher source. Being, as we are, a match for whatever evils actually confront us, we rather prefer to think of them as endowed with reality, and as being absolutely alien, but, we hope, subjugable powers. (61-2)

He then makes a contrast that is found in his father's writings between the healthy- and morbid-minded, a contrast that figures prominently in his *The Varieties of Religious Experience* some seventeen years later. The morbid-minded dwells on the fact "we are all potentially sick men. The sanest and best of us are of one clay with the lunatics and prison inmates" (62). Like his father, they must escape this sort of existential angst by postulating some absolute being or God who gives assurance of salvation and safety. But the healthy-minded, among whom James includes himself, "turn a deaf ear to the thought of being" in the form of some Absolute and accept the challenge of "philosophic moralism" to lead the morally strenuous life. He concludes his introduction with one of the most tender and diplomatic, yet cutting, sentences ever written in which he contrasts himself with his beloved father.

> Meanwhile, the battle is about us, and we are its combatants, steadfast or vacillating, as the case may be. It will be hot fight indeed if the friends of philosophic moralism should bring to the service of their ideal, so different from that of my father, a spirit even remotely resembling the life-long devotion of his faithful heart. (63)

What is especially appealing about meliorism is that its conditional prophecy, R. If we collectively exert our best moral effort, good will win out over evil in the long run, presents an ideal target for a will-to-believe type faith. This is James's most cherished (at least by his healthy-minded self) and promethean doctrine. It says, roughly, that it is both rational in the pragmatic sense and morally permissible to believe a proposition upon insufficient evidence just in case reason cannot in principle or practice decide the issue and our believing can help to bring about the truth of some morally (or even just prudentially) desirable proposition.[14] In the case of a will-to-believe type faith in meliorism, the proposition believed upon insufficient evidence and which reason cannot decide is R and the morally desirable proposition that we can help to bring about is its consequent

$R_1$. Good will win out over evil in the long run.

And this we do by morally exerting ourselves so as to actualize its antecedent

$R_2$. We collectively exert our best moral effort.

James, anticipating contemporary chaos theory, stresses that tiny differences in the cause can make for great differences in the final outcome; thus, our moral efforts, tiny though they are in comparison to the rest of the universe, could just tip the balance in favor of outcome $R_1$ ("Some Reflections on the Subjective Method" 338).

James is not consistent in the way in which he spells out the prophecy of meliorism. While he gives the R-type conditional formulation in P (and SPP 115-6), in his 1897 "The Will to Believe" (in WB, p. 25) he gives a categorical formulation that leads to serious problems for his pragmatic justification of faith. It is that "the best things are the more eternal things...the things in the universe that throw the last stone...and say the final word," which is a stylistic variant of

$R_1$. Good will win out over evil in the long run.

Herein, it is *one and the same* proposition that both is morally desirable to make true and must be believed by us if we are to succeed in making it true. For rather complicated reasons that are given in my article and book mentioned in note 14 it turns out that among our reasons for trying to make $R_1$ true in this case is our belief that it is true. But, on conceptual grounds, it is absurd to have among our reasons for trying to make a proposition become true that we believe that it will become true, thereby rendering our altruistic actions to help make $R_1$ truly irrational. This is a very serious matter, since it involves a significant limiting of the scope of our rational actions, and, since freedom requires rationality, of our free actions as well. According to my moral intuitions, the evil of this outweighs whatever good might be brought about by our altruistic actions induced by our belief in $R_1$. One's moral permission to believe upon insufficient evidence when doing so will help to bring about something morally desirable is defeasible, and herein we are confronted with a defeating condition.

This problem is easily circumvented by conditionalizing the proposition that must be believed so that it will be distinct from the categorical one that we desire to make true, as in the above formulation of meliorism, in which it was R that had to be believed for the purpose of helping to make $R_1$ true. James's you-will-like-me case in "The Will to Believe" also can be handled in this manner. Instead of saying that in order to make it true that you will like me I must first believe that you will like me, say only that I must believe the *conditional* proposition that if I act in a friendly manner you will like me.

But even when James's will-to-believe justification of religious faith is understood in this conditionalized manner, it faces the serious objection that it relativizes being morally permissible to persons, in violation of the moral principle of universalizability, that if it is morally permissible (right, obligatory, etc.) for one person to do X, then it is morally permissible (etc.) for any person in the same situation to do X. The problem arises because some people are so psychologically constituted that they can act in an all-out altruistic manner so as to help make $R_1$ true without believing that R (or even $R_1$) is true. Since their prior belief in R is not a causally necessary condition for their acting so as to make $R_1$ true, it looks as if they are not morally permitted to believe R upon insufficient evidence, whereas their less strong-willed brethren who cannot act so as to make $R_1$ true without first believing R have such moral permission. Thus, one's moral permission to perform some action, that of believing R, depends on her psychological quirks in regard to whether she can act so as to try to make $R_1$ without first believing R. One might counter that the fact that the psychologically weaker person is morally permitted to do something that a stronger person is not, does not violate the principle of universalizability, since there is a relevant difference in the circumstances in the two cases, viz. their psychological makeup. Is this a morally relevant feature of the circumstance? I think that it is no more morally relevant than is the fact that an agent suffers from cowardice. Certainly, we don't want to accord to the coward moral permissions that are denied to the courageous person.[15]

## The Anti-Promethean Mysticism of James

Hopefully, it has been shown that James's pragmatism, broadly conceived, is highly promethean, especially when combined with the will-to-believe doctrine. While James continued to espouse these doctrines up to the end, his last two books (*A Pluralistic Universe*, hereafter PU, and SPP) still defending the will-to-believe, there nevertheless is a marked shift beginning in the late nineties to an anti-promethean type of mysticism that challenges these doctrines.

The shift comes about through a change in his emotional response to evil. In 1870 James suffered a severe depression in which he came close to suicide. While he had experiences of existential angst, as we soon will see, the main source of the depression was his inability to function in a sufficiently promethean manner as a moral agent. This probably was due to the fact that he was now a doctor but couldn't get himself to actively pursue this profession nor any other.

Basically, James was deeply imbued with his father's belief that a man's true vocation is to bring down the tablets from on high so that we might be saved. Only philosophy could afford him this opportunity, but it was not yet a "live option" for him. Because of this inability to make a career-choice, James despaired whether he possessed free will, which widened into a despair over whether he could function as a moral agent at all, since he believed that free will is a presupposition of moral responsibility. He broke out of this depression by a promethean act of will in which he declared (in his diary entry of April 30, 1870—TC 121) that he is free and will do everything in his power to induce a real belief that he is, his public performatory utterance of declaring that he is free being just one aspect of this attempt to self-induce belief.[16] Not surprisingly, that we are free became one of the prized candidates for a will-to-believe type faith, serving as a cornerstone for his promethean faith.[17]

The religion of meliorism, as we saw in the above quotations, had great emotional appeal to the promethean James, who was now wallowing in his new-found belief in his freedom and was just spoiling to engage in a Texas death match with evil, which clearly is evident at the end of his Introduction to LR. But, by the time of *The Varieties of Religious Experience*, hereafter VRE, he completely and decisively rejects this beloved meliorism as being superficial and unsatisfying. There is one particularly dramatic point at which James seems to enter into a dialogue with his former self of the 1884 Introduction to LR and decisively reject its meliorism because it cannot "help him make it through the night." To understand this key passage we must begin with his famous existential angst experience of 1868 (as reported in TC 363-4 and anonymously in VRE 134-5) of a horror that fell on him when he came upon a hideously looking epileptic youth in an insane asylum.

> *That shape am I*, I felt, potentially. Nothing that I possess can defend me against that fate, if the hour for it should strike for me as it struck for him. There was such a horror of him, and such a perception of my own merely momentary discrepancy from him, that it was as if something hitherto solid within my breast gave way entirely, and I became a mass of quivering fear.

In the Introduction to LR (62) James alludes to this experience when he says: "we are all potentially sick men. The sanest and best of us are of one clay with the lunatics and prison inmates." His response, as we saw in the above quotations, is to suck it up and courageously follow the melioristic route of living the morally strenuous life without any assurance of success. On pp. 45-6 of VRE he repeats verbatim these quoted sentences about our being of one clay with the lunatics but now draws an opposite conclusion, viz. that our salvation must be found not in living the morally strenuous life but rather in finding an abiding sense of safety and peace through absorption into a higher surrounding spiritual reality. It is as if he is treading the same path as his former self but now goes in a diametrically opposed direction when he gets to the crucial fork in the road at which sits the epileptic youth.

This theme of the insufficiency of meliorism and the healthy-minded outlook in general is repeated over and over again in VRE. We are told that "the breath of the sepulchre surrounds" our natural happiness (118), that the advice to the morbid-minded person upon whom there falls "the joy-destroying chill" of "Cheer up, old fellow, you'll be all right erelong, if you will only drop your morbidness!" is "the very consecration of forgetfulness and superficiality" (118-9). What we need is a "life not correlated with death, a health not liable to illness, a kind of good that will not perish, a good in fact that flies beyond the Goods of nature" (119).[18]

On the final two pages of VRE James inconsistently endorses his old meliorism, as he does five years later in P, using it in the final lecture as his specimen religion in his attempt to reconcile religion with science and, in general, tender- with tough-mindedness. Why this blatant inconsistency? I can think of several possible explanations. The first is that since it was his intent in P to establish his reconciliation thesis he purposely hand-picked his specimen of religion so as to make his task easier. James was a one-problem-at-a-time philosopher, as seen in his remark on p. 286 of PP, "sufficient to that day will be the evil thereof." Since meliorism gives us a nice conditionalized empirical prediction, R, it satisfies the same pragmatic theory of meaning and truth as does science and also is suitable for a will-to-believe type faith. But this would not explain why he endorses meliorism at the end of VRE, since he was not intent on pushing the reconciliation thesis in VRE but rather that of synthesis and unity. To explain this further fact we might have to resort to James's deeply divided self, which approaches that of the split personalities that so fascinated him in the work of Janet and Binet. It might have been the case that what James would say on any given day depended on what side of the bed he woke up on—the state of his nerves, back, eyes, digestion, etc., etc. If the Broadway subway on which he rode uptown to give his P lectures at Columbia had been as cruddy in 1907 as it is today, he might very well have had one of his father's 1844 Swedenborgian vastation experiences and as a result spent the final hour chanting "O-M" instead of defending meliorism. James, after all, was a philosophical wheel of fortune, and, to push the analogy further, whatever doctrine he happened to point to reaped a rich payoff, since every one of his many philosophies was espoused with incredible brilliance and passion, it often being the best version we have of the doctrine.

James's ambivalent attitude toward evil, his both wanting and not wanting to believe that we have absolute assurance that we are safe because all evils are only illusory or ultimately conquered, finds a parallel in his views on the status of the good, his both wanting and not wanting to believe that it already is objectively determined what is good. His essay on "The Moral Philosopher and the Moral Life" (in WB) begins with the typical promethean theme of everything, in this case what is morally good, being relative to and created by our interests (189-91). His oft-repeated existential doctrine that existence precedes essence is marshalled to reject the platonic view that there are preexistent, objective moral truths. In spite of his initial relativistic stance, James goes on to recognize one objective moral truth, which he calls an "unconditional commandment"—that we should always act so as to maximize desire satisfaction, in which all person's desires are accorded equal weight except for the fact that their strength or intensity is to enter into the maximizing equation, so that my very strong desire to have the window remain shut would outweigh and take precedence over the quite mild desires of five other people to have it opened. A consequence of this highly counterintuitive desire maximizing rule is that since God is infinite his desires "are the greatest in amount" and thereby ought to be satisfied (193 and 213). (Imagine the field day Plato's Socrates of the *Euthyphro* would have had with that.) If this inconsistency with his initial ethical relativism isn't bad enough, toward the end of the essay James says that the answer to the ultimate casuistic ethical question of how to maximize desire satisfaction must already have an answer within God's mind. The absoluteness of God's moral judgments seems to be presupposed by his claim in PP (301) that each of us seeks to become "an ideal social self, of a self that is at least *worthy* of approving recognition by the highest possible judging companion" and "this judge is God, the Absolute Mind, the 'Great Companion.'" This goes back on his earlier promethean anti-platonism because it requires our ethical ideals to agree with some preexistent code, viz. the one in God's mind, thereby being a form of scholastic conceptualism. This is another case of James wanting it both ways, in this case that good both is created by men and also has a preexistent, objective status.

If solace from existential angst cannot be found in meliorism for James, in what can it be found? It will be shown that he found it in mysticism, of both a fancy, religious variety and a common, backyard sort. The former is worked out in VRE, the latter in PU, and to a lesser extent in SPP. The common message of the two forms of mysticism is that ultimate reality is some kind of unity within which the individual finds reassuring absorption.

## I. Religious Mysticism

The major thesis of VRE, and one which I think is successfully maintained to James's everlasting credit, is that the basis of religion, be it institutional, its theology, or personal religious feelings, is rooted in religious experiences of a mystical sort in which the individual has a feeling or direct, non-sensory perception of a "More," an "Unseen" supernatural or purely spiritual reality into which she is totally absorbed or from which spiritual energy flows into her. It is this experiential union that gives "an assurance of safety and a temper of peace, and, in relation to others, a preponderance of loving affection" (383).

James claims not to have had any mystical experiences himself— "my own constitution shuts me out from their enjoyment almost entirely, and I can speak of them only at second hand" (301). If this is so, is not my underlying thesis that James had a mystical self who clashed with his promethean pragmatic self, especially in regard to the challenge posed by evil, wrong? How can one be a mystic, or even be so sympathetically inclined to mystical experiences as to accept their cognitivity, as did James, without having mystical experiences? I have two replies.

My first response is that even if it were true that James did not have any mystical experiences, at least of the more developed type, it could be the case that he had a deep sensitivity to and appreciation of them and what they seemingly reveal, just as someone who lacks the musical genius to compose an *Eroica* symphony can esthetically resonate to it. As Walter Stace, a virgin to mystical experience who nevertheless was one of the greatest expositors and defenders of mysticism, was fond of pointing out, people are possessed of varying degrees of mystical intuition in ways analogous to their possession of varying degrees of musical sensitivity and talent. James's claim that "we all have at least the germ of mysticism in us" can be seen as making this point (P 76).

Second, James is not levelling with his audience. Mystical experiences for him cover a broad spectrum of cases, going from the relatively undeveloped experiences of a heightened sense of reality, an intensification of feeling and insight, such as occurs under the influence of alcohol, drugs, nitrous oxide, art, and even the raptures of nature, to the fully developed monistic experience of an undifferentiated unity in which all distinctions are obliterated. James never had an experience of the latter kind but he did have more than his share of the less developed ones, given his penchant to experiment on himself with nitrous oxide and mescal. Needless to say, being Irish, he was no stranger to alcohol and gives such glowing descriptions of its effects (307) that I can only check my urge to go on a binge by reading his remark to a group of school teachers that the best way to deter people from drink is to stress "the blessing of having an organism kept in lifelong possession of its full youthful elasticity by a sweet, sound blood, to which stimulants and narcotics are unknown, and to which the morning sun and air and dew will daily come as sufficient powerful intoxicants" (TT 114). God bless William James! He even had a fairly developed Wordsworthian type of nature mysticism experience in the Adirondaks in 1898 shortly before he caused irreparable damage to his heart, from which he eventually died, by overtaxing himself on a trek. James's four mystical experiences reported in the 1910 "A Suggestion about Mysticism," in which he seemed to become aware of experiences not his own, occurred in 1906, four years after the writing of VRE. Furthermore, it will be shown that these are not really mystical experiences.

Why was James so reticent to own up to his having had mystical experiences? The answer might be that James was very sensitive to the suspicions that his tough-minded scientific colleagues had of his interests in disreputable types of paranormal and mystical experiences and went to considerable pains to appear tough-minded, rather than some sentimental apologist for the wild claims elicited by these experiences. His deepest fear was to wind up like his father, an eccentric whose writings everybody safely neglected. His efforts to appear tough-minded come out in the severity of his investigations in psychical research. The only exception is that he investigated a certain medium, one Madame Blavatsky, and, although he unmasked her as a fraud, that he even investigated her, rather than ruling her out a priori on the basis of her name, shows some gullibility (*Essays in Psychical Research*, hereafter PR, p. 96).

Another example of his misrepresenting himself so as to disarm the suspicions of the tough-minded in his audience is in his 1898 lecture, "Human Immortality: Two Supposed Objections to the Doctrine" in ERM. He begins by saying that he cannot understand why the Ingersoll Committee chose him to give this lecture, since he is no friend of the doctrine of human immortality and has little personal concern for it. He then goes on neutralize the two major objections to it, mount an inference to the best explanation argument, about which more will be said, in support of it, and end with a will-to-believe justification for believing in it! With opponents like this, a doctrine doesn't need any defenders.

Granted that James had every right to be a sympathetic expositor and defender of mysticism, we can now consider the specifics of his account. The first question concerns whether our apprehension of the supersensible reality is conceptual or via some direct presentation. Throughout VRE James works with a perceptual model of mystical experiences, likening them to ordinary sense perceptions in that they involve direct acquaintance, though unlike the latter in being devoid of any sensory content. "Mystical experiences are...direct perceptions...absolutely sensational...face to face presentations of what seems to exist" (336).

James tries to take a neutral stance on whether mystical experiences support a monistic or pluralistic view of the More or Unseen reality, in spite of his own strong emotional commitment to the pluralistic version, which he liked to summarize in Blood's wonderful "ever not quite" phrase in his 1910 "A Pluralistic Mystic." At one place he seems to come down on the side of the modern-day mystical ecumenicalists, Suzuki, Stace and Merton, who contend that there is a common phenomenological *monistic* core to all mystical experiences that gets interpreted differently according to the culture of the individual mystic. "In mystic states we both become one with the

Absolute and we become aware of our oneness. *This is the everlasting and triumphant mystical tradition, hardly altered by differences of clime or creed"* (VRE 332, my italics). Some of James's major contentions in VRE, however, require a dualistic experience of the sort called "theistic" by R. C. Zaehner in his *Concordant Discord*. For example, James says that prayer is "the very soul and essence of religion," and then describes prayer as involving two-way interaction between two subjects. (For someone who takes such a strong anti-essentialist stance in Lecture II, James managed to say a lot of things about the essence of religion.) James's strong Protestant leanings cause him, for the most part, to give a dualistic interpretation of mystical experiences.

One of the features of mystical experiences, as well as conversion experiences in general, that James stresses, so much so that it is used as one of the four defining conditions of a mystical experience, is that the subject is passive in respect to them. While persons can take steps, such as following the mystical way, to help induce the experience, its coming is viewed by religious mystics as the bestowal of a gift upon them. Through the experience the subject feels that her conscious will is held in abeyance as she finds absorption in a higher unity. "The mystic feels as if his own will were grasped and held by a superior power" (303). James finds an interesting connection between the mystic's use "of negation as a mode of passage towards a higher kind of affirmation" and the subjugation of "the personal will...and the finite self and its wants" (331). In both cases there must be a canceling out of the finite so as to open ourselves to the infinite. This resignation and abandonment of the finite self and its conscious will is found in the mystical and conversion experiences of both the once- and twice-born, or healthy- and morbid-minded.[19]

James, no doubt with his own morbid-minded needs in mind, stresses how such mystically-based resignation cannot "fail to steady the nerves, to cool the fever, and appease the fret, if one be conscious that, no matter what one's difficulties for the moment may appear to be, one's life as a whole is in the keeping of a power whom one can absolutely trust" (230). The mystical experiences that are occasioned by such submission of the conscious will and self are "reconciling and unifying states" (330) that "tell of the supremacy of the ideal, of vastness, of union, of safety, and of rest" (339). In such mystical union there is a "life not correlated with death, a health not liable to illness, a kind of good that will not perish, a good in fact that flies beyond the Goods of nature" (119). Sounds like just what the doctor ordered for James's bad case of existential angst. Maybe he can now view the epileptic youth without "quivering fear," though I wouldn't bet on it.

Already we see James rejecting some of the important promethean themes in his pragmatism. Mysticism is where the trail of the human serpent stops. The true self, that "self of all the other selves," no longer is identified with the active aspect of a person, their free conscious will. Quite the contrary, it is that very self, along with its promethean will to believe and the meliorism it favors, that must be surrendered if we are to find a peace and safety rendering salvation. Rather our true or higher self is that aspect of us, identified by James with the subconscious or transmarginal self, that is able to enter into a complete or partial union with a supersensible reality, which is a "More" of the same kind as it, and this it does through ceasing to identify with its active conscious self. This More also fails to fit the doctrine of neutral monism, being spiritual through and through, rather than only in some relational sense. Given that it is, in James's words, "transcendent" and "invisible," i.e. non-sensory, it is hard to see how it could possibly qualify as physical, even in his relational manner. Herein, the mental or physical status of some reality is in no way dependent on how we *take* it and thereby what we *make* it. But the status of this mystical reality poses an even greater challenge to the protheanism of pragmatism. "The worst is yet to come!"

Mystical experiences not only have a noetic quality (another of James's four defining conditions of a mystical experience) in that they seem to their subjects to be revelatory of reality, but revelatory of an ultimate or absolute reality—the really real in comparison with which everything else is a mere illusion or emanation of some sort. They definitely do not accord to this reality the sort of person- or interest-relative status that James articulates in PP. To do so would award this reality an ontological status on all fours with Ivanhoe and Pegasus, certainly a booby prize. Another way of putting the mystic's anti-relativism claim is that their assertion that there is a oneness or unity is not modified by any *"qua"*-clause (recall the PP-claim that everything exists *qua* something), e.g. *qua* subject of discourse, spatio-temporal system, causal order, and so on for the other qualified or restricted senses of oneness that James recognizes on pp. 66-70 of P.

There is not in VRE even a hint of the promethean PP account of reality, though it is interesting to note that it does make its way into one of the drafts for Lecture II.

> What...determines our living attitudes has *reality* for us in so far
> forth. In fact, if you open some of the books on psychology, you
> will find them saying that the way in which the feeling of the thing
> grasps us and decides our living attitudes is all that we *mean* by its
> reality. What thus grasps us is by that very fact believed in, is real.
> That is all that the word real signifies,—you hear these
> psychologists insist. (Appendix II of VRE 483-4)

James dropped this PP-account of reality in the final draft. Why? One
would like to think that it was because he realized that it commits
the James Fallacy, but that is unlikely. A more likely explanation
is that he saw how much the mystic's noetic feelings clashed with
it. James, of course, could have continued to make use of the person-
relative doctrine of existence, along with its companion doctrine of
the ontological parity between the many worlds, and said that the
reality-claims of mystics, pace what they believe, are relative to their
passions and interests and that their mystical world or reality is not
ontologically privileged in a way in which the others are not simply
because it happens to be of special interest to them. But, if he were
to say these things, he could no longer sympathetically endorse the
reality claims of the mystics, for there then would be an inconsistency
between his meta-ontology—the interest-relative nature of reality
with its ontological parity between the many worlds—and his endorsement of the reality claims made on behalf of mystical experiences. Even without this endorsement James's meta-ontology runs
into the problem that it legitimates the claims made within each of
the many worlds or points of view—that of science, common-sense,
etc., but some of these claims, such as those made from the mystical
point of view, clash with this meta-ontology's relativization of existence to points of view. His meta-ontology legitimates too much.

There are still other features of pragmatism that get over-ruled by
mysticism. The claims of the mystic are not put forth as being fallible.
James, as we shall see, thinks that they should be, but this is to back
off from the sort of apodictic certainty that mystics think their special
experiences afford. Furthermore, without this sense of absolute
certainty there would not accrue the feeling of peace and safety which
James's morbid self needed so much. His MT-version of humanism,
which also is the generalized conclusion of his radical empiricism—
that the different parts of experience hang together without any need
of a transcendent or trans-empirical support or ground—clashes with

the mystic's claim that the sensible world as a whole is unsubstantial, being either a mere illusion or an emanation from their transcendent reality, such as in the manner described by Plotinus. They purport to have direct experiential authority for both this claim and their anti-fallibilism.

Mysticism's most striking challenge to pragmatism, however, is over meaning and truth. Pragmatism understood our conception of X *solely* in terms of the manner in which a believer is disposed to act toward X or the experiences that are anticipated if certain actions are performed, truth being a matter of whether these anticipations are satisfied. But the mystic's conception of the Absolute, the undifferentiated unity, the eternal one, God, etc. is not based on how we can ride herd on it, for there is nothing that we do to or with this mystical reality, or ways in which it is expected to behave if we do certain things. It doesn't dissolve in aqua regia! It simply *is*, and is just what it *appears* to be in the immediate experience of the mystic. A door to door salesman of mystical reality, therefore, would be stymied when asked, "But what does it do?" or "What can I do with it?" Herein the content of the proposition that this reality exists is not reducible to any set of actions on our part and their experiential consequences. The star performer finally gets into the act, unlike the case in the above pragmatically favored moralistic religions which were wholly consequentialistic in meaning, e.g. good will win out over evil if we do our best, believe this and you'll feel optimistic, safe, etc. and will feel justified in taking a moral holiday. It should now be obvious why James chose meliorism in P as his example of how religion could be reconciled with science: there was no clash with his pragmatic theory of meaning and truth.

Since the meaningful content of the mystic's assertion that there exists an undifferentiated unity, etc. is based on how she is appeared to, the truth of the assertion will depend primarily on whether her experience is objective or cognitive. The spiritual and moral benefits that the experience occasions, as we shall see, become relevant, but only as a means of indirect verification, there now being, as there wasn't for moralistic religions, a distinction between direct and indirect verification, with an assertion's meaning being identified primarily with the former, that being the content or apparent object of the mystical experience. James seems to recognize this when he says (in a footnote!! on 401) that "the word 'truth' is here taken to mean something additional to bare value for life..." Not surprisingly, we find James making the issue of the cognitivity or objectivity of mystical experiences a central issue in VRE. Concerning them, he asks about their "metaphysical significance" (308), "cognitivity" (324), "authoritativeness" (335), "objective truth" (340), "value for knowledge" (327), their "truth" (329), and whether they "furnish any *warrant for the truth* of the...supernaturality and pantheism which they favor" (335) or are "to be taken as *evidence*...for "the actual existence of a higher world with which our world is in relation" (384). James is quite explicit that the answer to the "objectivity" question is quite independent of the biological and psychological benefits that accrue from mystical experiences (401).

James concludes in the lecture aptly called "Conclusions" that there is a generic content of the many different type of mystical experiences which "is literally and objectively true" (405). His arguments for this, to say the least, are not made very explicit, so much so that many commentators claim that James gave no arguments at all.[20] With a little sympathetic imagination and anachronistic hindsight, I believe that we can detect two arguments in James: the argument from analogy with sense experience and the argument from an inference to the best explanation. The former is far more important and will be considered first.

This argument has been very ably defended in recent years by Wainwright, Swinburne, Gutting, and especially William Alston, whose forthcoming *Perceiving God* is certain to become a classic. By beginning first with an overview of their argument, I believe that we shall be able to locate it, or at least the germ of it, in James without being anachronistic to the point of developing a private history of philosophy, as has one very prominent contemporary interpreter of James. The argument goes as follows. Mystical and sense experiences are analogous in cognitively relevant respects; and, since the latter are granted to be cognitive, we should grant the same status to the former, in which a cognitive type of experience is one that counts as evidence or warrant for believing that the apparent object of the experience objectively exists and is as it appears to be in the experience. In regard to sense experience there is a presumptive inference rule that if it perceptually appears to be the case that X exists, then it probably is the case that X exists, unless there are defeating conditions. If mystical experiences are to be subject to this kind of presumptive inference rule, they must be analogous to sense experiences in having defeating conditions. Since a defeating condition is a test or check that is flunked, they must have tests and checks for their veridicality that are sufficiently analogous to those for sense experience. The analogical argument then proceeds by showing that this is for the most part the case, the cases in which their tests are disanalogous being explicable in terms of a difference in the categoreal nature of the apparent object of the two types of experience.[21] Among the important tests that they share in common are the agreement and prediction tests. For example, the fact that there is widespread agreement among mystics, as well as the fact that they show a favorable moral and spiritual development as a result of their experience, should count as evidence for the objectivity of their experience.

With a little imagination we can find all of the elements of this argument in VRE. In the first place, James makes a prominent use of a perceptual model of mystical experience, which is the analogical premiss of the contemporary argument. He comes right out and says:

> Our own more 'rational' beliefs are based on evidence exactly similar in nature to that which mystics quote for theirs. Our senses, namely, have assured us of certain states of fact; but mystical experiences are as direct perceptions of fact for those who have them as any sensations ever were for us. The records show that even though the five senses be in abeyance in them, they are absolutely sensational in their epistemological quality. (336)

Furthermore, like the contemporary defenders of the analogical argument for the cognitivity of mystical experiences, James goes on to fill out the analogy by showing that there are analogous defeating conditions for mystical experiences as there are for sense experiences. What is apparently revealed by mystical experiences "must be sifted and tested, and run the gauntlet of confrontation with the total context of experience just like what comes from the outer world of sense" (338). Mystical experiences are also likened to "windows through which the mind looks out upon a more extensive and inclusive world" than is revealed by our senses, and just as we have checks and tests for mediating between rival sensory-based claims there are analogous ones for mediating between rival mystically-based claims. Because of these defeating conditions, it will be possible for mysticism to have "its valid experiences and its counterfeit ones, just as our world has them...We should have to use its experiences by selecting and subordinating and substituting just as is our custom in this ordinary naturalistic world; we should be liable to error just as we are now" (339). Further indication of just how close James is to the contemporary analogical arguers is his claim that mystical experiences "establish a presumption" in favor of things being as it appears to be in them (336), which sounds very much like their presumptive inference rule.[22]

Like these contemporaries, James also recognizes a mystical analogue to the sensory agreement and prediction tests, though he adds a third one—the immediate luminosity test. Here, in brief, is how they work.

James makes a very broad application of the agreement test so that it concerns not only whether there is agreement among the mystics themselves but whether their reports agree with ordinary sensory-based ones. In regard to the former, he first says that there is a consensus among mystics and that "it would be odd...if such a unanimous type of experience should prove to be altogether wrong" (336). However, he immediately counters that "the appeal to numbers has no logical force" and that there is considerable disagreement among the monistic and pluralistic mystics, not to mention their collective disagreement with demoniacal mysticism. Not only doesn't the agreement test support the objectivity of mystical experience when only mystical experiences are considered, it counts against this when the sensory-based experiences are brought in. Mystical experiences "do not come to everyone; and the rest of life makes either no connexion with them, or tends to contradict them more than it confirms them" (22). And, against the claims of monistic mystics, James says that the "eaches" of the pluralists "are at any rate real enough to have made themselves at least appear to everyone, whereas the absolute has as yet appeared immediately to only a few mystics, and indeed to them very ambiguously" (PU 62).

James, I believe, tries to soften this clash between mysticism and sense experience by giving a very understated conclusion concerning what mystical experiences ultimately proclaim.

> As a rule, mystical states merely add a supersensuous meaning to the ordinary outward data of consciousness. They are excitements like the emotions of love or ambition, gifts to our spirit by means of which facts already objectively before us fall into a new expressiveness and make a new connexion with our active life. They do not contradict these facts as such, or deny anything that our senses have immediately seized. (338)

(The same protective strategy seems operative in James's bizarre initial set of defining characteristics of mystical experiences on pp. 302-3 in which he fails to include being a unitive experience, this being the feature of them that might clash with the deliverances of sense experience.) This aptly could be called the "comic book" theory of mystical experiences, since they are supposed to function as do the field of force lines that comic books place around an object that is perceived or thought in a specially intense manner. This at best fits the experiences at the undeveloped end of the mystical spectrum, such as drunkenness, but not those unitive experiences at the developed end, which not only report new facts, e.g. the existence of James's higher dimensions of reality, but also sometimes seem to contradict our sensory-based beliefs concerning the reality of space, time and multiplicity. James does not want us to have to serve on a jury and decide whether to believe the testimony of the mystics or that of the vast majority of mankind, but he does not map out any strategy for preventing the matter from going to trial. William Wainwright's discussion in his *Mysticism* could help James here.

Whereas the agreement test did not offer any support to the objectivity claim of mystics, quite to the contrary, the prediction test does. Because of the passive and transitory nature of mystical experiences, we are not able to predict their occurrence, and, to this extent, the prediction test counts against their objectivity. But this is more than offset by the fact that so many mystics grow morally and spiritually as a result of their experience. In attacking reductivistic causal explanations of mystical experiences he says that must "inquire into their fruits for life," rather than their causes (327). This is an on-going theme in VRE, especially in Lectures I, XIV and XV.

Unfortunately, James does not clearly distinguish between these good consequences being epistemologically confirmatory of the *proposition* believed and their pragmatically justifying in the will-to-believe manner our *believing* it. The following is a typical example of this unclarity.

> Believing that a higher power will take care of us in certain ways better than we can take care of ourselves, if we only genuinely throw ourselves upon it and consent to use it, it finds the *belief*, not only not impugned, but corroborated by its observation (of good consequences. RG). (103 my italics)

—"belief" here being ambiguous between the psychological state or act of believing and the what-is-believed, the proposition. This opens James to the standard objection that he ran together the psychological benefits of belief with the confirmation of what is believed. It is here that James is far outstripped by his contemporary analogical arguers, such as Alston, who make clear in their use of the prediction test that the good consequences for the mystic and her community are confirmatory of the objectivity of a mystical experience in virtue of a conceptual or categoreal link between these consequences and the nature of the apparent object of the experience. E.g. since God is essentially good, it is probable that those who have had an objective experience of him will benefit morally and spiritually.

Immediate luminosity, the subject's intense feeling of delight and reality, figures prominently in James's network of confirmatory tests, sometimes being accorded pride of place over good consequences (23) and at others taking second place to them (21-2). An interesting question is why James, unlike his contemporary analogical arguers, used this test. The answer might be that the PP interest-relative account of existence, although not explicitly endorsed in VRE, still weighs heavily in James's thinking. This might account for James's seeming relativization of *being evidence for* to persons in his first two conclusions regarding mystical experiences.

(1) Mystical states, when well developed, usually are, and have the right to be, absolutely authoritative over the individuals to whom they come.
(2) No authority emanates from them which should make it a duty for those who stand outside of them to accept their revelations uncritically. (335)

This makes it look as if the occurrence of mystical states constitutes evidence for their objectivity for those who have them but not for those who do not, which clearly violates the principle of universalizability of *being evidence for* among persons (as well as times, as seen above), i.e. if E is evidence for person X that proposition p is true, then E is evidence for anyone that p is true. No doubt those who have mystical experiences will be caused to believe in what they seem to reveal, whereas no such causal compulsion will operate on the non-mystic, but this is a psychological issue and of no epistemological interest. Further, mystics will be more certain of the occurrence of mystical experiences than non-mystics, but this makes no difference to the evidential status of mystical experiences, only to the certainty of their occurrence. It is not my purpose to critically evaluate James's argument from analogy with sense experience for the cognitivity of mystical experiences (this I do at length in my aforementioned book), but only to show that this argument can be found in James if we read him with a bit of anachronistic imagination.

The inference to the best explanation argument, like the analogical one, is only hinted at in VRE (see 303, 304 and 381), being more fully developed in other works. Mystical states, like many other paranormal phenomena, among which James recognized telepathy and alternative or secondary personality, such as prophetic speech, automatic writing, hypnotic and mediumistic trances, all admit of explanation if we follow Frederic Myers and Fechner and posit

> a continuum of cosmic consciousness, against which our
> individuality builds accidental fences, and into which our several
> minds plunge as into a mother-sea or reservoir...Not only psychic
> research, but metaphysical philosophy and speculative biology are
> led in their own ways to look with favor on some such 'panpsychic'
> view of the universe as this. (PR 374)

In certain exceptional states the ordinary threshold of consciousness is lowered so that we become aware of what is contained or going on in this surrounding sea of consciousness, the super mind or minds, since there might be more than one mother-sea. He employed this mother-sea hypothesis to explain his 1906 mystical experiences in which he seemingly became aware of mental states not his own—free floating states within this surrounding consciousness. He distinguished his experiences from the full-blown mystical states he featured in VRE by pointing out that "in my case certain special directions only, in the field of reality, seemed to get suddenly uncovered, whereas in classical mystical experiences it appears rather as if the whole of reality were uncovered at once" ("A Suggestion about Mysticism," in EP, p. 160). For other formulations of the mother-sea hypothesis see PR 98 and 195ff, PU 134-5, 140, and "Human Immortality..." 92-4.

There are some outstanding difficulties with this inference to the best explanation for the objectivity of mystical experiences. The subconscious is far too motley a crew of odd-ball states and actions to warrant an inference to the objectivity of any given subconscious state or experience.Some of them are non-cognitive, such as hysteria (also assigned by James to the subconscious), while others, such as hypnotism and a secondary self's perceptions, are explicable in terms of ordinary sensory ways of gaining (though not processing) information, there being no need to postulate a surrounding mother-sea(s) containing free-floating bits of consciousness. Furthermore, there are problems about the compounding of conscious involved in the idea that a finite consciousness is part of a larger, enveloping consciousness, which are pointed out Gerald Myers' excellent book on William James. The major problem, which goes much deeper than the lemonade and chord cases that worried James, in which what gets compounded are sensory qualia within a single consciousness, is how the intentional states of one person can be included within another person's mind. Could a person be part of another person in the way in which a doggie-door is part of another door! This should be especially worrisome for James, who was attracted to a pluralistic mysticism or panpsychism, in which there is more than one surrounding mother-sea, because he wanted to make room for separate persons as moral agents so that they could lead the morally strenuous life. Nevertheless, his inference to the best explanation argument is not without interest.

## II. Backyard Mysticism

James's mystical needs find a handier outlet in a far more commonplace type of mystical experience consisting in a unifying intuition of the perceptual flux. Like the bluebird of happiness, it has been in our own backyard all along, but we have been blinded to it by our inveterate pragmatic bent of thought—What is to be done with this crab grass? Are the coals hot enough to put on the burgers? Again, it is his promethean pragmatism that must be overcome in his quest for a mystical type of salvation from his existential angst.

The roots of James's backyard mysticism are found in his account of inter-personal relationships in the late 1890's, particularly in "On A Certain Blindness in Human Beings" and "What Makes a Life Significant." Each person is a Sartrian type of for-itself possessed of a rich and unique inner core of consciousness. (Recall James's dissatisfaction in MT with the mechanical sweetheart because he doubts that it is good for her too.) Through an act of empathetic intuition one person can penetrate to this conscious inner core of another person and experience the world through them. This goes even further in the direction of mysticism than does Cole Porter's "I've Got You Under My Skin." James fully anticipates in these articles Buber's I-Thou relationship, which, it should be noted, also requires overcoming one's pragmatic stance to the world and the people in it—the I-It relationship. James even wanted to I-Thou the beasts and fishes. In a note of 1873 he writes:

> Sight of elephants and tigers at Barnum's menagerie whose existence, so individual and peculiar, yet stands there, so intensely and vividly real, as much as one's own, so that one feels again poignantly the unfathomableness of ontology, supposing ontology to be at all. (TC 224)

Not to slight the fishes, in a letter of 1899 to his wife, he says:

> four cuttle-fish in the Aquarium. I wish we had one of them for a child--such flexible intensity of life in a form so inaccessible to our sympathy. (Reported in Gay Wilson Allen, *William James* (Viking, NY: 1967), p. 309.)

Maybe James would have had more luck with a cat, as did Buber. James wanted to go all the way and I-Thou the entire universe, which is what underlies his pluralistic pantheism or piecemeal supernaturalism. Clearly, James is personalizing the universe when he writes:

> The Universe is no longer a mere *It* to us, but a *Thou*, if we are religious; and any relation that may be possible from person to person might be possible here ("The Will to Believe" 27).

He later contrasts theoretic or scientific knowledge, which "touches only the outer surface of things," with a "living contemplation or sympathetic acquaintance with them" (PU 111). (See also his "Emerson" oration in ERM.)

James's pure Bergsonian intuition of the perceptual flux is his way of I-Thouing reality at large in PU and SPP. Just what does it reveal about the true nature of reality? James's initial response is a close paraphrase of his "specious present" in PP—"the short duration of which we are immediately and incessantly sensible" (594)—but oddly enough he does not explicitly mention this earlier work, the possible reason being that this name made an invidious distinction between the durational present of perception and the "strict" punctal present of physics and he had become convinced in the interim that Zeno's paradoxes showed that the invidious distinction must go the other way.

> The literally present moment is a purely verbal supposition, not a position; the only present ever realized concretely being the 'passing moment' in which the dying rearward of time and its dawning future forever mix their lights. (PU 113. See also 128 and 147.)

If this is his considered account, our perception of the flux turns out to be very blurry and muddy but not very mystical. When I hear the final note of a melody that falls within the duration of my musical auditory present I also am hearing all of the previous notes with a degree of loudness that is a function of how much earlier they are than the "strict" present. (If Mozart really had a specious present of thirty minutes because he could "hear" one of his symphonies all at once, he must have had some terrible headaches.) Likewise, when I see an arm rise, I am really seeing a Hindu god whose arms vary in their degree of vividness. Maybe the damage to James's eyesight as a result of his contraction of small-pox in 1865 was more severe than even he led on, and he really did perceive things in this fuzzy manner.[23] At any rate, there is nothing mystical about the contents of a specious present, for, although they are perceived at one fell swoop, they are perceived as being quite distinct, otherwise we would not be directly perceiving the relations of temporal precedence between the successive notes of the melody, which was the reason for introducing the specious present in the first place. A perception of a spatial or temporal field of related objects is unifying in the sense of presenting them as a unified whole but it is not unifying in the mystical sense of presenting them as identical with each other, which is a point that James misses in the above quotation from "A Suggestion about Mysticism."

Fortunately, the specious (suspicious) present isn't James's considered account of what is revealed by our pure intuition of the perceptual flux. Rather, "it presents, as if they were dissolved in one another, a lot of differents" (114). "Reality always is, in M. Bergson's phrase, an endosmosis or conflux of the same with the different: they compenetrate and telescope" (114; see also 121). Again, he speaks of "the through-and-through union of adjacent minima of experience, of the confluence of every passing moment of concretely felt experience with its immediately next neighbors" (147). This gives us a "manyness-in-oneness" with "each one of these terms being one with its neighbors, and yet the total 'oneness' never getting absolutely complete" (147). "Whatever is real is telescoped and diffused into other reals; that, in short, every minutest thing is already its hegelian 'own other,' in the fullest sense of the term" (121; see also 53 and SPP 49 and 54). Herein there is synthesis, not the mere reconciliation supplied by the "corridor" of pragmatic method in which we first do this and then do that.

These descriptions are counter-logical because they speak of a oneness between immediately successive neighbors but, pace the transitivity of identity, still insist on a numerical distinction between temporally separated contents of the perceptual stream. James is aware of this because he immediately adds that "Of course, this sounds self-contradictory" (121). The fault lies with our conceptualizing intellect and its law of identity. We must learn "to think in non-conceptualized terms" (131) by falling "back on raw unverbalized life as more of a revealer" of reality than is our "discursive thought" (121). Our conceptual distinctions, along with the hallowed laws of logic that they presuppose, are a product of our promethean self and must be overcome if we are to have the saving backyard, Bergsonian mystical experiences. "I must deafen you to talk," he says (131), and he does this, not by requiring us to follow the traditional mystical way of meditation and asceticism but rather by contemplating the koans supplied by the arguments of Zeno and Bradley and other absolute idealists to show the contradictory nature of our ordinary conceptual scheme.

The latter arguments, especially the vicious regress argument against relations (Bradley obviously never looked at a chain and saw that its links hang in each other, as the *Tractatus* tells) are at the top of the all-time El Stinko hit parade; and, when the mystical fever was not upon his brain, James refuted them by the technique of clearly stating them (e.g. see ERE 52 and PU 30-9). But, shocking as it might be, we find James embracing these very arguments in both PU and SPP for their value as koans.

> No real activities and indeed no real connexions of any kind can obtain if we follow the conceptual logic...The work begun by Zeno, and continued by Hume, Kant, Herbart, Hegel, and Bradley, does not stop till sensible reality lies entirely disintegrated at the feet of 'reason.' (PU 110. See also 115.)

Concepts not only do not completely capture the nature of reality—a trivial point—"they falsify...and make the flux impossible to understand" (SPP 45). James's endorsement of the El Stinko arguments is not unqualified. The arguments work on the assumption that concepts adequately portray reality. This requires, according to James impossibly high standards, that they be isomorphic in every way with this reality. (Like Bergson, he was dissatisfied with the physicist's vector diagram of a movement because it did not jump off the blackboard and run around the room.) Since the concepts are distinct from each other, so must be the realities they portray. But these concepts, being distinct from each other, cannot stand in relations to each other for the reasons given by the El Stinko arguments, and thus neither can the realities they portray. Thus, James really agrees with Bradley, et. al. that realities, be they percepts or concepts, cannot stand in any relations if they be distinct from each other!! So strong are James's mystical needs that he is willing to make a pact with the devil to find the bluebird of happiness in his own backyard.

This completes our account of James's mysticism and how it clashes with his promethean pragmatism. What are we ultimately to make of this deep-seated inconsistency that arises from his deeply divided self? This inconsistency, along with numerous other ones, comes from James's strength as a philosopher. He was the Don Juan of philosophy, a philosophical nymphomaniac who went for everything, because his perception and understanding were deeper and wider than those of your run-of-the-mill consistent philosophers. If you live in a crazy, mixed up world, such as this one, maybe the proper philosophy to embrace is an inconsistent one. Just what is wrong with being inconsistent? What is wrong with someone composing *Aida* on Monday and *The Rites of Spring* on Friday? It is surprising, and unfortunate, that James never turned his own pragmatic test on the acceptance of the law of non-contradiction. Like Quine, whose web of belief is a close cousin of his, James assumes without further consideration that whenever a contradiction breaks out within our system of beliefs we must go back to the drawing board and reject some of our former beliefs. Maybe he should have pushed his pragmatism further.[24]

### Notes

1. References will be to the *Briefer Version* (Harvard University Press, Cambridge: 1948), hereafter TC. See especially pp. 122 and 359.
2. *Pragmatism* (hereafter P), p. 37. All references to James's writings are to the ACLS-sponsored Harvard University Press editions of *The Works of William James*, the only exception being *The Will to Believe* (Dover, NY: 1956), and will be included in the body of the text. An interesting question is why James chose a pejorative way of designating his beloved doctrine. Both he and his father used at various places in their writings the unqualified phrase "the trail of the serpent" to designate something as evil (At P 16, for an example, he speaks of "the trail of the serpent of rationalism"), so why should "the trail of the *human* serpent" represent something we should be happy about? I can think of two possible

explanations that can be used singly or together. His usage was a tongue-in-cheek ploy to disarm his rationalist or intellectualist opponents by diplomatically letting them know that he is aware that they will see a form of evil in it and, furthermore, expressing some sympathy for their point of view. Another explanation is that he himself, or at least one of his many selves, aspired after objective truth and thereby viewed his brand of humanism as a booby prize. We shall see that the later mystical side of James did reach out for just such a truth about the true nature of reality.

3. James also used "humanism" to mean that "though one part of our experience may lean upon another part to make it what it is in any one of several aspects in which it may be considered, experience as a whole is self-containing and leans on nothing" (*The Meaning of Truth*, hereafter MT, p. 72). James failed to notice that this definition is logically distinct from the Schillerian one in that someone could be a thorough-going materialist, and thus qualify as a humanist in the MT-sense, and yet be an ardent scientific realist, and thus not qualify as a humanist in the Schillerian sense.

4. This gloss on the given in James tries to resolve some surface inconsistencies among his different presentations. In his "G. Papini and the Pragmatist Movement in Italy," in *Essays in Philosophy* (hereafter EP), p. 148, he first claims that we cannot separate off the subjective from the objective factors in the development of truth, but then goes on to say that by studying this development in the past we can see how subjective factors were involved, thereby implying that we can separate off the subjective contribution from the objectively given. Again, he says that "what we grasp is always some substitute for it (an independent reality) which previous human thinking has peptonized and cooked for our consumption...wherever we find it, it has already been faked" (P 119-20), but then attempts to illustrate this through the use of presented figures, such as star configurations and geometrical shapes, that can be grouped together or interpreted in more than one way and says that "in all these cases we humanly make an addition to some sensible reality..." (P 121), which seems to imply that we can distinguish between the objective and subjective factors.

5. See p. 1144 of PP and p. 375 of the *Briefer Course* version. This raises the burning question, cowardly overlooked so far by all of the commentators, as to why Latins turned into Slavs in the intervening two years. It seems to me that there are the following explanations: (a) James had a precognition of the mad Pole, Lutoslawski, whom he was to meet in 1893; (b) the Italian Defamation League made James an offer he couldn't refuse; or, (c), which is more likely the case according to Nick Rescher, he got to know Santayana better.

6. The James Fallacy also is evident in his account of negation. He again starts out with a claim about psychological genesis—"we never disbelieve anything except for the reason that we believe something else which contradicts the first thing" (PP 914)—from which the corresponding semantic and ontological propositions eventually are inferred. There

is a subtle inconsistency in James's adherence to this incompatibility theory of negation and his claim in *Some Problems of Philosophy* (hereafter SPP, pp. 26-30) that there is an ultimate mystery of existence in that we cannot explain why there is something rather than nothing. As Bergson showed in his *Creative Evolution*, the incompatibility theory of negation, when interpreted ontologically, entails, pace the mystery of existence, that it is necessary that some positive reality exist, since something can fail to exist only if there exists in its place some positive reality that logically excludes it. James read this book in 1907 and heaped lavish praise upon it, but he still adhered to the mystery of existence in SPP, which he began to write *two years later*. Maybe he had ceased to accept the ontological version of the incompatibility theory of negation. For a full discussion of this issue see my "Bergson's Analysis of the Concept of Nothing," *The Modern Schoolman* 51 (1974), 269-300.

7. Again we see James committing the James Fallacy. He opens his inquiry by asking what are the empirical grounds of our "sense of personal identity" (PP 314) and, after giving a Locke-Hume type analysis, draws the ontological and semantical conclusions respectively that "Resemblance among the parts of a continuum of feelings...thus constitutes the real and verifiable 'personal identity' which we feel" and that "the meaning of personal identity" is constituted of this "empirical and verifiable thing" (PP 319). A very striking instance of the James Fallacy is his claim that "the reasons why we call things true is the reason why they *are* true" (P 37).

8. Obviously, this is James's translation of the Italian "di capo di tutti di capo," which shows a strong Mafia influence as early as 1890 and thereby supports the (b) explanation in note 5 above of why explosive Latins turned into explosive Slavs in the 1892 *Briefer Course*.

9. The generalized conclusion is James's alternative sense of "humanism" in MT to the Schillerian one. See note 3 above. This conclusion, that the "apprehended universe needs...no extraneous trans-empirical connective support," might seem to clash with his espousal of "the mystery of existence" in SPP (see note 6 above). But, we could understand the former as denying that we need to appeal to any "transempirical" reality in order to explain only the fact that relations obtain among empirical objects, not the further fact that this entire aggregate of empirical objects exists or that there exist any empirical objects at all.

10. James's dispute with Hume over the givenness of relations is a queer one; for, while James agrees with Hume that we do not have a *sensible idea* of a relation, he contends that nevertheless we *feel* them, which sounds a bit like Berkeley saying that although he did not have an idea of his soul he had a notion of it. Would Hume want to deny this? It would seem that what results are derived from the application of a certain method of phenomenological analysis or introspection is determined in advance by how we define the permissible contents of such a search. Hume was performing only a mock search when he introspected his mind to see if it contained the idea of his self or a necessary connection

(just as Berkeley's Hylas was when he searched his mind for an idea of a triangle in general), for he so defined the possible contents of such a search so as to ensure that he would not stumble on such queer birds. James, on the other hand, has a more liberal definition that ensures he will.

11. For a discussion of this issue see my "Dewey and the Problem of the Paradox of the Alleged Futurity of Yesterday," *Philosophy and Phenomenological Research* 22 (1962).

12. This is the 1904 reprint in the *Journal of Philosophy, Psychology, and Scientific Method* of the 1898 California address, "Philosophical Concepts and Practical Results," in which James first formulates his pragmatism. Its discussion of the no-future case is identical with his account in P with one important exception that soon will be indicted.

13. One wonders what sort of perversity permitted James, knowing its flaw, to repeat this discussion eight years later in his P. The only explanation I can offer is that James had an incredibly low threshold of boredom (as witnessed by his abhorrence of reading proof) and just couldn't get himself to chew over an earlier discussion. There is something to be said in favor of the Germans, about whose method of investigation in psychology James said that it "taxes patience to the utmost, and could hardly have arisen in a country whose natives could be *bored*" (PP 192).

14. For an account of the complete set of necessary conditions for being morally permitted to believe upon insufficient evidence see my "William James and the Ethics of Belief," *American Philosophical Quarterly* v. 17 no. 1 (1980), and Chapter 9 of my book, *On the Nature and Existence of God* (Cambridge University Press, Cambridge: 1991). There is a conceptual problem of whether we can believe at will or voluntarily, as is required by the will-to-believe doctrine. James's account of belief has the consequence that we can when through an effort of concentration we are able to be conscious of a certain propositional-type content for a sufficient time, with sufficient intensity, and without any competitors. For those propositions that we cannot believe at will in this manner, James is willing to go along with a Pascalian account of how we can do things that will help to induce the belief (see PP 948-51). Herein we should not speak of having an option to believe them but only of having an option to do those things that will help to induce belief. At times James presents his will-to-believe in a trivial way that does not challenge the moral prohibitions of those like Clifford and Huxley who have mounted a "Just Say No to Epistemically Unwarranted Belief!" crusade. ("Sure, kid, your epistemically unwarranted belief that the Penguins will win the Stanley Cup may give you some short-range comfort, but it will make you turn into Joe Isuzu—"the liar and the cheat"—and this will create a plague that will cause humanity eventually to fall back into barbarism, so reasoned Clifford, the crazed act utilitarian.) What is required is not belief but the adoption of a proposition as a working hypothesis to guide our conduct, as happens when we adopt a proposition as a working hypothesis in science for the purpose of setting up new experiments or choose to travel along one of several paths that might

lead us to safety, as in the Fitz-James Stephen mountain pass example with which "The Will to Believe" ends. In "Reason and Faith" in *Essays in Religion and Morality*, hereafter ERM, p. 125, he says that he will accept the melioristic prophecy "as if it were true so far as my advocacy and actions are concerned." And, again, "To sum up, faith and *working hypothesis* are here one and the same." ("Some Reflections on the Subjective Method" 337. See also "The Sentiment of Rationality," in EP, p. 36, for a similar remark.) But for the most part James requires good old-fashioned sweating-with-conviction type of belief. This is especially evident in his confidence-building type cases, such as the one on p. 332 of "Some Reflections on the Subjective Method" in which a person's prior belief in her ability to leap a certain chasm is a causally necessary condition of her succeeding in jumping it—quite different from the mountain pass example in which your success in finding your way to safety by selecting in the manner of Buridan's ass some path is not dependent in any way upon your belief that it is the right path.

15. One way to square James's will-to-believe with the moral principle of universality is to interpret him as giving only a sufficient, not, as I interpreted him, both a sufficient and necessary, condition for being morally permitted to believe upon insufficient evidence. This would have the consequence that the stronger willed person no longer is forbidden to believe R, now having the same rights and privileges as the weaker-willed person. Whatever might be the merits of this way out of the problem, it does not agree with the text. See in particular pp. 19 and 29 of the WB.

16. John McDermott, in his *Introduction to The Writings of William James* (University of Chicago Press, Chicago: 1977) speculates that the cause of James's depression was that his father served as a poor role model by eschewing having any profession throughout his life. If I am right, this can't be the whole story. James would have despaired even if his father had been a bricklayer and pulled strings to get him in the union.

17. To make it such he had to show that our reason could not decide the issue. His strategy was to "argue" (though he actually gave us only question-begging "ball-and-chain" metaphorical descriptions of determinism) that freedom entails indeterminism and then show that it is impossible for our reason to choose between determinism and indeterminism, thus leaving it open to our passions to decide the issue. The way he defended the impossibility is quite different in his 1884 "Dilemma of Determinism" than it is in the 1890 PP and "The Will" chapter (which also features explosive Slavs in place of Latins) in the 1899 *Talks to Teachers on Psychology and to Students on Life's Ideals*, hereafter TT). In "Dil of Det" on p. 152 he claimed that the dispute concerns the truth of certain counterfactuals concerning whether or not things would always eventuate in the same way they actually did if the exact same state of the universe were to recur, though it doesn't. Following Peirce's account of counterfactuals in the 1878 "How To Make Our Ideas Clear" paper, which James first heard when it was presented to the Metaphysical Club in the early seventies, James claimed that there

is no fact of the matter, since "only facts can be proved by other facts," and thus there is nothing to be known. In PP he granted that there is a fact of the matter but claimed that our powers of mensuration could never be able to determine whether those brain events that are the correlates of our efforts to attend are fully determined (PP 1176). It is well that James changed his mind. The Peircean account of counter-factuals, in addition to being quite implausible, seems to offer no accusative for a will-to-believe since there is no fact of the matter. Certainly, James's pragmatic theory of meaning would have consigned such counterfactuals to the dung heap of the meaningless.

18. For a good account of James's rejection of meliorism in VRE see John Smith's splendid Introduction to VRE, especially pp. xxv-i, xxx, and xxlv.

19. James used this pair of distinctions as if they were interchangeable, but actually they sit askew of each other. The former is an *etymologically* based distinction that concerns whether or not one undergoes a rebirth along the way to salvation, the latter a *doctrinally* based distinction concerning the status that is accorded to evil in one's eventual world-view. Were the distinctions identified, it would result in cross-classifi-cations, since some healthy-minded persons are twice-born in that their eventual up-beat world-view concerning evil resulted from a rebirth or conversion experience. The French translator of VRE, Abauzit, wrote James about this difficulty, but James, with his typical abhorrence of rewriting, wrote back to go ahead with the book as is in spite of this flaw, giving the lame excuse that we should "Beware of logic in natural history" (Appendix VI of VRE 508).

20. Even so sensitive and sympathetic a critic as John Wild, in *The Radical Empiricism of William James* (Doubleday, Garden City: 1969), claimed that James's acceptance of the objectivity of mystical experiences "is not based on theoretical argument, nor on causal inference of any kind" (325), though he later inconsistently says that on the basis of the similarity between mystical and sense experience "James *concludes* that this object (the intentional accusative of a mystical experience) is real" (328 my italics). If there are no arguments, then there are no conclusions. Ayer, in his incompetent Introduction to P and MT, also fails to find any arguments in James, though he says that "There is a suggestion in VRE that he is willing to count religious experiences as evidence" for the existence of a supersensible reality (xx). This will be seen to be a radically misleading understatement.

21. I try my best to demolish this argument in chapter 8 on "Arguments from Religious Experience" in my book *On the Nature and Existence of God*.

22. If James did accept such a presumptive inference rule, he would not be committing the howler of inferring that the apparent object of a mystical experience objectively exists from the mere fact that it appears to exist to its subject, as he seems to do in the following: "the theologian's contention that the religious man is moved by an external power is vindicated, for one of the peculiarities of invasions from the subconscious region is that they take on objective appearances, and suggest to the

Subject an external control" (403; see also PU 139 for more of the same). He seemingly drops the intentional operator "take on" and "suggest" as he moves from the "seeming"-premiss to the "objectively is"-conclusion. Given the presumptive inference rule, the inference becomes valid provided the conclusion is weakened to, "*It probably is the case that the apparent object of a mystical experience exists.*"

23. But I doubt it. Rather his account of the specious present looks like a faked piece of voodoo phenomenology that is specially designed to undercut the dispute between the Humean atomists and the Kantian transcendentalists over the status of temporal relations by showing that they share a common diseased assumption—that we do not immediately perceive temporal relations between sensible contents. James is a veritable Jack Horner who can pull out of his phenomenological pie whatever is called for so as to dispel philosophical puzzlement. I am amazed at how widely James is praised as a phenomenologist. There is a failure here to distinguish between good phenomenology and good prose.

24. I am deeply indebted to James Conant for his help on this paper.

Philosophical Perspectives, 5, Philosophy of Religion, 1991

# THE PROSPECTS FOR NATURAL THEOLOGY

Alvin Plantinga
University of Notre Dame

## I. What is Natural Theology For?

What is natural theology, and what is it for? As to what it *is*, for present purposes we may take it, very simply, to be the attempt to provide proofs or arguments for the existence of God. More exactly, it is the project of producing proofs or arguments for *theism*, the view (roughly speaking) that there exists an all-powerful, all-knowing, wholly good person who has created the world. Clearly there are many things one might hope to accomplish by offering such arguments. You might be a believer in God yourself and might try to convince someone else to join you in this belief. Or you might be a wavering or troubled believer in God, and be trying to convince yourself. Or you might have no initial views on the subject and propose to come to a position on the matter by way of considering the evidence for and against. Or you might think theism useful in philosophy, in that it offers suggestions for answers to a wide range of otherwise intractable questions, and look for some arguments; you might then look for some arguments for theism, as part of your effort to deal with those questions.

### A. Fides Quarens Intellectum

But of course there are other, historically more prominent reasons for working at natural theology: to consider some of the more important ones we must make a brief historical *excursus*. According to one important strand of medieval thought, we begin with faith, but a faith that is seeking understanding: *fides quarens intellectum*. According to this tradition we have *understanding* when we have scientific knowledge, *scientia*, of the item in question; and we have *scientia* when we *see* that the item in question is true by seeing that it follows from what we see to be true. From this perspective, a central function of the theistic proofs would be to transform faith into knowledge, belief into *scientia*.[1] (Of course there is also the Augustinian-Bonaventurian medieval tradition; and for that tradition *fides quarens intellectum* is to be understood quite differently.) But in at least one important strand of the broadly Thomistic tradition, the central function of natural theology is that of transforming faith into knowledge. According to Aquinas, a person might be perfectly justified, perfectly within her rights, indeed, thoroughly meritorious in believing in God without the benefit of argument. Still, such a person does not have knowledge (*scientia)* of God's existence; she *believes* but does not *know*. He holds that it is possible for some of us, however—those of us who have the inclination, the ability, and the leisure—to *see* that God exists by way of the theistic proofs: the five ways, for example. Such a person *knows* that God exists, has *scientia* of that fact; and to have *scientia* is in general[2] a higher and better epistemic condition than merely to believe. Why so? On this way of thinking of the matter, what is self-evident (i.e., self-evident to us) has maximal epistemic status (for us); and what can be seen to be true by virtue of being seen to follow from what is self-evident has equivalent or nearly equivalent status. Suppose we say that *the deliverances of reason* are the propositions that are self-evident to us together with the propositions that we can see follow from them by way of arguments whose validity is self-evident for us. Then the deliverances of reason will have maximal (or near maximal) epistemic status for us; and to show that a proposition is among the deliverances of reason will suffice to show that its epistemic status is (almost) maximally great. A successful piece of natural theology, therefore, would be an argument that showed that the existence of God is among the deliverances of reason. It would start from premises that are self-evident; it would proceed by a self-evidently valid argument to the conclusion that indeed there is such a person as God; and it would thereby enable at least some of us to have *scientia* of the proposition in question. So another proposed reason for natural theology would be to make it possible for you yourself or someone else to *know* that God exists, to have *scientia* of this fact, to *see* that it is so, as opposed to merely believing it.

Can natural theology in fact perform such a function? I don't have the space here to go into this matter with the care it deserves: I shall have to be brief and dogmatic. First, on the view in question self-evidence is not a matter of degree; a proposition is self-evident to us or it is not. A proposition is self-evident (for us) only if it is such that we can simply see it to be true (and furthermore, says Aquinas, such that we couldn't so much as entertain it *without* seeing that it is true.) The fact is, I think (and here Aquinas need not disagree), that there are many degrees of intuitive warrant; and only a proposition that enjoys the highest degree of intuitive warrant for us is such that a person can't even entertain it without seeing that it is true. There are many degrees of self-evidence or intuitive warrant: it is self-evident *in excelsis* that $2+1 = 3$; it is nearly as clear that no propositions are both true and false; it is perhaps almost as obvious that every proposition is either true or false; it is less obvious (but still obvious) that (pace Meinong and Castañeda) there aren't any things that do not exist; it is still less obvious (but nonetheless obvious) that no propositions are sets.[3] The propositions that have intuitive warrant for us (what reason teaches us) have *varying* degrees of warrant, ranging all the way from cast iron certainty through great plausibility to substantial probability. If so, however, the deliverances of reason properly so-called will include propositions of varying degrees of warrant. And then it becomes less plausible to think that theism gains a really impressive epistemic status by being shown to be among the deliverances of reason. It would have that *maximal* degree of warrant or positive epistemic status only if it were shown to follow from what had maximal intuitive warrant by way of argument steps that themselves enjoyed that exalted status. It is doubtful, however, that any of the arguments of natural theology even approach that lofty and baronial condition. None of them, so far as I can see, measures up to the enormously high standards to which they would have to conform if they were to show that the existence of God has this maximal epistemic status. (Of course that is so far nothing against them; *no* philosophical argument of any significance measures up to those standards.) But then it seems unlikely that natural theology can serve the function of transforming faith into knowledge at least in the way outlined above.

## B. *Justifying Theistic Belief*

There is another historically important motive for engaging in natural theology. Many have held that to believe in God without believing on the basis of propositional evidence—without having an argument from other things you believe, for example—is somehow intellectually second-rate, intellectually improper, unjustified, out of order. (More subtly, the view might be that if there are no good arguments of that sort, then the believing community, to use Stephen Wykstra's term, is in "big doxastic trouble.") Under those conditions, belief in God would be *unjustified*; more exactly, the *believer* would be unjustified, doing something contrary to epistemic duty or obligation, doing something impermissible, something she has no right to do. Thus W. K. Clifford entitles his famous essay "The Ethics of Belief"[4] and loudly trumpets that "it is wrong, always, everywhere and for anyone to believe anything upon insufficient evidence." William James, in reply, entitles *his* essay "The Will to Believe"[5]; "The Right to Believe" would have been a more accurate title[6], since his central claim was that in some circumstances it is permissible, not contrary to duty or obligation, to believe even when you don't have evidence. The Cliffordian idea is that there is a sort of intellectual duty or obligation not to believe in God without having evidence, or sufficient evidence. If there is no evidence, or insufficient evidence, the believer is unjustified; she is flouting her epistemic duties. Clifford is not indulgent towards such dereliction of epistemic duty: "If a belief has been accepted on insufficient evidence, the pleasure is a stolen one. Not only does it deceive ourselves by giving us a sense of power which we do not really possess, but it is sinful, because it is stolen in defiance of our duty to mankind."[7] (Here one gets a whiff of that "robustious pathos" with which James credits him.)

Contemporary evidentialist objectors (for example, Brand Blanshard, Antony Flew, John Mackie, Bertrand Russell, Michael Scriven), though perhaps displaying less of that robustious pathos, nevertheless join Clifford in putting their objection in terms of obligations, permission and rights. Thus Brand Blanshard:

> Everywhere and always belief has an ethical aspect. There is such a thing as a general ethics of the intellect. The main principle of that ethic I hold to be the same inside and outside religion. This principle is simple and sweeping: Equate your assent to the evidence.[8]

The problem with the believer in God, they say, is that she holds her beliefs without having sufficient evidence; and the problem with *that* is that it goes contrary to our intellectual duties and obligations. Evidentialist objectors to theistic belief argue that there is insufficient evidence for theistic belief, and to believe something for which you have insufficient evidence is to go contrary to your epistemic duties. This view that there is a duty not to believe in God without propositional evidence has a long and distinguished history, going back at least to Locke[9] and possibly to Descartes; it has been popular ever since. As Locke sees the matter,

> Faith is nothing but a firm assent of the mind: which if it be regulated, as is our duty, cannot be afforded to anything, but upon good reason; and so cannot be opposite to it. He that believes, without having any reason for believing, may be in love with his own fancies; but neither seeks truth as he ought, nor pays the obedience due his maker, who would have him use those discerning faculties he has given him, to keep him out of mistake and error. He that does not this to the best of his power, however he sometimes lights on truth, is in the right but by chance; and I know not whether the luckiness of the accident will excuse the irregularity of his proceeding. This at least is certain, that he must be accountable for whatever mistakes he runs into: whereas he that makes use of the light and faculties God has given him, and seeks sincerely to discover truth, by those helps and abilities he has, may have this satisfaction in doing his duty as a rational creature, that though he should miss truth, he will not miss the reward of it. For he governs his assent right, and places it as he should, who in any case or matter whatsoever, believes or disbelieves, according as reason directs him. He that does otherwise, transgresses against his own light, and misuses those faculties, which were given him... .(*Essay* IV, xvii, 24)

Locke held that some propositions are *certain* for me: those that are self-evident, such as $2 + 1 = 3$, and those that are about my own immediate experience, such as *I feel a mild pain*, or *I seem to see something red*, or (to borrow Roderick Chisholm's terminology) *I am appeared to redly*. Here duty and obligation have no relevance; for, says Locke, it is not within my power to withhold a belief of that sort. As for other propositions, however—those that are *not* certain for me—duty requires that I believe them only if I have reason to do so: only if, that is, the belief in question is probable with respect to those beliefs that are certain for me.

So Locke holds that we rational creatures have epistemic (better, doxastic) duties: duties to regulate or govern our beliefs in the correct ways,[10] or duties to try to achieve a state in which they are thus properly ordered. Chief among these duties is that of believing a proposition only if it is probable with respect to what is certain for you; hence the claim that belief in God is permissible only if you have evidence for it (that is, only if it is probable with respect to propositions that are certain for you). To act in accord with these duties or obligations is to be within one's rights; it is to be approvable; it is to be *justified*. Clearly this deontological territory of duty and permission is where the whole notion of justification has its natural home. To be justified is to be without blame, to be within your rights, to have done no more than what is permitted, to have violated no duty or obligation, to warrant no blame or censure. The Lockean view, then, is that (1) you are justified if and only if you conform to your duties, and (2) among those duties is the obligation to refrain from believing a proposition that isn't self-evident or appropriately about your experience unless you have propositional evidence for it: evidence from other things you believe, and evidence that must trace back, ultimately, to what is certain for you.

This view has been enormously influential in western epistemological thought since the Enlightenment; indeed, it has achieved the status of epistemological orthodoxy. There is impressive testimony to our contemporary debt to Locke in the fact that we sometimes seem to use the expression 'justified in believing' just to *mean* 'has sufficient evidence for'. It is easy to see how this might come about. Suppose you begin by agreeing with Locke that among your duties is that of not giving "firm assent" to any uncertain proposition without having good reasons (i. e. propositional evidence) for it; then you will think that no one is justified in accepting such a belief without evidence or reason; and you may come eventually to use the term 'justified belief' as a synonym for 'belief for which one has good reasons'.

From this dominant Lockean perspective, then, a person is within her rights in believing in God only if she has propositional evidence for that belief. The evidentialist objector claims that none of us *does* have adequate evidence for that belief, so that those of us who do believe stand revealed as epistemic malefactors. On the other hand, you might think that one way to justify theistic belief, or bring it about that we *are* justified in accepting it, is by way of discovering and providing good theistic arguments. In this way natural theology could be used to provide *justification* for theistic belief. If I come up with a good theistic argument, I will thereby bring it about that I am justified in accepting theistic belief. I can also help others achieve justification in *their* theistic beliefs; for they can read and understand my argument, thus acquiring justification. (Alternatively, in a Wykstrarian vein I thus help protect the entire believing community from big doxastic trouble.) From this perspective, then, the central function of natural theology is to justify theistic belief, bring it about that it is permissible to accept it.

This alleged function of natural theology has more contemporary interest, in a way, than the Thomistic project of transforming faith into knowledge; for the idea that there is an epistemic duty to believe only if there is propositional evidence, like the evidentialist objection to theistic belief, is still very much with us.[11] But I shall argue briefly that this alleged function of natural theology doesn't need to be fulfilled. The basic reason is that there is no general intellectual duty to proportion one's belief, in this way, to the evidence, at least if my *evidence* is understood, Lockean fashion, as an assembly of beliefs—those beliefs that are self-evident to me or immediately about my own experience. Of course it is hard to *prove* that there is no such duty. But first, the whole history of modern thought from Descartes and Locke to Hume and Reid show that if there *is* such a duty, then we all constantly violate it in accepting memory beliefs, beliefs about other persons, beliefs about the ordinary physical objects of our environment, and so on. And why think, after all, that there is such a duty? Why am I not entirely within my rights, intellectual, or moral, or whatever, in believing with great firmness that I now see an ant on top of my computer—even if I can't produce much by way of noncircular evidence from self-evident propositions together with beliefs about how I am being appeared to? It isn't easy to take seriously this suggestion that in so doing I might be going contrary to epistemic duty. Why believe that I have any such duty? The proposition that there is such a duty is itself neither self-evident nor an account of how I am being appeared to; if there is such a duty, therefore, it is incumbent upon us to believe that there is only if there is an argument to the conclusion that there is such a duty from propositions that are self-evident or immediately about immediate experience: what would that evidence be?

But then we must raise the same question about belief in God: is there really a good reason for thinking that a believer in God who has no propositional evidence (no evidence from his other beliefs) is going contrary to his duty? Surely this is questionable *in excelsis*.[12] If, after careful and mature reflection, I find myself with the firm belief that there is such a person as God, how could I be violating my duty? Of course it is possible that I was undutiful *earlier on* and as a result now find myself believing in this way. But surely it is wholly implausible to suppose that belief in God either invariably is or results from epistemic iniquity. Conceivably there is *some* sort of problem for believers in God (or the believing community) if there aren't good arguments from natural theology; but it isn't surely, that under those conditions they would be flouting their intellectual duties. That is no more plausible than the claim that I am thus flouting duty in believing that the world is more than 5 minutes old (thus rejecting Bertrand Russell's fantasy that the world was created just 5 minutes ago, complete with all its dusty books, crumbling mountains, and other alleged evidences of a substantial past), despite the fact that I don't know how to give noncircular evidence for this belief. So this function of *justifying* believers in God, putting them in the right, putting them within their epistemic rights, bringing it about that they are or can be in conformance with their epistemic duties in believing in God—this function, I think, does not need to be performed. Those who believe in God without propositional evidence aren't necessarily falling into epistemic transgression.

## II. Warrant

I turn to still another function natural theology might perform, this one connected in an interesting way with the idea that the function of natural theology is to transform faith or belief into knowledge. No doubt Plato wasn't the first to recognize the important difference between mere true belief and knowledge; but his *Theaetetus* is the first known systematic and philosophically significant attempt to deal with that distinction. This question—the question what distinguishes mere true belief from knowledge—has been with us ever since, thus confirming Whitehead's view that Western philosophy is a series of footnotes to Plato. Suppose we use the term 'warrant' as a name for that quality, whatever exactly it is, that distinguishes knowledge from mere true belief. Thus you know what your name is; but if you get lucky and correctly guess that the Red Sox will win the pennant, then, while your belief is true, it does not constitute knowledge and does not have much by way of warrant for you. Warrant, obviously enough, comes in degrees; and a high (but not necessarily maximal) degree is necessary for knowledge. Now still another function natural theology might perform is that of providing warrant for belief in God. And here we must ask at least two questions: (a) Can belief in God have warrant apart from propositional evidence, apart from the arguments of natural theology? And (b) Can it have sufficient warrant to constitute *knowledge* apart from natural theology?

To answer those questions, naturally enough, we must know something about the nature of warrant. What is this quality or quantity, enough of which is sufficient to distinguish knowledge from mere true belief? At present there are really three main views as to what warrant is: Classical Internalism (represented at its contemporary best by Roderick Chisholm), Coherentism, and Reliabilism. Each of these, I think, suffers from crucial and debilitating difficulty. I can't take the time here to explain and explore them in detail;[13] but I must say a word about each.

## A. Chisholmian Internalism

Very briefly, Chisholmian Internalism follows[14] the received Lockean tradition in seeing warrant in terms of aptness for fulfillment of epistemic duty; a proposition has warrant for me if believing it is a good way to fulfill my epistemic duty or obligation.[15] Chisholm proposes different ideas as to what this epistemic duty is: perhaps it is that of trying to bring it about, for any proposition I encounter, that I believe it if and only if it is true; or perhaps it is that of trying my best to bring it about that I have a large set of logically independent beliefs in which true beliefs predominate; or perhaps it is something else. Chisholm's fundamental idea is that the rational creature, the being capable of beliefs, considers the various propositions that come to her attention at a time **t**, deciding which to accept and which to withhold. If she is appropriately dutiful, she will make these decisions in the service of an attempt to fulfill her epistemic duty; and a proposition will have warrant for her to the degree to which she can fulfill this obligation by accepting it.

Sadly enough, however, it is clear that warrant cannot be explained in terms of aptness for epistemic duty fulfillment. The problem is that I can be as dutiful as you please and still my beliefs might lack warrant. I may be trying my level best to fulfill my duty to the truth; fulfilling that duty may be the main aim of my life; I may be performing magnificent works of epistemic supererogation; a belief may be such that accepting it I do my duty and more; and yet my beliefs may utterly fail to have warrant for me. Perhaps, for example, I suffer from a deep and epistemically disastrous cognitive malfunction. Perhaps (due to genetic malfunction) I suffer from the following epistemic malady: whenever I seem to see another person, I form the belief that no human being is then in North Dakota. (More exactly, under those conditions that belief is produced in me.) Perhaps this belief is as utterly attractive and compelling, for me, as my most firmly held convictions; perhaps it has, for me, all the phenomenological *panache* of $2+1 = 3$ itself. Then the dutiful thing to do, of course, would be to accept that belief; but surely it would have little by way of warrant. Even if by some wild chance it happened to be true on an occasion when it is produced in me, I wouldn't have knowledge of it.

Alternatively, perhaps you think, in a Kantian vein, that what really goes with duty is doing what one takes to be right against one's inclinations. Very well; consider the following sort of case: having incautiously read too much Kant, I nonculpably acquire the deep conviction that it is unseemly for a free, autonomous, rational being such as I to be pushed around this way by his epistemic impulses. Indeed, as I see it, this is worse than unseemly; it is wrong, and I have a duty to do what I can to free myself from the tyranny of these impulses. I therefore undertake a regimen the aim of which is to enable me to withstand ordinary impulses to believe; when my experience is of the sort normally giving rise to the belief that there is another person before me, for example, I learn to resist that belief and form instead the belief that there is no one there, or only a cleverly constructed robot. This naturally leads to a certain amount of vexation; but despite the difficulties I heroically persist in doing my duty as I see it. My friends desert me; my wife finally leaves me for someone more in step, epistemically speaking, with the rest of the world; my family finally gets me committed; I spend the rest of my days doing my duty at great cost to myself. Despite my dutifulness, however, my beliefs have little warrant; they have little of that quantity enough of which (with truth) is sufficient for knowledge. Even if the belief happens to be true, by some improbable chance, it would be wrong to say that I knew that it was. Chisholmian internalism, therefore, doesn't offer an adequate account of warrant.[16]

## B. Coherence

A second popular current account of warrant sees it as essentially involving *coherence*. The historical credentials of Coherentism are not quite as august, perhaps, as those of Chisholmian internalism; still, it goes back essentially to the absolute idealists of the last century[17] and boasts such stalwart contemporary defenders as Keith Lehrer,[18] Lawrence BonJour,[19] and at least some Bayesians. The central thing to see about Coherentism is that it is what John Pollock calls a *doxastic* theory, a view according to which the warrant of a belief depends solely upon its relations to *other beliefs*. Perhaps those significant others are all of my other beliefs, or perhaps instead some significant subset of them—those that I would still have had, had I been an earnest seeker after truth, for example, or those that meet some other condition. In any event, what counts is the relation of the belief in question to other *beliefs*. And this is the Achilles' heel, the fatal flaw of Coherentism. For, clearly enough, proper relationship to other beliefs is not sufficient for a belief to have warrant for me: the belief in question must also be properly related to my *experience*. You and I are mountaineering; we are nearing the summit of the Matterhorn. I am struck by an errant burst of high energy radiation. This induces a cognitive disorder: my beliefs no longer respond to my experience in the usual way. Ordinarily, when I am appeared to in a certain way (including, for example, being appeared to bluely), I form the belief that the sky is blue; due to the disorder, however, when I am appeared to in that way (including being appeared to bluely) I now form the belief that the sky is not blue but red, and my other beliefs settle into a coherent pattern around this one. Despite its coherence with the rest of my beliefs, this belief still has little warrant for me.

So neither Chisholmian Internalism nor Coherentism provides a good answer to the question "What is warrant?" The third important contemporary view is the *Reliabilism* of Alvin Goldman,[20] Fred Dretske,[21] William Alston[22] and others. Reliabilism comes in many forms (and more than one of these forms are due to the seminal work of Alvin Goldman); but perhaps the basic idea, the guiding intuition of reliabilism is the notion that a belief has warrant if and only if it is produced by a reliable belief-producing process or faculty or mechanism—i.e., a belief-producing process or faculty or mechanism that for the most part produces true beliefs. I shall say no more about reliabilism here, partly because the view I want to present as the sober truth bears a close relationship to it.[23]

## III. The Truth About Warrant

Neither Chisholmian Internalism nor Coherentism provides a satisfactory account of warrant; it is worth noting, however, that on either account it would be perfectly possible for basic belief in God (belief not accepted on the basis of propositional evidence) to have warrant. On the Chisholmian account, a belief has warrant for me if believing it is a good way for me to fulfill my epistemic duty to try to bring it about that I stand in the right relation to the truth; but if a proposition seems overwhelmingly obvious to me (and I have no equally obvious reason for doubting it), then presumably the dutiful thing for me to do is to believe it, or to take whatever other sort of action is appropriate to promote my holding the belief. So suppose I am powerfully convinced of the truth of theism (and didn't violate my epistemic duty in coming to be so convinced); and suppose I know of no reason to doubt its truth. Then that belief will have warrant for me, whether or not I have arguments for it from other things I believe. Similarly for coherentism: there is no reason why belief in God can't be appropriately coherent with the rest of what I believe (or the appropriate subset of the rest of what I believe). On these two ways of thinking about warrant, therefore, natural theology wouldn't be necessary for my belief in God to have warrant. That belief could have warrant for me whether or not I have good arguments or propositional evidence for it. But of course these two ways of thinking of warrant are mistaken (as I see it); it is time to turn to a more adequate account. Then we shall have to look to see, from the vantage point furnished by that more adequate account, whether or not belief in God requires natural theology in order to have warrant.

Here there is room for no more than the barest sketch of a better view of warrant, but perhaps that will be adequate for our present purposes.[24] Recall Chisholm's dutiful epistemic agents and the coherent but mistaken climber. They came to epistemic grief; each had no warrant for his belief; and in each case it was because of cognitive pathology, because of *failure to function properly*. This suggests a necessary condition of warrant: your cognitive equipment, your belief-forming and belief-sustaining apparatus, must be free of such malfunction if your beliefs are to have warrant for you. **p** has warrant for you only if your cognitive apparatus is functioning properly, subject to no dysfunction, working the way it ought to work, in producing that belief in you.[25]

Working properly, however, is obviously not the whole story. I have just had a thorough epistemic checkup by the best cognitive scientists at the Mayo clinic; I receive a clean bill of health; everything is working splendidly. I then join an exploratory voyage to a planet near alpha Centauri. There epistemic conditions are wholly different from on earth; elephants are invisible to human beings, but emit a sort of radiation that causes human beings to form the belief that a trumpet is sounding nearby. We crack the hatch and emerge; an alpha Centaurian elephant wanders by; I form the belief that a trumpet is sounding nearby. Although my cognitive faculties are functioning properly, that belief will not have warrant for me. Even if a trumpet *is* sounding nearby (in a soundproof telephone booth, perhaps), I won't know that it is. So the fact that my faculties are functioning properly is not sufficient for my having warrant for my beliefs. The problem is that my cognitive faculties and the cognitive environment in which I find myself are not properly attuned. We must therefore add another component to warrant: your faculties must be in good working order *and* the environment must be appropriate for your particular repertoire of epistemic powers.

Now it may be tempting to say that warrant just *is* proper functioning, so that a given belief has warrant for me to the degree that my faculties are functioning properly (in producing and sustaining that belief) in an environment appropriate for my cognitive equipment. But this cannot be the whole story. At the moment I believe both *2 + 1 = 3* and *forty years ago I owned a blue jacket and work shoes that had been painted silver*. Both of these beliefs, I think, are produced in me by cognitive faculties functioning properly in a congenial epistemic environment; but one has a good deal more warrant for me than the other. The difference between them, in brief, is that the first seems much more obviously true than the second; I believe the first much more firmly than the second; the impulse to believe the first is much stronger than the impulse to believe the second. The beliefs that we accept are for the most part such that our nature impels us to accept them (in the circumstances in which we do); and this impulse is much stronger in some cases than in others. The strength of this impulse, I suggest, is what determines degree of warrant (given proper function in an epistemically appropriate environment). Putting these things together, we may say that

> **Warrant is a matter of a belief's being produced by faculties that are (a) working properly in an appropriate environment, and (b) aimed at truth; and if a belief has warrant for you, then the greater your inclination to believe it the more warrant it has.**

If we wish to introduce what is at this stage an undoubtedly spurious precision, we may say

> **A belief $B$ has warrant for $S$ if and only if that belief is produced in $S$ by epistemic faculties aimed at truth and working properly (in an appropriate environment); and (in those circumstances) $B$ has more warrant than $B^*$ for $S$ if and only if $B$ has warrant for $S$ and either $B^*$ does not or $S$ is more strongly inclined to believe $B$ than $B^*$.**

This is at best a provisional account of warrant, no more than a basic idea which stands in great need of development and qualification.[26] Here I shall mention just three such matters. First, the notion of proper function itself may be thought problematic: (a) unduly vague, or (b) improperly relative to our own aims and desires, or (c) such that while it fits in well with a theist's way of looking at things, it isn't available to others. As to (a), the notion *is* vague to some degree: but so is the notion of knowledge. There too there are many borderline cases, many cases where it simply isn't clear whether **S** knows **p** or not. My hope is that the vaguenesses of knowledge and proper function coincide, so that these notions waver, shimmy, or wiggle in tandem. As to (b) relativity to our own needs and desires, this just seems wrong. We can often tell whether a bird's wing or an enemy's pistol is functioning properly, even if we happen to prefer that wing or pistol to function in some other way.

And as to the third complaint, (that the notion of proper function isn't available to nontheists), again, the suggestion seems mistaken. Anyone, theist or not, can see that a horse is diseased, or that (due perhaps to a stroke) someone's facial muscles don't work properly. Anyone, theist or not, can agree that a malfunctioning heart can lead to shortness of breath or dizzy spells, and that exposure to asbestos can lead to respiratory disorders. It is possible, of course, that the notion of proper function is tied at a deep level to theism in such a way that the only satisfying *explanations* or *analyses* of it involve divine purpose and intention or something like it: perhaps a machine or organ is functioning properly when it is functioning in such a way as to achieve the purpose for which it was designed, and furthermore working the way in which it was designed to work by the being or beings that in fact designed and made it. If so, then there lurks in the neighborhood a strong theistic argument, not an objection to this account of warrant.

Second comment: a crucially important notion here is that of specifications, or blueprint, or *design plan*: there is a design plan for our cognitive faculties. Of course this terminology doesn't commit us to supposing that human beings have been literally designed—by God for example. Here I use 'design' the way, .e.g., Daniel Dennett (not ordinarily thought unsound on supernaturalism) does in speaking of a given organism as possessing a certain design: "In the end, we want to be able to explain the intelligence of man, or beast, in terms of his design; and this in turn in terms of the natural selection of this design... ."[27] When the organs (or organic systems) of a human being (or other organism) function properly, they function *in a particular way*. Such organs have a *function* or *purpose*; such an organ, furthermore, normally functions in such a way as to fulfill its purpose; but it also functions to fulfill that purpose in *just one* of an indefinitely large number of possible ways. Here a comparison with artifacts is useful. Your house is designed to produce shelter—but not in just any old way. There will be plans specifying the length and pitch of the rafters, what kind of shingles are to be applied, the kind and quantity of insulation to be used, and the like. Something similar holds in the case of us and our faculties; we seem to be constructed in accordance with a specific set of plans. Better (since this analogy is insufficiently dynamic) we seem to have been constructed in accordance with a set of *specifications*, in the way in which there are specifications for, say, the 1988 Buick. According to these specifications (here I am just guessing), after a cold start the engine runs at 1500 RPM until the engine temperature reaches 140 degrees F.; it then throttles back to 750 RPM, its warm idling speed.

Suppose we call these specifications a 'design plan'. It is natural to speak of organisms and their parts as exhibiting design, and such talk is exceedingly common: "According to Dr. Sam Ridgway, physiologist with the US Naval Ocean Systems Center in San Diego, seals avoid the bends by not absorbing nitrogen in the first place. 'The lungs of marine mammals,' Dr. Ridgway explains, 'are designed to collapse under pressure exerted on deep dives. Air from the collapsed lungs is forced back into the windpipe, where the nitrogen simply can't be absorbed by the blood.'"[28] And of course the design plan for human beings will include specifications for our *cognitive* faculties. According to this design plan, a person will form the belief that she sees something red when her experience is of the familiar kind that goes with perceiving a large London bus; she will not, under those conditions, form the belief that she is perceiving a small black horse. Of course the design plan also involves the sort of case where one forms a belief on the evidential grounds of another belief; here too, however, there is a specific way in which this goes on. Thus, for example, you will not form the belief that Feike can swim on the evidential grounds that 9 out of 10 Frisians can't swim and Feike is a Frisian.

This design plan, however, need not be such that every module of it is aimed at producing true belief. Someone may remember a painful experience as less painful than it was, as is sometimes said to be the case with childbirth. You may continue to believe in your friend's honesty long after evidence and cool, objective judgment would have dictated a reluctant change of mind. My belief that I will recover from a serious illness may be much stronger than is justified by the statistics of which I am aware. In these cases, the relevant faculties may be functioning properly, functioning just as they ought to, but nevertheless not in a way that leads to truth, to the formation of true beliefs. And the explanation, of course, is that the modules of the design plan involved aren't aimed at true belief, but at, e.g., willingness to have more children, or the possibility of loyalty, or recovery from disease. It is this notion of a design plan that is missing from the forms of reliabilism with which I am acquainted, and it is this deficiency that is the source of the counterexamples to reliabilism.

One final matter. It is clear, I think, that this is in fact how or nearly how we do think of warrant. We would not think of it in this way, however, if we weren't accepting a kind of *presupposition of reliability*; that is, we would not think of warrant in this way if we did not think that when our faculties function properly in appropriate circumstances, then (in particular when the beliefs in question are firmly held) for the most part they are true, or close to the truth. I said above that my way of thinking of warrant is closer to reliabilism than to coherentism or Chisholmian internalism; the reason, of course, is this presupposition of reliability. To put it more exactly: say that a belief is *proper* if it is formed by properly functioning faculties in an appropriate epistemic environment, where the modules of the design plan involved in its production are aimed at true belief. Then, according to the presupposition of reliability, the probability (objective or statistical) of a proper belief's being true or nearly true is high; and (in general) the higher the degree of belief involved, the greater the statistical probability of truth.

The view I mean to propose, therefore, incorporates a reliabilist element; and to this extent I am enthusiastic about reliabilism. The latter, however, neglects the crucially important matters of proper function and design plan. This opens it to counterexamples, as I said above; it also precludes its giving a sensible account of *degrees* of warrant.

## IV. Natural Theology Needed for Warrant?

Now suppose we return to our question: are the arguments of natural theology needed for belief in God to have warrant? Must it be the case, if my belief in God is to have warrant, that either I believe on the basis of good arguments, or I believe there *are* good arguments? Must it be the case (as Wykstra suggests) that at any rate there *are* good arguments lurking somewhere in the believing community, however *I* happen to believe? Say that a belief is *basic* for a person if she holds the belief, but does not hold it on the evidential basis of other beliefs she holds. Can my belief in God have warrant even if it is held in the basic way (and even if there are no good arguments for it in the believing community)? If so, then belief in God is more like, say, a deliverance of memory than a scientific hypothesis. From our present perspective this question is transmuted into another: when people accept belief in God in the basic way, is it the case that sometimes their faculties are functioning properly and the modules of the design plan governing the formation of this belief are aimed at truth? Or is there always, in these cases, either malfunction or inappropriate cognitive environment or guidance by modules not aimed at truth, but at survival, or ease, or social harmony, or whatever?

We must complicate the question just a bit. Clearly one source of belief in God, particularly in children, is *teaching* or *testimony*. In the typical case, what we learn on the basis of testimony we believe in the basic way; we don't typically argue to it from premises involving, say, the reliability of the testifier. But in asking whether basic belief in God has warrant we mean to ask more than merely whether belief in God is sometimes produced in human beings by way of the proper function of the faculties or mechanisms at work when I believe something on the basis of someone's testimony. The question is really whether belief in God is sometimes formed or strengthened by way of circumstances—experience of a certain kind, for example—*not* directly involving testimony.

The first thing to see, I think, is that there is a wide variety of circumstances—circumstances directly involving neither argument nor the testimony of others—in which as a matter of fact people *do* find themselves with new or renewed and strengthened belief in God. More exactly, what they find themselves with are beliefs immediately entailing that there is such a person as God. When I have done something I see as cheap or wrong, I may form the believe that God disapproves of what I have done; upon asking for forgiveness, I may feel forgiven and I may form the belief that God forgives me. Upon beholding the majesty of the mountains, or the glories of the starry heavens above, or the power of the ocean, or the marvelous, highly articulate beauty of a tiny flower, I may form the belief that it was good of God to have created all this. Upon reading and reflecting on the Bible, I may find myself convinced, e.g., that God really was in Christ, reconciling the world to himself. Overwhelmed by the dark splendor of Mozart's D Minor piano concerto, you may find yourself exulting in the beauty and power of the music; and you may see God as the source of that beauty and power. In these and a thousand other circumstances[29] many human beings do in fact find themselves with new or renewed or strengthened belief in God. According to William P. Alston,

> We sometimes feel the presence of God; we sometimes get
> glimpses, at least, of God's will for us; we feel the Holy Spirit at
> work in our lives, guiding us and strengthening us, enabling us to
> love other people in a new way; we hear God speaking to us in the

Bible, in preaching, in the words and actions of our fellow Christians.[30]

And according to Richard Swinburne,

> For many people life is one vast religious experience. Many people view almost all the events of their life not merely under their ordinary description, but as God's handiwork. For many people, that is, very many of the public phenomena of life are viewed religiously and so constitute religious experiences. ...What is seen by one man as simply a wet day is seen by another as God's reminding us of his bounty in constantly providing us with food by means of his watering plants.[31]

The above circumstances and experiences are common, and as ordinary as every day; at any time there will be millions of people in those circumstances, subject to those experiences, forming those beliefs. But of course there are also many vastly less common experiences: Moses and the burning bush; Paul on the road to Damascus; Samuel; Isaiah; a host of other biblical and extra-biblical examples. And the question, from our present perspective, is this: (a) do experiences of these kinds sometimes contribute to someone's feeling impelled to believe in God, so that she is more strongly inclined to believe than she would be simply on the basis of propositional evidence and testimony? and (b) if so, does this ever happen in the case of someone whose faculties are functioning properly?

Karl Marx would answer 'yes' (no doubt) to the first question but 'no' to the second:

> Religion...is the self-consciousness and the self-feeling of the man who has either not yet found himself, or else (having found himself) has lost himself once more. But man is not an abstract being. ...Man is the world of men, the State, society. This State, this society, produce religion, produce a perverted world consciousness, because they are a perverted world. ...Religion is the sigh of the oppressed creature, the feelings of a heartless world, just as it is the spirit of unspiritual conditions. It is the opium of the people. The people cannot be really happy until it has been deprived of illusory happiness by the abolition of religion. The demand that the people should shake itself free of illusion as to its own condition is the demand that it should abandon a condition which needs illusion.[32]

Marx speaks here of a *perverted* world consciousness. Religious belief, belief in God, thinks Marx, involves a perversion, a turning away from a healthy or natural condition. This perversion is brought about, somehow, by an unhealthy and perverted social order. So the believer suffers from intellectual or cognitive malfunction; her cognitive equipment isn't working properly. If it *were* working properly—if, for example, it were working more like Marx's—she would not be under the spell of this illusion. She would instead face the world and our place in it with the resolute and calm realization that there is no God, that we are alone, and that any comfort and help we get will have to be of our own devising. There is no Father in heaven to turn to; there is no comfort to be had outside ourselves and our own efforts.

Freud held similar if subtler views. He saw religious belief as an infantile strategy for coping with the intolerable situation in which mankind finds itself. Theistic belief, he says, arises out of wish fulfillment. We human beings find ourselves in the grip of overwhelming and impersonal forces that control our destiny—forces that take no notice, no account of us and our needs and desires; they just grind mindlessly along. Terrified, appalled, all but paralyzed, we invent a heavenly father of cosmic proportions—one who enormously exceeds our earthly fathers in power and knowledge, as in goodness and love. Beliefs of this sort, says Freud, are "illusions, fulfillments of the oldest, strongest, and most insistent wishes of mankind."[33]

According to Freud, we can see that the origin of religious belief lies in wish fulfillment as follows. "Religious ideas", he says, "are teachings and assertions about facts and conditions of external (or internal) reality which tell one something one has not discovered for oneself and which lay claim to one's belief." As it stands, of course, this is too broad; it would include not only the claims of religion but also what I learn by way of testimony: *there were 13 colonies at the time of the American Revolution, San Francisco is named 'San Francisco'* and *the population of Australia is about the same as that of metropolitan New York* are all assertions about facts of external reality which tell me something I have not discovered for myself, and which lay claim to my belief. On Freud's initial account, therefore, they too are "religious ideas." He goes on, however, to say that a difference between religious ideas and what we learn by testimony is that in the latter case we are also told how we can *find out* the fact in question for ourselves, in a way that is independent of testimony. That certainly seems to be stretching the truth: how could I find out for myself, in a way independent of testimony, that there were 13 colonies at the time of the American revolution? Wouldn't I have to rely on history books, for example, or what my teachers tell me? How could I find out *anything* about 18th century history without relying on testimony? And isn't the same true much more generally? I have never been told how I could find out that the population of Australia is about the same as that of metropolitan New York without relying on testimony, and I don't see how it could be done. How could I so much as know what geographical area the word 'Australia' denotes, apart from testimony—e.g., of maps and Atlases? In any event, Freud says that in the case of testimony we are told how to find out for ourselves; when it comes to "religious ideas," however, we are instead told three things: "Firstly, these teachings deserve to be believed because they were already believed by our primal ancestors; secondly, we possess proofs which have been handed down to us from these same primaeval times; and thirdly, it is forbidden to raise the question of their authentication at all" (p. 26).

It is this third point that enables us to see that religious belief has its origin in neurosis or wish fulfillment: "After all," he says, "a prohibition like this can only be for one reason—that society is very well aware of the insecurity of the claim it makes on behalf of its religious doctrines. Otherwise it would certainly be very ready to put the necessary data at the disposal of anyone who wanted to arrive at a conviction" (p.26). Religion, says Freud, is the "universal obsessional neurosis of humanity", and it is destined to disappear when human beings learn to face reality as it is, resisting the tendency to edit it to suit their fancies:

> I am reminded of one of my children who was distinguished at an early age by a peculiarly marked matter-of-factness. When the children were being told a fairy story and were listening to it with rapt attention, he would come up and ask: 'Is that a true story?' When he was told it was not, he would turn away with a look of disdain. We may expect that people will soon behave in the same way towards the fairy tales of religion,... . p. 29.

He adds that "...in the long run, nothing can withstand reason and experience, and the contradiction which religion offers to both is all too palpable."

Marx and Freud both see belief in God as *illusion*; Marx goes on to claim that such belief is a disorder, brought about by a disordered, improperly functioning social order. Freud, on the other hand, sees belief in God as wish fulfillment, as illusion, but it is not clear that he thinks it a *disorder*. Perhaps there is no cognitive dysfunction involved here at all; illusions, of course, have their functions too. Instead, perhaps Freud holds that the cognitive mechanisms that produce religious belief, unlike those that produce perceptual belief (or belief in psychoanalysis) are not "reality oriented". That is to say, the modules of the design plan involved in the production of such beliefs are not aimed at truth, at the production of true beliefs; they are aimed instead at psychological survival or comfort, at the possibility of carrying on in this daunting and intimidating world in which we find ourselves. So perhaps he doesn't see religious belief as resulting from malfunction; perhaps instead he thinks it is produced by mechanisms whose function is not that of producing true beliefs. Either way, of course, it lacks warrant.

Now the theist is not likely to agree that he displays either cognitive defect or illusion by virtue of being a theist, or even by virtue of believing in God in the basic way. As a matter of fact, he is likely to see the shoe as on the other foot; it is *unbelief, failure* to believe in God that is the diseased, unnatural, unhealthy condition. Unbelief results from an intellectual and spiritual disease, a cognitive dysfunction. Like all disease, it is ultimately a result of sin in the world[34] (although (like other diseases) not necessarily a result of sin on the part of the sufferer). As John Calvin, for example, sees the matter, God has created us with a nisus or tendency or disposition to see his hand in the world around us; a "sense of deity", he says, "is inscribed in the hearts of all". He goes on:

> Indeed, the perversity of the impious, who though they struggle furiously are unable to extricate themselves from the fear of God, is abundant testimony that this conviction, namely, that there is some God, is naturally inborn in all, and is fixed deep within, as it were in the very marrow... . From this we conclude that it is not a doctrine that must first be learned in school, but one of which each of us is master from his mother's womb and which nature itself permits no man to forget.[35]

It is only because of the results of sin, only because of this unnatural fallen condition, Calvin thinks, that some of us find belief in God difficult or absurd. If it weren't for sin and its effects, we human beings would believe in God with the same sort of natural spontaneity and to the same degree that we believe in the existence of ourselves, other persons, and the past. This is the *natural* human condition, the condition of a person all of whose cognitive faculties are functioning properly. The fact is, Calvin thinks, one who does not believe in God is in an epistemically defective position—rather like someone who, by virtue of some cognitive defect or other, does not believe that there really are other people with thoughts and feelings and beliefs, or believes that his wife is really an ingeniously constructed robot. The believer thus pays to Freud and Marx the compliment the latter paid to Hegel: he stands them on their heads. What they see as sickness, he thinks, is really health; and what they see as health is really sickness.

Here we come to an important point. Our question was: is natural theology needed for belief in God to have warrant? Alternatively: can belief in God taken in the basic way have warrant? And the important point is that this epistemological question is not ontologically neutral: it has ontological or religious roots. The answer you properly give to it will depend upon what sorts of beliefs you think will be produced by the faculties of a person whose epistemic faculties are functioning properly: more exactly, by properly functioning faculties or mechanisms whose purpose is the production of true beliefs. This is a question about the nature of human beings, a question the answer to which belongs in philosophical anthropology and hence in ontology. So if we trace the epistemological question back we find (with apologies to John Austin) an ontological question grinning residually up at us from the bottom of the mug. Your view as to what sort of creature a human being is will determine or at any rate heavily influence your views as to which basic beliefs have warrant; for your view as to what sort of creature a human being is will determine or at any rate heavily influence your views as to what sorts of beliefs will be produced in the basic way by properly functioning human cognitive faculties. So the dispute as to whether theistic belief needs argument—i.e. natural theology—to be warranted can't be settled just by attending to epistemological considerations; it is at bottom not merely an epistemological dispute, but an anthropological and thus ontological dispute.

Indeed, this question isn't merely anthropological; it is also theological. What you take to have warrant in the basic way is obviously dependent upon the sort of theological and religious stance you adopt. You may think humankind is created by God in the image of God— and created both with a natural tendency to see God's hand in the world about us, and with a natural tendency to recognize that we have indeed been created and are beholden to our creator, owing him worship and allegiance. Then you will be unlikely to think of basic belief in God as in the typical case a manifestation of wishful thinking or any other kind of intellectual defect; nor will you be likely to think that the appropriate modules of the design plan are not aimed at the production of true beliefs. On this view, basic belief in God will resemble sense perception, perhaps, or memory, or perhaps the faculty responsible for *a priori* knowledge. On the other hand, you may think we human beings are the product of blind evolutionary forces; you may think there is no God, and that we are part of a Godless universe. Then perhaps you will be inclined to accept the sort of view according to which basic belief in God is an illusion of some sort, to be traced to disease or dysfunction on the part of the individual or society. Our epistemological question is thus deeply intertwined with ontological and theological questions.

## V. The Function of Natural Theology

Now at long last we can return to our question about the need for natural theology. If I am right, it isn't needed for justification: one does not necessarily flout a duty in believing in God in the basic way, i.e, without believing on the basis of propositional evidence. Is it needed for warrant? This question, as we have just seen, isn't onto-logically neutral. If you think there is no such person as God, the question whether belief in God has warrant will be like the question, from a theistic perspective, whether atheism has warrant: an interesting (or uninteresting) side issue. If you think there is no such person as God, you will likely think theistic belief taken in the basic way does not have non-testimonial warrant. From this perspective, perhaps a given person's belief in God may have testimonial warrant, the sort of warrant a belief has for me when I accept it on the basis of testimony or teaching; but even that warrant will be slender and flawed. Consider a young tribesman whose elders fill him with false beliefs about the stars—that, for example, they are slits in a great canvas pulled over the earth every evening to permit us a good night's sleep. There is nothing wrong with his faculties; still his beliefs have little by way of warrant. From a nontheistic perspective, therefore, belief in God will have little or no warrant if it is held in the basic way. Still, it might have the sort of warrant enjoyed by a false belief for which there are convincing if ultimately unsound arguments. From a nontheistic perspective, then, it will be natural to think that the arguments of natural theology will indeed be needed for belief in God to have warrant.

From a theistic perspective—at any rate a Christian theistic perspective—on the other hand, things look quite different. On Calvin's view, properly functioning human cognitive capacities will indeed produce belief in God; the modules of the design plan governing the production of these beliefs are indeed aimed at truth; belief in God taken in the basic way, therefore, does indeed have warrant. Hence natural theology is not needed for belief in God to have warrant; the natural view here, in fact, will be that many people *know* that there is such a person as God without believing on the basis of the arguments of natural theology.[36] Of course it doesn't follow that natural theology has no role *at all* to play; there are lots of roles to play besides that of being the sole source of warrant.

And even if such arguments are not needed for theistic belief to have warrant (even if they are not the sole source of warrant for theistic belief), it doesn't follow that they cannot play the role of *increasing* warrant, and *significantly* increasing warrant. Here it may be useful to make a comparison with other beliefs that have warrant in the basic way. We all believe that there are other persons, other beings with thoughts, feeling and beliefs. I take it the belief that there *are* such persons (perhaps more specifically, beliefs *entailing* the belief that there are such persons, such as the belief that Paul knows how to prove the fundamental theorem of the calculus) have warrant for me, and have it in the basic way. Would the warrant this belief has for me be significantly increased if I discovered a successful (ultimately noncircular[37]) analogical argument for other minds? Well, perhaps a bit; but probably not much. No doubt I would have known that there are other persons before I encountered the argument in question. The increase in warrant, if any, wouldn't be very significant. In the case of belief in God, however, things aren't nearly so straightforward. As we saw above, an essential feature of the degree of warrant a belief has for me is the strength with which I hold the belief in question. My coming upon a good argument for other minds is not likely to strengthen my belief in other minds; I will already believe very firmly that there are other minds. In the case of belief in God, however, things might be different. Perhaps my belief in God, while accepted in the basic way, isn't firm and unwavering; perhaps it isn't nearly as firm as my belief in other minds. Then perhaps good theistic arguments could play the role of confirming and strengthening my belief in God, and in that way they might increase the degree of warrant belief in God has for me. Indeed, such arguments might increase the degree of warrant of that belief in such a way as to nudge it over the boundary separating knowledge from mere true belief; they might in some cases therefore serve something like the Thomistic project of transforming belief into knowledge.

Finally, I said above that natural theology may play these roles *if there are any good theistic arguments*. Are there? None of the traditional theistic arguments, I think, measures up to the standards traditionally applied to them. None starts from premises that are self-evident (or even accepted by every reasonable person who considers them) and proceeds inexorably by self-evident argument forms to the conclusion that theism is true; none of them meets the exalted standards traditionally applied to them.[38] But then no other philosophical arguments for interesting conclusions meet those standards either. Take your favorite philosophical argument: Quine's argument for the indeterminacy of translation, or Kripke's argument against the Russell-Frege account of proper names, or Searle's oriental argument against functionalism: none of these, nor any other philosophically worthwhile arguments, meets these standards. But of course there *are* good philosophical arguments. The problem isn't with philosophical arguments, but with those standards: they are wholly unrealistic. So suppose we apply more reasonable standards to natural theology (suppose we apply the same standards that we apply with other philosophical arguments): are any theistic arguments good arguments, as judged by those more reasonable standards? I think so; in fact I think there are *many* good theistic arguments. There are good arguments from the nature of sets, of propositions, of numbers, of properties, of counterfactual propositions. There are good arguments from the nature of knowledge, from the nature of proper function, from the confluence of proper function with reliability, from simplicity and from induction. There are good moral arguments; good arguments from the nature of evil; from play, enjoyment, love, nostalgia; and perhaps from colors and flavors[39]. There is no dearth of good theistic arguments; but this is not the place to explore them.[40]

**Notes**

1. Here I follow E. Gilson's *The Spirit of Mediaeval Philosophy*, trans. by A.C. Downes. (New York: C. Scribner's Sons, 1936), chapters 1 and 2;

and N. Wolterstorff's "The Migration of the Theistic Arguments: From Natural Theology to Evidentialist Apologetics" in *Rationality, Religious Belief & Moral Commitment*, ed. Robert Audi and William Wainwright (Ithaca: Cornell University Press, 1986).

2. In *general*; that is, there is a cognitive gain in the transition from faith to *scientia*. But there may also be *loss* of one sort or another, since according to Aquinas faith is a virtue; so it could be that (for a given person) on balance the transition from faith to knowledge wasn't a good thing.

3. See my "Two Concepts of Modality: Modal Realism and Modal Reductionism", in *Philosophical Perspectives, 1, Metaphysics*, 1987, ed. James Tomberlin (Atascadero: Ridgeview Publishing Co., 1987), p.207-208.

4. In *Lectures and Essays* (London: Macmillan, 1879).

5. *The Will to Believe and Other Essays* (New York: Longmans, Green, and Co., 1897).

6. As James himself remarks: see *James's Will-to-Believe Doctrine: A Heretical View* by James C.S. Wernham (Montreal: McGill-Queen's University Press, 1987) p. 6.

7. *Op. Cit.*

8. *Reason and Belief* (New Haven, Yale University Press, 1974) p. 401. See also the other citations in Plantinga, "Reason and Belief in God" in *Faith and Rationality* (Notre Dame: The University of Notre Dame Press, 1983) pp. 29 ff.

9. See Nicholas Wolterstorff's "The Migration of the Theistic Arguments: From Natural Theology to Evidentialist Apologetics" in *Rationality, Religious Belief & Moral Commitment*, ed. Robert Audi and William Wainwright (Ithaca: Cornell University Press, 1986) and see chapter I of what I hope is my forthcoming book *Warrant: the Current Debate*.

10. To see how, in more detail Locke thinks we are to regulate our belief and how such regulation fits in with irrational sources of belief and our lack of direct control over belief, see Wolterstorff, *Ibid.*

11. See my "Reason and Belief in God" in *Faith and Rationality*, ed. A. Plantinga and N. Wolterstorff (Notre Dame: the University of Notre Dame Press, 1983, pp. 25-ff.

12. See "Reason and Belief in God" pp. 42ff. and 47ff.

13. See my "Justification and Theism", *Faith and Philosophy* (special issue edited by Alvin Plantinga) Oct. 1987, "Positive Epistemic Status and Proper Function" in *Philosophical Perspectives, 2, Epistemology*, 1988, ed. James Tomberlin (Atascadero: Ridgeview Publishing Co., 1988) and *Warrant: the Current Debate*, chapters I-IX.

14. Though with a difference: for Locke epistemic duty doesn't involve propositions that are certain for me, but only those that are not; Chisholm doesn't make such a distinction.

15. See his *Theory of Knowledge* (Englewood Cliffs, N.J.: Prentice-Hall (first edition 1966; 2nd edition, 1977)) and *Foundations of Knowing* (Minneapolis: University of Minnesota Press, 1982).

16. I.e., what I shall call 'Classical Chisholmian Internalism'—the work of *Theory of Knowledge* and *Foundations of Knowing* does not. In some

of Chisholm's most recent writing there is a different account of warrant—an account that I believe is also wanting. (See his "The Place of Epistemic Justification" in *Philosophical Topics*, ed. Roberta Klein, vol. 14, number 1, and Chisholm's "Self-Profile" in *Roderick M. Chisholm*, ed. Radu Bogdan (Dordrecht: D. Reidel, 1986) p. 52 ff.; and see my *Warrant: the Current Debate* chapter III "Post-Classical Chisholmian Internalism".

17. E.g., F. H. Bradley, B. Bosanquet, and, as one born out of time, Brand Blanshard.

18. *Knowledge* (Oxford: Oxford University Press, 1974).

19. *The Structure of Empirical Knowledge* (Cambridge, Mass: Harvard University Press, 1985).

20. *Epistemology and Cognition* (Cambridge, Mass.: Harvard University Press, 1986).

21. *Knowledge and the Flow of Information* (Cambridge, Mass.: MIT Press, 1981).

22. "Concepts of Epistemic Justification" *The Monist* (January, 1985) and "An Internalist Externalism" *Synthese*, vol. 74, no. 3 (March, 1988).

23. I do think the prominent contemporary versions of reliabilism—for example, Goldman's, Dretske's, Alston's, Nozick's—all suffer from crucial problems. See my "Positive Epistemic Status and Proper Function" for animadversions on Dretske, Nozick and the early Goldman, and see *Warrant: the Current Debate* (chapter IX) for similar comments on Alston, Dretske and the later Goldman.

24. For a fuller account see "Positive Epistemic Status and Proper Function", "Justification and Theism", and chapters I and II of what I hope is my other forthcoming book, *Warrant and Proper Function*.

25. Of course this is not the same thing as one's cognitive equipment functioning *normally*, in the statistical sense.

26. See *Warrant and Proper Function*, chapters I and II.

27. *Brainstorms* (Montgomery, VT: Bradford Books, 1978) p. 12.

28. *National Geographic* vol. 171 no. 4 (April, 1987), p. 489.

29. Sometimes of the very sort often cited as counting *against* belief in God: thus Mother Teresa claimed that we see Christ in the faces of the poor and sick. What she meant, I think, (among other things) is that beholding intense and calamitous suffering can strengthen rather than weaken belief in God, can bring us closer to him rather than estranging us from him.

30. "Christian Experience and Christian Belief" in *Faith and Rationality* p. 103.

31. *The Existence of God* (Oxford: Clarendon Press; New York: Oxford University Press, 1979). pp. 252-253.

32. (*Introduction to a Critique of the Hegelian Philosophy of Right*, in K. Marx and F. Engels, *Collected Works* vol 3.)

33. *The Future of an Illusion* (New York: W.W. Norton & Co., 1961 (first German edition 1927)) XXI 30.

34. According to St. Paul (*Romans* 1) unbelief ultimately originates in an effort, as he puts it, to "suppress the truth in unrighteousness".

35. *Institutes of the Christian Religion*, tr. Ford Lewis Battles (Philadelphia: Westminster Press, 1960), pp. 43-44. (Here Calvin speaks of belief in God as "inborn in all, ... fixed deep within ..." What he means, I think, is not that belief in God is as such innate or inborn in all; what is thus inborn (in properly functioning human beings) is a tendency to *form* belief in God under appropriate circumstances; see "Reason and Belief in God" pp. 80-82.

36. And this need not contradict the Thomistic view that *scientia* of God, in our present condition, requires the arguments of natural theology; for scientia is a narrower notion than what goes with the contemporary ordinary use of 'knowledge'.

37. The argument *Paul has a fine mind; therefore there are other minds* is sound, but not ultimately noncircular for me.

38. See George Mavrodes, *Belief in God* (New York: Random House, 1970).

39. See Robert Adams' *The Virtue of Faith and Other Essays in Philosophical Theology* (New York: Oxford University Press, 1987), "Flavors, Colors, and God", pp. 243 ff.

40. My gratitude for sharp criticism and wise advice to Eleonore Stump and to the Calvin College Tuesday Colloquium, in particular Kenneth Konyndyk, Del Ratzsch and Stephen Wykstra.

Philosophical Perspectives, 5, Philosophy of Religion, 1991

# EPISTEMIC PARITY AND
# RELIGIOUS ARGUMENT

Philip L. Quinn
University of Notre Dame

It is requir'd
You do awake your faith.
*The Winter's Tale* v.3. 94-5

The notion of epistemic parity appears attractive from the outset. Every ethics should include fairness, and epistemic parity seems to do no more than introduce considerations of fairness into the ethics of belief. Initially the idea seems simple enough. One should demand no more, and no less, by way of justification for beliefs in one area of inquiry than one does in another. Equally stringent standards of rationality should apply in all cognitive domains. For example, belief in God should not have to satisfy higher standards in order to be rational or justified than does belief in the external world or other minds. What could be fairer than that?

The trouble is that initial simplicity is likely to turn into unmanageable complexity once a few realistic examples have been subjected to analysis. Consider this scenario. Smith is driving his new camper to his favorite fishing hole and comes to an old bridge. Though he has crossed this bridge often before in a car, he now wonders whether it is safe for a heavier vehicle such as his camper. Glancing about, he notices a sign that looks freshly painted and bears the seal of the state highway department; it says: SAFE FOR LOADS UP TO TEN TONS. Smith concludes that crossing will be safe, and he is justified in so doing. As he crosses in his camper, the bridge makes horrible groaning and creaking sounds. They frighten a nearby resident, who notifies the highway department. A decision is made to check the bridge for safety, and the highway department seeks the expert advice of a noted civil engineer. It is Smith. So when he gets back from vacation, he returns to the bridge and performs various tests, measurements and calculations. Smith then offers the highway department his justified expert opinion that the bridge is indeed safe for loads up to ten tons.

One thing the example is intended to suggest is that there is a division of cognitive labor with respect to certain technical questions. Specialists have to satisfy pretty high standards of justification if their beliefs on those questions are to count as justified expert opinion. Standards for expertise vary from one field of inquiry to another. If there is a consensus among the experts acting in their capacity as experts, it is rational for the laity to take what the experts tell them on trust. So those who are not experts may rationally believe what they remember their college professors taught them, what they read in magazines such as *Scientific American* or *Consumer Reports*, what the expert witnesses testify to in the courtroom and similar things. The standards for justified belief they must satisfy are different from and less stringent than those that apply to the experts when they are functioning as experts. But people who are experts do not always function as experts even with respect to matters within their areas of specialization. It is not that Smith's belief about the bridge being safe was not rational when all he had to go on was the sign; it is merely that it did not then satisfy the standards for being a justified expert opinion. And, of course, justified expert opinion can be false. Even very good civil engineers sometimes make mistakes in measurement or calculation without being culpable in any way.

As my talk about division of labor indicates, I take expertise to be, at least in part, a matter of socially defined roles. So the point of the examples can be put another way by saying that it looks as though standards for rationality of belief are, at least to some extent, role-relative. Depending on what our respective social roles are, it may be that my beliefs about a certain subject must satisfy more stringent standards than yours if they are to be rational, or *vice versa*. In a way, this thought should come as no surprise. One way to construe rationality in normative epistemology is deontologically, in terms of epistemic duty. A belief is rational just in case acquiring or sustaining it is contrary to no epistemic duty. But moral duties are famously role-relative. Recall the title of F.H. Bradley's celebrated essay, "My Station and its Duties." We all have special duties in virtue of the station or roles in life we occupy as children, parents, teachers, physicians, judges or confessors. You have a duty to care for your children; I normally do not. I have a duty to examine my students; you do not. And not all such duties result from choices we have made. We have duties to honor our parents, even though we did not choose them or contract with them to care for us in infancy and youth. More controversially, we have duties of obedience to God, our creator, though we did not choose to have God create us. A person who is both child and parent, teacher and advisor, friend and confessor will typically have many special duties; someone who is orphaned and childless, unemployed and isolated, friendless and mistrusted will normally have relatively few. Since moral duties are thus role-relative, it is only to be expected that epistemic duties will also turn out to be role-relative. Or, at any rate, this is the view the analogy proposes to us.

This is not the only analogy between ethics and epistemology that argues for a relativization to roles. Another has to do with similarities between ethical and epistemic virtues or excellences. There may indeed be virtues such as prudence that every human needs for the sake of successful living, but there are also moral virtues that are role-relative. Sentimentality may be a virtue in a romantic poet; it is not a virtue in a battlefield commander. Similarly, there may be virtues such as general intelligence that every human needs for the sake of successful cognizing, but there are also epistemic virtues that are role-relative. Barbara McClintock's celebrated intuitive feel for the organism clearly is an excellence in a plant geneticist; it would not be an excellence in a pure mathematician functioning in the role of mathematician.

But if different people have different epistemic duties in virtue of occupying different stations or roles in life, then different things will be contrary to epistemic duty for different persons in various roles. And if different things are contrary to epistemic duty for different persons in various roles, epistemic parity will not consist in applying exactly the same standards for rationality in believing to all persons in all roles. Moreover, if some people have more, or more stringent, epistemic duties than others in virtue of the stations or roles they occupy, neither will epistemic parity consist in applying standards of rationality in belief of exactly the same degree of stringency to all people in all roles. In other words, epistemic parity is not plausibly taken to require sameness or exact equality of standards for rationality across all potential beliefs and epistemic subjects. Fairness, of course, does not require complete equality; it permits justifiable differences. But what, then, does epistemic parity amount to? It is the purpose of this paper to consider in some detail answers to that question.

## Rationality

In order to fix ideas, I propose to focus attention on the family of concepts associated with the notion of epistemic duty. I shall take as primitive the idea of having a doxastic relation to a proposition being epistemically permissible for a person at a time. Epistemically permissible doxastic relations for a person at a time are just those doxastic relations that are not contrary to epistemic duty for the person at the time. I take it that the concept of epistemic permissibility is what certain philosophers have in mind when they speak of being within one's epistemic rights. Using the concept of epistemic permissibility, definitions of the two remaining ideas of epistemic deontology can be formulated. A doxastic relation to a proposition is epistemically forbidden for a person at a time if and only if that doxastic relation to the proposition is not epistemically permissible for the person at the time, and a doxastic relation to a proposition is epistemically obligatory for a person at a time if and only if it is not epistemically permissible for the person at the time not to have that doxastic relation to the proposition. So epistemically forbidden (or alternatively, prohibited or proscribed) doxastic relations for a person at a time are just those doxastic relations that are contrary to epistemic duty for the person to have at the time. And epistemically obligatory (or, alternatively, required or prescribed) doxastic relations for a person at a time are just those doxastic relations that it is contrary to epistemic duty for the person not to have at the time. The categories of the epistemically permissible and the epistemically forbidden are, by definition, mutually exclusive and collectively exhaustive. No doxastic relation to a proposition can be both permissible and forbidden for a person at a time. But the categories of the epistemically obligatory and the epistemically forbidden, though they are plausibly taken to be mutually exclusive, are not by definition collectively exhaustive. Some doxastic relations to propositions may be neither obligatory nor forbidden for a person at a time. Such doxastic relations are such that it is epistemically permissible to have them, since they are not forbidden, and also epistemically permissible not to have them, since they are not obligatory. They are, in other words, such that it is not contrary to epistemic duty to have them and also not contrary to epistemic duty not to have them. Such doxastic relations are, we might say, optional. Henceforth I shall be concerned primarily with the doxastic relation of belief.

According to one way of thinking about normative rationality, rational beliefs are to be identified with epistemically permissible beliefs. A belief is rational for a person at a time just in case it is not contrary to epistemic duty for the person at the time to have it. Irrational beliefs then become identified with epistemically forbidden beliefs. A belief is irrational for a person at a time if and only if it is contrary to epistemic duty for the person at the time to have it. On this view, there are two kinds of rational beliefs. First, there are those which are epistemically permissible but not obligatory. Such beliefs are rational to have, since it is permissible to have them, but it is also rational not to have them, since it is also epistemically permissible not to have them. They are rationally optional. And, second, there are those which are both epistemically permissible and epistemically obligatory. Such beliefs are rational to have, because it is epistemically permissible to have them, and irrational not to have, because it is not epistemically permissible not to have them. They are rationally mandatory. Beliefs of the first of these kinds are such that it is not contrary to epistemic duty to have them and also not contrary to epistemic duty not to have them. Beliefs of the second are such that it is not contrary to epistemic duty to have them but is contrary to epistemic duty not to have them. I shall, for reasons that will become clearer in what follows, adopt this way of thinking about rationality in this paper.

There are, I concede, other ways in which normative rationality might be aligned with our concepts associated with epistemic duty. One could, for instance, identify rational beliefs with epistemically obligatory beliefs and irrational beliefs with epistemically forbidden beliefs. On such a view, beliefs which were epistemically permissible but not obligatory would turn out to be neither rational nor irrational. But I shall make no use of such alternative possibilities in this paper. And there is, I also concede, a difficulty for the very idea of epistemic duty generated by the fact that it seems we are unable to acquire or abandon beliefs at will. If a belief is epistemically obligatory for a person at a time, then it must be within that person's power to bring it about that she has that belief at that time. This appears to be a legitimate instance of the intuitively appealing ought-implies-can principle. But suppose, for example, that my best friend today acquires conclusive evidence that I have betrayed her. Isn't she henceforth epistemically obliged to have the belief that I am unfaithful to her? Imagine, though, that she has the agreeable characteristic of not being able to bring herself to believe that I am unfaithful to her. Doesn't that show that she is not epistemically obliged to believe that I am unfaithful to her? I think this difficulty has a straightforward solution. If there is literally nothing my friend can do to bring it about that she has the belief that I am unfaithful to her, then it remains epistemically permissible for her, despite the conclusive evidence of my betrayal, not to have that belief. However, if there is something she can do to bring it about that she has that belief and if it is epistemically important enough that she have justified beliefs about my fidelity and not too costly in epistemic terms to her and to others to alter her doxastic state, then sooner or later, but not necessarily henceforth from today, it will become epistemically obligatory for her to have the belief in question. There are, of course, other difficulties of this sort that deserve consideration, but I know of none that is an insurmountable obstacle to making use of the notion of epistemic duty. And so, because I have other fish to fry in the present paper, I propose to pass over them without further discussion.

It is important to note that rationality construed as epistemic permissibility need not coincide with epistemic justification. Following Chisholm and Plantinga, I take justification to involve positive epistemic status. Positive epistemic status, in turn, is that which, when enough of it is coupled with true belief, yields knowledge. According to an externalist story that has recently been gaining popularity, justification derives from or supervenes upon reliability. Philosophers of the reliabilist persuasion differ over exactly what it is that reliability is to be attributed to. Some speak of belief-producing processes; others talk about belief-acquisition mechanisms; still others discuss belief-forming faculties; and others yet favor faculties operating as designed in environments for which they were designed. But all agree that, roughly speaking, an item is reliable just if it yields more true beliefs than false ones. By insisting that beliefs are justified only if reliably generated, this story gives hostages to statistical success in the enterprise of seeking truth. Hence it leaves room for tales of skeptical possibilities concerning justification.

It may be that ultimately we have no nonskeptical alternative to presupposing that many of our rational beliefs are also justified beliefs. But the skeptical possibilities are not ruled out by logical or conceptual necessities. On the ninth Antarean planet, let us suppose, the first astronauts from earth discover among the fauna what appear to their senses and instruments to be gigantic bufo toads. Unbeknownst to them, their senses and instruments are not reliable on Antares IX. Those creatures are actually small rodents akin to *rattus rattus* which exude a subtle chemical aura, undetectable by human senses or the instruments in the astronauts' possession, that fools both instruments and senses. The astronauts from earth come to believe that there are gigantic bufo toads on Antares IX. Surely this is a rational belief for these astronauts to acquire and hold. They act contrary to no epistemic duty in forming or having it; it is epistemically permissible for them. Yet it is not a justified belief for the astronauts. Since it was unreliably generated, it has little if any positive epistemic status for them. So there could be beliefs that are rational for a person at a time without being justified for that person at that time. Rationality and justification might pull apart.

With these distinctions and clarifications in mind, we are now in a position to ask some interesting questions about religious belief. Consider, for the sake of definiteness, belief in God, that is, belief that God exists. Is it rational, in the sense of not being contrary to epistemic duty, for any person at any time? If so, is it merely epistemically permissible but not also epistemically obligatory for some persons at some times, or is it epistemically both permissible and obligatory for some persons at some times? Is belief in God justified for some persons at some times? If so, does it have enough positive epistemic status to be knowledge if true? If belief in God is irrational, can it be shown to be so by being proved to be epistemically on a par with some other beliefs known to be irrational? If belief in God is rational, can it be proved to be so by an argument that it is epistemically on a par with some other beliefs known to be rational? These are some of the main questions of religious epistemology. Obviously I could not even begin to address them all within the confines of a single paper. In the remainder of this paper, I shall concentrate on some issues related to the last of them.

## Parity

If we are to make progress toward answering the question of whether belief in God can be shown to be rational by an argument from its epistemic parity to some other belief known or presumed to be rational, we need to have in hand some principles governing epistemic parity. I now turn to the task of formulating such principles.

In addition to the concepts I have already introduced, I will need to make use of two other quasi-technical ideas. The first is the notion of an epistemic situation. I am not in a position to give a precise, formal characterization of this concept, but I think I can explain informally something about what an epistemic situation is. Intuitively, the idea is to build into epistemic situations things to which standards of rationality need to be relativized. So, for instance, epistemic situations will include those roles in the cognitive division of labor I drew attention to previously. They will also include, I suppose, various perspectival factors that make it the case that a person is epistemically privileged with respect to certain kinds of beliefs *de se*. I think they will include broadly experiential or phenomenological factors, such as ways of being appeared to, which serve to ground properly basic beliefs, and facts about the extent to which acquisition and maintenance of various beliefs are directly or indirectly under the control of the person in the situation. And they may well include certain kinds of intellectual abilities, such as the ability to grasp propositions of certain orders of complexity, and logical capacities, such as the capacity to do computations of a certain level of difficulty, as well. Using the notion of an epistemic situation, I can then say something about what it is for a pair of epistemic situations to be equivalent relative to a pair of propositions. If, relative to proposition p, epistemic situation E is equivalent to epistemic situation E', relative to proposition p', then believing p is, respectively, epistemically obligatory, permissible or forbidden for anyone in E if and only if believing p' is, respectively, epistemically obligatory, permissible or forbidden for anyone in E'.

Next we may proceed to formulate several parity principles. The first of these I shall call the General Rational Parity Principle (or GRPP, for short). It goes as follows:

(GRPP): If epistemic subject S is in epistemic situation E at time t and epistemic subject S' is in epistemic situation E' at time t′ and E relative to proposition p is equivalent to E′ relative to proposition p′, then believing p is rational for S at t if and only if believing p′ is rational for S′ at t′.

GRPP does not mark the distinction between the two grades of rationality noted in the previous discussion. Since that distinction will subsequently be of some importance, it is useful to have before us two finer-grained subprinciples of GRPP. I call the first the Prescriptive Rational Parity Principle (or PRPP1, for short). It goes as follows:

(PRPP1): If epistemic subject S is in epistemic situation E at time t and epistemic subject S′ is in epistemic situation E′ at time t′ and E relative to proposition p is equivalent to E′ relative to proposition p′, then believing p is epistemically permissible and obligatory for S at t if and only if believing p′ is epistemically permissible and obligatory for S′ at t′.

And I call the second subprinciple of GRPP the Permissive Rational Parity Principle (or PRPP2, for short). It goes as follows:

(PRPP2): If epistemic subject S is in epistemic situation E at time t and epistemic subject S′ is in epistemic situation E′ at time t′ and E relative to proposition p is equivalent to E′ relative to proposition p′, then believing p is epistemically permissible but not obligatory for S at t if and only if believing p′ is epistemically permissible but not obligatory for S′ at t′.

Finally, for the sake of completeness, I formulate the parallel principle about irrationality. I call it the Prohibitive Rational Parity Principie (or PRPP3, for short). It goes as follows:

(PRPP3): If epistemic subject S is in epistemic situation E at time t and epistemic subject S′ is in epistemic situation E′ at time t′ and E relative to proposition p is equivalent to E′ relative to proposition p′, then believing p is epistemically forbidden (irrational) for S at t if and only if believing p′ is epistemically forbidden (irrational) for S′ at t′.

And, of course, the actual principles in question are the universal closures of these schematic formulas, that is, they are those formulas prefixed with universal quantifiers for all their schematic letters.

These principles have, I realize, an air of daunting complexity about them. But they are meant to be trivially true because there is by stipulation packed into the equivalence of situation asserted by their antecedents whatever factors and conditions are needed to guarantee the parity asserted by their consequents. And I think we need principles of at least this order of complexity if we are to do a thorough job of analyzing some of the current work in philosophy of religion that makes explicit or implicit use of the notion of epistemic parity. I shall try to build a case for this claim by employing them to help clarify some of the issues involving parity that come up in Terence Penelhum's recent book *God and Skepticism*.[1]

## Humean Inconsistency

One of the most interesting features of Penelhum's book is his discussion of what he calls the "Parity Argument." As Penelhum uses it, this term applies to a family of arguments, all of which proceed by "arguing that many of the secular beliefs of common sense or science with which faith is contrasted are themselves beliefs which we cannot justify by reason either, so that the contrast is a bogus one for that reason" (p. 30). Which beliefs of science or common sense does the parity arguer propose to show cannot be justified by reason? Likely candidates spring to mind; they are the beliefs that are the traditional targets of skeptical attack. They include such things as belief in the external world, other minds, causality and induction. For the sake of argument, let us suppose that the skeptic can show that some or all of such beliefs are unjustifiable by reason. What, exactly, is supposed to follow from this concession? Are we to conclude that such beliefs from common sense and science are on a par with religious beliefs in that beliefs of both sorts are epistemically forbidden or irrational for us? Or, by contrast, are we to infer that parity dictates that beliefs of both sorts are epistemically permissible or rational for us? And how, precisely, do such arguments go? What are their premises, and what are their conclusions?

The technical machinery we have elaborated enables us to give answers to some of these questions. I propose that we take to be a parity argument any deductive argument that has one of our parity principles GRPP, PRPP1, PRPP2 or PRPP3 as its major premise. A valid parity argument will have the following minor premises: (1) premises which assert that certain epistemic subjects are in certain epistemic situations at certain times; (2) a premiss which asserts that some of these epistemic situations are equivalent relative to certain propositions; and (3) a premiss which asserts that believing some of those propositions is rational or epistemically permissible and obligatory or epistemically permissible but not obligatory or epistemically forbidden (irrational) for some of those epistemic subjects at some of those times. The conclusion of a valid parity argument will then assert that believing others of those propositions is also rational or epistemically permissible and obligatory or epistemically permissible but not obligatory or epistemically forbidden (irrational) for some of those epistemic subjects at some of those times. Of course parity arguments will not always be presented with full formal explicitness. Sometimes they will be enthymematic, with some of their premisses left unstated. Sometimes references to subjects, situations and times will be suppressed. And sometimes the propositions argued to be on a par will be only vaguely specified. But, unless such things can be gathered from context, it will be difficult, if not impossible, to evaluate parity arguments for soundness.

The first major piece of work the so-called "Parity Argument" does for Penelhum is to aid him in formulating a criticism of the position he attributes to Hume. On behalf of the parity arguer, Penelhum charges the Humean position with inconsistency. He observes that the version of the "Parity Argument" he uses against the Humean position only applies to someone in very specific circumstances. Such a person

> ...must be someone who agrees, as Hume does, with the Pyrrhonist tradition that at least some of the fundamental philosophical commitments of secular common sense are without rational foundation. He must, however, decline to follow the Pyrrhonist in espousing suspense of judgment with regard to them; instead, he will yield to our natural tendency to believe them. The Parity Argument suggests to such a person that he is inconsistent if he refuses to yield to the demands of religious belief merely because he considers that it, too, does not have a rational foundation (p. 139).

As Penelhum notes, such considerations do not apply to someone who, like Sextus, rejects both religious belief and secular common sense because both are without rational foundations. Nor does an argument of this sort apply to someone who, like the fideist, accepts both religious belief and secular common sense despite a belief that both lack rational foundations. And neither does such an argument apply to someone who holds that secular common sense beliefs have rational foundations while religious beliefs do not. But, at least at first glance, such considerations do seem to apply to Hume or, at any rate, to Hume as he is customarily interpreted. For Hume, in both the *Treatise* and in the *Enquiry Concerning Human Understanding*, argues that some of the fundamental beliefs of secular common sense, such as the beliefs in causality and induction, are without rational foundations. And Hume, in the *Dialogues*, argues that religious belief, or at least any religious belief that goes beyond a rather attenuated deism, is also without rational foundations. Yet Hume speaks with approval of our having such beliefs of common sense, if only because we cannot permanently rid ourselves of them, nature being too strong for us in this matter. But Hume does not, except perhaps by way of ironic teasing, recommend that we have religious beliefs that go beyond attenuated deism or, at any rate, this is the case according to a standard interpretation of Part XII of the *Dialogues*, one which Penelhum clearly endorses. So it is plausible to take Hume to be in the special circumstances sketched by Penelhum.

But where in all this is there any inconsistency? Two states of affairs are logically inconsistent just in case no possible world includes them both. By this criterion, Hume's believing on his deathbed in the existence of Boswell's body and Hume's not believing on his deathbed in the immortality of his own soul are not inconsistent. From what we know of Hume's death, it seems reasonable to infer that the actual world includes both these states of affairs. And even if traditional lore is in error on this point, it is quite clear that some other possible world includes both these states of affairs. So we confront at the outset a difficulty in making sense of the allegation that the Humean position is threatened by an inconsistency.

This difficulty is not too hard to deal with, however, if we are allowed a little interpretive latitude. We may take the charge of inconsistency to be tantamount to the claim that Hume, or at least the Humean position, is committed to all the premises of a valid parity argument and also to the denial of its conclusion. But which of the parity arguments that can be constructed from our theoretical resources shall we stick the Humean position with? I shall consider two possible answers to this question.

The first is that we should pin on the Humean position a parity argument whose major premiss is our principle GRPP. On this view, the Humean is committed to holding that he is in equivalent epistemic situations relative to, say, the propositions that material bodies exist and that God exists. And he is committed to holding both that believing that material bodies exist is rational for him and that believing that God exists is not rational for him. Hence, given his commitment to GRPP, he is committed to holding that for him believing that God exists both is and is not rational. The trouble with this answer is that it is not easy to see how we are to stick the Humean with a commitment to holding that believing in God is not rational for him. Penelhum portrays the Humean as refusing to yield to the demands of religious belief, and I have described him as not recommending religious belief that goes beyond attenuated deism. But these descriptions commit the Humean at most to holding that not believing in God is rational for him. On the conception of rationality we have adopted, it does not follow from the fact that not believing in God is rational for one that believing in God is not rational for one. For we have identified the rational with the epistemically permissible. And, from the fact that not having a certain belief is epistemically permissible it does not follow that having that belief is not epistemically permissible. It is consistent to suppose that a belief is such that it is both epistemically permissible to have it and epistemically permissible not to have it. Hence, the Humean may accept the parity argument whose major premiss is the principle GRPP and allow that belief in God is rational for him. He need only insist that not believing in God is also rational for him, and this he may consistently do. If he does all this, he will not be inconsistent or irrational when he refuses to yield to the demands of religious belief. But, of course, he would not be irrational if he yielded to those demands. The propositions that material bodies exist and that God exists are for him on a par in two ways. Neither is justifiable by reason, and each is such that it is rational for him to believe it and rational for him not to believe it. So he does nothing contrary to epistemic duty in believing that material bodies exist, which is fortunate because he cannot help having this belief. And he does nothing contrary to epistemic duty in not believing that God exists, which is also fortunate because, as he sees it, people who believe in God are likely to be miserable themselves and to do harm to others.

The second answer I shall consider blocks this escape route from the charge of inconsistency. It involves attributing to the Humean position a parity argument whose major premiss is our principle PRPP1. On this view of the matter, the Humean is committed, as before, to holding that he is in equivalent epistemic situations relative to, for instance, the propositions that material bodies exist and that God exists. But he is also committed, we suppose, to holding both that believing that material bodies exist is epistemically permissible and obligatory for him and that believing that God exists is not epistemically obligatory for him. Hence, given his commitment to PRPP1, he is committed to holding that for him believing that God exists both is and is not epistemically obligatory. However, this answer too has its problems. In its case, it is not easy to see how to pin on the Humean a commitment to holding that believing in material bodies is epistemically both permissible and obligatory for him. To be sure, the Humean should concede that believing in material bodies is epistemically permissible for him, since his circumstances are ones in which he proposes to yield to his natural and, perhaps, irresistible tendency to believe in them. But he need not also allow that believing in material bodies is epistemically obligatory for him. Since he agrees with the skeptic that belief in material bodies is for him without rational foundations, it seems plausible to suppose that he should believe commitment to material bodies not to be epistemically obligatory for him. Like belief in God, belief in material bodies is epistemically optional for the Humean. Because both beliefs are on a par in virtue of being without rational foundations, it is not contrary to epistemic duty for the Humean not to have one or both of them. Hence, he may allow that belief in material bodies, like belief in God, is epistemically permissible but is not epistemically obligatory for him, and so he may reject the parity argument whose major premiss is the principle PRPP1. And thus the threat of inconsistency evaporates.

One way of summarizing the position I claim the Humean can consistently adhere to goes as follows. The parity argument whose major premiss is the principle GRPP can be subjected to a more fine-grained analysis in either of two ways. It may be construed either as an argument whose major premiss is the principle PRPP1 or as an argument whose major premiss is the principle PRPP2. The consistent Humean rejects the first of these arguments and accepts the second. From the argument he accepts, he derives the conclusion that beliefs of secular common sense and religious beliefs are on a par in that both are epistemically permissible but not obligatory for him. Since beliefs of secular common sense are epistemically permissible for him, he does nothing contrary to epistemic duty by yielding to the natural tendency to have them. Because religious beliefs are not epistemically obligatory for him, he does nothing contrary to epistemic duty by refusing to yield to their demands. But there is nothing inconsistent in such behavior, for what the argument whose major premiss is the Permissive Rational Parity Principle, PRPP2, shows is that beliefs of both sorts are such that it is epistemically permissible for the Humean to have them but also epistemically permissible for him not to have them. So accepting that parity argument does not preclude the consistent Humean from holding both that having the beliefs of secular common sense is epistemically permissible or rational for him and that not having religious beliefs beyond attenuated deism is also epistemically permissible or rational for him. I conclude, therefore, that a parity argument to which the Humean position is committed does not show it to be inconsistent and that a parity argument which would show it to be inconsistent is not one to which it is committed. So, as far as I can tell, the charge of inconsistency fails to hold up under examination.

Perhaps it would be wise at this point to pause in order to consider an objection to my conclusion. It might be said that I have not yet even addressed the real difficulty in the Humean position. According to the objection, the real difficulty derives from the fact that the Humean concedes that the beliefs of secular common sense and religious beliefs are on a par in that beliefs of each kind are epistemically permissible for him and yet treats beliefs of the two kinds differently and hence unequally, accepting beliefs of the former sort and rejecting beliefs of the latter sort. One way of sharpening up the intuition behind this objection is to point out that the Humean's commitments, as I have interpreted them, violate the following principle:

(F): If believing p is epistemically permissible for epistemic subject S at time t and believing p' is epistemically permissible for S at t, then believing p if and only if p' is epistemically obligatory for S at t.

But, as I have portrayed the Humean, he is committed, because he accepts the parity argument whose major premiss is PRPP2, to holding both that beliefs of secular common sense are epistemically permissible for him and that religious beliefs are epistemically permissible for him. If the principle F is true, then the Humean is also committed, at least implicitly, to holding that believing the former if and only if the latter is epistemically obligatory for him. But the Humean is committed to yielding to the natural tendency to believe the former while refusing to yield to the demands of the latter. Hence, the Humean is implicitly committed to doing something that is, though not inconsistent in the strictly logical sense, contrary to epistemic duty by his own lights.

Fortunately for the Humean, the objection in this form cuts no ice. The principle F is plainly false, as can be shown by counterexample, and the Humean need not accept it. Archaeologists disagree about the causes of the Classic Maya Collapse, and historians disagree about the causes of the American Civil War. Having been interested in both events for quite a while, I have by now read a fair amount about them. Let us suppose that it is now epistemically permissible but not obligatory for me to believe that the main cause of the Classic Maya Collapse was the exhaustion of the soil by slash-and-burn agriculture. If I were so to believe, I would be following reputable, though controverted, scholarly opinion. Let us also suppose that it is now epistemically permissible but not obligatory for me to believe that the main cause of the American Civil War was the quarrel over slavery between North and South. If I were to believe this, I would again be in accord with some but not all of the experts whose works I have consulted. Is it now epistemically obligatory for me to believe that the main cause of the Classic Maya Collapse was the exhaustion of the soil by slash-and-burn agriculture if and only if the main cause of the American Civil War was the quarrel over slavery between North and South? I think not. Or consider the case of Joey who, driven by remorseless parental pressure, has just barely managed to get himself into medical school. Joey is in a Jamesian situation in which he can bring himself to believe that he has what it takes to succeed in medical school and can bring himself to believe that he does not have what it takes to succeed in medical school. When Joey goes to medical school, he will be confident and successful if he believes he has what it takes, and he will lack confidence and fail if he believes he does not have what it takes. Either belief would be for Joey a self-fulfilling prophecy. From the point of view of the purely epistemic goal of believing truths and not believing falsehoods, one would be as good for Joey as the other. So each is epistemically permissible but not obligatory for Joey as he prepares to set off for medical school. But because he was smart enough to get into medical school in the first place, it is clear that for Joey it is not epistemically obligatory to believe that he has what it takes to succeed if and only if he does not have what it takes to succeed. It is at least epistemically permissible, and probably epistemically obligatory, for Joey not to have that obviously contradictory biconditional belief. Hence that proposition does not satisfy the consequent of the principle F for Joey as he prepares to go to medical school. Thus the principle F is clearly false, and the objection in this form fails. Perhaps there is some principle other than F which both captures the intuition behind the objection and is not susceptible to being refuted by counterexample. But it is not obvious that this is the case, even though nothing I have said rules it out. So the onus is on the objector to come up with such a principle. Until this has been done, the objection remains ineffective and may properly be disregarded.

But maybe the objector will wish to make the following rejoinder. The Humean is committed to the principle that rational belief is proportioned to evidential support or warrant.[2] Since both religious belief and the beliefs of common sense are without rational foundations, both have evidential support to exactly the same degree, namely, degree zero. Hence, both are rationally believed to exactly the same degree, whatever that may be, and it is not epistemically permissible to have the one and also epistemically permissible not to have the other. My reply to the rejoinder begins by noting that the objector's argument contains some tacit presuppositions about what the proportionality principle requires. Specifically, one thing the objector assumes is that degree of rational belief is a single-valued function of degree of evidential support. Perhaps the objector has in mind a familiar picture of a graph which represents degree of rational belief as a continuous, monotonically increasing function of degree of warrant. But the Humean is not wedded to this picture. Another interpretation of the proportionality principle is more consonant with the conceptual machinery developed in this paper. I think it also has the advantage of realism. On this view, for any belief, there is a range of degrees of evidential support, including degree zero, such that, for any degree in that range, the proportionality principle permits having the belief, represented by degree one of rational belief, and permits not having the belief, represented by degree zero of rational belief. There are also, on this view, two other ranges of degrees of evidential support, one of which is lower than and the other of which is higher than the aforementioned middle range, such that, when the degree of evidential support is in the former, the proportionality principle requires not having the belief, represented by degree zero of rational belief, and, when the degree of evidential support is in the latter, the proportionality principle requires having the belief, represented by degree one of rational belief. On this interpretation of the proportionality principle, which I take it is available to the Humean, the objector's argument fails. Since both religious belief and the beliefs of common sense have evidential support to degree zero, both are in the middle range. Hence, the proportionality principle permits having and permits not having each, and so both need not be rationally believed to exactly the same degree. Thus, consistent with the proportionality principle so construed, it is epistemically permissible to have the one and also epistemically permissible not to have the other. The rejoinder, then, is inconclusive, and the onus remains with the objector.

Another way to make the charge of inconsistency would be to accuse the Humean of holding that belief in God is resistible and epistemically forbidden while belief in material bodies, being irresistible, is epistemically permissible. But if the suggestion that irresistibility is enough to make a belief epistemically permissible is correct, then whether or not a belief is irresistible has to be factored into epistemic situations relative to that belief. On this view, the situation of a subject for whom belief in material bodies is irresistible relative to belief in material bodies is not equivalent to the situation of a subject for whom belief in God is resistible relative to belief in God. Hence the equivalence premises of parity arguments about this pair of beliefs are false in such circumstances, and the Humean should deny them for the sake of consistency. To be sure, belief in material bodies and belief in God are in such circumstances similar in one epistemically relevant respect: both lack rational foundations. But they differ in another: one is irresistible and the other is not. So there is not real parity between them.

## Contemporary Parity Arguments

The second big job the so-called "Parity Argument" does for Penelhum is to help him interpret certain positions in contemporary religious epistemology. I shall restrict my attention to what he has to say about Plantinga's recent work. Penelhum takes Plantinga to be offering a permissive parity argument for the rationality of belief in God, that is, belief in the proposition that God exists or in some proposition which self-evidently entails that God exists. Formulated in terms of the technical apparatus of this paper, a permissive parity argument is, presumably, one whose major premiss is our principle PRPP2, the Permissive Rational Parity Principle. But how exactly does the argument continue? Is it a successful argument? And is it an argument we find in Plantinga's work?

I find it interesting that Plantinga once did give an argument for the rationality of belief in God that I think may be reconstructed in an illuminating way as a permissive parity argument. That is the general argument of his *God and Other Minds*.[3] In rough outline, it goes as follows. The major premiss is the principle PRPP2. There are two minor premisses. The first is that the epistemic subject who has read and understood the book is in equivalent epistemic situations relative to the propositions that other minds exist and that God exists; in both cases, there are arguments for the proposition in question that have some justificatory force but fall short of being conclusive proofs, and these arguments are known to the reader of the book. The second minor premiss is that believing that other minds exist is epistemically permissible and hence rational, though not epistemically obligatory, for the reader of the book. And the conclusion which is validly drawn from these premisses is that believing that God exists is also epistemically permissible and hence rational, though not epistemically obligatory, for the reader of the book. In short, the general argument of *God and Other Minds*, as I reconstruct it in rough outline, is to the effect that belief in God and belief in other minds are epistemically on a par. Both are supported by arguments that are inconclusive against the skeptic. But since, despite this, belief in other minds is rational for the reader of the book, so too is belief in God.

However, I do not think Plantinga proceeds in 'Rationality and Religious Belief,' which is the paper Penelhum discusses, to deploy a permissive parity argument.[4] As I interpret that paper, Plantinga's argumentative strategy is roughly as follows. He advances the claim that belief in God can be properly basic in the right circumstances. A belief is basic just in case it is not based on any other beliefs, and a belief is properly basic in certain circumstances just if its being basic in those circumstances is not contrary to epistemic duty. Hence, a properly basic belief is epistemically permissible and so rational. He then considers and rebuts some objections to this claim. One of them is the Evidentialist Objection. The Evidentialist holds that belief in God is rational only if it is properly based on evidence and that belief in God is not, and perhaps cannot be, properly based on evidence. But why, asks Plantinga, should we buy into Evidentialism? He suggests that Evidentialism derives whatever plausibility it has from a foundationalist criterion for proper basicality. According to that criterion, a belief is properly basic if and only if it is self-evident, incorrigible or evident to the senses. Plantinga argues that this criterion is self-referentially incoherent. From this he concludes that it must be rejected and that Evidentialism, since it lacks plausibility, may also be rejected. Other objections, including the celebrated Great Pumpkin Objection, are rebutted in other ways. All the objections considered having been rebutted, Plantinga concludes that his original claim that belief in God can be properly basic in the right circumstances is in the clear.

If my admittedly sketchy portrait of Plantinga's argumentative strategy in 'Rationality and Religious Belief' is roughly accurate, then he is not employing a permissive parity argument for the proper basicality and, hence, the epistemic permissibility and rationality of belief in God. Indeed, he is not arguing directly for the claim that belief in God is rational at all. Rather, the argument is indirect. It is a defense of that claim against a battery of objections.

Clearly valid parity arguments can be constructed from materials Plantinga provides in 'Rationality and Religious Belief.' One goes as follows. The major premiss is the principle GRPP. The first minor premiss is that some epistemic subjects are in epistemic situations in which certain perceptual beliefs are properly basic. The second minor premiss is that some subjects are in situations in which belief in God is properly basic. The third minor premiss is that the situations of the former subjects relative to those perceptual beliefs are equivalent to the situations of the latter subjects relative to belief in God; it is actually a consequence of the first and second minor premisses. The fourth minor premiss is that having those perceptual beliefs is rational for the former subjects; given Plantinga's understanding of proper basicality, it is a consequence of the first minor premiss. And the conclusion is that belief in God is rational for the latter subjects. If Plantinga is correct in thinking that belief in God is properly basic for some people, this is a sound argument, but in that case the appeal to parity is redundant. For given Plantinga's understanding of proper basicality, the conclusion is a consequence of the second minor premiss alone, and so if it is true there is a sound argument directly from it to the conclusion. But if the first and second minor premisses are weakened to the point that the conclusion is not a consequence of the second by itself, it is easy to see that the soundness of the revised argument is problematic. William P. Alston has recently pointed out significant disanalogies between the practice of forming perceptual beliefs in response to sensory experience and the practice of forming religious manifestation beliefs in response to religious experience.[5] These disanalogies lend urgency to the question of whether the situations of the subjects of certain perceptual beliefs relative to those beliefs are ever equivalent to the situations of subjects who believe in God relative to that belief. Since the revised argument does not assume that both perceptual beliefs and belief in God are properly basic in some situations, its third minor premiss cannot be assumed to be a consequence of its first and second minor premisses and so is problematic in the absence of other reasons for thinking that the situations of some subjects relative to certain perceptual beliefs are equivalent to the situations of some subjects relative to belief in God. In short, even if the conclusion of the revised argument is true, the argument might be unsound; perceptual beliefs and belief in God might both be rational despite disparity rather than because of parity.

Penelhum appears to disagree with me about the exegetical point. From Plantinga's rebuttal of the Evidentialist Objection he extracts the following conclusion: "Plantinga argues that to commit oneself to the positive view that self-evident propositions and incorrigible propositions are properly basic is to make a commitment which all non-skeptics do make but which is not itself open to justification" (p. 148). And he goes on to claim that "the permissive version of the Parity Argument shows that someone who *does* make such commitments, but does not include religious commitment among them, is in no position to accuse someone who does include religious belief among them of irrationality" (p. 152). I do not suppose my disagreement with Penelhum about whether Plantinga actually argues in this fashion will be of much interest to those who are not textual scholars concerned to read Plantinga aright. What may be of philosophical interest is the question of whether a permissive parity argument shows what Penelhum says it does.

In order to investigate this matter, we need first of all to spell out in some detail the permissive parity argument in question. I shall suppose that it has as its major premiss our principle PRPP2, though one might begin such an argument with the principle GRPP. We are to assume, I take it, that one epistemic subject is in the epistemic situation of not being able to justify to the skeptic's satisfaction the belief that self-evident propositions and incorrigible propositions are properly basic. We are further to assume, I suppose, that another epistemic subject is in the epistemic situation of not being able to justify to the skeptic's satisfaction religious beliefs such as the belief that God exists. We are to suppose that the epistemic situation of our first subject relative to the proposition that self-evident propositions and incorrigible propositions are properly basic is equivalent to the epistemic situation of our second subject relative to the proposition that God exists or similar religious propositions. And we are also to suppose that believing that self-evident propositions and incorrigible propositions are properly basic is epistemically permissible and, hence, is rational, though it is not epistemically obligatory, for our first subject. From these suppositions we may validly infer that believing that God exists or similar religious propositions is epistemically permissible and, hence, is rational, though it is not epistemically obligatory, for our second subject. And we are further to conclude that, if our first subject, for whom belief that self-evident and incorrigible propositions are properly basic is rational, believes that proposition but does not also believe that God exists or similar religious propositions, then he or she is in no position to accuse our second subject, for whom belief in God or similar religious propositions is rational, of irrationality in believing such religious propositions.

If this, or something like it, is the way the parity argument in question goes, then it seems to me that it does not establish its ultimate conclusion. For I am convinced that one need not accept the argument's supposition that our first subject's epistemic situation relative to the proposition that self-evident and incorrigible propositions are properly basic is genuinely equivalent to our second subject's epistemic situation relative to the proposition that God exists or similar religious propositions. One might support not accepting the claim of equivalence with the following considerations. Though our first subject admittedly cannot prove to the satisfaction of the skeptic that self-evident and incorrigible propositions are properly basic, it is not as though he or she is completely lacking good reasons for accepting it. Particular self-evident propositions such as the conditional corresponding to modus ponens tend to strike one who entertains them as obviously true and not in need of evidential support from other propositions. Indeed, a proposition would not really be self-evident if its being evident depended on its being based on some other evidential propositions. So the proposition that self-evident and incorrigible propositions are properly basic is inductively supported by such examples as the conditional corresponding to modus ponens, even if such support does not altogether preclude skeptical possibilities of the evil demon variety. But, the argument continues, things are otherwise with respect to the second subject's epistemic situation relative to the proposition that God exists or similar religious propositions. It is not merely that the second subject cannot prove to the skeptic's satisfaction that God exists. Rather, the second subject may, as Hume claimed, have no good reasons at all, inductive or otherwise, on which to base any religious belief beyond attenuated deism and, moreover, no good reason to suppose that any such religious belief is rational for him or her in the absence of such a basis. If this is a correct description of the second subject's epistemic situation, as I think it could be, then it seems to me there is a relevant disparity between the epistemic situations of the two subjects relative to the propositions that self-evident and incorrigible propositions are properly basic and that God exists, though their epistemic situations are alike to the extent that neither absolutely precludes skepticism. In the light of this disparity, it appears we may claim that this parity argument is unsound because its equivalence premiss is false. If so, the first subject remains in a position to claim that, while believing that self-evident and incorrigible propositions are properly basic is epistemically permissible and, hence, rational for him or her on account of the inconclusive but real inductive support he or she has for that belief, believing that God exists is not similarly epistemically permissible and, hence, is not rational for the second subject just because of the second subject's lack of parallel support, inductive or otherwise, for the belief that God exists.

In advancing this objection to the parity argument I have been considering, my purpose is not to show that belief in God cannot be rational for some epistemic subjects. Nor is it to show that belief in God cannot be properly basic in certain circumstances. I mean only to challenge the claim that the rationality of belief in God is established by a permissive parity argument of the sort I have constructed. It may be that there is no way to prove that the skeptic is mistaken, and so perhaps the only escape from skepticism is by means of a leap of faith. But even if this is so, it does not follow that all leaps of faith are, so to speak, equal in size. Some leaps of faith may be, as it were, bigger than others. Hence, it is consistent with this concession to skepticism to hold that not all commitments that cannot be justified to the skeptic's satisfaction are epistemically on a par. It may be that some commitments which require only little leaps are rational for an epistemic subject and others which require large leaps are not rational for an epistemic subject. Given only that two beliefs are alike in that both require leaps beyond skepticism, we should not jump to the conclusion that one is rational if and only if the other is. Hence, the possibility that beliefs of secular common sense are rational and religious beliefs are not is not precluded by the mere fact that beliefs of both sorts are alike in not being susceptible of being justified to the satisfaction of the skeptic. In other words, our permissive parity argument does not succeed in showing that those who make only little leaps away from skeptical suspension in the direction of secular common sense and are in a position to claim rationality for their commitments are, by parity, in no position to accuse others, who make large leaps away from skeptical suspension in the direction of religious faith, of having irrational commitments.

In this paper, I have begun to explore the rich complexity of the notion of epistemic parity. I have tried to show how the intuitive idea of fairness in the ethics of belief can be explicated with some precision using the deontological concepts of prescription, permission and prohibition. I have also tried to illustrate the philosophical utility of the technical apparatus I have constructed by employing it to interpret, analyze and criticize two claims Penelhum has recently made about things the so-called "Parity Argument" shows about the rationality of religious belief. But I have not given a full positive account of the respects in which beliefs of secular common sense and religious beliefs are epistemically on a par or of the respects in which there are disparities between them. And I have not said much about what the bearing of these epistemic parities and disparities on the permissibility or rationality of religious belief might be. These are projects that must be deferred to another paper.[6]

## Notes

1. Penelhum (1983). References to this book will henceforth be made parenthetically in the body of the paper.
2. Hume says that "a wise man, therefore, proportions his belief to the evidence." See Hume (1977), p. 73.
3. See Plantinga (1967) for details.
4. Plantinga (1982). As Penelhum notes, Plantinga has set forth similar arguments in other publications.
5. See Alston (1982) for details.
6. Earlier versions of this paper were discussed by the Society of Christian Philosophers' Workshop on Skepticism and Fideism, the 1986 NEH Summer Institute in Philosophy of Religion, the Philosophy Colloquium of the University of Wisconsin at Milwaukee, and the Notre Dame Epistemology Discussion Group. I am grateful to many colleagues for helpful criticism in those settings. I also owe thanks to Richard Foley, C. Stephen Layman, and Ernest Sosa for detailed written comments.

## References

Alston, William P., 1982, "Religious Experience and Religious Belief," *Nous* 16, pp. 3-12.

Hume, David, 1977, *An Enquiry Concerning Human Understanding*, ed. Eric Steinberg (Indianapolis: Hackett).

Penelhum, Terence, 1983, *God and Skepticism* (Dordrecht, Boston and Lancaster: Reidel).

Plantinga, Alvin, 1967, *God and Other Minds* (Ithaca: Cornell University Press).

Plantinga, Alvin, 1982, "Rationality and Religious Belief," in *Contemporary Philosophy of Religion*, ed. Steven M. Cahn and David Shatz (New York: Oxford University Press).

Philosophical Perspectives, 5, Philosophy of Religion, 1991

# AN ANTI-MOLINIST ARGUMENT

## Robert Merrihew Adams
## University of California, Los Angeles

### I. Middle Knowledge: The Issue

A vigorous debate about Luis de Molina's theory of divine providence[1] has developed in recent years in analytical philosophy of religion. Molina was attempting to reconcile providence with a firmly incompatibilist conception of human free will. (And I will accordingly assume throughout this paper that free actions are neither causally determined nor logically or metaphysically necessitated.) Molina held that God eternally[2] knows, with infallible certainty, about every possible free creature, exactly what that creature would freely do in any possible situation. Molina called this kind of knowledge "middle knowledge" (*scientia media*) because he thought it occupied a middle position, in certain respects, between two other components of the divine omniscience—between knowledge of necessary truths and knowledge of what depends on God's own will.

Middle knowledge would obviously be an immensely powerful resource for anyone trying to govern free creatures. If you knew exactly how every possible free creature would respond to every possible combination of incentives, you would probably not need omnipotence to establish yourself as emperor of the world, if that is what you wanted. Equipped with middle knowledge, an omnipotent God would be able to maintain providential control of the world without interfering with the freedom of creatures. Knowing under what circumstances and by what creatures a given action would be freely performed, God could bring about their performance of it, without directly causing it, by causing them to be in those circumstances.

There are results, of course, that God could not bring about in this way—the performance of given actions by given creatures in circumstances in which those creatures would not perform those actions (as God, by virtue of having middle knowledge, would know). Molinists differ as to how great a problem that might be for God. Suarez, focusing on the reconciliation of divine providence with human freedom, thought it "incredible" that God would not be able, with the use of middle knowledge, to obtain just about any free act of a creature.[3] Plantinga, devising a free will defense against the problem of evil, argues that the very most desirable patterns of creaturely free action might be unobtainable for God.[4]

Middle knowledge must be distinguished from simple *fore*-knowledge. The object of the latter is what will in fact happen, and is expressed by categorical propositions. The object of middle knowledge is what would happen under various conditions, many of which will never be actual. It is expressed by subjunctive conditional propositions, many of which are strictly counterfactual conditionals. It has become customary in the analytical philosophical literature on this subject to call all of them *counterfactuals of freedom*. A counterfactual of freedom is a subjunctive conditional stating what would be done *freely* by a certain possible creature (or by more than one) under certain possible circumstances.

Counterfactuals of freedom must be contingent. If they were necessary, then the circumstances stated in the antecedent would necessitate the action described by the consequent, and the latter would therefore not be free. Alone among contingent facts, however, true counterfactuals of freedom are prior to the will of God, in the order of explanation, according to the Molinist view. For they are data that God takes into account in deciding what to do. Moreover, God's causing their truth would amount to God causing the supposedly free actions of creatures to follow from the circumstances in which they are performed, and would thus seem to be inconsistent with the freedom of the creatures. Who or what, we may ask, does cause the truth of counterfactuals of freedom, if God does not? This is a good question, and forms in a way the topic of the present paper.

The controversy about middle knowledge is primarily about counterfactuals of freedom, and only secondarily about divine knowledge. Philosophical theologians generally agree that an omniscient God would know any true counterfactuals of freedom. But are there any? My admiration for Molina is great. His theory is one of the most brilliant constructions in the history of philosophical theology. But I think it fails because counterfactuals of freedom are in general false. More precisely, I believe that all counterfactuals of freedom about possible but non-actual creatures, and all that have false consequents, are false, and that if counterfactuals of freedom with true consequents about actual creatures are true at all, their truth arises too late in the order of explanation to play the part in divine providence that it is supposed to play according to Molina's theory.

One reason for doubting the truth of counterfactuals of freedom is that it is hard to see what would ground it. The categorical predictions involved in simple foreknowledge may be true by corresponding to future events, or so we may assume here for the sake of argument, in agreement with many philosophers. But in the case of counterfactuals of freedom that are about non-actual creatures or have false consequents, the conditionally predicted actions are not there to be corresponded with because they never actually occur. The truth of counterfactuals is commonly grounded in a logical or causal necessitation of the consequent by the antecedent, but such necessitation is incompatible with the freedom ascribed to actions in counterfactuals of freedom. So I do not see how these counterfactuals can be true.[5]

A quite different anti-Molinist argument, related to the question who or what brings about the truth of counterfactuals of freedom (if they are true) has been developed by William Hasker.[6] Molinists may wish to hold that in the case of a true counterfactual of freedom with a true antecedent it is the agent of the free action described in the consequent who brings it about that the conditional is true.[7] Ascribing this control to the agent seems obviously in keeping with an emphasis on the freedom of the agent. Hasker argues, however, that it follows from Molinist principles that "in general, it is not true that the truth of a counterfactual of freedom is brought about by the agent" (p. 48). He then (pp. 49-52) uses this conclusion to argue that Molinist views imply that if it is true that

In circumstances C, person P would freely do action A,

then, in circumstances C, P would not have the power not to do A, and thus would not be free after all with respect to doing A or not.

Hasker's argument is ingenious, and, if sound, constitutes, as he claims, a decisive refutation of Molinism.

I am strongly inclined to think that an argument along Hasker's lines is sound. Intuitive reasons for thinking so may be put very roughly as follows. Suppose it is not only true that P would do A if placed in circumstances C; suppose that truth was settled, as Molinism implies, prior to God's deciding what, if anything, to create, and it would therefore have been a truth even if P had never been in C—indeed even if P had never existed. Then it is hard to see how it can be up to P to determine freely whether P does A in C.

The detailed working out of Hasker's argument is quite complex, however, and involves some ideas that are potentially controversial as well as intrinsically interesting. I believe that by focusing on an idea that Hasker does not use in this context, the idea of *explanatory priority*, the argument can be simplified, and points of controversy avoided—though perhaps another is introduced. This recasting of Hasker's anti-Molinist argument is my project in the present paper.

## II. The First Stage of the Argument

The first stage of his argument, in which he tries to show that Molinism implies that we do not bring about the truth of counter-factuals of freedom about us, is sufficiently complicated that I will not try to reproduce it here. It depends on a thesis, for which Hasker argues and which may be correct, but on which I would rather not depend, that counterfactuals of freedom, on the Molinist view, must be more fundamental features of the world than particular events are, for purposes of the logic of counterfactuals (pp. 45-47).[8] This thesis is avoided by the following alternative argument.

(1) According to Molinism, the truth of all true counterfactuals of freedom about us is explanatorily prior to God's decision to create us.
(2) God's decision to create us is explanatorily prior to our existence.
(3) Our existence is explanatorily prior to all of our choices and actions.
(4) The relation of explanatory priority is transitive.
(5) Therefore it follows from Molinism (by 1-4) that the truth of all true counterfactuals of freedom about us is

explanatorily prior to all of our choices and actions.
(6) The relation of explanatory priority is asymmetrical.
(7) Therefore it follows from Molinism (by 5-6) that none of our choices and actions is explanatorily prior to the truth of any true counterfactual of freedom about us.
(8) Whatever we bring about is something to which some choice or action of ours is explanatorily prior.
(9) Therefore it follows from Molinism (by 7-8) that we do not bring about the truth of any counterfactual of freedom about us.

The central idea in this argument is that of explanatory priority, or an order of explanation. I think it is roughly the same as the idea that Scholastic philosophers expressed by the term *'prius ratione'* (prior in reason), but I do not mean to be committed here to any predecessor's version of it. Like the Scholastics, I do mean to distinguish this sort of priority from temporal priority. Even if there was no time before God decided to create us, or if God is timeless, God's knowing various things can be explanatorily prior to God's deciding to create us. And it is clear that according to Molinism (as claimed in premiss (1)), God's knowledge (and hence the truth) of all the true counterfactuals of freedom about us is prior in the order of explanation to God's deciding to create us, since (by the perfection of God's providence) they were all taken into account in that decision.

The most debatable point in this argument, in my opinion, is the assumption (6) that the relation of explanatory priority is asymmetrical. This assumption would not be plausible if applied to *all* sorts of explanations. Two theories, for instance, can mutually illuminate each other. More to the point, two decisions—two free decisions, indeed—made by the same person at the same time can help to explain each other. But with respect to the specific explanatory relationships among facts and events that figure in my argument, I think it is plausible to rule out the possibility of a closed explanatory loop. I will not claim more than plausibility for the assumption, however. The question of the possibility of closed explanatory loops is one that naturally arises in connection with issues about divine foreknowledge and providence; and our judgment about it is apt in any case to have some effect on our conclusions in this area.

Of the remaining premisses of the argument, (2) and (3) seem to me obviously correct. The transitivity of explanatory priority (4) is less debatable than its asymmetry.[9] And premiss (8) can be defended as a partial definition or analysis of bringing about.

## III. The Second Stage of the Argument

Having reached the conclusion that created, supposedly free agents do not bring about the truth of counterfactuals of freedom about them if Molinism is true, Hasker argues that it follows that such agents do not have the power to act otherwise than they in fact do, and hence are not really free. This argument employs a "power entailment principle,"

> (PEP) If it is in A's power to bring it about that $P$, and "$P$" entails "$Q$" and "$Q$" is false, then it is in A's power to bring it about that $Q$ (p. 49).

Now suppose A performs action X. Or in Hasker's concrete example, suppose Elizabeth accepts a research grant in circumstances C. Was it in her power to bring it about that in circumstances C she does not accept the research grant? Hasker thinks that on Molinist assumptions her non-acceptance in those circumstances would *entail* the counterfactual of freedom, "If Elizabeth were offered a research grant in circumstances C, she would not accept it." But given that we do not bring about the truth of counterfactuals of freedom about us, Hasker thinks "[i]t follows that Elizabeth does *not* have it in her power to" bring about the truth of this counterfactual about her, "and lacking this, she also—by (PEP)—lacks the power to reject the offer.

(PEP) is not only interesting, and highly relevant to other issues about divine foreknowledge. It is also a principle for which Hasker, drawing in part on work of Thomas B. Talbott, offers persuasive arguments (pp. 108-115). It seems correct to me. It may remain controversial, however;[10] and there are least two other points in the second stage of Hasker's argument that may be thought debatable (though probably not *very* debatable).

One is the premiss that on Molinist assumptions, Elizabeth's refusal of the grant would *entail* the counterfactual of freedom of which it constitutes the consequent. Behind this premiss lies the assumption that for Molinism it is a *necessary* truth that every counterfactual of freedom whose consequent is true is true. I think that is the normal interpretation of Molinism, and any other interpretation would imply that God might have lacked middle knowledge. But some Molinist, intent on refuting Hasker, might conceivably wish to fiddle with this assumption.

The other debatable point is Hasker's assumption that if Molinism implies, as he argued, that we *do not* bring about the truth of counterfactuals of freedom about us, it also implies that we do not have the *power* to bring about their truth. The assumption is plausible, but I am not sure it has been proved. In particular, I do not take it to have been proved by my recasting of the first stage of Hasker's argument.[11]

In order to avoid these points of potential controversy, I prefer to take a different line in this stage of the argument, making use again of the idea of explanatory priority. In doing so, indeed, I do not need the conclusion of the first stage of the argument, but only the first part of my argument for it:

(1) According to Molinism, the truth of all true counterfactuals of freedom about us is explanatorily prior to God's decision to create us.

(2) God's decision to create us is explanatorily prior to our existence.

(3) Our existence is explanatorily prior to all of our choices and actions.

(4) The relation of explanatory priority is transitive.

(5) Therefore it follows from Molinism (by 1-4) that the truth of all true counterfactuals of freedom about us is explanatorily prior to all of our choices and actions.

Thus far I follow my argument of the first stage. At this point I add a premiss articulating something that is undoubtedly a feature of Molinism:

(10) It follows also from Molinism that if I freely do action A in circumstances C, then there is a true counterfactual of freedom F\*, which says that if I were in C, then I would (freely) do A.

And I draw an obvious conclusion from (5) and (10):

(11) Therefore it follows from Molinism that if I freely do A in C, the truth of F\* is explanatorily prior to my choosing and acting as I do in C.

My key premiss in this stage of the argument expresses the idea that if my action is free in the incompatibilist sense, the action must be the first thing, in the order of explanation, that absolutely precludes my refraining from it:

(12) If I freely do A in C, no truth that is strictly inconsistent with my refraining from A in C is explanatorily prior to my choosing and acting as I do in C.

I put it this way, rather than saying 'If I freely do A in C, no truth that is strictly inconsistent with my refraining from A in C is explanatorily prior to my doing A in C,' in order to allow for a case in which I make several choices simultaneously, each of which helps to explain the others, and more than one of which is inconsistent with refraining from A. I think that would be quite consistent with my doing A *freely*. What is inconsistent with my acting freely is for my refraining to be excluded by something that is prior in the order of explanation to the totality of my voluntary action in the situation C.

The remaining premiss is obviously correct:

(13) The truth of F* (which says that if I were in C, then I would do A) is strictly inconsistent with my refraining from A in C.

Given these theses, it can be proved, by reduction to absurdity, that if Molinism is true, my doing A in C is not free:

(14) If Molinism is true, then if I freely do A in C, F* both is (by 11) and is not (by 12-13) explanatorily prior to my choosing and acting as I do in C.

(15) Therefore (by 14) if Molinism is true, then I do not freely do A in C.

Since this argument applies to any creature's doing any putatively free action in any circumstances in exactly the same way as to my doing A in C, it shows, if sound, that creatures do no free actions if Molinism is true—which is of course contrary to an essential tenet of Molinism.

One of the attractions of this version of the second stage of Hasker's argument is that in relying on only a part of my argument for the first stage, it appears to avoid relying on the assumption that the relation of explanatory priority is asymmetrical. It does depend on the transitivity of the relation (premiss 4), but I think that is hard to deny, as applied to this case. The premiss (12) in which I attempt to state a requirement of incompatibilism regarding free action is easily the most debatable assumption remaining in the argument. It will have strong intuitive appeal for some incompatibilists, I think, but Molinists can be expected to attack it. It is certainly incompatible with their aims regarding the relation of divine predestination to human freedom, as well as their views about middle knowledge.

One line of attack on it would begin with an argument that it covertly presupposes the asymmetry of explanatory priority. For it may be claimed that the intuition behind (12) could be equally well satisfied with

(12′) If I freely do A in C, my choosing and acting as I do in C is explanatorily prior to any truth that is strictly inconsistent with my refraining from A in C.

It would be hard, I think, for an incompatibilist to reject (12′). And since F* is strictly inconsistent with my refraining from A in C, (12′) implies that my choosing and acting as I do in C is explanatorily prior to the truth of F*. But if the relation of explanatory priority is not asymmetrical, then the priority of my deed is not inconsistent with F*'s (also) being explanatorily prior to my choosing and acting as I do in C; and my *reductio* argument for (15) collapses.

I could reply to this objection by maintaining that the asymmetry assumption is correct, as applied to the case at hand. And I do believe that the specific explanatory loop that must be postulated by a Molinist who relies on the objection is implausible. How can my acting as I do contribute to explaining a truth that is explanatorily prior even to God's deciding to create me?

I think I can mount a stronger defense, however, by refusing the substitution of (12′) for (12). The objection under consideration amounts to the claim that (12) owes its plausibility to (12′), and is (implicitly) derived from (12′) by way of the asymmetry assumption. But I believe the plausibility of (12) is not in fact reducible to that of (12′). The intuition that supports (12′) may be expressed by saying that if my action is free, it must contribute something to the explanation of my not acting otherwise, and hence to the explanation of any truth that is strictly inconsistent with my acting otherwise. That is an intuition that compatibilists may share, insofar as they generally agree that the choosing or doing of an agent acting freely must be causally efficacious (though acceptance of (12′) will involve compatibilists in explanatory loops if they believe that free actions are *strictly* necessitated, in the relevant sense, by their explanatory antecedents). But (12) expresses a more distinctively incompatibilist intuition, that the explanatory antecedents of the totality of my choosing and doing, in a situation in which I act freely, must leave the omission of the free action "open," at least in the sense of not being strictly inconsistent with the omission. (12'), in other words, is a thesis about what a free action must explain, or contribute to explaining; whereas (12) is a thesis about how a free action cannot be explained, and about the sense in which it must be true that I "could have done otherwise" when I act freely. So understood, (12) should appeal to incompatibilists and need not depend on (12'). It therefore also need not depend on an assumed asymmetry of explanatory priority.[12]

## Notes

1. Luis de Molina, *Liberi arbitrii cum gratiae donis, divina praescientia, providentia, praedestinatione et reprobatione concordia* [generally abbreviated, *Concordia*], ed. John Rabeneck (Oña and Madrid, 1953). The relevant portion (Part IV) of the *Concordia* has now been translated into English by Alfred J. Freddoso under the title *On Divine Foreknowledge* (Ithaca, N.Y.: Cornell University Press, 1988).
2. In the present paper I shall not attempt to answer the question whether 'eternally' is to be understood as meaning *timelessly* or *at all times*.
3. Francisco Suarez, *De scientia Dei futurorum contingentium*, bk. 2, c. 4, n. 4, in his *Opera omnia* (Paris, 1856-78), vol. 7, p. 354.
4. Alvin Plantinga, *The Nature of Necessity* (Oxford: Clarendon Press, 1974), ch. 9.
5. I have developed this argument more fully and carefully in "Middle Knowledge and the Problem of Evil," *American Philosophical Quarterly*, 14 (1977): 109-117, reprinted as ch. 6 of my book, *The Virtue of Faith and Other Essays in Philosophical Theology* (New York: Oxford University Press, 1987).
6. In several publications. I will be discussing the form it receives in his book, *God, Time, and Knowledge* (Ithaca, N.Y.: Cornell University Press, 1989). Parenthetical page references hereafter, if otherwise unidentified, will be to this work.
7. Hasker (p. 40) says he has heard this asserted by a noted friend of middle knowledge. I doubt that Molinists should maintain it. Freddoso (in the Introduction to his translation of Molina, *On Divine Foreknowledge*, p. 75f.) denies that it is part of Molinism—though he denies it only on the assumption that 'bring about' is used "in a straightforward causal sense"—which is not Hasker's assumption (p. 39n).

8. Freddoso selects this thesis for attack in the Introduction to his translation of Molina, *On Divine Foreknowledge*, p. 75f. He cites an unpublished paper by Thomas P. Flint as containing a fuller Molinist treatment of this subject.

9. This claim may itself be debated. Hasker has pointed out to me that transitivity of any relation, combined with its irreflexivity, entails its asymmetry. And initially we will surely think that the relation of explanatory priority is irreflexive—that nothing can be prior to itself. If we are seriously entertaining the hypothesis of a closed explanatory loop, however, a failure of irreflexivity may be exactly what we are envisaging. If a marvelous time machine transported me to the past, for example, and I there met my younger self and my older self talked my younger self out of committing suicide, the resulting explanatory loop could fairly be described, I think, by saying that my not committing suicide would be explanatorily prior to itself. (I do not mean to make a pronouncement here, either way, about the possibility of such an explanatory loop, or of time travel.) In any event I think it highly unlikely that the *transitivity* of explanatory priority fails in any way that would invalidate the inference from (1), (2), and (3) to (5).

10. It is the point in this stage of the argument that Freddoso selects for attack, on behalf of Molinism, in his Introduction to Molina, *On Divine Foreknowledge*, pp. 76-78.

11. The issue here would be whether the thesis ascribed in (1) to Molinism, if true, could nonetheless be falsified by us if we did something we will not in fact do—whether there are acts we could perform but won't that would reverse the order of explanation discussed in the first stage of the argument, by depriving the truth of counterfactuals of freedom of its independence of the truth of their antecedents. An affirmative answer to this question seems to me bizarre, and unlikely to be appealing to Molinists, but I'd rather not undertake here the burden of justifying its exclusion.

12. This paper grew out of discussion at a symposium on Hasker's book that I attended at the Pacific Division convention of the American Philosophical Association, March 30, 1990. The principal participants, besides Hasker, were Thomas Flint and Stephen Davis. I am indebted to their discussion, and to Hasker for comments on a version of this paper, as well as to Marilyn McCord Adams for discussion of this topic.

Philosophical Perspectives, 5, Philosophy of Religion, 1991

# SHAPSHOT OCKHAMISM

John Martin Fischer
University of California, Riverside

## I.

Three sorts of arguments triangulate on the conclusion that human beings might not have the sort of freedom which implies "freedom to do otherwise." Each sort of argument is really a family of arguments. The three families are: the argument for fatalism, the argument for the incompatibility of causal determinism and human freedom to do otherwise, and the argument for the incompatibility of divine foreknowledge and human freedom to do otherwise. And the three families are themselves related; the three nuclear families are members of an extended family of arguments with a common structure.[1]

The common structure involves a premise which claims that a certain feature of the past is "fixed"—unalterable and, in some specified sense, "out of our control". In the argument for fatalism, the relevant premise expressing the idea of the fixity of the past might be as follows: "It is now out of my control that yesterday it was true that I would go to the movies tonight." (One could make this more precise by eliminating the indexicals.) In the argument for the incompatibility of causal determinism and human freedom to do otherwise, the relevant premise might be: "It is now out of my control that in the year 1000 B.C. the universe was in state $U$ (where $U$ is a complete description of the intrinsic, temporally non-relational facts)." Finally, the relevant premise in the argument for the incompatibility of divine foreknowledge and human freedom to do otherwise might be: "It is now out of my control that in the year 1000 B.C. God believed that I would go to the movies tonight."

It seems to me that these three arguments (or families of arguments) are plausible to different degrees, and it is not the point of this paper to assess the relative plausibility of the various arguments. It suffices for my purposes here to point out that it is widely believed that a certain sort of distinction is an important tool for responding at least to some of the arguments. This distinction is between temporally non-relational, genuine, or "hard" facts about times and temporally relational, non-genuine, or "soft" facts about times.[2] It is alleged, for example, that one can successfully respond to the argument for fatalism by claiming that the relevant premise asserting the fixity of the past is false because the claim about the past in question is a *soft* fact about the past. This move seems to me to be entirely correct.

Further, it seems that there is a clear asymmetry between the argument for fatalism and the argument for the incompatibility of causal determinism and human freedom to do otherwise. As claimed above, in the former argument the relevant premise is false because it claims that some *soft* fact about the past is fixed. In contrast, in the latter argument the relevant premise is not false in virtue of claiming that some soft fact about the past is fixed; the pertinent fact is by hypothesis a temporally non-relational, hard fact. (Now it might turn out that in the latter argument the relevant premise *is* false, but it would not be for the reason in virtue of which the premise of the former argument is false. More specifically, some philosophers believe that even hard facts about past times need not be fixed, and such a philosopher could deny the relevant premise of the argument for the incompatibility of causal determinism and freedom to do otherwise. But it would be clear that this denial would be based upon different considerations from those which ground the denial of the parallel premise in the argument for fatalism.)

I believe that there is an interesting sense in which the argument for the incompatibility of God's foreknowledge and human freedom to do otherwise is "in between" the two arguments mentioned above. That is, whereas the status of the relevant premises in the first two arguments is relatively uncontroversial, the status of the relevant premise of the argument from God's foreknowledge is highly controversial. Recall that this premise is, "It is now out of my control that in the year 1000 B.C. God believed that I would go to the movies tonight."

Some philosophers believe that God's beliefs are soft facts about the times at which they are held. These philosophers would assimilate the argument for the incompatibility of God's foreknowledge and human freedom to do otherwise and the argument for fatalism. Other philosophers hold that God's beliefs are *hard* facts about the times at which they are held. These philosophers are inclined to assimilate the argument for the incompatibility of God's foreknowledge and human freedom to do otherwise and the argument for the incompatibility of causal determinism and human freedom to do otherwise (at least as regards the parallel premises asserting the fixity of some feature of the past).

What should be clear from the above remarks is that the distinction between hard and soft facts is an important tool for understanding and responding to the various arguments discussed above. (It certainly has not been established—or even suggested—that this distinction is *necessary* in order properly to come to grips with the extended family of arguments. But it at least seems to be clear that this distinction is *useful* in addressing the arguments. Also, it seems to me that other approaches to responding to the arguments employ tools which are importantly related to the basic distinction between hard and soft facts.)[3]

There is a clear point, then, to attempting to give a precise account of the distinction between hard and soft facts about times. In the next section of this paper I shall lay out a version of an account of the distinction proposed by Marilyn Adams. I shall then briefly summarize a criticism which I have offered of this distinction elsewhere. Next, I shall present David Widerker's defense of Adams' account of the distinction.[4] Finally, I shall develop a criticism of this defense. This critique, however, will lead to a constructive proposal, because I believe that the difficulties with Adams' criterion (even as modified in light of Widerker's insights) point us to a new approach to sketching an account of the distinction between hard and soft facts.

## II.

For the sake of simplicity, I shall present my own version of Adams' suggestion; it should be kept in mind that this is a simplification and that it differs from the actual form of Adams' suggestion as she presents it. I do not, however, think that my version of the criterion distorts it in any way relevant to a fair discussion of it. Adams' account of the distinction between hard and soft facts can, then, be presented as follows[5]:

> (A) (1) A fact $F$ is about a time $T1$ if and only if $F$'s obtaining entails that something occur at $T1$; (2) A fact $F$ about $T1$ is a soft fact about $T1$ if and only if $F$'s obtaining entails that something (contingent) occur at some later time $T2$; (3) A fact $F$ about $T1$ is a hard fact about $T1$ if and only if it is not a soft fact about $T1$.

What exactly is meant by "something's occurring at $T1$"? In effect, Adams would say that "something's occurring at $T1$" consists in "the happening or not happening, actuality or non-actuality of something at $T1$". Basically, then, Adams' account implies that a given fact $F$ is a soft fact about a time $T$ insofar as its obtaining at $T$ entails that a contingent fact obtains at a time later than $T$.

Of course, (A) is rather rough, but I believe that it is sufficiently precise to allow us to draw out some implications. On (A) the fact that God believed at $T1$ that $S$ would not do $X$ at $T2$ is deemed a soft fact about $T1$: its obtaining entails that $S$ does not do $X$ at $T2$. It is here obvious that (A) embodies an "Entailment Criterion of Soft Facthood": a soft fact about $T1$ *entails* that some contingent fact obtains at some later time $T2$.

(A) is initially attractive. Also, (A) has the implication that God's belief at a time (about the future) is a soft fact about the time at which it is held, and thus (A) is appealing to an Ockhamist. But I believe that (A) is defective. It will be useful to set out a fundamental problem with (A) here.

The problem with (A) is that is appears as though (A) must classify all facts as soft. Consider the fact, "Jack is sitting at $T1$". Intuitively, this should be classified as a hard fact about $T1$. But notice that "Jack is sitting at $T1$" entails that it is not the case that Jack sits for the first time at $T2$. Thus, in virtue of (A)'s embodying the Entailment Criterion of Soft Facthood, it must classify "Jack is sitting at $T1$" as a *soft* fact about $T1$. Because this sort of result is clearly generalizable, it appears as if (A) will classify all facts as soft, and it is therefore evidently unacceptable.

David Widerker has taken exception to my criticism of Adams' (A), saying that "Fischer's objection...cannot be deemed convincing".[6] Widerker notes that, whereas a fact such as "Jack is sitting at $T1$"

does entail the non-occurrence of the event, "Jack sits for the first time" at $T2$, it does *not* entail that $T2$ exist. In other words, "Jack is sitting at $T1$" does entail that it is not the case that the event, "Jack is sitting for the first time" occurs at $T2$, but it does not entail that $T2$ exist. The point is that there are two ways in which it might be true that it is not the case that the event, "Jack is sitting for the first time", occurs at $T2$. In the first way, $T2$ exists but at $T2$ either Jack is not sitting at all, or he is sitting and he has sat before. In the second way, the world has (atemporally) gone out of existence and $T2$ does not even exist. Obviously, it is a presupposition of this view that it is not logically or metaphysically necessary that time continue: it is presupposed that it is logically and in some sense metaphysically possible that time stop. Presumably, the picture is that time would stop if the world, including all of space, went out of existence.[7]

Exploiting Widerker's point, we could slightly modify (A) as follows:

> (A')(1') A fact $F$ is about a time $T1$ if and only if $F's$ obtaining entails both that $T1$ exists and that something occurs at $T1$; (2') A fact $F$ about $T1$ is a soft fact about $T1$ if and only if $F's$ obtaining entails that some later time $T2$ exists. (3') A fact $F$ about $T1$ is a hard fact about $T1$ if and only if it is not a fact about $T1$.

(A') appears to remain faithful to the idea of Adams' approach but to avoid the implausible consequence of (A) that all facts about $T$ are considered soft facts about $T$. Further, (A') has the consequence that "God believed at $T1$ that Jones would mow his lawn at $T2$" is a soft fact about $T1$; this is because God's belief here entails that $T2$ exists.

Widerker does not explicitly accept (A'), but it is my reconstruction of Widerker's interpretation of Adams' criterion. If (A') or something very like it is *not* what Widerker has in mind as Adams' criterion, then it is hard to see what Widerker *does* have in mind. Widerker's basic point is that I wrongly attribute to Adams the admittedly problematic (A). Rather, Widerker suggests that what Adams really has in mind is something like (A'), which is not problematic in the same way as (A). (Of course, Widerker does not explicitly say or commit himself to the view that (A') is not problematic in *any* way.)

In this paper I shall develop a problem for the account suggested by (although not explicitly endorsed by) Widerker. The problem with (A') is this. On (A'), a fact such as the fact that God believed at $T1$

that Jones would mow his lawn at *T2* (let us call this fact, "*F1*") is a soft fact about *T1*, as stated above. Now, consider the following fact, which is generated by simply counting all the persons who hold the belief at *T1* that Jones will mow his lawn at *T2*: "Exactly *N* persons believed at *T1* that Jones would mow his lawn at *T2*." (Let us call this fact,"*F2*".) I claim that if *F1* is considered a soft fact about *T1*, then *F2* should be considered a soft fact as well. That is, if God is actually one of the *N* believers, then intuitively *F2* should be considered a soft fact about *T1*. But whereas (A') implies that *F1* is a soft fact about *T1*, (A') implies that *F2* is a *hard* fact about *T1*: *F2* does not entail that time continue after *T1*. (To see this, remember that the possible-worlds definition of entailment is as follows: *P* entails *Q* if and only if *Q* is true in all the possible worlds in which *P* is true. And note that in *some* possible worlds in which *F2* obtains, time stops at *T1*; in such worlds, God is not among the *N* believers at *T1*.)

Above I claimed that if *F1* is considered a soft fact about *T1*, then *F2* should be considered a soft fact as well. Further, I said that, if God is actually one of the *N* believers, then intuitively *F2* should be considered a soft fact about *T1*, if *F1* is so considered. I need to say a bit more about these claims. Notice that facts can be more or less abstract, and a fact such as *F2* is relatively abstract. That is, *F2* can be "made true" by various more "basic" facts. Now my claim is that, if *F2* is made true by a set of believers including God, then *F2* should be considered a soft fact about *T1* (on the assumption that *F1* is considered a soft fact about *T1*). Another way of putting the point might be as follows. In a possible world in which *F2* is made true by a set of believers including God, *F2* should be considered a soft fact about *T1* (if *F1* is so considered); one might even say that *F2* is a soft fact *relative to the world in question*. But (A'), as stated, does not have the consequence that *F2* should be considered a soft fact about *T1* or that it should be so considered relative to any particular possible world.

The above considerations raise the question of whether (A') might be easily revisable in such a way as to avoid the problem just discussed. What if we revised (A') so that it would apply to facts *as made true in particular ways* rather than facts simpliciter? I believe that there are a number of problems with this approach. First, note that *F2* is a different fact from *F2\**: "Exactly *N* persons including God believed at *T1* that Jones would mow his lawn at *T2*." They are apparently different facts insofar as they have different entailments.

But the revised version of (A′) would not be able to preserve this distinction; indeed, it would not seem to allow any space for the fact *F2* apart from *F2\**.

Further, the whole point of the enterprise of providing a precise account of the distinction between hard and soft facts (within the context of this paper) is to *employ* it in a certain way, *i.e.*, to apply it to facts about God's beliefs such as *F1* in order to determine whether such facts are hard or soft facts. But if (A′)—or whatever account one ultimately adopts—is to apply only to facts *as they are made true*, the question will arise as to exactly what makes true a fact such as *F1*. It seems to me that it is essentially controversial, within the context of debates about Ockhamism, exactly what state of affairs makes true a fact such as *F1*. That is, it is controversial whether Jones' mowing his lawn at *T2* is part of the state of affairs that makes true *F1*. Given this sort of consideration, I do not think that it is fruitful, within the context of debates about Ockhamism, to employ (at least in the way suggested above) the notion of what states of affairs "make true" certain facts in attempting to generate an account of the distinction between hard and soft facts.

Since (A′) classifies *F1* but not *F2* as soft, (A′) does not capture our intuitive judgments about softness (i.e., about temporal relationality). I believe that this problem in itself shows that (A′) is deficient. But I shall now point out why this sort of problem makes it impossible for an Ockhamist to employ (A′) in defense of his position. (Marilyn Adams endorses some version of Ockhamism in her paper. Ockhamism is the doctrine that God's prior beliefs are both (a) soft facts about the times at which they are held and (b) not fixed after the times at which they are held. Of course, the fact that (A′) cannot be employed by an Ockhamist does not in itself constitute a reason to think that (A′) is inadequate; but this fact is, nevertheless, an interesting fact to the extent that the hard fact/soft fact distinction is a necessary component of Ockhamism.)

Imagine that Jones mows his lawn at *T2* and that (*F1*) and (*F2*) obtain. It follows that (*F3*) obtains: Exactly *N-1* persons other than God believed at *T1* that Jones would mow his lawn at *T2*. Assume further that Jones is free at *T2* to refrain from mowing his lawn at *T2*. Now it seems to me that there are the following two possibilities:

(I) If Jones were to refrain from mowing his lawn at *T2*, then no person who failed to believe at *T1* that Jones would

mow his lawn at *T2* would have held this belief at *T1*, or
(II) If Jones were to refrain from mowing his lawn at *T2*,
then some person(s) who failed to believe at *T1* that Jones
would mow his lawn at *T2* would have held this belief.

Assume first that (I) is true. It follows that, if Jones were to refrain from mowing his lawn at *T2*, then *F2* would not obtain. And *F2* is deemed a hard fact about *T1* by (A'). Assume now that (II) is true. It follows that if Jones were to refrain from mowing his lawn at *T2*, then *F2* or *F3* would not obtain. And both of these facts are deemed by (A') hard facts about *T1*.

Since either (I) or (II) is true, if Jones were free at *T2* to refrain from mowing his lawn at *T2*, then *some* hard fact about *T1* (according to [A']) would not have been a fact. And if one cannot at any time so act that a fact which is a hard fact about the past would not have been a fact, then Jones *cannot* (contrary to the original supposition) refrain from mowing his lawn at *T2*.

So even if God's belief at *T1* that Jones will mow his lawn at *T2* were a *soft* fact about *T1*, it would be a "hard-core soft fact."[8] That is, even if God's prior belief were a soft fact about *T1*, it would be such that the only way in which Jones could at *T2* so act that it would not have been a fact would be by so acting that *some* fact which *is* a hard fact about the past would *not* have been a fact. (A'), then, generates the problem of "hard-core soft facts"—an apparently lethal problem for Ockhamism. After all, the Ockhamist (unlike his metaphysically more extravagant counterpart, the Multiple-Pasts Compatibilist), believes that one *cannot* so act that a fact which is a hard fact about the past would not have been a fact. Thus, if an account (such as [A']) implies that God's prior belief is a hard-core soft fact, then it cannot be employed by the Ockhamist to vindicate human freedom. Whereas Adams' (A) generates too many soft facts, the interpretation of (A) suggested by Widerker's criticism, (A'), generates hard-core soft facts.[9]

## III.

Suppose an Ockhamist says this. "I should never have said—if I really did say this—that no agent can ever so act that some hard fact about the past would not have been a fact. This is because there are hard-core soft facts, and, in general, not all soft facts about past times are fixed. More specifically, since one can alter certain soft facts, one might be able to alter certain hard facts *in virtue* of altering the soft facts. (This approach might be called, "Bootstrapping Ockhamism".) So one man's hard-core soft facts might be another's hard facts with soft underbellies. Why should one focus on the hard elements of these facts and take them to be salient, rather than focusing on the soft elements and taking *them* to be salient?"

The Ockhamist cannot, however, get away with this. Quite clearly, it is *not* in general true that it suffices for an agent's being able to do a certain act that in so acting the agent would be falsifying some soft fact. There are some soft facts about the past which are beyond an agent's power to control. Further, whenever it is the case that an agent is free to perform some action which he does not in fact perform, he is free so to act that *some* soft fact about the past would not have been a fact. So whenever one considers whether an agent can perform some action (which he does not in fact perform), one is considering whether an agent can falsify *some* soft fact about the past. For example, imagine that causal determinism is true, the natural laws are fixed, and Jones goes to a Stanford football game in September, 1990. Let *C* be the total set of hard facts about the year 1900 which, together with the natural laws, entails that Jones goes to the football game in September, 1990. If Jones is free in September, 1990 to refrain from going to the football game, then it follows that Jones is free so to act that 1900 would not have preceded his going to the game in 1990. But this fact—that 1900 preceded Jones' going to the Stanford football game in September, 1990—is clearly a soft fact about 1900. But note that if Jones is free in September, 1990 to refrain from going to the game, he is free so to act that *C* would not have been the case in 1900. But "*C* obtains in 1900" is clearly a hard fact about 1900. If one believes that it is not in an agent's power so to act that hard facts about the past would not have been facts (as the Ockhamist does believe), then presumably this is as clear a case as one can get of an agent's being constrained in his power by the fixity of the past. So it does not *follow* from the fact that in performing some act one would be falsifying some soft fact that one can perform the act in question. Indeed, unless Ockhamism is to *collapse* into multiple-pasts compatibilism, the Ockhamist must *not* allow that one can falsify hard facts *simply* in virtue of falsifying soft facts. Thus, it is not clear how the Ockhamist can justify the claim that facts such as those pertaining to God's beliefs are hard facts with soft underbellies.

The problem can be put as follows. The Ockhamist suggests that facts pertaining to God's beliefs are hard facts with soft underbellies. That is, he claims that they are hard facts which can be "falsified" in virtue of falsifying some *soft* fact. But it does not in general *follow* from the truth that in performing some act one would be falsifying some soft fact about the past that one *can* perform it. Not only would this entailment issue in the collapse of Ockhamism into Multiple-Pasts Compatibilism, but it would result in implausible claims that agents can perform actions which even a compatibilist would admit that they *cannot* perform. If I am chained to my chair, I cannot leave my office, even though by leaving my office I would be falsifying some soft fact about the past: the fact that (at some prior time) I did something prior to not leaving my office. Thus, the claim that in performing some act one would be falsifying some soft fact is not sufficient to justify the claim that one can perform the act in question, and hence the Ockhamist needs to produce some other justification for his claim that God's beliefs are hard facts with soft underbellies. Bootstrapping Ockhamism needs further support.

The Ockhamist might attempt to wriggle out of the uncomfortable position in which he finds himself as follows. "You still fail to do justice to my position. I do *not* think that all hard facts about the past are unalterable. Rather, it is only a proper subset of the hard facts about the past which are unalterable—the "accomplished facts". Let us define the set of such facts as follows: A fact $F$ is an accomplished fact about $T$ just in case $F$ is a hard fact about $T$ and for any fact $G$ which is a hard fact about $T$, the conjunction $F \& G$ is a hard fact about $T$. Now I can say that, whereas 'Condition $C$ obtains' is an accomplished fact about $T$, $F2$ is clearly *not* such a fact. ($F2$) is a mere hard fact about $T$ since the conjunction of $F2$ and $F3$ is not a hard fact about $T$ (on a criterion such as [A' ])."

But how can our (admittedly persistent) Ockhamist justify his claim that only accomplished facts about the past need be considered fixed? Try this. Only accomplished facts are unalterable because only they can be members of a *complete* conjunction $C^*$ of facts about a time $T$ (describing the state of the world at $T$) which is such that it is possible that $C^*$ hold and the world end at the instant after $T$. But this is false, since a fact such as $F2$ can be *made true* in different ways; some ways do not include God as one of the $N$ believers. Thus, it *is* possible that this fact be a member of a complete conjunction of facts about *T* and the world end immediately after *T*.

What the Ockhamist needs to do is somehow to capture the fact that God is actually one of the *N* believers in the example discussed above. That is, what is needed is an account of soft facts which takes a snapshot of the world at *T*; the information recorded in the snapshot will tell us exactly how the facts are instantiated at *T*. Only a Snapshot Ockhamism can obviate the problem of hard-core soft facts.

## IV.

A Snapshot Ockhamist might start with the following simple intuition. A fact about some time *T* is a hard fact about *T* insofar as its obtaining is compatible with the world's ending right after *T*. This somewhat chilling and eschatological idea can be made more precise. The world would end at a time to the extent that no particulars which can have properties or stand in relations exist at or after that time. The claim that the world ends at a time is intended to entail that nothing happens after that time.

So, for example, "Jack sits at *T*" should be considered a hard fact about *T*, and it is so considered by the above suggestion: "Jack sits at *T*" is compatible with the world's ending right after *T*. Further, "Jack sits at *T* five days prior to his swimming" should be considered a soft fact about *T*, and it is so considered.

But this simple account needs to be refined in light of facts such as *F2*. As argued above, if God is one of the *N* believers, then a fact such as "Exactly *N* persons believe at *T1* that Jones will mow his lawn at *T2*" should be considered a *soft* fact about *T1*. But note that this fact is compatible with the world's ending right after *T1*. As pointed out above, a fact such as *F2* can be made true in different ways, and God need not be one of the believers in order for *F2* to obtain. Thus, *F2* is not considered a soft fact about *T1*, according to the Snapshot theorist's suggestion.

Above, I pointed out that Adams' suggestion for an account of the distinction between hard and soft facts is this: a fact is a soft fact about a time insofar as it entails some contingent fact about a later time. I claimed that this account implies that all facts are soft facts about the relevant times. It is clear that the Snapshot theorist's suggestion avoids this problem. However, the Snapshot account, as formulated so far, has the same problem as (A'), which is the revision of Adams' suggested by Widerker's remarks: it generates hard-core soft facts.

I shall now sketch a strategy which might be used by a Snapshot Ockhamist to avoid the problem of hard-core soft facts. Let us define a special notion of entailment: entailment*. A fact $P$ entails* a fact $Q$ just in case $P$ is a member of a set $S$ of truths minimally sufficient to entail $Q$. A set $S$ is minimally sufficient to entail some fact $Q$ if and only if

   (1) $S$ entails $Q$, and
   (2) there is no set of true basic propositions $S'$ such that
       (a) $S'$ is equivalent to $S$,
       (b) no proper subset of $S'$ is equivalent to $S'$, and
       (c) some proper subset of $S'$ entails $Q$.[10]

When a set $S$ is minimally sufficient for some proposition $Q$, there is no set $S'$ which is equivalent to $S$ and which is a non-redundant "mini-entailer" of $Q$; that is, when $S$ is minimally sufficient for $Q$, $S$ is a compact entailer of $Q$.

Here is an example of entailment* which is not an example of entailment, *i.e.*, an example in which some proposition $P$ entails* some proposition $Q$ but in which it is not the case that $P$ entails $Q$. Suppose that Alex Rosenberg and Peter van Inwagen are on a train to Syracuse, and that they are the only two passengers on the train. The proposition that Alex Rosenberg is going to Syracuse (call this proposition, $AR$) entails* (but obviously does not entail) the proposition that exactly two passengers are on the train going to Syracuse. This is because $AR$ is a member of a set $S$ of propositions minimally sufficient for the proposition that exactly two passengers are on the train going to Syracuse. The relevant set $S$ is the set of true propositions, {"Alex Rosenberg is a passenger on the train going to Syracuse", "Peter van Inwagen is a passenger on the train going to Syracuse", "There is no other passenger on the train going to Syracuse"}. This set $S$ is a compact entailer (in the sense specified above) of the proposition that exactly two passengers are on the train going to Syracuse.

Now the Snapshot Ockhamist's view can be stated more precisely. The view is that a fact $F$ is a hard fact about a time $T$ only if (a) $F$ is compatible with the world's ending at $T$, and (b) no fact $G$ which entails that time continue after $T$ entails* $F$. Let us call the conjunction of (a) and (b), "(SO)".

We can now apply the Snapshot account. Fact *F1*—the fact that God believed at *T1* that Jones would mow his lawn at *T2*—entails that time continue after *T1*. Further, *F1* entails* *F2*—the fact that exactly *N* persons believed at *T1* that Jones would mow his lawn at *T2*. This is because *F1* is a member of a set of propositions *S* which meets the conditions developed above: *S* is minimally sufficient for *F2*. The set *S* in question is the set of propositions saying of each person who believed at *T1* that Jones would mow his lawn at *T2* that he so believed plus the proposition that these were the *only* persons who so believed. I claim that this set *S* entails *F2* and that there exists no set *S'* of basic propositions such that *S'* is equivalent to *S*, no proper subset of *S'* is equivalent to *S'*, and some subset of *S'* entails *F2*. Thus, the Snapshot Ockhamist's account—(SO)— captures the information we wanted to capture about *F2*; it captures information about the way in which *F2* is made true in such a way that it implies that *F2* is a soft fact, if God is one of the *N* believers.

Not only does Snapshot Ockhamism crystallize the Ockhamist's intuition about *F2*, it has another advantage over an approach such as (A'). On (A') it is *not* generally true that, if some fact *F* is a hard fact about a time *T* and some fact *G* is a hard fact about *T*, then the conjunction *F & G* is a hard fact about *T*. That is, (A') does not preserve hardness under conjunction. For example, on (A') facts *F2* and *F3* are each considered hard facts about *T1*, but the conjunction *F2 & F3* is not so considered. In contrast, I claim that (SO) preserves hardness under conjunction.

Further, it should be the case that a proper Ockhamistic account entails that facts about God's prior beliefs (and such facts as *F2* when made true in certain ways) turn out to be soft facts about the relevant times while entailing that such facts as, "At *T* the world is in state *U* (where *U* is the complete set of temporally non-relational facts which obtain at *T*)", are hard facts about *T*. And this is precisely what (SO) entails.

To see this, suppose that causal determinism is true, and condition *U* (which obtained a some time *T* before you were born), together with the laws of nature, constituted a causally sufficient condition for your going to the movies at *T+n*. It is here assumed that the conjunction of a statement saying that *U* obtained at *T* and a statement of the laws of nature entails that you go to the movies at *T+n*, although the statement that *U* obtained at *T* alone does not have this implication. Now, does "You go to the movies at *T+n*" entail*

"$U$ obtained at $T$"? (If so, then by (SO) the latter fact would be a soft fact about $T$.)

Let us suppose that a kind of "two-way" causal determinism obtains according to which it is true that the natural laws entail that you go to the movies at $T+n$ if and only if $U$ obtained at $T$. Now the fact that you go to the movies at $T+n$ is part of a set $S$ which entails that $U$ obtained at $T+n$. This set $S$ consists of: {"You go to the movies at $T+n$", "If you go to the movies at $T+n$, then $U$ obtained at $T$"}. But notice now that there *is* a set $S'$ of true basic propositions which is such that $S'$ is equivalent to $S$, no proper subset of $S'$ is equivalent to $S'$, and some proper subset of $S'$ entails that $U$ obtained at $T$; this is the set, $S'$, {"You go to the movies at $T2$", "$U$ obtained at $T$"}. Hence, $S$ is *not* minimally sufficient for "$U$ obtained at $T$"; $S'$ is a non-redundant mini-entailer (equivalent to $S$) of "$U$ obtained at $T$."

Snapshot Ockhamism, then, provides a precise way of showing that causal determinism presents a deeper challenge to human freedom than does divine foreknowledge. If an agent is free so to act that God would not have held the belief he did actually hold, then the agent is free so to act that some soft fact about the past (according to [SO]) would not have been a fact. In contrast, if an agent is free at $T+n$ so to act that $U$ would not have been a fact about $T$, then the agent is free so to act that a hard fact about the past (according to [SO]) would not have been a fact. Snapshot Ockhamism avoids a potential collapse of Ockhamism into Multiple-Pasts Compatibilism.

## V.

In the context of a discussion of Widerker's critique, I have attempted to present a general problem for a class of Ockhamistic accounts of the distinction between hard and soft facts: this is the problem of hard-core soft facts. Given that no human agent is free so to act that hard facts about the past would not have been facts, the revision of Adams' account suggested by Widerker's critique is inadequate; although God's belief may not be a hard fact about the past, one's freedom so to act that it would not have been a fact would require so acting that *some* hard fact about the past would not have been a fact.[11]

I have sketched a new version of Ockhamism—the Snapshot approach. Snapshot Ockhamism does not spawn hard-core soft facts, and it preserves hardness under conjunction. Further, Snapshot

Ockhamism is a device strong enough to protect compatibilism about freedom and foreknowledge (against certain worries), but not so strong as to yield compatibilism about freedom and determinism. Whereas I certainly have not argued here that Ockhamism is ultimately tenable, I have at least presented one way in which the theory can be formulated precisely. I have had a minimal project in this paper: to develop a sketch of some tools with which the Ockhamist could formulate his position. But even if these tools render it possible for the Ockhamist to avoid the result that God's prior beliefs are hard-core soft facts, they do not appear to render it possible for the Ockhamist to avoid the (equally mortifying) result that God's beliefs are hard-type soft facts.[12,13]

## Notes

1. I have set out various versions of these arguments and discussed their structural similarities in: "Introduction: Responsibility and Freedom", John Martin Fischer, ed., *Moral Responsibility*. (Ithaca: Cornell University Press, 1986); and "Introduction: God and Freedom", John Martin Fischer, ed., *God, Foreknowledge, and Freedom*, (Stanford: Stanford University Press, 1989).
2. For a selection of discussions of this distinction and its role in incompatibilist arguments, see: Fischer, 1989.
3. On one such approach, a distinction is made between temporally non-relational and temporally relational *properties* (rather than facts): David Widerker, "Two Forms of Fatalism", in Fischer, 1989, pp. 97-110.
4. David Widerker, "On A Fallacious Objection to Adams' Soft/Hard Fact Distinction" *Philosophical Studies* 57 September 1989, pp. 103-107.
5. Marilyn Adams, "Is the Existence of God 'Hard' Fact?", *Philosophical Review* 76 (1967), pp. 492-503, reprinted in Fischer, 1989.
6. Widerker, 1989
7. For discussions of the issue of whether time can stop, see: Arthur Prior, "On the Logic of Ending Time", in *Papers on Time and Tense* (Oxford: Oxford University Press, 1968); W.H. Newton-Smith, *The Structure of Time* (London: Routledge and Kegan Paul, 1980); and Quentin Smith, "On the Beginning of Time", *Nous* 19 (1985), pp. 579-584.
8. For a discussion of hard-core soft facts, see: John Martin Fischer, "Ockhamism", *Philosophical Review* 94 (January 1985), pp. 81-100.
9. David Widerker develops examples which involve what I would call "hard-core soft facts" in: Widerker, 1989; and "Against the Eternity Solution", forthcoming.
10. First, a set of propositions R is equivalent to a set R* just in case the conjunctions of the members of the sets are necessarily materially equivalent (or equivalent in the "broadly logical sense"). Second, the

restriction of $S'$ to basic propositions is essential. This can be seen by considering the following argument. Suppose $S$ is a non-redundant set {A1, A2, ..., An} which entails $Q$. We could *always* find a set $S'$ which satisfies the account without the restriction. Such a set would be: $S' = $ {A1, A2, ..., An or not-Q, Q, An + 1, ..., An}. This set $S'$ is equivalent to $S$, non-redundant, and a proper subset of it entails $Q$. Thus, the account requires the restriction to basic propositions. I should point out that all other accounts of the relevant distinction with which I am familiar require some sort of similar distinction; indeed, it is plausible to conjecture that Ockhamism requires (or at least is associated with) atomism—the doctrine that facts (propositions, states of affairs, etc.) can be divided into basic (atomic) and non-basic (molecular) entities.

11. This is precisely the same problem as the one I identified in an approach suggested by Nelson Pike. For this debate, see: Nelson Pike, "Fischer on Freedom and Foreknowledge", *Philosophical Review* 93 (October 1984), pp. 599-614; and Fischer, 1985.

12. John Martin Fischer, "Hard-Type Soft Facts", *Philosophical Review* 95 (October 1986), pp. 591-601. One might distinguish two ways of dividing up facts: into smaller facts and into individuals and properties. The first method of division yields "hard-core soft facts". The second method of division yields "hard-type soft facts". A hard-type soft fact is a soft fact whose falsification would require that some individual who actually possessed some *temporally non-relational property* would not have possessed this property. And it is plausible to suppose that, if hard facts about the past are fixed, then so are hard-type soft facts about the past.

13. I have benefitted from discussing a previous version of this paper with the members of the seminar (on God and Freedom) taught by Nelson Pike and me during the winter quarter of 1990 at UC Riverside and UC Irvine. Also, a version of this paper has been read at the University of North Carolina, Greensboro; on that occasion I greatly benefitted from the comments of Joshua Hoffman, Gary Rosenkrantz, and Jarrett Leplin. Finally, I am very much indebted to Carl Ginet for helping me to develop an ancestor of the idea behind "entails*".

### References

Marilyn Adams, "Is the Existence of God a 'Hard' Fact?", *Philosophical Review* 76 (1967), pp. 492-503, reprinted in Fischer, 1989.

John Martin Fischer, "Ockhamism", *Philosophical Review* 94 (January 1985), pp. 81-100.

John Martin Fischer, "Hard-Type Soft Facts", *Philosophical Review* 95 (October 1986), pp. 591-601.

John Martin Fischer, ed., *Moral Responsibility*. (Ithaca: Cornell University Press, 1986); and "Introduction: God and Freedom".

John Martin Fischer, ed., *God, Foreknowledge, and Freedom*, (Stanford: Stanford University Press, 1989).

W. H. Newton-Smith, *The Structure of Time* (London: Routledge and Kegan Paul, 1980).

Nelson Pike, "Fischer on Freedom and Foreknowledge", 93 (October 1984), pp. 599-614; and Fischer, 1985.

Arthur Prior, "On the Logic of Ending Time", in *Papers on time and Tense* (Oxford: Oxford University Press, 1968).

Quentin Smith, "On the Beginning of Time", *Nous* 19 (1985), pp. 579-584.

David Widerker, "Two Forms of Fatalism", in Fischer, 1989, pp. 97-110.

David Widerker, "On A Fallacious Objection to Adams' Hard/Soft Fact Distinction", *Philosophical Studies*, 57 September 1989, pp. 103-107.

David Widerker, "Against the Eternity Solution", forthcoming.

Philosophical Perspectives, 5, Philosophy of Religion, 1991

# MIDDLE KNOWLEDGE AND THE DOCTRINE OF INFALLIBILITY

## Thomas P. Flint
## University of Notre Dame

The thesis that God possesses middle knowledge has become a renewed point of dispute in recent discussions in the philosophy of religion. Originally promulgated in an explicit fashion by the 16th century Spanish theologian Luis de Molina, the claim at issue is that there are contingent propositions which are such that God has absolutely no control over their truth value. Central to Molina's claim is the thesis that, for any person who does or might have existed, not only does God know with certainty what that person would have freely done in any situation in which that person might have been placed, but *what* God so knows is in no sense under his control, for God cannot determine how his creatures freely act. Thus, God might know by his middle knowledge that a certain *counterfactual of creaturely freedom* (e.g., "If Edward Kennedy had received the Democratic nomination for the Presidency in 1980 and been free to choose his running mate, he would have chosen Lloyd Bentsen") is true, but its truth would not be something that is or ever was up to him; he couldn't have simply decided to make that very counterfactual false, for its truth or falsity is something over which he has no control.[1]

Advocates of middle knowledge (who will be referred to herein simply as Molinists) contend that it is only by accepting this view that we can reconcile the robust orthodox notion of divine providence with a genuine libertarian account of human freedom. This contention has not gone uncontested; numerous general grounds for rejecting middle knowledge have been proposed.[2] While Molinists have attempted to respond to such criticisms, little in the way of a consensus has thusfar been reached.

Despite this lack of agreement, I think the time has come for Molinists to move beyond the rather general objections which have thusfar consumed much of their energy. The major thrusts against middle knowledge have, I think, been parried successfully.[3] Further discussion of such criticisms is surely appropriate, but I suspect that little will be gained and much might well be lost should Molinists concentrate exclusively on what is in large measure a purely defensive battle. Were the scholarly objections to the general Molinist account of providence more compelling, or were the everyday believer's concept of providence seemingly at odds with the Molinist suggestion, such an apologetic program might well be in order. But the objections aren't compelling, and the everyday believer's view of providence simply is rough-hewn Molinism. This being the case, the time for an obsession with defense is past.

What is needed in its stead, I believe, is an attempt to apply the concept of middle knowledge to the many particular types of exercisings of divine providence which Molinists have claimed can be illuminated by such an application. In recent days, such claims have often taken the form of literary promissory notes which suggest that one *could* employ middle knowledge to analyze one or another element of providence (such as predestination, prayer, or prophecy), but which actually refrain from so employing it in a detailed or extended way.[4] The time for cashing in such notes has come. Only by applying middle knowledge to particular areas of providence can we reach a mature assessment of its usefulness as a concept in philosophical theology.

This paper can be seen as a first installment in the redemption plan proposed in the previous paragraph. My focus will be a particular element of the Roman Catholic view of providence—the doctrine of papal infallibility. After reviewing what the doctrine does and does not contend, I will present an obvious philosophical objection which might be raised against the doctrine. I will then suggest that middle knowledge might initially be seen as a concept that offers a ready answer to such an objection, thereby illuminating the manner in which infallibility is secured. A problem with this middle knowledge account of infallibility will then be discussed, along with the two ways in which Molinists might try to amend their account so as to deal with it. Having endorsed the second of these ways and examined two objections to it, I will conclude the paper with a brief discussion of the overall utility of middle knowledge for defending the doctrine of infallibility.

A word of explanation is probably in order before we proceed further. Even if one accepts my recommendation that Molinists focus upon particular doctrines, one might find my choice of infallibility as a rather peculiar place to begin—rather like beginning a discussion of Great American Heroes by focussing on Richard Nixon. For it is no secret that many Christians, including some who at least call themselves Roman Catholics, reject the doctrine of papal infallibility. Even among those who accept it, it is sometimes treated as a bit of an embarrassment, an odd and obstreperous old uncle whose membership in the family is not denied but about whom well-mannered members maintain a decorous silence while in public. Given this state of affairs, why focus on infallibility?

Well, for a number of reasons. As a Roman Catholic, I feel a special obligation to examine those elements of providence which my faith recognizes but which Molinists of other denominations do not; papal infallibility would surely rank high on such a list. Secondly, insofar as the doctrine of infallibility continues to divide Christians, and insofar as that division may be based in part on philosophical (as opposed to historical, scriptural and other such) objections to the doctrine, the cause of Christian unity may be advanced by our looking at the doctrine philosophically. Thirdly, many of those Christians who reject the notion of papal infallibility nevertheless endorse other notions (e.g., indefectibility, conciliar infallibility, inspiration and the like) regarding God's guidance of his church which engender questions similar to those raised by infallibility. Given that the notion of papal infallibility is, as these things go, a fairly simply and clearly delineated one, applying middle knowledge to it first may be seen as engaging in a controlled experiment which should prove instructive for anyone interested in applying it to the comparatively murky issues mentioned above. Hence, a discussion of infallibility may prove eminently relevant even to those who reject the Roman Catholic belief. And finally, many of the issues surrounding a Molinist explication of the doctrine of infallibility will, I am convinced, also arise in Molinist explications of other dimensions of providence. For all these reasons, starting with infallibility seems as good a place as any.

# I

The doctrine of papal infallibility, though explicitly affirmed by theologians at least as far back as the thirteenth century, was first declared to be part of Catholic belief by the First Vatican Council.[5] The relevant section of the dogmatic constitution *Pastor Aeternus* reads as follows:

> Therefore, faithfully adhering to the tradition received from the beginning of the Christian faith, for the glory of God our Saviour, the exaltation of the Catholic Religion, and the salvation of Christian peoples, the Sacred Council approving, We teach and define that it is a dogma divinely revealed: that the Roman Pontiff, when he speaks *ex cathedra*, that is, when in discharge of the office of Pastor and Doctor of all Christians, by virtue of his supreme Apostolic authority he defines a doctrine regarding faith or morals to be held by the Universal Church, by the divine assistance promised to him in blessed Peter, is possessed of that infallibility with which the divine Redeemer willed that His Church should be endowed for defining doctrine regarding faith or morals: and that therefore such definitions of the Roman Pontiff are irreformable of themselves, and not from the consent of the Church.[6]

This doctrine was explicitly reaffirmed by the Second Vatican Council's dogmatic constitution *Lumen Gentium*:

> This infallibility with which the divine Redeemer willed His Church to be endowed in defining a doctrine of faith and morals extends as far as extends the deposit of divine revelation, which must be religiously guarded and faithfully expounded. This is the infallibility which the Roman Pontiff, the head of the college of bishops, enjoys in virtue of his office, when, as the supreme shepherd and teacher of all the faithful, who confirms his brethren in their faith (cf. Lk. 22:32), he proclaims by a definitive act some doctrine of faith or morals. Therefore his definitions, of themselves, and not from the consent of the Church, are justly styled irreformable, for they are pronounced with the assistance of the Holy Spirit, an assistance promised to him in blessed Peter. Therefore, they need no approval of others, nor do they allow an appeal to any other judgment. For then the Roman Pontiff is not pronouncing judgment as a private person. Rather, as the supreme teacher of the universal Church, as one in whom the charism of the infallibility of the Church herself is individually present, he is expounding or defending a doctrine of Catholic faith.[7]

Several points are worth noting with regard to the doctrine these two statements promulgate. First, the pope is held to be infallible only when speaking *ex cathedra*—that is, only when speaking (as Vatican II puts it) "as the supreme shepherd and teacher of all the faithful." Popes can and do sometimes speak in other capacities (e.g., as private theologians), but when doing so are not said to be infallible. Furthermore, since one can speak *ex cathedra* only when one speaks, it follows that the pope's private, unexpressed opinions are a *fortiori* not said to be infallible. Second, papal pronouncements are held to be infallible only when they define a doctrine—only when they embody an intention on the part of the pope to decide a question once and for all. Even when speaking as pope, many popes have not spoken in this definitive fashion, and thus have not exercised their charism of infallibility. Third, the pope is declared to be infallible only with regard to faith and morals; though neither council declares him to be fallible in other areas, the suggestion that he is seems patent. Fourth, the charism of infallibility is said to be one which is given to the Church as a whole, not simply to the pope. Fifth, papal definitions which meet the conditions stipulated above are "irreformable of themselves": no council need approve them, and no successor to the papacy can abrogate them. Finally, the guarantor of papal (and, more generally, of Church) infallibility is held to be the Holy Spirit, though the manner in which he effects this guarantee is left unspecified.[8]

The doctrine of papal infallibility has, of course, been subject to numerous criticisms, most of which rest on theological or historical claims which one would expect others to be better equipped to adjudicate than are philosophers. But there is one type of objection to the doctrine which lies squarely within the domain of philosophy— an objection which deals with the question of papal freedom. Let us now turn to this objection.

## II

According to Vatican I and Vatican II, the pope cannot err when he makes a pronouncement, provided that certain conditions are satisfied. But how exactly can this be if the pope is, like you and me, a free human being? Let us say that a pope who fulfills the various conditions laid down by the Councils (i.e, one who speaks publicly and definitively as pope on a question of faith or morals) speaks *ex cathedra*. Isn't a pope who speaks *ex cathedra* speaking freely? If so, then couldn't the pope who speaks *ex cathedra* resist the assistance of the Holy Spirit? And if he did, couldn't he fall into error even when speaking *ex cathedra*? So isn't it simply false to say that a pope who speaks *ex cathedra* speaks infallibly?

Though rarely articulated in so blunt a form, this objection, or something much like it, surely lies behind much of the opposition to the doctrine of papal infallibility. It is, of course, really an objection to *any* notion of Church infallibility: we can't obviate the problem raised by the Bishop of Rome's freedom simply by throwing in a few more, equally free bishops. Indeed, if the objection has force, it's not easy to see how even so amorphous a thesis as that of the Church's indefectibility can be maintained. If to err (or more precisely, the potential to err) is, so to speak, ineluctably human, then many divines (and not just those at the Vatican Councils) require forgiveness for having claimed a stronger form of providential guidance of the Church than reason can allow.

There is one obvious way to defuse this objection which I will mention only to dismiss. The objection presupposes that a person acts freely only if the full set of circumstances in which a person acts do not determine one particular course of action. If we dispense with this libertarian notion of freedom, the objection against papal infallibility can be dispensed with as well, for we could then say that the circumstances in which the pope acts are determinative of his action (most likely because the grace brought by the Spirit determines the action) even though the act performed is a free one. While it is, I suspect, true that we could meet the objection to papal infallibility in this way, it would not be a very plausible approach, for the kind of compatibilist or crypto-compatibilist account of freedom required for such a defense of papal infallibility seems quite unlikely to be true.[9] The rock of infallibility claimed by Peter's successors would be ill-supported indeed were it grounded in the uncertain sand of compatibilism.

If we accept the libertarian notion of freedom presupposed by our objection to papal infallibility, it might appear that there are but two ways in which one might respond. On the one hand, one might endorse the objection—that is, one might say that the pope, being free, is not immune from error even when speaking *ex cathedra*. On the other hand, one might uphold papal infallibility by surrendering papal freedom. In other words, one might say that God guarantees that papal *ex cathedra* pronouncements are infallible by simply determining what it is that the pope pronounces in such situations.

Needless to say, neither of these alternatives will appear particularly appealing to the orthodox Catholic. The first response allows us to hold on to papal freedom, but only at the unacceptable cost of forcing us to reject outright the teaching of Vatican I and Vatican II. The second response allows us to hold on to papal infallibility, but only by saying that the pope isn't free when speaking *ex cathedra*. Not only does such a view seem somewhat implausible (or so it would surely appear, one would think, to the pope himself when in the act of speaking *ex cathedra*), but it also at least appears rather demeaning both to God and to the pope to suggest that the only way God can infallibly guide his Church is by playing Edgar Bergen to the pope's Charlie McCarthy. What the orthodox Catholic would like, clearly, is some way of holding on to *both* papal infallibility and papal freedom. But, in light of our objection, how *can* one hold on to both?

## III

It is here that the concept of middle knowledge seems to come to the rescue.[10] For if God has middle knowledge, why can't he arrange things in such a way that the pope always freely follows his guidance? How, one might ask, can he do so? By seeing to it that the *right* person *becomes* pope. If God has middle knowledge, then he knows how any candidate for the office would act—would *freely* act—if elected pope. Using this knowledge, God would then direct the cardinals to select as pope one of those men who God knows would freely cooperate with his guidance and thereby safeguard the church from error; he would also lead them away from selecting any of those men who he knows would not freely cooperate with his guidance and consequently lead the Church into error. By then guiding the man selected in the ways that, as his middle knowledge tells him, will elicit a free but positive response from him, God can insure that the pope is infallible even though he respects his freedom. This respect for human freedom would presumably extend to the cardinals as well. God's direction of them toward certain candidates and away from others would most likely be accomplished, not by God's determining their actions, but by his arrangement of circumstances which he knows via middle knowledge will lead to the result he desires.

An example of how this might work will perhaps be of some help here in making the Molinist suggestion more concrete. Suppose that a conclave to elect a new pope has begun, and that two prime candidates for the office have emerged—Cardinal Elfreth and Cardinal Filbert. Suppose also that the choice between these two will be influenced enormously by the way in which an elderly and well-respected Italian cardinal (call him Cardinal Rotundo) decides to vote. Finally, suppose that among the infinite number of true propositions God knows via middle knowledge are the following two (where $t$ represents the time of the conclave and $h$ the history of the world prior to $t$):

> (A) If Elfreth were elected pope at time $t$ in a world with history $h$, he would freely follow divine guidance and keep the Church safe from error.
> (B) If Filbert were elected pope at time $t$ in a world with history $h$, he would freely reject divine guidance and proclaim *ex cathedra* a falsehood.

Given this knowledge, God decides to act. While Rotundo is at prayer, God causes him to concentrate upon the various virtues of Elfreth. This leads him (as God knew it would) freely to come to the conclusion that Elfreth would make the better pope. Acting on this conviction, Rotundo enthusiastically throws his considerable weight behind Elfreth. As a result, Elfreth is indeed elected, and the Church is saved from the errors that Filbert would have proclaimed.

No doubt the election of a pope is not often as simple as in our example. Seldom are there only two viable candidates; rarely is there but one kingmaker such as Rotundo; and only infrequently are people persuaded to a certain course of action in the rather blunt way we created for Rotundo. Even so, I think the essentials of the matter are captured adequately in our simplified case. And most essential of all, from the Molinist point of view, would be counterfactuals such as (A) and (B). Provided God has knowledge of true counterfactuals of each of these kinds, he can guide the conclave toward those who would freely serve the Church unerringly and away from those who would freely proclaim a falsehood.

## IV

Although I believe that this Molinist answer to our problem with infallibility is on the right track, I fear that it may need to be shunted off to a siding for repairs before it can safely reach its intended destination. For there is a problem with this attempted solution: one of the counterfactuals upon which it is based seems to collapse.

Consider again the second of the two counterfactuals the truth of which we assumed would guide God's actions vis-a-vis the cardinals—namely,

> (B) If Filbert were elected pope at time *t* in a world with history *h*, he would freely reject divine guidance and proclaim *ex cathedra* a falsehood.

Letting E stand for "Filbert is elected Pope at *t* in a world with history *h*" and R for "Filbert freely rejects divine guidance and proclaims *ex cathedra* a falsehood," and using the single-line arrow for the counterfactual connective, we can represent (B) as

> (B) $E \rightarrow R$.

The problem with (B) is simply this: if B is true, how could God possibly allow Filbert to be elected? Having established his Church in the way he has, and having allowed (indeed, guided) that Church through its two most recent councils to proclaim papal infallibility as a dogma, how could God then permit the cardinals to elect as pope a man whom he knew with certainty would make an erroneous *ex cathedra* pronouncement? Isn't it impossible for God to allow Filbert's election if he knows that (B) is true?

What is being suggested here is that the truth of (B) entails the falsity of (B)'s antecedent. Letting the double-line arrow stand for strict implication, we can represent this suggestion as

> (1) $(E \rightarrow R) \Rightarrow \sim E$.

If (1) is true, then (B) is what we might call a *collapsing counterfactual*—a counterfactual which entails that its own antecedent is false. Now, as we have seen, there seems to be a strong *prima facie* case for Molinists to view (B) as a collapsing counterfactual. Unfortunately, there would be something rather embarrassing in their doing so. For one can make a strong case for thinking that (B) is false if it collapses. Since the story told above as to how God might arrange for a free but infallible pope required that (B) be true, that story would have to be amended if (B)'s falsity does follow from its collapsing.

Why, one might ask, think it does follow? Intuitively, because in saying that God couldn't allow Filbert to be elected if (B) were true, we seem to be saying that it's impossible for someone elected to the papacy to reject God's guidance and proclaim a heresy; but if we do hold this to be impossible, it's hard to see how we could also hold (B) to be true. Let's try to spell out these intuitions a bit more formally. Suppose that (B) collapses—i.e., that (1) is true. Adding E to both the antecedent and the consequent of (1), we can derive

(2) [E & (E→R)] $\Rightarrow$ (~E & E)

from (1). Now, the standard analyses of counterfactuals maintain that a counterfactual is true in every world in which both its antecedent and its consequent are true, and though one might have cause to question whether this is a general truth (e.g., does it hold in cases where the antecedent and consequent are utterly unrelated?), there would seem to be little doubt of its applicability to (B). Hence, we seem to be well justified in asserting:

(3) (E & R) $\Rightarrow$ [E & (E→R)].

From (3) and (2) it follows that

(4) (E & R) $\Rightarrow$ (~E & E),

which in turn entails

(5) ~◇(E & R)

and the equivalent

(6) (E $\Rightarrow$ ~R).

On reflection, we probably shouldn't be surprised by the fact that (5) and (6) follow from (1), for the very considerations which led us to think that (B) collapses should lead us just as readily to think that (5) and (6) are true. E, recall, is a *complete* antecedent, one which includes the entire history of the world prior to the time in question. How, one might ask, could there be a world with such a history—a history which includes God's establishment of the papacy and his councils' pronouncements on the charism of infallibility—in which one of the popes proclaims *ex cathedra* a heresy? So if we are at all inclined to concede that (B) collapses, the fact that (5) and (6) follow from that collapse should hardly strike us as unexpected.

But if (5) and (6) do follow from (1), it's hard to see how we can still hold (B) to be true. If Filbert's election to the papacy *entails* that he *doesn't* freely reject God's guidance and proclaim a heresy, how could his election *counterfactually imply* that he *does* so reject and proclaim? Admittedly, if E were impossible, there would be no difficulty in holding both (6) and (B) to be true. But there's no reason at all to think that E *is* impossible. If Filbert is perverse enough, it might perhaps just conceivably be the case that there's no feasible world (i.e., no world which God has the power to actualize) in which he's elected pope, simply because there's no such world in which he always freely refrains from proclaiming an error. (Were Filbert this obstinate type of character, we might say that he was *transworldly deprived* of the papacy.) Yet even if this were true, it would show only that there's no *feasible* world in which E is true; in no way would it challenge the obvious fact that there are *possible* worlds in which E is true. So, given that (6) is true, there doesn't seem to be any way in which (B) could also be true.

As we have already noted, the ramifications of (B)'s being false are serious indeed. For our story of how middle knowledge is supposed to be action-guiding for God, leaving him room for a pope who is both free and infallible, collapses if (B) is false. That story, recall, requires both that there be true counterfactuals such as (A) and (B) which God knows via middle knowledge and that this knowledge guide him as he guides the cardinals. If (B) and other such counterfactuals are not true, then of course God cannot know them to be true via middle knowledge, and cannot employ his knowledge of them to lead the cardinals away from the Filberts of the world. In short, if (B)-type counterfactuals are one and all false, the Molinist answer to our problem with papal infallibility seems to dissolve.

As I see it, there are two ways in which Molinists might try to resurrect their solution. On the one hand, noticing that all of our troubles seemed to arise when we granted that a counterfactual such as (B) collapses, they might question this assumption and attempt to rebuild the middle knowledge position on the foundation of a solid, non-collapsing (B). On the other hand, they might concede that (B) collapses, but suggest that there are other counterfactuals in the vicinity which don't collapse and which could thus serve the same action-guiding purpose which (B) served in our original story. Let us consider each of these alternatives in turn.

384 / Thomas P. Flint

## V

To deny that (B) collapses is to say that (1) is false—i.e., that (E→R) doesn't entail ∼ E. But if (E→R) doesn't entail ∼ E, then it's possible that both (E→R) and E be true. Since [(E→R) & E] entails R, it follows that [(E→R) & E] is possible only if [(E→R) & E & R] is also possible. Therefore, to deny that (B) collapses is to say that it's possible that [(E→R) & E & R]—in (other) words, it's to say that it's possible that Filbert be elected and proceed to proclaim *ex cathedra* a falsehood.

But if *this* is what the denial of (1) entails, then doesn't that denial ultimately amount to nothing less than a rejection of the doctrine of infallibility itself? Surely, one would think, the doctrine entails at least that no one in a world where God has allowed the doctrine of infallibility to be proclaimed will as pope proclaim *ex cathedra* a falsehood. Since holding (1) to be false would commit us to endorsing a possibility which the doctrine of infallibility excludes, denying that (B) collapses would seem to be a fruitless means of attempting to defend that doctrine.

Of course, there are ways of making the means in question at least appear fruitful. For example, one could point out that denying (1) is compatible with affirming the similar but weaker conditional

(1*) (E→R)→ ∼ E.

Now, one might continue, isn't (1*) really all that we need to endorse infallibility? For (1*) tells us that God as a matter of fact would not allow Filbert to be elected if he saw by his middle knowledge that Filbert would proclaim *ex cathedra* a falsehood. Presumably there would be many other true conditionals like (1*) relating to other persons, times and histories. And the truth of all these conditionals might well underwrite the truth of even so broad a statement as

> (7) If a pope in a world such as ours (i.e., a world in which papal infallibility has been defined) says *ex cathedra* that p, then it's not the case that p is false.

Since (7) can be seen as simply stating in a nutshell the doctrine of infallibility, it might well appear that the doctrine is indeed defensible even if (1) is rejected.

Tempting as such a response might appear, I think it is susceptible to several serious objections. In rejecting (1), this response tacitly grants that it is possible that a pope make an erroneous *ex cathedra* pronouncement. Hence, while it can accept (7), it can view (7) as only a contingent truth; it must grant that there are possible worlds in which a pope who has been defined to be infallible makes an erroneous *ex cathedra* pronouncement. It seems to me exceedingly unlikely that many defenders of the doctrine would be willing to grant this possibility. Though they may well grant that there are possible worlds with fallible popes, they would insist that such worlds would have different histories from our own, and would not include the kind of biblical and later historical events upon which the doctrine of infallibility is grounded. In a world where that doctrine has been proclaimed, though, there simply is no possibility of a papal *ex cathedra* error. If there were, one might ask, what would be the point of the doctrine? If there are worlds with histories just like ours in which the pope makes an erroneous *ex cathedra* pronouncement, then what confidence could one place in papal *ex cathedra* pronouncements in our own world? What confidence could one have that this isn't one of those possible worlds in which the pope goes awry?

Of course, if (1*) and other conditionals like it were known by us to be true, perhaps we would have a sufficient base for such confidence. But once we have rejected (1), what grounds do we have for thinking that (1*) is true? (1) seems to be supported by the belief that an all-good, non-deceiving God could not allow both that the doctrine of infallibility be proclaimed and that a pope make an *ex cathedra* error. Those who reject (1) would presumably deny that there is any such necessary connection between God's perfect nature and what he allows to happen in a world where infallibility has been defined. But if there is no such necessary connection, why think that even (1*) is true? If nothing in God's nature prevents him from putting a Filbert in Peter's chair, why should we believe that he hasn't done so?

It seems clear, then, that the rejection of (1) leads inexorably toward a vitiation of the doctrine of infallibility. If we are to defend a robust understanding of the doctrine, I think we are going to have to do it while accepting (1)—that is, while acknowledging that counterfactuals such as (B) collapse, and thus offer us no help in reconciling papal infallibility with papal freedom.

## VI

Suppose, then, that we grant that (B) collapses, and hence can't be known via middle knowledge to be true. In that case, the only clear way to repair our story reconciling infallibility and freedom would be to find a replacement for (B). That is, we must find a counterfactual of creaturely freedom which God could use in the action-guiding way we envisaged for (B), but which, unlike (B), can plausibly be held to be true by the defender of the doctrine.

It seems to me that a promising candidate is not all that hard to draft. For consider what happens to (B) if we alter its consequent to make it similar to the consequent of (A), but negate that consequent. The result would be:

(B*) If Filbert were elected pope at time $t$ in a world with history $h$, it's not the case that he would freely follow divine guidance and keep the Church safe from error.

Notice that, while the consequent of (B) entails that Filbert doesn't keep the Church free from error, the consequent of (B*) has no such implication; it entails only that Filbert doesn't *freely* keep the Church free from error. This distinction, I believe, is of crucial importance to the Molinist reconciliation of papal infallibility and papal freedom. For the upshot of this distinction is that, while (B) collapses, and thus is false, (B*) doesn't collapse, and thus could be one of the true counterfactuals which comprise God's middle knowledge.

Why think that (B*) doesn't collapse? Because the Molinist need not be a zealot with regard to the range of free actions. The core of the Molinist project in discussing infallibility is the attempt to show that papal freedom and papal infallibility are compatible—i.e., that there is no inconsistency in a pope's being both free and infallible. But nothing in this project (and, to the best of my knowledge, nothing in Church doctrine) commits the Molinist to thinking that a pope has to be both free and infallible. Thus, the Molinist should have no trouble granting that, in some possible worlds, the pope's infallibility is safeguarded at the expense of his freedom. But if this is so, then there's no reason to think that (B*) collapses. There are indeed worlds in which (B*) is true, Filbert is elected pope, and Filbert doesn't freely follow divine guidance *re* doctrinal proclamations. But these are not worlds in which Filbert makes an erroneous *ex cathedra* pronouncement. Rather, they are worlds in which Filbert's freedom to do so is somehow blocked—by some natural occurrence (such as death), by the free action(s) of some other created agent(s), or perhaps even by the direct action of God. Since Molinists have no reason that

I can see to doubt that such worlds are possible, they have no reason to doubt the truth of a counterfactual such as (B*).[11]

If (B*) is true, though, it could well play just as important a role in guiding God's actions as we had earlier ascribed to (B). For though God does not have to permit his creatures the freedom in each instance to act in the manner they intend to act, it seems fair to assume that, *ceteris paribus*, God would prefer to respect his creature's freedom rather than to frustrate it. If we don't make such an assumption, reconciling God's creation of free creatures with his goodness would seem to be all but impossible. Hence, though God could protect the Church from error even with a Filbert as pope, it would seem to be more fitting for him to do so by guiding the Church toward an Elfreth. Given his knowledge of both (A) and (B*), then, it seems not at all unlikely (other things being equal—we are, remember, greatly simplifying things by considering only Elfreth and Filbert) that God would have ample reason to move Rotundo in just the way we described.

Indeed, one might go so far as to argue that God might not have a choice in the matter. For it could be that other elements in God's middle knowledge tell him that Elfreth would in *all* respects (not just concerning *ex cathedra* statements) be an exemplary pontiff, whereas Filbert would in all respects be a pope worthy of disdain. In that case, one might argue, God would have no choice but to lead the Church to Elfreth. If we let (M) stand for the conjunction of all the counterfactuals other than (A) and (B*) which make up God's middle knowledge, we can represent this argument as suggesting that

(8) [(A) & (B*) & (M)] ⊃ ~(Filbert is elected pope at time *t* in a world with history *h*

is true.

Though I'm not convinced that we should hastily accept the argument for (8)—after all, don't we often point with pride to God's ability to bring a bounty of unforeseen good out of willful wickedness?—I see no reason to doubt that some propositions of the form of (8) are true. In other words, the totality of God's middle knowledge may place limitations upon his actions which individual elements of his middle knowledge do not place. Even if this is so, though—indeed, even if (8) itself is true—the crucial distinction between propositions such as (B) and those such as (B*) remains. For as it is only a conjunction of propositions in (8) which entails that the antecedent of (B*) is false, the truth of (8) would give us no reason to think that (B*) itself collapses. Hence, whether or not we think that there are true propositions such as (8), the usefulness of propositions such as (B*) for reconciling papal freedom and papal infallibility remains.

## VII

Before concluding, I would like briefly to consider a couple of objections to our attempt to resurrect the Molinist reconciliation of papal freedom and papal infallibility. The first objection focusses on the credentials of (B*) as a candidate for an element in God's middle knowledge; the second asks whether our solution has not come at the cost of too great a surrender of papal freedom.

Since it's commonly said that what God knows via his middle knowledge are counterfactuals of freedom, one might question whether (B*) qualifies for inclusion in middle knowledge. For (B*) doesn't say what Filbert would do; all it tells us is that there's a free action he wouldn't perform. Therefore, since it's doubtful that (B*) should be considered a counterfactual of freedom, it's doubtful that our strategy can succeed.

Perhaps it is sufficient in reply to point out that this objection relies upon a rather coarse conception of what middle knowledge is. As Molina conceived of it, and as I do as well, middle knowledge is that part of God's knowledge which consists of contingent truths which are at all times beyond God's power to control. Counterfactuals of creaturely (though not of divine) freedom would undoubtedly be counted in this class, but there's no reason to think that they exhaust this class. Hence, so long as a proposition such as (B*) is true, contingent, and not such that its truth value is dependent upon what God does, that proposition belongs to God's middle knowledge, whether or not it qualifies as a counterfactual of freedom. Since (B*) passes all three of the relevant tests, it clearly would be included in God's middle knowledge.

It may be worth pointing out in addition, though, that (B*) itself might qualify as a counterfactual of creaturely freedom, depending upon precisely how we define such counterfactuals. In any event, it is clear that (B*) might be based upon some other counterfactual which undeniably is one of creaturely freedom. For example, there could well be worlds in which Filbert is elected and in which he freely decides to resist God's grace and to make a false *ex cathedra* pronouncement. Though God or some other free being would in some way prevent this decision from flowering into an actual erroneous proclamation, the important point is that, since Filbert in such a world would indeed have acted freely in deciding as he did, there clearly would be a counterfactual of freedom describing this action. So while (B*) will (if true) be part of God's middle knowledge whether or not it qualifies as a counterfactual of freedom, it may well at least have such a counterfactual lying behind it.

The tendency to equate middle knowledge with knowledge of counterfactuals of freedom, then, is a dangerous one, one we need strenuously to avoid. Indeed, if we extend our story of Filbert just a bit further, we can see that there may well be constituents of middle knowledge which are even further distanced from counterfactuals of freedom than is (B*). Suppose God knew that, if Filbert were elected, he would indeed decide to declare *ex cathedra* a falsehood. Let

(9) $E \rightarrow D$

represent this counterfactual. Suppose God also knew that no free action on the part of any of his creatures (including Filbert) would block this Filbertian decision from issuing in an erroneous declaration. Let

(10) $(E \ \& \ D) \rightarrow B$

represent this counterfactual. Given his knowledge of (9) and (10), God would also know that

(11) $E \rightarrow B$.

And since (11) entails

(12) $E \rightarrow (E \ \& \ B)$,

God would know (12) as well. But, as we have seen, it seems impossible that God allow a pope, in a world where infallibility has been declared, to actually proclaim *ex cathedra* a falsehood. If no other free creature would step in to block Filbert's decision from turning into an actual proclamation, then God would have no choice but to block Filbert from making the proclamation he intends to make. That is,

(13) $(E \ \& \ B) \ \ni \ G$,

where G stands for God's acting to block Filbert, is true. But from (12) and (13) it follows that

(14) E→G.

So if things were as we depicted them in our story, (14) would also be true.

(14), of course, is not a counterfactual of creaturely freedom, for its consequent describes what God does, not what one of his creatures does. Indeed, it seems odd to view (14) as a counterfactual of freedom at all, for the story as we have described it seems to be one in which God has no choice but to block Filbert, not one in which he freely elects to do so. Nevertheless, (14) would still qualify as an element in God's middle knowledge. It couldn't be included in God's natural knowledge (i.e., his knowledge of necessary truths) because (14) isn't necessary. And it couldn't be included in God's free knowledge (i.e., his knowledge of contingent truths whose truth is dependent upon his creative activity) because God could know that (14) is true prior to his deciding upon any creative activity whatsoever. As we saw, (14) follows from (9) through (13). But the first four of these five conditionals are either constituents of God's middle knowledge or entailments therefrom, and thus would be known prior to creation, while the last of the five is a necessary truth and thus would also be known prior to creation. So (14), too, would be known prior to creation. And since it is clearly a contingent truth, it would have to be counted as part of God's middle knowledge.

With a bit of ingenuity, I suspect, we could easily concoct other, even stranger candidates for inclusion in middle knowledge. But none of this, of course, is really necessary to respond to our first objection. So long as we realize that middle knowledge need not be limited to counterfactuals of freedom, we'll have no problem acknowledging propositions such as (B*) as included in God's middle knowledge.

The second objection to our solution can be both stated and handled more briefly. One might charge that our attempt to defend both papal freedom and papal infallibility has resulted in too great a diminution of the former. For we have granted that God might maintain the infallibility of a pope only by stripping that pope of his freedom. In defending infallibility from the Scylla of its detractors, have we not in effect fallen into the Charybdis of divine determinism we had sought to evade?

I think not. All that we have granted is that there are possible worlds in which God maintains the infallibility of the pope by limiting the pope's freedom. But it hardly follows from this that papal freedom has thus been denied. In the first place, there's no reason at all to think that the kind of divine limitation on the pope which we are entertaining has in fact ever occurred. Indeed, if God has middle knowledge, one would expect that he would generally have more than enough Elfreths available to him, and hence little need to resort to a Filbert. More importantly, though, even if this type of divine activity has occurred, it hardly follows that the pope must henceforth be thought of as a robotic extension of his divine programmer. For the kind of divine intervention we have imagined, the kind which seems most likely to occur, is purely preventive in nature. Rather than determining the pope to speak in a particular way, it blocks him from following through on a decision he has come to freely. Hence, though the solution we have suggested clearly does countenance the possibility of God's circumscribing the pope's power in order to maintain papal infallibility, the charge that it constitutes too great an infringement of papal freedom seems to me unfounded.

## VIII

In sum, then, I think at least this one promissory note has been redeemed: the concept of middle knowledge can indeed play an important role in defending the doctrine of papal infallibility. The role is, perhaps, a bit more difficult to play than many of us Molinists would have suspected, and the final production perhaps a bit less polished than we would have liked; and, of course, there are more promissory notes (on prayer, prophecy, predestination, and the like) which remain. Still, it seems to me that the contribution of the concept of middle knowledge in explicating this niche of the notion of providence is quite significant, and should give Molinists confidence that the concept will exhibit the kind of fruitfulness they have envisaged.[12]

### Notes

1. *Why* think that such counterfactuals are beyond God's control? The simple answer is the one suggested in this paragraph: if libertarianism is true, God cannot cause his creatures freely to act in a certain way. If God could simply decide to make a certain counterfactual of creaturely

freedom true, then his doing so (in conjunction with his actualizing the antecedent of the counterfactual) *would* entail that the agent freely act in a certain way. For a fuller account of the Molinist position, see Flint (1988) and Freddoso (1988).

2. For the more prominent contemporary criticisms of middle knowledge, see Adams (1977), Hasker (1986), chapter 2 of Hasker (1989), and Kenny (1979), pp. 62-71.

3. In addition to the works cited in note 1, see Plantinga (1985), pp. 372-382; Otte (1987); Basinger (1987); and my "In Defense of Theological Compatibilism" (forthcoming in *Faith and Philosophy*) and "Hasker's 'Refutation' of Middle Knowledge" (unpublished).

4. For two such promissory notes, see Freddoso (1988), p. 61, and Flint (1988), p. 162.

5. For an informative (though hardly unbiased) look at the early history of the notion of infallibility, see Tierney (1972).

6. Translation in Butler (1930), vol. II, p. 295.

7. Translation in Abbott (1966), pp. 48-49.

8. Many Catholic commentators on the doctrine of infallibility have suggested that much of the dispute over papal infallibility stems from misconceptions (by both proponents and opponents of the doctrine) concerning what the doctrine actually is. For example, one prominent Catholic theologian contends that, though the doctrine "is and will always remain a matter of much theological and pastoral importance," it is already becoming "much less an ecumenical problem" insofar as it is being "[d]isengaged from exaggerations of papal authority." See McBrien (1981), p. 842.

9. The crypto-compatibilist account I have in mind is that offered by certain Thomistic opponents of Molinism. It differs from the more common brand of contemporary compatibilism in that it sees the determining divine influence as simultaneous with the action. Hence, it agrees with contemporary incompatibilists in holding *prior* determination to be incompatible with freedom. Still, insofar as it holds freedom to be compatible with *external* determination, it seems to me to be a view clearly outside of the libertarian fold. For more on this point, see Flint (1988), pp. 170-179.

10. My remarks here should not be taken to imply that we can solve this problem *only* if we say that God has middle knowledge. The point, rather, is that the Molinist seems to be able to offer a particularly attractive and plausible solution, one not available to those who deny God middle knowledge.

11. One of the early proponents of the doctrine of infallibility, Guido Terreni, argued in much the way I have suggested here. As Brian Tierney notes, Terreni was convinced that if a pope "formed the intention of defining a false doctrine, ...God would intervene to stop him from doing so. 'God would impede such a pope from his evil intention either by death or by the resistance of others or in other ways.'" See Tierney (1972), p. 250.

12. I would like to thank the members of the Notre Dame Center for

Philosophy of Religion discussion group for comments on an earlier draft of this paper.

## References

Adams, Robert M. (1977), "Middle Knowledge and the Problem of Evil," *American Philosophical Quarterly* 14, pp. 109-117.

Abbott, Walter M., ed. (1966), *The Documents of Vatican II* (New York: Corpus Books).

Basinger, David (1987), "Middle Knowledge and Human Freedom: Some Clarifications," *Faith and Philosophy* 4, pp. 330-336.

Butler, Cuthbert (1930), *The Vatican Council* (London: Longmans, Green and Company).

Flint, Thomas P. (1988), "Two Accounts of Providence," in Thomas V. Morris, ed., *Divine and Human Action* (Ithaca, N.Y.: Cornell University Press, 1988), pp. 147-181.

Freddoso, Alfred J. (1988), "Introduction," *On Divine Foreknowledge* (Ithaca, N.Y.: Cornell University Press).

Hasker, William (1986), "A Refutation of Middle Knowledge," *Nous* 20, pp. 545-557.

Hasker, William (1989), *God, Time and Knowledge* (Ithaca, N.Y.: Cornell University Press).

Kenny, Anthony (1979), *The God of the Philosophers* (Oxford: Oxford University Press).

McBrien, Richard (1981), *Catholicism*, study edition (Minneapolis: Winston Press).

Plantinga, Alvin (1985), "Replies," in James Tomberlin and Peter van Inwagen, eds., *Profiles: Alvin Plantinga* (Dordrecht: D. Reidel).

Otte, Richard (1987), "A Defense of Middle Knowledge," *International Journal for Philosophy of Religion* 21, pp. 161-169.

Tierney, Brian (1972), *Origins of Papal Infallibility, 1150-1350* (Leiden: E.J. Brill).

Philosophical Perspectives, 5, Philosophy of Religion, 1991

# PROPHECY, PAST TRUTH, AND ETERNITY

Eleonore Stump
Virginia Polytechnic Institute
Norman Kretzmann
Cornell University

## 1. Introduction

In an earlier article[1] we presented, defended, and applied the traditional doctrine of divine eternity, the doctrine that God's mode of existence is timeless, characterized essentially by "the complete possession all at once of illimitable life".[2] The traditional conception of God as the absolutely perfect being has included eternity as his mode of existence. In keeping with the traditional conception, the necessarily beginningless and endless life of a perfect being must also be possessed perfectly. No life, even a sempiternal life, that is imperfect in its being possessed with the radical incompleteness entailed by temporal existence could be the mode of existence of an absolutely perfect being. A perfectly possessed life must be devoid of any past, which would be no longer possessed, and of any future, which would be not yet possessed. The existence of an absolutely perfect being must be an indivisibly persistent present actuality.

Our article prompted some criticisms that attacked the concept of eternity directly, by focusing on difficulties in the notion of atemporal duration, which we take to be at the heart of the concept, or on difficulties in the epistemic and causal relationships between eternity and time, relationships presupposed by all traditional theological applications of the doctrine. We reply to these criticisms elsewhere.[3]

The applications of the doctrine of eternity that originally concerned us most were aimed at resolving the apparent incompatibility of divine immutability with divine omniscience and with the efficacy of petitionary prayer. But the application that has historically been most important to philosophers is the use of the doctrine of eternity in a purported solution to the problem of divine foreknowledge and human freedom.[4] Some critics have attempted to discredit this application, thereby weakening the doctrine's psychological support, since the apparent usefulness of the doctrine in this application of it has provided one important motive for continuing to struggle with its complexities. The problem of foreknowledge and freedom was not, however, the original reason why philosophers and theologians concluded that God must be eternal;[5] even if the doctrine of eternity were of no practical value in resolving the foreknowledge problem, it would for other reasons continue to be an important ingredient in perfect-being theology. But, in any case, we think these criticisms of its application to the problem of foreknowledge and freedom do not succeed.

In this article we examine three attempts to show that the doctrine of eternity fails to contribute to a solution to the foreknowledge problem. Since its purported contribution consists in providing a basis for arguing that God's eternal omniscience cannot include foreknowledge and so cannot threaten human freedom, critics sometimes set out to show that even eternal omniscience is either compatible with foreknowledge or, indeed, must include it. The first of these lines has been taken very recently by David Widerker, who finds problems for the eternity solution in the traditional doctrine that God occasionally reveals to prophets truths about the future.[6] The second received a classic presentation in the eighteenth century at the hands of Jonathan Edwards, who based his objection on the mere possibility of prophecy.[7] The third criticism we will examine, Alvin Plantinga's, appears to take a different tack, arguing that even though eternal omniscience is compatible with human freedom, the problem of foreknowledge and freedom cannot be resolved simply by appealing to that aspect of the doctrine of eternity.[8]

In fact, as we will try to show, none of these three criticisms succeeds. In the process of arguing against them we hope to throw some light on the relationship that must obtain between an eternal God and temporal creatures.

## 2. Widerker's objection

Suppose that God knows, timelessly, that in 1995 Corazon Aquino introduces land reform in the Philippines. God's eternal, timeless knowledge cannot be knowledge of the event ahead of time. That is, given the doctrine of eternity, God's knowledge of that event, an event future to us in 1990, cannot be foreknowledge; and so the standard arguments showing an incompatibility between foreknowledge and freedom cannot apply to this case.[9] Just as your mere observation of what is going on in the street outside your window could not threaten the freedom with which that activity is being carried on, so the supposition that God eternally knows Aquino's 1995 action provides no basis for inferring that that action of hers isn't freely done.

But the traditional belief that God sometimes reveals true prophecies to certain human beings raises a difficulty for this strategy for dealing with the foreknowledge problem. A prophecy brings some of God's eternal knowledge into time, thus converting at least the revealed bit of it into foreknowledge. So, if we suppose, further, that God reveals to some prophet in 1990 the proposition that Aquino will introduce land reform in 1995, and reveals as well that it is God from whom this revelation comes, then regarding the 1995 action that prophet in 1990 has genuine foreknowledge. Even though it is not God who has the foreknowledge generated in this way, the standard arguments against the compatibility of foreknowledge and freedom would apply to the prophet's foreknowledge, which stems from God.

According to Widerker, a case of this sort presents defenders of the eternity solution with a trio of unpalatable options:

(1) They can deny the doctrine of prophecy and claim that God never reveals to prophets any of his eternal knowledge; or
(2) They can concede that prophesied human actions are inevitable, are not done freely; or
(3) They can deny the principle of the fixity of the past.

The principle of the fixity of the past (PFP) captures the virtually universal intuition that it is never in anyone's power at time $t$ to bring it about that some actual state of affairs that is past with respect to $t$ did not in fact occur.[10] If defenders of the eternity solution reject options (1) and (2), it seems they can maintain that Aquino is free to do otherwise in 1995 only by conceding that it is within her power in 1995 to bring it about that what was the prophet's 1990 foreknowledge was, after all, *not* the prophet's 1990 foreknowledge. Thus in making that move they would be denying PFP.

Widerker takes options (1) and (2) to constitute denials of basic religious beliefs, and so he supposes that defenders of eternity will indeed find themselves embarrassedly committed to rejecting PFP— an outcome that shows, he maintains, that the doctrine of eternity does not provide a solution to the foreknowledge problem.

We share Widerker's view that option (3), denying PFP, is intolerable, and we agree with him that options (1) and (2) are incompatible with beliefs which defenders of the eternity solution are very likely to hold. Nevertheless, we still include ourselves among those defenders. In order to say how we think the solution escapes Widerker's criticism, it will be helpful, first, to say what we take free will and free action to consist in, and then to look more closely at the nature of prophecy.

## 3. Free will and free action

An agent, $S$, has freedom of will with respect to some volition, $V$, or $V$ is an instance of free will on $S$'s part, just in case $V$ meets these two conditions:

FW1. $V$ is not causally determined; and
FW2. $V$ is $S$'s own volition.

These two conditions are to be understood in the following way. (FW1) $V$ is not causally determined only if $V$ is not the result of an unbroken causal sequence that (a) originates in something other than $S$'s own beliefs and desires and that (b) makes $V$ unavoidable for $S$. (FW2) $V$ is $S$'s own only if (a) $S$'s intellect represents the state of affairs that becomes the object of $V$ as (under some description) a good to be pursued by $S$ at that time and (b) $S$ forms $V$ in consequence of that representation on the part of $S$'s intellect.[11] FW1 excludes as unfree any volition that is caused by something external to the agent, and so FW1 rules out compatibilist interpretations of free will.[12] FW2 excludes as unfree any volition ascribable to the agent only superficially—e.g., one resulting from some unconsidered, ungoverned passion or from some pathological state of the agent, such as a volition that the agent would not have had in the absence of hallucinogenic drugs the agent chose to take.

It is worth noting that these conditions, taken singly or together, do not entail the intuitively appealing principle of alternate possibilities. One form of this principle is that an agent who acts with free will always could *do* otherwise than she does. Consider, for example, a sane, loving mother who is casually invited to torture her baby to death just for fun, and suppose that in this particular instance God would in fact intervene to prevent the mother from accepting or even ignoring the invitation, although neither the mother nor her sadistic interlocutor know or believe this. Then as a matter of fact it is not possible for the mother to do otherwise than she does, when she rejects the invitation. But it is easy to suppose that her volition to reject it nevertheless satisfies conditions FW1 and FW2, and is thus an instance of free will on her part.

Conditions FW1 and FW2 also do not entail a weaker form of the principle of alternate possibilities, that an agent who acts with free will could always *will* otherwise than she wills. It is psychologically impossible for a sane, loving mother to agree to torture her baby to death just for fun; that's part of what it means to describe her as sane and loving. But there is no incoherence in supposing that the volition on which she acts in rejecting the insane invitation satisfies conditions FW1 and FW2 for freedom of will.

There are good reasons to adopt conditions for free will that do not *entail* the principle of alternate possibilities.[13] But, particularly in view of the principle's intuitive appeal, it should also be noted that conditions FW1 and FW2 are *compatible* with the principle. And, just because of its intuitive appeal, the principle of alternate possibilities is adopted in this article as a rule of thumb. That is, we proceed on the assumption that if there is no particular reason for questioning the applicability of the principle to a particular case, then an action that lacks alternate possibilities, an action that is inevitable for an agent, is not an action that the agent does freely.

We define free action in terms of the account of free will.

> An action, *A*, is a free action of an agent, *S*, just in case these two conditions are met:
> FA1. The volition on which *S* acts in doing *A* is an instance of free will on *S*'s part; and
> FA2. In doing *A S* is doing what he wants to do when he wants to do it.[14]

FA1 excludes as unfree any action stemming from a volition excluded as unfree by our definition of free will. FA2 excludes coerced actions as unfree even if they satisfy FA1.[15] In that same way, some actions done out of passion, obsession, or addiction might also be assessed as unfree—e.g., taking the drug to which one has become addicted.

## 4. The nature of prophecy

Since defenders of the eternity solution are unlikely to consider accepting Widerker's first option—i.e., denying that divinely revealed prophecy ever occurs—the heart of his criticism of the eternity solution is his claim that its adherents must admit that prophesied actions are unfree unless they are willing to deny PFP. Because he is, understandably, drawing on religious tradition, he takes his examples of prophecy from the Bible.

The first thing to notice about biblical prophecies is that they vary considerably in form. For instance, some are categorical, but others are conditional—such as this one regarding the throne of David: "If thy children will keep my covenants and my testimony that I will teach them, their children shall also sit upon thy throne for evermore" (Psalm 132:12). Obviously prophecies conditional in this way do not render any action inevitable or unfree.[16]

Even categorical prophecies are sometimes so vague that they cannot be taken as rendering any particular action unfree. Consider, for example, this prophecy from the book of Daniel: "And in the latter time of their kingdom, when the transgressors are come to the full, a king of fierce countenance, and understanding dark sentences, shall stand up. And his power shall be mighty, but not by his own power: and he shall destroy wonderfully, and shall prosper, and practise, and shall destroy the mighty and the holy people" (Daniel 8:23-24). This prophecy leaves vague the identity of the king, and the nature, victim, time, and place of the king's action. Consequently, it renders no particular action inevitable or unfree. Its central claim might be presented in this form:

> It will be the case that some king destroys some people at some time.

Such a prophecy could have threatened freedom only in case one or more of the elements compounded within the scope of 'It will be the case that' had been brought out and separately identified in, e.g., this form:

There is or will be some king, K, and there will be some time, T, such that it will be the case that K destroys some people at T.[17]

Of course, the vagueness of any particular form of words cannot be a feature of God's perfect knowledge itself, and even a vague prophecy brings some eternal knowledge into time. So, someone might think, what we have done to dismiss this prophecy as a threat to freedom has no bearing on the bit of divine knowledge conveyed, however obscurely, by the vague prophecy. But our present concern is just with the alleged threat to freedom in the expressed prophecies themselves. The further possibility, that there is a threat to freedom in the divine knowledge itself that stands behind the prophecy, is the one raised by Jonathan Edwards and considered in the next section of our paper.

Not every traditionally recognized prophecy is characterized by the degree of vagueness that renders the prophecy in Daniel unthreatening to freedom. Some categorical prophecies unmistakably identify certain elements of the prophesied event. In the story of Oedipus, the oracle says that Oedipus will kill his father and marry his mother. But even if we suppose that the ultimate source of the oracle is an infallible and perfectly truthful deity, and that consequently the oracle makes it inevitable that that particular agent will behave in those particular ways to his father and his mother, we need not conclude that the actual killing and the actual marrying are not free actions for Oedipus. What is rendered inevitable is, at most, the occurrence of such actions sometime between the pronouncement of the oracle and the deaths of the people mentioned in it. Nothing in that constraint entails that any particular action of Oedipus's will be inevitable or unfree. It is compatible with the prophecy that any particular instance of his killing his father or marrying his mother—the ones related in the story or any others—meet conditions FA1 and FA2 for free action and even satisfy the principle of alternate possibilities. Instead of killing his father when and as he did, for instance, he might have freely refrained from fighting on that occasion, and the prophesied event might have occurred another time, another way. Although crucial elements of this prophecy are unmistakably identified (the agent and the nature and objects of his actions), the vagueness of its other elements (e.g., time, place, and manner) leaves it compatible with the agent's freedom.

Still, it is easy to imagine a prophecy in which no crucial elements are left vague; and, more important in the context of our consideration of Widerker's position, there appear to be biblical prophecies of this sort. In Acts 9:10-12, for instance, a Christian named Ananias has a vision in which God says to him, "Arise, and go into the street which is called Straight, and enquire in the house of Judas for one called Saul, of Tarsus: for, behold, he prayeth. And hath seen in a vision a man named Ananias coming in, and putting his hand on him, that he might receive his sight." Saul has had a prophetic vision that stipulated not only the agent and the nature and recipient of the action, but also the place where and the way it will be done: Ananias will go to Judas's house in Straight Street and put his hand on Saul so that Saul's sight may be restored. In telling Ananias about it God does not say whether the prophecy to Saul mentioned any particular time, but the fact that God is commanding Ananias to go to Saul at once is at least consonant with the prophecy's having specified a time in the very near future, and, for the sake of the example, we will suppose that it did.[18] This prophecy, then, seems to be the sort that would render Ananias's particular prophesied action inevitable and unfree.

But Ananias's reply to the command is a version of 'If it's all the same to you, God, I'd rather not'—suggesting that he, at any rate, does not think of this prophesied action of his as inevitable. "Lord," he says, "I have heard by many of this man, how much evil he hath done to thy saints at Jerusalem; and here [in Damascus] he hath authority from the chief priests to bind all that call on thy name" (Acts 9:13-14). Ananias seems to view the situation as one in which his own volitions might, after all, be efficacious. Is this attitude of his just naive?

The most that may be said to have been rendered inevitable by the prophecy is that before this day is over (supposing the time to have been specified in that way) Ananias will put his hand on Saul, while Saul is in Judas's house, and that Saul's sight will be consequently restored. Now, that might take place against Ananias's will. For example, Judas, waiting for the promised event, might become impatient and, in order to rid himself of an incapacitated houseguest, kidnap Ananias and force him to put his hand on Saul. On the other hand, the inevitable event might take place not at all against Ananias's will but rather because he freely wills to do what he believes the prophecy has rendered inevitable.[19] Nothing in the prophecy or in the circumstances in which Ananias fulfills it is incompatible with supposing that in doing so he meets both conditions for freedom of will: it is certainly possible that he act as prophesied but on a volition that (FW1) is not causally determined and (FW2) is his own. The prophecy renders his action inevitable, but from the fact that an action is inevitable it does not follow that the volition the agent has as he does the action is inevitable. An action that is inevitable and unfree because in doing it the agent is not (FA2) doing what he wants to do when he wants to do it may nevertheless be an action in which (FA1) the agent acts with free will.

But in order to decide in what respects Ananias's will and action may or may not be free it helps to see how the story continues. Ananias's reply, indicating temerity and reluctance, is followed by God's saying to him "Go thy way: for he is a chosen vessel unto me, to bear my name before the Gentiles, and kings, and the children of Israel: for I will show him how great things he must suffer for my name's sake" (Acts 9:15-16). In letting Ananias see that his mission will help rather than endanger God's saints, God presumably dispels Ananias's reason for objecting to doing what he has been told to do. In this way God strengthens Ananias's natural inclination to cooperate in furthering God's work. "And Ananias went his way, and entered into the house; and putting his hands on him said, Brother Saul, the Lord...hath sent me, that thou mightest receive thy sight..." (Acts 9:17). In the circumstances, there is good reason to think not only that (FA1) Ananias did freely what the prophecy had rendered inevitable, but also that in going to Saul (FA2) he was doing what he wanted to do when he wanted to do it.

So not only can an inevitable action be done by an agent acting with free will, it is also possible for an action to be inevitable and yet a free action. Cases of this sort will be cases in which the agent himself has a powerful desire to do the action, his will is not causally determined by anything external to him or by pathological factors within him, and the inaccessible alternatives to his inevitable action are alternatives the agent has no desire to do or even some desire not to do.[20]

## 5. Reply to Widerker's objection

The story of Ananias and the other examples of prophecy we have been considering suggest that if Widerker's criticism is to succeed in showing that prophecy is incompatible with freedom, it will have to be construed quite narrowly as regards both the prophecy and the freedom. The prophecy will, in the first place, have to specify all the pertinent details of the prophesied action: the agent, the patient, the nature and manner of the action, and its time and place. In the second place, in order to block the sort of opening left for freedom in the story of Ananias, the prophecy will have to be about an act of will rather than an overt act. Finally, the prophesied act of will cannot be such that the agent finds every recognized alternative to it unthinkable for him. A prophecy predicting in all requisite specificity an act that has no acceptable alternatives recognized by the agent still leaves open the possibility that (FA1) the agent does it with freedom of will and that (FA2) the act is precisely what the agent wants to do just then.

A prophecy in which an act of will is specified in all requisite detail and has at least one alternative that the agent does not find unthinkable for him is what is needed to substantiate Widerker's charge. Faced with such a prophecy, defenders of the eternity solution should, we think, simply grant Widerker's point and accept his second option: in such a case the agent of the prophesied action does not act with free will, and so his action is not free. But we are also inclined to think that no biblical prophecies are of this sort.[21] If that's so, it's very likely to be so *just because* such prophecies would render the prophesied action unfree. If, as Christian theologians have often observed, a perfectly good God would not directly nullify the nature he has given his creatures, then neither would he deliver prophecies that would have that effect.

## 6. Edwards's objection

Jonathan Edwards recognized no *problem* of foreknowledge and free will. Instead, he fully accepted what he considered to be the well-reasoned conclusion that God must have foreknowledge and that human actions are consequently necessitated: "Having proved, that God has a certain and infallible prescience of the acts of the will of moral agents, I come now...to shew how it follows from hence, that these events are *necessary*, with a necessity of connection or consequence."[22] He therefore saw the doctrine of eternity not as a putative solution to a troubling problem but as an attempted evasion of an indubitable truth. In his view, even if God's knowledge were not temporal, "God knows the future voluntary actions of men in such a sense beforehand, as that he is able particularly to declare, and foretell them, and write them, or cause them to be written down in a Book, as he often has done; and that therefore the necessary connection which there is between God's knowledge and the event known, does as much prove the event to be necessary beforehand, as if the divine knowledge were in the same sense before the event, as the prediction or writing is. If the knowledge be infallible, then the expression of it in the written prediction is infallible; that is, there is an infallible connection between that written prediction and the event. And if so, then it is impossible it should ever be otherwise, than that that prediction and the event should agree: and this is the same thing as to say, 'tis impossible but that the event should come to pass: and this is the same as to say, that its coming to pass is necessary. So that it is manifest, that *there being no proper succession* [i.e., no temporality] *in God's mind, makes no alteration as to the necessity of the existence of the events which God knows.*"[23]

Although in this passage Edwards alludes to actual prophecies (e.g., "as he often has done"), he does so in order to establish his principal claim, that God "*is able* particularly to declare" "the future voluntary actions of men", which are consequently necessitated even if God's knowledge is timeless—i.e., without any "proper succession"—just "*as if* the divine knowledge *were* in the same sense *before* the event, as the prediction or writing is". And so the sort of reply we make to Widerker, which depends on considerations of actual prophecies, cannot be extended to Edwards, whose assessment of eternity as making no difference to divine determinism depends on a consideration of eternal knowledge itself. What must its nature be if divinely revealed prophecy is to be possible?

Edwards bases his answer to that question on his view that God's omniscience, even if understood as timeless, entails a necessary connection between God and the known event; it is this connection that he takes to render the event necessary "beforehand":

[A]ll certain knowledge proves the necessity of the truth known...Though it be true, that there is no succession in God's knowledge, and the manner of his knowledge is to us inconceivable, yet thus much we know concerning it, that there is no event, past, present, or to come, that God is ever uncertain of; he never is, never was, and never will be without infallible knowledge of it; he always sees the existence of it to be certain and infallible. And as he always sees things just as they are in truth; hence there never is in reality anything contingent in such a sense, as that possibly it may happen never to exist. If, strictly speaking, there is no foreknowledge in God, 'tis because those things which are future to us, are as present to God, as if they already had existence: and that is as much as to say, that future events are always in God's view as evident, clear, sure and necessary, as if they already were. If there never is a time wherein the existence of the event is not present with God, then there never is a time wherein it is not as much impossible for it to fail of existence, as if its existence were present, and were already come to pass.

God's viewing things so perfectly and unchangeably as that there is no succession in his ideas or judgment, don't hinder it but that there is properly now, in the mind of God, a certain and perfect knowledge of the moral actions of men, which to us are an hundred years hence: yea, the objection [raised by supporters of the doctrine of eternity] supposes this; and therefore it certainly don't hinder but that, by the foregoing arguments, it is now impossible these moral actions should not come to pass.[24]

Edwards's rejection of eternity as an attempted evasion of foreknowledge and its consequences relies on the fact that the doctrine of eternity includes the claim that God knows future events. Eternity would otherwise be incompatible with prophecy, and defenders of eternity would be forced to accept Widerker's first option. Edwards acknowledges that God's eternal knowledge of future events would not be *fore*knowledge but, rather, certain and infallible knowledge of the future that is grounded in the fact that events future to temporal creatures are present to eternal God. But present events, like past events, are as they are and cannot be otherwise. So, since on the doctrine of eternity as Edwards construes it our future is now present to God, our future now has the sort of unalterability or inevitability that undeniably characterizes our present. Consequently, even on the doctrine of eternity nothing about our future is genuinely contingent or evitable for us. It is in this way that Edwards argues that eternal knowledge would be just as incompatible with free will as foreknowledge is, starting from his correct observation that even those who claim God is eternal generally admit that he has the power to reveal true prophecies.

## 7. Edwards's misunderstanding of eternity

We think Edwards's argument is spoiled by his failure to appreciate certain implications of the doctrine of eternity.[25] The language that has always been associated with the doctrine makes expressions such as 'present' and 'now' ambiguous between applications to time and to eternity. In the context of the doctrine, the present tense, too, is ambiguous between indicating present time and timelessness. Furthermore, on the doctrine of eternity there will be one sort of simultaneity relating temporal things and another sort that obtains when the relata include both eternal and temporal things. Since being temporally simultaneous with some thing or event may be understood (roughly) as occurring, existing, or obtaining *at the same time as* it,[26] a different account of simultaneity is obviously required when not all the relata are in time. It is in that connection that we developed our notion of ET-simultaneity to portray the relationship presupposed by causal or epistemic interaction between eternal and temporal beings.

ET-simultaneity may be defined in this way: For every $x$ and for every $y$, $x$ and $y$ are ET-simultaneous if and only if

(i)  either $x$ is eternal and $y$ is temporal, or vice versa (for convenience, let $x$ be eternal and $y$ temporal); and

(ii)  with respect to some A in the unique eternal reference frame, $x$ and $y$ are both present—i.e., (a) $x$ is in the eternal present with respect to A, (b) $y$ is in the temporal present, and (c) both $x$ and $y$ are situated with respect to A in such a way that A can enter into direct causal relations with each of them and (if capable of awareness) can be directly aware of each of them; and

(iii)  with respect to some B in one of the infinitely many temporal reference frames, $x$ and $y$ are both present— i.e., (a) $x$ is in the eternal present, (b) $y$ is at the same time as B, and (c) both $x$ and $y$ are situated with respect to B in such a way that B can enter into direct causal relations with each of them and (if capable of awareness) can be directly aware of each of them.[27]

Like temporal simultaneity, ET-simultaneity is symmetric: $x$ is ET-simultaneous with $y$ if and only if $y$ is ET-simultaneous with $x$. Unlike temporal simultaneity, however, ET-simultaneity is neither reflexive nor transitive. Because $x$ can be ET-simultaneous with $y$ only in case one of them is eternal and the other is temporal, nothing can be ET-simultaneous with itself: ET-simultaneity is irreflexive. And the requirement of different domains for the relata of ET-simultaneity also guarantees its intransitivity. If the requirement of different domains is fulfilled in the premises of the transitivity schema, it must be violated in the conclusion (where 'R' = 'is ET-simultaneous with'):

$$x \; R \; y, \; y \; R \; z; \; \therefore \; x \; R \; z.$$

On this basis it is clear that many of the claims crucial to Edwards's argument are ambiguous. For instance, his claim that "there is properly now, in the mind of God, a certain and perfect [eternal] knowledge of the moral actions of men, which to us are an hundred years hence" is ambiguous between (at least) these two readings (where '$A$' designates some particular "moral actions of men" and '$t$' designates a time one hundred years from now):

E1. It is now (in the temporal present) the case that God eternally knows $A$-at-$t$.
E2. It is now (in the eternal present) the case that God eternally knows $A$-at-$t$.

And there is an analogous ambiguity in the tense of the main verb in Edwards's claim that "those things which are future to us, *are* as [eternally] present to God, as they already had existence", which can be read in either of these ways:

E3. It is now (in the temporal present) the case that $A$-at-$t$ is eternally present to God.
E4. It is now (in the eternal present) the case that $A$-at-$t$ is eternally present to God.

Although E2 and E4 provide no insight into the nature of the eternal present, the little they say is altogether in keeping with the doctrine of eternity. But since the eternal present can have no temporal relations with anything, no truths (such as E2 and E4) about the state of God's knowledge in the *eternal* present could show "the [future 'contingent'] event to be necessary *beforehand*", as Edwards thinks present-tense truths about God's eternal knowledge do. The readings that appear to generate the conclusion Edwards needs are E1 and E3, which tie God's eternal knowledge to the temporal present.

In one respect Edwards seems entitled to E1 and E3. Consider E5 and E6, which may well appear to be the contradictories of E1 and E3:

E5. It is *not* now (in the temporal present) the case that God eternally knows *A*-at-*t*.

E6. It is *not* now (in the temporal present) the case that *A*-at-*t* is eternally present to God.

It looks as if defenders of eternity would want to reject these apparent contradictories of E1 and E3. After all, E5 might be read as simply denying that God is omniscient. And E6 might be read as denying that the eternal present is ET-simultaneous with *A*-at-*t* although the doctrine of eternity entails ET-simultaneity between the eternal present and absolutely every time.

However, these readings of E5 and E6, which lend Edwards's argument the support it needs, depend on treating the expression 'now (in the temporal present)' as idle—just an awkward, pointless show of precision. In fact, omitting it entirely shows more clearly why defenders of eternity would be likely to reject E5 and E6. But that fact about E5 and E6 is enough to suggest that they are not unmistakably the contradictories of E1 and E3. For in E1 and E3 the expression 'now (in the temporal present)' is *not* idle but, rather, does the all-important work of tying God's eternal knowledge to the temporal present, the crucial move in Edwards's argument.

The phrase 'It is now the case that...' of course implies that what is within its scope describes something that currently obtains or occurs. But God's knowing, or having certain things present to him, is *not* a currently obtaining state of affairs if what is meant is that it obtains in the temporal present, and the '(in the temporal present)' rider attached to 'It is now the case that...' in E1 and E3 restricts their meaning in just that way. So, because the basis on which defenders of eternity ought to reject E1 and E3 is the general inapplicability of temporal specifications to eternal states of affairs, the proper contradictories of E1 and E3 require negations of broader scope than those in E5 and E6; they require negations that more clearly negate 'now (in the temporal present)':

E1n. It is not the case that it is now (in the temporal present) the case that God eternally knows *A*-at-*t*.

E3n. It is not the case that it is now (in the temporal present) the case that *A*-at-*t* is eternally present to God.

## 8. Edwards's position and ET-simultaneity

Still, the concept of ET-simultaneity might seem to offer Edwards's position a new lease on life. Since the eternal present is ET-simultaneous with every time, it is ET-simultaneous with the temporal present. And perhaps the notion of currently obtaining in the temporal present could be broadened to include obtaining ET-simultaneously with the temporal present.

On this generous interpretation, E3 may be read as telling us that there are relations of ET-simultaneity (a) between certain events future to us and God's eternal present, and (b) between God's eternal present and the temporal present. Similarly, E1 may be read as telling us that God's eternal knowledge, characterized by his ET-simultaneity with certain temporal events future to us that are objects of his knowledge, is itself ET-simultaneous with the temporal present.[28] Edwards's position becomes more formidable, then, if we interpret it in terms of ET-simultaneity and take this claim of his to be its central thesis: "If there never is a time wherein the existence of the [future 'contingent'] event is not present with God, then there never is a time wherein it is not as much impossible for it to fail of existence, as if its existence were present, and were already come to pass."

If it is now the case that God knows $A$-at-$t$, this is in virtue of the fact that the moral actions of those men a hundred years from now are present to God. But if it is now the case that $A$-at-$t$ is present to God, those events are not really contingent, those actions are not really free; $A$-at-$t$ is fixed and inevitable, like anything else that is currently obtaining, and so it is "impossible for it to fail of existence". In other words, Edwards thinks that from

E1′. It is now the case that God knows the particular sins Tom, Dick, and Harry commit one hundred years from today

we can infer

E7. It is now the case that Tom, Dick, and Harry will commit those sins one hundred years from today.

His warrant for thinking so is that we surely could infer E7 from E1′ if 'God' in E1′ were replaced by the name of some temporal knower—'Theresa', let's say. When the stipulated knower is temporal, prefacing these claims with 'It is now the case that' in no way affects the validity of the inference. When the knower is eternal, however, 'It is now the case that' (or Edwards's 'there is a time wherein') makes a crucial difference. On the interpretation we are supplying for Edwards, E1' says that there is a relationship of ET-simultaneity between God's eternal present and those future sins, the relationship that essentially characterizes his eternal knowledge of temporal events, *and* that God's eternal present, in which God's knowing *A*-at-*t* occurs, is likewise ET-simultaneous with our temporal present. On that interpretation, does E1' entail E7? E7 says that one of the states of affairs currently obtaining in the temporal present is Tom's, Dick's, and Harry's future sinning. E7 would follow from E1' if, but only if, ET-simultaneity were transitive. In that case, from the two claims of ET-simultaneity conveyed in E1' Edwards would be entitled to conclude that the future sinning is ET-simultaneous with the temporal present. (That is, (a) Now [*t* - 100] is ET-simultaneous with God's eternally knowing *A*-at-*t*, (b) God's eternally knowing *A*-at-*t* is ET-simultaneous with *A*-at-*t*; therefore (c) Now is ET-simultaneous with *A*-at-*t*.) But, as we have pointed out, ET-simultaneity is an intransitive relationship. From the facts that some past or future state of affairs is ET-simultaneous with the eternal present and that the eternal present is ET-simultaneous with the temporal present, it does not follow that that past or future state of affairs is ET-simultaneous (or simultaneous in any other respect) with the temporal present. The intransitivity of ET-simultaneity invalidates all inferences of the form 'It is now the case that God knows *p*; therefore, it is now the case that *p*', where '*p*' ranges over contingent propositions. Even on the generous interpretation that helps out Edwards's position with the concept of ET-simultaneity, his objection to the eternity solution fails.

Edwards pretty clearly assumes that if future events are really present to God, then, since God sees things as they really are, future events are somehow really present for us with all the infinitely detailed features God discerns in them. For that reason the future, present to God, is in all its details inevitable for us.

On the doctrine of eternity, however, if future contingent events are really present to God, it is because the time in which they happen to occur is ET-simultaneous with God's eternal present. From that explanation it doesn't follow that those events are somehow really present *temporally*, even though the eternal present is also ET-simultaneous with the temporal present. *A fortiori* it doesn't follow, as Edwards claims, that since God "always sees [future] things as they are in truth...there never is in reality anything contingent in such a sense, as that possibly it may happen never to exist". The supposition that Corazon Aquino's introducing land reform in 1995 is ET-simultaneous with God's eternal present is compatible with her action's being free, stemming from earlier free volitions and contingent causes, each of which is itself ET-simultaneous with the eternal present.[29] Analogously, each event leading up to Aquino's overthrowing Marcos in 1986 was simultaneous with our temporal present then as that event was occurring and was or might well have been the object of someone's direct temporal awareness. But nothing in those relationships of simultaneity or direct awareness makes those events inevitable rather than contingent.

Understanding that ET-simultaneity is intransitive blocks Edwards's attempt to infer the inevitability of temporal events from God's unquestioned ability to reveal prophecies about them. And, finally, there is nothing in the doctrine of eternity's account of time, eternity, and their interrelationship to support Edwards's basic conviction, that future events eternally present to God are as temporally determinate as if they had "already come to pass".

## 9. Plantinga on past truth and eternity

In dealing with the problem of foreknowledge and freedom, Plantinga understandably focuses his attention on Edwards's "particularly perspicuous" formulation of it.[30] Accordingly, Plantinga dismisses the eternity solution just because he thinks that "the claim that God is outside of time is essentially *irrelevant* to Edwardsian arguments",[31] a position at least superficially much like Edwards's own attitude towards the eternity solution. But Plantinga's dismissal of the solution, unlike Edwards's or Widerker's, depends not on assumptions about actual or possible prophecy but only on the past truth of claims about God's knowledge, regardless of whether that knowledge is or can be communicated to any person in time.

In view of the similarity between Edwards's and Plantinga's dismissals of the concept of eternal knowledge as inefficacious or irrelevant, it is not surprising that Plantinga characterizes the argument on which he bases his dismissal as a restatement of Edwards's argument.[32] Here is the argument:

Suppose in fact Paul will mow his lawn in 1995. Then the proposition *God (eternally) knows that Paul mows in 1995* is now true. That proposition, furthermore, was true eighty years ago;[33] the proposition *God knows (eternally) that Paul mows in 1995* not only *is* true *now*, but *was* true *then*. Since what is past is necessary, it is now necessary that this proposition was true eighty years ago. But it is logically necessary that if this proposition was true eighty years ago, then Paul mows in 1995. Hence his mowing then is necessary in just the way the past is. But, then it neither now is nor in future will be within Paul's power to refrain from mowing.[34]

It will be convenient to lay out Plantinga's argument in this way:

Suppose (1) Paul will mow his lawn in 1995.
∴ (2) The proposition *God eternally knows that Paul mows in 1995* is true now.
[∴] (3) The proposition *God eternally knows that Paul mows in 1995* was true eighty years ago.[35]
(4) What is past is necessary.
∴ (5) It is now necessary that *God eternally knows that Paul mows in 1995* was true eighty years ago.
(6) Necessarily, if *God eternally knows that Paul mows in 1995* was true eighty years ago, then Paul mows in 1995.
∴ (7) Paul's mowing in 1995 is necessary.
∴ (8) It neither now is nor in future will be within Paul's power to refrain from mowing in 1995.

Since this argument makes use of the notion of God's *eternal* knowledge and nevertheless leads to the conclusion that Paul's "mowing [in 1995] is necessary in just the way the past is..., the claim that God is outside of time is essentially irrelevant to Edwardsian arguments" presenting the problem of divine determinism.

## 10. Plantinga on hard facts

The first thing to notice about this argument is that (4), an old, familiar, and particularly troublesome version of the principle of the fixity of the past (PFP), is what makes it go. We have all learned to be cautious about the notion of the necessity of the past. In particular, it is commonly maintained that only "hard facts" about the past are "necessary", with the accidental necessity that accrues to what is genuinely past, and Plantinga endorses that position. He doesn't provide a definition of hard facts—a notoriously hard thing to do—but he does make clear which sorts of facts about the past he thinks *can't* be hard facts: "(17) [God knew eighty years ago that Paul will mow in 1995[36]] is not a hard fact about the past; for...it entails

(18) Paul will mow his lawn in 1995;

and no proposition that entails (18) is a hard fact about the past. ...No proposition that entails *(18)* is a hard fact about the past, because no such proposition is *strictly* about the past. We may not be able to give a criterion for being strictly about the past; but we do have at least a rough and intuitive grasp of this notion. ...First, no conjunctive proposition that contains (18) as a conjunct is (now, in 1986) strictly about the past. Thus *Paul will mow his lawn in 1995 and Socrates was wise*, while indeed a proposition about the past, is not *strictly* about the past. And second, hard facthood is closed under logical equivalence: any proposition equivalent (in the broadly logical sense) to a proposition strictly about the past is itself strictly about the past. But any proposition that entails (18) is equivalent, in the broadly logical sense, to a conjunctive proposition one conjunct of which is (18); hence each such proposition is equivalent to a proposition that is not a hard fact about the past, and is therefore itself not a hard fact about the past."[37]

Plantinga uses this negative account of hard facts against Edwards's argument for the incompatibility of foreknowledge and free will. In Plantinga's view, the claims about the past that are said to be necessary in Edwards's argument are not hard facts and so do not qualify as necessary under the principle of the necessity of the past.

## 11. Reply to Plantinga's argument

But, as we have seen, Plantinga's own argument for the irrelevance of the doctrine of eternity takes the form of an argument for the incompatibility of eternal knowledge and free will. As such, it is vulnerable to the same objection he brings against Edwards. In explaining that no proposition entailing (18) is a hard fact, Plantinga is out to show in particular that these two propositions are not hard facts:

(13) Eighty years ago, the proposition *Paul will mow his lawn in 1995* was true;

(17) God knew eighty years ago that Paul will mow in 1995.[38]

On this basis, supplied by Plantinga himself, it is easy to see that a crucial step in his argument against the eternity solution is not a hard fact either.

(3) The proposition *God eternally knows that Paul mows in 1995* was true eighty years ago

entails

(3a) God eternally knows that Paul mows in 1995;[39]

and (3a) entails (18) just as (17) does.[40] Since, on Plantinga's view, no proposition that entails (a proposition that entails) (18) is a hard fact, (3) is not a hard fact.

But if (3) is not a hard fact, Plantinga's version of the principle of the necessity of the past in (4) does not apply to it. In that case, the derivation of (5) is invalid, and so the argument is invalid. The derivable version of (5) is simply (3) all over again, and so the derivable version of (7) is simply (7R) 'Paul mows in 1995', or (1), the original supposition, all over again. And from (7R) or (1) it does not follow that (8) 'It neither now is nor in future will be within Paul's power to refrain from mowing in 1995'.

So if Plantinga is right in thinking that Edwards's argument against the compatibility of foreknowledge and free will fails, then his own argument against the compatibility of eternal knowledge and free will fails also, and for just the same reasons as those he alleges against Edwards.

## 12. The role of the argument in Plantinga's project

Edward Wierenga, in commenting on an earlier version of this paper, claimed that our objection against Plantinga's argument shows a misunderstanding of his project.[41] Wierenga pointed out that Plantinga thinks that a version of the hard-fact/soft-fact distinction is enough to solve the problem of foreknowledge and freedom, without recourse to the doctrine of eternity.[42] Since the argument we are objecting to is intended to show only that the concept of God's eternal knowledge by itself is not enough to solve the problem, it is of course an argument that deliberately ignores the hard-fact/soft-fact distinction. And so our criticism, which depends on introducing the distinction, is misconceived.

But the fact that the argument ignores the distinction means that it is trading on a false and misleading view of the applicability of PFP, as our objection shows. It is, therefore, not an argument that could show the insufficiency or irrelevance of the eternity solution considered on its own, because it doesn't consider it on its own but burdens it with a false view of the necessity of the past. As our discussion of Edwards should help to show, the eternity solution developed on its own has no need of the hard-facts/soft-facts distinction. We have recourse to it in objecting to Plantinga's argument only because the argument's deliberate avoidance of it unfairly couples the concept of God's eternal knowledge with a concept of the necessity of the past that Plantinga himself regards as crude and mistaken. No argument that burdens the doctrine of eternity in such a way could succeed in showing that the doctrine is irrelevant to the problem of divine determinism.

### 13. Past truth and ET-simultaneity

Someone might suppose that even if this particular argument from past truth fails, the idea behind it is generally sound and simply needs to be presented differently. That is, someone might suppose that the past truth of a proposition about God's eternal knowledge of a future event does show that the event is somehow fixed or inevitable *now*, before the event occurs. If that aspect of the future were *not* fixed in such a way, one might think, how could it be true now, or in the past, that God *knows* it?

But this way of raising the problem of past truth is just a variation on Edwards's objection to the eternity solution. Like Edwards's argument, it trades on the transitivity of simultaneity in a context in which the only appropriate simultaneity relationship is intransitive. God's eternal knowledge of an event that is future to us is characterized in part by the fact that the time at which that event actually occurs is ET-simultaneous with God's eternal present. Now consider this claim:

(A) The proposition (g) 'God eternally knows *p*' (where *p* is some future contingent event) is now true.

Proposition (g) of course entails *p*, but does it also entail this further claim?

(B) It is *now* the case that *p*.

Claim (B) is required for the argument that God's eternal knowledge shows future events to be fixed *now*, before they actually occur. Now a proposition is true only if things are as the proposition says they are. But the state of affairs presented in proposition (g) is an eternal state of affairs, God's eternally knowing *p*. What basis is there for saying, with (A), that (g) is *now* true, where 'now' is clearly intended to pick out the temporal present?

The only basis, as far as we can see, is the relationship of ET-simultaneity between that eternal state of affairs and the temporal present. If that's right, then the truth of (A) depends on two relations of ET-simultaneity: one between the future event and the eternal present (*p* is ET-simultaneous with God's eternal knowing), the other between the eternal present and the temporal present (God's eternal knowing is ET-simultaneous with *now*). But since ET-simultaneity is intransitive, the truth of (A) doesn't entail that *p* is in any way fixed or inevitable *now*, in the temporal present. So although (A) entails *p*, (A) doesn't entail (B) 'It is *now* the case that *p*'; and without (B) there is no basis for claiming that any future event is now inevitable simply in virtue of God's eternally knowing it.

Restated in this way, then, the thought presumably behind Plantinga's argument from past truth collapses into Edwards's objection to the eternity solution, which we have already provided grounds for rejecting.

## 14. The trouble with examples

The natural tendency to think that future events are inevitable, somehow already present for us if they are really present to God, seems to stem at least partly from the way examples have to be constructed in order to be pertinent to this discussion. In order to talk concretely about God's atemporal awareness of some future contingent event, we have to begin by saying something of the sort we've been saying in this paper: 'Suppose that in 1995 Corazon

Aquino will introduce land reform legislation; in that case that free future action of hers is ET-simultaneous with God's eternal present'. And there is a natural inclination to think that anyone who maintains that *p* is thereby committed to maintaining (or at least not denying) that it is now the case that *p*. As long as we're operating on this supposition about Aquino we can't with a straight face deny that we know what the future of Philippine land reform will be or insist that that aspect of the future isn't yet determined. Such suppositions are designed to give us some sense of the nature of an eternal being's knowledge of time. To the extent to which they succeed, they tend to confuse God's eternal viewpoint with our natural temporal viewpoint regarding future contingent events. The example puts us in God's position, or in the position of prophets to whom he has revealed a bit of his atemporal knowledge. So the natural, almost unavoidable way of presenting this material makes it hard to avoid thinking that if future contingent events are really present to God, they are somehow also really present for us.

But the doctrine of eternity recognizes time and eternity as two distinct real modes of existence. We in 1990 cannot be in a relationship of simultaneity with an event in 1995, because the latter event isn't occurring now. God's situation is different, however, because the beginningless, endless, persistent eternal present encompasses all of time. Any particular temporal event is earlier than, simultaneous with, or later than the temporal present; but every temporal event *as it is when it is temporally present* is ET-simultaneous with God's eternal present.

A rough analogy may help here. God is eternally aware of just what you are aware of now, and of just what you were aware of at noon yesterday, and of just what you will be aware of at noon tomorrow, but only *as you are directly aware of those things on those occasions*, not as you may be aware of them afterwards in memory or beforehand in anticipation. Omnipresent timeless awareness of time is direct awareness *at once* of *every* present time somewhat as you are aware of *this* time, in something like the way you can be directly aware of this time only when and because it is present.

The real existence of temporal events coincides precisely with their being temporally present. The perfection of God's knowledge entails his being aware of the real existence of temporal events; the atemporality of God's knowledge entails his being aware non-successively, at once, of the real existence of every temporal event. For God, who timelessly sees contingent events future to us when and as they are temporally present, those events have the sort of inevitability that accompanies presentness, and only that sort. For us, relative to whom they are future, those events are as evitable now as the presently occurring contingent events were evitable when they were future. Nothing in God's relationship to those events determines them in advance any more than our observing Aquino's present actions would render those actions of hers unfree.

So, the claim in the doctrine of eternity that all contingent events really future to us are really timelessly present to God does not entail that they are somehow really present for us, so that it is now determined what the future will be. Edwards's and Plantinga's positions, along with the many others of that sort, gain plausibility from the fact that merely presenting the kind of case to be considered involves pretending, probably without realizing it, to a view of future contingent events that is naturally unavailable to a temporal observer. And the central claims of Edwards's and Plantinga's arguments, even when they are helped out by an application of the notion of ET-simultaneity, are seen to trade on a mistaken view of that relationship as transitive.

## 15. Conclusion

We think eternity is a hard concept. We also think that conceiving of God as the absolutely perfect being entails recognizing that his mode of existence must be eternity rather than time. All the same, philosophers and theologians are rightly inclined to be suspicious of a concept whose coherence is repeatedly challenged. And so the alleged efficacy of eternity in resolving the problem of theological determinism has always been an important practical consideration on the side of persisting in the effort to provide a clearly coherent account of eternity. Those who are engaged in that effort therefore have a special obligation to look carefully at objections purporting to show that the best-known, most-valued practical application of eternity is, after all, of no value. In this article we have examined three such objections, representing the most formidable lines of thought we know of against the eternity solution, and we have found that none of them provides good reasons for abandoning the solution or giving up the attempt to understand eternity.[43]

## Notes

1. "Eternity", *The Journal of Philosophy* 78 (1981) 429-458; reprinted in Thomas Morris, ed., *The Concept of God* (Oxford: Oxford University Press, 1987), 219-252.
2. Our translation of Boethius's definition, on which see "Eternity", pp. 429-434.
3. In "Atemporal Duration: A Reply to Fitzgerald", *The Journal of Philosophy* 84 (1987) 214-219, and in "Eternity, Action, and Awareness", forthcoming in a volume edited by Thomas Tracy.
4. When divine omniscience is conceived of as temporal, it apparently entails divine foreknowledge, which apparently entails that human beings never can act or choose to act otherwise than as God has always foreknown they would. For a recent but already classic presentation of the problem, see Nelson Pike, "Divine Omniscience and Voluntary Action", *The Philosophical Review* 74 (1965), 27-46. In fact it was in connection with a discussion of this problem (beginning in V, Pr. iii) that Boethius developed his classic account of eternity in *The Consolation of Philosophy* V, Pr. vi. And recently William Hasker has laid down a stringent but tolerable "criterion for an acceptable doctrine of [divine] timelessness: such a doctrine must solve the problem of free will and foreknowledge" (*God, Time, and Knowledge* [Ithaca and London: Cornell University Press, 1989], p. 148). As further evidence of the problem's revived capacity to stimulate philosophical investigation, see, e.g., John Martin Fischer, ed., *God, Foreknowledge and Freedom*, Ithaca and London: Cornell University Press, 1989.
5. For a summary of the reasoning that gave rise to the concept see our "Eternity" (n. 1 above), pp. 444-445.
6. David Widerker, "A Problem for the Eternity Solution", forthcoming in *International Journal for Philosophy of Religion*. We are grateful to Professor Widerker for showing us his paper in typescript. Objecting to the eternity solution on the basis of considerations of prophecy is certainly not new, nor does Widerker claim that it is. For some sophisticated earlier disputation over problems of just this sort, see Rita Guerlac's translation of Leon Baudry's collection of a connected series of fifteenth-century texts: *The Quarrel over Future Contingents (Louvain 1465- 1475)*, (Dordrecht, Boston, London: Kluwer Academic Publishers, 1989).
7. Jonathan Edwards, *Freedom of the Will* (1754), II, 12 (see n. 22 below); reprinted in Baruch A. Brody, ed., *Readings in the Philosophy of Religion* (Englewood Cliffs, N. J.: Prentice-Hall, 1974), pp. 393-403. Although Widerker focuses his attention on examples of prophecy, like Edwards he insists that an objection of this sort can also be based on the mere possibility of divine intervention, in the form of prophetic revelation or otherwise, based on eternal knowledge of future contingent events.
8. Alvin Plantinga, "On Ockham's Way Out", *Faith and Philosophy* 3 (1986) 235-269; reprinted in Thomas V. Morris, ed., *The Concept of God* (Oxford: Oxford University Press, 1987), 171-200.
9. See, e.g., William Hasker, op. cit. (n. 4 above), Ch. 4: "Two Arguments

for Incompatibilism", pp. 64-74.

10. PFP is variously formulated in the literature. Widerker (see n. 6 above) presents it in more than one form, among which this form is basic: "No agent has it within his power at a given time T to bring about the non-obtaining of a fact about the past, relative to T."

11. For further explanation of these conditions and an argument for them see Eleonore Stump, "Intellect, Will, and the Principle of Alternate Possibilities", in Michael Beaty , ed., *Christian Theism and the Problems of Philosophy*; Notre Dame: University of Notre Dame Press, 1990.

12. As Hasker remarks, "if one takes a compatibilist view of free will, most of the problems considered here [concerning divine knowledge in relation to time and human free will] are rather readily resolved and a whole battery of new problems arises to take their places", op. cit., p. x.

13. As recent work by Harry Frankfurt and others has shown, the principle does not hold in every case that satisfies intuitive criteria for free will. (For bibliography and a discussion of these issues, see Stump, "Intellect, Will, and the Principle of Alternate Possibilities" [n. 11 above].)

14. This definition is adapted from one given by Harry Frankfurt (see "Freedom of the Will and the Concept of a Person", *The Journal of Philosophy* 68 [1971] 5-20). Frankfurt's definition is significantly different from ours because he is concerned to broaden the division between free will and free action. For instance, his definition has the result that an agent could act freely while not acting with freedom of will; our definition rules out that possibility. On the other hand, on our definitions of free action and free will an agent could act with free will in doing an unfree action. In a case of coercion, for example, the coerced agent might well meet the requirement in FA1 but not the requirement in FA2 of the definition of free action—acting with free will but not doing what he wants to do. (For more on coercion, see n. 15 below. For an interesting argument that it is possible to act with free will in doing an unfree action, see Rogers Albritton, "Freedom of Will and Freedom of Action" (*Proceedings and Addresses of the American Philosophical Association* 59 (1985), 239-251.) Part of the reason for the difference between Frankfurt's definition of free action and ours is that he is working with an unusually demanding notion of free will, interesting in itself and useful in certain contexts (as his work has shown) but irrelevant to our immediate concerns in this article.

15. We take coerced actions to include cases in which one person successfully threatens or intimidates another into acting in some way—e.g., Maggie is going to Chicago because David is holding a gun to her head and insisting that she go—but not cases in which one person exercises force over another to such an extent that what happens thereafter is in no sense the forced person's action—e.g., Maggie is going to Chicago because David has tied her up, put her in his car, and is driving her there.

16. Ockham dealt with the problem of preserving contingency in view of God's foreknowledge by taking all biblical prophecies as conditional:

"I maintain that no revealed future contingent comes to pass neces-sarily.... Consequently [what was revealed] could have been and can be false. Nevertheless the Prophets did not say what is false, since all prophecies regarding any future contingents were conditionals. But the condition was not always expressed. Sometimes it was expressed—as in the case of David and his throne—and sometimes it was understood— as in the case of [the prophecy of] the destruction of Nineveh by the prophet Jonah: 'Yet forty days, and Nineveh shall be overthrown' [Jonah 3:4]—i.e., unless they would repent; and since they did repent, it was not destroyed" (Marilyn Adams and Norman Kretzmann, *William Ockham: Predestination, God's Foreknowledge, and Future Contingents*, 2nd edn. [Indianapolis: Hackett Publishing Company, 1983], p. 44). Cf. Calvin Normore's discussion in Ch. 18, "Future Contingents" (pp. 358-381 in Norman Kretzmann, Anthony Kenny, and Jan Pinborg, eds., *The Cam-bridge History of Later Medieval Philosophy*, Cambridge: Cambridge University Press, 1982), pp. 370 ff.; also A. Edidin and C. Normore, "Ockham on Prophecy", *International Journal for Philosophy of Religion* 13 (1982), 179-189.

17. In terms of a convenient distinction familiar to medieval philosophers, the first of these forms presents the compounded sense of the prophecy, while the second presents one of its divided senses.

18. If we suppose that the prophecy left even just the time unspecified, then this example, too, might, through a crucial vagueness, avoid particular inevitability.

19. Some of the actions attributed to Jesus in the gospels seem to have been done by him because he chose to act as he believed he had been prophesied to act. Consider, e.g., Matthew 21:1-5; 26:52-54; Mark 14:48-49; John 19:28-30.

20. Certainly the most famous precise biblical prophecy and the one that figures most in philosophical discussions is Jesus' prophecy of Peter's denial (Matthew 26:34; Mark 14:30; Luke 22:34; John 13:38). (For in-genious examples of such discussions see Guerlac's translation of Baudry's medieval texts, n. 6 above.) Peter's denial, unlike Ananias's visit to Saul, seems clearly to be a case of freedom of will that is not also freedom of action: FA1 without FA2.

21. The biblical prophecies that look most like cases of this sort are those that involve the hardening of hearts, on which see Eleonore Stump, "Sanctification, Hardening of the Heart, and Frankfurt's Concept of Free Will", *The Journal of Philosophy* 85 (1988), 395-420.

22. Jonathan Edwards, *A Careful and Strict Enquiry into the Modern Prevailing Notions of that Freedom of Will, which is Supposed to be Essential to Moral Agency, Vertue and Vice, Reward and Punishment, Praise and Blame* (Boston, 1754); ed. Paul Ramsey, *The Works of Jonathan Edwards*, Vol. 1 [New Haven, Conn.: Yale University Press, 1957], Part II, section 12, 257-269), p. 257; reprinted in Brody (see n. 7 above), p. 393. The final clause of this passage, explaining that these events are necessary "with a necessity of connection or consequence", suggests that Edwards is relying on the distinction between *necessitas*

*consequentiae* and *necessitas consequentis*. Almost certainly he does have the distinction in mind, but he is not invoking *necessitas consequentiae* as many contributors to this discussion have done, in order to show that the necessity at issue here does not bind the agent. The other passages we quote make this clear.

23. Op. cit., p. 267; Brody, p. 401.
24. Op. cit., pp. 266-267; Brody, pp. 400-401.
25. The passages we have quoted contain several indications that he is at least careless in his description of eternity as an atemporal mode of existence: God, he says, "never is, never was, and never will be without infallible knowledge", and God "always sees things just as they are in truth"; "there is no event...that God is ever uncertain of". But our concern here with his understanding of divine timelessness is only with its effect on his treatment of God's knowledge as necessitating human action.
26. In "Eternity" we provide a slightly more sophisticated account of temporal simultaneity, pp. 435-438.
27. For more on this definition, see our "Eternity, Action, and Awareness" (n. 3 above).
28. The truth in Edwards's misleadingly expressed claim that eternal God "never is, never was, and never will be without infallible knowledge" of any temporal event (see n. 25 above) lies in the fact that the eternal present, in which God's eternal act of knowing every temporal event takes place, is ET-simultaneous with every time.
29. Of course, the suppositions (i) that Aquino's introducing land reform in 1995 is ET-simultaneous with God's eternal present and (ii) that Aquino does not introduce land reform then are incompatible. Necessarily, if her introducing land reform in 1995 is present to God, in 1995 she is introducing land reform. But that observation no more threatens freedom or contingency than does this one: 'Necessarily, if you are looking at this page, you are looking at this page'.
30. "On Ockham's Way Out" (n. 8 above), p. 237.
31. Op. cit., p. 240; emphasis added.
32. He introduces it by saying that if "the thesis that God is both atemporal and such that everything is present for him...*is* coherent, ...Edwards' argument can be restated in such a way as not to presuppose its falsehood" (p. 239). As we have seen, Edwards himself presents a version of his argument for divine determinism that does not presuppose the falsity of the doctrine of eternity.
33. Plantinga recognizes that the notion of a proposition's being true at a time is controversial, and so he offers a parallel argument based on the notion of a sentence's expressing a truth at a time. The parallel argument depends on this claim: "eighty years ago the sentence

(5) God knows (eternally) that Paul mows in 1995

expressed the proposition that God knows eternally that Paul mows in 1995... . But if in fact Paul will mow in 1995, then (5) also expressed a truth eighty years ago" (p. 240). In the interest of brevity, we will confine our discussion to his first formulation of the argument. Nothing in our discussion turns on the difference between the two formulations.

34. Op. cit., p. 239. This argument is coming in for considerable criticism in the literature (see, e.g., Linda Zagzebski, forthcoming; Brian Leftow, *Time and Eternity* (Ithaca and London: Cornell University Press, forthcoming); and David Widerker, op. cit. [n. 6 above]). Although these criticisms succeed in pointing out flaws in the argument, we think there is more to be said.

35. Plantinga leaves the status of this step in his argument unclear, but we assume that he takes it to derive from (2) along with certain tacit claims about eternal knowledge.

36. After the first few pages of his article Plantinga (apparently inadvertently) changes the date in his central example from 1995 to 1999. To avoid confusion, we silently change '1999' back to '1995'.

37. Op. cit., p. 248.

38. Op. cit., pp. 246 and 247.

39. Our (3a) appears as (5) in Plantinga's article; see n. 33 above.

40. The facts that (18) is in the future tense while (3a) uses the tenseless 'mows', appropriate to a description of eternal knowledge, is no obstacle to the inference. Sticklers may fill it out with such premisses as 'God eternally knows that 1995 is later than 1990' and 'God eternally knows that future-tense verbs are appropriate only in sentences intended to express propositions regarding events later than the time of utterance'.

41. Plantinga himself also made this claim in responding to an earlier draft, and William Alston said the same sort of thing in discussing the paper with us.

42. For an important criticism of this line of thought, see John Martin Fischer, "Hard-Type Soft Facts", *The Philosophical Review* 95 (1986), 591-601.

43. We are grateful for helpful comments on earlier drafts from William Alston, William Hasker, Nelson Pike, Alvin Plantinga, Richard Purtill, David Widerker, and, especially, Edward Wierenga.

Philosophical Perspectives, 5, Philosophy of Religion, 1991

# PROPHECY, FREEDOM, AND THE NECESSITY OF THE PAST

## Edward Wierenga
## University of Rochester

One of the strongest arguments for the incompatibility of divine foreknowledge and human free action appeals to the apparent fixity or necessity of the past. Two leading responses to this argument—Ockhamism, which denies a premiss of the argument, and the so-called "eternity solution", which holds that strictly speaking God does not have foreknowledge—have both recently come under attack on similar grounds. Neither response, it is alleged, is adequate to the case of divine prophecy. In this paper I shall first state the argument in question and the two responses to it. I shall then consider objections to these responses, focusing primarily on how they deal with prophecy.

## I. Accidental Necessity, Foreknowledge, and Free Action.

Thomas Aquinas considered an argument for the incompatibility of divine foreknowledge and human free action contained in the following passage:

> Further, every conditional proposition, of which the antecedent is absolutely necessary, must have an absolutely necessary consequent. For the antecedent is to the consequent as principles are to the conclusion: and from necessary principles only a necessary conclusion can follow, as is proved in *Poster*. i [Aristotle's *Posterior Analytics*, I, 6]. But this is a true conditional proposition, *If God knew that this thing will be, it will be*, for the knowledge of God is only of true things. Now the antecedent of this conditional proposition is absolutely necessary, because it is eternal, and

> because it is signified as past. Therefore, the consequent is also absolutely necessary; and so the knowledge of God is not of contingent things.[1]

The species of necessity Thomas has in mind here is a kind of necessity that attaches to propositions, but it is clearly not logical necessity; rather it is a kind of necessity that attaches to propositions that are "signified as past." Ockham called this modality necessity *per accidens* or accidental necessity.[2] Intuitively, even if a proposition such as *It was, is, or will be the case that Ockham goes to Munich in 1328* has always been true, prior to 1328 there were various things that could have been done to make it false. After 1328, however, this proposition has become fixed or unalterable; there is nothing anyone can do to make it false. More generally, if a proposition is accidentally necessary, no one can act in such a way as to render it false.

The argument suggested by the passage from Aquinas makes the following assumptions:

(1) Propositions reporting God's past beliefs are now accidentally necessary.

(2) Any (contingent) proposition that is entailed by an accidentally necessary proposition is itself accidentally necessary.

(3) If it is accidentally necessary that a person perform a certain action, then, since there is nothing the person can do to avoid it, the action is not free.

By employing these assumptions, we can construct an argument for the conclusion that any action that God foreknows will be performed is not free.

Suppose, to take an example that is familiar from recent literature, that Jones will mow his lawn tomorrow, and assume that God has foreknowledge of this action. Then, presumably,

(4) Eighty years ago God foreknew that Jones will mow his lawn tomorrow.

From (4) and (1) we may deduce that

(5) It is accidentally necessary that eighty years ago God foreknew that Jones will mow his lawn tomorrow.

Now (4) entails

(6) Jones will mow his lawn tomorrow;

thus by (2), the principle that accidental necessity is closed under (contingent) entailment,[3] and (5) it follows that

(7) It is accidentally necessary that Jones will mow his lawn tomorrow.

But from (7) and (3) it follows that

(8) Jones' mowing his lawn tomorrow is not free.

So from the assumption that God foreknows that an action will be performed, it follows that it is not free.[4]

## II. Ockhamism.

Ockhamists respond to the foregoing argument by denying assumption (1), namely, the claim that all propositions reporting God's past beliefs about the future are accidentally necessary.[5] They hold that a proposition such as (4) is only *apparently* about the past; it is not *wholly* about the past because it depends in a way upon the future. According to Ockham, "some propositions are about the present as regards their wording only and are equivalently about the future, since their truth depends on the truth of propositions about the future,"[6] and he presumably holds a similar view about propositions about the past. In more recent terminology: (4) is a *soft fact* about the past, and it is only *hard facts* about the past that are necessary *per accidens*.[7]

The Ockhamist response may be seen as a natural extension of a plausible response to an analogous argument for fatalism. Fatalism is the doctrine that it is a conceptual truth that no one is able to act otherwise than he or she does.[8] If we replace the first assumption of the argument with the stronger thesis that

(1′) Propositions about the past are now accidentally necessary,

and we replace premiss (4) with

(4′) Eighty years ago it was true that Jones will mow his lawn tomorrow,

we have an argument for fatalism.[9] For it again follows, by an argument exactly parallel to our original argument, that

(8)  Jones' mowing his lawn tomorrow is not free.

That is, from (4'), which asserts that

(6)  Jones will mow his lawn tomorrow

was true in the past, it follows that Jones is not free with respect to mowing his lawn tomorrow.

It is eminently reasonable, it seems to me, to reply to this fatalistic argument by denying that (4') is strictly about the past. Since (4') entails a proposition about the future,[10] it is merely a soft fact about the past, and thus not accidentally necessary. But just as (4') depends upon the future, so does (4). So (4), too, is only a soft fact about the past.

### III. A Molinist Alternative to Ockhamism.

Alfred Freddoso, who formerly was an eloquent defender of Ockhamism, has recently endorsed an alternative due to Luis de Molina.[11] Freddoso's conversion was occasioned in part by his concern with prophecy, about which more below. For now let us briefly consider the Molinist alternative. The Molinist concedes that

(5)  It is accidentally necessary that eighty years ago God foreknew that Jones will mow his lawn tomorrow.

But the Molinist denies that accidental necessity is closed under (contingent) entailment and, in particular, denies that

(7)  It is accidentally necessary that Jones will mow his lawn tomorrow.[12]

How plausible is it to deny that accidental necessity is closed under (contingent) entailment? It is difficult to give a compelling answer to this question simply because the concept of accidental necessity is notoriously difficult to explicate.[13] Nevertheless, if we agree that the apparent fixity of the past can be represented by a modal operator on propositions, then it is plausible to hold, as Freddoso had earlier written, that this modality is "respectable and well-behaved."[14] And part of what is required for respectability, I think, is that accidental necessity obey the following two principles. The first is that

(9) Any proposition that is logically equivalent to an accidentally necessary proposition is itself accidentally necessary.

If a proposition *p* is fixed and unalterable in virtue of what has happened, if there is nothing anyone can do that would render *p* false, then it is hard to conceive how a proposition *q* that is logically equivalent to *p* is not similarly fixed and beyond anyone's ability to render false. The second principle is that

(10) Any conjunction that has as a conjunct a contingent proposition that is not accidentally necessary is itself not accidentally necessary.

Suppose there is something you could do that would make *p* false. If you were to do it, then for any proposition *q*, the conjunction *p & q* would be false, too; so the truth of the conjunction is not fixed or unalterable.

If accidental necessity satisfies these two modest and intuitive principles, then it is closed under (contingent) entailment. To see this, suppose that *p* is accidentally necessary and that it entails a proposition *q* (where *q* is possibly false). Since *p* entails *q*, *p* is logically equivalent to the conjunction of *p & q*. By (9), then, this conjunction is accidentally necessary. But if this conjunction is accidentally necessary, then by (10) it does not have any contingent conjuncts that are not accidentally necessary. By assumption, *q* is a contingent conjunct of the conjunction *p & q*. So *q* is accidentally necessary. Hence, if *p* is accidentally necessary and entails a contingent proposition *q*, then *q* is accidentally necessary. So accidental necessity is closed under (contingent) entailment. Since I am persuaded by this argument, I do not regard the Molinist alternative to Ockhamism as a live option.

## IV. The Doctrine of Eternity.

According to a venerable tradition, God is outside of time; his perspective is that of eternity. The classic definition of eternity was provided by Boethius, who held that "eternity...is the complete, simultaneous and perfect possession of everlasting life."[15] On this view, everything that ever happens is present to God all at once. The doctrine of eternity, moreover, is often presented as a response to the claim that divine foreknowledge is incompatible with human freedom: it was so used by Boethius, that is how Aquinas replies to the argument in the passage quoted in Section 1, and recently Stump and Kretzmann have defended what they call "the eternity solution."[16]

The way in which the doctrine of eternity provides a "solution" to the alleged incompatibility, however, is by conceding it. This solution is thus a sort of skeptical solution:[17] divine foreknowledge is indeed inconsistent with human freedom, but God does not have foreknowledge. Since his knowledge is had in his own eternal mode of existence, strictly speaking, he does not have it before events that occur in time. There are thus two parts to this solution. The first is the concession that

> (11) Divine foreknowledge is inconsistent with human freedom.

The second is the insistence that

> (12) Divine eternal knowledge *is* consistent with human freedom.

## V. An Objection to the Eternity Response.

Let us call the argument for the incompatibility of divine foreknowledge and human free action presented in Section 1 above "The Original Argument". In the course of discussing a variant of The Original Argument, Alvin Plantinga considered the response that God is eternal and concluded, that "the claim that God is outside of time is essentially irrelevant to [such] arguments."[18] This is because an exactly analogous argument can be constructed from the premiss that God has eternal knowledge. If Jones will mow his lawn at $t$, some time tomorrow, then, on the view that God is eternal,

> (13)  God knows eternally that Jones mows his lawn at $t$.

This last claim is not only true now; it was true eighty years ago. So

> (4′′) Eighty years ago it was true that God knows eternally that Jones mows his lawn at $t$.

But, as in our original argument, (4′′) is a truth about the past, so it is accidentally necessary. Hence, what follows from it, that Jones mows his lawn at $t$, is also accidentally necessary, and so Jones is not free with respect to mowing his lawn at *t*. Let us call this argument against the compatibility of divine eternal knowledge and human free action "The Adapted Argument".

This objection to the eternity solution has been widely endorsed[19], but it has recently begun to attract some criticism. According to Linda Zagzebski, "it is a mistake to look at the past truth of propositions rather than the past occurrence of events as the entities to which accidental necessity applies."[20] Thus, even though (4′′) is a truth about the past, it is not accidentally necessary, because it is events (or states of affairs in some unspecified narrow sense) and not propositions that are accidentally necessary. Zagzebski attempts to support her contention by noting that "a proposition is not tied to moments of time as an event is. Its truth is usually thought to be either timeless or omnitemporal. If omnitemporal, then if it is true at one time, it is true at all times, and there is no asymmetry between past and future. If timeless, then it is not true at moments of time at all, and again there is no asymmetry between past and future. So there is not, or at least ought not to be, a temptation to think of propositions as becoming fixed at some time as there is with events."[21] It may well be, although this is a matter of controversy,[22] that propositions do not change over time with respect to truth value. It does not follow from this, however, that they display no asymmetry over time. In particular, it does not follow that they have no temporal asymmetry with respect to being fixed or unalterable. Indeed, we introduced accidental necessity above by noting that even if a proposition such as *It was, is, or will be the case that Ockham goes to Munich in 1328* has always been true, prior to 1328 (but not after that year) there were various things that could have been done to make it false. So lack of temporal asymmetry with respect to truth seems no barrier to a proposition manifesting temporal asymmetry with respect to unalterability.[23]

Stump and Kretzmann also object to Plantinga's argument against the adequacy of the eternity solution as a response to the Original Argument.[24] They note, in effect, that presupposition (1) of the Adapted Argument is a version of what they call the principle of the fixity of the past (PFP). They add, "We have all learned to be cautious about the notion of the necessity of the past. In particular, it is commonly maintained that only 'hard facts' about the past are 'necessary', with the accidental necessity that accrues to what is genuinely past, and Plantinga endorses that position."[25] Stump and Kretzmann then note that the reasoning Plantinga gives for holding, in response to the Original Argument, that

> (4) Eighty years ago God foreknew that Jones will mow his lawn tomorrow

is not a hard fact about the past and accordingly is not accidentally necessary can be adapted to yield the conclusion that

> (4′ ′) Eighty years ago it was true that God knows eternally that Jones mows his lawn at $t$,

too, is neither a hard fact about the past nor accidentally necessary. Stump and Kretzmann thus conclude that "if Plantinga is right in thinking that [the Original Argument] against the compatibility of foreknowledge and free will fails, then his own argument against the compatibility of eternal knowledge and free will [the Adapted Argument] fails also, and for just the same reasons as those he alleges against [the Original Argument]."[26]

Despite the explicitly conditional form of their conclusion, it is clear (see the next paragraph) that Stump and Kretzmann do intend to reject the Adapted Argument on the grounds that it fails to exempt soft facts about the past from being accidentally necessary and it therefore is mistaken in assuming that (4′ ′) is accidentally necessary. But responding to the Adapted Argument in this way is to concede Plantinga's claim that the doctrine of eternity is irrelevant as a reply to the Original Argument. This is because the doctrine of eternity plays no role in the reply. Rather, it is the claims that (4) is a soft fact about the past and that only hard facts are accidentally necessary that are being used to rebut the Original Argument.

Stump and Kretzmann attempt to dismiss this criticism by claiming that "the fact that the [Adapted] argument ignores the distinction [between hard and soft facts] means that it is trading on a false and misleading view of the applicability of PFP, as our objection shows. It is, therefore, not an argument that could show the insufficiency or irrelevance of the eternity solution considered on its own, because it doesn't consider it on its own but burdens it with a false view of the necessity of the past. ... No argument that burdens the doctrine of eternity in such a way could succeed in showing that the doctrine is irrelevant to the problem of divine determinism."[27] We should note first that Plantinga's claim was not, as the last sentence of this quotation suggests, that the doctrine of eternity is irrelevant to the problem of *divine determinism*. Rather, his contention was that the doctrine is irrelevant as a response to the Original Argument. But secondly, by accusing the Adapted Argument—and by extension, the Original Argument—of failing to distinguish between hard and soft facts and of assuming a "false view of the necessity of past," Stump and Kretzmann appear to repeat their concession that it is the Ockhamist claims that disarm the argument. The doctrine of eternity is not only not required to escape the Original Argument, it is not even helpful.

Of course, the defender of the doctrine of divine eternity is certainly free to adopt an Ockhamist response to the Adapted Argument. Doing so does not *discredit* the doctrine; at most it eliminates a consideration in favor of it.[28] In the reminder of this paper we shall attempt to determine how Ockhamism and the doctrine of eternity each deal with the problem of prophecy.

## VI. Prophecy.

Several authors have recently claimed that the fact of prophecy poses a problem for attempts to defend the compatibility of divine knowledge and human freedom. David Widerker, for example, claims that the occurrence of the kinds of prophecies common in the Jewish and Christian scriptures requires the adherent of eternity to violate what Widerker regards as a true version of the principle of the fixity of the past.[29] And Alfred Freddoso alleges that "Ockhamism simply cannot deal adequately with genuine prophecy of future contingents."[30]

How exactly does prophecy pose a problem for these attempts to defend the compatibility of divine knowledge and human freedom? Stump and Kretzmann suggest that it is because "a prophecy brings some of God's eternal knowledge into time, thus converting at least the revealed bit of it into foreknowledge." And they add, "Even though it is not God who has the foreknowledge generated in this way, the standard arguments against the compatibility of fore-knowledge and freedom would apply to the prophet's foreknowledge, which stems from God."[31] Now some of the standard arguments on this topic presuppose an important difference between divine and human knowledge, holding that it is only the former that is incompatible with human freedom. In Nelson Pike's influential version of the argument, for example, it is claimed that *essential* omniscience is incompatible with human freedom; human knowers—even prophets—fall far short of that epistemic standard.[32] And John Fischer concedes that past *knowledge* is a soft fact about the past. It is past *belief*, he claims, that is fixed, and it is only *divine* past belief that is incompatible with human free action.[33] So at least some of the standard arguments permit prophets to have foreknowledge without impinging on human freedom; but, of course, other arguments may treat human foreknowledge differently.

There is, however, another way of conceiving of the problem posed by prophecy. It is that a past prophecy involves the creation of some object or the occurrence of some event—an inscription or an utterance, for example—that has entered into causal relations with other objects in the past. As Freddoso puts it, "the past physical utterance of a given string of words is a paradigmatic instance of a 'hard' fact about the past."[34] So if

(14) Christ uttered (Aramaic words whose translation into English is), "Tonight before the cock crows you will disown me three times,"

addressing himself to Peter, then, immediately afterwards, that Christ made such an utterance would seem to be accidentally necessary. And if it follows from (14) that Peter will disown Christ three times, then immediately after Christ's utterance

(15) Peter will disown Christ three times

was also accidentally necessary. But then Peter's subsequent denials were not free. So a genuine prophecy involves some particular thing that not only is *in time* but is plausibly thought to be accidentally necessary and which provides the premises for yet another version of the Original Argument. Let us call this latest version of the argument the "Prophetic Argument".

## VII. Prophecy and Eternity.

Stump and Kretzmann's reply to the Prophetic Argument, which consists primarily of arguing against the conclusion of that argument rather than identifying a flaw in it, has two main strands.[35] First, they implicitly assume an ontology of actions as particulars, as opposed to actions taken as abstract or as act types.[36] A *particular* action, as I understand it, is a datable, nonrepeatable event. By contrast, an act *type* is general in the sense that it could be exemplified by a variety of different particular actions. For example, the act type *Peter's denying Christ* is a general action that could be exemplified by various specific actions—particular actions in which Peter utters different words or even the same words at different times. Second, they rely on a proposed account of free action. According to Stump and Kretzmann

(16) An action, *A*, is a free action of an agent, *S*, just in case (FA1) the volition on which *S* acts in doing *A* is an instance of free will on *S*'s part, and (FA2) in doing *A S* is doing what he wants to do when he wants to do it.[37]

And they add that a volition, *V* of a person, *S*, is an instance of free will only if, roughly, *V* is not caused by something outside of *S*'s beliefs and desires and *V* is a volition for some object that *S*'s intellect represents as a good.

Stump and Kretzmann appeal to these features, both singly and jointly, in mounting a reply to the Prophetic Argument. They say with respect to the nonbiblical, oracular prophecy that Oedipus will kill his father and marry his mother that "even if we suppose that...the oracle makes it inevitable that that particular agent will behave in those particular ways to his father and mother, we need not conclude that the actual killing and the actual marrying are not free actions for Oedipus. What is rendered inevitable is, at most, the occurrence of such actions sometime between the pronouncement of the oracle and the deaths of the people mentioned in it. Nothing in that constraint entails that any particular action of Oedipus's will be inevitable or unfree."[38] Putting this point in terms that they themselves do not use, Stump and Kretzmann hold that an act type can be inevitable even though a particular act that instantiates it is not inevitable: the type *killing one's father* was inevitable for Oedipus but the particular action in which he killed his father was free. I shall call this thesis that an action type can be inevitable even though a token of it is free the *generality response*.

Stump and Kretzmann also apply their second assumption to this case. They claim that "it is compatible with the prophecy that any particular instance of his killing his father or marrying his mother— the ones related in the story or any others—meet conditions (FA1) and (FA2) for free action..."[39]

This appeal to their account of free action, which I shall call the *volitional response*, is developed in greater detail by reference to another example. They take the blinded Saul's vision (Acts 9:12)—a man named 'Ananias' comes to Judas' house on Straight Street and lays his hands on Saul to restore his sight—as a prophecy, and they imagine that it is quite specific about what Ananias will do and when. Stump and Kretzmann first appear to repeat the generality response: they claim that "the most that may be said to have been rendered inevitable by the prophecy is that before this day is over (supposing the time to have been specified in that way) Ananias will put his hand on Saul, while Saul is in Judas's house, and that Saul's sight will be consequently restored."[40] But then they discuss God's effort at motivating Ananias and conclude, "In the circumstances, there is good reason to think not only that (FA1) Ananias did freely what the prophecy had rendered inevitable, but also that in going to Saul (FA2) he was doing what he wanted to do when he wanted to do it."[41] So Ananias' action satisfies the conditions specified by (16) for being free.

Despite the ingenuity of Stump and Kretzmann's response to the Prophetic Argument, I think that it is in fact unconvincing. This charge can be made in an intuitive way by reference to the generality response, but I will later try to state it more precisely and in a way that applies to both the generality and the volitional responses. There is some plausibility to the thesis that an act of a very general type can be inevitable even though no particular instance of it is. To take a trivial example, it may be inevitable *that I do something* without there being something that it is inevitable that I do. Or, less trivially but also less obviously, it may be inevitable that I make a mistake within the next ten years without there being some particular action of mine that is a mistake and inevitable. But if a considerably more specific act type is inevitable, it is much less plausible to suppose that an instance of it is not inevitable. This seems particularly to be the case in the example of Ananias. Assume, as Stump and Kretzmann suppose for the sake of example, that the prophecy was as specific as to say that Ananias will go to Judas' house within the next few minutes, and suppose that it is thus inevitable that he do so. I find it hard to reconcile these assumptions with the claim that Ananias' actual going to Judas' house was free; pointing out that it is up to Ananias whether he goes right away or after a minute or two seems not to make his actual going any less inevitable.

This somewhat vague animadversion can be made more precise

by focusing on the following sort of questions: What *makes* it inevitable that Ananias go to Judas' house? Is there a causal or some other deterministic mechanism at work? If not, it is hard to see how the action is inevitable. But if there is some such mechanism, we need to know more about it. In particular, we need to know whether it works by making some particular action inevitable. Or, to state the issue in a way that more clearly applies to the volitional response, we need to know whether whatever makes Ananias' action inevitable also makes his act of will or volition inevitable. Again, if this mechanism does not ensure that Ananias engage in an act of will of the right sort, then it is hard to see how it could ensure that he will do the action. But if the mechanism does make Ananias' volition inevitable, then it would seem that the condition that Ananias' act of will be caused by nothing other than his own beliefs and desires would not be satisfied. And if this condition is not satisfied, then on Stump and Kretzmann's own account, neither Ananias' act of will nor his action is free.

In addressing Stump and Kretzmann's response to the Prophetic Argument, I have assumed for the sake of discussion that having been prophesied does render such acts as Ananias' going to Judas' house inevitable. This is an assumption, however, that deserves critical scrutiny. Providing such scrutiny will be one of the aims of the next section.

### VIII. Prophecy and Ockhamism.

According to the Prophetic Argument, a past (genuine) prophecy to the effect that a certain action will be performed is a hard fact about the past and entails that the action will be performed. In terms of the example we used above, if

(14) Christ uttered (Aramaic words whose translation into English is), "Tonight before the cock crows you will disown me three times,"

addressing himself to Peter, then that Christ made such an utterance was thereafter accidentally necessary. And if it follows from (14) that Peter will disown Christ three times, then thereafter

(15) Peter will disown Christ three times

was also accidentally necessary. So Peter's subsequent denials were not free.

By an *Ockhamist response* to this argument I mean a response that, like the Ockhamist response to the Original Argument, appeals to Ockham's distinction between hard and soft facts and, furthermore, holds that, like past divine knowledge, past prophecies need not be accidentally necessary.[42] Before presenting such a response to the Prophetic Argument, it would be useful to make two preliminary remarks. First, let us assume throughout that in our example Christ speaks in his divine nature.[43] That will help rule out the possibility of the prophecy being mistaken. Secondly, let us strengthen the argument by revising (14), for (14) does not, as it stands, entail (15).[44] Christ could utter those words without intending to assert what they express, if, for example, he were testing his voice, auditioning for a play, or reading a scroll that someone else had written. So Christ could utter those words without them expressing a truth.

What is needed to replace (14) is a proposition satisfying several conditions. It should report the existence of a physical object or the occurrence of an event whose existence or occurrence is plausibly thought to be a hard fact about the past, thereby justifying the assumption that the proposition in question is accidentally necessary. Furthermore, the replacement should entail that the one making the prophecy *asserts* a proposition about the future action. To rule out mendacious or insincere prophecy, we could require that the prophet believe the proposition so asserted. And, finally, the proposition asserted should be one that clearly entails (15), for that entailment is required in order to derive that (15) is accidentally necessary. We can accommodate all of these conditions by substituting the wooden but explicit proposition

(14′) There was a token $T$ such that (i) Christ used $T$, and (ii) as used by Christ $T$ expressed $p$, the proposition that Peter will disown Christ three times, (iii) Christ believed $p$, and (iv) Christ intended to assert $p$ with $T$.

Now (14′) seems to have the requisite features: It explicitly asserts the existence of a token, perhaps an act of utterance or a string of words uttered, which is such that if Christ used it, it must now be accidentally necessary that he did. And according to (14′), the token so used expressed (15). If, moreover, Christ believed (15) and intended to assert (15), then it follows that (15) is true.[45] So (14′) entails (15).

According to the Revised Prophetic Argument, then, (14′) became accidentally necessary as soon Christ issued his prophecy. Since (14′) entails (15), (15) was thereafter accidentally necessary, too. But then Peter was not able to refrain from disowning Christ and so his later denials were not free.

It will come as no surprise that the Ockhamist response to this argument denies that (14′) is accidentally necessary.[46] It may be that it is accidentally necessary that Christ uttered the words he did and accidentally necessary that those words expressed (15). But it is not apparent that (14′) as a whole is accidentally necessary. It was clear from our discussion in Section 2 above that the Ockhamist is already committed to holding that God's past *knowledge* of the contingent future need not be accidentally necessary. Of course, the same holds for God's past *belief*, for, necessarily, God believes a proposition if and only if he knows it. So the Ockhamist will naturally want to deny that the third clause of (14′), that Christ believed that Peter would disown him three times, is accidentally necessary, for this is a belief about the contingent future. It is not a very large step to hold the same thing about other divine mental states (or other aspects of the divine mental state). In particular, the Ockhamist can deny that the fourth clause of (14′), that Christ *intended* to assert that Peter will disown him, is accidentally necessary. What Christ intends to assert is closely tied to what he thinks is the case. And if what he thinks to be the case is not fixed and inevitable, then what he intends to assert is not, either.

So far, I have represented the Ockhamist as denying that the last two conjuncts of (14′) are accidentally necessary. The remaining step is easy. We saw in Section 3 above that it is plausible to hold that

(10) Any conjunction that has as a conjunct a contingent proposition that is not accidentally necessary is itself not accidentally necessary.

By applying (10) to the case at hand, it follows that (14′) is not accidentally necessary. So the Ockhamist can reply to the Prophetic Argument by a natural extension of his or her reply to the Original Argument. Divine prophecy of the future, like divine knowledge of the future, is not fixed, inevitable, or accidentally necessary.

I shall conclude by considering two objections to the Ockhamist response. First, Freddoso claims that "Ockhamism commits one to having to choose between the Scylla of claiming that God can undo the causal history of the world and the Charybdis of claiming that divine prophecies might be deceptive or mistaken."[47] By allowing that the token used in making a prophecy can be a fixed part of the past, the Ockhamist intends, I believe, to deny that God can undo the causal history of the world. So the Ockhamist will indeed want to steer clear of the Scylla of Freddoso's dilemma. But is the Ockhamist thereby trapped in a whirlpool of admitting that

(17) It is possible that some divine prophecy is mistaken?

The answer, I think, is that the Ockhamist is not committed to (17) but only to

(18) Some divine prophecy is such that it is possible that it is mistaken.

That is, the Ockhamist will insist that nothing could be both a divine prophecy and mistaken. Something that is a divine prophecy, however, might not have been a divine prophecy, and, hence, could have been false: Christ's utterance might have been mistaken, but if it had been, it would not have been intended by him to express (15), and so would not have been a prophecy.

A second objection alleges that the Ockhamist account credits Peter with the ability to bring it about that Christ told a lie; but according to traditional theology, God cannot lie. The Ockhamist, however, does not credit Peter with this ability. Peter had it within his power to do something, namely, refraining from disowning Christ, which is such that if he had done it then (15) would have been false. But it does not follow that Peter was able to do something which is such that if he had done it then Christ would have told a lie. For if Peter had refrained from disowning Christ, then Christ would not have believed that Peter was going to disown him, and Christ would not have intended to assert (15). In that case, then, Christ would not have intended to deceive, and so he would not have told a lie.

## IX. Conclusion.

Ockhamism remains a viable response to the Original Argument that divine foreknowledge is incompatible with human free action; and introducing the complexity of prophecy does not diminish that viability, for the Ockhamist response has a natural and straightforward extension to prophecy. The attempt by Stump and

Kretzmann to provide a response to the Prophetic Argument on behalf of the doctrine of divine eternity seems to me unconvincing. Nevertheless, just as the Ockhamist response to the Adapted Argument is not only available to, but seems to be needed by, the defender of the doctrine of eternity, the Ockhamist response to the Prophetic Argument is also available to the defender of divine eternity. However, if the adherents of the doctrine of eternity choose thus to avail themselves of Ockhamism, it would be somewhat misleading to speak of the eternity "solution".

## Notes

1. Thomas Aquinas, *Summa Theologica*, Ia, 14, 13, obj. 2, in *Basic Writings of Saint Thomas Aquinas*, Vol. 1, Anton C. Pegis, ed. (New York: Random House, 1945), p. 154.
2. William Ockham, *Ordinatio*, Prologus, q. 6, quoted in his *Predestination, God's Foreknowledge, and Future Contingents*, 2nd ed., Marilyn McCord Adams and Norman Kretzmann, trans. (Indianapolis: Hackett, 1983), p. 38.
3. By "closed under (contingent) entailment" I mean *closed under entailment of contingent propositions*.
4. The recent literature discussing variants of this argument is voluminous. A good selection of essays, together with a useful bibliography, may be found in John Martin Fischer, ed., *God, Foreknowledge, and Freedom* (Stanford: Stanford University Press, 1989). I have discussed this argument at some length in Edward Wierenga, *The Nature of God* (Ithaca and London: Cornell University Press, 1989), chs. 3 and 4.
5. Ockhamists include, in addition to Ockham himself, the temporal segment of Alfred Freddoso who authored "Accidental Necessity and Logical Determinism," *Journal of Philosophy* 80 (1983): 257-278, reprinted in Fischer, ed., *God, Foreknowledge, and Freedom*, and "Accidental Necessity and Power over the Past," *Pacific Philosophical Quarterly* 63 (1982): 54-68, as well as Alvin Plantinga, "On Ockham's Way Out," *Faith and Philosophy* 3 (1986): 236-237, reprinted in Fischer, ed., *God, Foreknowledge, and Freedom*.
6. William Ockham, *Predestination, God's Foreknowledge, and Future Contingents*, p. 46.
7. Nelson Pike introduced the terms 'hard' and 'soft' facts in "Of God and Freedom: A Rejoinder," *Philosophical Review* 75 (1966): 369-379.
8. Peter van Inwagen, *An Essay on Free Will* (Oxford: Oxford University Press, 1983), p. 23.
9. In van Inwagen's term, we have a "fatalistic argument in a narrow sense," for it is an argument for fatalism that depends on the notions of time and truth. See ibid.
10. *Entailing a proposition about the future* is an intuitive but not an entirely

adequate test for a proposition failing to be a hard fact about the past. For details, see John Martin Fischer, "Freedom and Foreknowledge," *The Philosophical Review* 92 (1983): 67-79, reprinted in Fischer, ed., *God, Foreknowledge, and Freedom.*

11. For some of Freddoso's earlier work, see the references in note 5. The recent alternative is found in the fine introduction to his translation of Luis de Molina, *On Divine Foreknowledge (Part IV of the Concordia)* (Ithaca and London: Cornell University Press, 1988).

12. Alfred Freddoso, "Introduction," pp. 57ff.

13. I have attempted to evaluate some of the leading attempts in *The Nature of God*, ch. 4.

14. Alfred Freddoso, "Accidental Necessity and Logical Determinism," p. 258.

15. Boethius, *The Consolation of Philosophy*, V. E. Watts, trans. (Baltimore: Penguin Books, 1969), Book V, Prose 6, p. 163. The doctrine of eternity has been defended by Eleonore Stump and Norman Kretzmann is a series of articles, including "Eternity," *Journal of Philosophy* 78 (1981): 429-458, "Atemporal Duration: A Reply to Fitzgerald," *Journal of Philosophy* 84 (1987): 214-219, "Prophecy, Past Truth, and Eternity," this volume, and "Eternity, Action, and Awareness," (forthcoming). The doctrine has been seriously challenged in recent years. Critics include Stephen Davis, *Logic and the Nature of God* (Grand Rapids: Eerdmans, 1983) and Nicholas Wolterstorff, "God Everlasting," in Clifton Orlebeke and Lewis Smedes, eds., *God and the Good: Essays in Honor of Henry Stob* (Grand Rapids: Eerdmans, 1975), pp. 181-203, reprinted in Steven Cahn and David Shatz, eds., *Contemporary Philosophy of Religion* (New York: Oxford University Press, 1982), pp. 77-98. I have attempted to reply to these critics in *The Nature of God*, ch. 6.

16. "Prophecy, Past Truth, and Eternity."

17. Cf. Saul A. Kripke, *Wittgenstein on Rules and Private Language* (Oxford: Basil Blackwell, 1982), pp. 66ff.

18. Alvin Plantinga, "On Ockham's Way Out," p. 240.

19. Alfred Freddoso, "Introduction," p. 57, Wierenga, *The Nature of God*, p. 115, Linda Zagzebski, "Divine Foreknowledge and Human Freedom," *Religious Studies* 21 (1985): 279-298, p. 282. Zagzebski has recently retracted her endorsement.

20. Linda Zagzebski, *The Dilemma of Freedom and Foreknowledge* (New York and Oxford: Oxford University Press, forthcoming), ch. 2.

21. Ibid., ch. 1.

22. See Wierenga, *The Nature of God*, 175-190.

23. Zagzebski also argues that accidental necessity is rooted in the distinction between act and potency and that the relevant sort of potency is not had by propositions. I am not sure that I understand this argument, but I think that it is sufficient to note that whether a proposition is accidentally necessary need not depend on any potency that *it* has; what is relevant is the potency that *agents* have to render it false.

Compare David Widerker, "A Problem for the Eternity Solution," *International Journal for Philosophy of Religion* (forthcoming), who suggests in response to Plantinga's objection that accidental necessity applies only to statements that ascribe a property to an object in the past. But Widerker does not succeed in showing that statements like (4′′) and variants thereof do not ascribe a property to an object.

24. "Prophecy, Past Truth, and Eternity," this volume, Section 10.
25. Ibid., Section 10.
26. Ibid., Section 11.
27. Ibid., Section 12.
28. However, compare William Hasker, *God, Time, and Knowledge* (Ithaca and London: Cornell University Press, 1989), who holds that a "criterion for an acceptable doctrine of timelessness...is that it solve the problem of free will and foreknowledge" (p. 148).
29. David Widerker, "A Problem for the Eternity Solution."
30. Alfred Freddoso, "Introduction," p. 61. As Freddoso makes clear in his discussion of Molina's treatment of the topic, the problem is an old one. See also Calvin Normore, "Future Contingents" in Norman Kretzmann, Anthony Kenny, and Jan Pinborg, eds., *The Cambridge History of Later Medieval Philosophy* (Cambridge: Cambridge University Press, 1982), pp. 358-381, esp. pp. 373-381, and Aron Edidin and Calvin Normore, "Ockham on Prophecy," *International Journal for Philosophy of Religion* 13 (1982): 179-189.
31. "Prophecy, Past Truth, and Eternity," this volume, section 2.
32. Nelson Pike, "Divine Omniscience and Voluntary Action," *The Philosophical Review* 74 (1965): 27-46.
33. John Martin Fischer, "Freedom and Foreknowledge."
34. Alfred Freddoso, "Introduction," p. 60 n. Compare Widerker's concern with the past hearing of a voice or the past coming to believe an item of revelation in "A Problem for the Eternity Solution."
35. Although Stump and Kretzmann do not explicitly address the question of what is wrong with the Prophetic Argument, what they do say can be used against the argument. In particular, if we extend what they say about inevitable actions to accidental necessity, then they appear to deny the presupposition

> (3) If it is accidentally necessary that a person perform a certain action, then, since there is nothing the person can do to avoid it, the action is not free,

at least for the case in which the action in question is not specifically an act of volition.
36. "Prophecy, Past Truth, and Eternity," see esp. Section 3.
37. Ibid., Section 3.
38. Ibid., Section 4.
39. Ibid.
40. Ibid., Section 4.
41. Ibid., Section 4.
42. Ockham himself apparently gave two quite different responses to the Prophetic Argument. In his *Predestination, God's Foreknowledge, and Future Contingents* Ockham concedes that past prophecies are after-

wards necessary, but he holds that "all prophecies regarding any future contingents were conditionals. But the condition was not always expressed. Sometimes...it was understood—as in the case of [the prophecy of] the destruction of Nineveh by the prophet Jonah: 'Yet forty days, and Nineveh shall be overthrown'—i.e., unless they would repent; and since they did repent it was not destroyed" (Q. I, ad. 8), p. 44.

In *Quodlibeta* IV, q. 4, Ockham gives a different response—more like the one I defend in the text—according to which, as Normore puts it, "after God has revealed a future contingency it is necessary that the physical or mental things he used to reveal it have existed, but what is revealed is not necessary." See Calvin Normore, "Future Contingents," p. 373. Normore quotes Ockham's Latin text, ibid., n. 37. The same passage occurs in English translation in Edidin and Normore, "Ockham on Prophecy," p. 185.

My aim in the text is to defend what I call an Ockhamistic response to the Prophetic Argument. I do not pretend to exegete Ockham's actual position.

43. Anyone who objects to this assumption may substitute an example in which it is God who issues a prophecy.
44. *Pace* Freddoso, "Introduction," p. 61.
45. Recall our assumption that we are speaking of Christ in his divine nature.
46. Strictly, the Ockhamist holds that (14') did not become accidentally necessary as soon as Christ made his prophecy. It may be that since the time of Peter's denials (14') has been necessary. I shall not always trouble to insert this qualification, pretending that we are evaluating (14') during the interval between Christ's utterance and Peter's denial.
47. Alfred Freddoso, "Introduction," p. 61.

## References

Boethius, *The Consolation of Philosophy*, V. E. Watts, trans. (Baltimore: Penguin Books, 1969).

Davis, Stephen, *Logic and the Nature of God* (Grand Rapids: Eerdmans, 1983).

Edidin, Aron, and Calvin Normore, "Ockham on Prophecy," *International Journal for Philosophy of Religion* 13 (1982): 179-189.

Fischer, John Martin, "Freedom and Foreknowledge," *The Philosophical Review* 92 (1983): 67-79, reprinted in Fischer, ed., *God, Foreknowledge, and Freedom*.

Fischer, John Martin, ed., *God, Foreknowledge, and Freedom* (Stanford: Stanford University Press, 1989).

Freddoso, Alfred, "Accidental Necessity and Logical Determinism," *Journal of Philosophy* 80 (1983): 257-278, reprinted in Fischer, ed., *God, Foreknowledge, and Freedom*.

Freddoso, Alfred, "Accidental Necessity and Power over the Past," *Pacific Philosophical Quarterly* 63 (1982): 54-68.

Freddoso, Alfred, "Introduction," to Molina, *On Divine Foreknowledge*.

Hasker, William, *God, Time, and Knowledge* (Ithaca and London: Cornell

University Press, 1989).

Kripke, Saul A., *Wittgenstein on Rules and Private Language* (Oxford: Basil Blackwell, 1982).

Molina, Luis de, *On Divine Foreknowledge (Part IV of the Concordia)*, Alfred Freddoso, trans. (Ithaca and London: Cornell University Press, 1988).

Normore, Calvin, "Future Contingents" in Norman Kretzmann, Anthony Kenny, and Jan Pinborg, eds., *The Cambridge History of Later Medieval Philosophy* (Cambridge: Cambridge University Press, 1982), pp. 358-381.

William Ockham, *Predestination, God's Foreknowledge, and Future Contingents*, 2nd ed., Marilyn McCord Adams and Norman Kretzmann, trans. (Indianapolis: Hackett, 1983).

Pike, Nelson, "Divine Omniscience and Voluntary Action," *The Philosophical Review* 74 (1965): 27-46.

Pike, Nelson, "Of God and Freedom: A Rejoinder," *Philosophical Review* 75 (1966): 369-379.

Plantinga, Alvin, "On Ockham's Way Out," *Faith and Philosophy* 3 (1986): 236-237, reprinted in Fischer, ed., *God, Foreknowledge, and Freedom*.

Stump, Eleonore and Norman Kretzmann, "Atemporal Duration: A Reply to Fitzgerald," *Journal of Philosophy* 84 (1987): 214-219.

Stump, Eleonore and Norman Kretzmann, "Eternity," *Journal of Philosophy* 78 (1981): 429-458.

Stump, Eleonore and Norman Kretzmann, "Eternity, Action, and Awareness," (forthcoming).

Stump, Eleonore and Norman Kretzmann, "Prophecy, Past Truth, and Eternity," this volume.

Thomas Aquinas, *Summa Theologica*, in *Basic Writings of Saint Thomas Aquinas*, Vol. 1, Anton C. Pegis, ed. (New York: Random House, 1945).

van Inwagen, Peter, *An Essay on Free Will* (Oxford: Oxford University Press, 1983).

David Widerker, "A Problem for the Eternity Solution," *International* Journal *for Philosophy of Religion* (forthcoming).

Wierenga, Edward, *The Nature of God* (Ithaca and London: Cornell University Press, 1989).

Wolterstorff, Nicholas, "God Everlasting," in Clifton Orlebeke and Lewis Smedes, eds., *God and the Good: Essays in Honor of Henry Stob* (Grand Rapids: Eerdmans, 1975), pp. 181-203, reprinted in Steven Cahn and David Shatz, eds., *Contemporary Philosophy of Religion* (New York: Oxford University Press, 1982), pp. 77-98.

Linda Zagzebski, *The Dilemma of Freedom and Foreknowledge* (New York and Oxford: Oxford University Press, forthcoming).

Linda Zagzebski, "Divine Foreknowledge and Human Freedom," *Religious Studies* 21 (1985): 279-298.

Philosophical Perspectives, 5, Philosophy of Religion, 1991

# THE POSSIBILITY OF POWER
# BEYOND POSSIBILITY

Earl Conee
University of Rochester

## Introduction

Omnipotence is one of the extraordinary attributes that are traditionally ascribed to God. This gives theists reason to ponder the nature of omnipotence. Some philosophers of religion have developed accounts of omnipotence guided by the idea that omnipotence is identical to the extent of God's power. Often these accounts are interesting and impressive. But this guiding assumption is dangerous, particularly when it is coupled with the assumption that God exists. The principal danger is that omnipotence will be misconstrued in order to insure that it is compatible with God's other assumed attributes. Such an analysis may explain how powerful it is possible for God to be, instead of explaining omnipotence. This risk would be worth taking if we had no other initial conception of omnipotence except as the extent of God's power. But we do have an independent conception of omnipotence, and it has exciting philosophical ramifications in metaphysics and in epistemology, as well as in the philosophy of religion.

Let us pose our question as follows: Theological considerations aside, what would it take to be omnipotent? There is a compelling intuitive answer to this question: to be omnipotent is to be all-powerful, where the "all" is utterly unrestricted. Omnipotence includes being able to do anything that could possibly be done, and being able to do the impossible. Omnipotence is absolutely unlimited power.

The purpose of this paper is to argue that this conception of omnipotence is philosophically fruitful. It is a consistent concept. In fact, there is no good reason to deny that it might have been exemplified. In defense of the coherence of this notion it will be clarified and defended against challenges to its intelligibility. Then it will be compared to Descartes' view of the power of God. Philosophical issues involving omnipotence will be discussed in terms of this notion. The issues to be discussed are the problem of evil, the stone paradox, the question of how many omnipotent beings there could be, and a new epistemic issue concerning impossibility and actuality. These applications show the philosophical value of the notion.

## I. Clarification

Being omnipotent is being able to do anything. This simple formulation conveys the intuitive conception of omnipotence pretty well. But elaboration is needed to avoid interpretive difficulties and to make it clear that an omnipotent being would have the power that intuition requires. One interpretive problem arises because things of most sorts are neither possible nor impossible deeds, because they are not deeds at all. In a sense, an omnipotent being would be able to "do anything." But not even an omnipotent being would be able to "do" e.g. a physical object. Only deeds can be done by any being, even an omnipotent being. When a sentence purports to ascribe to a being an ability to do something which is not a deed, the sentence fails to make any assertion (except on irrelevant readings of "do"). This is not a limit on any being's powers. It is a limit on meaningful expressions. The claim that an omnipotent being would have the ability to "do anything" must be understood in accordance with this semantic restriction. When it comes to deeds, though, an omnipotent being would be able to do all of them.

Abilities to act do not exhaust the power that is needed to be omnipotent. Intuitively, omnipotence goes beyond this. It is absolute power over how things are. It is not merely unlimited power to act. An omnipotent being would be able to have things be any way at all. This includes abilities to have things any given way without doing anything to make things that way.

One efficient means of identifying the full range of abilities that is intuitively required to qualify as omnipotent is to make use of the notion of an agent's having power over the truth-value of propositions. Having an ability can be construed as being in a certain relation to a proposition, a proposition that would be made true by exercising the ability.[1] The relation is that of having control over the proposition's truth-value. An individual is in this relation to a given proposition just when the individual is able to have the proposition be true, and also able to have it be false. In other words, the individual has the power to be such that the proposition is true, and has the power to be such that the proposition is false.[2]

By use of this relation it is simple to express clearly the intuitive view of omnipotence. Being omnipotent is having control over the truth-value of every proposition. An omnipotent being is one who has an ability with respect to each proposition to have it be true and to have it be false. This account will be called here "the intuitive view of omnipotence."

The intuitive view of omnipotence implies that in the relevant sense an omnipotent being would have the power to "do anything." With respect to each being and every deed, there is a proposition to the effect that the being does the deed. In the intuitive view of omnipotence, any omnipotent being would be able to have any of these propositions be true. Thus, the being would be able to perform any act, since to be able to have any such proposition be true is to be able to have obtain any state of affairs that consists in some act being performed by the being.

This view of omnipotence as control over the truth-value of every proposition also bears out the intuitive requirement that the being be able to have things its way without acting to make them be that way. This is born out because there exist propositions to the effect that things are each given way without anyone ever doing something to make them that way. In the intuitive view of omnipotence, any omnipotent being would be able to have any such proposition be true.

The intuitive view of omnipotence requires an omnipotent being to be able to bring about all sorts of impossibilities. There are propositions that assert all sorts of impossibilities, e.g., the physical impossibility that something travels seven trillion miles in seven seconds, the metaphysical impossibility that Richard Nixon is a photon, and the logical impossibility that something is nothing. An omnipotent being would be able to have any of these propositions be true.

## II. Argument

The requirement of totally unrestricted power is substantiated by reflection on omnipotence: there is no intuitive limit on the "all" in the gloss of "omnipotent" as "all-powerful." But reflection on omnipotence is not the only way to defend this requirement of having thoroughly unrestricted power. The requirement can be established by argument. The argument has two premises about the abilities of any omnipotent being. Each premise is plausible for reasons that are independent of intuitions about the universality of the "all" in the paraphrase of "omnipotent" as "all-powerful."

The first premise of the argument asserts that omnipotence implies an unlimited ability to will. The premise asserts that in order to be omnipotent a being must have abilities to will the truth and the falsehood of every proposition. If there is any proposition that a being is unable even to will to be true, or unable to will not to be true, then the being is ipso facto lacking in will-power. Intuitively, any lack of will-power precludes omnipotence. This includes willing the truth of impossibilities, since it is incompatible with being omnipotent to have less will-power than some of us actually have. Some of us are able to will the truth of impossibilities. So the omnipotent must be able to do likewise. Here is the argument's first premise:

$P_1$ If a being is omnipotent, then the being is able to will any proposition to be true and able to will any proposition to be false.

The argument's other premise asserts that whatever any omnipotent being is able to will, it is also able to achieve.[3] It seems clear that any omnipotent being would be able to succeed at whatever it could will. If there were something that a being could will that it was entirely unable to achieve, then it would lack the power to carry out all of its intentions. This is clearly a weakness. The being would fall short of omnipotence. Thus, the other premise of the argument is this:

$P_2$ If an omnipotent being is able to will a given proposition to be true, and able to will the proposition to be false, then the being is able to have the proposition be true and able to have the proposition be false.

From $P_1$ and $P_2$ we can infer:

C  If a being is omnipotent, then the being is able to have any proposition be true and able to have any proposition be false.

An omnipotent being would be unlimited in its power to control the truth-value of propositions. We have previously seen that this range of abilities is supported by direct reflection on the concept of omnipotence. Now we see that the same range of abilities follows from plausible assumptions about the will-power and the capacity to succeed that are required to be omnipotent.

## III. Intelligibility

Simply as a concept and apart from any question of its exemplification, the intuitive view of omnipotence seems clear. But in effect its intelligibility has been questioned by Harry Frankfurt and by C. Anthony Anderson.[4] Let us see whether either of these philosophers successfully disputes the intelligibility of this concept.[5]

Frankfurt makes the familiar attribution to Descartes of the two views that God has infinite power and that this implies that God could have made mathematical and logical necessities false. Frankfurt claims that "the assertion that a state of affairs could have been brought about ordinarily entails that state of affairs is logically possible."[6] Frankfurt contends that Descartes' position concerning what God could have done appears to entail the logical possibility of the logically impossible. Frankfurt notes that this "appears to make very little sense."[7] Shortly thereafter Frankfurt claims that if the assertion that God has infinite power is construed to entail the logical possibility of the logically impossible, then on this construal the assertion that God has infinite power "seems itself unintelligible."[8]

The intuitive view of omnipotence implies that an omnipotent being would be able to have any logically or mathematically necessary proposition be false. This is the ability from which Frankfurt infers the unintelligibility of Descartes' conception of God's power. So Frankfurt's charge of unintelligibility is equally applicable to the intuitive view of omnipotence.

Alvin Plantinga defends Descartes against Frankfurt's objection.[9] It will help to elucidate the intuitive view to compare it with the position that Plantinga attributes to Descartes. Plantinga construes Descartes to be advocating "universal possibilism"—the doctrine that every proposition is possibly false and possibly true, including each logical truth and each logical falsehood. Plantinga finds this doctrine suggested in Descartes' thesis that God created the eternal truths. This thesis indicates that according to Descartes God could have refrained from creating each eternal truth. This in turn suggests that God could have made true instead the negations of the eternal truths. Plantinga infers from the ascription of this ability to God that in Descartes' view even the eternal truths are possibly false. Since according to Descartes God created absolutely everything, no truth would be exempt from possible falsehood on the same grounds, and likewise, no falsehood would be exempt from possible truth.

This interpretation of Descartes does put him in a position to rebut Frankfurt's charge of unintelligibility. Frankfurt takes Descartes to be committed to the claim that logical impossibilities are nonetheless possible. Plantinga's Descartes can reply that it is no part of his view that there are any logical impossibilities. Each proposition is possibly true, because God could have made it true. As Plantinga remarks, this universal possibilism may be clearly false, but it is not unintelligible. It is not committed to any impossible possibilities.

A mistaken inference underlies both Frankfurt's accusation of unintelligibility and Plantinga's reply on behalf of Descartes. Frankfurt begins with the Cartesian thesis that God could have made an eternal truth false. Frankfurt questions this sort of claim by asking what is meant here by "could." It is at this point, seemingly in order to develop the problem of how to interpret this "could," that Frankfurt writes:

> The assertion that some state of affairs can be brought about ordinarily entails that state of affairs is logically possible.[10]

It is not clear what Frankfurt intends by "ordinarily entails." On one reading, the idea is that to assert in any ordinary sense that a certain state of affairs "can be brought about" entails that the state of affairs is logically possible. This is true. But it is true because of an aspect of the ordinary meaning of the word "can" which is not shared by the meaning of the word "could." Notice that Frankfurt shifts from a Cartesian thesis about what God "could have" done to a claim about what "can be" brought about. "Could" works differently from "can". Some epistemic possibilities expressible with "could" are logically impossible. For example, consider the following assertion about some complex tautologous proposition, an assertion made by someone who understands the proposition without yet realizing that it is a tautology: "This proposition could be true, and also, its negation could be true." This sentence is a natural way to express the epistemic possibility of a proposition and its negation. The sentence so construed expresses a truth, even though the negation of a tautology is not logically possible. But the result of replacing "could" by "can" everywhere in the sentence is not plausible.[11]

Nothing of final importance here turns on a difference in meaning between "can" and "could." The use of "could" is inessential. The intuitive view of omnipotence is equally well expressed in terms of "ability" or "power". Whichever of these terms is used, Frankfurt's point might seem to apply. But the point is mistaken. Admittedly, there is a sense in which it is true that a claim that someone could, or is able, or has the power, to bring about a state of affairs does "ordinarily entail" that the state of affairs is logically possible. If this means that virtually all ordinary instances of such claims assert control over states of affairs which are logically possible, and metaphysically must be logically possible, then it is true. When the claimed possessor of the capacity, ability, or power is a mere mortal and not some supernatural being, the state of affairs said to be subject to control is rarely a logical impossibility. Notice that the state of affairs is also virtually always something that is physically possible too, and technologically feasible as well. This is not because part of what is conveyed in an ascription of a capacity, ability, or power to do something asserts that the deed is a physical and technical possibility. Intelligible ascriptions of ability clearly go beyond those boundaries, and Frankfurt does not suggest that there is any such further limit on intelligible claims concerning what God could do.

In ascriptions to human beings of capabilities, abilities, or powers, we ordinarily take it for granted that they are unable to do what is logically, mathematically, physically, or technically impossible. It is this entirely reasonable assumption of limited human ability that justifies us in ordinarily making such claims only about such possibilities, rather than the use of terms such as "could," "able," and "power". To claim that someone has an ability to make some proposition true is to claim that the person has what it takes to make the proposition true. The claim asserts nothing about the nature of the proposition concerning which the ability is had. When the person is a human being, we reasonably assume that for a proposition to be under the person's control it must be at least a logical and physical possibility. The reason for this assumption is that we obviously lack any ability to surmount the obstacles of logical and physical impossibility. It should be acknowledged that we could not understand an attribution to some being of an ability to do something that is an impossibility, if our understanding this required our knowing how the being is able to accomplish the impossible. But knowing how an ability would be exercised is not required for understanding a claim that someone has the ability. This can be seen by again noting that we clearly understand claims of abilities to do what is beyond current technology, although by hypothesis we lack knowledge of how to do such things. Frankfurt's challenge to the intelligibility of the intuitive view of omnipotence can thus be met.

These considerations show that Plantinga's ascription to Descartes of universal possibilism also rests on a mistake. Again, Plantinga infers from Descartes' claim that God could have made the eternal truths false that Descartes is committed to the possible falsehood of the eternal truths. But we have seen that a claim about a being's ability to render some proposition false asserts nothing about the modal status of the proposition. Descartes can consistently assert that the eternal truths are necessarily true and not possibly false, while maintaining that God "could have made them false" in the sense of God's having had the ability to do this. The claim that God could have done this ascribes to God power over the truth-value of the eternal truths. It does not also assert that the eternal truths are possibly false. The Cartesian position can be stated as follows: Prior to creation, God was able to render false propositions which are logically or mathematically necessarily true. The fact that God had this ability is compatible with the fact that they are not possibly false. Since these propositions are necessarily true, it follows that God does not *exercise* this ability to have them be false under any logically or mathematically possible circumstances. But this does not imply that God did not *have* the ability. It does imply that the ability to have these propositions be false includes the ability to have obtain states of affairs that are logical or mathematical impossibilities.

Claiming this ability for God does not commit Descartes to the view that the falsehood of eternal truths is a possibility of any sort. Likewise, a proponent of the intuitive view of omnipotence who holds that an omnipotent being is possible is not thereby committed to universal possibilism.

C. Anthony Anderson's question about the intelligibility of being able to do the impossible can be asked here. Again the topic is an omnipotent being's alleged power over logical impossibilities. Anderson asks how to understand any claim to the effect that something can be done, when the doing of the deed is something that cannot be.[12] In response to this question we can begin by noting that the following claim has a sense in which it is clearly true:

CBP (short for "Can-Be Principle"). Whatever deed can be done is logically possible.

If the "can be" is to read to express logical possibility, then CB says only:

CBPa. Any deed that is logically possibly done, is logically possibly done.

The claim that even logical impossibilities "can be done" by an omnipotent being, when read to assert only that the being possesses an ability to bring them about, is not incompatible with CBPa. This claim *is* incompatible with:

CBPb. Whatever deed some being is able to do is logically possibly done.

Unlike CBPa, CBPb is not true on logical grounds alone. One thesis of the present paper is that CBPb is at most contingently true. CBPb may be actually true because nothing nearly as powerful as an omnipotent being actually exists. But there is no good reason to deny that CBPb could have been false. As has been argued above, the fact that what is at issue is an ascription to an individual of an ability does not by itself entail that exercise of the ability is a possibility of any sort. The attribution to an individual of any particular ability is simply the claim that the individual has what it takes to get a certain thing done. This may include having what it takes to see to it that some impossibility is true. That would be an incredible claim to make about any of us. This last fact itself shows that the claim is intelligible: what it asserts about us goes too far beyond our actual accomplishments to be believed. It is not an incoherent claim, and it is not an inconsistent claim that asserts the possibility of something that it also asserts to be impossible.

It is impossible to do the impossible. On one reading of the scope of the initial "impossible", it is also impossible to do anything that is not done: just as there is no possible case in which anything impossible is done, there is no possible case in which anything that is not done is done. It is nonetheless clearly intelligible to claim that someone has an ability to do something that is not done. This is to claim that someone has of an ability that is not exercised. It is equally intelligible to claim that someone has an ability to do the impossible. This is to claim that someone has an ability that is not exercised under any possible circumstances. There is no problem in understanding such a claim. It is not as clear that it is possible for someone to have an ability to do the impossible as it is that someone might have an ability to do something that the person never does. But that is a different issue, one that is addressed in section V below.

## IV. Omnipotence and Descartes on the Power of God

The intuitive view of omnipotence is clearly similar to Descartes' account of the power of God. But there is an important difference concerning how much power is required in order to retain omnipotence. Richard LaCroix gives the account of Descartes' view of God's power that I believe to be most faithful to the Cartesian texts.[13] In outline, this is the position that LaCroix attributes to Descartes: Prior to the creation of the world, God could have made absolutely any proposition true, including those that are actually necessarily false. The reason that God was able to do this is that prior to creation only God existed. There was nothing to limit God's choice of what to create—no necessities and no possibilities, no truths and no falsehoods, and no reasons and no values. God created everything. God had the power to create anything else under any conditions.

The abilities of God prior to creation on this account render God omnipotent according to the intuitive view of omnipotence. God had every sort of control over every proposition.[14]

LaCroix presents convincing textual evidence that Descartes also held that in the act of creation God brought it about that there are some things that God is unable to do. God made certain propositions immutable: the eternal truths. After creation, God is no longer able e.g. to make accidents exist independently of a substance, or to bring it about that things that were done are undone.[15] Thus, in Descartes' view God's creation limited God's power. God brought it about that there are propositions that God is not able to render false.

In the intuitive view, an omnipotent being would have the ability to limit its power in any way. For convenience of illustration, let us have a name for an omnipotent being. Let us call her "Genie." Genie is able to do anything, including to change the past. There is a proposition asserting that Genie is unable to alter the past. Because she is omnipotent, Genie is able to make the proposition true, and thus to reduce her abilities as did Descartes' God. But it is not possible for Genie, or any other omnipotent being, to exercise such an ability and remain omnipotent. If she exercises this ability, she renders herself unable to do something. Once there is something that she is unable to do, she is not omnipotent.

In LaCroix's reading Descartes ascribes to God continued omnipotence after God created truths which God was then unable to make false. As evidence for this view, LaCroix quotes:

> For we do not take it as a mark of impotence when someone cannot do something we do not understand to be possible, but only when he cannot do something which we distinctly understand to be possible.[16]

LaCroix notes that according to an account of lacking power where only an inability to do something that is possibly done is a lack of power, God need not lack any power after having become unable to bring about logical impossibilities.

Descartes seems to be right about our judgments of impotence. If someone cannot do something that we see to be impossible, we are not inclined to count this inability as a weakness of any sort. But we can observe on behalf of the intuitive view of omnipotence that any loss of ability leaves a being with something less than wholly unlimited power. Any loss of ability by a formerly omnipotent being implies that the being is no longer all-powerful. It follows that

Descartes' God does not remain omnipotent subsequent to the creation of truths that God is unable to render false.

LaCroix conveys a Cartesian argument intended to support the view that God continues to be omnipotent after creating eternal truths that God is then unable to render false:

> [Descartes] believes that it is no defect of power in God not to be able to countermand the eternal truths because through his power *and* will God brought it about both that the eternal truths exist and that he cannot countermand them; that is, Descartes believes that through his own power and will God *determined himself* by creating what he created.[17]

This argues for the conclusion that God's inability to alter the eternal truths is not a defect in God's power. That conclusion does not imply that God remains omnipotent. It may be no flaw in God that God's powers no longer include this ability. But Descartes' God has undergone a reduction in power. The fact that the reduction was self-imposed does not alter this. It would not be a loss of power simply to refrain from taking an alternative. But to be deprived of an alternative, whether inadvertently or by one's own choice, is to lose an ability. Omnipotence survives no such loss. It may be reasonable to say that Descartes' God gave up omnipotence without becoming any worse for the loss.[18] This should not blind us to the fact that it is a loss of omnipotence.

## V. The Stone Paradox

Application of the intuitive view of omnipotence to the Stone Paradox is simple.[19] Is it metaphysically possible for an omnipotent being, say Genie, to create a stone that the being is unable to life? Well, being omnipotent, Genie is able to do anything. So of course Genie is able to create such a stone, and of course Genie is also able to lift such a stone.

Let us use "TO" as short for "Truly Omnipotent," which in turn is to be construed as short for "able to have any proposition be true and also able to have any proposition be false (including logical, mathematical, and metaphysical impossibilities)." It is metaphysically possible for something to be TO. Various versions of the Stone Paradox might appear to show otherwise. In this section it will be argued that this is not shown, and it cannot be shown because it is not true. Rather than to formulate and attack assorted versions of the Stone Paradox that apply to the hypothesis that a TO being is possible, the relevant facts about a TO being will be simply asserted. The goal of this section is to make it evident that these facts are adequate to refute applicable versions of the Stone Paradox.

Any TO being would be able to create a stone that it would be unable to lift if the stone were to be created, since any TO being would be able to make true a proposition asserting that it has created a stone that it is unable to lift. Indeed, any TO being would have to be able to have it be true that there exists a stone that the being is *already* unable to lift, even though this would be impossible because a TO being is able to lift any stone. TO beings are able to make any proposition true, including these. Since Genie is TO, she is able to have it be true that there is a stone that Genie is unable to lift. We can hypothesize that Genie is contingently TO. If so, then her co-existence with a stone that she is unable to lift is not a metaphysically impossible state of affairs. If Genie is contingently TO, then it is metaphysically possible for Genie to lack various abilities, including the ability to lift a stone. There are metaphysically possible cases in which Genie has been TO, she has created a stone that she is unable to lift, and because of this creation she is no longer TO.

It may be that some TO beings are essentially TO. Generally, arguments to the effect that a certain apparently contingent property might have been essential seem to do no more than to render this an epistemic possibility. Such arguments show only that we do not know anything that excludes the property from being essential to something under some possible conditions. On the other hand, there is no reason to suppose that the property of being TO must be essential to whatever can have it, and there is reason to deny this. Clearly, we can render ourselves unable to do certain things. It does not seem that merely having more power to the point where one's abilities are absolutely unlimited would have to make it the case that all of one's abilities are impossible to give up. If these appearances of contingency are veridical, then an exercise of Genie's ability to create a stone that she is unable to lift would, if exercised in some metaphysically possible situation, render her no longer TO. If she is contingently TO, then creating such a stone in any possible situation would change her into someone who is unable to lift a certain stone,

460 / Earl Conee

and thus no longer TO.

The alternative assumption that Genie is essentially TO also yields no contradiction, however. If Genie is essentially TO, then for her to have the ability to bring about the state of affairs of there being a stone that she is unable to lift would be for Genie to be able to bring about a metaphysical impossibility, because being essentially omnipotent she is essentially able to do anything. It is thus metaphysically impossible that Genie exercise this ability. But Genie's having this ability does not imply any contradiction. Since we are assuming that Genie is essentially TO, she would be able to make true the impossible proposition that Genie is TO and yet unable to lift some stone, and she would be able to make true the impossible proposition that she is not TO. Any TO being must by definition be able to have any proposition be true and these are not exceptions. Such abilities are not necessarily exercised. Because of this, the claim that an essentially TO being has the ability to create a stone that the being is unable to lift implies no contradiction.

There is one apparently good reason for denying that a TO being is a metaphysical possibility. The reason is based on a principle requiring the possibility of exercising any ability that it is possible to have. Here is the principle:

The Having-Exercising Principle ("HEP" for short). If it is in some way possible (e.g., physically possible, metaphysically possible) to have some ability, then it is in the same way possible to exercise the ability.

Clearly if HEP is true, then no TO being, whether essentially or contingently TO, is metaphysically possible, since being TO requires having abilities that are not possibly exercised. HEP can be reasonably defended on the following grounds. It is intuitive that in order for a being really to have the ability to make some proposition true, there must be nothing that prevents the being from exercising the ability, except self-imposed restraint. Yet if any exercise of some alleged ability would be impossible, then the states of affairs that constitute the relevant necessity, e.g., in the case of physical necessity the laws of nature, would seem not to be self-imposed restraints. Rather, they would seem to be external barriers to any exercise of the ability. It might be inferred from such considerations that no one could have any ability unless it was possible for the person to exercise the ability.

The intuition concerning the lack of any external barrier to the exercise of an ability can be born out without commitment to HEP. The laws of nature, metaphysics, and logic are not relevantly "external" to a TO being. Like the Cartesian God, a TO being has a choice about which laws obtain, since a TO being is able to have true instead the negations of the propositions asserting the laws. And unlike the Cartesian God, a being who is TO has not deprived itself of any ability, including the ability to have any law cease to obtain. However, there are possible situations in which a TO being allows the existing laws always to obtain. In these situations, a TO being has an ability to break the laws that is not exercised anywhere within the range of possibilities that are allowed by those laws. Yet only self-imposed restraint stops a TO being from exercising the ability. Thus, the argument in defense of HEP fails. What is plausible in the argument is compatible with the denial of HEP.

It is more extreme to claim that someone's abilities to act might extend beyond the limits of logical possibility than it is to make the familiar claim that someone, namely God, is able to do things that are physically impossible. But the plausibility of the familiar claim can serve to render HEP dubious. God is supposed to have an ability that is not exercised in any physically possible situation. This seems at least to be possible. Yet HEP denies it. So much the worse for HEP. Without HEP, there is no good reason to deny the more extreme claim that it is possible to have an ability to do the impossible.[20]

## VI. A Problem of Evil

The problem of evil can be raised in terms of the intuitive view of omnipotence. It seems to be metaphysically possible for a TO being also to be omniscient and morally flawless. But could a being who has these three properties allow evil to exist? This does not seem to be metaphysically possible. It seems that it would be morally necessary for any such being to exercise its ability to make it true that no evil ever exists. Since the being would be morally flawless, it would always comply with this moral necessity, and thus it would never be accompanied by the existence of evil under any metaphysically possible circumstances.

We should consider a free will defense of the compatibility of the existence of evil with the existence of an omniscient, morally perfect TO being. Suppose that the morally valuable sort of free act must be an act that no being other than the agent of the act brings about. If so, then it is metaphysically impossible for any being to bring it about that some other being act in the morally valuable free way. Alvin Plantinga's version of a free will defense is based partly on this supposition about the morally valuable sort of freedom.[21] Plantinga argues that a certain omniscient, morally perfect, omnipotent being, namely God, metaphysically might have been in a position where, whichever other free agents God created, some of them would produce evil by free action. Suppose also, as Plantinga does, that God's abilities are limited to metaphysical possibilities. Utilizing the additional assumption that it is metaphysically possible for the existence of free acts to be morally valuable enough to outweigh some freely caused evil, Plantinga infers that it is metaphysically possible for such a God and evil to exist together.

If the intuitive view of omnipotence is correct, then Plantinga's free will defense does not succeed. An indispensable assumption of the defense is that it is metaphysically possible for an omnipotent God to have been in a position where some free agents would use their freedom to act with evil results, no matter which free agents God created from among those that God was able to create. But it is not metaphysically possible for a TO God to be in such a position. A TO God would be able to bring it about that there are free agents and no evil ever exists. There is a proposition that asserts this and any TO being would be able to make this proposition true, no matter what position the TO being was in.

Plantinga argues that there is a metaphysically possible position for an omnipotent God to be in prior to creation, from which it would be metaphysically impossible for God to create free agents without evil ensuing. It can be granted that this is true while maintaining the intuitive view of omnipotence. In such a possible situation God would face the obstacle of metaphysical impossibility to creating free agents with no evil. Metaphysical impossibility is not an insuperable obstacle to a TO being. A TO God would always be able to create free agents without evil. If an omniscient, morally perfect, TO God were to create free agents from the position that Plantinga describes, where creating them while allowing no evil would be a metaphysical impossibility, such a God always would create free agents without evil, in spite of the impossibility of this. Such a God would have to prevent all evil in order to remain morally perfect. It is not possible for an omniscient, TO being who is morally flawless to allow evil to exist, since under any possible circumstances it would be a moral flaw for any being knowingly to allow evil for the sake of something that the being is knowingly able to achieve without evil.[22] An omniscient TO being would knowingly possess abilities to achieve anything without evil. Thus, it is metaphysically impossible for an omniscient, morally perfect being who is Truly Omnipotent to allow evil for the sake of creating free agents. In the case of such a being, the free will defense fails.

## VII. Knowledge That The Actual Is Not Impossible

Since the free will defense fails if being omnipotent implies having control over the truth-value of every proposition, it might seem that our knowledge that evil actually exists would enable us to establish directly that no TO, morally perfect, omniscient being actually exists. But establishing this may not be simple at all. The above objection to a free will defense asserts that a TO, morally perfect, omniscient being would, when in certain situations, bring about something impossible. It was argued that it would be impossible for such a being to co-exist with evil. But then an omniscient, morally perfect, TO being may actually co-exist with evil if the actual world is an impossible world.[23] And perhaps it is! That is, perhaps the actual world is an impossible world where all that we ordinarily think we know is true, including that evil exists, and it is also true that it is metaphysically necessary that an omniscient TO being is morally required to prevent all evil. Perhaps the actual world is an impossible world, impossible precisely because evil nonetheless does exist in the presence of a TO, morally perfect, omnipotent being.

It might seem easy to know that these "perhapses" are not the case. After all, it seems obvious that we know the actual world to be a world in which only possibilities obtain. But in fact it is not clear that we have this knowledge and, more remarkably, it is hard to see how this knowledge would help us here even if we do have it. The difficulty in knowing that the actual world is metaphysically possible can be conveyed as follows. We can take it for granted that we know that evil exists and that we know all of the other ordinary non-modal facts that we think we know. It can be taken for granted that we know that these facts are jointly possible, and that we know that it is metaphysically impossible for anything actual to be impossible. The trouble is that all of these things would be true if this were an impossible situation in which some impossibility was also true. All of the knowledge that we have taken for granted is present in such an impossible situation, just as it is present in various possible situations. Thus, all such knowledge seems insufficient to enable us to distinguish which sort of situation we are actually in. And if it is insufficient, then how can we know that only possibilities actually obtain? [24]

It is difficult to see what, if anything, enables us to know that the actual world is possible. In one familiar sense our assumed knowledge "entails" that the actual world is possible: in every possible world where we know these things, only possibilities obtain. But this entailment is useless toward establishing the conclusion that only possibilities actually obtain. Knowledge of this entailment can be used to learn that conclusion only if it is supplemented with the knowledge that the actual world is a possible world. And that is precisely what is in question here.

Worse, suppose that we do know that the actual world is possible. We know too that nothing can possibly be both possible and impossible. These two items of knowledge might prompt us to infer that the actual world is not impossible. But what follows is that it is impossible for the actual world to be both possible and impossible, or in other words, it follows that for the world actually to be both possible and impossible is an impossible situation. So we have established that it is impossible. But the question remains: What enables us to know that this impossible situation does not actually obtain?

Such considerations constitute an epistemic puzzle that is independent of the topic of omnipotence. But we can address the puzzle by continuing to pursue the question of what the problem of evil enables us to know about the existence of an omniscient, morally perfect TO being. We seem to be rationally required to draw the conclusion that there is no way to know on the basis of entailments of other things we know that a morally perfect, omniscient, TO being does not actually exist, since we seem unable to know in this way that nothing impossible is true. It might be inferred that we must know this non-inferentially, or not at all. Since the former alternative seems hopeless, the knowledge seems to be unattainable.

This skeptical conclusion is not justified. First we should be clear about how much is at stake. All knowledge by inference is subject to the same challenge: How do we know that this is not an impossible situation where the premises of the deduction are true and yet the conclusion is not true?

This problem is somewhat diminished by the observation that if this challenge presents the only obstacle to knowing a conclusion by deductive inference, then there is no obstacle to knowing at least this: it is impossible for the conclusion not to be true. Similarly, if our assumed knowledge establishes that there is no possible situation where what we actually know is true and an omniscient, morally perfect, TO being exists, then we can thereby know at least that the existence of such a being is impossible.

It will be informative to turn for a time from knowledge to reasons. We have reasoned roughly as follows. Known preventable evil is morally tolerable only when it is needed for the sake of gaining something of overriding moral value. For a TO being, all evil is preventable and no evil is needed in order to bring about anything. An omniscient TO being would know these things. Such considerations provide good reason to believe that a omniscient TO being would be morally required to prevent all evil. We have no reason to deny that this is a moral requirement. Also, we have good reason to believe, and no reason to deny, that some evil has not been prevented. Each of us has learned about enough suffering to have good reason to believe that evil actually exists. These considerations give us good reason to believe that no omniscient, morally perfect, TO being actually exists.

These are rational grounds for denying the existence of such a being. At least, intuitions about reasons provide good reason to believe, and no reason to deny, that they are rational grounds for accepting this conclusion. None of these propositions for which good reason has just been claimed is being held to be true in every last world, possible or impossible, where our reasons are true. Rather, a certain defeasible reason-giving relation is being held to obtain between the reasons and what they support. The reasons do not guarantee the truth of what they support in all possible worlds, much less in all worlds whatsoever. They are support, not proof. Thus, it is no refutation of this sort of reasoning to point out that in certain impossible worlds the reasons are true while what they support is not true. The same point applies to the claim that they are good reasons in the absence of overriding defeaters. This claim is not true in various impossible worlds. But that fact by itself is no refutation of the intuitive case for the reasons actually being good and undefeated reasons.

Such reasoning is never irrefutable. Metaphysically possible refutations take the form of evidence that argues against what the reasons support or evidence that the support is unreliable. In the absence of such a refutation, we have what can be called a "doubly fallible" rational case for the truth of the conclusion. The double fallibility of such reasons consists first in their supporting falsehoods in some possible cases where they are not overridden and second in their being no good as reasons even when not overridden in some impossible cases. Yet such doubly fallible reasons are good reasons, if they are not overridden and this is not an impossible world. In the absence of a successful objection to the problem of evil as it affects an omniscient, morally perfect, TO being, our reasons for thinking that no omniscient, morally perfect TO being exists are not overridden. So they are good reasons for thinking this, if the actual world is not impossible.

We have the same fallible sort of good reasons for thinking that the actual world is not impossible. The intuitive credibility of the principle of non-contradiction is a good reason for thinking that no logical impossibility is true. Logical paradoxes provide prima facie counter-evidence. Some of these paradoxes have no compelling solution, but all have solutions that are more reasonable to believe than is any contradiction. There are purported non-logical impossibilities, propositions asserting states of affairs contrary to seeming metaphysical necessities, such as a proposition asserting the existence of a sleeping universal. None of these propositions is reasonably thought to be both genuinely impossible and actually true. Considerations like these constitute good reason to believe that nothing actual is impossible. Again this is fallible reasoning. The reasons hold in impossible worlds where they are misleading and they hold in impossible worlds where they are not even reasons. But intuitively they are good reasons to believe the conclusion and we have no reason either to deny this or to think that they are unreliable.

We can now return to the topic of knowledge that nothing actual is impossible. It is a familiar point in epistemology that our knowledge of the external world is based on what are at least "singly" fallible reasons, if we have such knowledge on the basis of reasons. The reasons that we have for believing any contingent proposition about the external world all include some proposition that is supported without being entailed by its support. These reasons must give knowledge without guaranteeing the truth of what they support. If they can confer knowledge of some external world proposition, this is only because the support that the reasons provide confirms the proposition, or engenders for the proposition a coherent system of beliefs, or renders the proposition probable, or the like. This deductively invalid sort of support exists in some possible situations where what is supported is not true. The reasons fail to provide knowledge in such possible worlds. Thus they are fallible in at least this way. But still, it is plausible that external world skepticism is false, and that such reasons do give knowledge of the external world. They are not always overridden and they do not always otherwise fail us.

Our reasons for thinking that nothing actual is impossible are fallible in a different way. They do "entail" that the actual world is not impossible, but only in the previously mentioned unhelpful sense: any possible world where our reasons obtain is not impossible. The problem is that these reasons fail in impossible worlds where they obtain. But now we are able to see that this shows only that the reasons do not relevantly "guarantee" that the world is not impossible. Unlike the case of fallible external world evidence, this lack of a guarantee is not a lack of entailment. But the epistemic relationship of reasons to what they support seems fully analogous to the way in which our reasons for external world beliefs fail to guarantee the truth of those beliefs while nonetheless providing justification for them. In both cases the supported propositions are false in some worlds where the reasons obtain and are not overridden. But the analogy indicates that this sort of failure is not ruinous. Both sorts of reasons seem capable of giving knowledge where they do not fail us. If our fallible reasons do give us knowledge of external world propositions, then our reasons for believing that nothing actual is impossible seem equally suitable for giving us knowledge of this. Likewise, our reasons for believing that no omniscient, morally perfect, being TO actually exists, though they too are fallible reasons, seem good enough to enable us to know that no such being exists.

## VIII. Multiple Omnipotent Beings

Suppose that it is metaphysically possible for a TO being to exist. Is it also metaphysically possible for two or more TO beings to exist?[25]

There is no good reason to deny that the answer to this question is "yes." TO beings metaphysically might have existed in any number. The only reasonable consideration that suggests otherwise concerns potential conflicts between omnipotent beings. Would multiple omnipotent beings limit one another's power?

It seems plain that no conflict between TO beings need arise. Numerous TO beings might exist together without making any attempt to have incompatible propositions be true. Any number of TO beings might entirely concur about how things are to be.

Could there be a true "conflict of wills" between TO beings? This has several interpretations. First, one TO being might exercise an ability to have true the proposition that tigers exist while another TO being wants, or even wills, that no tigers exist. This is a metaphysically possible case, as long as the other TO being is able in some way to have it be the case that there are no tigers.[26] A second sort of conflict of wills occurs where one TO being exercises its ability both to be such that there are tigers and also to be such that another TO being is rendered unable to prevent the existence of tigers. There is no good reason to deny the metaphysical possibility of one TO being rendering another no longer TO by depriving the other of an ability. Since the deprivation is suffered by a TO being, it follows that the being is able to resist the deprivation. But it also follows that the being is able not to resist, and thus to be deprived in this way.

Another sort of case is one in which one TO being exercises its ability to be such that there are tigers and another TO being exercises its ability to be such that there are no tigers. This sort of case is not a metaphysical possibility, since if any being exercises an ability to have something true, this metaphysically necessitates that it is true.

But there is no reason to think that, if there metaphysically might have been two TO beings, then they metaphysically might both exercise abilities to make incompatible propositions true. To see that this is not implied by the possibility that two TO beings exist, it is helpful to compare the case with ordinary cases in which two individuals each have some ability to alter the same thing. It might be that you are able to be the one who picks up the book from the table, and so am I. In some possible situations one of us exercises this ability; in other possible situations neither of us does. These possibilities give no good reason to believe that it is metaphysically possible for us each to exercise simultaneously the ability to be the one who picks up the book. It need not be possible for us each to retain the ability, come what may, in order for it to be possible that we both have the ability. Likewise, the possibility that multiple omnipotent beings exist does not imply the possibility of some impossible mutual exercise of power.

## Conclusion

We initially conceive of omnipotence as absolutely unlimited power. It has been argued here that there is no good reason to modify this conception. The intuitive view of omnipotence is a fully defensible view. Its application to philosophical issues involving omnipotence shows that the concept rewards philosophical attention.[27]

### Notes

1. The exact nature of this connection between an ability and the corresponding potentially true proposition depends on controversial metaphysical facts about the relation between true propositions and states of affairs. In one view, a state of affairs is a concrete entity constituted by objects and their properties. The state of affairs of Richard Nixon being the U.S. President consists of Nixon having the property of being U.S. President. When Nixon has this property, the state of affairs that is so constituted makes true the proposition that Nixon is U.S. President. When the state of affairs does not exist, the proposition is made false, either by the absence of this state of affairs or by the existence of the state of affairs of it not being the case that Nixon is U.S President. The proposition that Nixon is U.S. President is an abstract entity which asserts the existence of the state of affairs and which exists whether or not this assertion is factual. In this view of how propositions

relate to states of affairs, the potential to make true the proposition that corresponds to having a certain ability is most naturally understood as an ability to bring into existence the truth-making state of affairs. This is the ability is to bring into being what is asserted by the proposition. In this view, by being able to do this one can have control over the truth-value of the proposition.

The other main view of the relation of a proposition to its corresponding state of affairs is an identity view. Each proposition is identical to a state of affairs. The proposition is true when, and because, the state of affairs obtains. If the state of affairs does not obtain, it is a false proposition. But the proposition, and hence the state of affairs, exists when it is not true. In that case, the state of affairs, i.e., the false proposition, exists but does not obtain.

According to this view as well, a person's having an ability implies that a certain proposition is potentially true. But in this case exercising the ability does not consist in rendering true the proposition via bringing into being a truth-making state of affairs. Rather, the proposition itself is a state of affairs. An ability to make the proposition true is an ability to make the state of affairs obtain.

2.  In order to account for every ability by a relation of an agent to a proposition, we can assume that there is a single proposition either made true by, or identical to, any state of affairs of any complexity and detail, including states of affairs so detailed and complete as to constitute whole alternative realities. That is, we can assume that for each world, whether the world is possible or impossible, there is a single proposition that asserts exactly what is true in the world. We can ensure a sufficient abundance of worlds, possible and impossible, by counting each combination of truth-values for every proposition as yielding a different world. Notice that we are thereby provided with an endless diversity of impossible worlds as well as possible worlds.

3.  Though this is not essential to the argument, it is worth noting that being able to do anything includes being able to fail at anything. It might be thought that an omnipotent being would have to have an inevitably effective will. That is, it might be thought that any omnipotent being would invariably succeed at whatever the being wills. But if it were necessary that an omnipotent being achieved whatever it willed, then it would be impossible for an omnipotent being to launch an ineffective attempt. This would be a limit in ability. Unlike we who are able to try and fail, omnipotent beings would be unable to fail in their attempts. Having an ability to fail is not often desirable. But failing is something that we do, and intuitively an omnipotent being would have to be able to do anything that we do. This requires having an unlimited ability to fail. Concerning any goal, an omnipotent being would have to be able to try to attain that goal and yet fail. (Of course, to be omnipotent the being would also have to be able to succeed.)

4.  Frankfurt's objection is given in section V of his "Descartes on the Creation of the Eternal Truths," *The Philosophical Review* vol. LXXXVI,

no. 1 (January, 1977); Anderson's objection is given in section 2 of his "Divine Omnipotence and Impossible Tasks," *International Journal for the Philosophy of Religion* vol. 15, no. 1 (January 1984).

5. Frankfurts's challenge to the coherence of the intuitive view arises as he develops his interpretation of Descartes work concerning God's power over the eternal truths. Anderson's challenge arises as he examines the tenability of one position that might be taken in an attempt to solve the stone paradox. Both Descartes' view of divine power and the stone paradox are discussed below in sections IV and V, respectively. This section conveys just those fragments of Anderson's and Frankfurt's work that bear on the intelligibility of the intuitive view of omnipotence.

6. Frankfurt, op. cit, p.43.

7. Ibid.

8. Ibid., p. 44.

9. Plantinga's defense occurs in section IV of his *Does God Have A Nature?* (The Aquinas Lecture, 1980) Marquette University Press (Milwaukee, 1980).

10. Frankfurt, op. cit., p. 112.

11. Thus, epistemic cases illustrate that asserting that some state of affairs "could" be true does not entail that that state of affairs is logically possible. And only "could" is definitely relevant here. Descartes' claim under discussion is that God could have made an eternal truth false. For the sake of Cartesian scholarship at least, the semantic difference between "could" and "can" may be crucial. Perhaps, as Richard LaCroix argues, Descartes differentiates between what God *could* have done prior to creation and what God *can* do after creation. This is discussed section IV below.

12. Anderson, op. cit., p. 112.

13. Richard LaCroix, "Descartes on God's Ability To Do The Logically Impossible," *The Canadian Journal of Philosophy* vol. XIV, no. 3 (September 1984), pp. 455-475. LaCroix's paper includes an extensive critique of Harry Frankfurt's interpretation in "Descartes on the Creation of the Eternal Truths," op. cit. For another interpretation of Descartes' position, see E.M. Curley, "Descartes on the Creation of the Eternal Truths" *The Philosophical Review* vol. LCII, no. 4, (October 1984) pp. 569-597.

14. There is a significant metaphysical difference between the Cartesian God's wholly unaccompanied situation prior to creation and the circumstances needed to be omnipotent in the intuitive view. But the difference does not affect the power that is needed to be omnipotent. It has been taken for granted here that propositions exist independently of the creative activities of any being. This seems to be a safe assumption for the purpose of conveying the intuitive view of omnipotence. Attributing control over the truth-value of every proposition is an expedient way to identify what is included in having control over absolutely everything. It does not seem also to be required in order to be omnipotent that the being create the propositions themselves (though

it is required than any omnipotent being be *able* to do this, since there is a proposition asserting that the being does so). According to LaCroix's interpretation of Descartes, prior to creation Descartes' God had nothing with which to work. God created all truths, made them true, and gave them their modal status. Any proposition that God actually made true or false, God could have made false or true and could have given any modal status. This much power is clearly sufficient for being omnipotent in the intuitive view. Whether it is also necessary for omnipotence is a different matter. It seems not to be necessary. It seems that the mere existence of uncreated propositions is no limit on a being's power, as long as their truth-values are wholly in the being's control. In any case, in LaCroix's reading Descartes' God prior to creation clearly has all it takes to be omnipotent in the intuitive view.

15. LaCroix gives citations for these examples and his case for his interpretation to them on p. 463 and p. 464 of "Descartes on God's Ability To Do The Logically Impossible," op. cit.

16. This citation is from Antony Kenny's translation of *Descartes - Philosophical Letters* (Oxford: Clarenden, 1970) p. 241. The citation and LaCroix's discussion of it occur in "Descartes on God's Ability To Do The Logically Impossible," op. cit., p. 464.

17. Ibid, p. 451. LaCroix's text for this argument is Descartes' Sixth Replies, as given in Haldane and Ross's translation of *The Philosophical Works of Descartes* (New York: Dover, 1955). p. 250. The Sixth Replies commit Descartes to the view that in creation God freely determined himself. Where it goes beyond this, the argument is by LaCroix on Descartes' behalf.

18. But see Section VI below, where it is argued that exercising this ability might have served a morally necessary purpose.

19. For literature on the Stone Paradox, see selections 20-25 of Urban and Walton's anthology, *The Power of God* (New York: Oxford, 1978).

20. There is a plausible apparent rival to the intuitive view of omnipotence. The rival account asserts that being omnipotent is identical to being as powerful as it is possible to be. We are now in a position to see that this account is reasonably thought to be extentionally equivalent to the intuitive view. We now see that there is no good reason to deny that is it possible to have abilities to do all of those deeds that are not done under any possible circumstances. If this is possible, then in order to be as powerful as it is possible to be, a being would have to be able to do the impossible as well as the possible, just as is required in the intuitive view of omnipotence.

21. Plantinga's fullest exposition of his version of the free will defense is in section IX of *The Nature of Necessity* (Oxford, Clarendon, 1974). This is my source for subsequent attributions.

22. If it were the case that something impossible was true, perhaps this very impossibility would be something evil about the world (as Edward Wierenga has suggested to me). It is not plausible that impossibility is a moral evil. It does not seem that impossibility might morally outweigh

the evil of suffering with the result that it would be morally better to allow suffering than to bring about an impossibility. But even if impossibility is a moral evil, a TO being is not stuck with that fact. A TO being would be able to make it true that the existence of an impossibility is not at all evil. This too would be a morally required part of its creative work.

23. Alvin Plantinga and Edward Wierenga independently suggested (in private communications) that the problem of evil for a TO being might be solved, or at least dissolved, by the hypothesis that the actual world is an impossible world that includes evil and yet, though this is impossible, it is nonetheless created by a TO, omniscient, morally perfect being.

24. Some philosophers might think that we can acquire this knowledge by engaging in the following reasoning. Either the world is possible or it is impossible. If the former, then by definition only possibilities obtain. If the latter, then every proposition is true, since there is only one impossible world. It is the world where every proposition is true. Thus, either way, it is true that only possibilities obtain. Q.E.D.

This reasoning relies on the objectionable premise that there is only one impossible world. The idea that impossible worlds are comprehensive ways that things could not have been does not support this view, nor does the method of individuating worlds that is described in note 2 above. There are endlessly many different comprehensive ways that things could not have been, and there are endlessly many different impossible combinations of truth-values for the propositions. It might be observed that it is logically necessary for all propositions to be true if any logical impossibility is true. This can be granted while defending the multiplicity of impossible worlds. This point is accommodated by the fact that logical necessities do not hold in all worlds. States of affairs that are contrary to logical necessity are some of the impossibilities that obtain in various impossible worlds. In some of these impossible worlds, some but not all logical impossibilities obtain, and not every proposition is true.

Thinking about impossible worlds can be vexing. The fact that a world involves some sort of impossibility can seem to constitute some sort of refutation of any view that is committed to such a world. But no. That is just how impossible worlds are.

25. The question of how many omnipotent beings can exist together is discussed in sections 13-15 of Urban and Walton, op. cit. See also Mele and Smith, "The New Paradox of The Stone." *Faith and Philosophy* vol. 5, no. 3 (July 1988) pp. 283-290.

26. In note 3 above it is argued that TO beings are capable of unsuccessful attempts.

27. I am grateful for comments and correspondence on topics in this paper from C. Anthony Anderson, Richard Feldman, Gareth Matthews, Alvin Plantinga and Edward Wierenga.

Philosophical Perspectives, 5, Philosophy of Religion, 1991

# TEMPORAL ACTUALISM AND SINGULAR FOREKNOWLEDGE

## Christopher Menzel
## Texas A&M University

Suppose we believe that God created the world. Then surely we want there to have been some rational basis for its creation. We don't want it to have been a divine *accident* that, say, the laws of motion are as they are, or that there are people. Rather, we want to say, God *intended*, in some sense at least, to create *this* world.[1] Along the same lines, most theists want to hold that God didn't just guess or hope that the world would take one course or another, but rather that he *knew* precisely what was going to take place in the world he planned to create. Call this familiar conception of divine knowledge and, more generally, intentionality, the *standard* conception.

Now, among the facts that make up the world there are particular, or *singular*, facts—facts involving specific individuals. Thus, one might reason, since God intended that this world exist, then among the things that he intended before creation was that *Reagan* exist; and among the things he knew was that *Prior* would be a philosopher. Indeed, scripture itself appears to lend support here: "all things were known to the Lord God before they were created," one reads in Ecclesiasticus.[2] At the same time, however, it seems that, before creation, God could not have intended or known any such things. For at the time there just *wasn't* any such person as Reagan to serve as the object of God's intentions; there *wasn't* any such person as Prior for God to know anything about.

So the standard conception appears to be at odds with the appealing and commonsensical view that there are no "future" individuals beyond those that already exist in the present. Call the latter view *temporal actualism*, or *actualism* for short. This is of course not a new problem. But past solutions to it involve metaphysical commitments that are, by my lights anyway, wholly unbecoming. In this paper, after canvassing previous approaches, I will propose a solution that seems to preserve both actualism and a suitably robust form of the standard conception while avoiding the pitfalls of the past.

## A Timeless Solution

Before digging in too deeply, though, we should consider the idea that this is a specious dilemma. One might simply argue that the problem dissolves if we take God to be "outside of time." For if he is—if he sees the entire history of the created universe in a single transtemporal glance, so to say—then he is eternally aware of any object that exists at any time. Thus, one could say on this view that God intended that Reagan exist before his creation in the sense that, at that time (no less than at present), it was nonetheless eternally true that God intended that Reagan exist, and he knew before creation that Prior was to be a philosopher in the sense that, at that time, God eternally grasped Prior's being a philosopher.

Well, maybe. But there are two difficulties with this move that make it of dubious worth here. First, it is not at all clear what to make of the idea that God is outside of time—not that it is pellucidly clear what it is to say he's *in* time either, but at least we've got pretty good intuitions about what *that* is like. Second, though, it's not clear that the move to timelessness really buys us anything, since the same issue that spawns the move seems to arise anew in a modal guise. Specifically, theists characteristically hold that God could have created some other world than this one, and hence that he knew prior to creation (or knew eternally) not only what was going in fact to happen, but what *could* have happened as well. This seems a natural extension of the standard conception. However, it could have happened that there were things other than the things that actually exist. Had that happened, there would have been singular facts about those things, and hence such singular possibilities are among the things that could have been. Thus, by the standard conception, God knew those possibilities prior to creation (or eternally).[3] But as above, timelessness notwithstanding, it doesn't seem that God could have known any such thing, since there would never have been a time when the subjects of those purported possibilities existed; they would never have *been there* at any time to be the subjects of the modal information in question. So, timelessness notwithstanding, the standard conception appears to be at odds with the appealing and commonsensical view—*modal* actualism—that there are no "possible" individuals other than those that actually exist.

The transtemporalist may be tempted to respond that possible facts are somehow different from future facts: future facts *really will* obtain, whereas modal facts won't; there is thus a certain unreality about possible facts, a certain ungroundedness in actuality that doesn't afflict future ones. But this is a confusion. Of course possible facts *won't* (in general) obtain; that's why they are only possible and not future. But just as future facts *really will* obtain, so possible ones *really could have* obtained. Possible facts are no less (and no more) real relative to the actual world than future ones are relative to the present moment. There just is no relevant asymmetry that warrants any such invidious distinctions.

Now, of course, the defender of timelessness could suggest, heroically, that God is not only outside of time, but "outside of modality" as well—that he takes in not only the history of the actual world but the histories of all possible worlds in a single transmodal glance. Most, I suspect, would shy away from so daring—not to mention marginally coherent—a move, and seek a solution elsewhere. It appears to me, however, that any solution that might be found to the modal case would generate an analogous solution to the temporal case, thus rendering the initial move to timelessness otiose (assuming, of course, one has no *other* reasons for taking God to be timeless). Even if not, though, since we have to broach the same kinds of issues either way, we are better off simply avoiding the complications of eternality, retracing our steps, and considering the dilemma in its original temporal guise.

## Possibilism Reconsidered

But what after all is so bad about possibilism? The standard conception in all its glory can be preserved and the obscurities of timelessness (and the specter of transmodalism) can be neatly sidestepped if only we take the possibilist plunge. For then God's knowledge of the future, indeed of all possible futures, in all their singular detail prior to creation is easily explained, since all the singular information that could ever be already falls within the divine purview at any time.

Indeed, some of the medievals argued that possibilism *had* to be true in order to explain the existence of, hence also the existence of future facts about, contingent particulars. For in creating the world, the argument seems to have been, God had to actualize something, i.e., there had to *be* something actualiz*able*. Avicenna, for example, seems to suggest this in the following passage:

> [i]t is necessary with respect to everything that came into existence that before it came into existence, it was in itself possibly existent. For if it had not been possibly existent in itself, it never would exist at all. Moreover, the possibility of its existence does not consist in the fact that an agent could produce it or that an agent has power over it. Indeed, an agent would scarcely have power over it, if the thing itself were not possible in itself...[4]

Okay, so it's not a very *good* argument. Geach diagnoses the error here—correctly, I think—as a sort of scope fallacy.[5] To explain how there could be particulars at all, a given man, say, we need only hold that God brings it about that $\exists x\mathbf{M}x$, i.e., that God brings it about that a man exist (with such and such other properties presumably), which doesn't force a possibilist reading of the quantifier; it requires only that we attribute sufficient conceptual resources to God (about which much more below). It doesn't follow, in particular, that therefore, in creating a man, $\exists x$(God brings it about that $\mathbf{M}x$), i.e., that there is some $x$ such that God brings it about that *it* be a man, which does seem to force possibilism. As Prior puts it, there is no Barcan formula for 'God brings it about that'.[6] Avicenna's error then is in thinking that God requires some power over pre-existent possibilia in order to create any particular thing at all; to the contrary, he needs only the power to create things of a given *sort*, and it is simply in exercising that power that a particular individual of that sort comes to be.

However, even if we grant that it is a confusion to suppose that there had to be some pre-existent substance for God to actualize in order for him to create, one might still argue that the theoretical power of possibilism in the present context is sufficient justification for the view. Nonexistent possibilia are not needed to explain the existence of particulars, but rather to preserve, powerfully and elegantly, the standard conception.

There are of course familiar objections to possibilia that can be raised here—most notably the dubious distinction between being and existence—to which I am more than sympathetic. However, more relevant in this context are theological difficulties.

The first of these is that possibilism seems to undercut the doctrine of creation *ex nihilo*. For if the possibilist account is accurate, then the creation of the physical universe was not *really* creation from *nothing*, but mere change, a mere (well, perhaps not exactly *mere*) matter of conferring the property of existence on previously subsisting possibilia.

Moreover, if this is how it works, then presumably possibilia subsist *necessarily*, since God knows all singular possibilities necessarily, and there wouldn't be such possibilities without the possibilia they involve. But this raises a dilemma. For either God creates—hence necessarily creates—the possibilia or he doesn't. If he doesn't, then this seems to compromise his sovereignty, his aseity. God then is not the source of all being, the creator of all that is other than himself. Rather, he is just one more necessary being among countless others, all subsisting independent of the divine will, and beyond the reach of the divine power. On the other hand, if he does create them necessarily, then this raises a problem for divine freedom: God had no choice but to create subsisting possibilia, a consequence at once undesirable and unintuitive. It is no doubt possible to live with these difficulties. But they are uncomfortable at best; we are certainly warranted in casting about for feasible actualist alternatives.

## St. Thomas on Divine Ideas

There's something right about possibilism. For there had to be some sort of antecedent to an existing thing within the divine purview, something that could serve as the subject matter of God's creative choices, else his creation would be nonrational and unmotivated. Avicenna's use of possibilia is out of step with creation *ex nihilo*, as we just noted. There is no antecedent stuff to which God adds the property of existence. But there do have to be some sort of antecedent *models* that guided the divine mind in its decision making, and grounded its knowledge of the world's future course.

Geach's reply to Avicenna hints at a solution. The idea there was that, to avoid possibilism, one need only to attribute to God sufficient conceptual resources. This is the line that Thomas pursued. For

Thomas, the conceptual resources in question were *divine ideas*, beings of reason dwelling in the divine mind. Divine ideas were typically invoked in response to the problem of how God, who first and foremost knows his own essence, could ever even conceive of anything other than himself, and hence could ever have any rational basis for creation in the first place. The answer, championed by most medievals in one form or another, was that among the things God must know in knowing his essence is the infinitely many ways in which his essence is imitable. But for his essence to be imitable is for it to be such that it is possibly imitated in something *else*. In this way, then, God is able to conceive of things other than himself. Thus Thomas:

> Inasmuch as God knows His own essence perfectly, He knows it according to every mode in which it can be known. Now it can be known not only as it is in itself, but as it can be participated in by creatures according to some kind of likeness. But every creature has its own proper species, according to which it participates in some way in the likeness of the divine essence. Therefore, as God knows His essence as so imitable by such a creature, He knows it as the particular model and idea of that creature.[7]

Indeed, since nothing can exist without imitating the divine essence, in virtue of his conceiving all the ways in which his essence is imitable God can be said to conceive all possible beings.

The suggestion, then, is that, rather than ontologically independent subsistents, possibilia are products of the divine intellect, secreted as it were by God's conceptual activity, and hence, analogous to our own thoughts, rightly thought to depend on him for their existence—in a sense, to be created by him.[8] Since God's cognitive powers are necessarily as they are, he necessarily conceives every possible way in which his essence is imitable, and hence necessarily creates every *possibile*. This move therefore grasps the second of the above dilemma's two horns. However, construed in this way, the necessity of possibilia is a natural consequence of God's cognitive perfection—he cannot fail to conceive every way in which his essence is imitable—and hence the necessity of their creation cannot be considered any more of an infringement on God's freedom than can his inability to sin. Where divine freedom *is* relevant is in the matter of which if any of the infinitely many possibilia shall be *exemplified*. And there is nothing in the doctrine at hand to suggest that God's choices here are anything less than free and contingent.[9]

Furthermore, on this proposal, creation of the physical universe remains genuinely *ex nihilo*: God does not confer existence on antecedently subsisting possibilia, but rather (at the beginning of creation anyway) creates substantial particulars modeled on the relevant ideas from nothing. And finally, there is no need for the distinction between being and existence: divine ideas exist plain and simple, albeit in the divine intellect. The role of unactualized possibilia in the possibilist's account is taken over by unexemplified ideas.

So there seem to be distinct theoretical advantages to this move. But how, exactly, does the doctrine of divine ideas solve the problem at hand? How, exactly, does the doctrine make sense of the claim that God intended or knew prior to creation that certain future individuals were to exist? To explore the answer, the first task is to get a better handle on the notion of a divine idea. Thomas often speaks of the ideas—at least, those at issue here—serving as *models* (as in the quote above), *exemplars*,[10] or *likenesses*[11] of the objects that exemplify them. These metaphors are not in themselves particularly helpful, though, as Thomas himself was fully aware. For, first of all, one thing might well be considered a model or likeness of another in so broad and general a way that it is similarly a likeness of many other things as well, indeed, perhaps, of everything. Thus,

> as fire, if it knew itself as the principle of heat, would know the nature of heat, and all things else in so far as they are hot; so God through knowing Himself as the source of being, knows the nature of being, and all other things in so far as they are beings.[12]

Clearly, however, this will not do to explain God's singular knowledge of future individuals; mere knowledge that two things shall have being is not of itself sufficient to distinguish one from the other; it is not, as Thomas puts it, a *proper* knowledge of the two things.[13] What is needed, then, at least, is a *distinct* likeness in the divine intellect for each of the infinitely many ways in which the divine essence is imitable in order to ground the idea that God can have anything approaching singular knowledge of each future existent. Thus, Thomas concludes,

> we must therefore say that God knows things other than Himself with a proper knowledge, not only in so far as being is common to them but in so far as one is distinguished from the other.[14]

That is to say, since the ideas are the basis of God's proper knowledge of things other than himself, each likeness must have a certain sort of richness that reflects every detail of a corresponding thing's character, everything at least that might distinguish it from some other thing. Thomas speaks in terms of a thing's *perfection*, i.e., the sum of perfections that "belong" to it, i.e., all the ways in which a thing manifests actuality, all the multifarious *forms* associated with its nature. Thus,

> whatever perfection exists in any creature wholly pre-exists and is contained in God in an excelling manner. Now not only what is common to creatures—viz., being—belongs to their perfection, but also what makes them distinguished from each other; [such] as living and understanding, and the like, whereby living beings are distinguished from the non-living, and the intelligent from the non-intelligent...Hence it is that all things pre-exist in God, not only as regards what is common to all, but also as regards what distinguishes one thing from another.[15]

The picture that Thomas suggests here is thus something like this. The perfections, such as life and intelligence, are, like full-blown likenesses, ideas pre-existing in the divine intellect as various reflections of God's essence. Since likenesses are the ground of God's proper knowledge of creatures, in knowing a likeness, God knows all the perfections that would be exemplified were that likeness instantiated. It is therefore natural to think of likenesses as rich, complex clusters of perfections that are in a certain sense "maximal", i.e., clusters of perfections joined together in appropriate measure (no creature, of course, could exhibit the full measure of any perfection) and such that possibly, something has all those perfections in those measures and has in addition no other perfections. The set of likenesses is thus the set of all such clusters, the set of all maximal combinations of perfections, the set of all ways in which the divine essence is imitable in creation. It is then this set which grounds God's knowledge of things insofar as they are distinct from one another:

> Since therefore the essence of God contains in itself all the perfection contained in the essence of any other being,...God can know all things in Himself with a proper knowledge. For the nature proper to each thing consists in some particular participation of the divine perfection. Now God could not be said to know Himself perfectly unless He knew all the ways in which His own perfection can be shared by others...Hence it is manifest that God knows all things with a proper knowledge, according as they are distinguished from each other.[16]

Since of course the perfections exist in God at all times, before creation in particular, God can be said to have proper knowledge of "future" things no less than of actual. For prior to creation, though Reagan did not yet exist, his likeness did. God's knowledge of Reagan's future existence thus consisted in his knowing that the likeness in question was to be instantiated.

There still seems to be a problem, though. The perfections as discussed by Thomas all seem to be universals. Thus, thought of as clusters of perfections, likenesses turn out to be clusters of universals. But if so, it is dubious whether any collection of them can be *essentially individuating*; that is, if likenesses are composed of universals, then it seems that for any given likeness **L**, necessarily, if x exemplifies **L**, then it is at least possible that there be something y distinct from x that exemplifies **L**. And if that is so, then likenesses don't seem to do the work of possibilia in grounding God's singular knowledge of the future.[17] Rather, if they are not essentially individuating, then God didn't know prior to creation that *Reagan* was to exist in virtue of the likeness that Reagan was in fact to exemplify; he knew only that there was to be *such* a person as Reagan, someone with the general character that Reagan in fact instantiated, albeit down to the last qualitative detail.

A response that leaps to mind here is just to deny that likenesses are not essentially individuating, and rather to defend a strong form of the identity of indiscernibles (call it SII), viz., that, necessarily, for any object x, it is not possible that there be an object y distinct from x that has exactly the same perfections (in the same measures) as x; that is, any two "possible objects," so to speak, must differ with regard to some perfection, and hence with regard to the likenesses they instantiate. Thomas does indeed hold something like SII explicitly in the case of divine beings. Thus, he argues that there can only be one god, since if there were more than one "they would necessarily differ from each other. Something, therefore, would belong to one which did not belong to another,"[18] in which case, whether perfection or privation, one of the two alleged gods would have to be less than perfect, a contradiction.

This doesn't settle the issue, though. For it follows on Thomas's hylomorphic principles alone that distinct *immaterial* beings in general necessarily differ with regard to form, hence with regard to perfection: since matter is the principle of individuation for material beings, it follows that distinct immaterial beings must differ in form, else they would not be distinct. (This is why, e.g., each angel is its own species for Thomas.[19]) Thus, assuming that divine beings are necessarily immaterial, there are special considerations that warrant holding SII with regard to them that do not generalize to all creatures.

But even aside from that, the picture is bleak for SII as a general Thomistic principle, at least so long as perfections are understood to be universals, and likenesses clusters of perfections. For, so understood, Thomas appears to reject SII overtly in *De Veritate*, where he writes that "from a number of universal forms gathered together—no matter how great this number may be—no singular can be constituted, because the collection of these forms can still be understood to be in many."[20] If, then, likenesses are thought of as clusters of perfections, and perfections are universals, it follows that, on Thomas's own view, they cannot be essentially individuating, and hence cannot be a ground for God's singular knowledge about the future.

Despite our initial impression, however, a closer reading of Thomas reveals that he did not think of likenesses solely as clusters of universals. What he did think is a little obscure, but he provides enough material for at least a rational reconstruction. For Thomas, recall, it is the parcel of "designated" matter—matter with determinate spatial and geometrical attributes[21]—in which a thing's form inheres at any given time that individuates it, makes it distinct from every other thing.[22] Like any principle of individuation worth its salt, Thomas's is also a principle of identity:[23] its matter is what makes a given material singular *that very thing*;[24] its form alone, consonant with its universality, could be exemplified by different individuals. Now, although matter is pure potentiality for Thomas, nonetheless it has being, albeit in a primitive and rudimentary way, and thus is to that extent a reflection of the divine essence. Hence, like all other such reflections, there must be a likeness of matter in the divine intellect. This, Thomas claims, is the source of God's knowledge of singulars. So, for example, in responding to an argument he attributes to al-Ghazali that God cannot know singulars because things knowable by an intellect must be separated from matter, Thomas writes:

> Although a singular as such cannot be separated from matter, it can be known [by God] by means of a likeness separated from matter, namely the likeness of matter itself.[25]

Thomas relies on analogy to flesh out the picture. The divine artisan, like creaturely artisans, models that which he creates after likenesses in the intellect—that is what makes creation rational. A human artisan, however, can possess intellectual likenesses of form only, which is universal. Hence, by the form alone, without the aid of sense experience, a human artisan cannot have singular knowledge of her work. In particular, she has no singular knowledge of future work she has only designed but has not yet produced.[26] However, the divine artisan, as creator of both the form and the matter of his art, antecedently possesses likenesses of both, and by this means he is able to know singulars:

> since divine art produces not only the form but also the matter, it contains not only the likeness of form but also that of matter. Consequently, God knows things in regard to both their matter and their form; and, therefore, He knows not only universals but also singulars.[27]

And since, of course, divine ideas exist necessarily, and in particular, prior to their being exemplified, by the same means God was able to have singular knowledge of future individuals prior to creation.

We need to expand on a couple of things to exploit Thomas's picture here. First, Thomas's remarks above and elsewhere suggest that it is the idea of mere matter *per se* that grounds God's singular knowledge, an idea exemplified by all *parcels* of designated matter. But that idea is just one more universal, and so by Thomas's principle in *De Veritate* it would not provide a solution to the problem at hand: the result of adding a universal to a cluster of universals is still a universal. Nor, for the same reason, would God's ideas of the spatial and geometric properties of parcels of designated matter suffice to ground God's singular knowledge, since different parcels could presumably exemplify the same spatial and geometric properties. Rather, there must be distinct divine ideas of the specific parcels of designated matter themselves that do the individuating.

Second, Thomas would no doubt want to hold that some variation in one's designated matter is possible over time without loss of identity; the matter of one's body, for example, seems to change significantly through the years without parallel changes in identity. The bald thesis above—that a material singular is individuated by *the* parcel of designated matter that constitutes its physical nature—on its face might suggest that a given thing is made essentially of exactly the same matter at every moment of its existence. Obvious facts of metabolism, for example, would then suggest that the span of most creatures' existence is alarmingly brief—either that, or that Thomas's notion of matter has precious little connection with our ordinary notion.

A simple fix would be that it is a thing's matter *at each moment* that individuates it at that moment. In fact, to ground the individuation of material singulars in (designated) matter, Thomas need only hold the following, somewhat weaker thesis:

> (1) Necessarily, for any time $t$, and for any material singular $S$, there is some parcel of matter $m$ such that $m$ is a part of $S$'s matter at $t$, and it is not possible that $m$ be a part of the matter of any other singular at any time.

That is, he need hold only that there must always be a material part $m$ of any material singular $S$ that couldn't have been a part of anything else. Call such a part an *individuating material part* of $S$.

Combining this with the first point, then, we have the following reconstruction of Thomas's view: vulgarly put, that there is a divine idea for every possible individuating material part of any possible material singular; more precisely, that,

> (2) Necessarily, for any material singular $S$, and for any individuating material part $m$ of $S$, there is a divine idea **I** such that, necessarily, (i) **I** exists, and (ii) **I** is exemplified only if it is exemplified by $m$.

Now, as noted, despite its ontological distance from the divine essence, matter manifests at least a rudimentary degree of being. Thus, since a perfection is simply a way of manifesting being (hence, a way of imitating the divine essence), having a particular material part is itself a perfection, and so by (1) such perfections will be among the perfections exhibited by any material singular. Thus, since likenesses as we defined them are maximal clusters of perfections, likenesses of material singulars (or likenesses that would be of material singulars if they were exemplified) must include ideas of individuating material parts (or ideas that would be ideas of individuating material parts if they were exemplified). Contrary to our initial impression, then, it turns out that for Thomas—on our reconstruction, anyway—not all perfections are universals; some perfections are such that having them entails having a certain individuating material part. But then it follows from the definition of an individuating material part that likenesses are essentially individuating,[28] and hence provide a sufficient foundation for divine singular foreknowledge after all.

This understanding of Thomas's view seems at least to be coherent. Its plausibility is perhaps another thing. The first difficulty, anticipated by Scotus,[29] is that designated matter, while perhaps an acceptable ground for *de facto* individuation alone, just doesn't seem to be a plausible ground for identity; in general at least, there doesn't seem to be anything about matter *per se* that prevents any chunk of it belonging to a given thing from being instead the matter of some other thing, or at least, some other thing of the same species.

But second, and perhaps more seriously, the source of ideas of designated matter that are sufficiently fine-grained in the divine intellect is a bit of a mystery. The problem is this. Matter *per se* is pure potentiality. There is therefore nothing to distinguish the idea of one individual parcel of designated matter in itself, *qua* matter, from any other. Hence, it would seem that ideas of designated matter can only be distinguished in terms of the spatial and geometrical properties of the parcels of matter that exemplify them. Thus, ideas of designated matter that do not differ with respect to those properties are identical. But, as already noted, it seems at least possible that different parcels of matter could have exactly the same spatial and geometrical properties (e.g., material counterparts in symmetrical universes). Thus, for at least some (and more likely, all) parcels of designated matter $m$, it does not seem possible on Thomas's own views for God to have an idea that only attaches to $m$ whenever it is exemplified. Rather, it would seem in addition that, if it is possible that there be a distinct $m'$ with the same spatial and geometrical properties as $m$, God's idea of $m$ would also attach to $m'$.

One could of course just bite down hard here. The divine intellect's ability to formulate distinct ideas that attach to designated matter in the requisite way, it might be said, is just the sort of thing that distinguishes the Creator. To be a creator is, among other things, to be able to have ideas such as this that are ordered toward production, rather than the mere intellectual blueprints of which we creatures are capable.[30] Perhaps it is sheer hubris to entertain anything less. But once again, until there are convincing reasons for adopting such a view as this that ultimately appeals *ad hoc* to God's unique status in the universe, the incentive to find an alternative, to my mind anyway, remains strong.

## Haecceitism

A somewhat less puzzling, and more contemporary, approach to the problem moves away (however slightly) from Thomas's metaphysics of matter and form to a metaphysics of objects and properties. On this approach, the role of individuating material parts in our reconstruction of Thomas's metaphysics is taken over by a certain class of properties, viz., *haecceities*, or *individual essences*. Analogous to such material parts, a property **P** is a haecceity just in case (i) it is possible that some object *S* have **P**, and (ii) it is not possible that anything other than *S* have **P**. **P** is a haecceity *of* some object *S* just in case **P** is a haecceity, and it is possible that *S* have **P**.[31] *Haecceitism*, then, is the view that

(3) Necessarily, for any time *t*, and for any object *S*, there is a property **P** such that *S* exemplifies **P** at *t*, and **P** is a haecceity of *S*.

Since they play a role analogous to Thomas's individuating material parts, then, haecceities offer promise of a solution parallel to Thomas's without the associated difficulties engendered by his metaphysics of matter. If in addition we take properties to be divine ideas, we can also retain Thomas's high view of God as the sole source of being in the universe. For the sake of the theologically faint of heart, however, I'll not overtly make the additional leap.[32]

In and of itself haecceitism is not terribly controversial. It is not implausible, for example, to hold that, for every object *S*, there is the property **being *S***, or **being identical to *S***. But that view of itself does not provide an answer to the question of singular foreknowledge, since from the fact that I now have a haecceity, it doesn't follow that there would have been any such thing if I hadn't existed, and in particular, it doesn't follow that there was any such thing before creation under the divine purview. Some haecceitists, however, Plantinga most notably, argue that since haecceities are properties, they exist necessarily. Combining this with (3) (and ignoring times for brevity), this yields the stronger thesis that

(4) Necessarily, for any object *S*, there is a property **P** such that (i) *S* exemplifies **P**, (ii) **P** is a haecceity of *S*, and (iii) **P** exists necessarily.

In particular, prior to creation there were the haecceities that were to be the haecceities of all the individuals that were to exist. Divine singular foreknowledge is thus assured as in Thomas's solution. Call this *strong* haecceitism.

Though less problematic than Thomas's solution, strong haecceitism is not without difficulties of its own. There are two forms of strong haecceitism to consider: *qualitative* and *nonqualitative*. The difference between the two is rooted in the idea that there is an important distinction to be drawn between properties that are "about" particular objects in some intuitive and direct way, and properties that are not. This distinction, as with most of our metaphysical distinctions, is grounded in a parallel linguistic distinction, one between two types of property-denoting expressions: those that involve names, demonstratives, or other devices of "direct" reference, and those that do not. Thus, on the one hand, we have properties like **being identical with Reagan, being as tall as that man**, and **being married to her**, and on the other such properties as **being self-identical, being taller than every other man**, and **being married to someone or other**.[33] Properties of the latter sort are usually called *purely qualitative* properties; those of the former sort we can, accordingly, refer to as *impure*. The distinction between the two types of haecceitism, then, is this: according to qualitative haecceitism, all unexemplified haecceities are purely qualitative; according to non-qualitative haecceitism, all (or at least most) unexemplified haecceities are impure.

To appreciate the difference between the two forms of haecceitism, as well as their difficulties, it will be useful to consider the distinction between pure and impure properties in some detail. What then, exactly, *is* an impure property? At this level of philosophical art, of course, we can only trade in stories; but in this case there's a pretty good one. Consider the so-called "iterative" conception of sets. The idea is that one begins with some initial bunch of individuals, and that the sets are "built up" layer by layer out of those things: first all the sets that can be formed out of the initial individuals, then all the sets that can be formed from those sets and the initial individuals together, and so on.[34]

Complex properties, relations, and propositions (PRPs)—impure properties in particular—can be thought of along similar lines. Only now, along with our initial bunch of individuals we also include all the logically simple (hence, on this story, purely qualitative) PRPs.[35] And alongside the sets that are built up from them, logically complex PRPs are constructed out of less complex entities, including, perhaps, concrete individuals. Given the property **P**, for example, there is, at the next level, so to speak, its complement **being non-P**; given two properties **P** and **Q**, there is the conjunctive property **being P and Q**; and so on.[36] Say that a complex PRP *involves* the less complex entities that it is constructed out of.

The properties most relevant to the current issue, of course, are those that involve individuals. Frege was the first to suggest the idea that properties and relations have an argument structure. They are, metaphorically once again, "gappy," and these gaps can be "plugged" by individuals to yield PRPs with fewer gaps. In particular—the punch line—impure properties, properties that are directly about certain objects, can be thought of as the result of plugging individuals into $n$-1 of the argument places of an $n$-place relation.

This appealing picture raises serious problems for strong non-qualitative haecceitism. Whether or not we take impure properties to be literal metaphysical composites of individuals and relations, the upshot of the picture is that a logically complex property *presupposes* the less complex entities it involves, in the sense that it would not be the property that it is without them; it couldn't have involved any entities other than the ones it does in fact, nor could it have failed to involve them. But if so, then presupposition in this sense seems to entail ontological dependence: if the objects an impure property involves hadn't existed, it wouldn't have had the logical structure it has in fact; and since a property's logical structure is essential to it, it wouldn't have existed either.[37] As there could be no singleton set {Reagan} without Reagan, likewise there could be no such singular property as **being identical with Reagan** without him either.

Given the picture, then, there is no ground for the assertion that impure haecceities of future individuals existed before creation, hence no ground for singular foreknowledge. This leaves strong non-qualitative haecceitism with little room to maneuver. On the one hand, one might reject the idea that impure haecceities are logically complex; like Thomas's ideas of individuating material parts, perhaps there just *are* logically simple nonqualitative properties—**Socrateity, Reaganhood, Priorness**—that necessarily attach to the same thing whenever they attach to anything at all, but which do not *involve* those individuals in any way that entails ontological dependence. The view is actualist, since (given the background Platonism) properties exist, plain and simple. But does it really take us all that far from possibilism? For when all is said and done, there is little to distinguish such nondescript properties from possibilia save the bare assertion that they *are* in fact properties. Possibilia seem at best to have been traded for entities scarcely less problematic and obscure.[38]

On the other hand, one might simply reject the picture straight-away. But that is unpromising as well. For any plausible theory of the nature of impure properties has got to account for their "about-ness;" and, short of introducing logically simple haecceities all over again, it is difficult to imagine how that could be done in a way that doesn't entail their ontological dependence upon the individuals they are about.

These difficulties have moved some strong haecceitists to quali-tative haecceitism, to the view, roughly put, that "all possible objects" have purely qualitative haecceities.[39] On the picture presented here, the purely qualitative PRPs consist of the logically simple PRPs, and whatever logically complex PRPs can be built up from them. Most friends of qualitative haecceitism take qualitative haecceities to be large sets, conjunctions, or disjunctions of purely qualitative prop-erties[40] (*Q- properties,* for short). It will be useful both now and below if we spell out an appropriate version in some detail.

Let's concentrate on my haecceity. To make sure we include enough of my properties, the safest idea for purposes here is to build the largest Q-property we can that includes all of my Q-properties (and no Q-properties that I lack).[41] The first thought that springs to mind is just to take the conjunction of all my Q-properties. But that won't quite work. If by 'all my Q-properties' we mean all the ones I have *now*, then we've fallen far short of all that can be said about me qualitatively. And if we mean all the ones I have at some time or other, then the conjunction will be inconsistent, since, e.g., I have had both the property of being under six feet tall and the property of being over six feet tall.

But, if we avail ourselves of the elaborate resources of (typical) qualitative haecceitism, there is a relatively straightforward fix available. Let $t$ be a time. Say that a property (relation, proposition) is *almost qualitative* if it is of the form **being P at** $t$ **(bearing P to at** $t$**, P at** $t$**)**, where **P** is purely qualitative. Then, recursively, call a PRP *qualitative\** if it is either purely qualitative, almost qualitative, or involves only qualitative\* PRPs. Say that a property of mine is *permanent* if I have it at all times (i.e., all times at which I exist[42]), and let **C\*** be the conjunction of all my permanent qualitative\* properties (*Q\*- properties*, for short). Call **C\*** a *maximal Q\*-conjunction* for me. **C\*** is consistent, of course, since it includes only my permanent properties. No information is excluded, however, since **C\*** includes all the appropriate time-indexed counterparts of such impermanent properties as **being under six feet tall** and **being over six feet tall**. Furthermore, **C\*** is a complete qualitative\* characterization of me, and hence looks like just the sort of property the qualitative haecceitist needs. (The move to Q\*-properties, of course, requires us to broaden the definition of qualitative haecceitism slightly: it is now to be taken to be the thesis that all unexemplified haecceities are qualitative\*.)

The defender of strong qualitative haecceitism might argue that we've still not gone far enough. For we need to account for all of my *modal* properties as well, not just my actual properties. More specifically, my qualitative haecceity must depict not only how I am in fact, but how I might be, completely, in any other "possible world." It must include complete qualitative characterizations of all the ways I might have been if things had been different.

Modalizing a Q\*-property, of course, does not make it any less qualitative; if **P** is a Q\*-property, so are **being possibly P** and **being necessarily P**. And furthermore, modal properties are properties that I *actually* have. The desired properties are therefore already included in **C\***. To see this more explicitly, suppose I was different in some way. Then there is some conjunction **C'** of all the permanent Q\*-properties that I would have exemplified had I been different in that way. Hence, **C'** is *possibly* a maximal Q\*-conjunction for me. Thus **being possibly C'** is a property I actually have. It is, moreover, a permanent Q\*-property, and hence a conjunct of **C\***. The same holds for any other way I might have been. **C\*** therefore includes the required modal properties.

If the amount of effort needed to reject a view were proportional to the effort expended in defining it, we should have our work cut out for us. But the matter seems to me straightforward. Despite the immense amount of qualitative detail in **C\***, the same problem that Thomas had noted for likenesses construed as clusters of universals still arises: no conjunction of purely qualitative properties seems to be essentially individuating. There just seems no reason why something couldn't be just like me qualitatively—both actually and modally—in every respect without *being* me.[43] If so, strong qualitative haecceitism is false.

It is possible, I think, to defend the consistency of qualitative haecceitism.[44] But mere consistency here is not enough; like Berkeley's immaterialism, it does not produce conviction. Both versions of strong haecceitism, then, fail to take us far enough from the shortcomings of Thomas's view. The search continues.

## Particularism and the Generality of the Possible

Let's take stock. We've examined four attempts to provide foundations for the doctrine of God's singular foreknowledge: timelessness, possibilism, divine ideas, and haecceitism. Timelessness was rejected primarily because it seemed to be open to an analogous problem with regard to God's modal knowledge. The remaining accounts provided authentic solutions, but the cost of each was deemed unacceptably high.

It is useful to see these latter three—possibilism, the doctrine of divine ideas, and haecceitism—as species of a single genus that we can call *particularism*, or *proxyism*. According to particularism, for any possible object, there is necessarily some sort of proxy to which God has access, a conceptual handle that can play the role of the object in the deliberations and cogitations of the divine mind. More exactly,

(5) Necessarily, for any object $x$, there is necessarily something $y$ and some relation **R** such that possibly **R**$yx$, and necessarily, for any $z$, if **R**$yz$, then $z = x$.

That is, for the particularist, roughly put, for any object $x$ there could be, there is necessarily something $y$ that goes proxy for $x$ in the sense that $y$ bears some relation to $x$ whenever $x$ exists that it could not bear to anything else. For the possibilist, $y$ is just $x$, and **R** is the identity relation; for Plantinga, $y$ is a haecceity and **R** the exemplification relation; for Thomas, $y$ could either be a likeness and **R** exemplification, or $y$ could be an idea of an individuating material part, and **R** the relation that holds between an object $S$ and an idea **I** just in case $S$ has a material part that exemplifies **I**.

We've found problems with particularism in three incarnations. But what seems most to trouble many philosophers about particularism— myself among them—is not the specific problems, but the overarching picture: the idea that the merely possible, or merely future, is none-theless entirely determinate with regard to its singular details, even when the individuals allegedly included in those details don't exist. The contrasting intuition is that the merely possible, or the merely future, is entirely general, except insofar as it involves actual, presently existing things. Peirce captures the intuition vividly:

> The possible is necessarily general; and no amount of general specification can reduce a general class of possibilities to an individual case. It is only actuality, the force of existence, which bursts the fluidity of the general and produces a discrete unit.[45]

In the terms at hand, that is, nothing within the merely possible and the merely future is essentially individuating, beyond what can be specified in terms of things that actually exist.[46] Contrary to the particularist vision, a definite individual is not determined until it is actual.

Clearly, this vision leaves us with our original dilemma. For if the future is general, then before creation there were no proxies by means of which God was able to have determinate singular knowl-edge of the future. He knew the future in all its *qualitative* detail; he knew to the last detail that the *sort* of person we now know Prior to have been was to be. But there was at the time no singular knowledge of *Prior* to be had in any sense.[47]

Nonetheless, I think that God knew that *Prior* was to be a philosopher.

## A General Solution

Contrary to appearances, my solution is not to develop a fancy for contradiction. I think the remarks above are consistent, and I'll try to say how. For all its simplicity, the solution seems to me to rectify actualism, the generality of the possible, and the standard conception of divine knowledge and intentionality.

Note to begin with that proxies play a dual role for the particularist: a metaphysical role, and a semantical role. In their metaphysical role, proxies serve as the ontological ground of divine singular fore-knowledge: God's knowledge of future individuals consists in his knowledge of proxies and their future properties. Semantically, they ground the *meaning* of our present day assertions about God's singular knowledge of future individuals prior to creation. Thus, to

say that God knew that Prior was to be a philosopher is to say that
God knew that a certain proxy—the one that was to be Prior's—had
a certain property: for a possibilist, that Prior himself, *qua possibile*,
was going to exist and be a philosopher; for haecceitists, that **being
Prior**, say, was to be coexemplified with the property **being a
philosopher**; for Thomas, that a certain likeness which was to be
exemplified contained the perfections exhibited by all and only
philosophers; and so on.

So, more generally, and a little more formally, let '*B*' be the operator
'Before creation', '*F*' the future tense operator, and '*K*' the operator
'God knows that'. Let α be the name of some contingent being, and
let ref(α) be the referent of α. Semantically, then, for the particularist,
sentences of the form $BKF\pi(\alpha)$—Before creation, God knew that it
would be the case that $\pi(\alpha)$—are evaluated solely in terms of God
(of course), a proxy of the appropriate sort for ref(α), the property
$\exp(\pi)$ expressed by $\pi$,[48] and a relation **R** (e.g., coexemplification)
appropriate to *p* and $\exp(\pi)$: $BKF\pi(\alpha)$ expresses a truth iff there is
a *p* such that (i) *p* is a proxy for ref(α), and (ii) before creation God
knew that *p* would stand in the relation **R** to $\exp(\pi)$.

Pulling apart the metaphysical and semantical roles of proxies helps
us to see that there are really two issues here: what God knew prior
to creation, and the meaning of our assertions about what God knew.
The particularist's fallacy, I think, lies in identifying the metaphysical
ground of the former with the semantical ground of the latter. More
specifically, it lies in the assumption that assertions about God's
singular foreknowledge before creation must be evaluated solely in
terms of entities existing at that time. But that isn't always how things
work, even in much more mundane cases.

Consider the following passage from Thomas:

> [a]n agent does not act for the sake of [a] form except in so far as
> the likeness of the form is in the agent; which may happen in two
> ways. For in some agents the form of the thing-to-be-made pre-
> exists according to its natural being, as in those that act by their
> nature; as a man generates a man, or fire generates fire. Whereas
> in other agents the form of the thing-to-be-made pre-exists accord-
> ing to intelligible being, as in those that act by the intellect; and
> thus the likeness of a house pre-exists in the mind of the builder.
> And *this may be called the idea of the house*, since the builder
> intends to build his house like the form conceived in his mind.[49]

I don't want to make any strong claims about Thomas's actual intent here, especially given the absence of definite articles in Latin. But a straightforward reading of the translation contains a crucial observation. A builder builds his house on the basis of a certain idea, a certain design. As with all creaturely ideas, this idea is universal; it is not essentially individuating. Thus, before any house is built, the idea might attach to any number of "possible houses." Nonetheless, after a definite house is built, from that temporal perspective looking back, so to say, the idea can be said to have been an idea of *it*.

Consider a further example along the same lines that is suggested by Thomas's artisan analogy above. A sculptor, a friend of yours, sets about creating a great work that she has been planning for many years. During this time she has meticulously developed and refined every detail of the conception on which she will base the work. Finally, she purchases a block of marble and sets about giving her conception substance. Upon completion, she sees that it is indeed all she had imagined. Entering her studio, you remark, "So *this* is the piece you were intending to create." To which she replies, "Yes; I knew that it would be my masterpiece."

Metaphysically, if the possible is general, then there was nothing essentially individuating about your artistic friend's conception.[50] Though meticulously detailed, it was—as Thomas would affirm—entirely general; it could have been instantiated in any number of other pieces of marble, and hence could have issued in any number of numerically distinct sculptures. There was thus, prior to its instantiation, nothing such that *it* was the thing the artist intended to create; and nothing such that she knew that *it* would be her masterpiece. Nevertheless, semantically, your assertions apparently to the contrary *after* its instantiation are clearly and unambiguously true.

The straightforward semantic lesson here is that some ascriptions of singular knowledge and, more generally, intentional attitudes *de re*, to an individual $S$ with respect to past times $t$ depend for their meaning in part on contingent facts that have transpired since $t$. Put another way, the content of $S$'s intentional state at $t$ can be legitimately redescribed at a later time $t'$ in light of facts unknown, or unavailable, to $S$ at $t$ in such a way as to reflect those facts. If, in particular, it turns out that

(a) $S$'s original state at $t$ includes a general conception of a kind of object with certain definite properties,

(b) those properties attach to a unique object $a$ that exists at or before a later time $t'$, and

(c) *a* is related appropriately to *S* (e.g., causally),

then the original state can often be legitimately redescribed at $t'$ as having been singularly directed toward *a*.

Before the creation of her masterpiece *m*, then, the content of your artistic friend's intention was only that she create *such* a sculpture as the sculpture *m* turned out to be; the intentional object of her state, so to say, was something satisfying a certain detailed but nonetheless general conception. Similarly, the content of her knowledge (at best) was only that *such* a thing was to be her masterpiece.[51] In light of the fact that *m* turned out to be such a thing, and the fact that it came to be as a result of that intention, your singular redescriptions of her original intentional states as directed toward *m* are true.

My proposal, which should be obvious enough by now, is that most ordinary assertions about God's singular foreknowledge before creation—those that give rise to the standard conception in particular—should be understood in exactly the same sort of way.

To elaborate. First, call a property **P** a *Q-proxy* if it is possible that there be some object *S* such that **P** is a maximal $Q^*$-conjunction for *S*. Then before creation, by virtue of the Q-proxies, God possessed an infinitely detailed but nonetheless *general* conception of every object there could possibly be,[52] and in particular, of the objects that were to be (though of course they wouldn't have actually been conceptions *of* anything at the time). Thus, there was nothing before creation such that God intended that *it* should exist; nothing such that he knew that *it* was to be a philosopher. Nor were there any proxies to play an analogous role. He intended only that something (uniquely) instantiate, say, $P_r$, where $P_r$ is the Q-proxy that, as it happens, Reagan exemplifies; he knew only that whatever was to instantiate $P_p$ was also to be a philosopher, where $P_p$ is the Q-proxy that, as it happens, Prior exemplified.

But clearly the requisite conditions hold here for ascribing singular intentions and singular knowledge to God before creation. Indeed, things are rather simpler in this case than above. The divine artisan creates each thing in perfect accord with an antecedent general conception that attaches only to that thing.[53] As in (a) and (b), God's knowing and intending before creation involve general conceptions—Q-proxies—of objects with certain properties—those entailed by Q-proxies—and, at a later time, those properties attach to unique objects. Clause (c) can be ignored, since it was added only to avoid

498 / Christopher Menzel

Gettier-style cases in which something, unbeknownst to the agent, has the properties the agent includes in her general conception.[54] This is presumably not relevant with regard to divine knowledge and intentionality.

So I propose the following semantics for our ordinary ascriptions of singular foreknowledge to God before creation: a sentence of the form $BKF\pi(\alpha)$ expresses a truth iff there is a Q-proxy $\mathbf{C}$ such that (i) God knew before creation that $\mathbf{C}$ would be exemplified, (ii) ref($\alpha$) exemplifies $\mathbf{C}$, and (iii) $\mathbf{C}$ entails the property exp($\pi$).

Note that I restrict this semantics to "ordinary" ascriptions of singular foreknowledge, the one's that typically undergird the standard conception of divine knowledge and intentionality. For in more reflective moments one's intent—as in clause (i) above, for example—may be to describe the literal content of God's knowledge before creation, the literal structure of the propositions known at the time. On the semantics appropriate for that sort of discourse, one refers only to entities existing at that time, as in particularist semantics, and hence statements of the above form invariably come out false (unless perhaps $\alpha$ is a name for God). My purpose is thus to provide a semantics that makes sense of ordinary statements of that form, and hence which preserves the standard conception—or at least, all of the standard conception that is warranted by what we ordinarily say.[55]

In sum, then, the account I propose is actualist—it does not appeal to nonexistent possibilia; it preserves the generality of the possible—there are no (creaturely) proxies before creation; and, I claim, it preserves all we need of the standard conception.

In particular, God knew that Prior was to be a philosopher.

## Three Objections

Objections seem to revolve around one of the following three lines. The first sort of objection is easily dispatched. According to me, before creation God didn't know that Reagan was to exist. But then there was something that God didn't know, which contradicts his omniscience.

There are two ambiguities in the premise 'before creation God didn't really know that Reagan was to exist' to sort out here. First, to make it come out true, we must interpret the premise so as to be describing the literal content of God's knowledge before creation, and hence evaluate it entirely in terms of semantic objects existing at that time. (Otherwise, if we interpret it on the proposed semantics—from the present perspective looking back, so to say—it is straightforwardly false.) So interpreted, it is indeed true that God didn't know that Reagan was to exist. However, in terms of its form alone, this statement can be true for at least three different reasons: (i) before creation, **Reagan will exist** was not true; (ii) the proposition **Reagan will exist** was true at the time, but God didn't know it; and (iii) there was no such proposition as **Reagan will exist** to be known. (i) is irrelevant. (ii) entails the objection's theologically jarring conclusion. But of course, the premise is true not for that reason, but because of (iii): there simply was no such singular proposition as **Reagan will exist**, and hence no such singular truth to be known. Hence, on the only interpretation of the premise that makes it true, the conclusion doesn't follow.

A more subtle argument charges that my account impinges on God's omnipotence, that, on my account, something which ought to have been within God's control was not. Let **P** be my Q-proxy. Since **P** is not essentially individuating, it follows that God might have acted in precisely the same way before creation, and yet something other than me might have instantiated **P**, i.e., more precisely, $\Diamond \exists y (y \neq$ me & **P**$y$). Thus, God didn't have control over whether or not I would come to be; it was, so to say, a *surprise* for God that *I* came to be rather than someone else.[56] But surely, if God is omnipotent, he ought to have control over what contingent things exist.

One is tempted to respond like this. A state of affairs **s** is under God's control at *t* just in case it is within God's power at *t* to actualize **s**. So what was it exactly that was supposed to have been out of God's control before creation? What possibility was he unable to actualize? Presumably, whether or not *I* exist. But, once again, that was not a genuine possibility at the time. There was not a range of choices open to God between me and my possible "doppelgängers," for there were no such singular possibilities; there was only the possibility that *something* instantiate **P**. Hence, God's omnipotence is not compromised; for he cannot be held responsible for not being able to actualize nonexistent possibilities.

But this won't do. In the case of knowledge, at least when literal description of the content of the agent's knowledge is desired, the thing known must coexist with the knower.[57] But in the case of what is within one's control, one can legitimately be said, after the fact, to have brought about certain present states of affairs in virtue of past actions. Hence, one can be said, after the fact, to have had it in one's power at a past time $t$ to bring it about that **s** obtain— even if **s** didn't exist at $t$—just in case it was within one's power at $t$ to act so as to guarantee that **s** would obtain, i.e., to act in such a way that it was not possible that **s** fail to obtain at some time thereafter. In particular, it might be said, even though there was no such singular possibility as **Menzel's existing** before creation, none-theless, there must have been something an omnipotent God could have done to guarantee that, after creation, I would exist. Thus, appealing to the fact that there was no such singular possibility before creation as **Menzel's existing** does not of itself escape the objection.

The real crux of the matter is the generality of the possible. Haecceitists make precisely the claim at the end of the previous paragraph. For the haecceitist, no less than for me, there was no such singular possibility as **Menzel's existing** before creation, *in the sense that* there was no state of affairs that included *me* (as opposed to some proxy) among the entities it involved. However, there was still something God could do that would guarantee that I would exist, viz., actualize my haecceity. But in affirming the generality of the possible, that is exactly what is denied on the present account. Because there were no haecceities, no proxies generally, it was not in God's power before creation to act in such a way as to guarantee that I would exist.

It must therefore be admitted that, before creation, it was outside of God's control to bring it about that I exist. And perhaps that conclusion is what some philosophers find objectionable. Again, though, this is ambiguous. For, parallel to the above, a state of affairs **s** can be outside of God's control at $t$ for one of three reasons: (i) **not-s** is necessary at $t$ and all times thereafter (logically or *per accidens*[58]); (ii) there is some action **A** such that it is possible that **A** be in someone's power at $t$, and doing **A** at $t$ guarantees that **s** obtain, but it is not within God's power to do **A** at $t$; and (iii) there is no possible action such that performing it at $t$ guarantees that **s** obtain. (i) is irrelevant. (ii) is theologically unacceptable. But, of course, my existence was not outside of God's control for that reason, but because of (iii): there was, by the generality of the possible, simply no action that could guarantee that I, rather than someone else just like me, would exist. My existence—singular existence generally was thus uncontrollable before creation not because of any lack of power on God's part, but simply by the nature of the matter; singular existence is essentially uncontrollable. And that does not compromise God's omnipotence in the least; not even an omnipotent being can be held responsible for having no control over a state of affairs that is by its very nature uncontrollable.

The word 'uncontrollable' here is unfortunate, connoting as it does such unruly events as nuclear meltdowns and fits of bad temper. Such connotations, I think, are what give rise to the idea that God must have been *surprised* that I rather than someone else came to be. But clearly, the uncontrollability of singular existence notwithstanding, he was not. For one can be surprised by an event only if it does not match one's expectations. But God's expectations—his expectation that someone instantiate my *de facto* Q-proxy **P** in particular—were met down to the last detail. The only logical room for surprise here would be if, for example, *per impossibile*, God had intended that something instantiate **P**, and, as a result of that intention, something turned out to instantiate another Q-proxy **P′** instead.[59]

A final objection attacks the semantics directly. Granted, the objection goes, the proposed semantics preserves our *talk* of God's singular intentions and singular foreknowledge. But it is really a cheat: it only interprets such talk in a way that preserves its surface form while evacuating it of genuine content, the way some theologians preserve talk of faith in God by translating it into talk of, say, openness to the future.[60] The simple fact of the matter is that, on the proposed account, God didn't *really* intend for me to exist, just someone, anyone, like me, and that is all one is warranted in saying. A clear-eyed assessment thus shows that the proposed semantics is hollow.

I see no ground for this objection. For first, unlike the clumsy retranslations of the theologians, the proposed semantics has not been developed *ad hoc* simply to avoid undesired metaphysical or theological commitments. To the contrary, the semantics is proposed as an instance of a more general semantic phenomenon, and is motivated by a powerful and pervasive metaphysical understanding of possibility.

Furthermore, surely it is no accident that we are semantically licensed to recharacterize certain past general intentional states as singular in the manner pointed out above. For even though the propositional content of such states is general, there is nonetheless, psychologically, a sort of singular directedness to them in virtue of the fact that what is conceived in general is a state of affairs that will (typically) involve a single individual. Natural language itself reveals this "quasi-singular" character of such states, especially in the use of pronouns to describe the contents of states such as those in question; your artist friend in the story above, for example, might have told you, "I intend to create a new work, and *it* will be my masterpiece," the pronoun conveying a redolence of singularity.[61] All the same, the content of the artist's intention is general. Thus, the pronoun, considered at the time of utterance, cannot be understood to be referential, but rather, e.g., a bound variable. Nonetheless, the resulting work is rightly said to be the *fulfillment* of that intention, and hence, after its creation, the artist's earlier attitude is, from that perspective, quite rightly redescribed as singular, and as directed toward the later work.

There is, I think, no reason not to model God's own intentions before creation along precisely the same lines. God's general creative intentions had the same sort of quasi-singular character—more so, given the detail of the conceptions with which he worked and the certainty of the outcome. Our singular redescriptions of his intentions and knowledge are thus similarly warranted. Furthermore, there seems no reason not to believe that God anticipated the singular outcome of his intentions with proportionally greater joy and expectation. I just don't see any gaps; semantically, metaphysically, and psychologically, there seems to me no need to suppose that the numerical identity of the products of God's creative activity had to have been fixed in the divine intellect ahead of time.[62]

## Notes

1. The qualification here stems from the fact that many theists might want to say that God intended that the world be exactly as it is only in some derivative sense that does not entail that God *desired* that the world be exactly as it is; in particular, most theists would not want to hold that God desires the evil that result from the actions of free creatures.
2. Ecclesiasticus 23:29; see also Jeremiah 1:5, where God affirms to the prophet that "before I formed thee in the bowels of thy mother I knew thee."
3. See, e.g., L. Zagzebski, "Individual Essence and the Creation," in T. Morris (ed.), *Divine and Human Action: Essays in the Metaphysics of Theism* (Ithaca, Cornell University Press, 1988), pp. 119-144; see esp. p. 136.
4. Quoted in M. Adams, *William Ockham* (Notre Dame, University of Notre Dame Press, 1987) p. 1068. St. Thomas discusses this argument in *De*

*Potentia Dei*, Q. 3, Art. 1, Obj. 17.

5. P. Geach, "Causality and Creation," *Sophia* 1 (1962), pp. 1-8.
6. A. Prior, *Past, Present, and Future* (Oxford, Clarendon Press, 1967), p. 140.
7. *Summa Theologica* (hereafter *ST*), Q. 15, Art. 2; see also *Summa Contra Gentiles* (hereafter *SGC*) I, 49 [3]. For Henry's position, see M. Adams, op. cit., pp. 1068-1072.
8. Though 'generated' would probably be more appropriate than 'created' here, since (as Fred Freddoso pointed out to me) the mechanism by which the ideas come to be in Thomas is analogous to, perhaps even itself the mechanism for, the generation of the Son by the Father, and Thomas would shrink from any hint of the idea that the Son is a creature. See, e.g., *DV*, Qu. 2, Art. 4. Also most medievals would want to qualify the doctrine of divine ideas so as to play down the apparent plurality of ideas in God, since a plurality of ideas does not sit well with the doctrine of divine simplicity. For more on this issue, see T. Morris, *Anselmian Explorations* (Notre Dame, University of Notre Dame Press, 1987), ch. 6.
9. See M. Adams, op. cit., p. 1072.
10. *ST* 1, Q. 15, Art. 3.
11. E.g., *ST* 1, Q. 14, Art's. 5, 11, 12; Q. 15, Art. 3.
12. *ST* 1, Q.14, Art. 6.
13. On proper knowledge, see *De Veritate* (henceforth *DV*) Q. 2, Art. 4 (1'): "No one can distinguish between things if he does not have proper knowledge of them. But God has that kind of knowledge of creatures which distinguishes between them; for He knows that this creature is not that creature...Therefore, God has proper knowledge of things." Also *ST* 1, Q. 14, Art. 6: "To have a proper knowledge of things is to know them not only in general, but as they are distinct from each other."
14. Ibid.
15. Ibid. Although in this passage Thomas speaks only of a thing's perfec*tion*, in the singular, elsewhere he speaks frequently of virtue, intelligence, etc. individually as perfections, and thus it seems reasonable to construe the perfection of a creature, or indeed perhaps of God (though not, for Thomas, so as to imply intrinsic plurality in God), as the sum of its perfections. See, e.g., *ST* 1, Q. 4, Art. 2; *SCG* I, 28 [3]; 36 [2]; 44 [6];
16. *ST* 1, Q.14, Art. 6.
17. Zagzebski, op. cit., can be taken to be arguing to the contrary. I discuss her view briefly below.
18. *ST* 1, Q. 11, Art. 3. Strictly speaking, the most Thomas can be said to be defending here is the principle that, necessarily, for any object $x$, there is no (as opposed to: necessarily, there is no) object $y$ distinct from $x$ that has exactly the same perfections (in the same measures) as $x$.
19. *ST* 1, Q. 50, Art. 4.
20. *DV*, Qu. 2, Art. 5, Reply.
21. See, e.g., *DV*, Qu. 2, Art. 6, answer to difficulty 1; see also E. Anscombe and P. Geach, *Three Philosophers* (Ithaca, Cornell University Press, 1961), pp. 74-5.
22. *DV*, Qu. 2, Art. 6, answer to difficulty 1; *DV*, Qu. 10, Art. 5, reply.

23. My reasoning: if a principle of individuation $P$ is not also a principle of identity, then it is superfluous. For if $P$ is not a principle of identity, then whatever it is in virtue of which a thing has its identity, in virtue of which it is that very thing, is simultaneously something in virtue of which it is distinct from every other thing. Hence $P$ is superfluous.

   Note also that there do seem to be individuating principles that are not principles of identity. Indeed, *pace* Thomas, it seems to me that having the matter one has at any given moment is just such a principle.

24. Else, if for no other reason, God would not know whether the singular he knows in virtue of its matter (see below) was that thing rather than some other thing which has or could have had the same form; e.g., a counterpart in a symmetrical universe.

25. *DV*, Qu. 2, Art. 5, reply to Obj. 14.

26. Cf. *DV*, Qu. 2, Art. 5: "[A]n artist knows a product of his art by means of the form which he has in himself and upon which he models his product. However, he produces his work only with respect to its form—nature has prepared the matter for the work of art. Accordingly, by means of his art, an artist knows his works only under the aspect of form. Now, every form is of itself universal; and, consequently, by means of his art, a builder knows, indeed, house in general, but not this house or that house, unless he acquires other knowledge of it through his senses."

27. Ibid.

28. To prove this using possible worlds lingo (and, for simplicity, ignoring times), suppose $L$ is a likeness and that $S$ exemplifies $L$ in some possible world $W$. By (1), $S$ must have an individuating material part $m$ in $W$. Having that particular part is a perfection $P$, hence it is included within $L$, by maximality. Suppose now that $S'$ has $L$ in some other possible world $W'$. Then $S'$ has $P$ in $W'$, and hence has $m$ as part of its matter in $W'$. But then, by definition of an individuating material part, $S = S'$.

29. See M. Adams, op. cit., p. 678.

30. Fred Freddoso suggested this pious response to me in conversation.

31. Unlike the more familiar definition, this notion of haecceity does not require that a haecceity $H$ be essential to the object, if any, that exemplifies it. Suppose, for example (implausibly, perhaps—it's only an example, after all), that there is a mental state that only one person $S$ is capable of having, but, like most mental states, is not one that $S$ is always in. Then the property of being in that state is a haecceity of $S$, on my definition, even though it is not essential to him (though of course possibly being in that state presumably is). For the more familiar definition, see, e.g., in R. Chisholm, *Person and Object* (London: Allen and Unwin, 1976), ch. 1, and A. Plantinga, *The Nature of Necessity* (Oxford: Clarendon Press, 1974)) ch. 5.

32. For a contemporary defense of the coherence of the doctrine of divine ideas with respect to properties, relations, and propositions, see T. Morris and C. Menzel, "Absolute Creation," *American Philosophical Quarterly* 23 (1986), pp. 353-363. A more detailed version of the view is extended to numbers and sets in C. Menzel, "Theism, Platonism, and the Metaphysics of Mathematics," *Faith and Philosophy* 4 (1987), pp. 365-382. The latter is reprinted with corrections and revisions in P. Grim et al. (eds.), *The*

*Philosopher's Annual: Volume X—1987* (Atascadero: Ridgeview Publishing Company, 1987), pp. 91-112.

33. See R. Adams, "Primitive Thisness and Primitive Identity," *Journal of Philosophy* 76 (1979), p. 7.

34. See G. Boolos, "The Iterative Conception of Set," *The Journal of Philosophy*, 68 (1971), pp. 215-231.

35. It is perhaps plausible to think that all propositions are logically complex. If there are logically simple propositions, they would presumably be ones like **It is raining**, though this is perhaps better taken to be the attribution of a property to a given piece of the world, and hence to be logically complex, involving the property of raining and the given piece.

36. Theories of PRPs that work out ideas along these lines in formal detail are found in G. Bealer, *Quality and Concept* (Oxford: Oxford University Press, 1982), E. Zalta, *Abstract Objects* (Dordrecht: D. Reidel, 1983), and C. Menzel, "A Complete, Type-free, 'Second-order' Logic and Its Philosophical Foundations," Report #CSLI-86-40, Center for the Study of Language and Information, Stanford University, 1986.

37. Fine makes this sort of move in "Plantinga's Reduction of Possibilist Discourse," in J. Tomberlin and P. van Inwagen, *Alvin Plantinga* (Dordrecht: D. Reidel Publishing Company, 1985), pp. 158-160.

38. For related complaints, see, e.g., R. Adams, "Actualism and Thisness," *Synthese* 49 (1981), pp. 3-41; R. Coburn "Individual Essences and Possible Worlds," in P. French *et al.* (eds.), *Midwest Studies in Philosophy, XI: Studies in Essentialism* (Minneapolis: University of Minnesota Press, 1986), pp. 165-183; A. McMichael, "A Problem for Actualism about Possible Worlds," *Philosophical Review* 92 (1983), pp. 49-66; and C. Menzel, "Actualism, Ontological Commitment and Possible World Semantics," *Synthese* 85 (1990).

39. Plantinga himself has appealed to qualitative haecceitism in the face of such difficulties in conversation, though he emphasizes that he has not abandoned its nonqualitative cousin.

40. See, e.g., Zagzebski, op. cit., p. 131.

41. Actually, I don't think this idea is very safe at all, since I'm adopting the freewheeling, informal approach to the theory of properties characteristic of the friends of haecceitism. On this approach, rather extravagant assumptions are made about the nature and existence of properties that are very difficult to justify in a more formal, and more judicious, setting. Natural reconstructions of those assumptions lead, at best, to considerable formal complications (e.g., infinite conjunctions, properties built up from themselves, etc.), and at worst, to paradox. Nonetheless, the approach has a very strong and, in the context, helpful, intuitive appeal, so I'll not cavil over the deeper logical issues here.

42. I thus assume the doctrine known as *serious actualism*, i.e., that an object can have properties only when it exists. For a complete modal logic that incorporates this assumption, and a discussion of surrounding issues, see C. Menzel, "The True Modal Logic," *Journal of Philosophical Logic*, forthcoming.

43. Adams has argued this very cogently and at great length in "Primitive Thisness and Primitive Identity."

44. I believe Zagzebski, op. cit., has accomplished this. However, I find her arguments for strong qualitative haecceitism to be unsuccessful, though it would take some work to show this. My apologies to Professor Zagzebski for not being able to give her interesting paper the attention it deserves.

45. C. Hartshorne and P. Weiss, *Collected Papers of C. S. Peirce*, vol. IV (Cambridge: Harvard University Press, 1933), p. 147 (4.172). Prior and Adams have been perhaps the most rigorous champions of the generality of the possible of late. Adams defends and develops the view at length in "Actualism and Thisness." Prior argues for the view throughout his writings, but the clearest statements are found in his paper "Identifiable Individuals," in *Papers on Time and Tense* (Oxford: Clarendon Press, 1968), ch. 7, and ch. 8, "Time and Existence," in *Past, Present, and Future* (Oxford: Clarendon Press, 1967).

46. E.g., of course, haecceities of actual individuals, and, perhaps, properties like **being the person resulting from the union of *these* zygotes**.

47. Compare Adams, "Actualism and Thisness," pp. 9-10.

48. For simplicity, I suppose here that $\pi$ expresses a purely qualitative property.

49. *ST* 1, Q.15, Art 1, my emphasis.

50. Indeed, I think that is so even if possibilism or haecceitism is true, since there is nothing in the artist's conception that could enable the sculptor to get hold of a single *possibile* or haecceity; it could determine at best a class of qualitatively identical ones.

51. There are of course epistemological problems here with creaturely knowledge of the future, but these don't affect the argument, since they presumably don't apply to God.

52. I'm supposing we can make precise sense of maximal $Q^*$-conjunctions formally (cf. my doubts in note 41). I assume, though, that something along these lines will do the job.

53. I am supposing that God has not done anything tricky like create a symmetrical universe, i.e., a universe with two halves that are qualitatively identical across an axis of symmetry, and hence one in which every instantiated Q-proxy is instantiated by two things. Even if this were the case, though, the semantics proposed below could easily be modified to accommodate it by imposing certain restrictions on the domain of discourse to one's own qualitatively corner of the universe.

54. P. Grim argues there are in fact Gettier-style problems for God in "Some Neglected Problems of Omniscience," *American Philosophical Quarterly* 20 (1983), pp. 265-276. These arguments are addressed in J. Kvanvig, *On the Possibility of an All-knowing God* (London: MacMillan Press, Ltd., 1986), pp. 35-37.

55. My proposal, of course, does not preserve the idea that God had singular knowledge of objects that don't in fact exist, which was suggested above in the discussion of timelessness to be part of the standard conception; nor should it. However, it isn't obvious that it preserves modal knowledge in general even of singulars that do exist. For example, ask yourself if the following should come out true: If God hadn't created Reagan, he would still have known that he could have created him. My own intuitions waffle.

56. George Mavrodes expressed this objection to me.

57. But see Adams, "Time and Thisness," *Midwest Studies in Philosophy, Volume 11: Studies in Essentialism* (Minneapolis, University of Minnesota Press, 1986), pp. 315-329, where he suggests that knowing can be a transtemporal relation between a knower and the proposition known. It's an intriguing idea, but I don't find his arguments convincing.

58. I.e., "accidentally" necessary because it has already obtained in the past; see A. Freddoso, "Accidental Necessity and Logical Determinism," *Journal of Philosophy* 80 (1983), pp. 257-278.

59. Indeed, opponents of this view who are partial to the principle of sufficient reason have a problem here. For if God had a range of qualitatively indistinguishable proxies to choose from before creation, what could possibly have motivated his choice of one over another? Creation, it would then seem, could never have gotten off the ground. Thanks to my colleague Michael Hand for bringing up the issue of sufficient reason in this context.

60. See, e.g., A. Plantinga "Two Concepts of Modality: Modal Realism and Modal Reductionism" in J. Tomberlin, *Philosophical Perspectives, 1, Metaphysics, 1987* (Atascadero: Ridgeview Publishing Co., 1987), pp. 189-231; see esp. p. 219, and note 41.

61. This phenomenon is made explicit in recent approaches to the semantics of attitude reports based on Kamp's work. See, for example, N. Asher, "Belief in Discourse Representation Theory," *Journal of Philosophical Logic* 15 (1986), pp. 127-189.

62. I am deeply indebted to Fred Freddoso for his generous assistance and scholarly advice throughout the writing of this paper, which he freely offered despite his misgivings that he was contributing to the perversion of philosophical theology. Thanks also to my colleague Jon Kvanvig for comments, and to Jim Tomberlin for providing the opportunity to write the paper, and for his patient and indulgent dealings with a tardy author.

Philosophical Perspectives, 5, Philosophy of Religion, 1991

# ON THE LOGIC OF THE
# ONTOLOGICAL ARGUMENT*

Paul E. Oppenheimer
Thinking Machines Corporation
Edward N. Zalta
Stanford University

Saint Anselm of Canterbury offered several arguments for the existence of God. We examine the famous ontological argument in *Proslogium* II. Many recent authors have interpreted this argument as a modal one.[1] But we believe that Jonathan Barnes has argued persuasively that Anselm's argument is not modal.[2] Even if one were to construe the word 'can' in the definite description 'that than which none greater can be conceived' in terms of metaphysical possibility, the logic of the ontological argument itself doesn't include inferences based on this modality. In this paper, we develop a reading of Anselm's *Proslogium* that contains no modal inferences. Rather, the argument turns on the difference between saying that *there is* such a thing as x and saying that x has the *property* of existence. We formally represent the claim that *there is* such a thing as x by '$\exists y(y=x)$' and the claim that x has the property of existence by '$E!x$'. That is, we represent the difference between the two claims by exploiting the distinction between quantifying over x and predicating existence of x. We shall sometimes refer to this as the distinction between the being of x and the existence of x. Thus, instead of reading Anselm as having discovered a way of inferring God's actuality from His mere possibility, we read him as having discovered a way of inferring God's existence from His mere being.

Another important feature of our reading concerns the fact that we take the phrase "that than which none greater can be conceived" seriously. Certain inferences in the ontological argument are intimately linked to the logical behavior of this phrase, which is best represented as a definite description.[3] If we are to do justice to Anselm's argument, we must not syntactically eliminate descriptions the way Russell does. One of the highlights of our interpretation is that a very simple inference involving descriptions stands at the heart of the argument.[4]

## The Language and Logic Required for the Argument

We shall cast our new reading in a standard first-order language. It contains the usual two kinds of simple terms: constants $a_1$, $a_2$,... ($a$, $b$,... as metavariables) and variables $x_1$, $x_2$,... ($x$, $y$,... as metavariables). It also contains predicates $P_1^n$, $P_2^n$,...($n \geq 1$) ($P^n$, $Q^n$,... as metavariables). In addition to atomic formulas of the form $P^n\tau_1...\tau_n$ and identity formulas of the form $\tau = \tau'$ (where the $\tau$s are any terms), the language consists of complex formulas of the form $\sim \phi$, $\phi \supset \psi$, and $\forall x\phi$.[5] We shall suppose that where $\phi$ is any formula, then $\iota x\phi$ constitutes a complex, though primitive, term of the language. We read $\iota x\phi$ as 'the (unique) $x$ such that $\phi$' and we refer to these terms as definite descriptions. Note that primitive descriptions (in complex formulas) do not have 'scope.' For example, in a complex formula such as $P\iota xQx \supset S\iota xTx$, there is no option of asking whether the descriptions have wide or narrow scope (or primary or secondary occurrence), since the formula is not an abbreviation of, or eliminable in terms of, any other formulas.

In what follows, we use '$\tau$' to range over all terms: constants, variables, *and* descriptions. We use '$\phi_x^\tau$' to designate the result of substituting term $\tau$ for each free occurrence of the variable $x$ in formula $\phi$.

The models of this simple language are standard. A *model* **M** is any pair $<$**D**,**F**$>$, where **D** is a non-empty set and **F** is a function defined on the constants and predicates of the language such that: (1) for any constant $a$, $\mathbf{F}(a) \in \mathbf{D}$, and (2) for any predicate $P^n$, $\mathbf{F}(P^n) \subseteq \mathbf{D}^n$. In the usual way, we define an *assignment* to the variables (relative to model **M**) to be any function **f** that maps each variable to an element of **D**. And since our language contains complex terms, we define in the usual way by simultaneous recursion the *denotation* function for terms (relative to model **M** and assignment **f**) and the *satisfaction* conditions for formulas (relative to model **M**) (we shall suppress the subscripts that relativize these notions throughout). The denotation function shall be that function $\mathbf{d}(\tau)$ meeting the following conditions:[6]

1. Where $a$ is any constant, $\mathbf{d}(a) = \mathbf{F}(a)$
2. Where $x$ is any variable, $\mathbf{d}(x) = \mathbf{f}(x)$
3. Where $\iota x \phi$ is any description,

$$\mathbf{d}(\iota x \phi) = \begin{cases} \mathbf{o} \ (\in \mathbf{D}) \text{ iff } (\exists \mathbf{f}')(\mathbf{f}' \overset{x}{=} \mathbf{f} \ \& \ \mathbf{f}'(x) = \mathbf{o} \ \& \ \mathbf{f}' \text{ satisfies } \phi \\ \qquad \& \ (\forall \mathbf{f}'')(\mathbf{f}'' \overset{x}{=} \mathbf{f}' \ \& \ \mathbf{f}'' \text{ satisfies } \phi \supset \mathbf{f}'' = \mathbf{f}')) \\ \text{undefined, otherwise} \end{cases}$$

Notice that the clause governing descriptions packs, in a semantically precise way, Russell's analysis of definite descriptions into the conditions that must obtain if a description is to have a denotation. Notice also we do *not* assign some arbitrary object outside the domain of quantification to descriptions $\iota x \phi$ for which $\phi$ fails to be uniquely satisfied; rather, we assign them nothing at all.

Now to complete the simultaneous recursion, we define $\mathbf{f}$ *satisfies* $\phi$ (i.e., $\phi$ is true (under $\mathbf{M}$) relative to assignment $\mathbf{f}$) as follows:

1. $\mathbf{f}$ satisfies $P^n \tau_1 ... \tau_n$ iff $\exists \mathbf{o}_1 ... \mathbf{o}_n \in \mathbf{D}$ ($\mathbf{d}(\tau_1) = \mathbf{o}_1 \ \& \ ... \ \&$ $\mathbf{d}(\tau_n) = \mathbf{o}_n \ \& \ <\mathbf{o}_1, ..., \mathbf{o}_n> \ \in \mathbf{F}(P^n))$
2. $\mathbf{f}$ satisfies $\tau = \tau'$ iff $\exists \mathbf{o}, \mathbf{o}' \in \mathbf{D}$ ($\mathbf{d}(\tau) = \mathbf{o} \ \& \ \mathbf{d}(\tau') = \mathbf{o}' \ \& \ \mathbf{o} = \mathbf{o}'$)
3. $\mathbf{f}$ satisfies $\sim \psi$ iff $\mathbf{f}$ fails to satisfy $\psi$
4. $\mathbf{f}$ satisfies $\psi \supset \chi$ iff either $\mathbf{f}$ fails to satisfy $\psi$ or $\mathbf{f}$ satisfies $\chi$
5. $\mathbf{f}$ satisfies $\forall x \psi$ iff for every $\mathbf{f}'$, if $\mathbf{f}' \overset{x}{=} \mathbf{f}$, then $\mathbf{f}'$ satisfies $\psi$

Finally, in the usual way, we define: $\phi$ is true (under $\mathbf{M}$) iff every assignment $\mathbf{f}$ satisfies $\phi$. $\phi$ is false (under $\mathbf{M}$) iff no $\mathbf{f}$ satisfies $\phi$.

Notice that our definitions of satisfaction and truth are well-defined even for atomic and identity formulas that may contain non-denoting descriptions. Clauses 1 and 2 of the definition of satisfaction guarantee that an atomic or identity sentence will be true if and only if each term in the sentence has a denotation and the denotations stand in the right relationship.[7] Thus, atomic and identity sentences containing non-denoting descriptions are simply false. The truth conditions for the molecular and quantified sentences are the usual ones. Notice that from a semantic point of view, primitive descriptions occurring in molecular and quantified formulas are interpreted as if they have narrow scope. For example, the sentence $P \iota x Q x \supset S \iota x T x$ is true just in case: if there is a unique thing in $\mathbf{F}(Q)$ which is also in $\mathbf{F}(P)$, then there is a unique thing in $\mathbf{F}(T)$ which is also in $\mathbf{F}(S)$. It is a consequence that molecular sentences may contain non-denoting descriptions but nevertheless be true, since they may be true solely in virtue of their logical form. Thus, $P\imath xQx \supset P\imath xQx$ is true regardless of whether the description $\imath xQx$ has a denotation.

We may associate with these semantic definitions a very simple logic for our language. All of the axioms and rules of classical propositional logic apply to the formulas, and all of the classical axioms and rules of predicate logic (with identity) apply to the constants and variables. However, the predicate logic of descriptions must be 'free', since these terms may fail to denote. This means that one cannot generalize upon a description $\imath x\phi$ without first asserting $\exists y(y = \imath x\phi)$. Specifically, one may not infer $\psi_z^{\imath x\phi}$ from $\forall z\psi$ without first assuming $\exists y(y = \imath x\phi)$, nor may one infer $\exists z\psi$ from $\psi_z^{\imath x\phi}$ without this same assumption. Without such restrictions, one could infer $P\imath xQx$ directly from $\forall zPz$, for example. But such an inference would move one from truth to falsehood in models where everything is in the extension of the predicate '$P$' and nothing (or more than one thing) is in the extension of the predicate '$Q$.' Consequently, $\exists y(y = \imath xQx)$ is required before one may infer $P\imath xQx$ from $\forall zPz$.

It is important to recognize that *we could have avoided the use of free logic for descriptions*, by assigning some arbitrary denotation to descriptions $\imath x\phi$ for which $\phi$ fails to be uniquely satisfied. It turns out that given the premises of the ontological argument described in the next section, we shall be able to prove that the description 'that than which none greater can be conceived' has a denotation.[8] Since this is the only description studied in this paper, and it provably has a denotation, we don't really have to make allowances for non-denoting descriptions as far as this paper is concerned.

So why, then, do we employ free logic for descriptions? Mainly for psychological reasons. By using free logic, we remove any suspicion that it is the models of our language, or the semantic definition of denotation, which force descriptions to have a denotation. We want our readers to be assured that it is not a formal device embodied by the very logical set-up that guarantees that the description 'that than which none greater can be conceived' has a denotation. Any demonstration that this description does have a denotation will not be a matter of logic alone, but must depend on additional non-logical premises.

Moreover, we would like to stress the fact that our use of free logic does not commit us to any arguments used to justify this logic. Indeed, we explicitly reject a certain argument that free logicians have used to conclude that the logic of constants must be free. They argue, from the fact that in standard quantification theory it is a theorem that $\exists y(y=a)$, for any constant $a$, that the *existence* of the things denoted by the constants becomes a matter of logic. But, of course, in a logic that separates being (or quantification) from existence, the only thing that the theorem in question shows is that the things denoted by the constants have being, not that they exist. This simply means that we can talk about and quantify over the thing denoted by '$a$' without presupposing that this thing exists.

Finally, note that a single logical axiom governs the behavior of definite descriptions. Where $\psi$ is an atomic formula or identity formula in which $z$ occurs free, the axiom governing descriptions may be formulated as follows:

*Description Axiom:* $\psi_z^{\iota x \phi} \equiv \exists y(\phi_x^y \ \& \ \forall u(\phi_x^u \supset u=y) \ \& \ \psi_z^y)$

To see what this says, consider the following instance, in which $\psi$ is '$Rz$' and $\iota x \phi$ is '$\iota x Q x$':

$R \iota x Q x \equiv \exists y(Qy \ \& \ \forall u(Qu \supset u=y) \ \& \ Ry)$

This simply says: the thing which is $Q$ is $R$ iff there is something $y$ such that (a) $y$ is $Q$, (b) everything that is $Q$ is identical to $y$, and (c) $y$ is $R$. This axiom expresses in our language Russell's analysis of the definite description without eliminating descriptions from the language.[9]

To state our first important theorem governing descriptions, let '$\exists! y \phi$' be an abbreviation for '$\exists y \forall u(\phi_y^u \equiv u=y)$.' Thus, we may read '$\exists! y \phi$' as 'there is a unique $y$ such that $\phi$.' Note that the following is a simple consequence of the *Description Axiom*:

*Description Theorem 1:* $\exists! x \phi \supset \exists y(y=\iota x \phi)$[10]

Semantically, *Description Theorem 1* tells us that if condition $\phi$ is uniquely satisfied, then the description "the $x$ such that $\phi$" is guaranteed to have a denotation. So if one knows that a condition $\phi$ is uniquely satisfied, one may *introduce* a description to denote the thing that uniquely satisfies it. It will soon become clear that this is something that Anselm does implicitly in his argument. Moreover, this theorem tells us that such descriptions may be generalized— they can be instantiated into universal claims or replaced by existentially quantified variables.

The following lemma is also a consequence of the *Description Axiom*:

*Lemma 1:* $\tau = \imath x\phi \supset \phi_x^\tau$, for any term $\tau$.[11]

Given *Lemma 1*, it should be easy to see that the following is a theorem:

*Description Theorem 2:* $\exists y(y = \imath x\phi) \supset \phi_x^{\imath x\phi}$

*Proof:* Assume the antecedent, namely, $\exists y(y = \imath x\phi)$. So there must be some object, say $c$, such that $c = \imath x\phi$. But by Lemma 1, it follows that $\phi_x^c$. So $\phi_x^{\imath x\phi}$. ∎

Here is a simple instance of this schema: $\exists y(y = \imath xQx) \supset Q\imath xQx$. In other words, if there is something that is *the* $Q$-thing, then it (i.e., the $Q$-thing) must have the property $Q$. We believe that this simple theorem plays a central role in the Ontological Argument.

## Non-Logical Predicates and Meaning Postulates

In order to represent the premises of Anselm's argument, we must add to our formal language some non-logical predicates and meaning postulates. Since our view is that the argument turns on the distinction between being and existence, we begin by discussing how this distinction is to be represented. Our plan is simply to add the special predicate '*E*!' to denote the property of *existence*. Note that there is a difference between formulas of the form '$\exists x\phi$' and formulas of the form '$\exists x(E!x\ \&\ \phi)$'. We read the former as "there is an $x$ such that $\phi$," or "some $x$ is such that $\phi$." We read the latter as "there is an $x$ having the property of *existence* which is such that $\phi$," or "there *exists* an $x$ such that $\phi$." In other words, we are not reading the quantifier '$\exists$' as existentially loaded. Unfortunately, there is a tradition of calling '$\exists$' the 'existential' quantifier, and in what follows, we conform to that tradition. But we want to make it clear that we do not use the existential quantifier to assert existence.[12]

We therefore absolutely reject the definition of '*E*!$x$' as '$\exists y(y = x)$'. This definition would collapse the very distinction that proves crucial to the argument. Indeed, the rejection of this definition has led to some rather interesting and exciting new developments in metaphysics. Recently, Terence Parsons ([1974], [1979], and [1980]) has developed a precise and fruitful new theory of nonexistent objects.

Parsons' theory asserts that there are objects that don't exist, and this assertion is captured formally as: $\exists x(\sim E!x)$. Now if '$E!x$' were defined as '$\exists y(y=x)$', Parsons' theory would assert a manifest logical falsehood, namely: $\exists x \sim \exists y(y=x)$.[13] So, in his metaphysical framework, the distinction between quantifying over $x$ and predicating existence of $x$, reflecting the difference between being and existence, is crucial. Parson's theory offers clearcut responses to the standard objections to theories of nonexistent objects and has interesting applications, which include the problem of negative singular existential statements and the problem of analyzing statements in and about fiction.

In addition to Parsons' work, one of the present authors has developed a metaphysical theory of abstract objects that also utilizes the distinction between the quantifier and the existence predicate. In Zalta [1983] and [1988], one finds '$E!$' used as a predicate denoting the property of existence. An object $x$ is defined to be *abstract* ($A!x$) iff $x$ couldn't possibly exemplify the property of existence ($\sim \Diamond E!x$). Zalta's metaphysical theory entails that there are such abstract objects ($\exists x A!x$), which in turn entails that there are objects that don't exist ($\exists x \sim E!x$). Zalta's abstract objects are then used to model such things as monads, possible worlds, fictional characters, Fregean senses, and mathematical objects, as part of the applications of the theory.

There are two points to be made by referring to the work of these authors. The first is that their work demonstrates that distinguishing being from existence is not only coherent but also useful. If Parsons and Zalta are right, then that difference underlies and explains many of our commonsense beliefs. The second is that, whether or not one accepts their theories of objects, the metaphysical framework they presuppose, that of a realm of objects about which one can talk and over which one can quantify *whether or not they exist*, is very similar to the framework Anselm presupposes. Here is why.

Inspection of Anselm's language in *Proslogium* II reveals that he explicitly contrasts objects that have being in the understanding (*esse in intellectu*) with those that have being in reality (*esse in re*) as well. Anselm sometimes refers to these two kinds of being as 'existence in the understanding' and 'existence in reality'. For example, line 12 of *Proslogium* II begins with '*Existit*', as opposed to '*Esse*', and concludes that God exists both in the understanding and in reality.[14] Let us, just for the moment, continue to speak with Anselm, and use the phrases 'being in the understanding' and 'exists in the understanding' interchangeably (and similarly for 'being in reality' and 'exists in reality'). Note also that Anselm speaks as if one and the same thing can have being (exist) either solely in the understanding, or can simultaneously have being (exist) both in the understanding and in reality. This is presupposed by his view that it is greater to have being (exist) both in the understanding and in reality than to have being (exist) in the understanding alone.

In summary, Anselm believes that there is a difference between the two metaphysical states of being in the understanding and being in reality. His use of the verbs 'to be' and 'to exist' is unregimented. He relies, rather, on the qualifying phrases 'in the intellect' and 'in reality' to reflect that difference. Parsons and Zalta rely on a regimented use of 'there is' and 'there exists' to reflect a similar difference.

Now if we were to represent Anselm's manner of speaking in a strict way, we would need three distinct notions. A quantifier '∃' would be needed to represent Anselm's notion 'there is' (*esse*) or 'there exists' (*existit*); a predicate '*U*' would be needed to represent the property of being in the understanding; a predicate '*E*!' would be needed to represent the property of being in reality. We would then be able to represent Anselm's quantification over two kinds of objects by the distinction between '∃x(Ux & ...)' and '∃x(E!x & ...)'. The former reads 'there is (exists) an $x$ in the understanding such that...', while the latter reads 'there is (exists) an $x$ in reality such that...'.

However, for reasons that will become plain, we shall simplify the formula '∃x(Ux & φ)' to '∃xφ', and read the latter as 'there is an $x$ such that φ', where this is to be distinguished from 'there exists an $x$ such that φ' ('∃x(E!x & φ)'). We thus assimilate Anselm's language to that used by Parsons and Zalta, for Anselm's notion of 'being (existence) in the understanding' corresponds to Parsons' and Zalta's notion of being or quantification, and Anselm's notion of 'being (existence) in reality' corresponds to Parsons' and Zalta's notion of existence. These correspondences establish an analogy between the metaphysical picture presupposed by Anselm, on the one hand, and that described by Parsons and Zalta, on the other. Both pictures include two realms of objects, one having a greater degree of reality than the other. In both pictures, an object can "inhabit" both realms simultaneously: Anselm concludes on line 12 of *Proslogium* II that God exists both in the intellect and in reality; for Parsons and Zalta, the existence of an object $x$ (*E*!x) entails the being of $x$ (∃y y=x).

Moreover, in both frameworks, one can talk about an object $x$, predicate things of $x$, and quantify over $x$, regardless of whether $x$ inhabits one or both of the ontological realms.

So by adopting Parsons' and Zalta's regimented use of 'there is' and 'there exists' and letting '$\exists x \phi$' go proxy for '$\exists x(Ux \& \phi)$' we shall be able to simplify the formulas that will be used in the argument. As the reader will soon be able to verify, this simplification has no untoward consequences. For our reconstruction of Anselm's argument, the notion of 'being' works just as well in opposition to the notion of 'existence (in reality)' as does the notion of 'being in the understanding'. However, if perfect faithfulness to Anselm is desired, then it is a routine exercise to add the conjunct '$Ux$' in the appropriate places of the argument that we present in the next section.

We turn, then, to an analysis of the premises of Anselm's ontological argument. These premises require the following special predicates and meaning postulate. First, '$C$' is to be a one-place predicate and '$Cx$' is to be read as: $x$ can be conceived. Second, '$G$' is to be a two-place predicate and '$Gxy$' is to be read as: $x$ is greater than $y$. For reasons that will become apparent, the relation denoted by '$G$' must be *connected*. In other words, $G$ obeys the following meaning postulate (which constitutes a non-logical axiom): $\forall x \forall y(Gxy \lor Gyx \lor x=y)$. We shall discuss this requirement in greater detail in the next section.

### The Premises of the Argument

We believe that the first premise of Anselm's main argument in the *Proslogium* II is: there is (in the understanding) something than which nothing greater can be conceived. This premise doesn't occur until line 8. In lines 1 through 7, Anselm works his way through a subargument designed to marshal agreement on this claim. He concludes: "Therefore even the fool is bound to agree that there is at least in the understanding something than which nothing greater can be imagined."[15] We believe that the conclusion of the subargument in lines 1 through 7, when stripped of the operator "even the fool is bound to agree that," serves as the first premise of the Ontological Argument.

From our discussion in the previous section, it should be clear that a strict representation of Anselm's words would be: $\exists x(Ux \& \sim \exists y(Gyx$

& $Cy$)). Although this is a perfectly good representation of the first premise, we have found that it is more elegant to formulate the first premise as follows:

*Premise 1:* $\exists x(Cx \ \& \ \sim \exists y(Gyx \ \& \ Cy))$

*Premise 1* simply asserts that there is a conceivable thing which is such that nothing greater can be conceived. There is one basic difference between this formulation and the former one: the clause '$Cx$' replaces '$Ux$' as the first conjunct of the quantified claim. Given our discussion in the previous section, it should be clear why we have dropped the conjunct '$Ux$' from our representation of this premise. And little justification is needed for adding the clause '$Cx$'. It makes explicit what is implicit in the clause 'nothing greater can be conceived,' namely, that any such object is itself conceivable.

Further evidence that our formulation of *Premise 1* with the formula '$Cx \ \& \ \sim \exists y(Gyx \ \& \ Cy)$' is a good one comes from the fact that it now follows, by the non-logical axiom for *greater than* alone, that if something satisfies this formula, then something *uniquely* satisfies this formula. In other words, if there is some conceivable thing such that nothing greater can be conceived, there is a *unique* conceivable thing such that nothing greater can be conceived. To see this, let us use '$\phi_1$' to abbreviate the open formula '$Cx \ \& \ \sim \exists y(Gyx \ \& \ Cy)$.' Now consider the following lemma:[16]

*Lemma 2:* $\exists x \phi_1 \supset \exists! x \phi_1$

*Proof:* If we assume the antecedent, all we have to prove is that at most one thing satisfies $\phi_1$. So assume: $\exists x(Cx \ \& \ \sim \exists y(Gyx \ \& \ Cy))$. So there must be some object, say $a$, such that: $Ca \ \& \ \sim \exists y(Gya \ \& \ Cy)$. Recall that all we have to show is that no other conceivable thing distinct from $a$ is such that nothing greater can be conceived. Suppose, for *reductio*, that: $\exists z(z \neq a \ \& \ Cz \ \& \ \sim \exists y(Gyz \ \& \ Cy))$. Let us call such an object '$b$.' We derive a contradiction from this as follows. We know, by the non-logical axiom governing $G$ that $Gab \lor Gba \lor a=b$. Since $b \neq a$, either $Gab \lor Gba$. But both disjuncts lead to contradiction. Suppose $Gab$. Then, since $Ca$, it follows that: $Gab \ \& \ Ca$. So $\exists y(Gyb \ \& \ Cy)$, contrary to the *reductio* hypothesis. But then suppose $Gba$. Again, since by hypothesis $Cb$, it follows that: $Gba \ \& \ Cb$. Again, it follows that $\exists y(Gya \ \& \ Cy)$, contrary to our initial assumption. By *reductio*, then, it follows that $\sim \exists z(z \neq a$ & $Cz$ & $\sim \exists y(Gyz$ & $Cy))$. ∎

It would serve well to explain semantically just why it is that *Lemma 2* is true. To do this, let us consider an arbitrary model that makes the antecedent of *Lemma 2* true and see why it is that the consequent of *Lemma 2* must also be true. In any model of the antecedent of *Lemma 2*, there must be a set of objects called the *conceivable* objects amongst the members of which the *greater than* relation sometimes holds. To picture these models, suppose that an arrow points *away* from conceivable object $a$ to conceivable object $b$ whenever $a$ is greater than $b$. Now, in any model in which '$\exists x \phi_1$' is true, i.e., in which there is a conceivable object such that no conceivable object is greater, there has to be at least one object *having no arrows pointing towards it*! Such an object is called a 'maximal element,' and of course, there may be several such maximal elements. Let us suppose that there are indeed several. Now the model also has to make the non-logical axiom expressing the connectedness of the *greater than* relation true as well. So anytime you find a pair of maximal elements $a$ and $b$, where $a \neq b$, *connectedness* requires that an arrow go from $a$ to $b$ or $b$ to $a$ or both. Note that there can't be *both* an arrow going from $a$ to $b$ and from $b$ to $a$, for otherwise, $a$ and $b$ would both cease to be maximal (the antecedent of *Lemma 2* requires that there be at least one maximal element). Consequently, either an arrow goes from $a$ to $b$ or from $b$ to $a$ (but not both), and so at most one of these two elements will be a maximal element (having no arrows pointing towards it). Since this reasoning applies to any pair of candidate maximal elements, it follows that there is a unique element having no arrows pointing towards it. Thus, the consequent of *Lemma 2* is true, that is, there is a unique conceivable object such that no conceivable object is greater.[17]

Another interesting fact about *Lemma 2* is that its truth doesn't require the stipulation that *greater than* be an *ordering* relation on the conceivable objects. Recall that a relation '$R$ *partially orders* a set $S$ just in case $R$ is anti-symmetric and transitive on the members of $S$.[18] $R$ *totally orders* $S$ whenever $R$ partially orders $S$ and $R$ is connected. But a connected relation $R$ doesn't have to be either transitive or anti-symmetric. To see this, consider the relation $R = \{<a,b>, <b,a>\}$. $R$ is connected, but to make it transitive, you need to add the pairs $<a,a>$ and $<b,b>$; to make it anti-symmetric, you have to delete either the pair $<a,b>$ or the pair $<b,a>$.

Now we believe that only one other premise is used in the Ontological Argument. It occurs in the following line of *Proslogium* II: "For if it is at least in the understanding alone, it can be imagined to be in reality too, which is greater." One way of expressing Anselm's point here is as follows: if that than which none greater can be conceived doesn't exist (in reality), then something greater than it can be conceived. In order to represent this premise formally, note that the description '$\iota x \phi_1$' is the proper translation of "that (conceivable thing) than which none greater can be conceived." We now take the following to be *Premise 2* of the argument:

> *Premise 2:*  $\sim E! \iota x \phi_1 \supset \exists y (G y \iota x \phi_1 \ \& \ Cy)$

In our interpretation of this premise, we don't explicitly identify the object that satisfies the matrix quantified in the consequent. Anselm, however, identifies that object as one just like the nonexistent object of the antecedent but existing. Our slightly weaker interpretation suffices for the argument.

It is worthwhile to note here how *Lemma 2* and *Description Theorem 1* connect *Premises 1* and *2*. From *Premise 1* and *Lemma 2*, it follows that $\exists! x \phi_1$. From this and *Description Theorem 1*, it follows that $\exists y (y = \iota x \phi_1)$. This chain of reasoning shows that there is such a thing as *the* thing than which none greater can be conceived. Such a proof that '$\iota x \phi_1$' has a denotation justifies the introduction and use of this description in any argument based on *Premise 1*. In particular, it justifies the introduction and use of the description in *Premise 2*.

Finally, let us define:

> $D_1$ God ('$g$') $=_{df} \iota x \phi_1$

So, with Anselm, we have defined 'God' to be "the conceivable thing than which no greater can be conceived." One might think that definition $D_1$ introduces the constant '$g$' as a mere abbreviation of the definite description. However, if the constant '$g$' is utilized in an argument *after* it is shown that the description '$\iota x \phi_1$' has a denotation (for example, as shown in the previous paragraph), then $D_1$ doesn't simply provide a way to abbreviate the description, but rather introduces the logical fact that '$g$' is a genuine constant that has the same denotation as the description.

## The Ontological Argument

From *Premise 1*, it follows that $\exists!x\phi_1$, by *Lemma 2*. From this, it follows that $\exists y(y = \iota x\phi_1)$, by *Description Theorem 1*. From this, it follows that: $C\iota x\phi_1$ & $\sim \exists y(Gy\iota x\phi_1$ & $Cy)$, by *Description Theorem 2*. Now, for *reductio*, assume: $\sim E!\iota x\phi_1$. Then, by *Premise 2*, it follows that $\exists y(Gy\iota x\phi_1$ & $Cy)$, which is a contradiction. So $\sim \sim E!\iota x\phi_1$, i.e., $E!\iota x\phi_1$. And by $D_1$, it follows that $E!g$, i.e., God exists. ■

## Features of Our Interpretation

This is a valid argument. It is simple, elegant, and faithful to the text. Our reading has certain virtues not found in other readings in the literature, and in particular, the readings offered by Plantinga, Lewis, Adams, and Barnes. Though Plantinga, Lewis, and Adams do distinguish between quantification and existence, modal inferences play a central role in their readings, and none of these authors takes definite descriptions seriously. Of the four, Barnes is the only one to have eliminated modality from the argument, though we think that his treatment of the definite description is not as satisfying as ours.[19] Here, then, is a list of some new and interesting features of our interpretation of the argument.

First, the validity of our interpretation doesn't depend on the validity of modal inferences. It depends solely on the distinction between being (quantification) and existence, the logic of descriptions, and two premises having at least some *prima facie* plausibility. We represent the phrase 'that than which none greater can be conceived' as a definite description, which is what Anselm took the phrase to be.

Second, our interpretation reveals that *Description Theorem 2* is crucial to the argument. If the description '$\iota x\phi$' denotes, then one may legitimately substitute it for each free $x$ in $\phi$, no matter how complicated $\phi$ is. This principle of 'turning the description upon itself' makes the *reductio* argument possible.

Third, our interpretation *justifies* Anselm's introduction of a definite description into the argument. That is, his first premise is simply that there is *something* such that nothing greater can be conceived. But then he begins talking in terms of the description "that than which none greater can be conceived." *Lemma 2* and *Description Theorem 1* together justify this move.

Fourth, our interpretation reveals that the *connectedness* of the *greater than* relation suffices for the purposes of the argument. The appeal to the connectedness of *greater than* is made in *Lemma 2*. So *greater than* doesn't have to be an ordering relation! This is quite an unexpected result. Besides being connected, the only constraint on *greater than* is that it be a relation that makes *Premises 1* and *2* true.

Fifth, our interpretation seems to make better sense of the commentary on the argument by St. Thomas Aquinas. Aquinas took Anselm to be arguing that the existence of God is obvious.[20] Our reading shows how very simple Anselm's argument is, yet if it had relied on a lot of modal technicalities, then Aquinas would hardly have thought that Anselm takes the existence of God to be self-evident.

Sixth, unlike modal interpretations, our reading makes sense of Kant's criticisms of the argument. In the first *Critique*, Kant argues that 'existence' is not an (analytical) predicate of a thing.[21] It doesn't really matter, for the present purposes, whether one believes that Kant was right or wrong about this. What matters is that his criticism presupposes that the argument is formulated with 'existence' as a predicate. On our conception, the argument is so formulated.

Last, and most interesting of all, on our interpretation, the argument may be transformed into an argument schema for conclusions of the form *God exemplifies F*, for any perfection *F*. To see how, note that one can substitute for the existence predicate in *Premise 2* any predicate that denotes a perfection and the premise remains true. For example, if you let *F* be *omnipotence*, then *Premise 2* asserts: If $\iota x \phi_1$ is not omnipotent, then something greater than $\iota x \phi_1$ can be conceived. Now the argument, and in particular, the *reductio*, will proceed in the same way. The conclusion will be, God exemplifies *F*, no matter which perfection *F* is used in the argument. We take this to be an insight into the structure of the ontological argument.[22]

This last feature of our reading establishes a link between Anselm's argument and Descartes' argument in *Meditation V*. Recall that one of Descartes' arguments in *Meditation V* is a deduction of God's existence from the claim that God is a being with every perfection and the claim that existence is a perfection. But, to get this result, it looks as though Descartes has to *define* God to be that being having every perfection, whereas Anselm's argument appears to be general enough for us to *derive*, for every perfection *F*, that God has *F*. Thus, defining 'God' the way Anselm does allows us to derive facts about God which for Descartes have to be assumed in the definition. This puts Anselm's and Descartes' arguments in better perspective. Philosophers have often wondered whether Descartes' definition of 'God' as 'that Being having all perfections' is equivalent to Anselm's definition as 'that than which none greater can be conceived.' Our answer is 'No!,' for the above considerations suggest that Descartes' definition is derivable from Anselm's, but not vice versa. It appears that the only way to derive Anselm's definition from Descartes' is to add additional hypotheses.

The above considerations suggest that our interpretation has much to offer philosophers interested in Anselm, in the history of philosophy, and in the nature of the ontological argument in general. Before we conclude, however, it is instructive to enquire why this conception of the argument has just now surfaced. The reason is that it has only been in the past ten years that logical systems have been constructed in which the logic of descriptions and the distinction between being and existence have been combined. After [1905], when Russell introduced his method of eliminating descriptions, few logicians took descriptions seriously as genuine terms. In [1956], H. Leonard began the investigation of free logic, and descriptions began to be taken seriously as genuine terms. They were analyzed as terms "free of existence assumptions." But the free logicians followed Russell's [1908] assumption that the formula '$E!\iota x\phi$' is just equivalent to the formula '$\exists x \forall y (\phi_x^y \equiv y=x)$.'[23] For example, this equivalence appears as a valid law in H. Leonard's [1956].[24] Consequently, these logicians just identified 'being' and 'existence,' and read the formula '$\exists x\phi$' as "there exists an $x$ such that $\phi$." But in [1980], T. Parsons developed a coherent system of *nonexistent* objects, in which it makes sense to say "there *are* things that don't *exist*", or '$\exists x \sim E!x$.' Moreover, in Parsons' system, descriptions are taken seriously as genuine terms, so that they may denote objects even though the objects denoted do not exist; '$\exists y(y=\iota x\phi)$' and '$E!\iota x\phi$' express different things. We believe that this kind of formal system holds the key to the logic of Anselm's ontological argument. It is, therefore, a recent innovation in intensional logic that has made our reading of the argument possible.[25]

In the *Proslogium*, St. Anselm meditates on how we can be sure by natural reason alone that God exists. His focus is on the eminence of God. Everyone has the idea of that than which no greater can be conceived. In order not to prejudice the issue, he doesn't assume that everything that is exists. Some things can be merely in the understanding, without existing in reality as well. This is just to avoid assuming the desired conclusion. One of the things we show is that a very simple point about the logic of descriptions, namely *Description Theorem 2*, and a simple point about *greater than*, namely, that it is connected, is all the technical apparatus Anselm really needs. Anselm's argument for the existence of God doesn't depend on a sophisticated theory about multiple possible worlds. The logical mechanisms and metaphysical assumptions of Anselm's *Proslogium* II argument are paradigms of simplicity.

### Appendix: Anselm's *Proslogium* II

1. Therefore, Lord, who grant understanding to faith, grant me that, in so far as you know it beneficial, I understand that you are as we believe and you are that which we believe. (*Ergo, Domine, qui das fidei intellectum, da mihi, ut, quantum scis expedire, intelligam quia es, sicut credimus; et hoc es, quod credimus.*)
2. Now we believe that you are something than which nothing greater can be imagined. (*Et quidem credimus te esse aliquid, quo nihil majus cogitari possit.*)
3. Then is there no such nature, since the fool has said in his heart: God is not? (*An ergo non est aliqua talis natura, quia dixit insipiens in corde suo: Non est Deus?*)
4. But certainly this same fool, when he hears this very thing that I am saying—something than which none greater can be imagined—understands what he hears; and what he understands is in his understanding, even if he does not understand that it is. (*Sed certe idem ipse insipiens, cum audit hoc ipsum quod dico, aliquid quo majus nihil cogitari potest; intelligit quod audit, et quod intelligit in intellectu ejus est; etiamsi non intelligat illud esse.*)
5. For it is one thing for a thing to be in the understanding and another to understand that a thing is. (*Aliud est enim rem esse in intellectu; aliud intelligere rem esse.*)
6. For when a painter imagines beforehand what he is going to make, he has in his understanding what he has not yet made but he does not yet understand that it is. (*Nam cum pictor præcogitat quæ facturus est, habet quidem in intellectu; sed nondum esse intelligit quod nondum fecit.*)
7. But when he has already painted it, he both has in his understanding what he has already painted and understands that it is. (*Cum vero jam pinxit, et habet in intellectu, et intelligit esse quod jam fecit.*)
8. Therefore even the fool is bound to agree that there is at least in the understanding something than which nothing greater can be imagined, because when he hears this he understands it, and whatever is under-

stood is in the understanding. (*Convincitur ergo etiam insipiens esse vel in intellectu aliquid, quo nihil majus cogitari potest; quia hoc cum audit, intelligit; et quidquid intelligitur, in intellectu est.*)

9. And certainly that than which a greater cannot be imagined cannot be in the understanding alone. (*Et certe id, quo majus cogitari nequit, non potest esse in intellectu solo.*)

10. For if it is at least in the understanding alone, it can be imagined to be in reality too, which is greater. (*Si enim vel in solo intellectu est, potest cogitari esse et in re; quod majus est.*)

11. Therefore, if that than which a greater cannot be imagined is in the understanding alone, that very thing than which a greater cannot be imagined is something than which a greater can be imagined. But certainly, this cannot be. (*Si ergo id, quo majus cogitari non potest, est in solo intellectu, id ipsum, quo majus cogitari non potest, est quo majus cogitari potest: Sed certe hoc esse non potest.*)

12. There exists, therefore, beyond doubt something than which a greater cannot be imagined, both in the understanding and in reality. (*Existit ergo procul dubio aliquid quo majus cogitari non valet, et intellectu, et in re.*)

*translated by Jonathan Barnes*

## Notes

*The authors would like to thank Chris Menzel for encouraging us to write this paper and William Uzgalis, Edgar Morscher, and Marleen Rozemond for some excellent suggestions on how to improve it. We would also like to acknowledge generous support from the Center for the Study of Language and Information at Stanford University.

1. See the works by Malcolm, Hartshorne, Adams, Plantinga, and Lewis cited in the Bibliography.

2. See Barnes, [1972], Chapter 1, §III. Morscher, in [1990], also takes the argument to be a non-modal one.

3. D. Lewis, in [1970], says:

> We will also not have to worry about the logic of definite descriptions. If I say "That which is red is not green" I might just mean "Whatever is red is not green," neither implying nor presupposing that at least or at most one thing is red. Similarly, we can construe Anselm's "that, than which none greater can be conceived" not as a definite description but rather as an idiom of universal quantification.

This phrase might be construed as an idiom of universal quantification. Such a construal, however, would not capture its use by Anselm as a definite description.

4. This inference is labeled *Description Theorem 2* in what follows.

5. We frequently drop the quotation marks by which we mention expres-

sions of our object language whenever our intent is clear.

6. In what follows, we use '$\mathbf{f}' \stackrel{x}{=} \mathbf{f}$' to mean that $\mathbf{f}'$ is an assignment function just like $\mathbf{f}$ except perhaps for what it assigns to $x$.

7. Note the trivial modification of the standard base clause in the definition of satisfaction which allows for the possibility that some terms may not have denotations. The standard base clause in the definition of satisfaction is: $\mathbf{f}$ satisfies $F^n\tau_1...\tau_n$ iff $<\mathbf{d}(\tau_1),...,\mathbf{d}(\tau_n)> \in \mathbf{F}(F^n)$. This clause would be undefined for descriptions that fail to denote. Our revised clause requires both that all terms have denotations and that the denotations stand in the right relationship for $\mathbf{f}$ to satisfy an atomic formula.

8. This is not to be confused with the proof that the object denoted by the description *exists*, which we take to be the main point of the Ontological Argument—recall we are distinguishing $\exists y(y = \iota x\phi)$ from $E!\iota x\phi$.

9. The restriction on the *Description Axiom* merely reflects the fact that the correspondence theory of truth applies only to logically simple formulas! The correspondence theory of truth, which presumes truth to be a kind of correspondence between language and the world, places the following constraint on the truth of atomic and identity formulas $\phi$: $\phi$ is true if and only if every term in $\phi$ has a denotation and the denotations stand in the correct relationships. Otherwise, how could an atomic or identity formula having a non-denoting term be *true* in virtue of some feature of the world? Note that this constraint doesn't apply to logically complex formulas. Consider a molecular formula $\phi$, say $\psi \supset \chi$, where $\psi$ is an atomic formula having a non-denoting term. $\phi$ is true, because the antecedent is false (given the constraints of the correspondence theory and two-valued logic). Complex formulas, even those containing non-denoting terms, may be true in virtue of their logical form. So the constraint doesn't apply to logically complex formulas. The restriction on the *Description Axiom* simply acknowledges this fact.

   An example we've already considered makes this vivid. Note that the formula '$Pz \supset Pz$' is a logical truth, and remains a logical truth even when '$z$' is replaced uniformly by a non-denoting description, say '$\iota xQx$.' Without the restriction on the *Description Axiom*, the following biconditional would be an instance:

$$(P\iota xQx \supset P\iota xQx) \equiv \exists y[Qy \,\&\, \forall u(Qu \supset u=y) \,\&\, (Py \supset Py)]$$

However, for models in which '$\iota xQx$' doesn't denote, this biconditional is *false*, since the left side would be true (in virtue of its logical form) while the right side would be false. So without the restriction, the *Description Axiom* would constrain the descriptions in true complex formulas to have denotations. That is, without the restriction, the *Description Axiom* extends the constraints of the correspondence theory to logically complex formulas. This, as we saw in the previous paragraph, can not be done.

10. *Proof:* Assume the antecedent, that is: $\exists x\forall u(\phi^u_x \equiv u=x)$. So there must be some object, say $a$, such that: $\forall u(\phi^u_x \equiv u=a)$. And since $a=a$, it

follows that $\phi_x^a$. But we now know: $\phi_x^a$ & $\forall u(\phi_x^u \supset u = a)$ & $a = a$. So by Existential Generalization, this yields: $\exists y(\phi_x^y$ & $\forall u(\phi ux \supset u = y)$ & $a = y)$. And by the *Description Axiom*, it follows that $a = \iota x \phi$. ∎

11. *Proof:* Assume the antecedent. Now if we let $\psi$ be '$\tau = z$', our antecedent has the form $\psi_z^{\iota x \phi}$. So by the Description Axiom, it follows that: $\exists y(\phi_x^y$ & $\forall u(\phi_y^u \supset u = y)$ & $\tau = y)$. So, there must be some object, say $b$, such that: $\phi_x^{b y}$ & $\forall u(\phi_y^u \supset u = b)$ & $\tau = b$. If so, then, it follows that: $\phi_x^\tau$. ∎

12. We should also remind the reader to distinguish the symbols '∃!' from 'E!'. The former is used as a quantifier that asserts *uniqueness*, whereas the latter is just the existence predicate.

13. The language and semantics we have developed is therefore similar to Parsons' in the following respects: '$\exists x(\sim E!x)$' may be consistently asserted (in formal terms, this formula is satisfiable), and '$\exists x \sim \exists y(y = x)$' is false in every model (and thus a logical falsehood).

14. The reader may wish to examine the Appendix, where the original Latin and a line by line translation (by Barnes [1972]) may be found.

15. See the Appendix.

16. If you prefer to represent *Premise 1* as '$\exists x(Ux$ & $\phi_1)$,' then let $\phi_2$ be '$Ux$ & $\phi_1$', and replace $\phi_1$ by $\phi_2$ everywhere in what follows.

17. In this semantic proof, we began with a model in which the antecedent of *Lemma 2* is true, and looked at what happened when the connectedness of *greater than* is added. Alternatively, we might have started with a model in which *greater than* is a connected relation, and then looked at what happens when you add the antecedent of *Lemma 2*. This is an exercise left for the reader.

18. $R$ is *anti-symmetric* $=_{df} \forall x \forall y(x \neq y \supset (Rxy \supset \sim Ryx))$.

19. Compare his proof (Barnes, [1972], p. 88-9) with ours, and especially his Step 26 with our use of *Description Theorem 2*. Note also that *five* assumptions are required in his reading of the argument—though in all fairness it must be said that he assimilates both the subargument for *Premise 1* and the main argument into a single argument.

20. See Aquinas' *Summa Theologica*, Book 1, Question 2, Article 1, Second Objection.

21. See Kant's *Critique of Pure Reason*, translated by F. Max Müller, London: Macmillan, 1896, Chapter III, §4, of the Transcendental Dialectic.

22. The authors are indebted to Harry Deutsch for noticing that our argument is generalizable.

23. See Russell [1908], p. 93.

24. See Leonard [1956], p. 60, Law L4.

25. Actually, Parsons has a section on the ontological argument in [1980] (pp. 212-217), but nothing like our interpretation of the argument is to be found there. Instead, in footnote 1 (p. 214), he discusses the reading of the argument presented in Barnes [1972]. Parsons then goes on to say that a *de re/de dicto* ambiguity undermines Anselm's argument (p. 215). He says:

> Anselm's argument begins by establishing that the fool 'imagines that than which nothing greater can be imagined' in its *de dicto*

sense (for the justification is merely that the fool understands the words). But then he begins referring back to the alleged referent of the denoting phrase by means of singular pronouns, as if it had been established that there is such a object imagined by the fool (*de re*)—a natural and reasonably subtle transition—but a question-begging one.

We don't believe that Anselm does commit the fallacy Parsons attributes to him in this passage. We have shown that Anselm is *justified* in using the anaphoric singular pronouns once he asserts *Premise 1*, for by *Lemma 2*, it follows that there is a unique object such that nothing greater can be conceived. So given that Anselm believes *Premise 1* to be true, his use of anaphoric pronouns is legitimate.

Parsons' objection is best taken not as directed at *Premise 1* but rather at Anselm's support for *Premise 1*. Here is what appears to be Anselm's subargument for *Premise 1*, where ψ stands for the phrase "none greater can be conceived":

*Premise:* Anyone (even a fool) can understand the phrase "that than which ψ."
*Premise:* If anyone (even a fool) can understand the phrase "that than which ψ," there is something in the understanding such that ψ.

These two premises entail *Premise 1*. Parsons' complaint concerns the *second* premise of this subargument, namely, that its consequent makes a *de re* claim although its antecedent is grounded on *de dicto* considerations. The antecedent asserts that anyone can understand a certain denoting phrase. The consequent, however, is a quantified *de re* claim the truth of which requires that there be a certain object (*res*) in the understanding. Parsons might argue that understanding a denoting phrase doesn't entail any *de re* claims. However, it seems certain that Anselm felt justified in thinking that to understand a phrase (even *de dicto*), there must be something in the understanding, such as an idea, that is grasped. Nevertheless, Parsons may be raising a legitimate question about whether there is a thing in the understanding which is such that ψ and which is grasped when the phrase "that than which ψ" is understood. The answer to this question depends on one's analysis of the intentionality of directed mental states and the intensionality of denoting phrases. Anselm has a philosophy of language, knowledge, and mind that provides such analyses in general, and in particular, how God's being in the fool's understanding follows from the fool's saying "there is no God." A discussion of these issues would take us beyond the scope of this paper. Consequently, any further comment on Anselm's support for *Premise 1* must be postponed.

## References

Adams, R. M., 1971, "The Logical Structure of Anselm's Arguments," *The Philosophical Review* LXXX (1971): 28-54.

Alston, W., 1960, "The Ontological Argument Revisited," in Plantinga, 1965, *op. cit.*

Aquinas, T., 1285, *Summa Theologiæ.*

Barnes, J., 1972, *The Ontological Argument*, London: Macmillan.

Brody, B., 1974, (ed.) *Readings in the Philosophy of Religion*, Englewood Cliffs, NJ: Prentice Hall.

Descartes, R., 1641, *Meditations on First Philosophy*, translated by E. Haldane and G. Ross, in *The Philosophical Works of Descartes*, Vol. 1, London: Cambridge University Press, 1970.

Hartshorne, C., 1962, *The Logic of Perfection*, LaSalle, IL: Open Court.

Hartshorne, C., 1965, *Anselm's Discovery*, LaSalle, IL: Open Court.

Hartshorne, C., 1961, "The Logic of the Ontological Argument," *The Journal of Philosophy* LVIII (1961): 471-73.

Kant, I., 1787, *Critique of Pure Reason*, translated by F. Max Müller, London: Macmillan, 1896.

Leonard, H., 1956, *Philosophical Studies* VII/4 (June): 49-64.

Lewis, D., 1970, "Anselm and Actuality," *Nous* 4: 175-88.

Malcolm, N., 1960, "Anselm's Ontological Arguments," *The Philosophical Review* LXIX (January 1960): 41-62.

Morscher, E., 1990, "Was Sind und Was Sollen die Gottesbeweise? Bemerkungen zu Anselms Gottesbeweis(en)," forthcoming in, Friedo Ricken (ed.), *Klassische Gottesbeweise in der Sicht der gegenwärtigen Logik und Wissenschaftstheorie*, Stuttgart.

Parsons, T., 1980, *Nonexistent Objects*, New Haven: Yale University Press.

Parsons, T., 1979, "The Methodology of Nonexistence," *Journal of Philosophy* LXXVI: 649-61.

Parsons, T., 1974, "Prolegomenon to Meinongian Semantics," *Journal of Philosophy* LXXI: 561-80.

Plantinga, A., 1965, (ed.) *The Ontological Argument*, Garden City, NY: Anchor Books.

Plantinga, A., 1974, *The Nature of Necessity*, Oxford: Oxford University Press.

Plantinga, A., 1967, *God and Other Minds*, Ithaca: Cornell University Press.

Russell, B., 1908, "Mathematical Logic as Based on the Theory of Types," reprinted in R. C. Marsh (ed.), *Logic and Knowledge*, London: Unwin and Hyman, 1956.

Russell, B., 1905, "On Denoting," *Mind* 14 (October): 479-493.

Zalta, E., 1983, *Abstract Objects: An Introduction to Axiomatic Metaphysics*, Dordrecht: D. Reidel.

Zalta, E., 1988, *Intensional Logic and the Metaphysics of Intentionality*, Cambridge: Bradford Books/The MIT Press.

Philosophical Perspectives, 5, Philosophy of Religion, 1991

# DIVINE SIMPLICITY

Nicholas Wolterstorff
Yale University

Once upon a time, back in the so-called middle ages, theologians, Jewish, Christian, and Muslim alike, in developing their doctrine of God, gave extraordinary prominence to the attribute of simplicity. God, they said, is simple; in God there are no distinctions whatsoever. I am not aware of any theologian in these three traditions contending that God's simplicity ought to be prominent in one's religious consciousness, in the way, for example, that it appears to have been prominent in the religious consciousness of Plotinus. It was, instead, theoretical prominence that they gave it.

For one thing, they recognized its *theoretical fecundity*. If one grants God's simplicity, then one also has to grant a large number of other divine attributes: immateriality, eternity, immutability, having no unrealized potentialities, etc. Aquinas, in his earlier *Summa contra gentiles*, still argued for God's eternity, immateriality, and lack of passive potency before he introduced God's simplicity. By the time he wrote his later *Summa theologica* he had fully recognized the theoretical fecundity of this attribute and moved it up to the top of the list, introducing it immediately after he had established the existence of a first mover. Secondly, the doctrine of divine simplicity had, for the medievals, extraordinary *framework significance*. If one grants that God is simple, one's interpretation of all God's other attributes will have to be formed in the light of that conviction. Of course the fecundity of this attribute for deriving others of God's attributes, and its framework significance, are quite beside the point unless one has good reason for holding that God is simple. The medievals thought they had such good reason.

A theology structured by moving from God's existence immediately to God's simplicity and then on to God's other attributes seems part of a quaint and bygone era for anyone reared on twentieth century theology. Contemporary theologians seldom speak of God's simplicity. And when they do, they rarely (if ever) give it a significant structural role in their doctrine of God—let alone giving it the preeminent role that it enjoyed in the articulated doctrine of God developed by the medieval school theologians.

I shall not on this occasion ask why this striking alteration has taken place in the mode of structuring theology—partly because, though I find the question intriguing, I am far short of knowing the answer. I suspect that a full answer would illuminate, down to a deep level, the differences between contemporary theology and medieval school theology. But I am more in need of illumination on that score than able to give illumination. On this occasion I want to pursue the answer to a different question suggested by the difference between medieval and contemporary attitudes toward the doctrine of simplicity. And from here on I shall speak mainly of *Christian* philosophical theology.

The doctrine that God is simple was understood by the medievals as the denial of any form of composition in God. In his *Summa theologica* Aquinas, before drawing the general conclusion that God is simple, dismisses various specific modes of composition. He argues, among other things, that

(1) God is not distinct from God's essence;

that

(2) God's existence is not distinct from God's essence;

and that

(3) God has no property distinct from God's essence.

Since I shall want to refer to these three theses rather frequently in what follows, let me, for convenience sake, call them the *theistic identity* claims.

In the Thomistic texts there is no sign—none of which I am aware, anyway—that Aquinas found anything ontologically problematic in these claims. He marshalls arguments for them. He does not toss them out as self-evident. But he gives no sign of bafflement over how it can be that something would be identical with its essence, nor over how it can be that that entity's existence would be identical with its essence, nor over how it can be that all its properties are identical with its essence (and hence, that its essence itself has no complexity).

Though Aquinas gave no sign of finding anything problematic in the theistic identity claims as such, when he combined those claims with certain other convictions of his, he experienced bafflement aplenty. Aquinas found himself, by virtue both of his construal of his biblical inheritance and his acceptance of certain arguments from his Greek inheritance, as committed to the propositions that

(4) God is omniscient

and that

(5) God is omnibenevolent.

Further, it seemed to him that in predicting omniscience of God, one is predicating of God something other, for example, then omni-benevolence; and that in predicating either of these of God, one is predicating of God something other than existence. But how can one give an intelligible account of these predications without assuming that there is in God God's goodness and God's wisdom, distinct from each other and from God's existence? To assume this, however, would be flagrantly to compromise God's simplicity. Aquinas strug-gled, then, to find a way of accounting for the predications that his biblical and Greek inheritance required him to make of God which would preserve the distinctness of these predications without com-promising God's simplicity.

Secondly, Aquinas struggled to show that the doctrine of divine simplicity is not in contradiction with other doctrines that he felt required to affirm. For example, Aquinas held, on the basis of his biblical inheritance, that

(6) God has free choice

But it was far from clear how this is compatible with the claim that God has no properties distinct from God's essence—i.e., that God has no accidents, either essential or contingent. Likewise, it was not at all clear how the doctrine of simplicity is compatible with the doctrine that

(7) God is triune.

To the best of my knowledge it was the same for all other medieval philosophers and theologians—though here I stand to be corrected by those whose acquaintance with medieval thought goes beyond my own. When Marilyn Adams, in her fine book on Ockham, reviews the medieval debates over simplicity through Ockham, the debates she reports occur, so far as I can tell, only at the point of Aquinas' bafflement. Some of the medievals gave a different ontological construal of the theistic identity claims than Aquinas gave; but none, so far as I can see, found anything especially baffling in those claims as such.

For most of us contemporary philosophers the situation is strikingly different. Our bafflement does not arise only when we reach the point where we have to find a theory of predication which, without compromising the doctrine of simplicity, accounts for how we can say a multiplicity of distinct true things about God, or when we reach the point where we have to show the compatibility of the doctrine of simplicity with other doctrines. It arises already with this trio of ontological claims. How could any substance possibly be its essence, we ask? Maybe a property could be its essence—though even that merits careful reflection. But how could something which is not a property be its essence? And how could such an entity's essence be its existence? And how could all its properties be identical with its essence? We have no difficulty in repudiating *some* modes of composition in God—for example, that God is composed of matter. But those three theistic identity claims seem to many, if not most, of us incoherent.

Admittedly there are some who do not confess to seeing any difficulty. Stump & Kretzmann in their article "Absolute Simplicity"[1] concentrate on the advantages and disadvantages of accepting the doctrine of divine simplicity. They think the most important reason for hesitating to accept it is the apparent incompatibility of the doctrine with God's free choice. They then argue that Aquinas had a way of harmonizing God's simplicity with whatever someone who accepts the biblical tradition would want to say about God's choice. As they see it, this leaves the theologian in the situation where there are no significant reasons for not accepting the doctrine, whereas there are significant theoretical advantages in accepting it.

Admittedly this is a considerably less ringing endorsement of the doctrine than the medievals customarily gave it. Nonetheless, in their discussion I find no sign that Stump & Kretzmann find the theistic identity claims problematic. For them the only question is whether those claims, and the other claims making up the doctrine of simplicity, should be accepted.

Why would a medieval thinker find the theistic identity claims ontologically non-problematic, whereas so many of us find them inscrutable or incoherent? That is the question whose answer I want to pursue. The answer I shall offer is that we have here a clash between two fundamentally different ontological styles; if we are to understand and engage the medievals on this matter, we shall have to enter imaginatively into their ontological style and then debate, among other things, the tenability of these two different styles. We need, if you will, a paradigm shift. Meta-ontology is what is needed. Possibly the reason Stump & Kretzmann find nothing problematic in the doctrine is that they, being medieval scholars, themselves do their thinking in terms of this alternative ontological style.

I am also inclined to think that we will never succeed in finding a satisfactory non-trivial formulation of the doctrine of divine simplicity in our own dominant contemporary ontological style. But I see no way of defending this thesis; for all I know, it might be the case that right over the horizon is a creative discussion by someone who proves that it can be done by doing it. Hence I shall content myself with the less daring thesis, that to understand the medievals we must enter imaginatively into a style of ontology different from that which is dominant among us.

But first, what exactly are the difficulties that we have with the identity claims? Alvin Plantinga has canvassed them lucidly in his book *Does God have a Nature?*[2] A substance's essence, says Plantinga, will be a certain one of its properties—that conjunctive property which includes as conjuncts those properties which the substance has in all possible worlds in which it exists. So if God is identical with God's essence, then God is identical with a property. But God, being a person, is not a property.

That is the most fundamental difficulty. But Plantinga also finds difficulties in roughly the region where Aquinas and most medievals found them. Let us suppose that God has the attributes of omniscience and omnibenevolence. Now the theistic identity claims entail that all God's attributes are identical with God, and hence with each other. But surely omniscience and omnibenevolence are not the identical property; and if either were identical with God, then, once again, God would be a property, which God is not (cf. p. 47).

These moves are so simple, swift, and decisive, that Plantinga acknowledges that what he has refuted must not be what the medievals meant. So he tries again. The medievals speak of God's goodness, God's existence, God's power, God's wisdom, etc. Maybe in speaking thus they did not mean to refer to *properties*. Maybe with the expression "God's goodness" they did not intend to refer to that property of goodness which God has, maybe with the expression "God's existence" they did not intend to refer to that property of existence which God has, etc. Maybe they intended to pick out entities of some other ontological category. Perhaps, says Plantinga, they intended to pick out states of affairs, relationships. Perhaps with the locution "God's wisdom" they intended to pick out the state of affairs of God's being wise; with the locution "God's goodness," the state of affairs of God's being good; etc.

One challenge facing us immediately, in working out this suggestion, is to find a criterion of identity/diversity for *states of affairs* which is both plausible in its own right and has the consequence that God's wisdom is identical with God's goodness, with God's existence, etc. Plantinga formulates a criterion, modifies it in the light of an objection, and raises an objection to the modification. Then he drops the matter. For even if we find a satisfactory criterion, we would be left with this deep difficulty: on this account, God is identical with a certain state of affairs. But, says Plantinga, "If God is a state of affairs, then he is a mere abstract object and not a person at all; he is then without knowledge or love or the power to act. But this is clearly inconsistent with the claims of Christian theism at the most basic level (52-53).

At the point where Plantinga drops the matter, William Mann picks it up in his paper titled "Divine Simplicity."[3] Perhaps, says Mann, we should look once again at what the medievals had in mind by their locutions "God's existence," "God's wisdom," God's goodness," etc. Perhaps it was not abstract objects like states of affairs that they had in mind. Perhaps they had in mind what may be called *property instances*. (Property instances are what I called *cases* in my *On Universals*; they are what D.C. Williams called *abstract particulars*, and *tropes*. They are Aristotle's *entities present in something*. And at least some of them are what the medievals called *qualia*). Suppose that Socrates had the property of wisdom. Then we can say that whereas Socrates was an *exemplification* of wisdom, Socrates' wisdom was an *instance* of it. And as to the relation of the person Socrates to the property instance, Socrates' wisdom, perhaps

Aristotle's phrase is as good as any: Socrates' wisdom is *present in* Socrates. As his reason for thinking that property instances are not states of affairs Mann says this: "It is claimed by the friends of states of affairs that all states of affairs *exist*, but only some of them *obtain* or are actual.This feature does not hold for property instances. In order for a property instance to exist, it must be actual: some existing thing must either exemplify it or be it" (p. 457).

Two fundamental challenges face this proposal. By now we can guess what they are. We need a criterion of identity/diversity for property instances which is both plausible in its own right and whose consequences are consistent with the theistic identity claims. And we must be assured that God's being a property instance is not incompatible with God's having the properties that we want to predicate of God. Mann faces up to both these challenges; but let me, on this occasion, rush past what he says about the identity and diversity of property instances to get to what he says on the issue of whether God's being a property instance would be compatible with our convictions as to what God is like. Mann formulates the challenge to his view thus: "this conclusion offends against deeply entrenched theistic belief that God is knowing, loving, and active. In brief, God is a person; no property instance is a *person*; therefore God is not a property instance. Given the theist's beliefs about the person-hood of God, the doctrine of divine simplicity must be rejected" (p. 465).

Mann's way of answering this objection is to argue that one of the principles assumed in the objection, viz., that no property instance is a person, is false. Take anything whatsoever, says Mann, and con-sider all its properties. From these, single out that conjunctive property which includes as its conjuncts all the properties of the thing. Call that the *rich property* of the thing. The thing itself, says Mann, is "an instantiation of the appropriate rich property." To generalize: "For anything whatsoever, there is an appropriate rich property. Therefore, everything is a property instance of some rich property or other. Therefore, every person is a property instance....It is certainly true that *most* property instances are not persons, yet every person is a property instance" (p. 467).

It appears to me that Mann has here fallen into an ontological trap. Let us once again have before us the distinction between an *exempli-fication* of a property and an *instance* of a property. Whereas Socrates exemplified the property, wisdom, Socrates' wisdom instantiated it.

Now a person certainly *exemplifies* its rich property. But what reason is there to think that the person also *instantiates* that property—that in this case the instantiation is the exemplification? What reason is there to think that Socrates' instantiation of his rich property just is Socrates? I see no reason at all to think this; nor does Mann offer any reason. I surmise that Mann, at this crucial point in his argument, momentarily lost sight of the distinction between an exemplification of a property and an instance of a property. Mann does not think that *Socrates' wisdom* is identical with Socrates, whereas he does think that the one and only instance of Socrates' rich property is identical with him. Presumably what was going through Mann's mind was the thought that Socrates' wisdom was not rich and complex enough to be Socrates. So he proposed taking a property instance which was as rich as necessary. But taking a more complex property instance does nothing to collapse this trio of ontological relationships into a solo: Socrates *exemplifies* his properties, his property instances *instantiate* those properties, and his property instances are *present in* him.

The most decisive consideration against identifying Socrates with Socrates' instantiation of his rich property is this: if Socrates were identical with his instantiation of his rich property, then his exemplifying of that property would of course be the same as his instantiating of it. But notice that Socrates might have exemplified a different rich property from that which he in fact exemplified; he only contingently exemplified the rich property which he did exemplify. By contrast, an instance of a property cannot instantiate different properties from those it does instantiate—on pain of losing its identity. Call Socrates' rich property, *SR*. That entity which is Socrates' instantiation of *SR* cannot have existed and not have been the instantiation of *SR*. Instances do not contingently instantiate the properties that they do instantiate.

In response to a criticism of his theory lodged by Thomas Morris, Mann, in a later article, has made some revisions and introduced some additions.[4] Morris' criticism was this: if God is an instance of a property, then "there is at least one property existing distinct from God as an abstract object on which God is, in some sense, dependent for what he is—an instance of that property."(302) But this violates the conviction that God exists a se. Mann's response, in the first place, is to combine a property account of divine simplicity with a property-instance account by proposing that God's property be taken as identical with God's instance of that property—that omniscience be taken as identical with God's omniscience, omnipotence as identical with God's omnipotence, etc.

What strikes one about this proposal, as Mann presents it, is its ad hoc character. One looks for a general discussion of properties and property instances in which it is shown that certain properties are self-instantiating (n.b., not self-exemplifying but self-*instantiating*), in which the general conditions under which that is the case are laid out, and in which it is shown that these conditions are satisfied in the case of omniscience, omnipotence, omnibenevolence, and the rest of God's properties. But Mann offers no such general ontological discussion. Instead he concerns himself entirely with a certain rather obvious objection to this theory.

The objection is this: if God is identical with the property instance, God's omniscience, and if that property instance is identical with the property, omniscience, then it follows that God is a property. But to hold that God is a property is to be confronted once again with Plantinga's objection: properties are abstract objects, incapable of having the personal attributes which belong to God. This objection, which formerly Mann regarded as decisive, he now tries to meet by questioning the assumption that properties are abstract objects. He suggests that the properties of objects are the *causal powers* of the objects (though he also speaks of a property's presence in some entity as *conferring* a causal power on that entity).

I myself fail to see, however, that this proposal secures Mann's goal. I presume that by the causal powers of objects, Mann means those capacities which objects have for causing one and another event. Water, for example, has the causal power of dissolving sugar. Mann himself speaks of causal powers as that in *virtue of which*. But if this is indeed what causal powers are, they seem to me clearly *abstract* entities. They are not concrete causal agents but abstract powers of agents. On the other hand, it is possible that I don't at all understand what Mann has in mind by "causal powers." For he speaks of *being triangular* as the same causal power of objects as *being trilateral*. I myself have considerable doubt as to whether these properties are correctly thought of as causal powers; but if one does so think of them, then it seems to me that they must be thought of as distinct causal powers. It is in virtue of the triangularity of this object, not its trilaterality, that I have these three bloody points in my hand. So also, though I find it difficult to think of omniscience as a causal power, it appears to me that if it is a causal power, it is a different causal power from omnibenevolence—whereas of course Mann, because of the pressures of the simplicity doctrine, holds that they are the same. Perhaps, then, I do not understand what Mann has in mind by causal powers. For as I think of causal powers, the theory that properties are causal powers does not have the consequence that properties are in general concrete.

Of course it would be open to Mann to argue that in the case of God, the causal powers of the agent just *are* the causal agent. That is to say, he could hold that though causal powers are in general abstract entities, that is not true of all of them. At least one causal power just is a concrete causal agent, that one being God. And perhaps this is Mann's actual line of thought. For though he uses words which suggest that he wishes to question Plantinga's assumption that properties, in general, are abstract objects, he also says the following, which appears to go in the other direction which I have suggested: "if properties are causal powers and if God is a property, then he is a causal power. Moreover, if the property that God is is variously identified as omniscience, omnipotence, moral perfection, and the like, then the property *cum* causal power that God *is* looks more and more analogous to the causal powers that ordinary persons *have*" (352). About this, I think we must simply say that the thought is too undeveloped for us to know whether Mann's theory that properties are causal powers meets Plantinga's objection to the identification of God with any property, or whether it merely presents the proposal to which Plantinga made his objection under a new guise. I might add that Mann himself stresses the inchoate character of his theory.

We have canvassed one of the recent attempts to offer a construal of the theistic identity claims which will both make those claims ontologically intelligible and not yield consequences patently unacceptable to theists. None of the attempts of which I am aware has made any significant advance in this endeavor. One possible explanation for this situation is that we are just much less intelligent than our medieval forebears; not only can we not devise an acceptable account of divine simplicity; we cannot even understand accounts presented to us by the medievals which they found non-problematic. I prefer another explanation. The theistic identity claims were put forward by thinkers working within a very different ontological style from ours. They worked within a style of ontology that I shall call *constituent ontology*. We typically work within a style that might be called *relation ontology*. We should expect that claims which are baffling within the one style will sometimes seem straightforward within the other. The theistic identity claims are a paradigm example of this.

I propose now to try to enter into that alternative way of thinking far enough to explain how a medieval, thinking within the style of constituent ontology, would have understood those theistic identity claims. One criterion of success in this endeavor will be that those claims cease to be baffling. Bafflement is to enter at the next point, where we try to show that divine simplicity is compatible, say, with God having free choice, and where we try to devise a theory of predication—note, not a theory of property-identity but a theory of predication—which, without compromising God's simplicity, accounts for the multiplicity of distinct predications that Jews, Christians, and Muslims want to make about God.

Let us start with the first of the theistic claims. But let us for the most part not use the word "essence" in our reflections, since for us it carries too many misleading connotations. Let us instead use the term "nature," and speak of the nature of a thing.

The nature of an entity, a medieval would have said, is *what-it-is-as-such*. An entity does not *have* a certain nature in the way it has a certain property. It *is* a certain nature. If an entity is something as such, then it is a certain nature. One has to add at once that, for most things, that isn't all they are. But with that qualification understood, everything is a certain what-it-is-as-such. I am something as such. I am not only that, indeed; but I am at least that. You too are something as such. So too are all the plants and animals in the world. So too are the angels. And so too is God. There is no mystery in how it can be that God is something as such—that God is a certain nature. Everything is something as such; everything is a certain something-as-such, a certain what-it-is-as-such. The only mystery about God—if mystery it be—is that we do not have to add, "but that's not all God is." For all other substances, we have to make this addition.

It has become habitual for us twentieth century philosophers, when thinking of essences, to think of things as *having* essences, and to think of these essences as certain properties or sets of properties. An essence is thus for us an abstract entity. For a medieval, I suggest, an essence or nature was just as concrete as that of which it is the nature. That is because everything, including every concrete thing, is a something-as-such. A medieval would have found the suggestion that that is not the case baffling—though, of course, plenty of later thinkers have made this suggestion. Naturally the medieval will speak of something as *having* a certain nature. But the *having* here is to be understood as *having as one of its constituents*. Very much of the difference between medieval and contemporary ontology hangs on these two different construals of "having." Whereas for the medievals, *having an essence* was, having an essence as one of its constituents, for us, *having an essence* is, having an essence as one of its properties: exemplifying it.

So far then, no problem. But now we come across a perplexity which generated enormous controversy among the medievals. Socrates appears to have the same nature as Plato—appears to have the same what-it-is-as-such, viz., human nature. Yet obviously Socrates is not identical with Plato. How are we to explain this?

Well, notice in the first place that both Socrates and Plato are made out of something; namely, out of a certain lump, or parcel, or bit, or quantity of matter (we don't have the right word in English). And the bit of matter out of which Socrates is made is distinct from the bit of matter out of which Plato is made. So let us think of Plato and Socrates as composites, articulated composites, with different constituents playing different roles. That composite which is Socrates will include his nature, but will also include his bit of matter. And what makes Socrates distinct from Plato is that he is made out of a different bit of matter. Admittedly that is not the only thing that makes him distinct; he also has different "accidents." But that's the basic thing.

Having said this, we had better look once again at that human nature which we found, or thought we found, in both Socrates and Plato. Is the situation really that there is a common human nature which enters into different substantive-composites? Or do the different bits of matter which enter into substantive-composites also, as it were, 'particularize' the natures? Does Socrates, contrary to initial appearances, have a distinct nature from Plato—similar but distinct? And if so, is it the matter out of which Socrates is made that makes his nature distinct from all others? Suppose it is. And suppose, further that we make Socrates' nature an object of thought, focussing just on the nature and abstracting from the bit of matter with which it is associated in that composite which is Socrates. Is that which we are thinking of in such a case distinct from what we would be thinking of if we thought about Plato's nature along the same lines, or is it identical with it?

All these questions, and many more in the same region, were posed and discussed by the medievals. It would serve no purpose in this essay to go into them farther. But notice that the difficulties are posed by material objects sharing, or being capable of sharing, or *apparently* being capable of sharing, their natures. In the case of immaterial entities, everyone agreed: everything is its own nature.

I have already suggested that what enters into the sorts of composites which you and I are is more than a certain nature and a certain bit of matter. We also possess various attributes which, though they are not involved in what we are as such, nonetheless characterize us. Some of these are essential to us; some, non-essential. We should not think of these attributes themselves as constituents of those composites which we are. But for each of these properties not belonging to a thing's nature, be they essential or non-essential, there will be a property instance which is present in that thing. Let us call these the *accidents* of the thing. The composite that I am will include my accidents. To say it once again: I am an articulated composite, with different sorts of constituents playing different roles in the composite, explaining different facts about me.

And now for our question: why should there not be a certain entity which, like everything else, just *is* a certain nature, but which, unlike most or all other entities, is nothing more than that—is not a composite? Such an entity will not be made out of matter. Nor will it have any accidents. It will be just a certain something-as-such, a certain what-it-is-as-such. That would be an extraordinary entity. We would know next to nothing about what it would be like to be such an entity. But there seem to be no ontological difficulties in the proposal that there is such an entity. Of course there will be a variety of things which such an entity is not, and there will be a variety of relations between that entity and others. But there seems no reason to think that these facts imply that the entity is, after all, a composite of constituents.

In the *respondeo* of the third article of question 3 of Part I of his *Summa theologica*, Aquinas gives a lucid exposition of the points I have been making. The *respondeo* in this case is a bit longer than most. Nonetheless it is worth having before us in its entirety:

> God is the same as His essence or nature. To understand this, it
> must be noted that in things composed of matter and form, the

nature or essence must differ from the *suppositum*, because the essence or nature connotes only what is included in the definition of the species; as, humanity connotes all that is included in the definition of man, for it is by this that man is man, and it is this that humanity signifies, that, namely, whereby man is man. Now individual matter, with all the individualizing accidents, is not included in the definition of the species. For this particular flesh, these bones, this blackness or whiteness, etc., are not included in the definition of a man. Therefore this flesh, these bones, and the accidental qualities distinguishing this particular matter, are not included in [humanity. Nevertheless they are included in] the thing which is a man. Hence the thing which is a man has something more in it than has humanity. Consequently humanity and a man are not wholly identical; but humanity is taken to mean the formal part of a man, because the principles whereby a thing is defined are regarded as the formal constituent in regard to the individualizing matter. On the other hand, in things not composed of matter and form, in which individualization is not due to individual matter—that is to say, to *this* matter—the very forms being individualized of themselves,—it is necessary the forms themselves should be subsisting *supposita*. Therefore *suppositum* and nature in them are identified. Since God is not composed of matter and form, He must be His own Godhead, His own Life, and whatever else is thus predicated of Him.[5]

There are interesting connections between that part of the Thomistic perspective which I have been expounding, and some of the things Mann says. It is Aquinas' view that humanity, i.e., human nature, has as its instances the various particularized human natures to be found in reality—Socrates' nature, Plato's nature, etc. Not human beings, but human natures, are the instances of humanity—each human being including in its composite a human nature but always more than that as well. But what, then, about the property of *being a human being*? What does this have as its instances? The instances of this property will be human beings. But obviously human beings are also the entities which exemplify this property. In the case of such "individuating" properties as this, then, exemplification and instance coincide—rather than for those properties that Mann calls "rich".

We are ready to look at the second of the three theistic identity claims. The first, that God is not distinct from God's essence, has proved to be non-problematic when considered within the medieval frame of thought; perplexities arise instead for certain of those entities not identical with their essences. But what about the claim that God's existence is not distinct from God's essence. Isn't God's existence an accident, or an accident-like entity? If so, how can it possibly be identical with God's nature?

Let us be sure that we have in hand the most felicitous way of putting the question here. I think it is not helpful to say that God's essence is to exist—as if what God is as such were just a lump or bit of existence. I think it is only slightly better to say that God's essence is identical with God's existence. The most felicitous way to put the claim, in my judgment, is the way Aquinas puts it in the first section of Chapter 22 of *Summa contra gentiles*: God's "essence or quiddity is not something other than his being." In other words, God's existence is not something distinct from God's nature. We have seen that God is a something-as-such, a certain what-it-is-as-such. The question before us now is whether God's existence is distinct from what God is as such.

If God existed contingently, then God's existence would be distinct from God's essence—it would not belong to what God is as such. But of course Aquinas holds that God does not exist contingently. Elucidating the point here is a bit tricky. For if we say that something belongs necessarily to some entity X just in case X has it in all possible worlds in which X exists, then everything which exists has its existence necessarily. But whatever difficulties there may be in elucidation or articulation, let us on this occasion agree that it is right to say that if an entity exists contingently, then its existence is distinct from what it is as such. Aquinas himself tries to articulate the point in terms of causation, or accounting for. If a thing exists contingently, then one cannot account for its existence just by referring to its essence; whereas, for example, to account for why a horse is an animal, one just points to its nature.

So what about entities which exist necessarily? Is their existence distinct from or identical with their essence? Perhaps for some it is distinct. For it may be that for certain necessarily existing entities, there is something external to the thing which accounts for why it exists. Aquinas was of the conviction that God accounts for the existence not only of contingently existing entities but of all necessarily existing entities distinct from God. To account for why they exist, we have to appeal to God—whereas appealing to them does nothing whatever to account for why God exists. Articulating the concept of account/explanation/cause which is operative here is a challenging intellectual task.[6] But suppose it can be done. Then it seems right to say that whether or not some entity X exists necessarily, if to account for its existence one has to refer to something other than its own nature, its existence is distinct from its nature—does not belong to what it is as such. Aquinas says that "that thing, whose existence differs from its essence, must have its existence caused by another" (S.Th.I, Q.3), art. 4 resp.). And clearly he intends to affirm the converse as well. It was the uniform conviction of the medievals that there is nothing other than God's nature which accounts for why God exists. Hence God's existence is not distinct from God's essence—as also, for example, Bucephalus' equinity is not distinct from Bucephalus' essence.

Aquinas was of the view that, for every non-divine nature, what belongs to the nature is not existence but *potentiality for existing*. What belong to what I am as such is not existence but being capable of existing. My existence is the realization, the actualization, of this potential. Thus for non-divine entities, their essence and their existence stand in a potentiality/actualization relation to each other. "Existence must be compared to essence, if the latter is a distinct reality," says Aquinas, "as actuality to potentiality" (ibid.). What makes God different from everything else is that it is not *potentiality for existing* which belongs to what God is as such, but *existing*.

There seems, then, to be nothing ontologically problematic in the second of the theistic identity claims, the claim that God's existence is not distinct from God's essence, when that claim is considered within the framework of the constituent ontology characteristic of the medievals. The principal problem in this area will be to explain how, for an entity which exists necessarily, there can yet be something which accounts for its existence.

The last of the theistic identity claims which we are considering is that God has no properties distinct from God's essence. Perhaps the best way to begin reflecting on this is to consider some necessary entity other than God—some number, say. So consider the number 9. The number 9 stands to me in the relation of just having been mentioned by me; we would conclude, in contemporary ontology, that it has the relational property of having been mentioned by me. We all feel, however, that this property is extrinsic to the number 9, in contrast, say, to the property of being odd, which is intrinsic to it. Though I think we all have some grasp of this extrinsic/intrinsic distinction, no one, to the best of my knowledge, has yet succeeded in articulating it. It's not the same as the contingent/necessary distinction. For take the two properties of having believed that God is simple, and having been mentioned by me. Aquinas possesses both of these properties. Clearly the former is intrinsic to him, the latter, extrinsic. Yet both are contingent properties of him.

Now it seems plausible to think that all the intrinsic properties of the number 9 are essential to it. It even seems plausible to think that they all belong to what the number 9 is as such, i.e., to the nature of 9. So I think there is also nothing especially problematic in the third identity claim, that none of God's properties is distinct from God's nature. Admittedly Aquinas would not have made the point in the way I just made it, in terms of a distinction between intrinsic and extrinsic properties of a thing. He would have denied that what I have called extrinsic properties are truly properties. Whatever I do when I assertively utter of something, "was referred to by me," Aquinas would not have described that as predicating a property of it. If he *had* conceded that they are extrinsic properties, he would have faced the question: in what are their property instances present? He would have been extremely reluctant to view those as constituents of that entity which purportedly possesses the extrinsic properties. (Furthermore, he would probably have thought it misleading to speak of anything other than the nature of the thing as *intrinsic* to it.)

The task I set myself in this article has been completed. I wanted to show that the three theistic identity claims, which to many of us who do ontology in the twentieth century seem so baffling, are, when approached within the ontological framework of the medievals, not at all baffling. The root of the difference, I have suggested, is that whereas the medievals worked within the style of constituent ontology, we typically work within the style of relation ontology and as part of this difference we work with a different view of essence. Of course not every constituent ontology will render the theistic identity claims non-problematic. The great exception to my generalization about the style of twentieth century ontology is Gustav Bergmann. Bergmann worked relentlessly in the style of constituent ontology.[7] His way of developing constituent ontology was such, however, that he would probably find the theistic identity claims as baffling as do the rest of us. So my point has not been that working in the style of constituent ontology automatically makes the theistic identity claims non-problematic, but rather that working in the style of relation ontology automatically makes them problematic.

According to the dominant style of twentieth century ontology, the essence of an entity is something to which it bears a certain relation—the relation of necessarily exemplifying it. Likewise a contingent property of an entity is something to which it bears a relation, the relation of contingently exemplifying it. And if we acknowledge property instances, these too are in relation: the property instances of those properties which some entity exemplifies are *present in* that entity. The pattern is clear: twentieth century ontology is relentlessly relational in its style. We don't think of entities as being composites of constituents but as standing in multiple relationships with other entities. And naturally God stands in relationships too. A medieval looking at our ontology would find acknowledgement of essence just missing. We talk about the properties of things; and some of those properties we call the *essence* of the thing. But nowhere do we give ontological acknowledgement to what an entity is *as such*. What we call the essence of an entity would by a medieval be regarded as something whose instance is a non-contingent accident of the entity.

It may be added that a characteristic feature of our contemporary way of practicing relation ontology which also plays a role in the discussions over simplicity is a clear-eyed denial of the Platonic thesis that properties are ideal examples of themselves—that justice is the ideally just entity, etc. We hold that, in general, properties are not self-exemplifying. Essential in Plantinga's argument is the assumption that knowledge does not know, that love does not love, that potency does not do anything, etc.

Shortly after noticing the difference of ontological style between us and the medievals, however, the thought comes to mind that the twentieth century ontologist actually has no difficulty at all with the doctrine of divine simplicity. True, he finds the three theistic identity claims to be baffling, if not incoherent. But these three claims emerged from the attempt of the medieval philosophers to articulate the doctrine of divine simplicity. They are not to be identified with the doctrine itself. The relation ontologist doesn't think of things as composites. In a way, then, he thinks of everything as simple. If one goes about the ontological enterprise trying to discern the constituents that each sort of thing must be acknowledged as having, then the claim that there is something with no constituents comes as an extraordinary limiting case to one's whole style of thinking. One can see why a theologian who is a constituent ontologist would feel compelled to lead off with this claim in his reflections on the nature of God. But if one's fundamental ontological model is that of entities standing in relation rather than of entities composed of constituents—well then, as it were, everything is simple, nothing is a composite. The doctrine of divine simplicity fits even more smoothly into the contemporary style of ontology than into the medieval. In the medieval style, simplicity is a limiting case—albeit, an intelligible one. In the contemporary style, simplicity is the general case.

Unfortunately, victory in the debate is not to be won so easily. For though the medievals deduced a great many of God's attributes from God's simplicity, they deduced that in turn from something else even more fundamental; namely, from God's self-sufficiency and sovereignty. As I read the history of medieval philosophy and theology, the medievals were ineluctably gripped by the Plotinian vision of reality as requiring something which is the unconditioned condition of everything not identical with itself; this they identified with God. Says Plotinus: "If there were nothing outside all alliance and compromise, nothing authentically one, there would be no Source. Untouched by multiplicity, it will be wholly self-sufficing, an absolute First, whereas any not-first demands its earlier, and any non-simplex needs the simplicities within itself as the very foundations of its composite existence" (Fifth Ennead IV,1). Anyone who is gripped by these convictions and arguments would see our twentieth century claim, that God has an essence—i.e., that God stands in the relation of exemplification to an essence—as an obvious violation of God's self-sufficiency. Thus in my judgment Plantinga is absolutely right in concluding that the fundamental issue facing us in our reflections— us, who think in the style of relation ontology—is whether God has a nature. And he is quite right in suggesting that in reflecting on this we will find ourselves dealing with a fundamental conflict of intuitions.

I hope I have shown, however, that that was *not* the fundamental perplexity facing the medievals. For them, as I have already suggested, the fundamental perplexities were two fold. The doctrine that God has no properties distinct from God's essence seems, on the face of it, incompatible with some of the things that Christians hold about God, e.g., that God has free choice. And secondly, the medievals found it difficult to devise a theory of predication which would adequately account for the multiplicity of distinct things that we find ourselves required to affirm of this simple being which is God. We say of God that God is wise, and that God is good, and that God is powerful. In speaking thus, we are not simply repeating ourselves. The general strategy of the medievals was clear: to interpret these different predications as expressing different "cognitive fixes" on God. What they could not say, however, was that the difference between these different cognitive fixes on God is grounded in some difference within God's essence or God's accidents; for that, of course, would introduce composition. But neither were they willing to give up the conviction that these predicates do indeed express some sort of cognitive fix on God. Their recourse was to say that our predications concerning God express either determinate negations concerning God, or refer to some relation of God to entities other than God. But working this out in detail proved difficult, and proposed solutions to the difficulties, almost always controversial.

Plotinus and Kant, wrestling with the same issues, gave up on the attempt to offer a cognitive construal of predications concerning God. We are, they said, to select and choose among ways of thinking and speaking of God by reference to some non-cognitive purpose. For Kant, the relevant purpose was the moral Life: it is conducive to the moral life to think of the transcendent as if it were a God related to us as a father. For Plotinus, the relevant purpose was the mystical vision: to think of the One as existing, as one, etc., is more conducive to the mystical vision than to think of it as not thus:

> ...when we speak of this First as Cause, we are affirming something happening not to it but to us, the fact that we take from this Self-enclosed: strictly we should put neither a This nor a That to it; we hover, as it were, about it, seeking the statement of an experience of our own, sometimes nearing this Reality, sometimes baffled by the enigma in which it dwells...
>
> Our way then takes us beyond knowing; there may be no wandering from unity; knowing and knowable must all be set aside; every object of thought, even the highest, we must pass by, for all that is good is later than This and derives from This as from the sun all the light of the day.
>
> "Not to be told; not to be written": in our writing and telling we are but urging towards it: out of discussion we call to vision: to those desiring to see, we point the path; our teaching is of the road and the travelling; the seeing must be the very act of one that has made this choice (Sixth Ennead IX, 3-4).

None of the medieval school theologians was willing to follow this non-cognitive strategy; only some of the mystics were willing to do so. Hence the perplexities.

It would require another paper to canvas and appraise the strategies that the medievals adopted in their struggle to explain how it can be that we can make a multiplicity of distinct true predications concerning the simple God. But I suggest that if we grant them their ontological style, the *constituent* style, then the place to engage them is not on the theistic identity claims as such. Those prove to be non-problematic. The place to engage them, in the first place, is on the tenability in general of constituent ontology. The place to engage them, in the second place, is on the general question of whether it is possible, while holding that God is simple, to develop a theory of predication which adequately accounts for the multiplicity of distinct things Christians wish to say about God. And the place to engage them, thirdly, is in their attempt to show that the doctrine of simplicity does not contradict other fundamental doctrines. As part of this third engagement, we shall want to look closely at their attempt to find something in the simple God and its relationships to other things which can be called knowledge, something else to be called love, something else to be called creating, something else to be called revealing, something else to be called redeeming, etc. We shall want to ask whether what they identify as knowledge, love, creation, revelation, redemption, etc., in the simple self-sufficient God, can be viewed as what the theist is speaking of when she says that God knows and loves what God has created, that God reveals to human beings God's will, and that God is working for the redemption of the cosmos. I have my doubts. But that, too, is another tale.[8]*

## Notes

1. In *Faith and Philosophy*, Vol. 2, No. 4, October 1985, 353-382.
2. Alvin Plantinga, *Does God have a Nature?* (Milwaukee, Marquette University Press; 1980).
3. William Mann, "Divine Simplicity" in *Religious Studies* 18 (1982), 451-471.
4. Morris' discussion is in "On God and Mann," *Religious Studies* 21 (1985), pp. 299-318. Mann's response is in "Simplicity and Properties," *Religious Studies* 22 (1986), pp. 343-353.
5. My colleague, Jan Aertsen, called my attention to the fact that there are some words in Thomas' Latin text for which the equivalents are missing in the Dominican translation which I have been using. I have inserted them in brackets. With the passage quoted, compare *Summa contra gentiles*, Book One, chapter 21, section 2: "There must be some composition in every being that is not its essence or quiddity. Since, indeed, each thing possesses its own essence, if there were nothing in

a thing outside its essence all that the thing is would be its essence, which would mean that the thing is its essence. But, if some thing were not its essence, there should be something in it outside its essence. Thus, there must be composition in it. Hence it is that the essence in composite things is signified as a part, for example, humanity in man. Now, it has been shown that there is no composition in God. God is, therefore, His essence."

6. Cf. Chris Menzel, "Theism, Platonism, and the Metaphysics of Mathematics" in *Faith and Philosophy* Vol. 4, No. 4 (Oct. 1987), pp. 365-382.
7. See my "Bergmann's Constituent Ontology" in *Nous*, May 1970.
8. I discussed some of the issues in my "Suffering Love" in Thomas V. Morris (ed.) *Philosophy and the Christian Faith* (Notre Dame, University of Notre Dame Press; 1988).

* I wish to thank Jan Aertsen for his very helpful comments on an early draft of this paper.

Philosophical Perspectives, 5, Philosophy of Religion, 1991

# GOD'S GENERAL CONCURRENCE
# WITH SECONDARY CAUSES:
# WHY CONSERVATION IS NOT ENOUGH

Alfred J. Freddoso
University of Notre Dame

## 1. Introduction

The sacred writings of Judaism, Islam, and Christianity proclaim with full voice that God is the transcendent and provident Lord of nature; as the First or Primary Cause, He has created the physical universe, sustains it in being, and is always and everywhere active in it by His power. Prompted by this basic conviction, theistic philosophers have through the centuries fashioned deep and subtle metaphysical accounts of God's causal activity in nature. Significantly, these accounts do not limit such activity to the miraculous. On the contrary, the dominant presumption has been that the metaphysics of miracles can be coherently expounded only against the backdrop of a philosophically and theologically adequate account of God's constant causal involvement in the *ordinary* course of nature. It is this more general component of a theistic philosophy of nature which will be the focus of my attention here.

To set the stage for what follows, I will first describe briefly and informally what have emerged from the historical debate as the three principal theistic accounts of God's causal influence in the ordinary course of nature.

a. *Occasionalism.* According to occasionalism, which was espoused by several important medieval and early modern thinkers, God alone causes effects in nature; natural substances, contrary to common opinion, make no genuine causal contribution at all to any such effect. In short, there is no creaturely or "secondary" causation in nature;

created substances are incapable of *transeunt* action, i.e., action that has effects outside the agent. So, for instance, the gas flame on your stove does not heat the kettle of water placed over it; rather, it is God alone who heats the water on the occasion of its being proximate to the flame. The flame counts as a "cause" only in the attenuated sense that God acts in accord with a firm, though arbitrarily decreed, intention to heat water when it is brought into proximity to a gas flame of a given type under a given range of circumstances; and so it is for *all* the effects produced in nature. (Occasionalism will figure only tangentially in this paper; I have, however, discussed it at some length in another.[1])

b. *Mere Conservationism.* Occasionalism is in many ways congenial to scientific anti-realism, according to which the natural sciences aim only to attain "empirical adequacy" and not to discover "real" causes and causal structures in nature. By contrast, mere conservationism is closer in spirit to some forms of scientific realism. According to mere conservationism, God contributes to the ordinary course of nature solely by creating and conserving natural substances and their accidents, including their active and passive causal powers. For their part, created substances are genuine secondary causes which can and do causally contribute to natural effects on their own, given only that God preserves them and their powers in existence. When such substances directly produce an effect, they alone are immediate causes of that effect, whereas God is merely an indirect or remote cause of the effect by virtue of His conserving action; consequently, the actions of created substances are in some straightforward sense their own actions and not God's actions.[2]

c. *Concurrentism.* Concurrentism, which flourished among the late medieval Aristotelian scholastics and certain figures in the early modern period, occupies a middle position between what its advocates perceive as the unseemly extremes of occasionalism and mere conservationism. According to concurrentism, a natural effect is produced immediately by *both* God *and* created substances, so that (*pace* occasionalism) the latter make a genuine causal contribution to the effect and indeed determine its specific character, but (*pace* mere conservationism) they do so only if God cooperates with them contemporaneously as an immediate cause in a certain "general" way which goes beyond conservation and which makes the resulting cooperative *transeunt* action to be in all relevant respects the action of both God and the secondary causes. This cooperation with secondary causes is called God's *general concurrence* or *general concourse*.

At first glance concurrentism appears eminently sane from a theistic standpoint, since it allows for secondary causation in a robust sense while at the same time sustaining a strong interpretation of the theological tenet that God is intimately involved in the production of effects in nature. However, lurking below the surface are some intricate philosophical problems concerning the nature of cooperative *transeunt* action. William Durandus, an early fourteenth-century Dominican bishop and theologian who espoused mere conservationism, argued in effect that any detailed explication of God's purported general concurrence with secondary causes will either suffer from incoherence or else collapse back into occasionalism or mere conservationism.[3]

I plan to deal elsewhere with Durandus's arguments and the concurrentist response to them. Here, however, I will concentrate instead on the arguments propounded by concurrentists against mere conservationism.

Although mere conservationism has enjoyed the status of an unspoken and unsupported assumption among some recent Christian thinkers, almost all the important figures in the history of philosophical theology have rejected it as philosophically deficient and theologically "unsafe". According to Albert the Great, writing in the thirteenth century, the opinion that secondary causes are sufficient by themselves to produce at least some effects without God's direct causal influence "has all but disappeared from the lecture hall and is regarded as heretical by many moderns."[4] Indeed, Durandus himself is the one and only well-known medieval proponent of mere conservationism, or at any rate the only one cited as a champion of this position by sixteenth- and seventeenth-century writers.

The four arguments I will examine are found in Francisco Suarez's *Disputationes Metaphysicae* [hereafter: *DM*], Disputation 22, with some parallels appearing in Part II, Disputation 25 of Luis de Molina's *Concordia*.[5] Although Suarez and Molina, both late sixteenth-century Spanish Jesuits, disagree sharply with their Thomistic opponents about the exact character of God's general concurrence, this disagreement is not reflected in the arguments I will be considering.[6] So these arguments can plausibly be taken to represent the reply of mainline Christian Aristotelians in general to what they see as Durandus's deviation from the truth about God's causal involvement in nature.

The first two of Suarez's arguments presuppose some relatively technical reflections on efficient causation in general and on creation and conservation in particular. On the whole, Suarez's metaphysics is broadly Aristotelian in the central role it accords to efficient or "agent" causation and broadly Thomistic in the pivotal use it makes of the notion of *esse* to develop an account of efficient causation and to clarify the concept of divine transcendence. I myself have become convinced that this metaphysics is fundamentally rightheaded and worthy of serious study by contemporary philosophers in general and philosophical theologians in particular. So in sections 2 and 3 I will take a first and admittedly halting step toward making some of the key concepts accessible to contemporary readers, not only in order to clarify Suarez's attack on mere conservationism but also with an eye toward recommending these concepts and the metaphysical framework in which they are embedded as fruitful and sound in their own right. This discussion will also enable me to give a fairly rigorous characterization of the difference between concurrentism and mere conservationism. Then, with this background in place, I will proceed in sections 4-7 to lay out Suarez's four arguments and briefly comment on them.

## 2. Efficient Causation and the Giving of *Esse*

The medieval Aristotelians, Durandus included, all take efficient causation to be a relation holding between substances which act (agents) and substances which are the recipients of actions (patients). In a typical case (excluding creation *ex nihilo* and divine conservation, which will be treated in section 3) one or more agents act upon a patient in such a way as to produce or conserve an effect, where the effect is itself either a substance or an accident, i.e., an intrinsic determination of a substance.[7] So both agents and patients may properly be said to contribute causally to the existence of various substances and accidents, and both acting and being acted upon may properly be thought of as modes of causal contribution. What's more, since causal contributions involve the complete actualization or exercise of causal powers, we can also distinguish active from passive causal powers. The active causal powers of a substance delimit the range of its "proper" effects, i.e., the effects the substance is capable of producing or conserving directly through its own power when it acts upon suitably disposed patients in appropriate circumstances; the passive causal powers of a subject delimit the range of effects that might be produced or conserved in it when it is acted upon by suitably situated agents in appropriate circumstances.

In what follows I will employ three undefined causal locutions. The *first* is 'x causally contributes to y's existing at t', where x is a substance, y either a substance or an accident, and t a time. As I am using this locution, it implies that y in fact exists at t. But note that, taken just by itself, this locution does not require that causal contributors be capable of acting freely, or that they be endowed with sentient powers, or even that they be living. Indeed, the medieval Aristotelians, sensibly to my mind, conceive of the *whole* created world, inanimate as well as animate, as a dynamic system of interrelated and interacting entities endowed by nature with causal tendencies and always poised to produce their proper effects in the appropriate circumstances. It follows that "agent causation" is a pervasive feature of the physical universe and is not limited just to substances endowed with freedom of choice.[8]

Again, this first undefined locution says nothing either about the time at which x makes its causal contribution or about the specific nature of that contribution. So, for instance, x might make its causal contribution to y's existing long before t and not even exist at any time proximate to t. Similarly, x's causal contribution to y's existing may be more or less direct or immediate, more or less closely connected with x's proper causal tendencies or (in the case of rational beings) intentions, and more or less determinative of the specific character of the effect.

Finally, x's causal contribution might be either wholly active, wholly passive, or active in one respect and passive in another. (This last alternative may occur, for instance, when a substance brings about changes in itself, or when a substance is deployed as an instrumental cause by some "principal" agent.) In this paper I will be interested mainly in active causation:

x is an **active cause** of y at t if and only if
    (a) x causally contributes to y's existing at t, and
    (b) x's causal contribution to y's existing at t is at least
        in part active.

Whereas occasionalists hold that God is the only active cause in nature, theistic Aristotelians all accept a form of naturalism according to which every created substance has and exercises its own active causal powers; some of these powers are "inseparable" accidents that flow directly from the substance's essence as definitive of its natural kind, and some of them are "separable" accidents that are consonant with its essence but not endemic to it.[9]

The *second* undefined locution is '*x* is an active cause of *y* at *t* only in virtue of the fact that *x* causally contributes to *z*'s existing at *t*\* (at or before *t*)', where it is assumed that *z* is distinct from *y*. This locution allows us to characterize more and less direct or immediate modes of causal contribution relative to a given effect, a desirable result in view of the fact that the dispute between concurrentism and mere conservationism hinges in large part on the question of whether or not God is an *immediate* cause of all natural effects. What the locution captures is a certain causal distance or indirectness in *x*'s causal contribution to *y*'s existing at *t*. So, for instance, *x* might be a *temporally* remote active cause of *y* at *t* by virtue of its having acted long before *t* to initiate or sustain a causal chain that terminates in *y*'s existing at *t*. In addition, *x* might be a *metaphysically* remote cause of *y* at *t* by virtue of its preserving *z* in existence while it is in a state of causal activity at *t*, with the result that *y* exists at *t*. More formally,

*x* is an **immediate cause** of *y* at *t* if and only if
 (a) *x* exists at *t*, and
 (b) *x* is an active cause of *y* at *t*, and
 (c) there is no set *M* such that (i) neither *x* nor *y* is a member of *M*, and (ii) each member of *M* is an active cause of *y* at *t*, and (iii) *x* is an active cause of *y* at *t* only in virtue of the fact that *x* causally contributes to the members of *M* existing at *t*\* (at or before *t*).

*x* is a **(merely) remote cause** of *y* at *t* if and only if
 (a) *x* is an active cause of *y* at *t*, and
 (b) *x* is not an immediate cause of *y* at *t*.

Concurrentists maintain that God is an immediate cause of every effect in nature, whereas mere conservationists contend that God contributes to effects in nature only remotely or mediately by virtue of the fact that He conserves the relevant agents in existence for as long as is required for them to be immediate causes of their effects.[10]

The *third* undefined locution is the Thomistic '*x* gives *esse* to *y* at *t*'. According to St. Thomas, *esse* is a principle of actuality or perfection, where the notion of perfection is broadly construed to encompass any sort of positive determination or 'form', including active and passive causal powers and the entities that come to exist through the exercise of such powers. So giving *esse* entails giving perfection of some sort or other, i.e., giving existence to a substance by actualizing a particular concrete nature with the set of "specifying powers" endemic to its natural kind, or giving existence to an intrinsic accidental determination of a substance.

A finite created entity is said to "participate in" or "have a part of" *esse* as such. This is because all created entities have some proper part of, or finite share in, the whole gamut of possible perfections; in other words, they have *esse* as limited by their natures to what we might in general call *such-esse* and to what in each particular case is the sort of *esse* proper to the entity's essence and accidental determinations. So, for instance, a white oak tree has *white-oak-tree-esse* and, subordinated to it, the sorts of *esse* proper to its various separable and inseparable accidents. Again, a human being has *human-esse*, a photon has *photon-esse*, and so on. This explains the spirit behind St. Thomas's claim that for a living organism to exist is for it to be alive, i.e., to have a sort of *esse* or actuality appropriate to living organisms. Thus the term '*esse*', unlike the term 'exists' in at least one common use, admits of degrees or at least of distinct grades, even though 'to have *esse*' and 'to exist' are equivalent in the sense that an entity exists if and only if it has some sort of *esse*.

Given this general metaphysical picture, one might naturally think of created entities as being partially ordered from the less perfect to the more perfect according to the type of actuality (including causal power) they have. Such an ordering reflects the degrees or grades of *esse*, i.e., lesser and greater shares in the plentitude of perfections. What's more, as "beings by participation" or "participated beings," created entities are such that they need not exist at all and hence must receive *esse* from causes distinct from themselves; in St. Thomas's terminology, there is in them a real distinction between *esse* and essence.[11] Only God is such that in Him there is no distinction between *esse* and essence; He is subsistent *esse* itself (*ipsum esse subsistens*), and so He cannot fail to exist and cannot fail to be "unparticipated"—or, as it were, "unpartitioned"—*esse*, a being with all possible perfections possessed to an unlimited degree.[12] Hence, the notion of *esse* enables St. Thomas to give a clear account of the ontological chasm that separates the transcendent creator of the world from His creatures. What's more, just as each created entity has its own proper effects, i.e., types of *esse* or actuality which it can be an immediate "principal" or "perfecting" cause of, so too God as unparticipated *esse*—*esse* that is not delimited to any particular species or genus—has His own proper effect, viz., *esse*-as-such. I will return to this point in section 3.

So giving *esse* to an entity is itself a form of active causal contribution. Indeed, Suarez's first two arguments presuppose that the production or conservation of *any* effect in nature involves some agent's giving *esse* of some sort to some recipient.[13] However, we must carefully distinguish *x*'s causally contributing to *y*'s existing at *t* from *x*'s giving *esse* to *y* at *t*, since even though every instance of causal contribution is either a withholding of or a giving of *esse* to *some* substance and/or accident, it is nonetheless possible for *x* to causally contribute to *y*'s existing by giving *esse* just to a substance or accident distinct from *y*.

Before I proceed to expound some further causal notions, I should say a few more words of clarification about the background ontology presupposed by my use of the locution '*x* gives *esse* to *y* at *t*'. As above, I am assuming that *x* is an agent and *y* a recipient of an action; *y* is either a substance or an accident, where an accident is conceived of as an intrinsic perfection or determination of a substance, a perfection or determination which is an individual entity in its own right with its own "accidental" (as opposed to "substantival") *esse*. In general, an entity which has accidental *esse* is apt by its nature to "inhere in" or "belong to" a substance that has substantival *esse* of a sort consonant with its being the subject of such an accident. In the present context I mean to circumvent disagreements about just what sorts of accidents there are or about whether every term associated with a given Aristotelian category signifies a distinct type of accident.[14] So I will simply assume (i) that terms which import intrinsic modes or states of a substance signify *some* accident or other, and (ii) that a genuine causal contribution involves the giving of *esse* unless it consists merely in the withholding or withdrawing of some action. (One consequence of this last assumption is that the corruption or dissolution, as opposed to annihilation, of a composite material substance occurs when active causes give *esse* to one or more entities with the result that the substance in question ceases to exist.) Also, when I speak of the "constituents" of a substance, what I have in mind are not only material constituents but also formal constituents, e.g., the internal organization of the material constituents, their functional interrelations with one another, various physically or mathematically describable structural features of a substance, and, generally speaking, any other characteristics that fall under the broad Aristotelian notion of a perfecting form.[15] I also assume that some accidents are spatially extended and thus have constitutive parts.

We are now in a position to articulate the notion of a *per se* cause. According to Suarez, "a *per se* cause is a cause on which the effect directly depends with respect to the proper *esse* that it has insofar as it is an effect...and this alone is a cause in the proper and absolute sense" [*DM* 17, sect. II, § 2]. Simply put, a *per se* cause of a given entity is an agent that gives *esse* to that entity. More precisely,

*x* is a ***per se* cause** of *y* at *t* if and only if
    (a) *x* exists at *t*, and
    (b) *x* is an active cause of *y* at *t*, and
    (c) *x* gives *esse* to *y* at *t*.[16]

So *per se* causation requires a certain intimacy between cause and effect that is not required for causal contribution as such. For even though every agent that contributes positively to a given effect *E* is a *per se* cause of something or other, it need not communicate the form or perfection that constitutes *E*.

According to concurrentists, God is a *per se* as well as an immediate cause of every effect produced in nature. Mere conservationists deny this, even though they do agree that God must give *esse* to entities *after* they have been produced if they are to remain in existence and causally contribute to effects of their own.

## 3. Creation and Conservation

As noted above, according to St. Thomas God's proper effect is *esse*-as-such rather than, as is the case with created agents, some limited type of *esse*. This claim stands at the heart of the Thomistic account of divine creation. Of course, no entity receives *esse* unless it receives *esse* of a determinate sort, and St. Thomas does not mean to imply otherwise. So what is it to give *esse*-as-such? The reply, as I understand it, is that the giving of *esse*-as-such involves both an intensive and an extensive aspect.[17]

The *intensive* aspect is this: To give *esse*-as-such to an entity is to give it *esse* from the bottom up, as it were, i.e., to give *esse* to it and to each of its constituents and accidents. It follows, according to St. Thomas, that only an agent which is, in Aristotelian terms, "pure actuality," i.e., lacking in any sort of perfectibility, can give *esse*-as-such. For an agent which is not pure actuality can be rightly understood to be composed of a perfectible subject and that which perfects this subject. For instance, a corporeal entity is a composite of material constituents and a formal principle according to which those constituents are organized, interrelated, and otherwise unified into a single substance. It follows, according to St. Thomas, that such a substance can be a *per se* cause only of perfections which, like its own substantival and accidental perfections, modify a perfectible subject. Consequently, a composite substance requires for its action an already existent subject that has an intrinsic capacity to receive the sorts of perfection or types of *esse* which the agent is able to give or communicate. Only an agent that is itself lacking in any perfectible element can produce effects outside itself without presupposing an already existent subject to act upon.

As for the *extensive* aspect, to say that an agent gives *esse*-as-such is to imply that it is not confined to causing just one or another limited range of perfections. That is, even though we might be able to conceive of or imagine an agent that is capable of giving *esse* from the bottom up just to, say, quarks or pigs and nothing else, it is, according to St. Thomas, metaphysically impossible that there should be such an agent.[18] It follows that an agent which gives *esse*-as-such must itself be, in the idiom of neo-Platonism, "unparticipated *esse*" and hence capable of giving *esse* to any possible participated being.

The following explication captures both the intensive and the extensive aspects:

$x$ gives **esse-as-such** to $y$ at $t$ if and only if
      (a) $x$ is a *per se* cause of $y$ at $t$, and
      (b) for any $z$ such that $z$ is either a constituent of $y$ at $t$
          or an accident of $y$ at $t$, $x$ is a *per se* cause of $z$ at $t$,

and
(c) *x* has the power to give *esse* to any possible
participated being.

St. Thomas simply identifies the doctrine that God is the creator of
all entities distinct from Himself with the claim that God gives *esse*-
as-such to all of them. That is why he can plausibly maintain that
the physical world would still be created *ex nihilo* by God even if
it existed from eternity. However, he also makes use of the more
restricted notion of *de novo* creation, which adds to giving *esse*-as-
such the condition that neither the entity in question nor any of its
constituents or accidents existed beforehand:[19]

*x* **newly creates** *y* **ex nihilo** at *t* if and only if
(a) *x* gives *esse*-as-such to *y* at *t*, and
(b) either (i) *y* is a substance and neither *y* nor any of
the constituents of *y* exists immediately before *t*, or
(ii) *y* is an accident and the substance which is the
subject of *y* at *t* does not exist immediately before *t*.

So *x* newly creates something *ex nihilo* only if *x* gives *esse* from the
bottom up to an entity that was literally nothing beforehand.

Let us now turn to conservation. Suarez, following St. Thomas,
distinguishes several modes of conservation, each of which incorporates the following basic notion:[20]

*x* **conserves** *y* at *t* if and only if
(a) *x* is an active cause of *y*'s existing at *t*, and
(b) for some temporal interval *i* that includes *t* but
begins before *t*, *y* exists throughout *i*.

In this broad sense of conservation, *x* may conserve *y* at *t* even without giving *esse* to *y* at *t*, since *x* may simply counteract or eliminate
agents whose action would otherwise result in *y*'s being corrupted
and thus passing out of existence. In such a case *x* would conserve
*y* but only, as it were, *per accidens*. A stronger mode of conservation
is *per se* conservation:

*x* **conserves** *y* **per se** at *t* if and only if
(a) *x* conserves *y* at *t*, and
(b) *x* is a *per se* cause of *y* at *t*.

However, this is still not sufficient by itself to capture the sense in which conservation is a divine prerogative, since, as Suarez points out, secondary causes can be said to conserve a created substance *per se* but *remotely* when they "bring about the influx or inpouring of certain dispositions or forms which are required in order for that thing to be conserved in *esse*" [*DM* 21, sect. III, § 2]. That is, such causes directly effect various formal or structural features through the mediation of which the type of *esse* characteristic of the substance in question continues to be sustained. Take the case of a living organism. Suarez has in mind, I take it, various agents (e.g., the sun and other providers of heat and light, oxygen, foods, liquids, etc.) which preserve the organism's health and well-being in a way required for the continuation of its life. In general, once a created entity exists, secondary causes—more specifically, secondary conservers—are able to cooperate with God in maintaining various internal dispositions and conditions without which the entity cannot long survive as a member of its natural kind.[21] As St. Thomas puts it, "In the very creation of things God institutes an order such that some of them depend on others through which they are secondarily conserved in *esse*."[22]

Still, even though secondary causes may conserve the whole thing conserved, they do not and cannot constitute the whole conserving cause of any created entity. Or so, at least, theistic philosophers have argued. According to Suarez, to get something akin to divine conservation properly speaking, we have to say that *x* conserves *y* *immediately* and not just by producing or conserving certain formal constituents of *y*. He himself characterizes this more direct type of conservation as "the persisting influx or inpouring of the very *esse* which was communicated through the production" of the entity in question [*DM* 21, sect. III, § 2].

But what exactly does *per se* and immediate conservation add to simple *per se* conservation? Is it sufficient to append to our account of *per se* conservation just the condition that *x* is an immediate cause of *y* at *t*, in the sense of 'immediate cause' defined above? I think not. First of all, it may well be that the secondary *per se* conservers of *y* at *t* themselves count as immediate causes in that sense.[23] Second, and more important, Suarez seems to be using the term 'immediate' here in order to emphasize the intimacy of the conserving action in question; the discussion following the passage just cited strongly suggests that an immediate and *per se* conserver of a given entity provides a type of conserving action in the absence of which that entity, along with all its constituents and accidents, would instantaneously be reduced to nothingness. We might reasonably conjecture that this can be so only if *per se* and immediate conservation is conservation "from the bottom up," the giving of *esse* to an entity and to each of its constituents. This conjecture would help explain why Suarez considers it utterly obvious that only God can be an immediate and *per se* conserver of those things which have no potentiality for undergoing dissolution or corruption, viz., immaterial substances (e.g., angels and human souls) and incorruptible material things (e.g., celestial bodies on an Aristotelian cosmology, physical atoms in the classical sense if there be such, and the more elusive "primary matter," i.e., principle of bare physical potentiality from which material substances are fashioned). Such things can cease to exist only if they are annihilated rather than corrupted, and so no secondary cause conserves them from potential extrinsic or intrinsic corrupters. In addition, Suarez argues at some length for the less evident thesis that only God can be a *per se* and immediate conserver of corruptible material substances, a position which seems at least plausible on the assumption that *per se* and immediate conservation involves the giving of *esse* to *all* the constituents of the conserved entity.[24] With this in mind, I propose to explicate *per se* and immediate conservation as follows:

$x$ **conserves** $y$ ***per se*** **and immediately** at $t$ if and only if
> (a) $x$ conserves $y$ *per se* at $t$, and
> (b) for any $z$ such that $z$ is a constituent of $y$ at $t$ or an accident of $y$ at $t$, $x$ is a *per se* cause of $z$ at $t$.

Condition (b) puts us in a position to see clearly the connection between divine conservation and God's giving *esse*-as-such to all created substances and accidents. In fact, we can delineate a special instance of the above formula for God's conserving action:

**God conserves** $x$ ***per se*** **and immediately** at $t$ if and only if
> (a) God conserves $x$ at $t$, and
> (b) God gives *esse*-as-such to $x$ at $t$.

This dovetails nicely with the traditional view of philosophical theologians that the same basic divine activity lies at the heart of both creation and divine conservation. Indeed, as will become more evident in the discussion of Arguments One and Two below, concurrentists conceive of God's general concurrence with secondary causes as yet another instance of God's giving *esse*-as-such, viz., His giving *esse*-as-such to an effect or form while it is being brought into existence by secondary causes.

We can now give a more precise characterization of the difference between concurrentism and mere conservation. Both accept the following principles of conservation and secondary causation:[25]

> (CON)  Necessarily, for any participated being $x$ and time $t$ such that $x$ exists throughout a temporal interval that includes $t$ but begins before $t$, God conserves $x$ *per se* and immediately at $t$.
>
> (SC)  In general, created substances causally contribute, both actively and passively, to the existence of various entities at various times.

What distinguishes mere conservationism is the claim that God is not an immediate and *per se* cause in the production of the effects of secondary causes:

> (MC)  Necessarily, for any entity $x$ and time $t$, if any created substance produces $x$ at $t$ as an immediate and *per se* cause, then God is a (merely) remote cause of $x$ at $t$ and not an immediate and *per se* cause of $x$ at $t$.

Concurrentists deny (MC) and affirm the following principle of divine general concurrence:

> (DGC)  Necessarily, for any entity $x$ and time $t$, if any created substance produces $x$ at $t$ as an immediate and *per se* cause, then it is also the case that God is an immediate and *per se* cause of $x$ at $t$.

We are now ready to look at Suarez's arguments.

### 4. Argument One: From the Symmetry between *Esse* and *Fieri*

Each of Suarez's first two arguments is aimed at showing that it is incongruous for mere conservationists to affirm (CON) while denying (DGC):

> [The true] position is that God acts *per se* and immediately in every action of a creature, and that this influence of His is absolutely necessary in order for a creature to effect anything...[This] truth can be proved sufficiently by natural reason. First, it seems to be clearly entailed by what has been said about conservation, in such a way that by this argument it is almost as certain in the faith that God effects all things immediately as that He conserves all things immediately. [*DM* 22, sect. I, § 6]

The thrust of the arguments is that (DGC) follows straightaway once we take the natural step of generalizing (CON) to

> (ESSE) Necessarily, for any created entity $x$ and time $t$ such that $x$ exists at $t$, God gives *esse*-as-such to $x$ at $t$.

Suarez will argue in effect that any good reason for accepting (CON) will also be a good reason for accepting (ESSE), and that any good reason for rejecting (ESSE) will be a good reason for rejecting (CON). But to accept (ESSE) is tantamount to rejecting (MC) and thus to affirming that God is an immediate and *per se* cause of any entity produced by secondary causes. For according to (ESSE) any entity produced by a secondary cause is such that God gives it *esse*-as-such at the very instant at which it comes into existence. In short, by means of the first two arguments Suarez tries to demonstrate that there is a deep tension between two of the defining principles of mere conservationism, viz., (CON) and (MC)—a tension that can be resolved only if mere conservationists abandon their position either for concurrentism on the one hand or some form of deism on the other.

The initial argument for what Suarez calls this "first line of reasoning" from conservation to concurrence is the more perspicuous:

> The first line of reasoning is proved, first, from the fact that if it is not the case that all things come to exist immediately from God, then neither is it the case that they are conserved immediately, since a thing is related to its existing (*esse*) in the same way that it is related to its coming to exist (*fieri*). For the existence of a thing cannot depend more on an adequate cause *after* it has come into existence than it did *when* it was coming into existence. Likewise, if the cause depends on God in its existing, then the effect will, too, since both are beings by participation...Therefore, every effect of a secondary cause depends on God in its coming to exist, and as a result a secondary cause can do nothing without God's concurrence. [*DM* 22, sect. I, § 7]

Molina presses the same general point in these words:

> No effect at all can exist in nature unless God by His influence in the genus of efficient causation immediately conserves it...But since that which is necessary for the *conservation* of a thing is *a fortiori* necessary for the *first production* of the thing, it surely follows that nothing at all can be produced by secondary causes unless at the same time the immediate and actual influence of the First Cause intervenes. [*Concordia*, pt. II, disp. 25, § 14]

Mere conservationists, recall, hold that God conserves each created entity *per se* and immediately once it has been produced. So they agree with Suarez and Molina that God gives *esse*-as-such to every created entity after it has come into existence. But their position entails the negation of the intuitively appealing principle of symmetry asserted here by the Jesuits, viz., that a created entity depends on God for its coming into existence in exactly the same way it depends on Him for its continuing to exist. So the alternative picture painted by mere conservationists must follow the lines suggested by Suarez:

> Perhaps Durandus will reply that...when the action of the secondary cause ceases, then God conserves the effect immediately by Himself even if it was produced immediately only by the secondary cause, since no created thing can either have or retain existence without an efficient cause; and, therefore, as long as the secondary cause is immediately acting, it suffices [by itself], but when it ceases to act, then in order for the thing to remain in existence it is necessary that God act by conserving it. [*DM* 22, sect. I, § 7]

How might Durandus arrive at this picture? We can imagine him reasoning as follows: "I am convinced that no coherent account of God's general concurrence can be given, but I do believe both (i) that there is genuine secondary causation in nature and (ii) that no created entity produced by secondary causes can continue to exist after its production unless God conserves it *per se* and immediately. Therefore, there must be an asymmetry between the sort of dependence it has on God *while* it is being produced and the sort of dependence it has on God *after* it has been produced. While it is being produced, its secondary causes are alone *per se* and immediate causes of it; afterwards, God conserves it *per se* and immediately."

But this will not do. Mere conservationists take their own theory to be the only one which coherently accommodates the naturalistic conviction that there is genuine secondary causation in nature. However, as intimated in section 3, the belief that there are secondary *conserving* causes is epistemically on a par with the belief that there are secondary *producing* causes. After all, it would be anomalous to assert that, say, the gas flame on your stove produces heat in the kettle of water placed over it and yet to deny that the food you eat or the air you breathe helps conserve you in existence. So if mere conservationists want to insist that when secondary causes *produce* an effect, God is not an immediate and *per se* cause of that effect, then the very same line of reasoning should lead them to admit that when secondary causes *conserve* an entity, God does not conserve that entity *per se* and immediately. In short, since secondary causation is found in both production and conservation, mere conservationists have no plausible epistemic grounds for treating secondary production and secondary conservation asymmetrically.

It follows that mere conservationists have no good reason to affirm the strong conservation principle (CON) once they deny the general principle (ESSE) in light of their account of secondary production. They should instead claim that a created entity requires God's immediate and *per se* conservation only when and to the extent that secondary causes are not sufficient to conserve it *per se*. But this is just to abandon mere conservationism for a more deistic account of God's causal influence in nature, an account that repudiates (CON) while retaining (SC) and (MC).[26]

## 5. Argument Two: From the Nature of *Transeunt* Action

The second argument for the "first line of reasoning," though ostensibly uncomplicated, plunges us deep into the fascinating, though recondite, scholastic controversy over the ontology of *transeunt* action, a controversy in which Suarez himself ends up taking a minority position. However, despite the fact that Suarez presupposes his own account of the nature of action in presenting Argument Two, the argument itself depends on only a certain feature which that account shares in common with most of the rival positions, viz., the existential claim that *transeunt* action essentially involves the existence of a participated entity that is distinct from the agent, from the agent's active power, from the patient, and from the effect or form produced in the patient. In order to provide some background here, I will begin with a brief sketch of Suarez's position on the ontology of *transeunt* action.

We can look at a created agent's *transeunt* action from two sides, that of the agent and that of the patient. From the side of the agent, the existence of an action requires the fully actualized state of, or exercise of, a certain accident, viz., an active causal power which inheres in the agent, and it is by virtue of this exercise of power that the effect is said to "emanate" or "flow" from the agent.[27] From the side of the patient, a *transeunt* action requires the passive reception by the patient of the causal influence of the agent, resulting in a real modification or form in the patient which is said to "terminate" the action. So a simple *transeunt* action such as the acid's turning the litmus paper red involves at one and the same time the exercise of an active power possessed by the acid and the reception by the paper of the acid's causal influence, resulting in the paper's redness, which terminates the action. These two aspects of a *transeunt* action are metaphysically inseparable. That is, it is metaphysically impossible for there to be an action emanating from an agent without there being a form which is produced in some patient and terminates the action. This is the basis for the common scholastic adage that a *transeunt* action exists in the patient ("*Actio est in passo*").

The competing positions on the ontology of *transeunt* action by and large agree with what has been said thus far. However, Suarez differs from some of his rivals in denying that the term 'action', taken just in itself, signifies a real accident (whether a quality or relation) that inheres in the *agent* and is distinct from the relevant active power. And he parts ways with the rest of his rivals by insisting that an action is "nothing other than that special sort of dependence which an effect has on its efficient cause" [*DM* 48, sect. I, § 15]. This same relation of causal dependence is signified, albeit in different ways, both by the term 'action' or 'acting' on the one hand and by the term 'passion' or 'being acted upon' on the other:

> I maintain...that the same dependence and emanation of the form from the agent is called (i) a *passion* insofar as it affects the subject intrinsically and (ii) an *action* insofar as it denominates the agent itself as actually acting. [*DM* 49, sect. I, § 8]

Suarez thus conceives of this relation of causal dependence as a participated being which is a real accident inhering in the patient but which nonetheless involves an intrinsic and essential reference to the agent as actually acting; therefore, it exists as long as, and only as long as, the agent is actually exercising the relevant causal power with respect to the patient. Accordingly, the relation of causal dependence is an entity distinct both from the agent and the agent's causal power on the one side and from the patient and the form produced on the other side. In contrasting his view with certain other accounts of the ontological status of an action, Suarez puts it this way:

> From what has been said here against the other opinions one is easily persuaded that an action is not the thing which does the producing, nor the thing produced (i.e., the terminus of efficient causality), nor is it those two things taken together, nor a denomination arising from their coexistence; rather, it is something that mediates between them. [*DM* 48, sect. I, § 15]

Other scholastics insist to the contrary that the relation of causal dependence, far from constituting the ontological reality of the action, is a further reality which presupposes the existence of the action and which itself continues to exist even after the completion of the action. However, I will leave this objection to one side, since my primary aim for now is to present Argument Two as Suarez understands it.

Given his own account of action, he begins by asserting the conditional thesis that if, as mere conservationists hold, the effect or entity produced does not require God's immediate and *per se* influence in order to come to exist, then the action itself, conceived of as an entity distinct from the agent and the effect, does not require God's immediate and *per se* influence in order to exist. For, according to mere conservationism, the action has its immediate origin solely from the secondary agent and not from God.[28] He then argues that if the action does not depend on God's conserving it *per se* and immediately while it exists, then by parity of reasoning there is no basis for insisting that the form or effect produced by the agent depends on God's conserving it *per se* and immediately in order for it to remain in existence once it has come into existence:

> Second,...the first line of reasoning is proved from the fact that if God does not have an immediate influence on every action of a creature, then a created action itself does not of itself require God's influence essentially in order to exist, even though it, too, is a certain participation in being; therefore, there is no reason why the form that comes to exist through such an action should require for *its* conservation an actual influence of the First Cause. For it does not require this influence in order to *come to exist* (*ratione sui fieri*), according to the position in question, since this coming to exist is not itself immediately from God. Nor does it require this influence in order *to exist* (*ratione sui esse*), since [if it did, this

would be] mainly because it is a participated being—but this reason is not judged sufficient, according to the position in question, in the case of the action itself; therefore, neither will it be sufficient in the case of the form, i.e., the terminus of the action. [*DM* 22, sect. I, § 9]

So whereas Argument One concentrated on the entity or form that terminates the action, Argument Two focuses on the action itself. But the theme is similar: If mere conservationists deny (ESSE) and affirm that some created entity or other can exist at some time without God's giving it *esse*-as-such at that time, then they will be hardpressed to maintain the strong conservation principle (CON).

Argument Two is less obviously compelling than Argument One just because it presupposes the controverted contention that a *transeunt* action essentially involves the existence of an entity that is distinct at once from the agent, from its active causal power, from the patient, and from the form produced in the patient. Still, as I noted above, the argument will have a purchase on those who accept this existence claim, even if they reject Suarez's own peculiar elaboration of it. For anyone who accepts the existence claim will be forced to concede the key premise that if the *transeunt* action of a secondary cause is its own immediate action and not God's immediate action, then God does not give *esse*-as-such to that action; and, once this premise is granted, the argument *is* compelling. So in order to uphold their position in the face of Argument Two, mere conservationists must construct and defend an account of the ontology of *transeunt* action which does not entail the existence claim in question. This in itself constitutes an interesting result, since it is by no means clear that any such account of the metaphysics of action can be made plausible. But if this is so, then the force of Argument Two will, once again, be to push mere conservationists toward giving up the strong conservation principle (CON) and adopting instead some form of deism.

## 6. Argument Three: From *Contra Naturam* Miracles

The final two arguments, both of which invoke deepseated theological postulates, are more indirect in intent than Arguments One and Two. Unlike the latter, these two arguments are not aimed at establishing that there is a deep tension among the defining tenets of mere conservationism. Instead, they purport to show that even if mere conservationism does not suffer from irremediable intrinsic defects, it nonetheless cannot do full justice to the theological tenet—affirmed by occasionalists, mere conservationists, and concurrentists alike—that God is absolutely sovereign over nature.

Argument Three is propounded by Molina as well as Suarez. Both draw attention to a certain proper subset of the miracles recorded in Sacred Scripture. The distinguishing feature of these miracles is that even while God produces the effect by Himself alone in the relevant circumstances, the secondary agents involved in those circumstances retain their causal tendency to produce an effect directly contrary to the effect produced by God. St. Thomas, in distinguishing such miracles from miracles that are *supra naturam* and miracles that are *praeter naturam*, labels them *contra naturam* miracles:

> [A miracle] is said to be *contra naturam* when there remains in nature a disposition that is contrary to the effect which God produces, as when He kept the young men unharmed in the furnace even though the power to incinerate them remained in the fire [Daniel 3], and as when the waters of the Jordan stood still even though gravity remained in them [Josue 3].[29]

Suarez and Molina both light upon the miracle of the three young men in the fiery furnace, arguing that mere conservationism fails to give a theologically satisfying metaphysical account of *contra naturam* miracles. For mere conservationism entails that in order to perform a *contra naturam* miracle, God must act to thwart His creatures by impeding their action *from without*, as it were. But this, the Jesuits claim, is demeaning to God's sovereignty over the created world. What we need instead is a theory which, like concurrentism or occasionalism, is consistent with the claim that God brings about such miracles by omission rather than by commission, even while all the relevant creatures remain in existence. Thus Suarez:

> Just as God can deprive a created thing of its existence simply by withholding His action, so too He can deprive a created thing of its natural action simply by withholding His concurrence; therefore, just as from the former power one infers evidently an immediate dependence in existing, so too from the latter power one infers an immediate dependence in the action itself. The antecedent[30] (as I certainly concede) is not evident from any natural experience. However, it is sufficiently evident from supernatural effects. For God deprived the Babylonian fire of its action

even though no impediment was set against it from without; therefore, He accomplished this by taking away His concurrence. For how else could He have done it? And this is what is meant in Wisdom 11 [16:23 in modern editions], when it is said that the fire was forgetful of its own power—since, of course, it was not able to exercise that power without God. And this is of itself wholly consonant with the divine power, since that power has within its control the *actions* of all things in the same way that it has within its control the *existence* of all things. [*DM* 22, sect. I, § 11]

Molina is more explicit about how mere conservationists are constrained to deal with *contra naturam* miracles:

If God did not cooperate with secondary causes, He clearly would not have been able to bring it about that the Babylonian fire did not burn the three young men except by opposing it, as it were, and impeding its action either (i) through some contrary action or (ii) by placing something around the young men or conferring on them some resistant quality which would prevent the fire's impressing its action upon them. Therefore, since this derogates both the divine power and also the total subjection by which all things submit to and obey that power, one should claim without doubt that God cooperates with secondary causes, and that it was only because God did not concur with the fire in its action that the young men were not incinerated by it. [*Concordia*, pt. II, disp. 25, § 15]

Notice, even though Argument Three assumes that the miracle of the fiery furnace is itself best construed as a miracle by omission, this specific assertion about how one ought to interpret the third chapter of Daniel is not absolutely crucial to the point that Suarez and Molina want to make. What *is* crucial is the claim that God at least *can* bring about *contra naturam* miracles by omission, i.e., by withholding His immediate causal concurrence with the action of those created substances that are poised to produce a contrary effect.[31]

To get a deeper understanding of the issues surrounding this claim, we should take note of the occasionalist charge that *any* form of Aristotelian naturalism will turn out to be inimical to the doctrine of God's sovereignty over nature. And it is precisely *contra naturam* miracles—or, more neutrally, what theistic naturalists call *contra naturam* miracles—which, in the eyes of occasionalists, undermine Aristotelian naturalism and its attendant essentialism.

We might imagine an occasionalist reasoning as follows: "Those who, like the Aristotelians, insist that the basic causal powers of a created agent are essential to it must hold that it is *metaphysically* necessary that under the appropriate conditions such agents produce their characteristic effects unless they are impeded from without. In the case of the fiery furnace, for example, the Aristotelian naturalists seem bound to hold that human flesh (the flesh of the three young men) is *essentially* or *by nature* such that if it is exposed to extreme heat (the heat of Nebuchadnezzar's furnace) in the absence of natural impediments (e.g., asbestos clothing, protective shields, etc.), it will be incinerated. So according to the Aristotelians, it is metaphysically necessary that, in the circumstances described in Daniel 3, the flesh of the three young men should be incinerated when brought into contact with the fire of the furnace.[32] (Remember, by the way, that according to the biblical story the soldiers who threw the three young men into the furnace were themselves incinerated.) What's more, it is not enough to reserve to God the power, say, to change the flesh into a heat-resistant substance for the duration of its sojourn in the fire or to miraculously interpose a natural impediment by, say, creating a heat-resistant shield between the flesh and the fire or by endowing the flesh with some special heat-resistant quality. Why is this not sufficient? For the very reason Molina cites. God does not have to *counteract* His creatures *from without* in order to make them do His bidding; He does not have to vie with them in order to exercise control over them. Rather, He controls them *from within* as their sovereign creator and governor. They are beholden to His word: He can command the fire not to incinerate the flesh even while it remains fire; He can suspend the flesh's susceptibility to being incinerated without changing it into a different substance or altering its natural kind."

Occasionalists, of course, go on to assert that the doctrine of the absolute subjection of creatures to God requires theistic philosophers to repudiate naturalism altogether and to subscribe instead to the theory that God is the *sole* active cause in nature. Only on such a theory is it clear that miracles like that of the fiery furnace occur when God refrains from being an immediate cause of effects that He would under ordinary circumstances produce. Or so, at any rate, occasionalists claim.

As we have just seen, Molina and Suarez agree that mere conservationists are vulnerable to this occasionalist objection. But they demur at the suggestion that naturalism must therefore be abandoned. They reply instead that naturalism and theism can coexist with and indeed complement one another as long as the theistic naturalist is careful to stipulate that God's immediate and *per se* concurrence constitutes a necessary condition for the action of any secondary cause. To return to the fiery furnace, what is metaphysically necessary is that, in the circumstances related in Daniel 3, the flesh should be incinerated by the fire in the absence of natural impediments *on the assumption that God grants His contemporaneous general concurrence to all the relevant secondary causes.* Once this stipulation is added, theistic naturalists can take the miracle of the fiery furnace to be a miracle by omission even while preserving the naturalistic claim that the fire remains fire and that the flesh remains flesh and that all of the relevant secondary causes retain their characteristic causal inclinations and susceptibilities. In this way the concurrentists can accommodate the occasionalist claim that God controls created agents from within, with the result that He is able to make them "forgetful of their power" even while they retain that power.

This strikes me as a very powerful objection to mere conservationism. However, at least some in my acquaintance remain unpersuaded by it. A large part of the problem, I believe, is that there are two distinct ways to understand the dialectical intent of the argument.

On what I will call the *strong* reading, Molina and Suarez are using Argument Three to show that *any* acceptable theistic philosophy of nature must have as a consequence the thesis that God does (or at least can) bring about *contra naturam* miracles by withholding His immediate causal influence with respect to the relevant effects. According to this reading, if the argument is successful, then, taken just by itself, it rules out mere conservationism as a viable philosophy of nature from a theistic perspective. It follows that if concurrentism can be shown to be false or incoherent, then theists will have no recourse but to abandon naturalism altogether and embrace occasionalism.

On the *weak* reading, by contrast, Molina and Suarez are using Argument Three to show only that a philosophy of nature according to which God does (or at least can) bring about *contra naturam* miracles by the sort of omission in question is, *ceteris paribus*, preferable from a theistic standpoint to one according to which this is not so. Thus Argument Three, taken just by itself, does nothing more than establish a defeasible presumption in favor of concurrentism over mere conservationism. So even if concurrentism were proven to be false or incoherent, theistic naturalists would still have a *prima facie* viable alternative to occasionalism, viz., mere conservationism.

The passages quoted above suggest that Molina undoubtedly has the strong reading of Argument Three in mind and that Suarez probably does, too. However, in reply to the argument so taken, someone might reasonably wonder just how obvious it is that the mere conservationist account of *contra naturam* miracles "derogates the divine power and the total subjection by which all things submit to and obey that power." While I myself think that it is obvious enough, I see no easy way to convince someone who disagrees.

I do believe, however, that the concurrentist can rest content with the weak reading of Argument Three. First of all, on this reading the argument invokes only the relatively plausible claim that the sort of sovereignty attributed to God by the thesis that *contra naturam* miracles are wrought by God's withholding His general concurrence is *prima facie* more impressive than the sort of sovereignty accorded Him by mere conservationism. And so, even on the weak reading, the argument, taken just by itself, provides anyone who accepts this claim with a powerful motive for not abandoning concurrentism too early in the game. Second, as we already know, Argument Three need not stand on its own, but can be seen as simply adding force to the already strong case against mere conservationism built by Arguments One and Two.

So the safest course is to see Argument Three as aimed at the modest goal of providing all theistic naturalists, those who lean toward mere conservationism as well as those who lean toward concurrentism, with a strong motive for seeking a coherent account of God's general concurrence. With Argument Four Suarez tries to strengthen this motive even further.

## 7. Argument Four: From the Breadth of the Divine Power

Argument Four is unquestionably aimed at establishing an *a priori* predilection for concurrentism over mere conservationism. The claim is that, in general, theistic naturalists should be antecedently disposed to countenance in nature the maximal degree of divine activity compatible with the thesis that there is genuine secondary causation. Suarez, in something of an overstatement, calls this his best argument:

> Finally, the best argument: This manner of acting in all things and
> with all agents pertains to the breadth of the divine power, and it
> presupposes on God's part a perfection untainted by imperfection;
> and even though it does bespeak an imperfection on the part of the
> creature (whether we are thinking of the secondary cause or of the
> action or of the action's effect), this imperfection is nonetheless
> endemic to the very concept of a creature or participated being as
> such—as the arguments already given make clear. And, for the
> rest, in this way a perfect and essential ordering intercedes
> between the First Cause and the secondary cause, and there is
> nothing impossible here, as will easily be seen from the replies to
> their arguments; therefore, this general influence should not be
> denied to God. And this is why it seems not to have been
> altogether ignored even by philosophers, as we intimated [above]
> concerning Aristotle's view; and in the *Liber de Causis*, whether
> this work be judged to belong to Aristotle or to Proclus, there are
> various propositions by which this truth is expressed...[*DM* 22, sect.
> I, § 13]

This argument does not require much comment; indeed, it is hard
to imagine mere conservationists resisting it. After all, their primary
purpose is to safeguard the claim that created substances are true
causal contributors. If they became convinced that a coherent version
of concurrentism were available, they would, it seems, lack any good
philosophical or theological reason for not embracing it. Of course,
this argument by itself does nothing to establish that such a version
of concurrentism is in fact available. But like Argument Three taken
on the weak reading, it does at least provide theistic naturalists,
including mere conservationists, with a powerful incentive to work
hard at the project of producing an adequate account of God's general
concurrence.

## 8. Conclusion

As the last two sections make clear, the concurrentist case against
mere conservationism must, in order to be complete, go beyond the
arguments discussed in this paper to deal adequately with the objections that mere conservationists raise against concurrentism itself.
This is the positive project that awaits concurrentists, a project which
I hope to explore historically and systematically in another place.

Nonetheless, it does seem to me that Arguments One and Two
go a long way toward establishing that mere conservationism is itself
plagued by grave internal tensions that push it forcefully in the

direction of a form of deism which, however weak, falls beyond the pale of theistic orthodoxy.[33] What's more, Arguments Three and Four establish, if nothing else, that concurrentism is theologically preferable to mere conservationism as long as it itself can be shown to be free of serious intrinsic deficiencies. In either case, mere conservationism appears not to be an attractive resting place for theistic naturalists. Indeed, I find it difficult to resist the conclusion that the arguments of Suarez and Molina have narrowed the field for theistic philosophies of nature to occasionalism and concurrentism. In short, it is not entirely surprising that in the history of the theistic debate over God's causal activity in nature mere conservationism has not been able to attract much of a following.[34]

## Notes

1. See my "Medieval Aristotelianism and the Case against Secondary Causation in Nature," pp. 74-118 in Thomas V. Morris, ed., *Divine and Human Action: Essays in the Metaphysics of Theism* (Ithaca, NY: Cornell University Press, 1988).
2. The common scholastic view is that actions are individuated by their effects and that, as will become clearer in section 5, an action is an intrinsic modification of the patient rather than the agent. Accordingly, it is possible for an action to emanate immediately from both God and a secondary cause, so that the action belongs to both of them in all relevant respects, even though they are acting by distinct powers.
3. See William Durandus de Saint-Pourçain, *In Sententias Theologicas Petri Lombardi* II, dist. 1, q. 5 (Venice, 1571; reprinted at Ridgewood, N.J., 1964), pp. 130d-131d.
4. Albertus Magnus, *Commentarii in II Sententiarum*, dist. 35, sect. I, art. 7, in *Opera Omnia* (Paris, 1894), vol. 27, p. 575. Albert's comment occurs within a discussion of whether every act, good or evil, is immediately from God. In order to exonerate God of any responsibility for evil acts, some had claimed that secondary causes produce evil effects on their own without God's immediate causal influence:

   "Some have claimed that the will is sufficient of itself for an evil act, but not for a good act...Since the moderns have seen that it is more perfect to act than to exist, they have seen that that which does not exist on its own (*a se*) cannot remain in existence on its own, either—and much less can it act on its own. And this is the reason why that other opinion has all but disappeared from the lecture hall and is regarded as heretical by many moderns."

5. The general references to Suarez and Molina are as follows: Francisco

Suarez, *Disputationes Metaphysicae*, vols. 25 and 26 of Suarez, *Opera Omnia: Nova Editio*, edited by Carolo Berton (Paris, 1866; reprinted in two volumes at Hildesheim, 1965); and Luis de Molina, *Liberi Arbitrii cum Gratiae Donis, Divina Praescientia, Providentia, Praedestinatione et Reprobatione Concordia*, edited by Johann Rabeneck, S.J. (Oña and Madrid, 1953).

6. In particular, these arguments are neutral with regard to whether God's general concurrence involves a "premotion" in the secondary agent itself by which God moves it to act; hence, the arguments do not presuppose the truth of the unrestricted principle, rejected by both Molina and Suarez, that whatever is in motion is moved by another.

7. Most scholastics agree that what is caused by an efficient agent is always some "form", i.e., formal perfection, be it a form which constitutes a substance as a member of a natural kind or a form which is an accident of a substance. However, the minority who insist upon a deflationary account of accidental being, which posits fewer types of accidents as distinct beings, will presumably prefer to say that intrinsic *states* of substances count as effects in many cases. (See note 14 below.) I will presuppose the majority view here. I am also presupposing the Aristotelian thesis that entities other than elemental ones are true substances and that living, sentient, and rational beings are in fact paradigmatic substances. There are possible versions of mere conservationism and concurrentism which are based on more reductionist ontologies, but I will leave it to others to defend them.

8. It does not follow that from an Aristotelian perspective talk about so-called "event causation" is utterly wrongheaded; it follows only that every instance of event causation involves, at the deepest metaphysical level, the exercise of causal powers by various agents and patients.

9. What I have just said should caution contemporary readers against assuming that substances have all of their accidents contingently rather than necessarily or essentially. According to the scholastics, a substance's inseparable accidents are such that the substance cannot exist without them. The scholastics thus use the term 'accident' in a way different from that in which the term 'accidental property' is normally used in contemporary analytic metaphysics, where an accidental property of a substance is one which the substance has but can lack even while remaining in existence.

10. A question: When a principal cause employs another substance as an instrumental cause in bringing about a given effect, is the principal cause itself a merely remote cause of the effect? The explication of an immediate cause given above allows for an ambiguity between what St. Thomas (*De Potentia*, q. 3, art. 7, corpus) calls an *immediacy of power* and an *immediacy of suppositum*, where, to answer the question just posed, the principal cause is immediate to the effect in the first mode but not in the second, and the instrumental cause is immediate to the effect in the second mode but not in the first. All concurrentists claim that God is an immediate cause of every natural effect, but they differ as to which of these two modes of immediacy is involved.

11. It does not follow that in a given creature *esse* and essence are separable; it follows only that it is metaphysically possible that there should be no such participation in *esse*. Also, I admit that what I have said here presupposes—and thus is not an argument for—the thesis that finite entities are radically contingent beings whose constituents would all revert to nothingness without a continuing "adequate cause" of their existence. For an extremely interesting, though to my mind not wholly successful, discussion of some of the relevant issues, see Jonathan L. Kvanvig and Hugh J. McCann, "Divine Conservation and the Persistence of the World," pp. 13-49 in Thomas V. Morris, ed., *Divine and Human Action, op. cit.*

12. The claim that God possesses all possible perfections requires careful unpacking, since there are many formal perfections, e.g., quantitative accidents, which can, strictly speaking, be possessed only by limited or finite beings. Nonetheless, the divine nature is said to contain such perfections "eminently" by virtue of the fact that (i) all such perfections are in some way or other reflective of the divine nature and (ii) God is able to produce all such perfections *ex nihilo*.

13. This is true even when a patient comes to suffer some sort of privation of *esse* as the result of an agent's causal influence—as, for instance, when someone is blinded by being struck in the eye. What occurs in such cases is the introduction into the patient of a form which is incompatible with the form that the patient is thus deprived of. Such examples should make us aware that even though every instance of active causal contribution involves a giving of *esse* or perfection, this does not mean that the patient is itself more perfect *absolutely speaking* as a result of the agent's influence.

14. Scholastic accounts of accidental being range from the highly inflationary (e.g., Scotus's) to the highly deflationary (e.g., Ockham's). While everyone agrees that causal powers are distinct accidents signified by terms in the category of *quality*, there is a dispute about whether terms in the categories of *quantity* and *relation* signify entities distinct from substances and qualities. For a fine treatment of this dispute as it bears upon relations, see Mark Henninger, S.J., *Relations: Medieval Theories 1250-1325* (Oxford: Oxford University Press, 1989), and for a revealing look at the internal dispute among Thomists over the status of accidental being in St. Thomas's metaphysics, see Barry Brown, *Accidental Being* (New York: University Press of America, 1985).

15. Of course, the material elements of a bodily substance are themselves composites, and so any such substance will include a nesting of appropriate material constituents. Indeed, according to almost all the scholastics, "primary matter" cannot exist as such, and so there can be no material constituent of a corporeal substance which is not itself formed in at least some primitive way. For each such constituent itself involves both a principle of perfectibility or potency (matter) and a principle of perfection or actuality which actualizes the relevant potentiality (form). I should note in passing that the Aristotelian distinction between matter and form is itself a species of the more generic distinction between

582 / Alfred J. Freddoso

potentiality (or perfectibility) and actuality (or perfection). So even if, as is sometimes alleged, the concept of matter/form composition has no place in the far reaches of contemporary particle physics, it does not follow forthwith that the more esoteric physical entities posited by contemporary physical theories cannot be understood as having a potency/act composition. I hope to develop this idea in more detail elsewhere.

16. Three points are in order here. First, even though characterizing causation in the proper sense as the giving of *esse* might initially sound impious to modern philosophical ears, some such account seems needed to undergird familiar distinctions like that between "real" changes and so-called "Cambridge" changes. Second, the present account is meant to apply both to what St. Thomas (*Summa Theologiae* I, q. 104, art. 1, corpus) calls a cause of coming to be (*causa secundum fieri*) and to what he calls a cause of being (*causa secundum esse*). This distinction will become more evident in section 4. Third, the notions of immediate causation and *per se* causation are not, as defined here, extensionally equivalent. For, as will be adumbrated below, an agent can be an immediate cause of an entity's continuing to exist without conserving that entity *per se*.

17. Here I follow St. Thomas's discussions in *De Potentia*, q. 3, arts. 1-4 and *Summa Theologiae* I, q. 45, arts. 1-5.

18. One might be tempted to ask the following rhetorical question in support of this claim of St. Thomas's: If such an agent could give *esse* to *something* from the bottom up, how could its creative power be limited at all? One possible reply is that the agent is deficient in knowledge and is hence incapable of directing its creative intention to more than just a limited range of creatable entities; or perhaps the agent acts by a necessity of nature and is limited by nature to a single effect or range of effects. St. Thomas himself was well acquainted with neo-Platonist emanationist cosmogonies in which the First Cause, acting by a necessity of nature, creates just a single effect, viz., the first intelligence. Against such cosmogonies, he tried to show that God has perfect knowledge and acts freely in creating.

19. In order not to beg any interesting questions, I have explicated *de novo* creation in such a way as to leave open the possibility that an entity might be newly created more than once.

20. In what follows I draw upon Suarez, *DM* 21, sect. III, §§ 1-13, and St. Thomas, *De Potentia*, q. 5, arts. 1-3 and *Summa Theologiae* I, q. 104, arts. 1-3.

21. It may not always be easy for us to distinguish cases of *per accidens* conservation from cases of *per se* conservation. For instance, while it is clear that the food ingested by a living organism conserves it *per se*, it is not clear what to say about the conserving action of an antibiotic.

22. *Summa Theologiae* I, q. 104, art. 2, ad 1.

23. The reason is that the forms and dispositions which they effect and which mediate their influence on the substance in question do not themselves seem to be further *efficient* causes of that substance.

24. See *DM* 21, sect. III, §§ 4-8. There remains, of course, the task of showing how God's action as a *per se* and immediate conserver is consonant with the action of secondary conservers. But this is just a special moment in the overall concurrentist project of laying out a coherent account of secondary causation. The concurrentist must try to show that, in general, God's giving *esse*-as-such to an entity, either to produce it or to conserve it, is not incompatible with a secondary agent's simultaneously giving it *esse*.

  Suarez maintains, by the way, that certain types of *accidents* can be conserved *per se* and immediately by secondary causes. These include, among others, thoughts conceived of as immaterial mental accidents; for thoughts exist only as long as the intellect that has them gives them *esse*. But God's action as a *per se* and immediate conserver is also required in such cases.

25. At one point in the discussion of Argument One below Suarez imagines Durandus giving up the strong conservation principle (CON) for the weaker principle that God conserves every created entity *either* immediately *or* mediately. However, in my reconstruction of this dialectic in section 4 I will assume that Durandus wants to hold on to (CON). The reason is that repudiating (CON) leads directly to at least a weak form of deism, according to which God conserves created entities only when or to the extent that secondary conservers are unable to.

26. Philip Quinn has suggested to me that Durandus might be able to escape deism by retreating in the face of Suarez's objection to a weaker version of (CON) on which God is a *per se* and immediate conserver just of substances and not of accidents. But this seems unpromising for two reasons. First of all, Suarez's argument talks about effects just insofar as they are participated beings, and both substances and accidents are equally participated beings. Second, even this weaker conservation principle would be in tension with (MC), since the mere conservationist is constrained to hold that God does not give *esse*-as-such to a substance while it is being produced by secondary causes. And no full-blooded naturalist will dispute the claim that secondary causes are capable of effecting substances as well as accidents.

27. Though Suarez freely uses terms like 'influx' and 'flow' to describe the causal influence of an agent on a patient, the scholastics generally deny that *transeunt* action involves the transfer of some entity from the agent to the patient. This is the way St. Thomas replies to one standard objection against *transeunt* action: "It is ridiculous to claim that bodies do not act because no accident passes from one subject into another. For a hot body is said to produce warmth not in the sense that numerically the same heat which is in the heating body passes into the heated body, but rather because by virtue of the heat which is in the heating body a numerically distinct heat comes to exist actually in the heated body—a heat that previously existed in it in potentiality. For a natural agent is not something that transfers its own form into another subject, but is instead something that brings (*reducens*) the subject which is acted upon from potentiality to actuality" [*Summa Contra Gentiles* III, chap. 69].

28. Neither Suarez nor his opponents claim that an agent causes its own *transeunt* actions in the sense that a *transeunt* action might itself be the proper terminus aimed at by the exercise of an active causal power. Instead, an agent gives *esse* to its own actions concomitantly with causing its proper effect.

29. *De Potentia*, q. 6, art. 2, ad 3. *Supra naturam* miracles involve effects that no created agent is capable of producing in any way, and *praeter naturam* miracles involve effects that created agents are capable of producing but not capable of producing as quickly or as directly or with as much abundance as God produces them.

30. The antecedent includes everything that precedes the semicolon in the preceding sentence.

31. Peter van Inwagen points out that mere conservationists can construe the miracles in question as wrought by omission if they claim simply that God ceases to give *esse* to the relevant creatures. For instance, in the case of the fiery furnace, "as the photons are on their way from the fire to the flesh, God ceases to sustain most of the energetic ones in existence" ("The Place of Chance in a World Sustained by God," pp. 211-235 in Thomas V. Morris, ed., *Divine and Human Action, op. cit.*, p. 216, note 7). One important reply to this suggestion is that the intellectual, scriptural, and liturgical traditions within which the present debate occurs place a premium on the idea that obedience to the will of God is a prerequisite for the flourishing of any created being; even inanimate substances give glory to God by being subject to His will and in this way fulfill the ends for which they were created. This general picture, it seems to me, fits best with the thesis that in *contra naturam* miracles God suspends the action of such entities rather than their *esse*. Perhaps a more philosophically satisfactory reply is that acting and existing are distinct perfections in a created entity and so, *ceteris paribus*, should be thought of as being subject to God's will in distinct modes, with the result that such an entity can become "forgetful of its power" even while it remains in existence. Also, the concurrentists' account of such miracles allows them to admit the truth of the occasionalist (and positivist) claim that there are no non-trivial conceptual constraints on what sorts of causal sequences are possible. For instance, the concurrentist can accept the Humean claim that it is metaphysically possible that when one billiard ball makes contact with another, the second ball simply stays put—and this precisely because God does not cooperate with the normal movement of the second ball. The mere conservationist must presumably claim that this can happen only if God withholds *esse* from the first ball (or from relevant parts of it) when it makes contact with the second ball.

32. Interestingly, this very same claim is insisted upon by the contemporary naturalists Rom Harré and Edward Madden in their book *Causal Powers* (Totowa, NJ: Rowman and Littlefield, 1975), pp. 46-47.

33. I am assuming as before that mere conservationism is the weakest account of divine causation which is even arguably compatible with theistic orthodoxy. Some may wish to contest this assumption. If so, it

seems evident that, in light of the religious and intellectual tradition handed down to us on this matter, the burden of proof lies with the dissenters.

34. Earlier versions of this paper were read to the Society of Medieval and Renaissance Philosophy and to the Notre Dame Philosophy Colloquium. I want to thank David Burrell, Michael DePaul, William Hasker, John Jenkins, John Nieto, John O'Callaghan, David O'Connor, Alvin Plantinga, David Quackenbush, Mark Webb, and especially Philip Quinn for their help.

Philosophical Perspectives, 5, Philosophy of Religion, 1991

# THE OCCASIONALIST PROSELYTIZER: A MODIFIED CATECHISM

Hugh J. McCann
Jonathan L. Kvanvig
Texas A&M University

On what is perhaps the most popular conception among believers, God created the world "in the beginning," and it has existed on its own ever since. No direct activity on God's part is needed to explain the world's persistence, and although the unfolding of its history is a matter of great concern to Him, it would take an extraordinary act of intervention on God's part for anything that occurs to count as a direct manifestation of His power. We have argued elsewhere that on the first score at least, this conception is mistaken.[1] The mere fact that there is a universe offers no guarantee, logical or scientific, that it will persist for another instant; rather, it is the direct activity of the Creator which conserves the world in existence at each moment. In this paper, we want to reflect on the second.part of the popular conception. We think there are good reasons for rejecting also the view that God is only indirectly involved in what occurs in the world. Some are based on the doctrine of conservation itself, while others arise from the concept of divine providence. To make the whole of universal history a direct manifestation of the power of God is, however, to court accusations of occasionalism—the view that nothing that occurs is owing to natural causes or the operation of scientific laws, and that apparent causal relations between events consist in nothing but the occurrence of certain sorts of events prompting God to see to it that others will follow. Such a view appears to deny the explanatory force of scientific laws, not to mention what seems obvious to experience: that the things in the world interact with one another, and that at least sometimes those interactions determine the course of future events. Part of our task will be to examine the extent to which such accusations are justified. We shall hold that the conservation doctrine is indeed incompatible with event causation, if by the latter we understand a relation in which one event is responsible for the existence of another. We hope to show, however, that no such productive relation between events is possible, and hence that this concept of event causation must be abandoned. Nevertheless, we think there are other ways of understanding event causation on which it remains a viable concept, and the explanatory force of scientific laws is preserved.

## 1. The Impulse Toward of Occasionalism

Occasionalism is often understood as involving a denial of some rather obvious truths: that heating the water makes it boil, for example, or that the cue ball's striking the object ball explains the latter's acceleration. Whether it should be so taken depends in part on our theories of causation and scientific explanation. Equally important, however, is the way in which occasionalism itself is defined, and the considerations that are seen to motivate it. Too often, the latter are misunderstood, and occasionalism is seen as prompted by a desire for some convenient metaphysical payoff, such as an easy solution to the problem of mind-body interaction. This is a serious underestimation. As we see it, the heart of occasionalism lies neither in its negative claims about the role of secondary causes, nor in the metaphysical consequences thereof, but rather in a positive thesis about the intimacy with which God is related to His creation.

The distinctive feature of occasionalism is its thoroughgoing anti-deism. Occasionalists hold not only that God brought the universe and all that is in it into being, but also that He sustains these things at every moment of their existence.[2] They go further, however, than affirming the doctrine of divine conservation. Occasionalists also hold that God is directly responsible for the things He has created having the characteristics they do, as well as for whatever changes they undergo. If we follow the convention of using the term "event" to refer to states along with changes, we may say that for the occasionalist, God is directly responsible not just for the complete existence of every substance, but also for that of every event that occurs within the created realm. This does indeed imply that an immediate exercise of the power of God occurs when water boils, and when billiard balls accelerate. For the occasionalist, however, these consequences are inevitable once the relationship between God and the created world is understood.

As has been indicated, part of what is involved here is the conservation doctrine itself: that the universe endures only because part of God's activity as Creator is to sustain it at every moment of its existence. Suppose this were not so, and that the universe had a beginning in time. In that case, the immediate effects of divine creation would be confined to the first moment of the universe's appearance, a moment "prior to which" there would have been nothing physical.[3] And it is only natural to include among those effects the characteristics of whatever things appeared first as well as those things themselves. *Ex hypothesi*, there is no prior state of the universe by which the presence of those characteristics can be explained, so there is only the activity of the Creator to fall back upon. Moreover, it seems impossible for a creative act to be responsible for the existence of a thing but not the characteristics it has at the moment it appears. To cite an example of Malebranche's, "...it is a contradiction that God should will the existence of the chair yet not will that it exist somewhere and, by the efficacy of his volition, not put it there..., not create it there."[4] The reason for this is simply that it is impossible for a chair to exist but not exist in a definite location; thus, given that there is no other way for the position of the chair to be determined, it is impossible for God to will its existence without seeing to its location as well. Needless to say, the same goes for the color of the chair, for whether it is in motion or at rest at the instant it appears, etc. The situation of God is like that of an artist executing a painting. What the artist conceives in her mind may be indeterminate as to its exact position on the canvas, its color, etc., but she cannot paint on the canvas an object that is indeterminate in these ways. The same applies *a fortiori* to an object created *ex nihilo*. If it is to appear at all, the object must be fully determinate: for every property $P$, it must either have $P$ or lack $P$.[5]

Clearly, then, if the universe had a temporal beginning, God must as Creator be responsible for its entire initial state, including whatever changes were underway when it first appeared. But now suppose the conservation doctrine is true, so that God is directly responsible for the continued existence of the universe, as well as any temporal beginning it might have had. If so, then every instant of the universe's existence has the same status as the initial one hypothesized above.

This is especially obvious if conservation is conceived as a kind of "continuous creation," in which the universe is newly brought into existence at each moment.[6] If this is correct then as Creator, God would have to be directly responsible for every aspect of being, including every event. But we need not think of the universe as appearing anew at each moment of its existence in order to reach this result. Suppose again that the universe has had but one temporal beginning, and that there were prior moments. Clearly, the transition from those earlier moments to the one at which the universe appeared involved a change. Notice, however, that this was not a change in which any *thing* changed, not one that involved any intermediate stages during which the world was only "coming to be." Rather, there is nothing short of the *being* of things that can count as the first effect of God's creative activity.[7] But then what God contributed to the universe in its inception—namely, its being—is precisely what, on the conservation doctrine, He contributes throughout its career. And if to provide for the being of things in their inception requires bringing it about also that they have the characteristics they do, then presumably the same holds when the being of things is sustained. Both in the beginning and thereafter, all that obtains does so as a direct consequence of God's will. But then the entire state of the universe at every instant, all that is and all that occurs, is directly owing to the creative activity of God. It appears to follow that there is no role left for secondary causes; God has, as it were, saturated the world with His own causal power so as to make all other causes otiose.

A second path to the same apparent outcome can be found in the doctrine of divine providence. Theists believe not only that God is responsible for the existence of the universe, but also that He providentially cares for all of His creation. At the very least, this implies divine control over the direction of history. The world is not left to its own devices, to work out in some unthinking fashion what its *telos* is. Rather, God Himself has prescribed the goal of history, and His providence insures that events in time interact so as to achieve that goal. Now perhaps the chosen path is ensured simply by God's having chosen the right conditions for our hypothesized initial state of the universe. But then again, perhaps there was no such state. And even if there was, perhaps no selection of initial conditions on God's part could have ensured that His chosen *telos* would be the natural end toward which all creation tended once left to its own devices.[8] So perhaps some level of miraculous involvement in the course of nature is required in order for God to exercise governance over the direction of history.

But this is only the beginning. God's providence is not exhausted by some remote, unfeeling ordering of the course of nature, even with an occasional miracle thrown in. Rather, it is of the essence of His governance that it display unbounded love for all that He governs. God's providential guidance of things is not something independent of His love for what He has created, but instead is subservient to it. He guides the course of nature precisely because He loves and cares for the offspring of His creative activity. At the very heart, then, of the doctrine of providence is unfathomable love; far from being a calculating manager, driven by efficiency considerations to achieve maximal governance from minimal involvement, God lavishes on His children His attention and concern in the process of ordering and directing His creation. Further, the display of His love is not any emaciated, truncated attention only in terms of conservation; it is not just our being, but our well-being, which concerns Him. Such love is not compatible with the ordering of things from afar; instead, it requires direct and immediate involvement—the kind of direct and immediate involvement humans know only rarely, in moments of true intimacy. The events and situations in which we find ourselves must be a part of this involvement; they cannot be hindrances or obstacles to the Divine intention, but must instead issue from the very hand of God as part of His active love for us. Here again, however, any contribution by secondary causes to the course of events seems to be overwhelmed. For if God's involvement in universal history is so direct, immediate, and active, what is left of that history which can be attributed to, or explained by, the nature of things?

Thus, from the direction of the doctrine of providence as well as from that of divine conservation, considerations appear to converge toward some version of occasionalism. Neither doctrine, moreover, is of a very radical sort; many theists would endorse both of them in much the form we have given, especially in preference to their deistic alternatives. The problem is, the endorsement is usually given without attention to the resultant threat to the integrity of science. If God is solely responsible for the existence of all that is, it would seem that our attempts to determine the nature of things through scientific investigation are at best superficial, and at worst downright misleading. The nature of things and the operation of scientific law, it might seem, have nothing to do with how things happen as they do; instead, it is only the hand of God at work. And that conclusion seems simply too wild to accept, however edifying the premises on which it is based.

## 2. The Elusiveness of Compromise

Perhaps it is for this reason that even philosophers who accept the doctrine of divine conservation have tended to resist any inference from it to the view that God is responsible for the existence of events. Philip Quinn, for example, holds that to accept the conservation doctrine is to be committed only to:

    (A) Necessarily, for all $x$ and $t$, if $x$ exists at $t$, God willing that $x$ exists at $t$ brings about $x$ existing at $t$,

where $x$ ranges over ordinary physical objects like tables and chairs. But the occasionalist is committed also to:

    (B) Necessarily, if $x$ is F at $t$, God willing that $x$ is F at $t$ brings about $x$'s being F at $t$.

Quinn objects to this second thesis, claiming we can have a theory of conservation that makes God directly responsible for the existence of things, but not for their character.[9] We question, however, whether attempts to affirm (A) while avoiding (B) can ultimately succeed. Granted, (B) is not entailed by (A) alone; but we have already seen reason to question whether God could will the existence of a thing at any point during its career without attending to its characteristics as well. Additional arguments are available. For example, any respectable theory of creation must make God responsible in *some* way for His creatures having the characteristics they do. And it may well be questioned whether the divine simplicity would permit God to engage in one sort of activity to create the world and quite another put in place a supposed cosmic mechanism for directing the course of events. The most important point, however, is that the result of accepting (A) while rejecting (B) is a theory that will satisfy neither the scientifically nor the theologically minded, much less those who are both.

To see why, we need to consider the metaphysical issue of the nature of substance. One way to uphold (A) while rejecting (B) is to adopt a theory according to which substances are radically independent of their attributes. On a Lockean view, for instance, a substance is a thing of which properties are predicated, and in which they inhere; taken strictly in itself, however, it is propertyless. Of a Lockean substance, therefore, it might be claimed that God is directly responsible for its existence, but leaves the issue of which properties are to inhere in it to the operation of natural or secondary causes. But this argument is no stronger than the notion of substance on which it depends, and the difficulty is that the notion of a propertyless substance is inconsistent. One can, of course, entertain the concept of substance in abstraction from any thought of its properties, but in reality every substance has to have at least some properties, and essential ones at that. Otherwise, the notion of a natural kind would be lost: the same substance that is, say, George Bush could as easily have been a frog, or an atom of hydrogen. But if a substance cannot be indifferent as to its natural kind, then God cannot create a substance with indifference to its kind. He must at least decide what sort of substance He will create. Thus if we make God directly responsible for the existence of substances, some concession to occasionalism is inevitable; He must at least be responsible for the existence of a substance's essential properties, for substances are intrinsically property laden. Concession does not, of course, mean complete surrender. The latter might be required if we adopt some sort of bundle theory, according to which substances are no more than sets, either of properties or of their instantiations. But there is a continuum of theories from those that treat substances as bare substrata to those that posit their full reducibility to property-like entities. How far one goes on this continuum determines the extent to which accepting thesis (A) pushes one in the direction of occasionalism.

One can also approach this issue from the semantic side. Suppose, for example, that Frege is right about existence: that it is a second order property, the property another property has of having an instance. In that case, for God to bring about the existence of a thing is for Him to bring it about that some property has an instance. What property might this be? Perhaps, again, the essence of that thing. But on semantical treatments, the concept of essence often has markedly different content from that found in traditional metaphysical theories. On one important set of accounts, George Bush figures in his own essence: that is, his essence is understood to be the property itself either of being George Bush, or of being identical with George Bush. On the other hand, there are accounts which impute a more qualitative character to the essence. Plantinga, for example, holds that an essence is a world-indexed version of any property a thing has uniquely.[10] Thus, if George Bush is the one individual with 3800 hairs on his head in 1990, then the property of having 3800 hairs on one's head in 1990 in alpha, where alpha names the actual world, is an essence of George Bush. Let us consider these views in turn.

The difficulty with the non-qualitative conception of essence is that it at least verges on circularity.[11] Indeed, this objection seems to be decisive against views on which the essence of Bush is the property of being identical with Bush. That property appears to have Bush as a constituent, since its logical representation employs a constant whose semantic value is Bush himself. But if this is correct then the property is ontologically dependent on Bush, in that it presupposes his existence. Now it is peculiar in itself to treat the essence of Bush as consisting in a property to which his existence is logically prior. But to appeal to this property to *explain* his existence would be ridiculous. That is what we do, however, if we make the instantiation of this property be what God wills when He sustains the existence of Bush. Furthermore, even if this were an acceptable move it would provide no assurance that, in bringing about Bush's existence, God does not bring about that of his accidental features as well. After all, if Bush's essence includes Bush *in toto*, why should it be otherwise?

The situation is somewhat less clear when one conceives of Bush's essence as the property of being Bush. In this case, the representation of the property might not employ a constant whose semantic value is Bush: perhaps the property of being Bush is a non-complex property best represented by a single predicate letter. If so, the circularity of the formulation which appeals to the concept of identity would at least be mitigated. But this advantage is won only at the expense of clarity. On the one hand, the property of being Bush is held to have different metaphysical status from that of being identical with Bush—so different that the first but not the second permits a non-circular explanation of God's bringing about Bush's existence. But if no qualitative content is constitutive of the property of being Bush, this becomes a suspect claim. For in the absence of qualitative content only a reference to Bush himself seems capable of providing the property of being Bush with any content whatever. On the other hand, if we accede to the idea that the property of being Bush lacks any reference to Bush himself, then it is hard to see how we can view it as without qualitative content. If, as we saw above, Bush himself cannot exist without the properties that keep him from being a frog, how can the property of being Bush fail to involve those properties? And if it does involve them, how will we be able to maintain that God is directly responsible for this property being instantiated without some concession to occasionalism?

Perhaps, however, the concession can be a limited one, so that in accepting (A) one is not driven all the way to (B), which makes all the features of things direct products of God's creative activity. The approach which treats essence in terms of world-indexed properties holds some promise here, since it allows the essence of an individual to be constituted even by what would traditionally be viewed as accidental features, provided they are held uniquely by that individual in our world. Here too, however, there are serious problems. One is that once essences like this are admitted, God's willing the existence of any particular thing becomes quite a complex matter. Having 3800 hairs on his head in 1990 in alpha can count as an essence of the individual that is George Bush only if God wills that that individual alone have this feature. But then He must also see to it that no other individual has that number of hairs. Plausibly, however, any strictly negative willing on God's part would be without creative effect; a negative result can be achieved only by His willing some positive state of affairs that is contrary to what is to be excluded. Thus, given that Reagan is to be alive in 1990, making sure he does not have 3800 hairs on his head at that time requires willing positively that he have some other number. And of course the same task must be carried out for every individual other than Bush, regardless of whether any of them sport an essence based on hirsuteness. Needless to say, this is not a very satisfying picture. Many even of the accidental features of things would have to be held directly owing to God's action; and the division of labor between divine and natural causation promises to be helter-skelter, to say the least.

There is, however, an even worse problem here, concerning the existence of world-indexed properties themselves. We may think of the complete abstract universe as a hierarchically ordered entity, each level of which is composed of items constructed from simpler entities found at lower levels. The important question then is; at what level do world-indexed properties appear? On one standard conception, a possible world is a very large collection of jointly realizable propositions, which represents a complete description of a way things might have been. It turns out, however, that in order for the description to be complete the collection must contain propositions drawn from throughout the abstract hierarchy. This being the case, a possible world cannot itself appear at *any* level of the hierarchy. Hence no possible world is ever available for use in constructing world-indexed properties. World-indexed properties must, in essence, be constructed after the entire abstract universe is in place.[12] Clearly, however, this picture is inconsistent. A defender of world-indexed properties must therefore resort to some other account, either of ontological complexity in general or of possible worlds—perhaps a Lewis-style view on which possible worlds are themselves primitive entities. It is almost superfluous to point out that such a route to accepting thesis (A) while rejecting (B) is not especially attractive.

If the criticisms we have raised are correct, both the Lockean and the semantic approach to saving (A) while rejecting (B) face serious difficulty. To be sure, nothing we have said shows that either approach will necessarily be driven to impute to God wholesale responsibility for the characteristics of the things He creates. Strictly speaking, defenders of these views can still claim success in avoiding (B). The trouble is, however, that either approach leads to an account of how the world gets to be the way it is that lacks credibility. For we do think our discussion shows that these theories cannot legitimately endorse (A) without ascribing to God *some* direct responsibility for the characteristics of things as well as their sustenance. And that makes what we might call "partial occasionalism" inevitable. God must be counted responsible for whatever events are demanded by the combination of thesis (A) and one's favorite theory of substance; only the events that are left over, it seems, can be left to natural causation.

Any such account, however, is intrinsically volatile, and likely to be unacceptable to both science and theology. On the scientific side, if we acquiesce in the assumption that anything caused directly by God lies beyond the reach of nature's laws, then the features of things that are entailed by God's conserving activity must be held to escape natural explanation. Yet surely the reach of scientific laws cannot be understood to be thus limited. Certainly there is no empirical argument for such a limitation, nor is it obvious that any argument, scientific or otherwise, could fix the supposed boundary in a fashion that, to our empirical sensibilities, would appear anything but strictly arbitrary. As for theology, the view under consideration appears to introduce an unreasonable complexity into God's attitude toward His creatures, and His ways of dealing with them. For some of their characteristics He is held directly responsible, and for others only indirectly, through the operation of natural causal processes. But what could be the reason for such a dualism? Nothing of theological importance is gained by it. Unlike the case with the free will defense against the problem of moral evil, there can be no hope of exempting God from the consequences of natural processes by placing Him at one level of causal removal from them. Furthermore, nothing in the views we have considered addresses the point made earlier, that God's providential love for all that He has created demands His intimate involvement with all creation, in all of its fullness. If this is correct then God should not be less concerned, say, with acceleration than with inertial motion, or less responsible for a thing's physical features than for its biological or psychological ones, or more involved in producing its essential properties than its accidents.

There are, then, theological as well as scientific reasons for rejecting the view that the occasionalist implications of the doctrine of conservation extend to some of the properties of created things but not others. If conservation has occasionalist implications, then either the conservation doctrine must be rejected, or we must find an accommodation with the scientific view of nature that does not seek to divide responsibility for what exists between divine and natural causation. We think such an accommodation is available. To reach it, it is necessary to distinguish two claims traditionally associated with occasionalism, but only one of which we endorse. The first is the claim we have been defending: that the existence of *all* that is— substances and their attributes alike, whether essential or accidental—is directly owing, not to any natural process, but rather to the creative activity of God. This is what we see as implied by divine conservation and providence. If those doctrines are to have teeth, there has to be something about the world the reality of which is not owing to natural causation, something whose *production* cannot be ascribed to the operation of scientific law. Short of this, a theory of sustaining and providential creation reduces to mere verbal obeisance: God's creative sustenance and providential love toward the world are held to be facts, but facts which, in the normal run of circumstances, make no visible difference. From a theological perspective this simply will not do. What could it be, then, about the world the existence or reality of which is not owing to the operation of scientific law? The occasionalist answer is: Everything. And here we see no room for a plausible compromise. If the theological doctrines at issue are correct, then not only is it "in Him that we live, and move, and have our being," it is also through Him and by His power that the universe and the things in it have their own distinctive character at each instant.

In certain ways, this claim is every bit as radical as it sounds. Nevertheless, it is a long way from it to a second claim associated with occasionalism: that scientific laws have no explanatory force, and that the apparent interactions among things in the world are illusory. Here we do think a line can plausibly be drawn, for depending on how scientific laws are understood, no such consequences need follow from the occasionalist's understanding of divine creativity. What makes it seem otherwise is that we tend, especially in our everyday thinking, to interpret scientific laws as recording natural processes whereby one event or set of events is *productive* with respect to another or others, in the sense of actually bringing about their existence. Usually, such processes are understood to be diachronic, and the supposed productive relation they involve is what is sometimes referred to as the "causal nexus." Now obviously, not everyone associates such processes with scientific laws: indeed, some philosophers have gone so far as to claim a mature science requires no concept of causation at all.[13] Once accepted, however, such processes appear to compete directly for the role occasionalism ascribes to divine creativity alone. Hence the tendency either to reject divine conservation, or to seek the kinds of uncomfortable compromise we have been considering.[14] But the correct move, as we hope to show in the next two sections, is to reject the causal nexus.

## 3. The Impossibility of a Diachronic Causal Nexus

On cursory reflection it might well appear that earlier events are responsible for the existence of later ones. How can it be otherwise, given that scientific laws may be used to predict and control the course of events? The laws governing heat transfer and vaporization *assure* us that the water will boil if heated sufficiently, and the laws of dynamics are what we exploit when, by controlling the motion of the cue ball, we determine that of the object ball. And surely the natural way to understand this is in terms of a model on which events that occur at one time are responsible for the *existence* of those that follow. Indeed, if we ignore such phenomena as quantum indeterminacy, then the operation of scientific laws seems to settle all questions as to how the future will go. The event of the water's being heated *makes* it boil, and by controlling the motion of the cue ball we *bring it about* that the object ball moves in a certain way. What is it to make such claims, if not to say that given the way they are acted upon, the water and the object ball must react as they do? And what is this if not to say that the events we count as causes are responsible for the reality of their effects? In short, the very idea that a sequence of events is lawfully governed appears to carry the implication that the later events in it owe there existence to the causal activity of earlier ones.

Upon closer scrutiny, however, this conception turns out to be fraught with problems, and not the least of them is the diachronicity it imputes to the causal relation. Historically, the leading proponent of this idea was Hume, who while no friend of the causal nexus, held that any cause must be temporally anterior to and contiguous with its effect.[15] But temporal contiguity is impossible to secure if, following the usual practice, we understand time as a densely ordered continuum. Consider a pair of events, $e$ and $e'$, and suppose the former occurs before the latter. The simplest way to interpret this supposition is take $e$ and $e'$ as point events, the first occurring at an instant $t$ and the second at $t'$. Now either there is an interval between $t$ and $t'$ or not. If there is, then $e$ occurs before $e'$, but the two are not contiguous; if there is no interval, then the density of time requires that $t=t'$, so that $e$ and $e'$ become simultaneous. If causation is diachronic, therefore, only the situation in which there is a temporal interval between $e$ and $e'$ would permit a causal relation between the two. Yet this seems impossible, at least if causation is to be construed as a relation wherein $e$ is responsible for the existence of $e'$. For if we take the relation to be direct, so that $e$ is held to produce $e'$ without the assistance of any intervening events, we are calling for $e$ to produce an effect—i.e., the existence of $e'$—at a time when $e$ no longer exists. Such temporal action at a distance is even more offensive than the spatial variety. Nothing can exercise direct productive efficacy if it does not exist at the time of the exercise. So if $e$ and $e'$ are point events occurring at different times, there is no direct productive relation between them.

Perhaps, then, the relation is indirect: perhaps, that is, the efficacy of e with regard to the existence of e' is mediated through intervening events. But this supposition simply raises the same problem again, at least if the events that are thought to intervene are themselves point events. For any pair of these will either be separated by a temporal interval or not. If so they cannot share a direct productive relation, and if not they must be simultaneous. In short, no pair of point events that occur at different times can enter into a direct relation whereby one is responsible for the existence of the other. If a productive relation obtains between point events at all, it has to count as simultaneous, not diachronic, causation. Furthermore, even if there are simultaneous productive relations between point events, that would still provide no reason for thinking our temporally *separate* events e and e' share *any* productive relation, even an indirect one. For indirect production is here conceived simply as a situation where the efficacy of e is, as it were, transmitted to the time at which e' appears, via diachronic productive relations among intervening point events. But there are no such relations. There cannot, then, be any diachronic productive relation, direct or indirect, among point events.

It might be thought that this problem is in some way connected with our having chosen to view events as point-like, rather than as having duration, or occupying stretches of time. And it has to be admitted that events properly so called are better portrayed along lines of the latter sort. It may be convenient to think of the states of entities—for example, this paper's being white—as events, but events in the strict sense are *changes*. For a change to occur, something has to go from having one property to having a contrary one: the paper could fade from white to yellow, a billiard ball could move from one position to another on a billiard table.[16] Since contrary properties cannot be held simultaneously, this means point events are in reality abstractions. Anything properly referred to as an event must involve temporal transition.[17] Is it possible that events conceived as involving temporal transition could enter into diachronic productive relations whereas point events cannot? We think not, but here the situation is more complicated.

Let us speak of events that involve temporal transition as "temporally extended."[18] As examples, consider the movements of a cue ball and an object ball respectively, the first from position $p_1$ to $p_2$, and the second from $p_3$ to $p_4$. We can imagine $p_2$ and $p_3$ as having whatever is the required degree of nearness to each other for a collision between the two balls to have occurred, and we then ask whether the first movement could have produced the second—in the sense of being responsible for its existence—diachronically.[19] The answer is again No, and for substantially the same reasons as were given for point events. Here, however, the argument is complicated by the fact that the temporal boundaries of an extended event need not necessarily be taken as internal to the event's duration. Let $t_1$ and $t_2$ be, respectively, the last instant at which the cue ball is in $p_1$ and the first at which it is in $p_2$; and let $t_3$ and $t_4$ be the last instant of the object ball's being in $p_3$ and the first of its being in $p_4$. The natural thing is to understand each pair of times as *internal to* the duration of the event they measure, so that the motion of the cueball begins *at* $t_1$ and continues through subsequent times up to and including $t_2$, and similarly for the motion of the object ball and the other pair of times.[20] But if we do this, it is quickly apparent that any claim of a diachronic productive relation between the two events faces essentially the same problem that occurred with point events.

The argument is substantially as before. The intervals of the two movements must either overlap—i.e., have at least one instant in common—or not. If they do not, then $t_2 < t_3$: the motion of the cue ball must end before that of the object ball begins. Given the density of time, however, $t_2$ and $t_3$ cannot be adjacent. There must be an interval between them, which, as before, requires that any productive relationship between the two events be either at a temporal distance or mediated through other events. The former is impossible, and the latter will only raise the same problem again, as long as the intervening events are assumed to be internally bounded and to display no temporal overlap. Consider, then, the possibility that the durations of the two movements do overlap, and let us make the simplifying assumption that the overlap is minimal—i.e., that $t_2 = t_3$. This at least produces the gain that the density of time no longer stands in the way of their being a productive relation between the events; and since the overlap between the events is not complete, a semblance of diachronicity is preserved. Unfortunately, however, it does not follow that the supposed productive relationship must *itself* be diachronic, and once temporal overlap is permitted any assurance of that is lost. Indeed, at least with regard to the present example, things seem to go the other way. The early stages of the cue ball's motion could not, it would seem, be directly efficacious with regard to any part of the motion of the object ball, since they no longer exist when the object ball moves; and for the same reason no part of the cue ball's motion could be directly responsible for later stages of the motion of the object ball. To deviate from this would only raise the difficulty of action at a temporal distance all over again. The most plausible assumption, then, is that any ontological relation wherein the movement of the cue ball could be held to produce that of the object ball would have to be confined, as far as its own reality is concerned, to the instant at which both exist. Obviously, such a situation has the look not of diachronic but of simultaneous causation.

The supposition that the temporal boundaries of extended events are internal to them does not, then, allow meaningful progress toward a plausible claim of diachronic productive relations. Perhaps, however, this supposition should be abandoned. It's guiding conception is that the times that mark the boundaries of an event belong to its duration, and hence constitute the first and last instants of that event. And it might be thought that it is only our insistence on this conception that stands in the way of our finding events that are temporally contiguous. Once we treat a pair of events as internally bounded we cannot speak of the termination of one and the onset of the other without specifying instants such as $t_2$ and $t_3$ as belonging to the events' durations, and once this is done the density of time makes it inevitable that they will either overlap or occur at a temporal distance. But, the argument continues, it is not necessary to treat the temporal boundaries of events as internal. Instead, we can say that the movement of the cue ball includes all that happens *between* the last instant when it is in $p_1$ and the first when it is in $p_2$, but not its actually being in either of those positions. To do so is not to leave the temporal location of the movement any less clearly fixed: $t_1$ and $t_2$ remain its temporal boundaries. The difference is simply that they are now *external* to its duration. And of course we can treat the movement of the object ball in the same way, making $t_3$ and $t_4$ external to its duration. The price of so doing is that, since none of these instants have adjacent ones, we may no longer say of either movement that it has a first or last instant. But, it is claimed, we *can* now hold that the events are contiguous. For now we can let $t_2 = t_3$ without danger of temporal overlap, since this instant belongs to neither event. Yet, since all the times surrounding this instant are times at which one or the other ball is in motion, there will be no temporal interval between the two movements. Hence we can now claim the first gives rise to the second without danger of the pro- ductive relation being either simultaneous or at a distance.

One way of responding to this suggestion is to point out that the assumption on which it is based—that events are externally bounded—is metaphysically implausible. It may be acceptable to treat intervals of time, considered abstractly, as externally bounded by instants. But events are supposed to be real changes in the world, in which an entity goes from having some property to having a contrary one. It seems unreasonable to define events as transitions between contrary properties and then exclude the having of either property from participation in the ontological makeup of the event.[21] But the proponent of productive relations between events need not be deterred. As long as we understand the externally bounded entities described above as the true participants in causal relations, she might argue, it doesn't matter what they are called. The point is just that they are bound together in a relation wherein one gives rise to the other.

Again, however, we question whether such a relation could exist. It must be remembered here that the productivity is supposed to be direct: the prior event must be responsible for the existence of the later one without intermediaries, without its efficacy being trans- mitted through intervening events. With this in mind, consider again the motions of the cue ball and the object ball, understanding these to be "separated" by the temporal discontinuity $t_2$ ($=t_3$). It is true that this separation introduces no interval between the events. But it is also true that *neither* the motion of the cue ball nor that of the object ball exists at $t_2$. And the directness of the supposed relation between them precludes there being some other event whose duration includes $t_2$, by means of which the supposed productive power of the first is transmitted. But then, we claim, the first event cannot produce the second, for there is a point in time at which neither exists, and yet nothing else occurs which may bind the two in a productive relation. That is, we hold that a temporal discontinuity like $t_2$ is, as far as the ontology of causation is concerned, the same as a temporal interval.[22] It renders any productive relation between the events it separates impossible. Furthermore, even if there were such a relation it could not, on the present supposition, extend to the states which terminate our two events—i.e., the states of the cue ball's first being at $p_2$ and the object ball's first being at $p_4$. Yet causality is regularly taken to be as much involved in the occurrence of states as in the transitions by which they are reached.

There is one last resort that might be suggested at this point: perhaps we should understand events to be bounded internally at one terminus and externally at the other. For example, we could take the first instant the cue ball is at $p_2$ as internal to its moving to that position, but then take the last instant of the object ball's presence at $p_3$ as externally bounding its motion. On this account $t_2$ and $t_3$ can be allowed to be identical *without* postulating a temporal discontinuity between the events. The instant in question is the last of the duration of the cue ball's motion, and the motion of the object ball is understood to have no first instant. Here at last, it might be thought, we have a pair of events that are temporally contiguous, and so can share a productive relation. We cannot, of course, think of that relation as obtaining between the last instant of the cue ball's movement and the first of that of the object ball, since we are committed to the object ball's movement not having a first instant. However, it might be claimed, we can treat the productive efficacy of the first event as extending ahead in time to nearby instants: that is, it may be held to operate from the last instant of the cue ball's movement to some arbitrarily close point in the future, enough to get the object ball's motion underway. Presumably, the latter would then be continued in some other manner—through inertia, perhaps—so that the efficacy of the cue ball's motion would no longer be needed to explain it.

Again, however, any initial plausibility this view may have disappears under scrutiny. Ignoring for the present the business about inertia, the position is in part objectionable for its sheer arbitrariness. One could as easily have made the reverse claim about how the two events are bounded, specifying a first instant for the object ball's motion but no last one for that of the cue ball. Productive efficacy would then be held to extend from the final stages of the first motion to the first instant of the second. There does not appear to be a way of deciding between these interpretations, and that in itself is reason for thinking the supposed productive relation is bogus. A further point of arbitrariness lies in the claim that the causal efficacy of the first event extends to some nearby point in the future. The reason for this seems clear. There is, on the one hand, no conceivable reason for assigning one specific duration rather than another to productive efficacy; yet to deny it any limit at all would be to allow events to be directly efficacious as far into the future as one might like—the very sort of thing we have been at pains to reject. And this is where the decisive failure of this view emerges. The truth is that to claim a direct productive relation extends from $t_2$—here taken to be the final instant of the cue ball's motion—to all temporal points in the arbitrarily near future is to make *nothing but* a claim that there is direct productive action at a temporal distance. What makes it possible to convince oneself otherwise is the supposition that as long as the productivity extends to *all* points in the near future it must extend to whatever point is adjacent to $t_2$, thence to the next, and so forth, so that no real action at a distance will have occurred. But that is wrong. The fact is, rather, that once $t_2$ is specified, *there is no adjacent point. Each and every* point in time to which the productive efficacy of the cue ball's motion might be held to extend is at a distance from $t_2$. The supposed productive efficacy of the cue ball's motion cannot, then, be manifested except at a temporal distance, and that is precisely what we have denied is possible.

We conclude that there is no direct, diachronic relation of productivity between events. Internally bounded events cannot be temporally contiguous, and so cannot share direct productive relations except on pain of the productivity operating at a temporal distance, which is impossible. The introduction of external boundaries can, if mixed with the internal variety, produce a situation in which pairs of events might be considered temporally contiguous, but the resulting picture of events seems arbitrary, and despite initial appearances the problem of temporal distance remains. So if there are any relations of direct productivity between events, they have to be simultaneous, not diachronic.

## 4. The Impossibility of a Synchronic Causal Nexus

It turns out, however, that there are excellent reasons for rejecting also the notion of a synchronic causal nexus—i.e., a productive relationship in which an event or set of events is held to be responsible for the existence or reality of another that occurs simultaneously. In fact, even a friend of productive relations between events might begin to find them unattractive if they could only be simultaneous. Part of the reason for postulating such relations is, after all, that they seem to be the only alternative to divine conservation for explaining the continuance of the universe. But if they cannot be diachronic, then that function appears to be lost; there does not seem to be any metaphysical glue that holds the universe together over time.[23] Moreover, if causal productivity can only be simultaneous it would seem that, lest all causal explanation of events be rendered ultimately circular, a certain amount of what goes on in the universe at any instant must be *uncaused*, at least as pertains to its existence at that instant. Or, we could opt for the theistic hypothesis that some of what goes on at any instant is caused by God's creative activity, and that it in turn produces the remainder. Here again, however, we are in the area of uncomfortable compromise. In the long run, neither of these outlooks is likely to prove acceptable either to science or to theology.

But perhaps we are moving too quickly. It might be argued that a synchronic causal nexus together with a diachronic conservation principle, such as the classical law of inertia, would solve our problem. And one could even claim empirical backing for such a view. To return to our example, classical physics is misrepresented by the supposition we have made so far, that the motion of the cue ball from $p_1$ to $p_2$ *directly* causes the subsequent motion of the object ball from $p_3$ to $p_4$. The more correct view is that interaction occurs only when the two spheres are in collision, and by Newton's third law action and reaction are supposed to be simultaneous. Perhaps, then, we should hold that the event which is the cue ball's striking the object ball is, by simultaneous causation, responsible for the existence of the object ball's acceleration. Thereafter, the first law takes over. It is inertia which, once the object ball is accelerated, carries it from $p_3$ to $p_4$; and we may suppose equally that inertial movement is what brought the cue ball into contact with the object ball. Here, it might be thought, is the ideal solution to our problem. By making productive relations between events simultaneous, we avoid the problem of action at a temporal distance. Yet we retain diachronicity, since motion is conserved inertially during the intervals from $t_1$ to $t_2$ and from $t_3$ to $t_4$. To be sure, there is some residual smudginess. In particular, we have to worry about the fact that the interaction itself takes time, and about how the events it involves are related to the two motions with which we began. But perhaps in the ideal case even these problems would disappear. For example, maybe collisions between ideally small particles could be held to involve an energy exchange that occurs instantaneously, at a temporal point boundary external to the motions of the two particles.

This would provide a situation in which the temporal discontinuity between the two motions is no longer devoid of a relevant occupant, and we could again appeal to conservation principles to handle the diachronicity on either side.

We think this view is mistaken not only in its acceptance of synchronic productive relations among events, but also in the appeal it makes to conservation principles. To deal with the latter point first, it is a mistake to think conservation principles can do what the causal nexus cannot: i.e., account for the ongoingness of things. Inertia is not a force or power that operates in or on physical bodies, so that they will keep going in the right direction and at the right speed. Hence it is a mistake to think it can explain, in any useful sense, why the states and events in which substances participate are apt to continue to exist once they are underway. Indeed, one way of understanding conservation principles is to view their inclusion in a theory as recording what the theory does *not* explain, but instead either presupposes or treats as requiring no explanation. On this type of view, the Newtonian principle of inertia might be taken as calling for the motions of our two billiard balls to continue once established, but as offering no explanation of why this should be so. But it is a mistake to think even this much follows from Newton's first law alone; the truth is that taken strictly in itself, the first law has no diachronic import whatsoever.

How could it? Consider again the cue ball in our example, and suppose it is moving with a certain velocity at $t_1$. Does the principle of inertia tell us it will have the same velocity at the next instant? Clearly not, for there is no next instant. Does it say, then, that the cueball will have this velocity at some instant further along—$t_2$, perhaps, or some point in between? Again no, for something could easily "cause" a change in the cue ball's velocity during the time that intervenes. Indeed, taken by itself the principle of inertia does not even guarantee that there will be at least *some* instant after $t_1$ at which the velocity will be unchanged. $T_1$ could, after all, turn out to be the last instant at which the cue ball has the velocity in question. That is, it could be the external boundary of a period of acceleration for the cue ball—an instant whose subsequent vicinity is filled with instants at which the ball is subject to some net force. If so then by the third law the cue ball must be undergoing acceleration at those instants, and hence have some other velocity. What, then, does the first law tell us by way of useful information about the cue ball?

Simply this: that if the cue ball is subject to no net force at $t_1$, then the velocity we supposed it to have is not changing *at* $t_1$. That is a very useful piece of information to have, but it tells us nothing at all about the velocity of the cue ball at any prior or subsequent moment. A fortiori, it can tell us nothing about the longevity of the motions those velocities define.

How is it, then, that we are at times able to make such confident predictions about the future by assuming the principle of inertia? The answer is that we make other assumptions as well. And the most important of them have a suspiciously occasionalist ring! The case of the cue ball is as telling as any. First, we must assume the ball will continue to exist, since otherwise it cannot be involved in any events. Second, we have to assume the ball cannot exist without being in some state of motion (rest being the limiting case) relative to other objects. Once these assumptions are made the principle of inertia becomes useful. For while it guarantees nothing about the existential future, it does describe *how* the dynamic characteristics of objects change, if they change at all. Specifically, it defines a relationship between changes in motion and the (simultaneous) imposition of physical force. This enables us, if we have independent knowledge of what forces are about to impinge on an object, to predict its motion. But none of this calls for any secret Newtonian mechanism for preserving the dynamic features of things. Indeed, the first law would be just as useful if it called for those features to change (and hence for present events to cease), provided only that the change were regular. Rather, the expectation that present events will be prolonged is owing, as far as the prolongation aspect is concerned, to the assumption that their subjects will enjoy continued existence. And that is an assumption we introduce. Scientific theory offers no foundation for it.[24]

The principle of inertia fares no better than the causal nexus, then, when it comes to guaranteeing a diachronic progression of events. And the prospects for the other part of the view we are considering— i.e., that the causal nexus is synchronic—are equally dim. Some of the problems here are empirical. Even if we accept the idea that cause and effect must occur at the same time, we would not expect them to occur in the same place. We think of the collision of two billiard balls, for example, as occurring at the place where the surfaces of the two are in contact, or perhaps in the entire spatial volume occupied by the two.[25] But the resultant acceleration of the object ball occurs only where it is located. Similarly, a subatomic particle that imparts energy to another is not thought to occupy the same position as the particle upon which it acts. As a matter of empirical fact, however, there can be no energy transfer between different spatial locations that does not require the passage of time, since the speed of light counts as the maximum rate at which such interactions occur.[26] So if we think of fundamental causal processes as involving transmission of energy, exchanges of particles or the like, we appear to have no choice but to consider them diachronic rather than synchronic. We have already seen, however, that there can be no diachronic relation wherein one event is responsible for the existence of another. So if we insist on making causation a productive relation we are forced either to give up the idea that it involves energy transfer, or to insist also that the events sharing the relation occur at precisely the same place as well as at the same time. But surely either move would strain credibility to the limit. Cases of energy transfer, such as our billiards example, are the most paradigmatic examples of causation we have. And to say that cause and effect must occur in the same place as well as simultaneously is to rule out their occurring in different physical objects, again in complete violation of expectation. Indeed, it would be no small irony were the causal relation, which is usually thought to be what allows commerce between different spatio-temporal locations, to turn out upon examination to do no such thing, but instead to isolate each point in space-time, monad-like, from every other.

Scientifically, then, it is hard to see what agenda is furthered by our thinking of causation as a simultaneous productive relation. And there are good metaphysical reasons for rejecting this view also. Indeed, the very idea of a simultaneous *productive* relation between events seems at least to border on the self-contradictory. "Production" bespeaks a process whereby something is brought about; but processes take time, and that is precisely what simultaneity rules out. In a way, this is as it should be. Causation cannot, after all, count as a process over and above the events it relates: if it were, we would simply be faced with a further event positioned between a cause and its effect, whose relation to each of them would be still more puzzling than causation itself is. If, on the other hand, causation is not a process and takes no time, it is hard to see how it can be productive at all, or in any way responsible for the existence of what is produced. This leads to what we think is the real metaphysical difficulty. Relations, or at least simultaneous ones, *presuppose* the existence of their relata, and so cannot *explain* the existence of either of them. That is why we do not think of overdetermined events as having a multiple or fuller existence as compared to others, and why it would be foolish, in the case of events that have complex causes, to try to divide the existence of the caused event into increments contributed by the various items making up the total cause. It is also why the search for an empirical foundation for any supposed causal nexus has always failed. The fact is that there is nothing one event can contribute to the existence of another, nothing that "goes on" when one event is said to cause another besides the events themselves. Synchronic productive relations between events are, then, just as impossible as diachronic ones. There is no nexus, no glue either diachronic or synchronic that holds the cosmos together, and whose secret workings are recorded in the laws of science.

## 5. Explaining Events

From a theistic point of view, the absence of a causal nexus is to be expected, for even if—as we think the foregoing arguments show is impossible—it could do its job, it would in the end explain nothing anyway. Indeed, the existence of any kind of cosmic glue would only require in its turn a God who, ever attentive to its viscosity, carefully maintains it in existence, so that his sustaining power can operate through the causal nexus to uphold the world. It is indeed the creative activity of God that is responsible for the existence of things, but He employs no means to see to their continued existence, or to make sure they have any of the character they do. Such a claim presumes, of course, that divine agency can be given a more credible account than the causal nexus, and this may of course be questioned. This issue is too complicated for treatment here, but at least where God's creative activity is concerned we have the model of human agency to fall back on. The workings of the human will may not be well understood, but they hold a great advantage over the causal nexus in that they are at least there to be studied. We see no a priori reason to be skeptical about their offering some glimpse of how divine agency works.

But what about event causation, and the integrity of scientific laws? We see every reason for optimism about these as well, once the superstition of the causal nexus is removed. As for laws, the fact that God is fully and directly responsible for the existence of all there is provides no reason for thinking that what He has created cannot be described, or that its workings will not fall under general principles. Nor need such principles be taken in a merely instrumentalist sense. That would be compatible with what we have said, but it is too weak: science is in the business of describing the nature of things, not telling a just-so story to enable us to predict experience. What it is to describe the nature of things has to be spelled out, of course, and that too is a complicated matter. In part, it is a question of the strength of scientific laws. Presumably, they are more than material conditionals, or expressions of "constant conjunction." But nothing we have said rules out analyzing laws in terms of counterfactual or even logical necessity, as long as the necessity is not held to involve productive relations.[27] Nor does our argument tell against theoretical explanations of the ways substances interact. It is perfectly compatible with an occasionalist account of the existence of events that there should be collisions between billiard balls, exchanges of subatomic particles, or transfers of energy from one substance to another.

Indeed, even the notion of event causation is perfectly bona fide, as long as it is kept clear of the error that one event can be responsible for another's existence. The concept of event causation arises out of the asymmetry that characterizes much of scientific explanation, and the fact that we are often able to control the future course of affairs by acting in the present. But these things too can be accounted for without supposing that causes are responsible for the existence of their effects. Some explanatory asymmetries are not between events anyway: the period of a pendulum depends on its length, rather than the other way around, because the period is a dispositional property, for which the basis is the length of the pendulum.[28] But even when real events are involved, as when the cue ball's striking the object ball causes the latter to move, the explanatory asymmetry bespeaks no causal nexus. In this case the asymmetry is largely temporal, in that the motion of the object ball continues after the collision is ended. And of course it is no accident that the object ball moves as it does. It is, rather, a part of the nature of things that when billiard balls collide, certain accelerations occur, and that as long as the billiard balls continue to exist thereafter the resultant motions will themselves endure until further interactions occur. But none of this is a matter of earlier events bringing later ones into existence. It is simply a question of the things God creates being what they are rather than something else.

We do not, then, think the integrity of science is in any way undermined by the doctrines of divine sustenance and providence. It is true that these doctrines have occasionalist consequences. Properly taken, they imply that God is responsible for the complete nature of things, for their essence as well as their existence, for their accidental characteristics along with their essential ones. But this in no way precludes there being general principles describing the nature and behavior of the things God creates, nor does it rule out any useful concept of event causation. All it precludes is the existence of a causal nexus, and the idea that earlier events are able to provide for the existence of later ones. Furthermore, if the arguments we have given are correct these are useless notions anyway; if they ever infected science, it is well rid of them. The order of things remains as real as ever without them, and it is still true that by understanding that order we are able to predict, and even to play a conscious role in determining, the sorts of events that will occur. But the existence of things is to be explained by the creative activity of God, which is direct and immediate, and owes nothing to the assistance of a causal nexus.

We wish finally to urge that the sort of view we have been defending is more important to theism than is usually recognized. It is one thing to say of God's wisdom that it is not always apparent to us, of His purposes that they are not always discernible, even to say of His goodness and love that they are at times not visible to us in the workings of nature. But the same must not be said about His role as creator. If God is the creator of heaven and earth, that fact has to make quite literally *all* the difference in the world. It cannot be hidden from our sight, or obscure to our understanding, or empirically neutral in the slightest way. On the contrary: correct understanding should make it manifest that the creative action of God is the only viable hypothesis, the only way of accounting for the being of anything that has a glimmer of a chance at being true. In part, our argument here has been that the heart of the competing hypothesis— i.e., that the existence of later events can be explained by the causal productivity of earlier ones—is hopelessly inadequate. We take this to be the positive import of occasionalism, and a legitimate accompaniment of the theories of divine sustenance and providence. The negative import often associated with occasionalism—that scientific

laws have no legitimate standing, and that there are no genuine
interactions among the things God creates—we do not defend. Such
a view does not follow from the doctrine of divine sustenance, or
even from the failure of event causation to explain the existence of
things.

## Notes

1. J. L. Kvanvig and H. J. McCann, "Divine Conservation and the Persistence
   of the World," in *Divine and Human Action: Essays in the Metaphysics
   of Theism*, ed. Thomas V. Morris (Ithaca, New York: Cornell University
   Press, 1988), pp. 1-37.
2. See, for example, Nicolas Malebranche, *Dialogues on Metaphysics*, trans.
   Willis Doney (New York: Abaris Books, 1980), p. 153.
3. This way of putting things presumes it makes sense to speak of times
   prior to the existence of the physical world—a suspect idea which we
   adopt only for ease of expression. In its essentials, the argument that
   follows would still hold if time were understood to appear only with
   the appearance of the world.
4. *Dialogues on Metaphysics*, p. 157.
5. Indeterminacy issues aside, that is. When such issues arise, an object
   is complete only if it is indeterminate with respect to both $P$ and its
   complement.
6. For more on the notion of continuous creation, see Philip Quinn, "Divine
   Conservation, Continuous Creation, and Human Action," in *The Existence and Nature of God*, ed. Alfred J. Freddoso (Notre Dame, Indiana:
   University of Notre Dame Press, 1983), pp. 55-80.
7. St. Thomas Aquinas, *Summa Theologica* I, Question 45, Article 2.
8. Besides the issues of quantum indeterminacy and human free choice,
   there are theological matters to contend with here. Christians, for
   example, are committed to a wholesale intervention by God in the course
   of human history in the person of Jesus Christ.
9. Philip Quinn, "Divine Conservation, Secondary Causes, and Occasionalism," in *Divine and Human Action: Essays in the Metaphysics of
   Theism*, ed. Morris, pp. 50-73.
10. Alvin Plantinga, *The Nature of Necessity*, (New York: Oxford University
    Press, 1974), p. 63.
11. For a discussion of some of the implications of this circularity see Robert
    M. Adams, "Time and Thisness," *Midwest Studies in Philosophy* 11 (1986),
    pp. 315-29.
12. Christopher Menzel, "Theism, Platonism, and the Metaphysics of Math-
    ematics," *Faith and Philosophy* 4 (1987), 365-382.
13. Most notably Bertrand Russell. See "On the Notion of Cause," *Proceedings
    of the Aristotelian Society* 13 (1912-13), 1-26.
14. Equally unsatisfactory would be to attempt to solve the problem simply
    by calling for wholesale overdetermination of natural events, making

614 / Hugh J. McCann / Jonathan L. Kvanvig

event causation as well as the direct action of God responsible for their existence. In effect, this is not a solution but a restatement of the problem. There is no reason for God to create a world in which natural causes bring events to pass if in fact His very creation of that world includes bringing about those events Himself.

15. Hume, *A Treatise of Human Nature*, ed. L. A. Selby-Bigge (New York: Oxford University Press, 1888), p. 170.

16. The theory of events as changes between contrary properties receives extensive development in Lawrence B. Lombard, *Events: A Metaphysical Study* (Boston: Routledge & Kegan Paul, 1986).

17. This goes also for what are sometimes offered as examples of instantaneous events—e.g., winning a race. If by winning a race we understand the change from not yet having won to being the winner, then the passage of time must be involved, even if it is only the transition from some arbitrarily close point in time to the first instant of being the winner. For more on this issue see Lombard, *Events: A Metaphysical Study*, pp. 140-144.

18. This is an oversimplification. There are in fact two quite different ways of conceiving the relation between events and temporal transition, and only on one of them do events turn out to be extended in the proper sense of the term. H. J. McCann, "Nominals, Facts, and Two Conceptions of Events," *Philosophical Studies* 35 (1979), 129-149. This complication can be ignored, however, since the argument that follows above has force on either conception.

19. It is legitimate to point out here that we are at least closer to an immediate causal relation if we think of the *collision* between the two balls as the cause, and the *acceleration* of the object ball as the effect. But thinking in terms simply of the two motions makes it is easier to visualize the problem being discussed, and does not affect the substance of the argument at this point. We shall have more to say about collisions and accelerations later.

20. Lombard, *Events: A Metaphysical Study*, pp. 134 ff.

21. It would, of course, be impossible to make such a move with instantaneous events, if the idea that they involve but one instant is taken strictly.

22. Lest it be thought that the argument we offer here depends too much on the assumption that time is a continuum, it should be pointed out that if it were a succession of discrete instants, a discontinuity of the sort represented by $t_2$ would intervene between each pair of them.

23. Indeed, Hume thought that any admission of simultaneous causation ultimately brings with it the impossibility of temporal succession, and hence "the utter annihilation of time." *Treatise*, p. 76.

24. It might be claimed that the foundation is provided by the principle of conservation of mass-energy. But if we take that principle as promising that the world will have a future, it has no warrant beyond sheer enumerative induction. An underlying theory to explain the persistence of mass-energy is utterly lacking. Furthermore, it is not in the least obvious what such a theory would look like, or how empirical discovery

could have any bearing on its truth. For all science could ever have to say, then, the persistence of the world might as well be the work of God. For this reason, we think it best for scientific purposes not to take the principle that mass-energy is conserved as promising any future. Rather, it makes the perfectly reasonable point that there is nothing in the nature of things that accounts for their existence or non-existence, and hence no "scientific process" either of creation or of destruction. See "Divine Conservation and the Persistence of the World," pp. 32 f.

25. The second supposition is by far the better. There is a problem about physical objects being contiguous in space that is precisely analogous to the difficulty over events being contiguous in time. Its historical importance has been considerable. See, for example, J. E. K. Secada, "Descartes on Time and Causality," *The Philosophical Review* 99 (1990), 45-72.

26. Henry Byerly, "Substantial Causes and Nomic Determination," *Philosophy of Science* 46 (1979), p. 62.

27. See Quinn, "Divine Causation, Secondary Causes, and Occasionalism" for a defense of the view that an analysis of causation in terms of conditionals is compatible with occasionalism.

28. It is perhaps worth noting here that when the length of a pendulum is changed, the period (conceived strictly as a dispositional property) changes instantaneously—a sure sign that the change is relational rather than real.

Philosophical Perspectives, 5, Philosophy of Religion, 1991

# JEPHTHAH'S PLIGHT:
# MORAL DILEMMAS AND THEISM

William E. Mann
University of Vermont

> Then the spirit of the Lord came upon Jephthah, and he passed through Gilead and Manasseh, and passed on to Mizpah of Gilead, and from Mizpah of Gilead he passed on to the Ammonites. And Jephthah made a vow to the Lord, and said, "If thou wilt give the Ammonites into my hand, then whoever comes forth from the doors of my house to meet me, when I return victorious from the Ammonites, shall be the Lord's, and I will offer him up for a burnt offering." So Jephthah crossed over to the Ammonites to fight against them; and the Lord gave them into his hand. And he smote them from Aroer to the neighborhood of Minnith, twenty cities, and as far as Abel-keramin, with a very great slaughter. So the Ammonites were subdued before the people of Israel.
>
> Then Jephthah came to his home at Mizpah; and behold, his daughter came out to meet him with timbrels and with dances; she was his only child; beside her he had neither son nor daughter. And when he saw her, he rent his clothes, and said, "Alas, my daughter! you have brought me very low, and you have become the cause of great trouble to me; for I have opened my mouth to the Lord, and I cannot take back my vow." And she said to him, "My father, if you have opened your mouth to the Lord, do to me according to what has gone forth from your mouth, now that the Lord has avenged you on your enemies, on the Ammonites." (Judges 11:29-36, Revised Standard Version)

An agent is in a moral dilemma if, no matter what he does, he does something wrong. This characterization can stand some refinement, but it is clear enough as it stands for us to ask the most controversial question about moral dilemmas: *Are* there any? I wish to rephrase that question from a particular perspective: Do theists have a special stake in whether there are moral dilemmas? My answer is quintes-sentially philosophical: Yes and No. Yes, the existence of moral di-lemmas should influence the way in which theists think about faith and morality. No, the existence of moral dilemmas does not pose a threat or a scandal to theism.

I think that there are moral dilemmas. Other philosophers disagree. It might seem that the way to settle our disagreement is to hunt for an example. If we find one, I am right; if we do not, after a thorough search, I am wrong. But things are never that simple in philosophy. For one thing, the question is really whether moral dilemmas are so much as *possible*. The literature on the topic abounds with discussions of cases drawn from fiction, and no one dismisses them as beside the point.[1] Thus the mission of the person who denies the existence of moral dilemmas is not merely to show that we have not yet uncovered one. It is rather to argue that their existence is somehow strongly precluded. Such a person might argue, for in-stance, that moral dilemmas are logically impossible, or incompat-ible with principles known to be true. A theist who denies moral dilemmas might argue that even if they would be possible in a world without God, they are nevertheless precluded in the actual world by divine providence. Therefore, any case put forward as a candidate for a moral dilemma will be avidly disputed.

I shall discuss two major issues concerning theism and the existence of moral dilemmas. This first is the thesis that if there are moral dilemmas, they are always the result of previous culpable wrong-doing. The thesis is attractive to theists because it appears to be a corollary of the more general claim that providential God will never force the righteous to sin. Even so, it seems to be false as a matter of fact. The thesis has been attributed to no less an authority than Saint Thomas Aquinas. I shall argue that he does not hold it. The second issue devolves from the first. I shall suggest that the denial of the thesis, rather than damaging theistic ethical theory, deepens our understanding of some of its most distinctive features. But first I need to set the stage.

## I. First Things

I have chosen for my example the plight of Jephthah, narrated in the Book of Judges. His rash vow and subsequent events would seem to place him in the following dilemma. If he sacrifices his daughter, then he does something wrong by violating the Decalogue commandment that forbids killing. If he does not sacrifice his daughter, then he does something wrong by not fulfilling his vow to the Lord. So no matter what he does, he does something wrong.

Or does he? In order to evaluate Jephthah's case from a theistic perspective, we need a somewhat more precise notion of a moral dilemma. And we need a specimen theist.

If there are any moral dilemmas, they might come in two varieties. On the one hand, a person might be in the position of being required to perform two actions whose joint performance is impossible. Having made two separate, simultaneous, symmetrical promises to Baker and Charlie to loan a sum of money, Abel may find that he is able to honor only one of the promises. There is nothing wrong in Abel's loaning the sum to Baker, but there is something wrong in his failing to loan the sum to Charlie. Abel's problem is that he has *too many obligatory* actions to perform. On the other hand, a person might confront a situation in which two courses of action are forbidden, yet the person cannot avoid performing one of them. Here the agent has *too few permissible* actions to perform. Jephthah's plight is a candidate for this sort of dilemma.

Let us define the notions of a "weak moral $n$-lemma" and a "strong moral $n$-lemma":

> An agent, $x$, is in a weak moral $n$-lemma if and only if (1) there are $n$ alternative actions open to $x$ and (2) for each alternative action, $\phi$, open to $x$, if $x$ does $\phi$ then $x$ fails to do something that $x$ ought to do.
> An agent, $x$, is in a strong moral $n$-lemma if and only if (1) there are $n$ alternative actions open to $x$ and (2) for each alternative action, $\phi$, open to $x$, if $x$ does $\phi$ then $x$ does something that $x$ ought not to do.

'N-lemma' is a barbarism whose only excuse for existing is to point out that moral dilemmas are but one family in a clan of predicaments: there could be moral trilemmas, tetralemmas, and so on. One might try to reduce all cases of $n > 2$ to cases of $n = 2$ by regimenting them into the form 'either alternative $\phi$ or alternative not-$\phi$,' where to choose not-$\phi$ just is to choose one of the other alternatives from the actions comprising the $n$-lemma. There is a problem, on the surface at least, with the reduction. Suppose that $x$ has an indivisible good and has promised simultaneously to give it to $y$, $z$, and $w$. Then to represent $x$'s predicament as a choice between, say, $y$ and not-$y$ is unfair to $z$'s and $w$'s chances if the predicament is to be resolved by a coin-flip. No doubt much more can be said about the prospects for the reduction, but we need not pursue the issues further here.

An alternative action is open to $x$ if it is in $x$'s power to perform the action in question, which implies that $x$ has the ability to perform the action (that sort of action is in $x$'s repertoire) and the opportunity to perform it on the occasion in question (nothing is preventing $x$ from exercising the ability). If one assumes that omissions are actions, then one may say that on some occasions an alternative to φ is just to do nothing.

Some may wish to argue that the distinction between weak and strong moral dilemmas is merely a surface distinction. Given three principles, one can show that every weak dilemma is really a strong dilemma. Suppose that every omission is an action; more specifically, that (i) if $x$ omits or fails to do some action, ψ, then $x$ does not-ψ. Suppose further that (ii) if $x$ ought to do ψ, then it is not permissible that $x$ do not-ψ. Finally, suppose that (iii) if it is not permissible that $x$ do not-ψ, then $x$ ought not to do not-ψ. Then consider the consequent in clause (2) of the definition of a weak moral dilemma: '$x$ fails to do something that $x$ ought to do'. Let ψ be any alternative action that $x$ fails to do but ought to do. By the first principle, $x$ does not-ψ. Since $x$ ought to do ψ, the second principle implies that it is not permissible that $x$ do not-ψ. But if it is not permissible that $x$ do not-ψ, the third principle implies that $x$ ought not to do not-ψ. Thus $x$ does something (namely, not-ψ) that $x$ ought not to do. Thus in virtue of the three principles, '$x$ fails to do something that $x$ ought to do' implies '$x$ does something that $x$ ought not to do', which is the consequent of clause (2) of the definition of a strong moral dilemma. Since the two definitions differ only in respect of this consequent, the three principles yield the result that every weak dilemma is a strong dilemma.

The three principles deserve more critical scrutiny than I shall give them here. Since I shall focus our attention on strong moral dilemmas in the remainder of the paper, it would not distress me if it turned out that every weak dilemma is a strong dilemma. Even so, one should not accept that result if it rests on dubious principles. It is not obvious that principle (i) captures the sense of the doctrine that omissions are actions. I am inclined to think that the converse of that doctrine, that actions are omissions, is false. Yet the converse of principle (i), if $x$ does not-$\psi$ then $x$ omits to do $\psi$, seems true. Principles (ii) and (iii) together give the biconditional principle that $x$ ought to do $\psi$ if and only if it is not permissible that $x$ do not-$\psi$. This biconditional is a variation of part of a familiar principle of deontic logic, the so-called interdefinability of 'is obligatory' and 'is permissible'. In the context of discussions of moral dilemmas, however, one ought to watch this principle carefully.[2]

There may be dilemmas that are irreducibly religious in character, that is, dilemmas that cannot be analyzed as moral or as any other kind of dilemma. There may also be dilemmas that pit a religious requirement against a moral requirement.[3] I believe that nothing in this paper precludes those possibilities. But the notion of $n$-lemma that I have defined is to be understood specifically as a moral notion. Moreover, the specimen theist I am about to introduce holds views that locate the source of morality in God.

The theist I have in mind—let us call her "Agnes"—believes that God exists and is the omniscient, omnipotent, perfectly good, and providential creator and sustainer of the world. Agnes further believes that there are absolute principles of rightness and wrongness, binding on all peoples at all times: love of one's neighbor is right; murder is wrong. Finally, Agnes believes that God's relation to these moral principles is not adventitious. It is not as if God merely sees the long-range good tendencies of neighborly love, the long-range bad tendencies of murder, and gives us helpful hints on which courses of action to follow. It is rather that the moral principles are part of the expressive content of the will of God, an all-knowing being whose will is perfectly good. Agnes thus holds a view about moral rightness and wrongness that is sometimes called theological voluntarism and sometimes called a divine command theory. Agnes may not be too happy with either title. "Theological voluntarism" can conjure up images of a God who might have approved of just any kind of action, including murder, and who might have disapproved of just any kind of action, including neighborly love. Agnes's view is that God's wisdom and God's love play an important role in shaping God's will. "Divine command theory," on the other hand, can suggest that commands are the only means God uses in communicating moral knowledge to us, along with the corollary that our having moral knowledge is simply a matter of our obediently accepting such commands. Agnes's view is that there are all sorts of ways in which God can make his will known to us, including the enablement of our capacity for practical reason. We need not specify Agnes's views in any further detail; it is better if we leave them in a fairly generic form.[4] What is important for Agnes is that the content of morality is dependent ultimately on God's willing, knowing, and loving activity.

The constellation of Agnes's views about God and morality should force her to think seriously about moral dilemmas, since it is not obvious that her views leave room for their possibility. When Agnes comes to read the Book of Judges, what should she think about the story of Jephthah's vow and its aftermath?

Agnes might begin by comparing Jephthah's plight with the story of Abraham and Isaac (Genesis 22:1-14). There are more differences than similarities, however. In both cases a father is placed in the position of having to sacrifice an only child in order to fulfill an obligation to God. In both cases it is obvious to the father that the sacrifice must be made. In both cases the certitude is vouchsafed by an intimate encounter between God and a righteous man. (Referring to Hebrews 11:32, Aquinas says that Jephthah is included among the saints.) Nevertheless, the obligations are incurred in different ways. Abraham is commanded directly by God to sacrifice Isaac. Jephthah's obligation arises from the vow he made to God. God (or his messenger) intervenes at crucial junctures of the episode of Abraham and Isaac. In Jephthah's case God's only overt role is to fill Jephthah with the enthusiasm to make the vow. The identity of the sacrificial victim is known from the start in Genesis, and discovered with anguish only at the denouement in Judges. Finally, Abraham's sacrifice is prevented by God, while God does nothing to stop Jephthah from sacrificing his daughter.

One might think that the salient similarity in both cases is that Abraham and Jephthah both know what they must do. Neither of them takes himself to be in a dilemma. Jephthah's behavior on seeing his daughter emerge from his house is the behavior of a person unable to face the horrible consequences of his act, not the behavior of a person caught in the toils of moral predicament. So it might seem that if Jephthah knows what he must do, then he cannot be in a dilemma.

But this conditional proposition comes close to begging the question. For if Jephthah is in a genuine dilemma, and he knows it, then he will know what he must do, namely, sacrifice his daughter, *and* he will know what he must *not* do, namely, sacrifice his daughter.

Thus the fact that Jephthah knows what he must do does not entail that he is not in a dilemma. In similar fashion, Jephthah's not taking himself to be in a dilemma is compatible with his being in a dilemma nevertheless, just as an agent can believe himself to be free when he is not.

There is a temporal difference between the episode of Abraham and Isaac and the episode of Jephthah and his daughter, a difference that might seem to be significant to someone like Agnes. P. T. Geach has claimed that Abraham was not in a "bind" with respect to God's command to sacrifice Isaac because "a schoolboy of Macaulay's day would know...that the Decalogue could not worry Abraham, since it was promulgated long after his death" (Geach 1980, p. 181). Perhaps Geach believes that a person cannot be confronted with a moral dilemma, that is, with a choice between alternative wrong courses of action, until God has promulgated the relevant commandments. Even if that belief were plausible, it would not help in Jephthah's case: a schoolboy of Macaulay's day would know that Jephthah's case *postdates* the promulgation of the Decalogue. Moreover, the belief is not plausible, not to a thoughtful defender of divine command morality. God punishes Cain for slaying Abel, even though the homicide antedates the promulgation of the Decalogue (and the existence of Abraham and Isaac). No defender of divine command morality need suppose that murder, adultery, theft, and perjury were permissible until the time of the promulgation of the Ten Commandments. Murder is wrong because it is contrary to the will of God, but that does not entail that one cannot know that murder is wrong until God does something as dramatic as issuing the Ten Commandments.

## II. *Secundum Quid*

At first blush it might seem to Agnes that a providential God could have arranged things so that his creatures would never have to face genuinely dilemmatic situations. At second blush it might occur to her that there are limits to what even an omnipotent God can do if he is going to have creatures who are significantly free. As providential, he will endow us with sufficient intellectual and moral capacities and furnish us with a commodious environment. He will give us moral principles that are within our capacity to follow. Our freedom, however, which is part of our endowment, entails the ability to ignore or flout those moral principles. Once an agent violates one of the principles, all bets are off about whether it will be possible for her subsequently to follow all the principles that she could have followed had she not initially violated one of the principles. "Oh, what a tangled web we weave, when first we practice to deceive," to which we may lamely add, "Or kill or covet, cheat or thieve."

A nonmoral analogy may be useful. Suppose you are consigned to playing second, or **O**s, in ticktacktoe. Your primary goal is not to lose; your secondary goal is to win, whenever possible. There is an algorithm which, if followed, will insure against losing. *Part* of the algorithm is given in the following two rules:

R1. Whenever it is your turn and your opponent has two **X**s in the same (horizontal, vertical, or diagonal) row, place your **O** so as to block your opponent from completing the row.

R2. If your opponent's first move is to place an **X** in the center cell, place your **O** in one of the four corner cells.

Suppose that your opponent places an **X** in the center cell and that you do not follow R2; instead, you place your **O** in one of the four side cells. If your opponent now plays optimally, you are doomed. There will come a point, after your opponent places the third **X**, at which you will be confronted with two unblocked rows, each containing two **X**s. You should block the first row, but you cannot do that without leaving the second row unblocked. You should block the second row, but then you leave the first row unblocked. No matter what you do, you leave something undone, something that results in your losing. Your ticktacktoe quandary is analogous to a weak moral dilemma. The fault is not with the rules constituting the algorithm. The problem is that your earlier failure to follow R2 brings about a situation in which you are stuck.

Your opponent need not play optimally, of course; your not following the algorithm only puts you at risk. Similarly, the world need not react in such a way that on every occasion of an agent's wrongdoing, the agent is subsequently confronted with a dilemma whose cause can be traced back to the wrongdoing. Some philosophers have maintained, however, that *all* moral dilemmas—weak ones and strong ones—are like your hypothetical predicament at ticktacktoe: something wrong done by the agent is responsible for the dilemma the agent now faces. Every moral dilemma is a dilemma *secundum quid*, it is said; no moral dilemma is a dilemma *simpliciter*. Present defenders of this strategy derive the terminology from Aquinas and claim him as a confrere.[5] Alan Donagan's articulation of the distinction is useful.

> A moral system allows perplexity (or conflict of duties) *simpliciter* if and only if situations to which it applies are possible, in which somebody would find himself able to obey one of its precepts only if he violated another, even though he had up to then obeyed all of them. For reasons already given, Aquinas held that any moral system that allows perplexity *simpliciter* must be inconsistent. By contrast, a system allows perplexity (or conflict of duties) *secundum quid* if and only if situations to which it applies are possible in which, as a result of violating one or more of its precepts, somebody would find that there is a precept he can obey only if he violates another. (Donagan 1984, in Gowans 1987a, p. 285.)

The thesis is, then, that every case of a moral dilemma for an agent has a causal ancestry containing at least one wrongdoing on the part of the agent which is connected in a relevant way, one presumes, to the ensuing dilemma. I take it that propounders of the thesis do not think that its truth is guaranteed by the doctrine of original sin. According to a common version of that doctrine, we are all in such a fallen state that, without supernatural aid, it is not possible for us always to refrain from acting sinfully. If the doctrine of original sin is true, then our fallen state is our common heritage, the lamentable, all-pervasive backdrop against which we play out our lives. It is one thing to say that all of us, left to our natural devices, are bound to sin. It is another thing to say that all of us are bound to end up in dilemmas *secundum quid*. Even if one believes the latter claim— and there is no indication that defenders of the thesis do—one can still insist that the proper explanation of *secundum quid* dilemmas must include reference to a personal wrongdoing, not merely to a faulty condition.

Agnes may wonder how to apply the thesis to the case of Jephthah. The salient action prior to Jephthah's homecoming is his vow to the Lord. Although the product of rash enthusiasm, the vow can hardly be counted as intrinsically wrong, especially since it was made after the Spirit of the Lord came upon Jephthah. Is it to be counted as wrong nevertheless, just because it led to the tragic denouement at homecoming? This approach has all the advantages of theft over honest toil. It makes the *secundum quid* thesis rousingly successful: the only *simpliciter* dilemmas it would not thus automatically convert into *secundum quid* dilemmas would be those—if any such are possible—in which an agent faces a moral dilemma having made no previous decisions whatsoever. The price of success is exorbitant,[6] although that is not to say that no consequentialist will pay it. Thus, it seems unpromising to attempt to categorize Jephthah's case as a dilemma *secundum quid*. But on the thesis that all moral dilemmas are dilemmas *secundum quid*, it then follows that Jephthah's plight is no dilemma at all. But Jephthah's plight certainly looks like a dilemma, and if it is not plausible to classify it as *secundum quid*, then it must be *simpliciter*.

The thesis that all dilemmas are *secundum quid* would have some claim on Agnes's credulity if it had been held by as profound a thinker as Aquinas. But in fact Aquinas does not hold the thesis. He does acknowledge that *some* dilemmas are *secundum quid*. Recent discussions of Aquinas's views cite four passages, one from the *Disputed Questions on Truth* and three from the *Summa Theologiae*.[7] The *De Veritate* passage discusses an example that recurs in the first of the three *Summa* passages. Thus, three different examples are supposed to provide the data for the thesis that Aquinas believes that *all* dilemmas are dilemmas *secundum quid*. Since the myth that Aquinas held the thesis has become pervasive in the recent literature, it is high time to debunk it. The three examples themselves are more subtle than the commentators seem to realize. And there are other examples to be found in Aquinas's writings which, when examined, have the cumulative effect of undermining the attribution of any reductionistic thesis to Aquinas.

Aquinas reserves the term *perplexus* for dilemmatic situations. But he does not apply it to all dilemmas; the last case we shall examine makes no use of that term or its cognates. Nine of the ten examples we shall examine occur in the context of "objections;" the other occurs in the context of a reply to an objection. Aquinas's policy with objections is to resolve them. That fact by itself, however, does not entail the conclusion that Aquinas thinks that there are no dilemmas, nor the conclusion that if there are any, they are all *secundum quid*. Quite often, as Aquinas recognizes, an objection rests on a valid point.

The three examples usually cited are the following:

> (A) Aquinas believes that any act of will that goes against the agent's reason, whether that reason is correct or mistaken, is evil.[8] Suppose, then, that a person sincerely

but mistakenly believes that he ought to commit adultery. If he commits adultery, then he does something wrong by violating a law of God. If he does not commit adultery, then he does something wrong by acting against his conscience. (*De Veritate*, Q. 17, a. 4, obj. 8 and reply; IaIIae, Q. 19, a. 6, obj. 3.)

(B) Restitution for what has been taken from another is necessary for one's salvation. Suppose that a person has ruined another's reputation by telling the truth, and that she can now only restore the reputation by lying. If she mendaciously restores the other's reputation in order to make restitution, then she does something wrong. If she does not restore the person's reputation, then she does something wrong by not making restitution. (IIaIIae, Q. 62, a. 2, obj. 2.)

(C) A priest in a state of sin sins in administering the sacraments. Suppose that a sinful priest is confronted with a dying, unbaptized baby. If he baptizes the baby, he sins by his administering the sacrament. If he does not, he sins by allowing the baby to die unbaptized. (IIIa, Q. 64, a. 6, obj. 3.)[9]

Let us consider cases (A) and (C) first. Edmund N. Santurri has recently argued that, so far from contributing to the thesis that dilemmas are merely *secundum quid*, Aquinas's treatment of cases like (A) and (C) shows that he does not regard these cases as dilemmas.[10] In both cases, Aquinas says, there is something the agent can do to extricate himself. The sincerely intending adulterer can give up his mistaken belief; the priest in a state of sin can repent. On Santurri's analysis, the agents are confronted not with dilemmas but rather with threefold choices, one option of which is a permissible alternative. But this analysis fails to appreciate the point of the *secundum quid* thesis. To say that a person faces a dilemma *secundum quid* is to say that the person faces a dilemma brought about by some culpable condition of the person, and that the dilemma endures as long as the person remains in that condition. The adulterer's culpably mistaken belief or the priest's sinful condition is the *quid* following which the agent faces a dilemma. What Santurri takes to be a third alternative just is the action that will rectify the condition and extricate the agent from the situation, thus showing it to be one kind of *secundum quid* dilemma.

An agent, $x$, is in a *secundum quid* dilemma if and only if $x$ faces a dilemma because $x$ is in a culpable condition for which $x$ is responsible. Sometimes, as cases (A) and (C) show, $x$ can reverse or put aside the condition. But case (B) is significantly different. Aquinas's resolution of case (B)—the case of one person's ruining the reputation of another by telling the truth—depends on a distinction between whether the agent told the truth justly or unjustly. If she told the truth justly, then she is not bound to make restitution. If she told the truth unjustly (by betraying a confidence, for example), and if she cannot now undo the harm done except by lying, then she must not lie, but must make compensation in some other way to be determined by an arbiter (IIaIIae, Q. 62, a. 2, *ad* 2).

If the agent told the truth justly, case (B) is not a dilemma *secundum quid* because it is not a dilemma of any kind. In that case, it is irrelevant to cite it as evidence. If the agent told the truth unjustly and cannot undo the harm done without doing something else that is wrong, then case (B) is unlike cases (A) and (C). In those cases the agent can dissolve the dilemma: there is something he can do now, the doing of which is permissible and will enable him to escape the horns of the dilemma *in prospect*, before he chooses one of the forbidden horns. In contrast, if the agent in case (B) is an unjust truthteller, then she is not confronting a dilemma in prospect; she is already immersed in a continuing dilemma from which she cannot inculpably extricate herself. She ought to restore the person's reputation, she cannot do that without lying, and she ought not to lie. Aquinas's solution, to make recompense in some other way, is not put forward as a way of dissolving the dilemma. It presupposes the dilemma's indissolubility—that is, the unavoidable continued wrongdoing of the agent—and proposes a way of repairing the rent thus created in the moral fabric.[11] There is thus an enduring feature to case (B). Nothing the agent does now or in the future can count as a permissible *restoration* of the other person's reputation. Compensation is thus a *pis aller*, a substitute for restoration. Its character as a substitute is a reminder of the permanent irreversibility of some dilemmas.

Let us say that an agent, $x$, is in a *soft* moral dilemma if (but not only if) (1) $x$ is in the dilemma only because of some wrongful or mistaken condition on $x$'s part, (2) $x$ can still do something, $\phi$, permissible in itself, to alter or renounce the condition, and (3) $x$'s doing $\phi$ would enable $x$ to avoid both horns of the dilemma. (It may be, for all of this, that *x* does not know that the dilemma is avoidable, or even that there is a dilemma.) Let us say that a moral dilemma is *hard* if and only if it is not soft. Thus if *x* is in a hard dilemma, then it is not the case that all three conditions apply to *x*'s situation. The agents in cases (A) and (C) are in soft *secundum quid* dilemmas. The unjust truth-teller in case (B) appears to be in a hard *secundum quid* dilemma, or, to put it more cautiously, if it is soft, it is not soft in virtue of the above sufficient conditions (1)-(3). There just is no relevant condition of the agent such that she can alter or renounce it and thereby avoid the dilemma.

The most we have shown so far is that there may be two kinds of dilemma *secundum quid*; this should not in itself disturb a defender of the *secundum quid* strategy. Let us turn our attention, however, to a family of four cases from near the end of the *Summa*. The cases involve unforeseen flaws in the celebration of the sacrament of the Eucharist.

(D1) A priest might suddenly recall, during the consecration, that he has not fasted, or not confessed a sin, or even that he has been excommunicated. He sins if he continues the consecration and he sins if he discontinues it. (IIIa, Q. 83, a. 6, obj. 2.)

(D2) A priest might discover, after consecrating the wine, that it has been poisoned. If he drinks the wine, he sins either by committing suicide or by tempting God, that is, by doing something in order to test God's power, goodness, or knowledge.[12] If he does not drink it, he sins by violating an ecclesiastical statute. (*Ibid.*, obj. 3.)

(D3) A priest might discover, after the consecration, that the server did not pour wine into the chalice. Once again, he sins if he continues and he sins if he stops. (*Ibid.*, obj. 4.)

(D4) A priest might not recall whether he has said the words of consecration. If he has in fact omitted them and does not say them, he sins by invalidating the service. If he has not omitted them and repeats them, he also sins by invalidating the service. (*Ibid.*, obj. 5.)

Case (D1) fits the pattern of cases (A) and (C). According to Aquinas, if after the consecration a priest recalls, for example, that he is in a state of sin, he ought to repent inwardly, with the intention of confessing and making satisfaction, and continue the sacrament (*ibid.*, *ad* 2). Consider, however, cases (D2), (D3), and (D4). If they are dilemmas at all, then they are dilemmas without fault on the part of the agent. What is absent from (D2), (D3), and (D4) is any mention of the *secundum quid* apparatus. By hypothesis, the priest has done nothing relevantly wrong; he is not in a sinful state. Aquinas describes each case as an apparent dilemma. In each case he prescribes a course of action for the priest to follow. (D2) The poisoned wine must not be drunk; it should be placed in a vessel and kept with the relics (*ibid.*, *ad* 3). (D3) If the priest discovers that there is no wine in the chalice, he should redo whatever needs to be done to ensure that the sacrifice is performed in perfect order (*ibid.*, *ad* 4). (D4) If the words the priest thinks he has forgotten to say are not necessary for the sacrament, he should not say them now; if they are, he should (*ibid.*, *ad* 5). Aquinas's prescriptions and the context in which they occur suggest that in each case he is prescribing the one course of action that will prevent a defective situation from getting worse. But that does not allow us to infer that he thinks that the situations are not genuine dilemmas. Nor does he say in the replies that it was a mistake to think of them as dilemmas. It is natural for a person to think that precisely because such genuine dilemmatic situations can arise, it is important to have prescriptions to cover them, even though the function of the prescriptions can only be to allow one to prevent things from worsening, not to allow one to avoid doing something that is wrong.

Suppose, as the evidence indicates, that Aquinas does regard cases (D2), (D3), and (D4) as genuine dilemmas. Then we could suggest another way in which a dilemma can be soft. Agent $x$ is in a soft dilemma if (but not only if) (1) $x$ is in the dilemma through no wrongful action or mistaken condition on $x$'s part, (2) there is some action, $\phi$, that $x$ can do such that $x$'s doing $\phi$ entails that $x$ grasps one horn of the dilemma, and (3) $x$'s doing $\phi$ prevents a defective situation from getting worse. (Once again we can say that if $x$ is in a hard dilemma, then not all three of these conditions hold true of $x$'s situation.) On the supposition that Aquinas regards cases (D2), (D3), and (D4) as dilemmas, we could say that they are *soft simpliciter* dilemmas. That is, they are dilemmas involving no fault on the part of the agent, to be handled by the agent's doing something that is wrong in itself but that stems further worse results.

The last three cases involve Aquinas's discussion of oaths and vows.

(E) Not to fulfill a promise made under oath is a case of the sin of perjury. Suppose that a person swears to commit murder. If she commits the murder, then she sins. If she does not commit the murder, then she sins by committing perjury. (IIaIIae, Q. 98, a. 2, obj. 1.)

If Aquinas had a general strategy that regimented all apparent *simpliciter* dilemmas into *secundum quid* dilemmas, one would have expected to see that strategy deployed especially in case (E). It would have been extremely plausible to say that the agent is in a dilemma *secundum* her wrongful oath. But in fact Aquinas does not analyze case (E) along those lines. His determination of case (E) is that it is not a dilemma because no legitimate oath has been sworn.

To swear an oath is to invoke God as a witness. A *declaratory* oath concerns past or present matters; a *promissory* oath is taken with regard to the future (IIaIIae, Q. 89, a. 1). An oath must meet three conditions in order to be good. The oath must be the result of *judgment* or discretion on the part of the oath-taker. The oath must not be false but *true*. And the oath must be *just*, not sinful or unlawful (*ibid.*, a. 3). Of the three conditions on oaths, truth—more precisely, its opposite, falsity—is essential and most important to perjury. Even the person who swears that something is true, believing it to be false when in fact it *is* true, has sworn to something formally false (false as apprehended by the person) but materially true (IIaIIae, Q. 98, a. 1, *ad* 3). Justice is the second most important condition, but in the case of perjury with respect to a promissory oath, Aquinas connects absence of justice to falsity: "For whoever swears to something unlawful incurs falsity by that very fact, because he is obligated to do what is contrary" (*ibid.*, *ad* 1).[13] I believe that what Aquinas has in mind is this. The notions of truth and falsity as they apply to promissory oaths have to do not with what *will* be so much as they have to do with what *ought* to be and what *ought* to be done. That is, Aquinas thinks that to swear to do something wrong is unjust because it is swearing to *make* true what ought to be left false.

We are now in a position to understand Aquinas's determination of case (E). The person who swears to commit murder by that very fact commits perjury through a defect of justice (IIaIIae, Q. 98, a. 2, *ad* 1). That is, she swears to make true what she ought to leave false. She is obligated not to keep the oath (*cf.* IIaIIae, Q. 89, a. 7; a. 9, *ad* 3). She is not in a dilemma, however, because she is not also obligated to keep the oath. Her failing to keep the oath is not a case of perjury, because what she swears to do is "not the sort of thing that could fall under an oath" (IIaIIae, Q. 98, a. 2, *ad* 1). It is not as if she swears an illicit oath which then places her in a dilemma *secundum quid*. It is rather that the oath, if sworn, has no binding force, because it lacks truth *cum* justice.

The promissory oath in case (E) is vitiated because what is sworn to is something intrinsically wrong. Such cases are not *secundum quid* dilemmas; swearing to something that is intrinsically wrong creates no dilemma at all. It sometimes happens, though, that an oath, whose content is not intrinsically wrong, would result in evil, if kept, because of unforeseen circumstances.

> (F) Herod, captivated by the dancing of Herodias's daughter, swears to grant to her whatever she asks. She asks for the head of John the Baptist on a platter. (IIaIIae, Q. 89, a. 7, *ad* 2.)

Aquinas says of the case, "This oath could be lawful from the beginning, given an understood, requisite condition, namely, if she asked for what it would be right to give; but the fulfillment of the oath was unlawful" (*ibid.*). It is wrong for Herod to carry out his oath, whose content began life as morally neutral. Is it also wrong for Herod *not* to carry out his oath? The determination of article 7 implies that it is not: "An oath should not be observed in that case in which there is sin or an obstacle to good."

Defenders of the *secundum quid* thesis might rejoice in Aquinas's determinations of cases (E) and (F). They might point out in particular that case (F) is very much like Jephthah's plight, inasmuch as they both involve a promise whose unguarded liberality is the source of ensuing tragedy. Their joy would be premature. Let me introduce as case (G), the tenth and last case to be considered, Aquinas's discussion of Jephthah.

Unlike Herod's case of an imprudent oath, Jephthah's case involves a *vow*, and that difference is significant for Aquinas. There are three parties entailed by the structure of a promissory oath, namely, the promisor, the promisee, and the confirmatory witness to the oath; the witness is always God. The structure of a vow, in contrast, entails two parties, the promisor and the promisee, who is always God (IIaIIae, Q. 88, a. 1).[14] In an obvious way, a promisor's relation to God is more direct when the promise is a vow than when it is an oath. For that reason vows are more binding than oaths.[15] To fail to keep a legitimate oath displays irreverence, but to break a vow is an instance not simply of irreverence but of infidelity to God, a form of betrayal that is the greatest kind of irreverence (IIaIIae, Q. 89, a. 8). It is not surprising, then, that Aquinas's pronouncement about vows admits no class of permissible exceptions. Other sorts of promises require certain conditions in order to remain binding. In contrast, every vow made to God that is still within the agent's power to keep must be kept (IIaIIae, Q. 88, a. 3). Thus Jephthah must keep his vow. Moreover, Jephthah's case cannot be assimilated to case (E)—a case of an oath vitiated by its content—because the content of Jephthah's vow is not something intrinsically wrong. In this respect, Jephthah's vow is more like Herod's oath. Indeed, Aquinas cites Jephthah's vow as an instance of a vow that is good considered in itself yet that has an evil result; such a vow should not be kept (IIaIIae, Q. 88, a. 2, *ad* 2). Thus in two adjacent articles Aquinas either says or implies that it is wrong for Jephthah to keep his vow and wrong for him not to keep his vow. There is no reason to think that we have caught Thomas nodding. He himself provides the grounds for undercutting any attempt to turn Jephthah's case into a *secundum quid* dilemma. Not only does he say that there is nothing intrinsically wrong with the vow, but he also explicitly adverts to the fact that Jephthah made the vow when the spirit of the Lord came upon him (*ibid.*). Finally, we may note that unlike the (D2), (D3), and (D4) cases, there is no prescription offered to prevent a defective situation from worsening. The very idea of trying to develop such a prescription to apply to Jephthah's tragedy is, of course, daft. In sum, I submit that Aquinas's treatment of Jephthah's plight recognizes it as a hard *simpliciter* dilemma.

Aquinas's views about moral dilemmas are thus considerably more complex than contemporary philosophers have thought. Recall that there are two ways in which a dilemma can be soft, and let us assume that a dilemma is hard if it is not soft in either way. Without undue distortion we can then map the results of our examination of the ten cases onto the following grid.

|  | Soft | Hard |
|---|---|---|
| *Secundum Quid* | (A), (C), (D1) | (B) (truth unjustly told) |
| *Simpliciter* | (D2), (D3), (D4) | (G) (Jephthah) |

(Cases (E) and (F) are not dilemmas.)

Defenders of the *secundum quid* thesis thus should not look to Aquinas for support. Nor should they rely on Donagan's claim that "Aquinas held that any moral system that allows perplexity *simpliciter* must be inconsistent." There are only two occasions on which, when discussing *perplexus*, Aquinas uses the term *impossibile*. One is the *De Veritate* discussion of case (A). The other is Aquinas's discussion of the same issue raised in case (A)—whether a false conscience is binding—in his commentary on the *Sentences* of Peter Lombard.[16] Both works are earlier than the *Summa Theologiae*. In the *Summa* the term used is not *impossibile* but rather *inconveniens*. *Inconveniens* can sometimes be rendered as 'inconsistent' when it occurs in medieval logical treatises, but in its garden-variety philosophical occurrences, it will bear no more weight than 'unsuitable', 'unfitting', 'inappropriate', 'discordant', or 'awkward'. I conjecture that Aquinas came to realize that *impossibile* was too strong a term to use to characterize dilemmatic situations: *ab esse ad posse valet consequentia*. To be sure, Aquinas thinks that dilemmas are occasions in which something has gone awry, perhaps horribly awry. He does not think, however, that the source of the wryness is always a wrongdoing on the part of the agent.

## III. *Tertium Datur*

What happens to theistic ethical theory if the prop of *secundum quid* dilemmas is removed? How should Agnes respond to the thought that there are genuine *simpliciter* dilemmas? There are two complementary strategies one might offer to Agnes. The first is to argue for the thesis that no adequate ethical theory, secular or theistic, will allow the existence of unresolvable moral dilemmas. (By the lights of the first strategy, to acknowledge that there are even *secundum quid* dilemmas is already a mistake.) The second strategy is to present a procedure whose application would show that all apparent dilemmas are only apparent. What I will suggest is that although Agnes may accept the strategies, she need not. I will then explore the consequences of her rejecting them.

We might think of ethical theory on the model of scientific theory. Two hallmarks of an adequate scientific theory are its capacities for prediction and explanation. The analogous functions in the realm of the practical would seem to be guidance and appraisal, respectively. Suppose that a particular scientific theory were such that with respect to some type of phenomenon, the theory's laws predicted logically incompatible outcomes. With respect to this type of phenomenon, the theory would be useless as a predictive device. Our natural inclination would be to reject the theory as it stands: at a minimum we would regard the theory's laws as incompletely expressed or flawed in some other way. Now suppose, by analogy, that an ethical theory were such that in a certain kind of choice-situation, the theory's principles told us that the agent ought to perform some action, φ, and ought to refrain from performing φ. Here we would be inclined to regard the theory as useless as a guide to the agent's behavior. The flaw in both cases seems to be a kind of inconsistency. It is then tempting to assimilate the practical inconsistency exhibited by the ethical theory case to the logical inconsistency exhibited in the scientific theory case. There is a popular argument used to effect the assimilation. Suppose that my ethical theory tells me that I ought to do φ and that I ought not to do φ. Then, by a seemingly obvious agglomeration principle and the principle that if one ought not to do φ, then one ought to do not-φ, it follows that I ought to do (φ and not-φ). Of course I cannot do (φ and not-φ). But 'ought' implies 'can', and so 'not can' implies 'not ought'. Thus, if I cannot do (φ and not-φ), then it is not the case that I ought to do (φ and not-φ). It is contradictory to be told both that I ought to do (φ and not-φ) and that it is not the case that I ought to do (φ and not-φ). So if my ethical theory ever tells me that I ought to do φ and that I ought not to do φ, I can be sure that my ethical theory is logically inconsistent.[17]

The second strategy picks up at this point, offering a technique or a set of techniques for the repair of defective ethical theories. Some of the more salient tactics at the disposal of a practitioner of the second strategy are the following. *Distinguish between levels of appraisal*. The 'ought'-judgments giving rise to the apparent dilemma may be based on intuitive ethical principles that are efficient but only approximate. In cases in which there is conflict between such principles, one can appeal to a supreme principle of morality, which itself licenses the intuitive principles and which can be applied directly to recalcitrant cases.[18] *Distinguish between different senses of the same moral term*. There may be a sense of 'ought' according to which it can happen that I ought to do φ and that I ought to do not-φ. But there is another sense of 'ought', tantamount to 'morally best', according to which if I ought to do φ, then it cannot be the case that I ought also to do not-φ.[19] One can go on to allege that dilemmas get off the ground only by confusing the first sense with the second. *Revise and refine moral principles.* Moral principles should be thought of as "open-textured;" they apply to situations *ceteris paribus.* The appearance of dilemmas is a symptom that certain principles may need further refinement. Perhaps important exceptions and exclusions need to be built into them. Or perhaps meta-principles should be developed that will either adjudicate between lower-order principles or lexically order them. The goal of such activity should be, *inter alia*, to eliminate moral dilemmas.[20]

Agnes might find it fascinating to explore the ramifications of the second strategy further if she found the first strategy especially compelling. But she need not. The first strategy has two components, an appeal to an analogy between the enterprises of scientific theorizing and ethical theorizing, and an assimilation of moral dilemma to logical inconsistency. A closer examination of the first component can result in one's denying the second.

The goal of predictive success in scientific theory is important but not paramount. For some sciences, such as paleontology and cosmology, prediction plays little or no direct role. Two rival scientific hypotheses might make the same predictions, yet one of them might do a better job of explaining the phenomena than the other. Explanation and understanding lie at the heart of science in such a way that an adequate scientific theory makes it clear why its predictions are successful and not just lucky guesses. If Agnes takes the analogy between scientific theory and ethical theory seriously, she should expect an adequate ethical theory not only to tell her what to do, but also, more fundamentally, to give an account of why she should do it. The latter function of the theory will be bound up with the theory's criteria of moral judgment and appraisal, that is, the criteria in terms of which the theory judges things, persons, and situations to be good or bad, and actions to be right or wrong, obligatory, forbidden, or permissible. Just as rationally acceptable scientific prediction must be embedded in an adequate explanatory framework, so rationally acceptable moral guidance must depend on an adequate theory of moral appraisal. Agnes may be a theological voluntarist, but remember that on her brand of voluntarism, God's will is informed by his love and wisdom.

Still, one might ask, how can a reasonable theory of moral appraisal ever issue in dilemmatic moral guidance? How can an adequate ethical theory ever tell us that one and the same action is right and wrong, or obligatory and forbidden, all things considered? The problem seems to be compounded for theistic ethical theory. It seems impossible that an omniscient God would inadvertently promulgate an ethical theory whose criteria of appraisal yield inconsistent guidance on occasion.

If Agnes has her wits about her, she will be able to see that appraisal and guidance can come apart, even in an ethical theory that is reasonable, adequate, and complete. In this respect the analogy between scientific theory and ethical theory fails. A scientific theory that predicts incompatible phenomena in some possible situation is a theory whose explanatory devices are somehow defective. In contrast, if an ethical theory's criteria of appraisal tell us that in a given situation, $x$ ought to do $\phi$ and $x$ ought not to do $\phi$, then that *might* be a sign that the theory is defective, but it *need* not be. The judgment in question might be the best, most complete assessment of the situation: anything less may be one-sided, tendentious, overly simplistic, or insensitive to the complexities of the situation. In such a case, the theory's ability to offer guidance breaks down, if guidance is supposed always to require the specification of a permissible course of action. Even though a reasonable, adequate, and complete ethical theory will include a general system of moral appraisal, it will lack a comprehensive procedure for moral guidance, understood as the identification of permissible alternatives, if there are genuine strong moral dilemmas.

The kind of breakdown between appraisal and guidance induced by moral dilemmas need not be a symptom of logical inconsistency. The argument for the assimilation of moral dilemma to logical inconsistency rests on two less-than-obvious principles, the agglomeration principle and the principle that 'ought' implies 'can', or what I shall call the ability principle.[21] I propose to leave the agglomeration principle undiscussed and focus instead on the ability principle. Let us consider first a special but easily overlooked case of a strong moral $n$-lemma, the case in which $n = 1$. In this case there is only one action, $\phi$, open to $x$, and $\phi$ is such that if $x$ does $\phi$, then $x$ does something that $x$ ought not to do. Call such a case a moral *monolemma*. It is obvious that consideration of the agglomeration principle is out of play here. So the issue of logical inconsistency in the case of monolemmas boils down to this question: if an ethical theory countenances the existence of monolemmas, does that show that the theory is inconsistent or that the ability principle is not universally true?

Let us have an example before us. Suppose that Jones kills a pedestrian while voluntarily driving drunkenly. The intuitive moral response is to say that Jones ought to have avoided hitting the pedestrian. But in his condition Jones was not able to. We may say of this case either that the intuitive moral response is mistaken or that the case constitutes a refutation of the ability principle. In an attempt to exercise the first option, there are those who would say that what Jones ought not to have done was drive while drunk. We need not gainsay that judgment, but it does not negate the fact that Jones also ought to have avoided hitting the pedestrian. Perhaps there are those who would say that in some sense of 'can', Jones, even in his inebriated condition, could have avoided hitting the pedestrian. No doubt there is some such sense of 'can', but to appeal to such a sense risks saving the ability principle at the cost of rendering it trivial. In the sense of 'can' with which we have been operating, involving both ability and opportunity, avoiding the pedestrian is not something Jones can do. At the time of the accident, he either lacked the ability or his condition prevented him from exercising it.

This example suggests that there are other sorts of monolemma, or cases in which the ability principle is not true. A segment of a person's behavior may be so habituated that even though she knows that she should not behave that way, she cannot avoid it. If occurrent mental judgments count as actions, then they comprise a rich source of counterexamples to the ability principle. Smith ought not to form biased opinions about the members of other racial groups, but he cannot directly prevent himself from doing so. (The best Smith may be able to do is not to act on those opinions and to take whatever steps he can indirectly to reform them.) It is mildly ironic that the etiological assumption of the *secundum quid* thesis is more plausible as an account of many cases of moral monolemma than it is of dilemma. But perhaps not all: Smith's biased opinions might have their origin in Smith's unlucky upbringing in a racist social environment.

If Agnes is a Christian theist, she will have additional reasons to regard the ability principle with suspicion, reasons that depend on beliefs about the function of God's grace. The Pelagians took Matthew 5:48 as a proof-text for the heretical claim that grace was not necessary for salvation: "You, therefore, must be perfect, as your heavenly Father is perfect." God would not have commanded us to become perfect if it were not possible for us to do so on our own. Therefore, the Pelagians concluded, we are capable of leading lives free of sin by means of our own natural abilities, without the assistance of divine grace. The argument obviously depends on the ability principle. Confronted with the argument, some orthodox Christian theists curtail the principle in a way that makes it compatible with the passage from Matthew. Aquinas, for example, says that although individual acts of sinning can be avoided, no one without grace can persevere against all acts of sinning for any great length of time (*ST*, IaIIae, Q. 109, a. 8). It is tempting to read into Aquinas's remarks an awareness of a fallacious quantifier-shift: 'Each individual act of sinning is such that the agent can avoid it' could be true while 'The agent can avoid all acts of sinning' be false.[22] Thus, even though it is plausible to interpret the injunction of Matthew 5:48 as requiring that you avoid sin at all times, anti-Pelagian orthodoxy maintains that it is not within your natural power to avoid sin at all times.

A defender of the ability principle can legitimately claim that the only curtailment imposed on it by the above consideration is on its *collective* use, not its *distributive* use. According to the collective version of the principle, 'You ought to avoid all sin' might not imply 'You can avoid all sin'. Even so, that would leave untouched the thesis that 'Each individual sin is such that you ought to avoid it' implies 'Each individual sin is such that you can avoid it'. It takes further considerations to dislodge the distributive version of the ability principle. The doctrine of God's grace provides one source of such considerations. There is, for example, the phenomenon of God's hardening the hearts of some, construed as his justly withdrawing his aid from someone who has turned away from him.[23] Many of the resultant individual sins committed by such a person are forbidden yet unavoidable.

Agnes thus has ample reason to doubt the truth of the ability principle in many cases of moral monolemmas. Or, to put it another way, Agnes's ethical theory displays no void of inconsistency in its escutcheon by acknowledging moral monolemmas; it simply provides grounds for denying the ability principle. And once released from the grip of the ability principle, what reason could Agnes have for not expecting to find moral *n*-lemmas for $n > 1$?

Do not think that this question is merely rhetorical. Even if an

ethical theory can be logically consistent while allowing moral dilemmas, Agnes's theistic ethical theory might not pass muster. There
might be particular theistic reasons for thinking that God would not
confront his creatures with *simpliciter* dilemmatic situations. J. L. A.
Garcia has recently put forward two arguments to this effect. The
arguments express what I think worries many theists about the
possibility of moral quandary. In responding to them, we will be able
to extract some more general lessons about theistic ethical theory.

Garcia's first argument appeals to God's (essential) rationality and
omniscience:

> Now a rational agent never wills each of two things she knows to
> be mutually exclusive. However, if there are situations in which
> one acts wrongly no matter how one acts and therefore situations
> in which one acts against God's will no matter how one acts, then
> it would seem God must will things which are, and which He
> therefore knows to be, mutually exclusive. Since God cannot act in
> such an irrational way, it appears we need to give up either some
> traditional Christian beliefs about God's will and knowledge or the
> thesis that there are situations in which one cannot but act
> wrongly. (Garcia 1990, p. 192.)

Garcia's second argument appeals to God's moral perfection:

> [I]t is a commonplace of both secular and Christian morality that it
> is immoral to will another to do evil. However, if God wills one to
> do something which she cannot do without doing evil, then God, it
> would seem, wills her to do evil. (*Ibid.*)

What credence should Agnes give the premise that "a rational agent
never wills each of two things she knows to be mutually exclusive"?
Agnes believes that God's will promulgates the principles that killing
is wrong and that vows must be kept. The principles are not mutually
exclusive, yet in their application to Jephthah's case, they yield
dilemma. Is it then that God, in foreseeing Jephthah's plight, should
not have promulgated one or the other of the two principles? If God
acts according to the policy that if a set of principles ever yields an
$n$-lemma, then at least one member of the set must not be promulgated, then God will promulgate a very short list of principles, perhaps
one at most.[24] It may be that Garcia's premise is better construed
as licensing any number of applications to particular cases, for example the denial that God wills both that Jephthah keep his vow and
that Jephthah not sacrifice his daughter. If in this context 'wills' is
tantamount to 'effectively chooses', then the application of the

premise is true but irrelevant to the campaign against moral dilemmas. Even omnipotent God cannot effectively choose both that Jephthah sacrifice and not sacrifice his daughter, but that fact does not constitute a tribute to God's *rationality*. Perhaps then 'wills' in the context should be interpreted to refer to an imperative expression of God's will, so that the application of the premise to Jephthah's plight results in the claim that God, *qua* rational, does not command or require of Jephthah both that he keep his vow and not sacrifice his daughter. This thesis is not obviously true.

Suppose that Lloyd has been taught by his parents that he ought to honor them by keeping the promises he freely makes to them and that he ought to remember the Sabbath by not laboring on that day. Suppose further that out of gratitude for what they have done for him, Lloyd spontaneously promises to cut the hay on their farm on the next dry day. Suppose that the next dry day turns out to be a Sabbath. Suppose, finally, that Lloyd turns to his parents for help. We can imagine several different ways in which they might respond. I want to have us focus on one possible and natural response *that only makes sense on the hypothesis that Lloyd's situation is a genuine dilemma.*

Lloyd's parents release him from his promise, suggesting that he defer cutting the hay. Lloyd's contrition in approaching his parents is evidence that he believes, as do his parents, that his failure to keep the promise would be wrong, just his failure to remember the Sabbath would be wrong. The parents' action is not to *advise* Lloyd, as if they thought that one alternative were preferable or somehow made permissible by the context. Instead, their action *extricates* Lloyd from his predicament by graciously waiving or deferring a requirement legitimately owed them in order that he might be able to fulfill his other, conflicting requirement. Their action achieves something *for* Lloyd that cannot be achieved *by* Lloyd. From the parents' and Lloyd's point of view, Lloyd is required to keep his promise and required to remember the Sabbath. To waive a requirement is not to make it not to have been. The parents, in waiving or deferring Lloyd's requirement to keep his promise, are willing to absorb a wrong done to them and forgive Lloyd in advance. They might also hope that their action will have the educative effect of encouraging Lloyd to be more circumspect about avoiding such predicaments in the future. Finally, if Lloyd's parents are sensitive and sensible, they will not dwell on the fact that they are waiving a requirement: nothing undermines gracious behavior so much as parading it. The parents' action can only be described in this way on the assumption that Lloyd is in a real, not just an apparent, dilemma. A diehard, committed to the impossibility of dilemmas, will have to say of this case that Lloyd and his parents are deluded, playing out a touching, benighted charade. It is obvious that we need not acquiesce in that judgment.

Agnes is thus entitled to believe that a being can be rationally required to do mutually exclusive things. But now one may be inclined to ask why God was not as gracious with Jephthah and his daughter as Lloyd's parents are with Lloyd. God could have intervened at Jephthah's homecoming and canceled the debt owed him. Or he could have arranged that the only thing that came out of Jephthah's doors was a superannuated chicken. How could a morally perfect God allow such a tragic denouement? Even if Agnes need not subscribe to the first of Garcia's arguments, it might seem as if the second is devastating when applied to Jephthah's plight. God apparently wills that Jephthah keep his vow, which Jephthah cannot do without doing evil, namely, killing his daughter.[25] Therefore, if Garcia is right, God wills Jephthah to do evil.

Garcia's argument must pass successfully through two stages. Suppose that

(1)  $x$ wills that $y$ do $\phi$ and [$x$ knows that] $y$ cannot do $\phi$ without doing evil.

The addition of the bracketed knowledge claim in (1) gives Garcia a stronger premise and makes (1) more obviously applicable to omniscient God. The first stage of the argument is that (1) is supposed to entail

(2)  $x$ wills that $y$ do evil.

The second stage of the argument is that (2) is supposed to entail

(3)  $x$'s willing that $y$ do evil is immoral.

One might think that (2) follows from (1) by means of a principle to the effect that to will the end is to will the means. But if we assume that to will that someone do evil is to will that the person do some evil action, then there are at least two readings that can be given to (2):

(2′) There is some action, $\psi$, such that $\psi$ is evil and $x$ wills that $y$ do $\psi$.

(2\*) *x* wills that there be some action, ψ, such that ψ is evil and *y* does ψ.

It is clear that (2\*) does not follow from (1). Lloyd's parents will that he remember the Sabbath, knowing that he cannot do that without breaking his promise. It does not follow, as (2\*) would have it, that they malevolently will that there be some action of his that is evil. If anything in the neighborhood follows from (1), it is more likely to be something like (2').[26] Lloyd's parents will that he break his promise, and Lloyd's breaking his promise is evil. On the (2') interpretation of (2), however, we cannot get to (3). There is nothing immoral about Lloyd's parents willing that he break his promise, because the promise was made to them and it is the sort of promise from which they may waive their claim. Garcia's second argument thus fails. Even if (1) entails (2'), (2') does not entail (3). And even if (2\*) entails (3), (1) does not entail (2\*). There is no plausible way to book passage successfully from (1) to (3).

We can now explicate a way in which dilemmas fit into Agnes's theism. The crucial concepts are offense, repentance, forgiveness, and mercy. Offense is distinct from harm. Although we cannot harm God, we can certainly do things that offend him. For very many—perhaps all—moral wrongdoings, offense is given primarily to God whether others are harmed or not. Offense can also be given to others. If Lloyd callously reneges on his promise to his parents, he may offend (and harm) them. Offenders can repent the wrong they have done. They can even, as in Lloyd's case, show contrition about an impending, unavoidable wrong. Such behavior provides an occasion for the wronged party to forgive the offender. There are three observations to be made here. First, the wronged party might forgive the offender even if the offender has shown no signs of repentance or contrition. Second, there may be circumstances in which the wronged party ought not to forgive the offender. Third, "the wronged party" may include a plurality of agents occupying different positions in the moral network. Forgiveness by one in the absence of forgiveness of the others may not be sufficient to achieve total forgiveness. Had he reneged on his promise, Lloyd would have offended both his parents and God, in which case his parents' forgiveness might or might not have been sufficient to settle God's grievance with Lloyd. In the ordinary course of events, forgiveness is a manifestation of an agent's loving mercy.

If Agnes believes that God is perfectly rational and good, she can believe nevertheless that his creatures may confront genuine dilemmas that are not of their own making, just as she believes that they confront suffering and evil. If Agnes believes that God is just, she can believe that God sometimes requires, with justification, contrary performance from them. If Agnes believes that God is merciful, the one who sacrificed *his* only begotten son so that we might have eternal life, she can believe that God will forgive those who genuinely repent, absorbing the offenses committed primarily against him in his infinite and all-encompassing love. Agnes's reflections on the story of Jephthah may make clear to her another dimension of her religious commitment. Jephthah's faith is commended to us by the author of Hebrews (11:32). Yet Jephthah's faith is overshadowed by the faith of his daughter, who remains nameless to history. Faith is a virtue, but so too is hope.[27]

## Notes

1. See the essays and references cited in Gowans 1987a. For a detailed discussion of a case drawn from fiction, namely, Shusaku Endo's novel, *Silence*, see Quinn 1989.
2. See Sinnott-Armstrong 1988, pp. 156-161 for an interpretation that falsifies part of the interdefinability thesis.
3. Quinn 1986 argues that the case of Abraham and Isaac is best viewed as a case of "Kierkegaardian conflict," in which an indefeasible religious requirement, imposed by God's command to Abraham to sacrifice Isaac, conflicts with a moral requirement—not to sacrifice an innocent child—that is not overridden by any state of affairs. On this interpretation, the Abraham and Isaac case is not a pure moral dilemma, but rather a dilemma between two incommensurable realms of value. This interpretation is compatible with the belief that there are moral dilemmas and compatible with the belief that there are not.
4. For a sampling of different views, see Quinn 1978; Quinn 1979; Adams 1987, essays 7 and 9; and Mann 1989.
5. Von Wright 1968, p. 81 attributes the strategy to Aquinas and credits Geach with calling his attention to it. Geach 1969, p. 128 endorses the strategy, attributing its truth to God's providence. Donagan 1977, pp. 144-145, Donagan 1984, in Gowans 1987a, pp. 285-286, MacIntyre 1984, p. 179, MacIntyre 1988, pp. 185-187, Gowans 1987b, p. 5, and Sinnott-Armstrong 1988, pp. 102-103 also attribute the strategy to Aquinas. Von Wright, Donagan, Gowans, and Sinnott-Armstrong cite the same passages from Aquinas in support of the attribution.
6. If the principle is that *any* action that leads to a moral dilemma is wrong, then God's allowing Jephthah to defeat the Ammonites is wrong. If the

principle is that any action *of an agent* that leads to a moral dilemma *for the agent* is wrong, then it runs afoul of any sort of case in which the action brings about a great good while leading to a trivial dilemma (such as being committed to mowing two lawns at the same time). If the principle is that any action of the agent that leads to a *great* moral dilemma for the agent is wrong, then we may ask whether that action remains wrong in circumstances in which choosing one horn of the dilemma leads to an even greater good. When, if ever, is an action irrevocably right or irrevocably wrong for a consequentialist?

7. The passages are in *De Veritate*, Q. 17, a. 4, obj. 8 and reply; *Summa Theologiae*, IaIIae, Q. 19, a. 6, obj. 3 and reply; IIaIIae, Q. 62, a. 2, obj. 2; IIIa, Q. 64, a. 6, obj. 3 and reply. (All subsequent references to the *Summa Theologiae* will cite only part, question, article, and objection numbers. I have used the Latin texts in Aquinas 1980.) See von Wright 1968, p. 81n (who does not cite the third passage); Donagan 1977, p. 254, n. 3; Donagan 1984, in Gowans 1987a, p. 290, n. 17; Gowans 1987b, p. 31, n. 2; Santurri 1987, p. 223, nn. 23 and 25.

8. *De Veritate*, Q. 17, a. 3; IaIIae, Q. 19, a. 5.

9. Aquinas discusses other variations on the type (C) example. Thus, it is not lawful for a priest to refrain altogether from consecrating the Eucharist, but it is also not lawful for a sinful or excommunicated priest to consecrate the Eucharist (IIIa, Q. 82, a. 10, obj. 2.)

10. Santurri 1987, pp. 91-94. Santurri infers, invalidly, that Aquinas's position is that there are no moral dilemmas *secundum quid* or *simpliciter*.

11. Note that case (B), cited but not examined by Santurri, cannot be assimilated to the analysis he proposes, even if the analysis were unobjectionable in other respects.

12. On the sin of tempting God, see IIaIIae, Q. 97.

13. The least important condition on perjury is lack of judgment, because it only puts one in danger of falsity (*ibid.*).

14. Oaths and vows may involve beneficiaries, who may be distinct from the promisee. Whether there are beneficiaries depends not on the structure but on the content of the promise.

15. It is unclear whether Aquinas means that a vow to do something is always more binding than an oath to do the same thing, or whether he intends the stronger thesis that any vow, no matter what its content, is more binding than any oath.

16. Book II, Distinction 39, Question 3, article 3, objection 5.

17. See (page references are to Gowans 1987a) Williams 1973, pp. 129-134, McConnell 1978, pp. 155-156, Marcus 1980, pp. 199-200, Foot 1983, p. 254, Donagan 1984, pp. 276-281; and Sinnott-Armstrong 1988, pp. 108-135.

18. Such a tactic is deployed, for example, in Hare 1981.

19. This tactic is suggested in Foot 1983, although Foot does not use the distinction to deny the possibility of moral dilemmas.

20. A version of this tactic is deployed in Donagan 1977 and Donagan 1984.

21. For doubts about the agglomeration principle, see (in Gowans 1987a) Williams 1973, pp. 132-134, van Fraassen 1973, pp. 148-150, Marcus

646 / William E. Mann

1980, p. 200, Foot 1983, p. 254; and Sinnott-Armstrong 1988, pp. 127-135. For doubts about the ability principle, see Marcus 1980, in Gowans 1987a, pp. 199-200; and Sinnott-Armstrong 1988, pp. 110-126.
22. Compare 'Each individual day of creation is such that I can live through it' with 'I can live through all the days of creation'. Note also that on the hypothesis that there are strong moral dilemmas, although the agent might be able to avoid each individual act of sinning, there will nevertheless be situations in which she will not be able to avoid sinning.
23. See Kretzmann 1988 and Stump 1988.
24. It is possible for a single principle to yield dilemma. See Marcus 1980, in Gowans 1987a, p. 192.
25. I for one would find it hard to deny that God wills that Jephthah kill his daughter; see Mann 1988. And I would be suspicious of any attempt to maintain that in these circumstances, what Jephthah does is not evil.
26. It is not clear to me that (2′) follows from (1), partly because it is not clear to me what proposition (1) is supposed to express. Even without the bracketed knowledge claim, '$y$ cannot do $\phi$ without doing evil' needs to be explicated. For the purposes of this paper, I will assume, without prejudice, that (2′) follows from (1).
27. An earlier version of this paper benefitted from the comments of Alan Donagan, J. L. A. Garcia, Scott MacDonald, and Philip L. Quinn. The University of Vermont and the National Endowment for the Humanities provided research support. I wrote most of the paper while enjoying the intellectual stimulation at the Center for the Philosophy of Religion at the University of Notre Dame. Alfred J. Freddoso wishes not to be acknowledged for the many discussions we had on these topics.

**References**

Adams, Robert Merrihew. 1987. *The Virtue of Faith and Other Essays in Philosophical Theology*. New York: Oxford University Press.
Aquinas, Saint Thomas. 1980. *Opera Omnia*. Edited by Roberto Busa. 7 vols. Stuttgart-Bad Cannstatt: Friedrich Frommann Verlag Günther Holzboog.
Donagan, Alan. 1977. *The Theory of Morality*. Chicago: University of Chicago Press.
Donagan, Alan. 1984. "Consistency in Rationalist Moral Systems." *The Journal of Philosophy* 81:291-309. Reprinted in Gowans 1987a.
Foot, Philippa. 1983. "Moral Realism and Moral Dilemma." *The Journal of Philosophy* 80:379-398. Reprinted in Gowans 1987a.
Garcia, J. L. A. 1990. "Love and Absolutes in Christian Ethics." *Christian Philosophy*. Edited by Thomas P. Flint. Notre Dame, Ind.: University of Notre Dame Press.
Geach, Peter. 1969. *God and the Soul*. London: Routledge & Kegan Paul.
Geach, Peter. 1980. Review of Quinn 1978. *The Philosophical Quarterly* 30:180-181.
Gowans, Christopher, ed. 1987a. *Moral Dilemmas*. New York: Oxford University Press.

Gowans, Christopher. 1987b. "Introduction: The Debate on Moral Dilemmas." In Gowans 1987a.

Hare, R. M. 1981. "Moral Conflicts." In Gowans 1987a.

Kretzmann, Norman. 1988. "God Among the Causes of Moral Evil: Hardening of Hearts and Spiritual Blindness." *Philosophical Topics* 16,2:189-214.

MacIntyre, Alasdair. 1984. *After Virtue*. Second Edition. Notre Dame, Ind.: University of Notre Dame Press.

MacIntyre, Alasdair. 1988. *Whose Justice? Which Rationality?* Notre Dame, Ind.: University of Notre Dame Press.

Mann, William E. 1988. "God's Freedom, Human Freedom, and God's Responsibility for Sin." *Divine and Human Action: Essays in the Metaphysics of Theism*. Edited by Thomas V. Morris. Ithaca: Cornell University Press.

Mann, William E. 1989. "Modality, Morality, and God." *Noûs* 23:83-99.

Marcus, Ruth Barcan. 1980. "Moral Dilemmas and Consistency." *The Journal of Philosophy* 77:121-136. Reprinted in Gowans 1987a.

McConnell, Terrance C. 1978. "Moral Dilemmas and Consistency in Ethics." *Canadian Journal of Philosophy* 8:269-287. Reprinted in Gowans 1987a.

Quinn, Philip L. 1978. *Divine Commands and Moral Requirements*. Oxford: Clarendon Press.

Quinn, Philip. L. 1979. "Divine Command Morality: A Causal Theory." *Divine Command Morality: Historical and Contemporary Readings*. Edited by Janine Marie Idziak. New York: Edwin Mellen Press.

Quinn, Philip. L. 1986. "Moral Obligation, Religious Demand, and Practical Conflict." *Rationality, Religious Belief, and Moral Commitment*. Edited by Robert Audi and William J. Wainwright. Ithaca: Cornell University Press.

Quinn, Philip L. 1989. "Tragic Dilemmas, Suffering Love, and Christian Life." *The Journal of Religious Ethics* 17:151-183.

Santurri, Edmund N. 1987. *Perplexity in the Moral Life: Philosophical and Theological Considerations*. Charlottesville, Va.: University Press of Virginia.

Sinnott-Armstrong, Walter. 1988. *Moral Dilemmas*. Oxford: Basil Blackwell.

Stump, Eleonore. 1988. "Sanctification, Hardening of the Heart, and Frankfurt's Concept of Free Will." *The Journal of Philosophy* 85:395-420.

Van Fraassen, Bas C. 1973. "Values and the Heart's Command." *The Journal of Philosophy* 70:5-19. Reprinted in Gowans 1987a.

Von Wright, Georg Henrik. 1968. *An Essay in Deontic Logic and the General Theory of Action*. *Acta Philosophical Fennica*. Fasc. 21. Amsterdam: North-Holland Publishing Company.

Williams, Bernard. 1973. "Ethical Consistency." *Problems of the Self: Philosophical Papers 1956-1972*. By Bernard Williams. Cambridge: Cambridge University Press. Reprinted in Gowans 1987a.